MEMORY

Sara Miller McCune founded SAGE Publishing in 1965 to support the dissemination of usable knowledge and educate a global community. SAGE publishes more than 1000 journals and over 800 new books each year, spanning a wide range of subject areas. Our growing selection of library products includes archives, data, case studies and video. SAGE remains majority owned by our founder and after her lifetime will become owned by a charitable trust that secures the company's continued independence.

Los Angeles | London | New Delhi | Singapore | Washington DC | Melbourne

MEMORY

Foundations and Applications

Third Edition

Bennett L. Schwartz

Florida International University

Los Angeles | London | New Delhi
Singapore | Washington DC | Melbourne

FOR INFORMATION:

SAGE Publications, Inc.
2455 Teller Road
Thousand Oaks, California 91320
E-mail: order@sagepub.com

SAGE Publications Ltd.
1 Oliver's Yard
55 City Road
London EC1Y 1SP
United Kingdom

SAGE Publications India Pvt. Ltd.
B 1/I 1 Mohan Cooperative Industrial Area
Mathura Road, New Delhi 110 044
India

SAGE Publications Asia-Pacific Pte. Ltd.
3 Church Street
#10-04 Samsung Hub
Singapore 049483

Printed in Great Britain by Bell & Bain Ltd, Glasgow

ISBN: 978-1-5063-2653-5

This book is printed on acid-free paper.

Acquisitions Editor: Abbie Rickard
eLearning Editor: Morgan Shannon
Production Editor: Libby Larson
Copy Editor: Karin Rathert
Typesetter: C&M Digitals (P) Ltd.
Proofreader: Alison Syring
Indexer: Will Ragsdale
Cover Designer: Candice Harman
Marketing Manager: Katherine Hepburn

18 19 20 21 10 9 8 7 6 5 4 3 2

Brief Contents

Detailed Contents

4 Episodic Memory 100

5 Semantic Memory 141

6   Visual Memory   171

9   Metamemory   285

12 Memory in Older Adults

Preface

It is hard to imagine an aspect of psychology more fundamental than memory. Without a functioning memory, all other cognitive functions—perception, learning, problem-solving, and language—would be impossible. Other aspects of life would also be difficult. Emotion is informed and influenced by memory. Many daily activities from walking to turning on our phones require learning, which require functional memory systems. Without intact memory, social interactions such as play, relationships, and work would be chaotic at best. For this reason, the study of memory has been important to psychologists from the very beginnings of psychology.

When I teach memory, the most common question that I receive from students is the following: How can I improve my own memory? However, memory textbooks seldom address this topic. Students learn about memory models, theories, a great many experiments, much about neuroscience, and the brain. These are all important if one is to understand how memory works, and these issues are well covered in this book. But *Memory: Foundations and Applications, 3rd Edition* is also designed to instruct students to apply these concepts to their everyday life and use them to improve their individual ability to learn and remember. The third edition includes an extended discussion of retrieval practice, a warning about the hazards of distraction, and a warning about the nature of stability bias, all of which can be used by students to improve the efficiency of their learning.

The classroom itself has changed drastically in the past few years of higher education. Classes have companion websites, and in many cases, entire classes are online—students may never see their professors. College students have been downloading information from the Internet since they were in elementary school. However, textbooks in memory exist as if these resources did not exist. I want *Memory: Foundations and Applications, 3rd Edition* to capitalize on these sources of information. Thus, the book contains references and links to websites where students can learn more about a particular topic or a particular individual's research. I believe that this approach will be conducive to the way modern students have grown accustom to learning. On the other hand, *Memory: Foundations and Applications, 3rd Edition* provides depth into the science and methodology of memory that may not be easily available from Internet sources. In the end, in many classes, there is still a professor in front of a classroom and a student reading a textbook. I wanted a textbook that provided depth and created interest in the field of memory—that is, a textbook that students would want to read. The balance between depth of understanding and ease of access is difficult in a world of super-information, but that is what I've strived for.

This book emphasizes the science of memory. It describes experiments, patients with memory disorders, the areas of the brain involved in memory, and the cognitive theory that links this research together. I have tried to write this book with students in mind—their concerns, interests, and curiosity. I hope at the same time that this book emphasizes the science of memory, that it also tells a story about our search to understand our own minds and how we can benefit from that understanding.

ORGANIZATION AND CONTENT

Memory: Foundations and Applications, 3rd Edition is an accessible textbook on memory science presented in clear and understandable language. Each chapter begins with a discussion or exercise that engages the reader with an example or real-life incident that helps illustrate the relevance and importance of each chapter. This opener provides students with an appreciation for the topic and why scientists consider the topic important. Examples and applications of key concepts are integrated throughout the text in a way that students can appreciate the relevance to their lives.

Instead of having separate neuroscience sections, each chapter integrates findings from neuroscience. Topics such as the time course of brain activation during autobiographical memory, the regions of the brain involved in encoding, and the regions of the brain involved in monitoring are included in the flow of the chapters rather than in a separate section at the end of each chapter or a separate chapter entirely. Neuroscience is not simply presented as a map as to where memory processes occur but also how the neuroscience data can shape how we construct our theories.

Memory: Foundations and Applications, 3rd Edition is unique in its emphasis on applications, in educational situations, police investigations, courtrooms, hospitals, memory clinics, and everyday life. These issues are also integrated within each chapter rather than kept separate from the development of theory and experiments. For example, the chapter on false memory discusses applications to legal proceedings. The chapter on memory and aging discusses the "use it or lose it" hypothesis. The chapter on amnesia discusses memory rehabilitation for patients with brain damage. And most chapters contain mnemonic hints, designed to help students become more efficient learners.

WHAT'S NEW TO THE THIRD EDITION

Memory: Foundations and Applications, 3rd Edition follows the same format as the first two editions. The chapters are ordered the same. However, *Memory: Foundations and Applications, 3rd Edition* is thoroughly updated. The third edition now has 207 new references to papers that were not in the first or second editions. The third edition is now the most up-to-date textbook in the field. Some of the pivotal changes from the second edition include a discussion of brain-stimulation techniques such as trans-magnetic stimulation and how these techniques are used in memory research, a discussion of white-matter tracts and their role in the neurology of memory, the use of n-back tasks to examine the central executive in working memory, more on semantic priming and its role in semantic memory, up-to-date discussion concerning the differences between line-ups and show-ups, changes in semantic memory in older adults, and the effects of distraction on memory efficiency. The biggest change is in the chapter on semantic memory, in which the discussion of semantic memory is increased, but the discussion of lexical memory and language is reduced to allow more focus on memory research.

PEDAGOGICAL FEATURES

1. Important terms are highlighted in bold. This is useful when students outline their textbooks while studying for exams. It directs them to the parts of the book that are important for studying after the material has been understood.

2. Mnemonic hints. Almost every chapter contains highlighted *mnemonic hints*. These hints state succinctly how a particular concept can be applied to memory improvement. Chapter 13 ends with a list of all the mnemonic hints provided in the textbook.

3. Interim summaries. Every chapter except for Chapters 1 and 13 have interim summaries. These review the main points of the section, emphasize the important points, and provide organization that students can use in study. In the third edition, each chapter has one additional interim summary.

4. After each interim summary is a section quiz. These short quizzes allow students to assess their comprehension of the previous section.

5. Key terms. At the end of each chapter, I list the important terms introduced or reviewed in the chapter. Key terms include new definitions, jargon, and concepts, as well as terms that may have been introduced in another chapter but are reviewed here. Students can use the "key terms" section as a way to review. Successfully defining the terms is the first step in mastering the material.

6. Review questions. At the end of each chapter are 10 review questions. Each question prompts the reader toward an understanding of one or more of the important ideas in the chapter. A student who can successfully answer all of the questions at the end of the chapter can be confident that he or she understands the main topics in that chapter.

ADDITIONAL RESOURCES

1. Online resources. Throughout each chapter are markers that indicate that there is additional content at sagepub.com. The links at sagepub.com will take readers to sites where they can get more information about a topic, learn about the research in a particular lab, or participate in a demonstration.

2. Test bank. Clear, unambiguous questions are available to professors using this textbook. Each question covers either factual knowledge from the text or conceptual knowledge based on the text. Many questions directly concern experiments discussed in the book.

3. PowerPoint package. A PowerPoint package has been designed to accompany the text. It parallels the textbook and highlights the important points. It can be modified by individual professors or used without modification.

ACKNOWLEDGMENTS

I need to thank many people at Sage Publications for their contribution to the development, writing, and production of *Memory: Foundations and Applications, 3rd Edition*. I thank Christine Cardone for guiding this book to the finish line and seeing it published in a timely manner. I thank Lisa Cuevas Shaw for overseeing the production of this book, promoting patience when I might be reckless, and ensuring that the book was always high quality. I thank Acquisitions Editor Erik Evans for his enthusiasm and for his insight into the world of textbook publishing, from which the book benefitted immeasurably. I thank Sarita Sarak for always being willing to help me with any aspect of the book—from permissions to the artwork. For the second edition, Reid Hester's encouragement and knowledge were beneficial. I thank him. I thank Sarita Sarak again. She was again always able to answer a question and help me with every aspect of the book. For the third edition, I thank Reid Hester and Lucy Berbeo for their help throughout the revision process. I thank Karin Rathert for thorough copyediting. I also thank Alex Helmintoller with his help with getting the book ready for production.

I also need to thank many colleagues and students who read parts of the first edition or second edition or gave me advice on what the important questions were in a particular topic. I thank my dissertation adviser Janet Metcalfe of Columbia University, who continues to advise and inspire me. I also thank George Wolford of Dartmouth College, a mentor par excellence. I thank Nate Kornell, Lisa Son, Bridgid Finn, John Dunlosky, Harlene Hayne, Rachel Herz, Steven M. Smith, Mike Toglia, Daniel Lehn, Anthony Prandi, Jeffrey Thomas, Leslie Frazier, and Endel Tulving for their advice and guidance in specific areas of the book. Jonathan Altman was always willing to be a sounding board for any idea, however silly, and give me technical advice. For the second edition, I thank the following people who read drafts or selected sections of the book: Anne Cleary, Hildur Finnbogadóttir, Ron Fisher, and Serge Nicholas. For the third edition, I thank the following people who read drafts or selected sections of the book: Bryan Auday, Elisabeth Bacon, Roberto Cabeza, Brian Cahill, and Jeffrey Neuschatz.

Finally, I wish to thank two special people whose love for me and pride in me inspire me every day to do my best. They are my wife, Leslie Frazier, and my daughter, Sarina Schwartz.

—*Bennett L. Schwartz*
August 11, 2016

CHAPTER 1

Introduction to the Study of Memory

Remembering is a part of our every moment. Nearly everything we do throughout the day, including dreaming at night, involves memory. Consider the act of waking up each morning. As the alarm goes off, you must remember whether you have an early appointment. If you do, you must get up right away, but if you do not, you can hit the snooze button and sleep a bit longer. Once you do get out of bed, even more is asked of your memory. Did you wear the same shirt on the same day last week? Would people notice? Are you going to the gym after classes? If so, do you need to bring workout clothes, or are they already in your car? If you live in a dorm, you might try to remember whether your roommate is in class already or trying to catch up on sleep. If you have a job, do you have any important meetings that you cannot afford to miss? These are just a few of the needs for memory that occur within just a few moments of waking up. As the day proceeds, you have to remember the directions to the university, the material for class that day, how to get from one class-room to another and what rooms classes are in, where your car is parked so you can drive home, and the best route to get home in afternoon traffic. You also have to remember which friend you are meeting for lunch and where. Did this friend just break up with her boyfriend, or are they back together? Remembering this is crucial in how you start your conversation with your friend. And yes, did you forget that you had an exam in your social psychology class? You need to remember all the material you have been studying for the past few days. Based on these examples, you can see how critical good memory perfor-mance is in everyday life.

Memory also forms the basis of our views of our selves and our personalities. Think of how crucial your memory is to your sense of self and personality. Most of us, for example, like to think of ourselves as generous. But when was the last time you engaged in a gener-ous act? Do you remember it? Being able to recall the characteristics of our own personal-ity and back it up with actual memories is an important part of developing our sense of self. Certainly, early memories from childhood tend to be an important part of personality and sense of self as well. Almost all of us can describe poignant memories that shaped who we are today. For example, on the positive side, it might be the memory of a grand-parent telling us to be confident and do our best, or it might be the memory of a teacher

1

who inspired us in high school. On the other hand, a memory of the first time you saw a dead body in an auto accident may be instrumental in keeping you a safe driver, or your memory of the first inauguration of President Obama may shape your view of world politics. Each of us has important memories like these.

Another way to view the importance of memory in our society is to search for the term *memory* on the Internet. I just did and got over one billion hits. Now some of these deal with computer memory, not human memory, but searching for *human memory* still elicits 35 million hits and *human memory improvement* over 3.5 million. That is a lot of information, confirming both how important memory is to us and the importance of understanding it. This text should serve to help readers understand both the science of human memory and how that science can be employed to improve the efficiency of our own learning.

Moreover, the thought of losing or forgetting certain memories is scary and painful. Imagine losing access to all the memories of your dear grandmother. These memories are "treasures" in a way more closely connected to our sense of self than physical objects, such as a bracelet or ring. Losing these memories, even the bad ones, is seen as devastating. Capitalizing on this fear, movies abound that tell fictional tales of amnesiacs who lose not just their ability to learn (common in amnesia in the real world) but also the memory of the personal past and hence their personalities (not common in the real world). What makes the amnesia plot compelling is the knowledge of how important the personal past is to the present self.

For students, memory is also one's livelihood. One's job is to learn and remember a myriad of information. Facts, dates, authors, concepts, methodologies, hypotheses, theories, and philosophies all must be learned and remembered. Doing so efficiently is important to the many students who have many conflicting obligations. One of the goals of this textbook is to help students use their memory more efficiently. Because learning and memory are a student's tools for advancement, memory is crucial to daily life.

For this reason, students can potentially perform better in school with training in the best ways to use their memory. However, students are seldom given any formal training in learning and memory, especially training supported by scientific research. Though we place tremendous demands on the memories of students, little scientific information is provided about how memory works and how we can improve upon our ability to encode, store, and retrieve information. One goal for this book is to provide students with some knowledge about the current state of memory science and what psychological science and neuroscience can tell us about the nature of human memory. Another goal is to provide students with concrete ways of applying memory science to improve their own abilities to learn and remember, a topic that is covered extensively in Chapter 13. Nonetheless, as important as advice is on how to improve memory, the science must come first. Thus, more words in this textbook will be devoted to the science of memory than the wherewithal of improving memory efficiency. But I hope you will be able to improve your own learning by gathering useful strategies from the sections on memory efficiency as well as generating personalized strategies through your own interpretations of theory and data. Indeed, the final chapter is completely devoted to improving memory efficiency. Some readers may want to read the last chapter first.

THE SCIENCE OF MEMORY

We approach the study of human memory from a scientific perspective. What does the term *scientific perspective* mean? In a broad sense, *science* refers to a particular view of the world, one based on systematic observation, experimentation, and theory. Critical to science is an unbiased attitude. A scientist needs to be open to different points of view but follow his or her data to the most logical conclusions, and these are based on evidence, not on the researcher's opinion. In science, a particular theory is useful only if careful and unbiased observations and experimentation support it. For psychological science, data derived from experiments constitute the building blocks of our theories. Our intuitions and guesses about the world have value, but to be science, they must be tested and verified via the scientific method. (For further information on this topic, go to study.sagepub.com/schwartz3e.[1])

Empirical evidence is the product of scientific research. To be empirical evidence, data must be verifiable; that is, another scientist should be able to get the same results by conducting the same or a similar experiment. The data from empirical studies are the building blocks of scientific theory. For example, in earth science, there is overwhelming empirical evidence

> **Empirical evidence:** The product of scientific research. To be empirical evidence, data must be verifiable; that is, another scientist must be able to get the same results by conducting the same or a similar experiment.

that, as of 2017, the world's climate is warming. Yes, there are global-warming deniers, but these deniers ignore the overwhelming empirical evidence. Note, however, that empirical evidence by itself does not inform us how to act. For example, with respect to global warming, some may advocate changing human industrial activity so as to reduce warming, whereas others may claim that we have to adjust to warming but do not need to eliminate this climate pattern. Both may agree on the basic empirical evidence—that global temperatures are rising—but disagree on what governments should do about it.

Similarly, in memory science, empirical evidence is the results of experiments, which can and should be replicable. Therefore, this textbook will devote much space to the methods and results of experiments. Interpretations of what these experiments mean may vary, and you may find different opinions in other textbooks, but you will find that we all rely on the same empirical evidence. These experiments form the basis of memory science.

In making recommendations about ways in which to boost memory performance, I will rely on only those methods that have been put to the scientific test and for which empirical evidence is available. This is not to deny that performance boosters may exist that we do not yet know about, but this textbook will only include empirically tested sources. I will also try to make scientific principles easier to understand by giving examples and telling a story or two. But although they may assist good pedagogy, stories and anecdotes do not constitute science. So please keep in mind the following: Experiments and empirical evidence form the basis of what we know about human memory from a scientific perspective.

The goal of memory science is to make generalizations about how memory works in the real world by studying it under careful and controlled laboratory conditions. Thus, a researcher might be interested in how witnesses remember what they saw during a crime and how accurate their memory is for that event. But memory researchers cannot follow the police around and interview witnesses at the crime scenes as the police are trying to do their jobs. This would be neither good science nor helpful to the criminal justice system. Nor can memory researchers "hang around" in places where crimes might occur. This would be dull and tedious work, because except in movies, convenience stores are mostly safe places, and brawls do not break out every night in every bar. Furthermore, witnessing a crime might be dangerous for that researcher. We can, however, ask people to come to labs, where they may see an acted film clip of a convenience store robbery or a bar brawl and then look at simulated mug shots. This, by and large, simulates the conditions that people might encounter when witnessing a crime in a safe and controlled manner. The control involved also allows for careful experimentation, which produces valuable empirical evidence. Control over the conditions is not just a safety measure; as we will see, it also allows us to make causal connections between variables.

Memory researchers are occasionally able to conduct field studies in which they study memory in the real world, including memories for crimes (Yuille & Cutshall, 1986). These studies generally confirm what has occurred in the lab. Some 130 years of laboratory research have yielded a strong body of knowledge that applies in the real world as well as in the lab. Thus, in this book, we will focus on scientific research and assume that, by and large, what we learn in the lab is applicable in everyday life.

So we will spend most of the book discussing the latest data and most up-to-date theories, but before we do that, let's take a quick look at the history of memory science.

THE HISTORY OF MEMORY RESEARCH

Human beings have most likely been wondering about their own memories and how they work since prehistoric times. Early human beings showed evidence of introspective behaviour at least as long as 40,000 years ago (Higham et al., 2012). We know from cave paintings as far afield as China, South Africa, and France that people were adorning themselves with body painting and jewelry, creating art, and presumably developing religious beliefs that long ago (see Figure 1.1). It is likely, though unproven, that some of their art re-enacts memories of great hunting stories. Thus, it is likely that some of these early Stone Age people thought about their own memories.

Certainly, people have been writing about memory since the beginning of writing itself. Some of the oldest writing in the world records information about human memory. An ancient Egyptian medical manual, known as the Ebers Papyrus, from 1500 BCE (that is, over 3,500 years ago) describes the nature of memory deficits after injury (Khalil & Richa, 2014). Nearly 2,500 years ago, in classical Greece, Plato and Aristotle described theories of memory that sound surprisingly modern. It is likely that many other ancient writings on memory have been lost to history. Certainly, many philosophers and medical professionals have written about the nature of memory during the ensuing millennia.

Memory metaphors are verbal models of how memory works. The great philosopher Plato (428–347 BCE) used two metaphors to account for memory. First, he compared human memory to a wax tablet, a common technology for showing the written word

Figure 1.1   Cave painting. It is likely that some prehistoric art re-enacts memories of great hunting stories. When you draw, do you call on events from your memory?

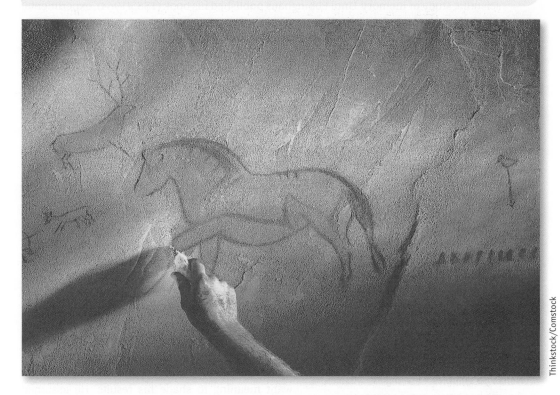

Thinkstock/Comstock

in his day. As learning occurs, information gets written into memory, as writing would get pressed into a wax tablet. Although the technology is outdated, this metaphor allows memory to be encoded, retrieved, and altered if the wax gets altered. Second, Plato compared human memory retrieval to a birdcage. We reach our hands into a cage to remove a bird, just as we reach into our memory to retrieve a particular event or item. Sometimes, the memory may be difficult to retrieve, just as the bird may be difficult to catch. Thus, 2,500 years ago, theorists were modeling human memory. More recently, your author compared memory to a teenager's room. It may appear disorganized, but the teenager knows where to find things because of his or her unique organizational schema. Roediger (1980) provides an excellent review of memory metaphors throughout history.

Particularly influential in the later development of a scientific approach to memory were the British associationists. Philosophers such as John Locke and George Berkeley emphasized how the mind creates associations between one idea and another. Their philosophy shaped much of the original science on human memory. However, the scientific method was not applied to the study of memory until a mere 125 years ago, when German psychologist Hermann Ebbinghaus (1885/1965) published a volume titled *Memory: A Contribution to Experimental Psychology.* So our history starts with him.

Hermann Ebbinghaus (1850–1909)

Hermann Ebbinghaus was a German psychologist and philosopher who pioneered the scientific study of memory. Until Ebbinghaus published his book (1885/1964), experimental psychology had confined itself to exploring the nature of sensation and perception. Ebbinghaus was the first person to use scientific methods to study memory and indeed, the first person to use the experimental method to address issues of higher cognition (Nicolas, 2006; Nicolas et al., 2015). Ebbinghaus is remembered today not only because he was the first memory psychologist but also because he established a number of principles of memory that are still relevant today, in terms of both theory and application. Indeed, a number of his findings are directly applicable to the goals of improving memory efficiency.

Most memory experiments today sample a large number of people. A memory experiment run on college students might test anywhere from 20 to 200 participants, depending on the nature of the experiment. Even studies on special populations (infants, older adults, individuals with brain damage, etc.) will try to get at least several participants. But Ebbinghaus used only one test participant—himself. Of course, we now know that simply testing one person leads to questionable generalizations and is not necessarily a good way to conduct science. Luckily, although Ebbinghaus was a pioneering memory scientist, his own memory was rather ordinary. The experiments that he conducted on himself have since been tested on many other individuals, and what Ebbinghaus found in his 1885 study generalizes to other people (Nicolas, 2006).

Ebbinghaus taught himself lists of **nonsense syllables**. These nonsense syllables consisted of consonant-vowel-consonant trigrams, which lacked meaning in Ebbinghaus's native German. In English, nonsense syllable trigrams might be TOB or HIF. They are pronounceable, as they follow the rules of English word formation, but they do not mean anything in everyday speech. Ebbinghaus chose nonsense syllables over words because he did not want meaning to shade his results. He assumed that meaningful stimuli would be more memorable than non-meaningful stimuli, and he wanted a set of material that did not differ with respect to meaning. Ebbinghaus created and studied more than 2,000 of these trigrams over the course of his experimental study.

Nonsense syllables: Meaningless syllables that can be given to participants to study that avoid the effect of meaning on memory (e.g., *wob*).

Ebbinghaus prepared lists of 6 to 20 nonsense syllables. He then studied a list until he could free-recall all of the nonsense syllables on the list. Later, he tested himself to see how many syllables he could remember from each list. Not surprisingly, he found it was easier to master the shorter lists than the longer ones. This is true of memory in general—shorter lists are easy to master than longer lists. I often wonder what his neighbors must have thought of this young, eccentric, long-bearded philosophy professor endlessly reciting nonsense syllables in his garret in Berlin.

His next experiment was to vary the **retention interval** between when he studied a list and when he retrieved that list. A retention interval is the time between when an item is initially learned or encoded and when it is retrieved or remembered. In Ebbinghaus's case, he varied the time between

Retention interval: The amount of time that transpires between the learning of an event or material and when recall for that event or material occurs.

his mastery of a particular list and testing himself again on that list. He found that the longer the retention interval, the more likely he was to forget items from a list. After a retention interval of just a few minutes, he might remember all of the syllables from a list, but if he waited a week, he might have forgotten a substantial number of syllables. This is another truism in memory—the longer the amount of time between learning and remembering, the more will be forgotten.

Ebbinghaus measured this forgetting by looking at the **savings score**. *Savings* meant the reduction in the amount of time required to relearn the list. If Ebbinghaus initially needed 10 repetitions per item to learn a list, he might need only 5 repetitions per item to relearn the list. Even if Ebbinghaus could no longer remember any items from a previously studied list, he demonstrated savings; it took him less time to relearn the list than to learn the list initially. Although savings diminished with longer retention interval, no matter how long the retention interval was, there was always some evidence of savings. Nearly 100 years later, Bahrick (1984) showed that there are savings in memory for high school Spanish and French vocabulary even 25 years after the last time a student took those courses. The choice of measurement, namely savings, allowed Ebbinghaus to examine some other characteristics of memory as well.

> **Savings score:** The reduction in time required to relearn a previously mastered list.

Ebbinghaus was keenly interested in measuring forgetting as well as learning. In fact, one of his important contributions was the idea of the **forgetting curve**. He noticed that forgetting happened rapidly at first. In self-tests just a few hours after study, he often found that he had forgotten over 50% of what he had learned. In later tests, though, the rate of forgetting declined. Testing himself a month later for a particular list would still reveal some memory for that list. Like many of his findings, the forgetting curve has been documented repeatedly since Ebbinghaus first studied it (see Schacter, 2001a). Ebbinghaus also found that some variables would affect the forgetting curve, with some making forgetting occur more rapidly, and others, like overlearning, preventing rapid forgetting.

> **Forgetting curve:** A graph that traces the decline of memory performance over time.

MNEMONIC IMPROVEMENT TIP 1.1

Overlearning: If you need to master material, particularly information without intrinsic meaning (e.g., the names of the parts of the brain), continue to study it even after you have mastered it completely. The additional study will ensure that you remember the information for a longer amount of time (the forgetting curve will not be as steep). This may reduce the time you need to restudy information later for a cumulative final exam.

Ebbinghaus investigated the phenomenon of **overlearning**. Overlearning is studying after material has been thoroughly learned. In some of his experiments, Ebbinghaus studied some lists until he mastered the list (that is, could recall all of the items), then put that list

Overlearning: Studying after material has been thoroughly learned.

aside until it was time to test himself for that list. For other lists, he continued to study the list even after he scored 100% on retrieving it during practice. He even varied the amount of time that he studied a list after he had achieved 100% performance on that list. He found that if he overlearned a list, his forgetting curve was less steep. That is, if he studied past the point of mastery, his forgetting of that list was slowed considerably. Thus, if he had studied a list on Day 1 to 100% accuracy and then stopped, his performance on that list might be 50% the next day. However, if he overlearned the list on Day 1, his performance would be better, perhaps 75% on the next day. Thus, studying past the point of mastery led to better long-term retention of that information. This principle has considerable generality and usefulness. If you want to minimize your chance of forgetting something, keep studying it even after you have "gotten it."

MNEMONIC IMPROVEMENT TIP 1.2

Spacing effect: To maximize learning, study the same information at different times. Don't "cram" all at once but space your study over time, both for individual items and for the entire set of material that you need to master. Spacing your study improves your learning efficiency.

Massed practice: When all study occurs in one block of time.

Distributed practice: When study is spread out over time.

Another variable that Ebbinghaus studied was the distribution of study time. For some lists, he studied the lists all at once until he mastered them (**massed practice**). For other lists, he distributed his study over a series of lists and a series of days (**distributed practice**). But he measured the amount of time and the number of rehearsals he needed to learn each list individually. Thus, even if he was distributing his practice over several lists on one day, he would record the time for each list separately. This allowed him later to compare how many rehearsals and how much time it took for him to master each list. Ebbinghaus found that if he had studied a list the same amount of time (but on different schedules) through massed practice or distributed practice, he experienced different savings scores for the lists. Even though equal amounts of time went into study, the distributed lists demonstrated higher savings scores than those that were studied all at once. This is now called the **spacing effect** or the advantage of distributed practice over massed practice (Gerbier, Toppino, & Koenig, 2015; Toppino & Cohen, 2010). Moreover, it took less total time to master a list that had been given distributed practice than one that received massed practice. This effect is also relevant today. Indeed, one of the crucial memory improvement hints given in the book is to

Spacing effect: More learning occurs when study trials on the same information are spread out over time than when they occur successively.

take advantage of the spacing effect. Modern studies show that distributed practice can produce enormous boosts in the amount remembered per amount of time studied relative to massed practice. Indeed, if students can do only one thing to help their learning, it would be this one. And Ebbinghaus discovered it in the 19th century.

As you can see, Ebbinghaus's work is still important and relevant and provides the basis for the first two mnemonic improvement hints. After finishing his studies on memory and writing his book on the topic, Ebbinghaus himself moved on to other interests. But for all those who followed, interested in the scientific pursuit of memory, Ebbinghaus laid the groundwork for memory science with solid methodology and important findings. (For the complete text of Ebbinghaus's book, you can go to study.sagepub.com/schwartz3e.[2])

Mary Calkins (1863–1930)

Shortly after the publication of Ebbinghaus's book, U.S. psychologist Mary Calkins began her seminal study on the nature of associative learning—how we pair new knowledge to existing knowledge. Calkins did this by examining **paired-associate learning**. Calkins (1894) had her participants study cue-target pairs of various types. In some cases, they were word-word pairs (e.g., *rain–cathedral*), but in others, they were syllables paired with words, syllables paired with pictures, and words paired with pictures. Calkins then gave the participant the first item from a pair and asked the participant to recall the second item in the association. For example, if the participant had studied a word-word paired associate, such as *rain–cathedral,* Calkins presented the first word in a word-word pair (*rain*), and the participant would have to respond with the target—the second word from the pair (*cathedral*).

> **Paired-associate learning:** Learning the association between two items, such as in language learning (e.g., learning the association *monkey–le singe*).

Shortly after Calkins published her study, the behaviorist tradition would become dominant in U.S. psychology. The behaviorists did not think memory was an appropriate topic of research, as memory is not a directly observable behavior. However, Calkins's methodology was easily carried over into this way of thinking, and thus learning research in this time period heavily relied on her methodology. Calkins's stimulus-response approach to memory preserved the importance of memory research in this period.

Calkins also made some significant discoveries concerning the nature of human memory. First, she found that the greater the overlap between meaning in cue-target pairs, the easier it was for the participant to learn and retain the information. Prior familiarity with the cue-target pairs also helped learning. Thus, for example, it was easier for her U.S. students to learn English-French word pairs than to learn English-Turkish word pairs, because the French words were more familiar to her students, even if they did not know the meanings prior to the study (see Bower, 2000). Second, in her investigations of short-term memory, Calkins discovered the **recency effect**—in immediate

> **Recency effect:** The observation that memory is usually superior for items at the end of a list; thought to be caused by the maintenance of those items in working memory.

recall (when the test occurs right after learning), items that were most recently learned are remembered better than items from the middle of the list.

Throughout her career, Calkins campaigned for equality for woman, particularly in academia. She became the first woman president of the American Psychological Association and then became president of the American Philosophical Association. Despite that, Harvard University never awarded her the PhD she had earned from its psychology department. (For more on the life of Mary Calkins, go to study.sagepub.com/schwartz3e.[3])

Behaviorism

In the early 20th century, **behaviorism** was the predominant approach in U.S. experimental psychology. Behaviorism took a somewhat paradoxical approach to learning and memory. Learning was a suitable topic of research, because it is directly observable. However, memory, the stored information in the brain, is not directly observable. Thus, behaviorism focused on learning but deliberately ignored memory. Starting with the work of J. B. Watson (1913), behaviorism stipulated that psychology should focus only on observable, verifiable behavior. Following Watson, behaviorism emphasized the nature of environmental stimuli and their influence on the observable behavior of humans and other animals. Behaviorists considered not only memory but also thought, concepts of mind, images, and emotions to be inappropriate issues for psychological science, because they could not be directly observed.

> **Behaviorism:** A school of psychology that focused on the relation of environmental inputs and the observable behavior of organisms, including human beings.

Although contemporary cognitive psychologists no longer agree with these assumptions, behaviorism made important contributions to the study of learning, particularly in the areas of **classical conditioning** and **operant conditioning**. Classical conditioning occurs when a neutral stimulus is continually presented along with a stimulus that has a particular association. After enough repetition, the neutral stimulus acquires some of the characteristics of the other stimulus. For example, in many people, riding a roller coaster may trigger a nauseous response. Initially, the smell of diesel may be a neutral stimulus. But if a person rides enough diesel-powered rides, he may get nauseous at the smell of diesel alone, even if there is no dizzying ride in sight. Similarly, an animal may learn that hearing a sound is associated with the release of food from a dispenser. Classical conditioning occurs when the animal moves to the food dispenser when hearing the sound.

> **Classical conditioning:** Learning that a relation exists between a stimulus (e.g., a ringing bell) and an outcome (e.g., getting food); the organism demonstrates a behavior or response (e.g., salivating) that shows that the organism has learned the association between the stimulus and the outcome.

> **Operant conditioning:** Organisms learn to perform responses or behaviors (e.g., pressing a bar) in response to a stimulus to achieve desirable outcomes (e.g., getting food) or avoid undesirable outcomes (e.g., getting an electric shock).

Operant conditioning means that an organism learns to respond in a particular way, because whenever the organism does respond in that way, it receives reinforcement or avoids punishment. Thus, a young child who makes requests without using the word *please* may have a request refused, but when she makes requests using the word *please,* the requests are granted. Both the punishment and the reinforcement will increase the likelihood that the child will utter "please" when making a request. Similarly, an animal such as a rat or a monkey will learn to press a lever when that lever causes the release of a desirable food item.

These learning methods appear to be widespread across animals from the most simple to the most complex, including humans. Because of its commonality across animals, behaviorists often speculated that all learning was based on classical and operant conditioning. Indeed, with respect to human verbal memory, an attempt was made to understand memory in terms of these principles; it was labeled S-R psychology for stimulus-response (Bower, 2000). By the 1960s, the S-R psychologists studying verbal learning started switching to cognitive models of memory. There were simply too many phenomena that classical and operant conditioning did not sufficiently explain and that required thinking about internal memory states to predict.

Frederic Bartlett (1886–1969)

Frederic Bartlett was a British psychologist who rejected the approach of behaviorism as well as the methodology of Ebbinghaus. In 1932, he published an important book titled *Remembering: A Study in Experimental and Social Psychology.* In contrast to Ebbinghaus, who emphasized "pure" memory uninfluenced by meaning, Bartlett considered the issue of meaning to be inseparable from the nature of human memory. As such, his studies focused on meaningful stimuli, such as stories, and how expectations could subtly distort people's memory of these stories. For example, he had Cambridge University students read Native American folktales. When the English students retold the stories, they were biased in their retelling in ways that revealed their particular cultural influences. Inexplicable and magical aspects of the story tended to be replaced by more rational versions of the stories, consistent with the mind-set of a Cambridge University student in the 1920s. Bartlett greatly influenced the increasing emphasis on real-world memory and everyday issues in memory research in the 1980s (Cohen, 1996; Wagoner, 2013), and his influence continues today. Bartlett's impact has also been felt in the recent interest in memory accuracy and its opposite, false memory. (For more information on Sir Frederic Bartlett, go to www.sagepub .com/schwartz3e.[4])

Endel Tulving (1927–)

Endel Tulving, a Canadian memory researcher, was originally born in Estonia (see Figure 1.2). Tulving served as a translator for the U.S. and Canadian armies during World War II in Germany before immigrating to Canada. There, he attended the University of Toronto. He then went to Harvard University to get his PhD. Eventually, he became a distinguished professor of psychology at the University of Toronto. Perhaps no scientist has made more meaningful and varied contributions to the science of memory than has Dr. Tulving, starting in the 1950s and continuing to the present. Taking first the perspective of cognitive psychology and later cognitive neuroscience, Tulving has introduced to the field many of the theoretical ideas

Figure 1.2   Endel Tulving.

on which all memory researchers now rely. He developed the encoding specificity principle, the idea that retrieval is better when it occurs in situations that match the conditions under which the memory was encoded.

He was also an early proponent of the idea that long-term memory involves multiple systems. When he introduced the concept of multiple systems, it was roundly criticized; today, it is universally accepted, in one form or another, by memory scientists. Tulving (1972) initially labeled these systems episodic memory (memory for personal events from one's life) and semantic memory (memory for facts). The theory has evolved considerably over the years, but the semantic/episodic distinction has stood the test of many empirical studies (Storm & Jobe, 2012; Tulving, 1983, 1993, 2002). Both episodic memory and semantic memory are considered long-term memory systems, but they differ in the content of their representations—that is, what they are about. Tulving also pioneered the study of the experience of memory, from how memories "feel" to us to the ways in which we monitor and control our own memory.

In recent years, Tulving has also become a leader in the field of cognitive neuroscience, focusing on the neural underpinnings of human memory. In this area, he has been instrumental in demonstrating the areas of the brain associated with remembering our personal past and exploring differences between the left and the right hemispheres. (For more on the life of Endel Tulving, go to study.sagepub.com/schwartz3e.[5])

Cognitive Psychology

By the 1960s, memory scientists were finding the behaviorist models unable to explain many of the phenomena that they were starting to study, including why different variables affected short-term and long-term memory (Atkinson & Shiffrin, 1968; L. R. Peterson & Peterson, 1959). Thus, memory scientists started switching from S-R models to models emanating from the new science of cognitive psychology, which emphasized the concepts of mind and internal representation of memories (Neisser, 1967). This change involved two big features. First, cognitive psychology reopened the "black box" and allowed mental processes and "mind" to become appropriate topics of study. Second, it postulated that mental states are causal, not simply the by-products of behavior.

Cognitive psychology: An approach to psychology that emphasizes hidden mental processes.

Cognitive psychology proved useful in addressing issues of language, attention, and decision-making as well as memory, and it continues to be a dominant force in psychological theory. For example, behaviorists were reluctant to address the issue of representation (or storage) in memory because it is a hidden process not directly observable through behavior. Theory in cognitive psychology has led to a variety of ways to address the issue of representation and study it through careful experimentation.

At the core of theory in early cognitive psychology was the idea of the flow of information (Atkinson & Shiffrin, 1968). For this reason, it often relied on an analogy to the computer, in which information also moves and is transformed over time. For example, the study of encoding became the study of how information is transferred from short-term memory to long-term memory and how this process unfolds over time. The idea of the flow of information remains controversial. Many modern cognitive psychologists disagree with this view, because the brain is a remarkably parallel device, doing many things at once as opposed to doing one thing at a time.

Elizabeth Loftus (1944–)

Elizabeth Loftus is an American psychologist, best known for her pioneering work on eyewitness memory and later for her work on false memory. Her groundbreaking work on the misinformation effect brought memory science into a number of applied domains, particularly into the courtroom and other legal settings. When she received her PhD from Stanford University in 1970, memory science was just emerging from behaviorist times, and most work was designed to test specific models of how memory worked in general. Loftus modified word-learning paradigms to the study of simulated crimes and accidents and tested to see if the same principles could be found both in the lab and in a more real-world setting. In her early work on the misinformation effect, Loftus showed that subtly introduced misinformation given after an event had been witnessed influenced people's memory of that witnessed event (Loftus, 1974, 1979; Loftus & Palmer, 1974). Loftus also testified in many trials, claiming that eyewitness memory may be error, thereby bringing empirical memory science into the legal systems of the United States and many other nations. Later, in the 1990s, Loftus became a leading proponent of the idea that memory is fallible in general, and that normal people have false memories (Loftus, 1992, 2004). This idea greatly impacted some forms of psychotherapy, which were based on the recovery of hidden memories. Loftus's view challenged the assumption of this approach. Loftus continues today to conduct important research on issues of memory and its implication for the legal system. To hear Loftus speak about her work, go to https://www.ted.com/speakers/elizabeth_loftus.

Cognitive Neuroscience

Cognitive neuroscience is the study of the role of the brain in producing cognition. Advances in neuroimaging techniques have led to tremendous gains in our knowledge of the biological processes involved in memory as well as the psychological processes of memory. Neuroimaging allows us to observe the intact living brain as it learns, remembers, communicates, and contemplates. The past

> **Cognitive neuroscience:** The study of the role of the brain in producing cognition.

20 years of neuroimaging research have provided great progress in understanding both the workings of the brain and why certain memory processes are the way they are.

Consider a recent study by Roland Benoit and his colleagues (Benoit, Hulbert, Huddleston, & Anderson, 2015). They were interested in the areas of the brain responsible for suppressing unwanted memories. For example, you may have embarrassed yourself by asking out a person who was not interested in you in return. When you think about this event, you may become embarrassed again, so you try not to think about it. In traumatic memories, one may not want to recall horrible things that happened, so such suppression may be critical to mental health, if a person has experienced trauma. Benoit wanted to know what was going on in the brain when people are suppressing memories.

In this study, Benoit et al. (2015) used a functional magnetic resonance imagery (fMRI), which allows the researchers to look at whether specific areas of the brain are active during particular memory activities—we will review the specifics of fMRI later in the chapter. For here, we only need to know that fMRI can pinpoint specific areas of the brain that are active while someone is engaging in a particular cognitive activity.

Benoit et al. were interested in traumatic memory—that is, memory for unpleasant events that a person may not want to actually recall. Benoit and his colleagues were also interested in why some people can suppress unwanted and unpleasant memories and why people with post-traumatic stress disorder (PTSD) cannot suppress these unwanted memories. Moreover, they were interested in the neural underpinnings of memory suppression. Thus, they asked participants to either recall or suppress the memory of specific faces or specific places while they were being monitored by the fMRI. After each trial, participants reported whether or not they had been successful at suppressing the unwanted memory (or recalling the wanted one). They found a particular area of the brain, the dorsolateral prefrontal cortex, was most active when unwanted memories occurred, even when the person was trying to suppress them. However, greater activity in this area also predicted better control over suppression on future trials. Thus, Benoit et al. concluded that the dorsolateral prefrontal cortex is an important area in the regulation—and suppression—of memory retrieval. Because the dorsolateral prefrontal cortex is also known to be involved in the regulation of many memory processes, Benoit et al. concluded that difficulty in memory suppression is a problem in the process of control over memory rather than with memory retrieval itself, a conclusion they could not have drawn from behavioral data alone. This study illustrates how cognitive neuroscience can tell us more than just information about where things happen in the brain: It can also tell us about how cognitive processes work. This dual nature of cognitive neuroscience makes it important from a psychological perspective as well as from a neurological one.

Cognitive neuroscience research such as this has great promise of answering many questions, both neurological and psychological. Nonetheless, a word of caution is needed here. All psychological scientists agree that the brain is responsible for cognitive processes. Thus, it is not surprising that particular brain processes are correlated with particular aspects of memory. It has to be so. From the point of view of cognitive neuroscience, it is important to know what those brain processes are and exactly how they correlate with memory. However, cognitive psychology endeavors to understand memory at the functional level—that is, how it works in terms of psychological processes. Thus, cognitive psychologists may not always find brain process research relevant to their understanding of the mind. The Benoit study is interesting from a psychological process, because it also implies that suppression is an attentional/control phenomenon rather than an automatic retrieval phenomenon. In this textbook, we take a "memory-science" perspective in which we draw from all psychological sciences that deal with memory. From this perspective, understanding brain processes involved in memory is important.

Figure 1.3   An MRI of a human brain. The top layer is the cerebral cortex. Also visible is the corpus callosum, which joins the left and right hemisphere.

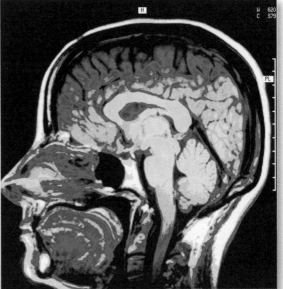

Thinkstock

Section Quiz

1. Empirical evidence is
   a. Generally recommended practices in employing recall to improve memory
   b. Any correlational analysis
   c. Data generated from experiments
   d. Dependent measures in psychological experimentation

2. Which of these historical figures is associated with discovering the savings score?
   a. Hermann Ebbinghaus
   b. Elizabeth Loftus
   c. Frederic Bartlett
   d. Mary Calkins

3. Endel Tulving is associated with which of these ideas?
   a. The semantic episodic memory distinction
   b. The study of how memories are experienced by us
   c. The encoding specificity
   d. All of the above

4. An approach to memory that emphasizes hidden mental processes is
   a. Behaviorism
   b. Cognitive Psychology
   c. Black box empiricism
   d. Double-blind procedures

5. A scientist who wants to understand the role of the certain areas of the brain in understanding memory would be most influenced by which approach to memory?
   a. Behaviorism
   b. Cognitive neuroscience
   c. Philosophy
   d. None of the above

1. c
2. a
3. d
4. b
5. b

METHODS OF STUDYING MEMORY

We all feel familiar with the workings of our own memories. One individual might report that she never remembers her family members' birthdays. Another individual might tell you that he is not good at remembering faces. Yet a third will tell you that she has "photographic memory" and can simply look at a page on a textbook and recite all the information on it from memory (this is typically illusory, but more on that in Chapter 6). As memory scientists, however, we cannot simply rely on people's stories and anecdotes. Instead, we conduct experiments, which measure memory abilities under different conditions. We test to see if all those who claim to have photographic memories really can remember what is on a page of text after one or more casual glances. We test to see how good people are, in general, at recognizing faces and then can objectively tell your friend whether he is indeed above or below the average in remembering faces. In short, to study memory objectively, we must apply the scientific method. By applying the scientific method, we can make generalizations about how memory works in human beings and get reasonable estimates of measurable individual differences. The key to this enterprise is the experiment.

An **experiment** is set of observations that occur under controlled circumstances determined by the experimenter. *Controlled circumstances* means that the researcher strives to maintain a situation in which he or she has control over what a participant sees, hears, or can potentially remember. The control

Experiment: Set of observations that occur under controlled circumstances determined by the experimenter.

allows the researcher to focus on one select issue at a time. Thus, a researcher interested in distributed practice and massed practice will conduct an experiment to determine which condition results in better memory performance. By keeping other conditions constant, the researcher can determine whether distributed practice is truly better than massed practice.

The experimenter does this by looking at the effects of independent variables on dependent variables. **Independent variables** are the factors that the experimenter manipulates across different conditions. To use a hypothetical example, if an experimenter is interested in whether coffee containing caffeine can improve memory, he or she can manipulate the amount of coffee given to individuals in different groups of participants. In this example, the amount of coffee consumed is the independent variable. Each group receives the same list of words to remember. Thus, one group of people does not get

> **Independent variables:** Independent variables are the factors that the experimenter manipulates across different conditions.

any coffee in advance of studying the list of words; this group is called the control group. A second group gets one cup of coffee before studying the list. And a third group gets four cups of coffee. The second and third groups are considered the experimental groups and are compared to each other and to the control group. Another way of saying this is that the experiment has an independent variable (amount of coffee consumed) with three levels (zero cups, one cup, and four cups). Sometime after the participants study the list, we test them to see how many words they can remember.

Dependent variables are the observations that we measure or record in response to the independent variable. In the coffee experiment, the dependent variable is the number of words the participants recall from the study list. As memory researchers, we are interested in the effects of the independent variable (amount of coffee consumed) on the dependent variable (number of words remembered). So we measure the number of words remembered for each participant

> **Dependent variables:** Dependent variables are the observations that we measure or record in response to the independent variable.

in each condition. We can then statistically compare the outcomes in each condition. This statistical comparison can inform us whether coffee (i.e., one cup) helps us remember words on lists and whether too much coffee (i.e., four cups) makes us too jittery to concentrate on anything (see Figure 1.4). In memory science, we will see a few dependent variables used extensively in the work described in this book. These dependent variables include recall, recognition, reaction time, and a variety of judgments (to be introduced soon).

A number of features must be included in an experiment to make it a good scientific study. First, **random assignment** means that any particular person is equally likely to be assigned to any of the conditions. Usually, a random-number generator assigns a given individual to one of the possible groups. In the coffee experiment, you would not want to put the people whom you know are good at memory in the four-cup condition,

> **Random assignment:** Any particular participant is equally likely to be assigned to any of the conditions.

Figure 1.4 Graph of memory as a function of caffeine consumed. This graph shows a potential hypothetical outcome. A small amount of caffeine boosts memory, but a larger amount hurts memory. In fact, research shows that caffeine can hurt memory even at relatively small amounts. The y-axis is the number of words recalled.

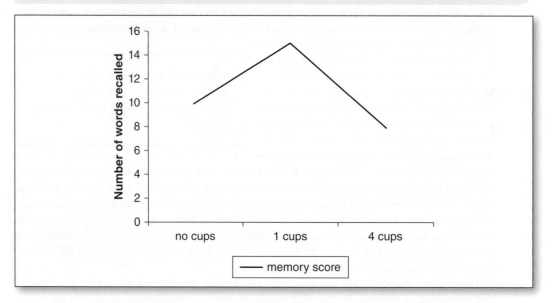

as their propensity to remember well would bias the results. You want a representative sample of people who are good and poor at memory in each condition. The best way to do this is to assign each person randomly to one of the conditions. Second, the participants should not know what you expect to find in the experiment until after the experiment is over. Even the most honest participants may slightly alter their concentration or attention to satisfy (or perhaps disrupt) the experiment if they know what the experimenter wants to find. Third, as best as possible, the person actually running the experiment should not know what condition each participant is in. The person administering the memory test to the coffee drinkers should not know if an individual had zero, one, or four cups of coffee, as this knowledge might introduce subtle bias into the experiment. These last two concerns inform what is called a **double-blind procedure**, in which neither the tester nor the participant knows what condition the participant is in.

Double-blind procedure: Experimental structure in which neither the tester nor the participant knows what condition that participant is in.

When these conditions are met, our experiment will test only the independent variable or variables that we are interested in studying. We can be sure that other extraneous factors have been controlled for by randomizing the assignment of participants to conditions and by keeping both the participants and the experimenters unaware of what condition participants are in. This allows us to be confident that any differences we get between conditions are a function of the independent variable. Then, we can safely draw conclusions about the effects of caffeine on the learning of a list of words.

In memory research, it is crucial to have good dependent measures. Thus, scientists have developed a large set of memory measures so that researchers can choose the right dependent variable for their experiment. The next section will review these common measures, which we will see throughout the book.

MEMORY MEASURES

Recall

Recall means that a person must generate the target memory. That is, **recall** is the production of a memory or a part of one that was not already presented. For recall, a person must speak or write the remembered items without seeing them in advance. In some cases, a recall test might involve re-enacting a physical event as well. Recall can be **free recall**, in which you are given a global cue to remember a particular memory or set of memories. "Tell me about your childhood," "What were all the words on the study list?" "Write two paragraphs about the Peloponnesian War," and "Describe everything you saw at the scene of the crime," are examples of prompts for free recall. The cue "Tell me about your childhood," provides no information about one's childhood. Thus, all the information recalled

> **Recall:** A person must generate the target memory based on cues, without seeing or hearing the actual target memory.

> **Free recall:** A person must generate memories with minimal or no cuing of the memories.

is freely selected by the rememberer. In memory experiments, free recall is more likely to be of the "Write down all the words from the study list," variety.

A second variant of recall is often used in memory experiments. **Cued recall** occurs when you are given a specific cue to remember a specific memory. Cued recall includes questions like "What is your middle initial?" "What word went with *pasture* on the study list?" "In what year was the Greek philosopher Aristotle born?" and "What color car were the bank robbers driving?" Cued recall is also a common technique in memory experiments. It is useful in looking at association in memory—that is, the connection between two ideas of two memories. Thus, for a student learning French, a person must

> **Cued recall:** A person is given a specific cue and must generate a target memory that corresponds to that cue.

associate the English and the French words, as in *walnut–le noyer*. In a cued recall test, you might receive the English word (*walnut*) and be asked to recall the French word.

Recognition

Recognition means matching one's memory to a presented choice. Rather than having to produce the item itself, the person must match what is stored in memory with what he or she sees on a list. Recognition can be **old/new recognition**, in which the person has to decide whether an item was on the study list. If the participants saw the word *pasture* on the study list, they would need to indicate that by saying "old," whereas if the participants had not seen the word, they would indicate that by saying "new." Recognition can also be **forced-choice recognition**, also known as *multiple-choice recognition*. In this case, a question is asked with a series of possible answers. Using the earlier examples, we could ask a recognition question such as "In what year was Aristotle born? (a) 502 CE, (b) 5 CE, (c) 384 BCE, (d) 672 BCE." (The correct answer is 384 BCE.) A police lineup is technically a recognition test, as the witness can see all of the possible suspects. Most police lineups, however, are not forced. The witness can say "not there" if none of the suspects match his or her memory. To summarize, the key difference between recall and recognition is that in recall, the person must generate the memory, whereas in recognition, the person must match what is in his or her memory with what he or she sees in front of them.

> **Recognition:** Person must identify the target memory from among a set of presented item(s).

> **Old/new recognition:** Person must decide whether an item was on the study list.

> **Forced-choice recognition:** Person must identify the answer from among a series of possible answers.

Implicit Memory Tests

Implicit memory tests draw on the nonconscious aspects of memory. Memory is tested without the person being conscious of the fact that his or her memory is being assessed. In some cases, the participant may not have conscious access to the memory at all, although this is not required for the task to be classified as implicit.

> **Implicit memory tests:** Tests that draw on the non-conscious aspects of memory.

To give an example, something as simple as a spelling test can be used as an implicit memory test. Eich (1984) presented two streams of stimuli, one to each ear of his participants. The participants were directed to attend to one of the two stimuli and to ignore the other. Decades of research on attention demonstrate that people are very good at focusing on one message and ignoring the other. However, in Eich's study, the focus was on implicit memory, not attention. Eich showed that in a test of free recall, the participants remembered very little to nothing at all of the unattended stimuli. In contrast, Eich found that, even though participants could not consciously recall the items presented to the unattended ear, there must have been some non-conscious processing of those items, because the processing biased their spelling of homophones (words with different meanings that sound the same but are spelled differently). Some of the items presented to the ignored ear were sentences such as "The men took photographs of the grizzly bear," and "The fencers flashed their swords of cold steel at each other." During the spelling test, participants were read aloud words to spell, including *bare/bear* and *steal/steel*. No instructions were given as to how to choose which of two spellings they should use. Participants who had heard these words in the unattended ear were more likely to spell them according to the context in which they had heard them, even though they could not consciously remember having heard the words. Relative to control participants who had not heard the words being presented to the unattended ear, those who had were more likely to spell *steal/steel* as *steel* and *bear/bare* as *bear*. Thus, even though the participants could not consciously recall what the words were, exposure to the words affected their performance in an implicit memory test. This increase (or decrease) in performance based on some prior processing is known as *priming* (see Jacoby, 1991). Such priming of implicit memory is often important in helping patients with impaired memory (Redondo et al., 2015).

Reaction Time

Reaction time is the measured amount of time required to perform a particular task. Different tasks will require different amounts of time to perform, revealing the time course of the underlying processes. Reaction time varies as a function of the number or difficulty of the underlying memory processes (Sternberg, 1969). Sprinters reacting to a starter's pistol initiate their sprint in less than 200 milliseconds.

> **Reaction time:** the measured amount of time required to perform a particular task.

Hitting a button as fast as possible if it is red may take about 200 to 400 milliseconds, but hitting a button if it is the same color as what you just saw may take a bit longer. The reaction time to determining whether a series of letters, such as potchbork, is a word or not may take nearly one second (Popov & Hristova, 2015). Thus, longer reaction times usually reflect more internal cognitive processing. With respect to retrieval from memory, Dewhurst and Conway (1994) looked at reaction times of old/new recognition judgments. They measured how long it took to decide whether or not a word had appeared in the experiment earlier. They found that if people felt as though they "remembered" the items from the earlier list, they had faster reaction times than if they felt as though they "knew" the items were from the earlier list. We will discuss the remember/know distinction later in Chapter 4.

Source Judgments

Source judgments are our attributions of where or from whom we learned something rather than the memory content itself. For example, a student may recall that it was the teaching assistant and not the professor who told her that a particular chapter would be on the exam. Or a person may recall that she imagined winning the U.S. Open Tennis tournament rather than recalling actually having done so in real life. With source

> **Source judgments:** Our attributions of where or from whom we learned something.

judgments, the task is to identify who told you the fact, not necessarily to remember the event or fact itself. In some cases, we may remember an event or fact but not remember the source. Thus, I know that the first European settlers introduced rabbits to Australia. However, I cannot recall who told me this, where I read it, or when or where I may have seen this on a television nature show. However, in many cases, remembering the source is vital to your appraisal of the memory. Consider a situation in which, while gossiping with a friend, you mention that the actress Jennifer Lawrence is having a baby. Your friend asks, "Where did you hear that?" In such gossip, the source of a memory is important. If you read it in a tabloid newspaper, such as the *National Enquirer,* it may be of dubious validity. However, if you saw it on CNN, it is more likely to be true (but no more your business).

Researchers test source judgments by asking people from whom they heard information (Foley & Foley, 2007). In some experiments, for example, two individuals, one male and one female, read a list of words. The two readers alternate, with one reading one word and the other reading the next word. Later, participants must recall not only the words but also which speaker said which one. Related to source judgments is the concept of **reality monitoring**. Reality monitoring refers to our ability to distinguish whether our memory is of a real or an imagined event. Each of us may have memories of fantasies (dating a movie star or being elected president, for example), but it is important to recognize these memories as being internally generated rather than based on real events. Recently, there has been work on whether we can identify whether other peoples' memories are real or imagined (Clark-Foos, Brewer, & Marsh, 2015).

> **Reality monitoring:** Our ability to distinguish whether our memory is of a real or an imagined event.

Metamemory Judgments

Metamemory means our knowledge and awareness of our own memory processes. Metamemory judgments are the ratings or decisions we make concerning what we know about our memory processes. Metamemory includes our knowledge of our own strengths and weaknesses about our memory. For example, when you say, "I am good at remembering faces," you are making a metamemory statement. A tip-of-the-tongue state is also a metamemory judgment; we are confident that an unrecalled word will be recalled (Cleary & Claxton, 2015). Usually, in memory experiments, the metamemory judgments refer to whether we think we can learn or retrieve a particular item. **Judgments of learning** are predictions of the likelihood of remembering an item that we make as we study the items. We can ascertain if these judgments are accurate by later correlating them with actual memory performance. Other metamemory judgments include ease-of-learning judgments, confidence judgments, feelings of knowing, and as noted, tip-of-the-tongue states. Metamemory will be covered extensively in Chapter 9.

> **Metamemory:** Our knowledge and awareness of our own memory processes.

> **Judgments of learning:** Predictions we make as we study items of the likelihood that we will remember them later.

Summary of Memory Measures

These six categories (recall, recognition, implicit memory tests, reaction times, source judgments, metamemory judgments) make up the vast majority of measures that memory scientists use to study human memory. Almost every behavioral experiment that we will cover in this book makes use of one of these six techniques. So make sure you know what they are and what they mean now! The next three methods are drawn from the neuroscience/neuroimaging perspective on memory research.

Neuropsychology

Neuropsychology is the study of patients with brain damage. The study of patients with brain damage has a long and distinguished history (Feinberg & Farah, 2000). As mentioned earlier, ancient Egyptian doctors noted that blows to specific areas of the head resulted in characteristic behavioral change. Nowadays, the goal of neuropsychological research is to correlate the specific area of brain damage with

> **Neuropsychology:** The study of patients with brain damage.

the cognitive or behavioral deficits seen in a particular patient. For example, damage to an area of the brain called the hippocampus can cause amnesia. Damage to an area of the brain called Broca's area causes deficits in the ability to produce speech. You can see the change in language behaviors based on damage to Broca's area (go to study.sagepub.com/schwartz3e[6]).

For many patients, the damage is too wide, too diffuse, or too minor to be of interest to research neuropsychologists. But if the damage is relatively restricted, whatever behavioral changes occur in a patient can be linked to that area of the brain. For example, those patients with damage to the hippocampus (a small part of the brain in the limbic system) will show deficits in learning new information but not in retrieving information that is already well learned. Thus, we can conclude that the hippocampus is involved in the encoding of new events. Other patients might have damage restricted to areas of the right frontal lobe, which will result in difficulties in remembering the source of information. We will discuss several famous neuropsychological patients in Chapter 2. By probing the nature of brain damage, we can develop a model of the relation between a particular brain region and memory function.

Animal Models

Many animals, including most mammals and birds, have complex brains. Many of the structures involved in memory are common across these animals. For example, the hippocampus is involved in memory in both mammals and birds, even though their common ancestor lived long before the dinosaurs went extinct. Animals can be used in simple behavioral experiments, because in general, their memory systems are less complex than ours. In the past, animals, particularly rats and rhesus monkeys, have been used for single-cell recording. In single-cell recording, electrodes are inserted into individual neurons in the animal's brain so that researchers can determine what kinds of stimuli elicit responses in a given cell. Animals have also been used for lesion studies, in which parts of their brain are surgically removed. Because both of these methods involve invasive and potentially painful procedures, they are now used only for medically critical experiments.

Neuroimaging

Neuroimaging techniques are advanced technologies that allow researchers to visually examine intact human brains as well as injured brains. This area has seen marked growth in recent years; it will be briefly introduced here but covered in much greater depth in Chapter 2. Neuroimaging techniques allow scientists to correlate cognition and behavior with function in normal, active brains. In fact, neuroimaging techniques allow us to trace the flow of information in the brain as individual people think. As of yet, researchers cannot tell what a person is thinking, but when a person reports what he or she is thinking, reliable correlations seem to exist between that person's reports and particular parts of the brain as well as the connections between them. Neuroimaging techniques have been used to investigate memory, perception, language, and emotion.

> **Neuroimaging:** Refers to a set of techniques that allows researchers to make detailed maps of the human brain and assign functions to particular regions in the brain.

Two goals of neuroimaging are to determine where things happen in the brain and how they unfold over time. To determine where in the brain a particular process is occurring, scientists can use neuroimaging to develop detailed spatial maps of the brain showing which areas are active during which cognitive task. To determine the flow of activity in the brain over time, scientists can use neuroimaging to take pictures of the brain in quick succession to determine the time course of processes. Examining the relation between brain processes and memory processes has led to a greater understanding of both how the brain works and the cognitive underpinnings of memory.

The field of neuroimaging is rapidly evolving, but five of the major techniques are reviewed here. It is important to note, however, that PET technology is rapidly being replaced by the better (and safer) MRI technologies. We will explore these techniques in greater depth in Chapter 2, but introducing them here will help you, via distributed learning (discussed earlier in this chapter in the section on Ebbinghaus), to understand them when you encounter them again later.

1. **EEG (electroencephalography).** In EEG, often as many as 128 electrodes are placed on various places on the scalp. Each electrode can then pick up an electrical signal from the brain's total electrical output. Because areas of the brain that are active will generate more electric output than those that are not active, we can see where things are happening in the brain by comparing these outputs. The electrodes pick up a continuous electric signal, so measurements can be made very quickly, on the order of every millisecond (1/1,000th of a second). Therefore, EEG provides an excellent way of measuring the changes that happen in the brain as a person engages in a memory task. In many memory science applications, EEGs are recorded repeatedly in response to specific stimuli. These recordings are then averaged to create an event-related potential (ERP). Many cognitive tasks produce ERP-identifiable patterns that mark a particular cognitive task.

> **EEG (electroencephalography):** Using electrodes to measure the electrical output of the brain by recording electric current at the scalp.

2. **MEG (magnetoencephalography).**
A magnetic sensor detects the small magnetic fields that are produced by the electrical activity in the brain. In this way, MEG is
similar to EEG in that it can detect rapid
changes in the brain, although its temporal
resolution is less than that of EEG. However,

> **MEG (magnetoencephalography):** Using
> a magnetic sensor to detect the small
> magnetic fields produced by electrical
> activity in the brain.

because the magnetic fields are less distorted by other parts of the body (e.g., bone), MEG
can produce better spatial maps of the brain than can EEG, though not as good as fMRI.
MEG is useful today because it represents a compromise between good spatial resolution
and good temporal resolution.

3. **PET (positron emission tomography).** PET is rapidly being replaced by fMRI and is
included here mainly for historical purposes. In PET, a small amount of radioactive tracer is
injected into a person's bloodstream. The tracer travels to all areas of the body, including the
brain. Areas of the brain that are active require
more blood than areas that are resting. This is
a fundamental assumption of neuroimaging—
that blood flows to areas of the brain that are
active. Therefore, more radioactivity will be
drawn to active regions of the brain. A complex X-ray-like camera measures the radioactive emissions and determines where they are

> **PET (positron emission tomography):**
> Radioactive chemicals are placed in the
> blood, allowing scientists to obtain a
> three-dimensional image of the intact
> brain.

coming from in the brain. From this, researchers can determine what areas of the brain are active
during different memory processes. PET is very good at making spatial maps of the brain and
pinpointing where in the brain activity is taking place. However, successive images can be made
only every 30 seconds, so it is not helpful in determining the flow of information in the brain.

4. **MRI** and **fMRI** (magnetic resonance imagery and **functional magnetic resonance
imagery**). In these techniques, people are put in large magnetic fields that align the molecules in the brain. Then, as blood flows into areas of the brain, the molecules' organization
is disrupted. A specialized camera detects this disruption. The fMRI technique traces oxygen
molecules in the blood, measuring which
areas of the brain are more active during any
particular cognitive task. Because fMRI can
take a picture every 50 milliseconds, the
researcher can determine both where in
the brain a particular memory function is
taking place and how it changes over time

> **fMRI (functional magnetic resonance
> imagery):** Magnetic fields create a three-
> dimensional image that can capture both
> the structure and function of the brain.

(Boyacioğlu & Barth, 2013). Thus, fMRI has an advantage over EEG, MEG, and PET, although
it is still slower than EEG and MEG. It is safer than PET because no radioactivity is involved.
In fact, research suggests there are no health risks associated with having an MRI. Its only
current drawbacks are its expense and that you cannot place an electronic device, such as
a computer, into the magnetic field without destroying the electronic device. This requires
scientists to obtain data from participants using a variety of mirrors and levers. (For a video
clip showing fMRI, go to study.sagepub.com/schwartz3e.[7])

TMS (transmagnetic stimulation): Using a magnetic coil to electrically stimulate particular areas of the brain. This stimulation causes cognitive changes in the participant.

5. **Transmagnetic Stimulation (TMS).** There are a number of technologies that we are grouping under the general label of TMS. All of these techniques stimulate the brain by electric current. In TMS, a magnetic field generator, often called a coil, is placed on the head of a willing participant. The coil induces electric currents in the region of the brain beneath the coil. TMS has a number of clinical applications, which we will discuss in the next chapter (Hickin, Mehta, & Dipper, 2015). For research, researchers can apply TMS to various parts of the head and observe the behavioral changes in the participant. These changes are relatively mild and short-lived, but allow researchers to experimentally examine brain region and function. In most cases, once the current is removed, the changes in cognition disappear, and there do not appear to be any long-term negative effects of TMS. For example, Pergolizzi and Chua (2015) using direct current TMS stimulated the parietal lobes of their participants. While under stimulation, the participants were more likely to falsely recognize words, as being seen previously, that were related in meaning to words seen earlier, but had not been seen earlier themselves.

Figure 1.5   Person having MRI. Despite appearances, having an MRI is painless. Without introducing any harm, the MRI can produce a detailed image of the intact human brain.

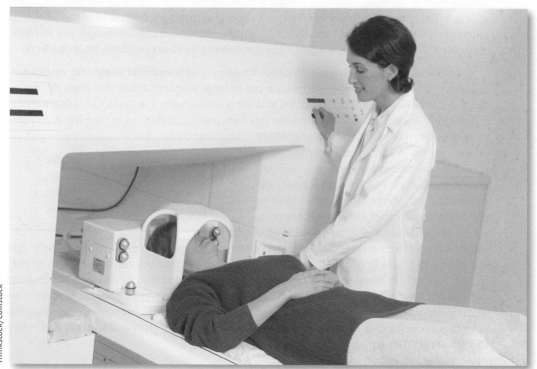

Thinkstock/Comstock

That is, participants were more likely to say that the word "lawyer" was on the list when they had seen the word "attorney" when they were getting TMS stimulation than when not. One of the important advantages that TMS technology has over other technologies is that the researcher has experimental control over where the TMS is applied. Thus, changes that result in a person's cognition are caused by the TMS. In fMRI, we can only correlate changes in cognition with changes in brain state. For a video clip of TMS, go to https://www .youtube.com/watch?v = xLiHRG9I9W4.

Throughout the book, we will be discussing research generated from each of these neuroimaging techniques. The fMRI technique is currently the state of the art in neuroimaging. It is providing insight into the workings of the brain not just for memory but for almost all areas of human thinking and emotion (see Figure 1.5).

Section Summary and Quiz

1. In a memory experiment, the researcher varies the amount of study time given to participants and measures how much they remember as a function of study time. Amount of study time is the _____, and how much they remember is the _____.
    a. Experiment; recognition quotient
    b. Independent variable; dependent variable
    c. Reaction time; source judgment
    d. Random assignment; experimental control

2. In an experiment, a participant is asked to determine on which of two projectors they saw a particular video. This task must map onto
    a. Recall
    b. Neuropsychology
    c. Source monitoring
    d. Implicit memory testing

3. A researcher induces a mild electric current into the frontal lobe of the brain of a participant in order to determine if source monitoring is affected. This technique is called
    a. Transmagnetic cranial stimulation
    b. Functional magnetic resonance imagery
    c. Positron emission tomography
    d. Neuropsychological testing

4. A person must decide if a word, such as *pasture*, was seen on an earlier list of words. This method is called
    a. Free recall
    b. Old/new recognition
    c. The tip-of-the-tongue phenomenon
    d. Reality monitoring

5. Judgments of learning are
   a. A neuroimaging technique that allows one to measure the brain directly
   b. A measure of free recall
   c. Predictions we make as we study items about future remembering
   d. Our ability to distinguish whether our memory is of a real or imagined event

1. b
2. c
3. a
4. b
5. c

IMPROVING MEMORY EFFICIENCY

One of the themes of this book is that you can use the principles advanced here to improve the efficiency of your own learning and remembering. Memory science has found a great many ways in which learning efficiency can be improved and memory can be enhanced. However, the first point to be made is that there is no memory magic bullet—no one sentence that I write will transform you, the reader, into a mnemonic marvel. Nor is there a pill that your doctor can prescribe that will radically improve your ability to remember information. To state bluntly a point that will be repeated throughout the book: Improving memory efficiency is hard work! Yet the hard work can be directed in thoughtful and informed ways to be more efficient. Memory science knows much about what makes for good learning and good remembering. The informed student can apply much of this information to his or her schoolwork or other aspects of daily life that require remembering.

When discussing memory improvement, it is important to begin with a discussion of types of memory. Chapter 3 will outline the current theories concerning how many different memory systems human beings have. Although there is some debate as to exactly where to draw the lines between one memory system and another, it is now abundantly clear that not all memory is alike. Indeed, the research suggests that there are a number of systems of memory with different neurological underpinnings (Schacter, 2007; Sun, 2012). For example, the learning and remembering required to play the violin is very different from the learning and remembering required to master the rules of spoken German (or any other language). The rules that govern remembering the individual events from our lives are quite different from the learning and remembering of facts in school. Thus, the principles that govern memory improvement are going to differ between one domain and another. Visual imagery mnemonics, for example, are useful for mastering new-language vocabulary (Thomas & Wang, 1996) but of little use in learning to play a new musical instrument. Similarly, linkword mnemonics are useful in learning name-face associations, but they will not help you remember the name of your kindergarten teacher when somebody asks you many years later. Having said that, a number of principles do apply across a wide domain of memory systems. The spacing effect, described in the section in this chapter on Ebbinghaus, is one such example. Spaced rehearsal is helpful for remembering facts about the world, learning a skilled task such as typing or playing a musical instrument, and remembering landmark events from one's life.

MNEMONIC IMPROVEMENT TIP 1.3

There is no magic bullet for memory. Good memory requires hard work.

Although students are usually concerned about ways in which they can improve their ability to remember school-based information, older adults are often more concerned about the failings of another aspect of memory, known as prospective memory. Prospective memory is memory for the things we need to do in the future. This is not some weird science fiction–type thing. It refers to the fact that we need to remember our future plans. Parents have to remember to pick up their kids at school, employees have to remember to pick up the mail from the mailroom, chefs have to remember exactly what time to take the soufflé out of the oven, and someone better remember to take out the garbage. And perhaps most important, individuals requiring medication must remember to take their medication at the prescribed time of day. In other words, prospective memory is about remembering intentions (McDaniel & Einstein, 2007; Oates, Peynircioğlu, & Bates, 2015). For example, McDaniel and Einstein made a series of recommendations as to how we can improve our prospective memory. However, most of their recommendations involve the extensive use of external cues. If you need to remember to pick up your kids at school (perhaps normally your spouse's task), you can carry around a photograph of them, perhaps by placing it in your pocket where you will keep coming across it. The constant reminder will help you to remember your intention even if you are a chef and busy with your soufflé. Similarly, if you have to remember to return a particular book to the library, place it by your car keys the night before. When you look for your keys to drive to school, you will also find the book you need to return to the library. Once you are in your car, place it in the passenger seat so you will see it and won't drive to school or work without stopping at the library. (For further information on this topic, go to study.sagepub.com/schwartz3e.[8])

Prospective memory: Memory for the things we need to do in the future.

We can improve the efficiency of our learning and remembering. In this book, I hope to offer a number of ways in which memory science has shown that memory can be made more efficient. However, I will reiterate the following point: Memory improvement is an active process. It doesn't just happen; we have to work to make it happen. We must think about how to distribute our learning; it requires a little planning. And taking advantage of external cues also requires us to work a little. We have to think about our routines and use them to our advantage.

In the last section of this chapter, I will present four themes, which will be returned to repeatedly throughout the book. Each theme represents an important concept in memory theory and practice. (For further information on this topic, go to www.sagepub .com/schwartz3e.[9])

MNEMONIC IMPROVEMENT TIP 1.4

External cues can help. But external cues require action. You must place them in your environment.

THEMES FOR THE BOOK

1. **Learning and remembering are active processes**. Human beings are learning animals. Learning is what we do best. Human beings can learn to knit sweaters in intricate patterns, and we can learn to negotiate small kayaks down ferocious white-water rapids that would drown the untrained person. Some human beings memorize the Bible or the Koran, whereas others can tell you the complex ingredients of a crème brûlée. But little if any of this learning happens passively. The person who learns and remembers best is the person who seeks out opportunities to learn, who rehearses the information, and who teaches it to others. Throughout this book, I will make note of how the active learner who employs strategies, relates information to himself or herself, organizes information, and employs metamemory strategies winds up learning a lot more than those who do not.

2. **Learning and remembering have a biological/neurological basis**. Our brains are our biological organ of learning and remembering. The past two decades, with the advent of neuroimaging, have seen tremendous growth in our understanding of how the brain works, particularly with respect to learning and memory. Our understanding of behavior, memory, and cognition has guided much of this neuroscience research, and in turn, neuroscience is now guiding the questions we ask of our memory systems. Chapter 2 will provide an overview of what we know of the neurological basis of memory, and then each chapter will discuss the specifics of a particular aspect of memory and how it plays out in the brain.

3. **Memory has multiple components, which act in different ways**. We have many different kinds of memory. We have memory for the individual events from our lives, for the words of our native languages, for the geography of our home and surrounding areas, and for the music we love. We hold some memories, like the phone number of the pizza place as we dial it, for very short periods of time; other memories, such as of a friend's wedding ceremony or the time you hit a home run in Little League, may last a lifetime. We have different neurocognitive systems to handle these different kinds of memory. Chapters 3 and 4 will explore the nature of these memory systems.

4. **The efficiency of learning and remembering can be improved**. By applying many of the facts, theories, and ideas of memory science, we can improve our ability to learn and remember. Many of these techniques involve managing our existing resources and efficiently using our time. We can apply a number of principles consciously to our efforts both to learn information and to remember it. Each chapter will offer memory hints, based on the research discussed, as to how you can improve some aspect of learning and remembering. And then, in Chapter 13, an entire chapter will be spent on this topic.

SUMMARY

Understanding the science and practice of memory is the overarching goal of this book. Memory is an essential component of our cognitive systems and indeed our sense of who we are. This book addresses the science of memory, what we know from both cognitive psychology and cognitive neuroscience. In both domains, established methodologies allow us to analyze and think about memory research. From this research, we can draw practical applications that will allow each of us to improve and make more efficient our own learning. We also reviewed the history of the field, starting with the seminal work of Hermann Ebbinghaus. Ebbinghaus established a number of key findings, including some that benefit memory performance. Following Ebbinghaus, other scientists such as Mary Calkins, Frederic Bartlett, Endel Tulving, and Elizabeth Loftus defined the future of memory along with bigger schools of thought, such as behaviorism, cognitive psychology, and cognitive neuroscience. This chapter also reviewed the fundamental techniques used to study memory from behavioral measures—such as recall, recognition, and metamemory judgments—to neuroscience methods—such as fMRI, EEG, and TMS. Four overarching themes were introduced, focusing on the active nature of learning and remembering, its status as a biological process, the multiple systems that comprise it, and the principles of learning and remembering we can use to improve our individual ability to learn and remember. With this in mind, we will begin our exploration of the fascinating world of human memory.

KEY TERMS

behaviorism	dependent variables	experiment
classical conditioning	distributed practice	fMRI (functional magnetic resonance imagery)
cognitive neuroscience	double-blind procedure	
cognitive psychology	EEG (electroencephalography)	forced-choice recognition
cued recall	empirical evidence	free recall

forgetting curve	nonsense syllables	reality monitoring
implicit memory tests	old/new recognition	recall
independent variables	operant conditioning	recency effect
judgments of learning	overlearning	recognition
massed practice	paired-associate learning	retention interval
MEG (magnetoencephalography)	PET (positron emission tomography)	savings score
metamemory	prospective memory	spacing effect
neuroimaging	random assignment	source judgments
neuropsychology	reaction time	TMS (transmagnetic stimulation)

REVIEW QUESTIONS

1. Who was Hermann Ebbinghaus, and what were his important contributions to memory science?

2. How can the spacing effect be used to improve memory?

3. How did the contributions of the science of behaviorism and cognitive psychology to modern understanding of memory differ?

4. What are the key components of a memory experiment?

5. What is the difference between recall and recognition?

6. What are source judgments? What are metamemory judgments?

7. How does studying neuropsychological patients aid in understanding the nature of memory and the brain?

8. Describe three techniques of neuroimaging? What are the advantages and disadvantages of each?

9. What is prospective memory?

10. What are the four themes of the book? Why are they important?

ONLINE RESOURCES

1. For a good website on the general philosophy of science, go to http://teacher.pas.rochester.edu/phy_labs/appendixe/appendixe.html.

2. For Hermann Ebbinghaus's book, see http://psychclassics.yorku.ca/Ebbinghaus/.

3. For more on Mary Calkins, go to http://www.webster.edu/ ~ woolflm/marycalkins.html.

4. For more on Frederic Bartlett, go to http://www.bartlett.psychol.cam.ac.uk.

5. For more on Endel Tulving, go to http://www.science.ca/scientists/scientistprofile.php?pID = 20.

6. To hear Loftus speak about her work, go to https://www.ted.com/speakers/elizabeth_loftus.

7. See a patient with Broca's aphasia at http://www.youtube.com/watch?v = f2IiMEbMnPM.

8. For an in-depth discussion of fMRI, go to http://science.howstuffworks.com/fmri.htm.

9. For a glimpse of TMS, see https://www.youtube.com/watch?v = xLiHRG9l9W4.

10. For the latest on memory research, go to http://www.human-memory.net.

11. For the latest research on applications of memory, go to http://www.sarmac.org.

Go to **study.sagepub.com/schwartz3e** for additional exercises and study resources. Select **Chapter 1, Introduction to the Study of Memory**, for chapter-specific resources.

Memory and the Brain

The word *brain* means different things to different people. In everyday usage, the word *brain* is nearly synonymous with the word *mind*. We say that we have something "in our brain," meaning we have been thinking about something. You call someone a "brain" if you think that his or her intelligence is that person's chief characteristic. Underlying this metaphor is the certainty that the brain is the biological organ responsible for thinking, memory, reasoning, and language. In this chapter, we will explore the science of how the brain produces memory. It is important, however, to keep in mind that our use of the word "brain" refers to the neural structures maintained inside the head and not to the various metaphorical roles that the word "brain" has acquired.

For a neurosurgeon, the brain is a mass of soft tissue inside the head that has to be handled very carefully when damaged. The brain itself has no pain receptors, so neurosurgeons are less concerned about anesthesia than other doctors. However, the brain is surrounded and infused with 400 miles of blood vessels, so surgeons must be very careful when probing the brain, lest they accidentally induce a hemorrhage. Neurosurgeons understand the critical nature of the human brain for what it is to be human, yet for a surgeon, its identity is as a biological tissue that needs to be treated very carefully.

For a cognitive neuroscientist, the brain is a complex assortment of separate areas and regions, each of which has its own unique function. For example, the prefrontal regions are for planning, thinking, and monitoring, whereas the back of the brain processes vision. The temporal lobe is involved in memory and language, whereas the parietal lobe directs attention. Increasingly, cognitive neuroscience is also considering the role of the various white-matter tracts that connect different regions of the brain, and this is considerably enhancing our understanding of the brain (Dick, Bernal, Tremblay, 2014). Viewed this way, the brain is not really one organ but many dozens of distinct regions, each with its own appearance, its own microanatomy, its own set of connections to other areas, and its own function.

Behind each way of looking at the brain, however, is the assumption that the biological organ located inside the skull is directly involved in memory, language, and thought. It was not always thus. Aristotle famously mistook the heart as the organ of thought and believed that the brain merely cooled the blood. This theory has long since been discredited; any physician who advanced such a notion today would find himself or herself without patients very quickly. Nonetheless, it is important to understand what the brain is and how it physically achieves its function in order to understand the relation of brain and memory in human beings.

We live in an age in which we are at the cusp of tremendous breakthroughs in our understanding of the relation of brain and cognition (Slotnick, 2012; Weldon, 2015). Recent technological advances have provided unrivaled methods for examining how the brain works and how memories are formed, stored, and retrieved. Most of these advances come from neuroimaging technology, which allows us to peer inside the normal functioning brain. Despite these advances, much still remains a mystery, and neuroscientists will be researching the correlation between brain function and memory processes for many years to come. Nonetheless, this chapter would have been much less detailed if it had been written 20 years ago. We are in the midst of a neuroimaging revolution, and we know much about brain function because of it. And for a number of reasons, research on the cognitive neuroscience of memory has been leading the way.

OLD QUESTIONS, NEW ANSWERS

To introduce the neuroscience of memory, we will start with one of the oldest questions in this area—namely, where in the brain are memories stored? This question is of interest for a number of reasons. First, it is a deeply philosophical question: How is it that this brain stuff (shortly to be called neurons) can contain information about the taste of oranges, the name of the 10th president of the United States, and the image of one's long-departed great-grandmother? Second, knowing where memories are stored would allow neuropsychologists to predict particular forms of amnesia. Third, it is an important practical question. If certain areas of the brain store memories, then we need to respect these areas when probing the brain during neurosurgery. The question thus is whether it is possible to pinpoint an area in the brain responsible for a particular memory (Quiroga, 2013).

The consensual wisdom on this topic is that memories are not stored in any particular location in the brain but are distributed throughout the brain. The memory of your great-grandmother is stored in many parts of the brain—her image is in your visual cortex, her voice is in your auditory cortex, and the emotions from childhood her memory elicits are in yet other areas of the cortex. However, this consensual wisdom has recently been challenged. We will briefly review some data that support the idea that specific areas of the brain are for specific memories. These data are based on neuroimaging techniques using the newest and most sophisticated technology.

Many years ago, Karl Lashley labeled this question the "search for the engram"—the **engram** being the physical unit of storage of a memory (Schacter, 2001b). For example, when you learn that "Bratislava is the capital of Slovakia," there must be some change in the brain that marks this new information. If somebody asks you what the capital of Slovakia is, the question activates the engram that stores the association between the names *Bratislava* and *Slovakia*. Lashley suspected that there might be specific cells or groups of cells that transform when

> **Engram:** The hypothetical physical unit of storage of a memory.

new information has been acquired, and he wondered if one's memory of the capital of Slovakia could be eliminated by excising a few cells. He spent his entire career looking for these memory-specific cells but never found any. His research focused on memory in rats, which probably did not know much about Slovakia but nonetheless can learn a great many things. Finally, at the end of his career, Lashley was forced into concluding that there are no engrams and that memory representation instead occurs because of a connection between disparate areas in the brain. Nowadays, there is good evidence to support this idea. For example, Addis et al. (2012) showed that visual areas of the brain are activated during autobiographical recall as well as more standard memory areas, such as the hippocampus. Thus, the current view is that that stored memories are distributed throughout the brain and that stored memories have more to do with connections across spatially separate areas of the brain than any specific area. Thus, the memory of your great-grandmother is the result of axonal connections among areas in the visual brain, auditory brain, emotion centers, and perhaps many others.

This was the conventional wisdom from Lashley's time and for many years. However, Quiroga, Reddy, Kreiman, Koch, and Fried (2005), using functional magnetic resonance imaging (fMRI) technology, which was never available to Lashley, claim to have found specific areas in the brain that seem to support very specific knowledge structures. In Quiroga et al.'s (2005) studies, people saw photographs or printed names of various celebrities while the fMRI was scanning their brains. In general, the photographs elicited greater responses in the visual areas of the brain, whereas the printed names evoked responses in areas of the brain involved in reading. But embedded in the temporal lobe, Quiroga et al. found areas of the brain that responded specifically to information about particular people. These areas of the brain responded selectively to either the picture or the name of one celebrity but not another celebrity. For example, many of Quiroga et al.'s participants actually had "Halle Berry" areas of the brain—that is, neurons that responded to the actress's name or her photograph, even across a range of characters from movies. Nearby the Halle Berry area is a "Harrison Ford" area, which responds to his name and his picture but much less so than to Halle Berry. The specificity of these areas to the recognition of individual people makes it look like there just may be engrams after all (see Bowers, 2009). The Quiroga study was done with single-cell recording of volunteers who were about to have brain surgery, and as consequence, some have challenged the generalizability of their findings. Moreover, there have also been failures to replicate this study as well. Thus, others think that there are other explanations of Quiroga et al.'s data and that citing their findings as support of an engram theory is premature (Plaut & McClelland, 2010). Most researchers continue to believe that memory storage is widely distributed across the brain and that distributed models, such as that of Plaut and McClelland, offer better explanations than do engrams.

BRAIN AND MEMORY

Understanding how the brain forms, stores, and retrieves memory has tremendous practical applications in educational and medical settings, because learning is such an important human process. First, consider the medical implications of understanding brain-memory relationships. In particular, knowing how the brain forms memories means that we may be better able to intervene in memory loss, especially memory loss associated with pathological aging, such as Alzheimer's disease. **Alzheimer's disease** is one of many dementia-type illnesses that are more common in older adults than they are in younger

> **Alzheimer's disease:** One of many dementia-type illnesses that are more common in older adults than in younger adults. Memory is the first deficit detected in this disease.

adults. It is likely that over 26 million people now have Alzheimer's worldwide, and that number is likely to quadruple in the next 40 years (Brookmeyer, Johnson, Ziegler-Graham, & Arrighi, 2007). As of 2015, there were 5.3 million people in the United States alone with Alzheimer's disease (see http://www.alz.org/facts/). Alzheimer's disease is a terminal illness; its initial signature is the development of amnesic (memory loss) symptoms. It affects the brain, clearly illustrating the brain-memory relation. In its early stage, Alzheimer's patients have trouble learning new information and retrieving recent events. During later stages, Alzheimer's involves the loss of knowledge of the past and eventually the identity of close relatives. Understanding the neural processes of memory will help medical research to be able to prevent Alzheimer's or alleviate the symptoms of those with the disease. Preventing Alzheimer's will have enormous consequences for untold millions and will also relieve fear among many who will never develop it. (Go to study.sagepub.com/schwartz3e[1] for more information on Alzheimer's disease.)

Normal aging is also characterized by memory loss, albeit mild compared to the ravages of Alzheimer's. Much of this loss is correlated to changes in the brain. Therefore, understanding brain-memory relationships could wind up benefiting normal older adults as well.

Memory deficits are also a common symptom of **traumatic brain injuries** (TBIs; for more information, go to www.sagepub .com/schwartz3e[2]). TBIs occur when the brain violently and suddenly hits a hard

> **Traumatic brain injuries:** Sudden and devastating injuries to the brain.

object, such as an automobile windshield. TBIs are often closed-head injuries, because the windshield seldom completely cracks the skull. TBIs often can occur in open-head injuries as well, such as when the brain is penetrated by a bullet. Closed-head injuries often result in greater damage to the brain than open-head injuries. According to the Centers for Disease Control and Prevention (Faul, Xu, Wald, & Coronado, 2010), 1.7 million people suffer TBIs every year. Most of these are minor, but 50,000 a year are fatal.

The biggest source of TBIs is motor vehicle crashes. In fact, 17% of TBIs result from motor vehicle crashes (Corrigan, 2015). TBIs are a leading cause of death among young adults, particularly among young male adults. In many severe auto accidents, the head strikes the windshield, causing damage to the prefrontal lobes of the brain. This damage to the frontal lobe can result in long-term deficits in memory, emotional complications, and difficulties in planning and organization. Temporal lobe areas may also be damaged, causing further memory complications. The countercoup (that is, the blow to the back of the head) may damage the occipital lobe, resulting in visual deficits as well. Better understanding of the nature of memory in the brain could bring much-needed relief to these individuals. In the near term, however, buckle up and don't disconnect your airbag!

Clinical neuropsychology: The practice of helping brain-damaged patients recover and cope with their injuries.

The care and treatment of patients with brain damage falls in the domain of **clinical neuropsychology**, which focuses on rehabilitation and restoration of cognitive skills for auto accident victims. Since most auto accident victims are young adults with long lives in front of them, the treatment and rehabilitation of TBIs is of tremendous social importance in our automobile-based culture. However, because of the usual pattern of widespread damage in an auto accident, auto accident victims are seldom used in research examining the relation of brain and behavior.

Alzheimer's and TBIs are two major sources of individuals with memory-related brain damage. But there are other sources as well. Strokes affect the brains of many older adults, as do tumors. Each of these may create deficits in memory. We will return to each of these phenomena in this book, as understanding memory deficits is an important part of memory science. But the primary goal of this chapter is to understand how the brain processes result in the cognitive processes of memory. It is therefore important to begin with an understanding of the underlying structure in the brain.

NEURONS

Our brains contain billions of microscopic cells called **neurons**. Neurons are biological cells that specialize in the transmission and retention of information (see Figure 2.1). As such,

Neurons: Biological cells that specialize in the transmission and retention of information.

neurons are the basic building blocks of both our brain and our entire nervous system. Neurons form huge communicating networks in the brain and connect to neurons in the muscles throughout the body. They innervate all of the sensory systems and muscular systems and allow us to move, see, think, and remember. Understanding memory or any other cognitive process requires a fundamental understanding of how neurons transmit information. To understand how they transmit information, you must first understand their basic anatomy.

Like all biological cells, the neuron contains a nucleus, which houses one set of the individual's chromosomes. The chromosomes contain the genes, which hold the individual's DNA. Surrounding the nucleus is the soma or cell body. The soma contains all the apparatuses that keep the cell working, such as mitochondria and other organelles. In this way, neurons are similar to all other cells of the human body. What makes neurons unique are the fibers that extend outward from the soma. These fibers allow neurons to transmit information from one part of the brain or nervous system to another part. There are two types of fibers, one that leads into the neuron and one that leads out of the neuron. Each of these fibers conducts electricity, although each type of fiber does so in a different manner. Indeed, the transmission of information within the brain occurs through small electric currents racing through the neurons there.

The part of the neuron that receives information from other neurons is the **dendrite**. Any neuron may have many hundreds of dendrites, each one receiving different pulses from other neurons. Some of these pulses may make the voltage higher within the cell, and some of the pulses may make the voltage lower in the cell. The voltage refers to the electrical potential of the cell. The various inputs sum at the soma and determine the electrical state of that neuron at any particular instant of time. This sum total of electric input at any given time can then cause that particular cell to start a signal to other cells. The message leaves the cell via the other unique fiber in the neuron.

Dendrites: The parts of the neuron that receive information from other neurons or directly from sensory receptors.

Each neuron has only one **axon**, which transmits messages to other neurons. The single axon may branch out and be connected to many hundreds of other neurons, transmitting the same electrical pulse to all of them. Transmission in an axon is an electrochemical process called an **action potential**. This is because transmission of electricity along the axon is not simply electrical, like electricity going through a wire. Chemical processes keep the message strong regardless of the length of the axon.

Axon: The part of the neuron that sends information to other neurons.

Action potential: The electrochemical process of transmission in an axon.

The axon of one neuron does not actually touch the dendrite of the next neuron. An extremely small gap, called the **synapse**, exists between the two neurons. Electricity does not pass from the axon of one cell to the dendrite of the next. Instead, the transfer of information between neurons occurs chemically, rather than electrically. At the end of the axon are little nodules called **terminal buttons**. When the electrical signal reaches the terminal buttons, the signal triggers them to release **neurotransmitters**, which are chemicals (such as dopamine) that cross the synapse and induce an electric flow in the next cell (see Figures 2.2 and 2.3). Thus, the flow of information in the neurons is both chemical and electrical.

Synapses: Gaps between the axon of one neuron and the dendrite of the next neuron, in which transmission occurs via neurotransmitters.

Terminal buttons: The ends of axon that hold neurotransmitters.

A few important things to note about this process are as follows. First, transmission of information along the dendrites is electrical. Therefore, longer dendrites experience a greater loss of electrical power than do shorter dendrites. This is similar to the transmission of electricity through power lines, in which more energy is lost when the electricity is transported over long distances than when transported over short distances. As such, dendrites tend to be very short to minimize this loss of information. Because the flow of information in the dendrite is electrical, it is also extremely fast. Indeed, in terms of the size of biological

Neurotransmitters: Chemicals (such as dopamine) that cross the synapse and induce an electric flow in the next neuron.

Figure 2.1   A typical neuron.

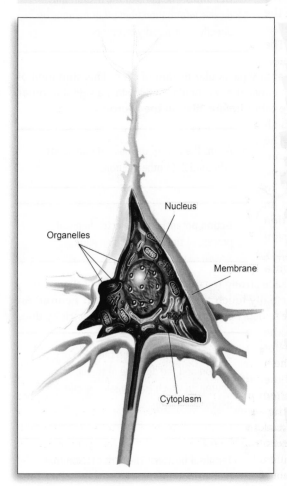

Organelles

Nucleus

Membrane

Cytoplasm

SOURCE: B. Garrett (2009).

organisms, transmission in the dendrites is said to be practically instantaneous.

Transmission of information in the axons, in contrast, is electrochemical. It is electrical over very short segments but then gets a power boost (the action potential) via a chemical process as it moves down the axon. This allows axons to be quite long (indeed, you have one-meter-long axons going up your spinal cord), as the action potentials keep the electric potential constant as it flows along the axon. However, because of these action potentials, information flow in the axon is relatively slow (sometimes as slow as 10 meters per second—that is the speed of an Olympic sprinter). Incidentally, it is likely the slowness of axon transmission that led to the evolution of a large ganglion ("a second brain") in the tail of such animals as dinosaurs.

Finally, transmission of information is completely chemical at the synapse, where neurotransmitters carry the information from one axon to the next dendrite. This transmission also slows down the general speed of neural transmission.

Most axons are coated with a myelin sheath, which speeds the flow of information in the axons. Myelin is a fatty substance that acts as an insulator does around a copper wire. The myelin, therefore, allows the electric signal to travel faster along the axon. The loss of myelin along human axons is associated with the disease known as **multiple sclerosis** (MS). The loss of movement and coordination seen in MS is due to the slowdown of information flowing through the axons.

Sensory systems have specialized neurons called receptor cells. These neurons have essentially modified dendrites. Instead of receiving information from other neurons, receptor cells transform physical energy, such as light, into an electrochemical neural signal. For example, the rods and cones on the retina of the eye respond to light by converting the light (electromagnetic energy) into a neural signal, which travels up the optic nerve and synapses in the brain. (Go to study.sagepub.com/schwartz3e[3] for more information.)

Multiple sclerosis: A disease that causes the loss of myelin along axons, resulting in movement deficits.

Figure 2.2   Components of the neuron.

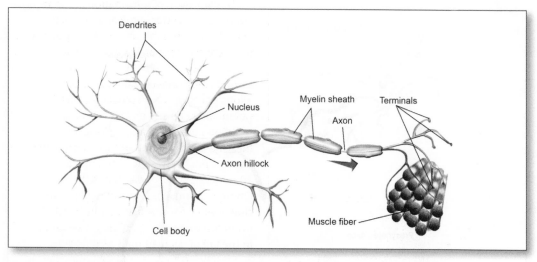

SOURCE: B. Garrett (2009).

Neurotransmitters

The brain and nervous system make use of many different neurotransmitters, depending on the type of neuron and the part of the brain. Neurotransmitters are proteins produced by the nervous system. To be classified as a neurotransmitter, the chemical must bridge the synapse and induce an electric current in a dendrite. Neurotransmitters may either excite the dendrite or inhibit it, and the same neurotransmitter may be excitatory or inhibitory in different neural circuits. Neurotransmitters that increase activity in the neuron are said to be excitatory. These neurotransmitters elicit more action potentials per unit of time. In contrast, neurotransmitters that decrease activity in the neuron are said to be inhibitory. Inhibition causes the neuron to make fewer action potentials rather than more. Common neurotransmitters include dopamine, acetylcholine, serotonin, gamma-aminobutyric acid (GABA), and norepinephrine. GABA is the most commonly found neurotransmitter in the human brain. Acetylcholine is used by neurons that innervate and control our muscles.

If some of these chemicals' names seem familiar to you, it is because of their importance. Many neurological diseases are associated with malfunction of the systems that produce these chemicals. Moreover, many psychiatric conditions are treated by altering the process by which neurotransmitters are produced in the body. Finally, orally consumed drugs can alter the functioning of many of these neurotransmitters. Indeed, many of the drugs we consume (both legal and illegal) affect the function of the brain by changing the chemistry at the synapse. This section will provide just a few examples of this. For more information on the topic, see Sheng, Sabatini, and Südhof (2012).

Figure 2.3   The synapse.

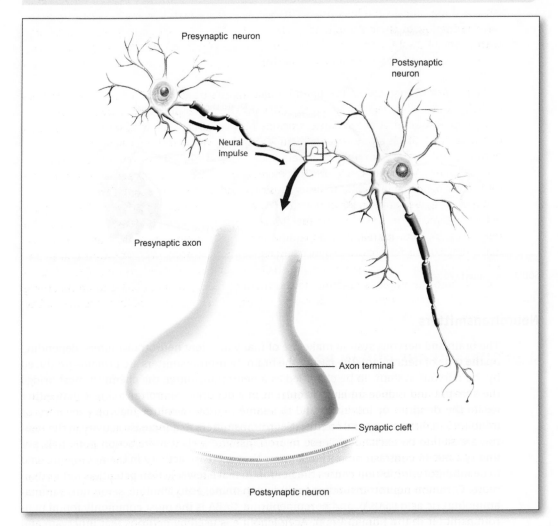

Presynaptic neuron

Postsynaptic neuron

Neural impulse

Presynaptic axon

Axon terminal

Synaptic cleft

Postsynaptic neuron

SOURCE: B. Garrett (2009).

Substantia nigra: A part of the brain that produces dopamine. In Parkinson's disease, this brain region does not produce enough dopamine.

In Parkinson's disease, for example, a part of the brain (the **substantia nigra**) is no longer able to produce enough dopamine. This loss of dopamine then results in the characteristic disorders of movement associated with Parkinson's. Patients with Parkinson's disease may have difficulty initiating movements, frozen facial expressions, and tics about which they are not aware. If left untreated, the symptoms get worse as the disease progresses. However, medicines are available that can control the symptoms, at least to some extent. The medicine given to patients with Parkinson's disease contains a precursor of dopamine, which the body can convert into dopamine and thereby replenish the dopamine in the synapses. This gives patients with Parkinson's disease short-term reduction of their symptoms. Although Parkinson's disease is mainly associated with physical disabilities, it may often affect areas of the frontal lobe, leading to decrements in certain aspects of memory performance, such as prospective memory (Costa et al., 2015).

Many illegal drugs affect the brain by altering the transmission of neurotransmitters at the synapse. The illegal drug ecstasy (MDMA) affects people's moods by modifying the release of serotonin at the synapse. Cocaine blocks the flow of dopamine. Lysergic acid diethylamide (LSD) is a powerful hallucinogenic drug, popular during the 1960s. It affects both dopamine and serotonin channels, increasing the release of neurotransmitters by axons in sensory areas of the brain. This increase of activity in sensory areas is responsible for the strong visual illusions, auditory illusions, and even illusions of balance.

Legal drugs also affect neurotransmitters. Caffeine—common in coffee and tea—affects neurotransmitters in the neurons that innervate our muscles. Caffeine also causes the release of the neurotransmitter dopamine in our prefrontal cortex. Nicotine, one of the main active drugs in tobacco products, increases the activation of the neurons that innervate our muscles. This is why some baseball players used to chew tobacco. The influx of nicotine into the nervous system allowed them to react just a tad faster to an incoming fastball. Chocolate induces the additional release of serotonin. Luckily, chocolate, unlike nicotine, is harmless.

STRUCTURES OF THE HUMAN BRAIN

The human brain is an incredibly complex biological organ containing more than 100 billion neurons (Murre & Sturdy, 1995). In addition to the neurons themselves, the brain consists of a greater number of other cells that support the functioning of neurons. In total, the human brain weighs about 1,300 to 1,400 grams (3 pounds), making it larger than all other primate brains but smaller than those of dolphins, whales, and elephants. Even though the brain represents only about 2% of the average human's body weight, it is an energy-intensive organ, accounting for about 25% of the body's oxygen use at any given moment. For this reason, the brain has a very large blood supply.

In earlier times, the brain was thought of as a single organ whose entirety was equally involved in all of its functions. This is not entirely true. We now know that the brain is composed of many separate anatomical and functional areas. In this section, we will review some of the main anatomical regions of the brain, explore what their functions are, and describe how they relate to learning and memory (see Figure 2.4). This is not a textbook in neuroanatomy; thus, our tour of the brain's anatomy will provide an incomplete sketch of the incredible complexity of the brain's organization.

Right hemisphere/left hemisphere: The brain is divisible into two symmetrical halves, oriented in the left-right direction.

The brain is divisible into two symmetrical halves, oriented in the left-right direction. These are the **right hemisphere** and the **left hemisphere**. The left and right hemispheres have some specific specializations, with the left hemisphere focused on language and with respect to memory, the interaction of language and memory. The right hemisphere is heavily involved in spatial cognition—that is, our understanding of space around us. The right hemisphere also has a greater role in the processing of music. Although hemispheric specialization is the rule in human brains, there is also great overlap in function and considerable cross talk between the two hemispheres.

Because of this overlap, the popular distinction between "left-brained people" (logical, verbal, and cold) and "right-brained people" (emotional, musical, and warm) has no reality in the brain. There is no evidence that people who are linguistically talented, for example, have larger or more neuronal connections in their left hemisphere than they do in their right hemisphere. Indeed, evidence now suggests that the right hemisphere is indeed critical to many aspects of language (Blake, 2016). Modern neuroimaging is showing that, although the left and right hemispheres are anatomically separate, there is less hemispheric functional specialization with respect to higher cognition than previously thought (Dundas, Plaut, & Behrmann, 2013). In the top-to-bottom direction, the brain is divided into cortical (surface of the brain) and subcortical (below the surface) structures. Subcortical structures are the many areas of the brain that rest below the brain's surface. These are "evolutionarily old" areas of the brain that we, by and large, share with nonhuman animals. Subcortical structures are critical in maintaining basic life functions. They control the regulation of heartbeat, breathing, hunger, thirst, sleep, and many aspects of movement. Some subcortical areas are also involved in memory and in emotion.

Figure 2.4 Gross anatomy of the human brain.

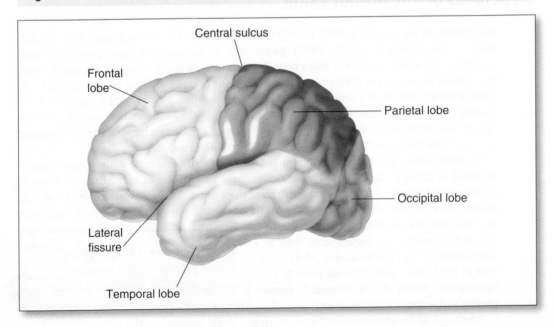

The thin top layer of the brain (see Figure 2.4) is the **cerebral cortex**, which is most closely associated with the processes that we study in psychology. Language, memory, complex emotion, creativity, problem-solving, and music (to name a few) are all largely a function of this thin crust of the brain. It is our large cerebral cortex that distinguishes our brains from those of other species. Suffice it to say that the brain regulates everything we do externally,

> **Cerebral cortex:** The outer layer of the brain most associated with higher cognitive and emotional functioning.

internally, consciously, and unconsciously, but we will consider only those areas of the brain that are involved in memory function. At the level of large-scale anatomy of the brain, memory functions appear to be most critical in the subcortical structures, the hippocampus, and the amygdala and in the frontal and temporal lobes of the cortex. We will review these areas next.

Subcortical Structures

Hippocampus

The **hippocampus** (see Figure 2.5) is part of a network in the brain called the **limbic system**, located in and below the medial temporal lobe (a part of the temporal lobe, which is just behind your ear). The hippocampus is considered a subcortical structure. Like most brain structures, it is bilateral—that is, there is one hippocampus on each side of the brain. To some, its physical shape is reminiscent of a seahorse; hence the name *hippocampus*, which means "seahorse" in Greek. The main function of the limbic system seems to involve both memory and emotion, but the hippocampus is a structure very much associated with

> **Hippocampus:** An area of the brain associated with learning and memory. Damage can cause anterograde amnesia.

> **Limbic system:** Set of brain structures located just beneath the cerebral cortex that includes the hypothalamus, the hippocampus, and the amygdala and functions as an important area for both memory and emotion.

memory. In particular, the hippocampus is an important part of the circuit that encodes new memories, both conscious and unconscious. It does not appear to be involved in the storage or representation of information in memory. However, when we retrieve information, the hippocampus does become activated.

Interestingly, the hippocampus is involved in memory across a wide range of species. Rats, monkeys, and songbirds all have hippocampi that are involved in memory. That such diverse species use the hippocampus for memory suggests that this brain structure served the function of memory in the common ancestor of mammals and birds, many millions of years ago. Moreover, among songbirds, the right hippocampus is associated with spatial memory and migration, whereas the left hippocampus is associated with song memory, in a manner similar to our hemispheric lateralization (Bailey & Saldanha, 2015; Sherry & Hoshooley, 2009). Birds with damage to either the left or right hippocampus

Figure 2.5 The location of the hippocampus.

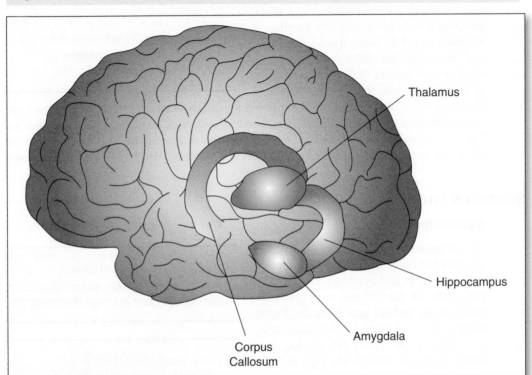

SOURCE: Copyright 2001 Ann L. Myers-Krusznis.

become "amnesic"; if the left hemisphere is damaged, they can no longer sing, and if the right hippocampus is damaged, they do not fly south properly in the winter (or whatever their migratory pattern is).

In humans, damage to the hippocampus can likewise cause **amnesia** (that is, memory deficits acquired through brain damage). In particular, damage to the hippocampus causes difficulties in acquiring new information. We will shortly discuss the patient HM, who had damage to both his left and right hippocampi and had a severe form of amnesia that prevented almost all new learning. Some research suggests that in humans the left hippocampus takes on more responsibility for verbal memory, whereas the right hippocampus is more involved in the memory for the spatial world around us and directions within the world (Hartzell et al., 2015). Data show that in humans, damage to the left hippocampus is more likely to affect memory for stories and words, but damage to the right hemisphere will affect memory for directions and pictures.

> **Amnesia:** Memory deficits acquired through brain damage.

Amygdala

The **amygdala** is also in the limbic system (*amygdala* means "almond" in Greek). The amygdala appears to play an important role in connecting features of memory with aspects of emotion. It is highly connected to the hippocampus, consistent with its role in memory, and with the **hypothalamus**, an area of the brain associated with basic emotions. Because of these connections, the amygdala is associated with both fear conditioning and emotional learning. In humans, the amygdala seems to have an important role in the symptoms of post-traumatic stress disorder. When people with post-traumatic stress disorder are asked to retrieve trauma-specific memories, significant activity can be seen in the amygdala (O'Doherty et al., 2015).

Amygdala: A part of the brain critical in emotional learning, fear, and memory.

Hypothalamus: An area of the brain associated with basic emotions.

Diencephalon

This part of the brain includes the structures known as the thalamus and the hypothalamus. The **thalamus**, in particular, is an area of the brain heavily connected to other areas of the brain. It appears to serve as a routing center, connecting disparate parts of the brain. Parts of the thalamus are crucial in the transmission of information from our sensory organs (eyes and ears, for example) to the cortical areas responsible for sensation. With respect to memory, the **diencephalon** includes massive connections between the medial temporal lobes and hippocampus with the prefrontal lobes, which are involved in memory as well. Damage to the diencephalon can incur tremendous costs in terms of memory deficits. The amnesic syndrome known as Korsakoff's disease is associated with damage to the diencephalon. Korsakoff's disease involves deficits in new learning, deficits in retrieving well-stored information, and an impairment in the ability to distinguish between true and false memories. We will discuss Korsakoff's disease at greater length in Chapter 10.

Thalamus: An area of the brain heavily connected to other areas of the brain. It appears to serve as a routing center, connecting disparate parts of the brain.

Diencephalon: The part of the brain that includes the thalamus and hypothalamus. It serves as an important relay point in human memory circuits.

Cortical Areas of the Brain Associated With Memory

The cerebral cortex is the evolutionarily most recent area of the brain and the area of the brain most different in humans compared to other animals. The cerebral cortex (also known as the neocortex or simply the cortex) consists of four main anatomical areas: the frontal lobe, the temporal lobe, the parietal lobe, and the occipital lobe (see Figure 2.6). Each area is named in concordance with the name of the skull bone under which it lies.

Each of these lobes is bilateral—that is, there is one on the left side and one on the right side of the brain. The cognitive-functional specialties of each area can be summarized as follows:

Frontal—higher emotion, decision-making, metacognition, memory

Temporal—audition, language, memory

Parietal—somatosensory, attention

Occipital—vision

Let's begin our discussion of the role of the cerebral cortex in memory with the parietal and occipital lobes.

Figure 2.6   The cortical lobes.

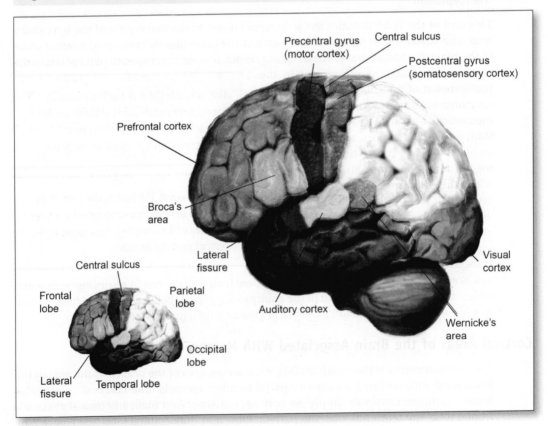

Parietal Lobe

The two main functions of the parietal lobe are somatosensory perception and attention. Somatosensory perception refers to our various senses of touch (fine touch, pain, heat, cold, and pressure) (Schwartz & Krantz, 2016). This perception is located toward the front of the parietal lobe, adjacent to the frontal lobe. Toward the back of the parietal lobe, near the occipital lobe, are networks engaged in spatial attention (in the right hemisphere) and attention to verbal material (in the left hemisphere). Though memory processes may be a secondary in the parietal lobe's set of tasks, increasing activity in the parietal lobe has been linked to memory. In particular, activity in the parietal lobe is critical to working memory tasks and prospective memory tasks—that is, memory of things to do in the future (Cona et al., 2015).

Occipital Lobe

The function of the occipital lobe is visual processing. With respect to memory, this area of the brain is important in providing visual imagery when people remember events from their lives or what people or visual scenes look like. Therefore, when you recall what Jennifer Lawrence looked like in *X-Men,* your visual cortex will become activated. Similarly, when you think about the time you saw the *Mona Lisa* at the Louvre Museum in Paris, your visual cortex will become activated. The occipital lobe is also involved in basic visual memory. V4 is an area of the brain involved in color processing. Patients with damage to this area forget the colors associated with objects. For example, a patient will forget that ripe bananas are yellow and that red lights mean for a driver to stop. V4 is seldom damaged in isolation from the rest of the occipital lobe, but there have been patients with selective V4 damage who show impaired color memory without other memory deficits.

Frontal Lobe

The **frontal lobe** particularly distinguishes humans from other primates; especially different is the area most anterior (i.e., toward the front) in the brain, usually referred to as the **prefrontal cortex** (also called the *prefrontal area*). The prefrontal areas of the frontal lobe are those most involved in memory. Their functions include initiating memory (starting the conscious process of remembering). They are also involved with source monitoring. Source monitoring means being able to distinguish if a memory is a personally experienced event or something someone told you. Source monitoring includes reality monitoring, which means distinguishing between fact and imagination. For example, one might have a vivid memory of surfing big waves in Hawaii but then realize this is a

Frontal lobe: The most anterior part of the cerebral cortex. It is associated with higher emotions, decision-making, metacognition, and memory.

Prefrontal cortex (prefrontal area): The part of the frontal lobe most associated with higher emotions (e.g., jealousy, respect) and memory.

memory of dreaming that one participated in such an activity rather than a memory of actually surfing. Patients with damage to the prefrontal lobes are known to confabulate (telling untruths but not knowing they are untrue), because they cannot distinguish real memories from fantasies. The prefrontal lobes are also associated with metamemory and self-regulation. Metamemory involves our awareness and knowledge of our own memory, and self-regulation involves our control of our memory system. The prefrontal lobes have other functions aside from the self-regulation of memory; they are also involved in higher emotion (e.g., jealousy, respect) and various aspects of problem-solving and creativity.

Temporal Lobe

The areas of the **temporal lobe** most involved in memory processing are those directly adjacent to the hippocampus. These areas are called the medial temporal cortex. Like the hippocampus, the **medial temporal lobe** appears to be involved in the encoding of information into memory but not in the storage or representation of that information. In humans, there is some evidence that the left temporal lobe is more involved in the processing of verbal information and the right temporal lobe is more involved in the processing of spatial information. Damage to the medial temporal lobe produces amnesia similar to that seen with hippocampus damage. Other areas of the temporal lobe are involved in language, auditory processing, and interpreting and labeling visual images.

> **Temporal lobe:** A part of the cerebral cortex associated with learning, memory, audition, and language.

> **Medial temporal lobe:** Area of the temporal lobes associated with learning and memory. Damage can cause anterograde amnesia.

That concludes our brief sketch of neuroanatomy. As we delve in greater detail into the cognitive psychology of memory, we will touch on the underlying neuroanatomy when the relation between memory function and brain anatomy is known and provide greater detail on anatomy-functional relations. Next we turn to the tools for learning about memory and the brain—namely, neuroimaging and neuropsychology.

INTERIM SUMMARY AND QUIZ

The brain is a remarkably complex organ, composed of many intersecting parts and layers. Fundamental to the study of memory are the brain's division into left and right hemispheres and its division into cortical and subcortical areas. The left and right hemispheres of the cortex have slightly different functions. The right hemisphere is more likely to take on roles related to spatial memory, imagery, and music, whereas the left hemisphere focuses on language and verbal learning. The cortical areas of the brain tend to be involved in higher levels of memory processing, whereas the subcortical areas, such as the hippocampus, are more directly involved in encoding or as in the case of the amygdala, emotion and emotional learning.

Quiz

1. Quiroga et al. did an experiment on neural representation with patients about to have brain surgery. They were interested in
   a. If the surgery would affect their ability to recognize faces
   b. If there are specific neurons in the temporal lobe associated with specific knowledge, such as individual people
   c. If neural representation occurs in cortical areas or subcortical areas
   d. The exact location of the pineal gland

2. Research on memory in Parkinson's patients shows that
   a. All Parkinson's patients show deficits in recognition
   b. There is some evidence that, because of compromise to the occipital lobe, some Parkinson's patients show global amnesia
   c. Because of damage to the prefrontal lobe, some Parkinson's patients show deficits in prospective memory
   d. All of the above are true

3. The importance of the synapse is that
   a. In order for a neural signal to be sent, an electric charge must surge over the synapse
   b. In order for a neural signal to be sent, neurotransmitters must move from the axon of one neuron to the dendrite of the next
   c. The synapse generates the axon potentials that travel from one neuron to the next
   d. Electrochemical processes stop at the synapse—only terminal buttons can cross the synapse

4. Which of these limbic system structures is most associated with emotion and emotional learning?
   a. The amygdala
   b. The thalamus
   c. The hyperthalamus
   d. The hypothermus

5. Self-regulation of memory is most associated with which lobe of the cerebral cortex?
   a. Parietal
   b. Occipital
   c. Frontal
   d. Temporal

1. b
2. c
3. b
4. a
5. c

METHODS IN COGNITIVE NEUROSCIENCE

The second theme of this book is that learning and remembering are biological processes based in the brain. Neuroimaging studies over the last quarter century have continually supported and elaborated on that statement. Improvements in technology and reductions in costs have allowed memory researchers to employ modern neuroimaging techniques to explore the relation between memory processes and the physical brain in ways in which researchers, even in the 2000s, would not have thought possible. We are beginning to get good snapshots of not only where various processes occur but how these areas are connected and how these processes unfold over time (Dick et al., 2014).

Neuroimaging: A set of techniques that allow researchers to make detailed maps of the human brain and assign functions to particular regions in the brain.

Neuroimaging is the technology that allows us to create images that demonstrate which regions of the brain are working during a particular memory or cognitive task. In this section, we will give a rudimentary description of how the technology works and then focus on what the technique can tell us about human memory. Six main neuroimaging techniques are outlined here: EEG, PET, MEG, MRI, near-infrared spectroscopy (NIRS) and stimulation techniques.

EEG (Electroencephalography)

EEG (electroencephalography) is the oldest of the neuroimaging techniques, dating back to the 1940s. EEG technology is based on the fact that neurons conduct electricity. This electrical conduction can be measured by sensitive electrodes, which are placed on the skull of a person. As electrical activity moves from one area of the brain to another, it can be measured as distinct "waves" of electrical activity (see Figure 2.7). During particular tasks, some areas of the brain will be more active. This activity will produce a larger wave of electricity, which EEG can detect. More important today is that, as noted in Chapter 1, the electrical activity of the brain can be measured every millisecond (1/1,000th of a second). Therefore, EEG is very sensitive to changes in time in the brain. However, even when the maximum of 128 electrodes are placed on the skull, EEG is not as good as the other techniques at developing maps as to where processes occur in the brain. During sleep, our brains produce characteristic electric waves, whose form can be captured by the EEG. These waves are associated with the various stages of sleep (Massimini et al., 2005). EEG is also important in the diagnosis of epilepsy.

EEG (electroencephalography): Using electrodes to measure the electrical output of the brain by recording electric current at the scalp. Also known as scalp EEG.

There is also a form of EEG called **intracranial EEG (also known as electrocorticography)**. Intracranial EEG means when electrodes are placed directly on the surface of the brain. This form of EEG only occurs during surgery or post-surgery if the brain is still exposed. We have already seen data from this type of procedure when discussing the engram (Quiroga et al., 2005). Because the recording is now occurring directly on the surface of the brain rather than through the skull and

Intracranial EEG: Measuring brain activity when electrodes are placed directly on the surface of the brain.

intervening fluid, intracranial EEG can get much more precise readings of electrical activities in particular areas. For example, Perez et al. (2015) used intracranial EEG to follow patterns in the brain while patients were driving car simulators in the hospital. Perez found activity in the motor areas of the brain prior to drivers making decisions about routes, suggesting the importance of motor planning in such decision-making.

Returning to scalp EEGs, researchers use a particular method called the **event-related potential** (ERP). In the ERP technique, EEGs are measured in response to particular stimuli (or events). The EEG starts recording when the stimulus is presented to a participant. It continues for the duration of the trial. The stimulus is then presented in many trials, and the EEGs are averaged across the trials to eliminate random activity that may be present during any given trial. What remains is a clear wave. Once the trials have been averaged together, the resulting data present a picture of how electrical activity changes over time in response to the stimulus. ERP can be used to probe the time course of cognitive processes in the brain. One example

> **Event-related potential:** The averaged EEG pattern across many trials of EEG recordings in response to a particular class of stimulus.

involves a brainwave known as the p300. When words are presented during a memory experiment, a specific wave occurs about 300 milliseconds after the stimulus is presented. It is called the *p300* because it is a positive change in voltage. In a famous paradigm (known as the von Restorff effect), a list of words is presented to a participant. All but one of the words are from the same category. The out-of-category word, called the von Restorff item or the oddball, might be the name of a city in California among a list of names of kinds of fish. The p300 part of the ERP is distinctly higher for the oddball item than it is for in-category items (Juckel et al., 2012; Shang, Huang, & Ma, 2015). Being able to see in the ERP exactly where the p300 is and how it correlates to the person's memory allows researchers to make a hypothesis about how memory is processed in the brain.

Magnetoencephalography (MEG)

Magnetoencephalography (MEG) allows researchers to measure brain activity by detecting magnetic fields that the brain produces. As with scalp EEG, the measurements take place at the scalp and do not require any invasive procedures. Also like EEG, MEG can record highly accurate timing of when events occur in the brain, down to the millisecond. However, it can also produce more detailed spatial maps of the brain. In this way, MEG is useful in tracking the pathway of information, as particular processes work their way from one part of the brain to the next. MEG presents no risk to the person being studied; indeed, it has been used with

> **MEG (magnetoencephalography):** Using a magnetic sensor to detect small magnetic fields produced by electrical activity in the brain.

infants (Sheridan, Matuz, Draganova, Esweran, & Preissl, 2010). In one study, Garrido, Barnes, Sahani, and Dolan (2012) showed that the amygdala is active when people are evaluating the emotional content of faces. In another study, Ueno, Masumoto, Sutani, and Iwaki (2015) showed that specific sensory areas of the brain were active when participants were recognizing words that had been presented to them either auditorily or visually.

Figure 2.7   EEG patterns. When an EEG is recorded on paper, it produces a pattern that looks like this. The specific pattern of the EEG shown is not relevant here. Rather, the illustration demonstrates that reliable readings from multiple areas of the brain over time can be obtained. Although the EEG measures the electrical activity of millions of neurons, it can be used to make reliable inferences about brain function.

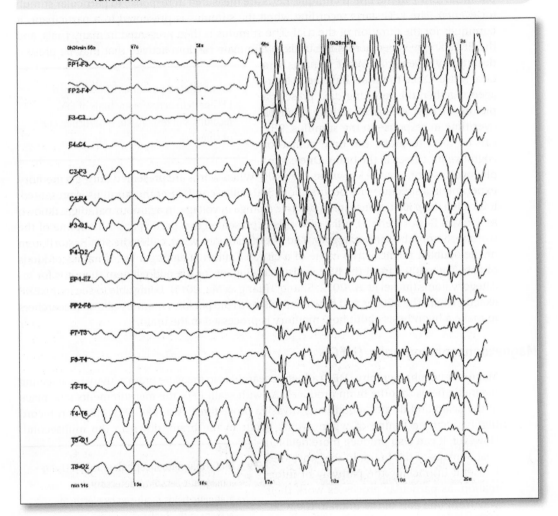

Positron Emission Tomography (PET)

Positron emission tomography (PET) technology allows scientists to get a detailed image of a living human brain without having to damage any living tissue. It does involve, however, injecting a small amount of a radioactive substance into a person's blood, which does have potentially negative effects. Therefore, it should not be done repeatedly. PET is useful for both medical purposes (it can pinpoint a tumor) and research, because it can isolate functional areas of the brain. PET offers, relative to earlier techniques, a superior ability to determine where in the brain a particular function is occurring. However, it does not allow for the detailed description of how information is changing over time in the brain, because it requires about 30 seconds of exposure to capture a good image. Thus, activity in the brain is blurred over a 30-second window.

PET is based on an assumption that areas of the brain that are being used require more blood. The brain is a biological organ that is powered by the oxygen and sugars supplied by blood. Because neurons that are active require more oxygen, the body should send more blood to those neurons that are engaged in any particular cognitive, emotional, or behavioral task. Therefore, if a researcher can trace where the blood is going during a particular memory or cognitive task, then he or she can correlate that area of the brain with that particular cognitive function.

In PET, a small amount of radioactive tracer is injected into the blood of a willing volunteer. The tracer travels through the bloodstream to all parts of the body and brain. Although all parts of the body receive the tracer, more active areas of the brain draw more blood from the circulatory system than less active areas. PET scans use complex measurements to determine which areas of the brain are emitting more radioactivity. Those areas that are more "radioactive" are associated with whatever cognitive task the volunteer is engaging in.

PET allows for very precise maps of the brain to be drawn. Increased activity is often restricted to very small regions of the brain, which the PET can show. Cabeza and Nyberg (1997) used PET technology to isolate hemispheric differences in memory processing. They showed that when people were actively trying to learn new information—as opposed to passively registering information—there was increased activity in both the hippocampus and areas of the left frontal lobe. During retrieval, however, right frontal regions were more active. Other studies show that the right prefrontal lobe is more involved in retrieving events from your personal past, whereas the left prefrontal lobe is more involved in encoding new verbal information. (Go to study.sagepub.com/schwartz3e[5] for more information on PET technology.)

Magnetic Resonance Imaging Technologies

As noted in Chapter 1, functional magnetic resonance imaging (fMRI) has advanced our understanding of the relation of brain and mind more than any other tool. MRI and fMRI, in particular, are safe and quick means of generating images of the structure and function of the brain. Moreover, the latest technology involves combining MRI methods to allow detailed spatial mapping, excellent temporal resolution, as well as the ability to look at white matter (axon connections) and gray matter (neuron cell bodies). MRIs and fMRIs also offer much greater spatial resolution of where events take place in the brain than any other neuroimaging technique. fMRI can rescan the brain every 0.2 seconds, thus offering a better time window than does PET, although still not as good as EEG.

Standard magnetic resonance imaging (MRI) is a medical tool commonly used to examine structural damage in internal organs, and it is routinely used to detect tumors, growths, and other damage in the brain. The term *MRI* means a structural MRI—these images are used to produce a detailed picture of the intact human brain. MRI works because different molecules in the brain react differently when placed in an extremely strong magnetic field. To generate structural images of the brain, the detector looks for changes in the structures of water molecules in the brain. fMRI is a variant that shows where in the brain particular functional components occur by tracking blood flow. In addition, the blood flow scan can be superimposed on an MRI to reveal the structure responsible, thereby providing researchers with both a structural map and a display of dynamic changes in the brain (see Figure 2.8).

Diffusion MRI or **diffusion tensor imaging (DTI)** is another MRI technique. DTI compares the pattern of movement of molecules, particularly water, within tissue in order to derive structural images. DTI is particularly useful for examining white-matter connections in the brain. As such, it is useful in delineating pathways in the brain rather than neural centers. For example, Dick et al. (2014) have looked at the white-matter pathways that connect areas of the brain associated with language. White-matter tracts, such as the arcuate fascilus, are particularly involved in these processes. DTI also is very useful in medical diagnoses, such as distinguishing Alzheimer's disease from other forms of dementia (Parra et al., 2015).

Research using MRI techniques has far-reaching consequences. In an example of the power of fMRI to answer previously unanswered questions, Koshino et al. (2008) were interested in the differences in working or short-term memory for faces in individuals with autism. Autism is a disorder in which people may have linguistic, social, and emotional problems. Working memory is the memory system that handles information over short periods of time and that we currently have accessible in consciousness. It turns out that individuals with autism have a deficit in remembering faces, and Koshino and colleagues wanted to determine whether it was a perceptual phenomenon or a memory phenomenon. If it is a perceptual phenomenon, the individuals with autism would have difficulty seeing the faces, and this difficulty would show up in the fMRI as decreased activity in the areas associated with vision. If it is a memory phenomenon, the individuals with autism would see the face but then have difficulty matching it later. This would show up in the fMRI as a decrease in activation in memory areas of the brain, such as the prefrontal lobe. Koshino et al. asked people with and without autism to match faces while being monitored by an fMRI. The researchers found that, relative to the normal controls, the individuals with autism showed lower levels of activation in areas of the left prefrontal lobe, known to be involved in working memory. Thus, the neuroimaging data support the memory interpretation of this deficit in autism. (For more on this study, go to www .sagepub.com/schwartz3e.[6])

Brain Stimulation Techniques

Another class of neuroscience techniques involves directly stimulating specific areas of the brain and observing the change in cognition that results from the stimulation. There are several techniques that stimulate the brain via different methods. The ones reviewed here are transcranial magnetic stimulation (TMS), transcranial direct current stimulation (tDCS), and deep brain stimulation (DBS).

In **transcranial magnetic stimulation (TMS)**, a magnetic charge is applied via the skull to a particular area of the brain. This is done by placing a magnetic coil near the surface of the scalp. This coil then produces electric currents, which surge into the adjacent areas of the skull and brain. TMS has a number of medical uses, including being an effective treatment for severe migraines (McWhirter, Carson, & Stone, 2015). In terms of research, TMS allows a small pulse of electricity to temporarily disrupt function in a small area of the brain. Researchers can then observe the changes in cognition and behavior that follow. In some cases, TMS will inhibit performance or decrease people's ability to do a task, but in some cases, it can

Figure 2.8   An image produced by MRI. In this view, we can see much of the cerebral cortex, the corpus callosum, and a number of subcortical structures.

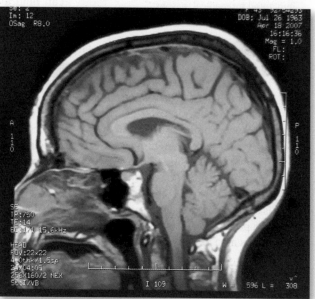

Istock/Allison Herreid

also enhance skills. In either case, the effects of the TMS wear off within a matter of minutes after the coil is removed from near the person's scalp. Because TMS allows true experiments, one can infer causation from the disrupted area rather than simply correlation, as in neuroimaging work. Some examples of TMS research on memory include a study by Desmond, Chen, and Shieh (2005), who showed that verbal working memory (short-term memory for words) was impaired after a single TMS pulse to an area of the brain called the cerebellum. In addition, Bonni

et al. (2015) applied a continuous TMS pulse to an area of the brain known as the precuneus. Stimulation of the precuneus led to a better ability to recognize the context of a particular memory—that is, participants were better able to recognize previously seen pictures and identify the color of the pictures.

In **transcranial direct current stimulation (tDCS)**, low current electricity is applied directly to the scalp in a continuous fashion. In TMS, the coil is kept away from the scalp and the current can either be a single pulse or continuous, but in tDCS, the coil is in contact with the scalp and the current is

Transcranial magnetic stimulation (TMS): a small magnetic pulse to create a small pulse of electricity, which temporarily changes function in a small area of the brain.

Transcranial direct current stimulation (tDCs): low current electricity is applied directly to the scalp in a continuous fashion. Used for both research and medical reasons.

> **Deep brain stimulation (DBS):** A device is implanted directly into the brain, which then sends electrical impulses to specific regions of the brain; used exclusively implanted for medical reasons.

continuous. This technique has a number of medical applications, including improving cognitive performance after stroke, alleviating depression, and reducing memory deficits in early Alzheimer's disease (Goldsworthy et al., 2015). In research, tDCS can help localize function in the brain. If current is applied to an area of the brain, and performance on a certain task improves (or gets worse), that area must be involved in that cognitive skill. For example, Schaal et al. (2015) administered tDCS to the right parietal cortex while participants were doing a memory task on music. Participants had to determine if a melody being played at the time of test was also one they heard during learning. Schaal et al. found that tDCS to the right parietal cortex decreased performance on the music-recognition task, suggesting a role of this area in music recognition.

In **deep brain stimulation (DBS)**, a device is implanted directly into the brain, which then sends electrical impulses to specific regions of the brain. DBS is exclusively implanted for medical reasons—it is useful for alleviating symptoms of Parkinson's disease and other brain-based motor disorders. It has also been successful in treating major affective disorders, such as obsessive-compulsive disorder and major depression (Mavridis, 2015). In research, it is only used with patients who have the DBS device implanted for medical reasons. However, in a population of severely epileptic patients, Miller et al. (2015) found that DBS pulses to the fornix area of the brain improved the patients' performance on a variety of memory tasks.

Section Quiz

1. If a cognitive neuroscientist wanted to determine the time course of an event recognition in the brain, which techniques would give that researcher the best temporal resolution?
   a. PET
   b. EEG
   c. DBS
   d. None of the above

2. Which correctly states the logic behind neuroimaging techniques?
   a. Blood flows to the areas of the brain being used; neuroimaging techniques can detect this flow.
   b. Electrical impulses cause chain reaction in the brain, which allow researchers to identify white-matter tracts.
   c. Electrical stimulation of the brain allows participants themselves to report which area of the brain is being used.
   d. Areas of the brain that are in use produce more metabolic correlates, which can be detected by deep brain stimulation and other sensors.

3. Diffusion tensor imaging is especially good at detecting
   a. White-matter tracts that are used in a particular cognitive task
   b. Whether a patient has Parkinson's disease or not

   c. Cognitive manipulations that work through the brainstem rather than the cortex

   d. All of the above

4. In transcranial magnetic stimulation (TMS), a coil is placed near the scalp, which generates an electrical current in the brain. Which statement is true about TMS?

   a. The coil is not placed directly on the skull.

   b. The stimulation can either improve performance or inhibit performance, depending on the task.

   c. Either a single pulse can be applied or a continuous current can be applied.

   d. All of the above are true.

1. b

2. a

3. a

4. d

NEUROPSYCHOLOGY: MEMORY DEFICITS AND AMNESIA

The oldest methodology for examining the relation between memory and the brain is to study patients with brain damage. This is because examining patients with neuropsychological deficits does not require technology. However, researchers must first locate patients who have suffered brain damage and then observe the cognitive and behavioral deficits in the patients. Going back to the famous case of Phineas Gage in 1848, research has been directed at how brain damage affects cognition and behavior (Fleischman, 2002). Gage, a foreperson on a railroad crew, was severely injured when a poorly timed dynamite blast shot a metal rod through his frontal lobe. Although he survived the accident and lived for many years afterwards, the resulting brain injury changed his cognitive and emotional abilities as well as drastically altered his personality. The study of the change in his behavior set the stage for the development of neuropsychology. The research goal of neuropsychology is to correlate behavioral deficits or cognitive changes with the area of the brain that is damaged. The assumption, then, is that the damaged area of the brain is normally involved in the function of the affected behavior or cognitive ability. Because damage to an area causes deficits in a particular function, such as working memory, then it is thought that the brain area must play some role in that function, in this case, working memory.

Just over 100 years after Gage, in September 1953, a 27-year-old man known to science as HM underwent risky experimental surgery to alleviate symptoms of debilitating epilepsy. During the surgery, parts of his medial temporal lobe, including most of both of his hippocampi, were removed on both sides. As a direct result of the surgical procedure, HM suffered from strong **anterograde amnesia**—that is, a deficit in learning and retaining new information. He could not learn new facts, such

> **Anterograde amnesia:** An inability to form new memories following brain damage.

Retrograde amnesia: An inability to retrieve memories of events prior to brain damage.

as memorizing a phone number. He also suffered some relatively mild **retrograde amnesia**—that is, the loss of memory of events before the injury. Although this surgery has never been repeated on any other human being, HM's memory was studied extensively for the next 50 years (Corkin, 2002). HM passed away in 2008 at the age of 82. Although his ability to encode new events into episodic memory was strongly affected, research showed that his working memory (short-term memory) and procedural learning (skills) were largely intact.

Many other patients have been studied since then. These patients have varied from having very mild amnesia, with memories just barely different from those of people without brain damage, to very severe amnesia. Moreover, the particular pattern of deficits is different in each patient, and the pattern of these deficits can be linked to where in the brain the damage occurs in that patient (Wilson, 2009).

Neuropsychological studies allow researchers to examine the relation of deficits in cognition and behavior with the locus of damage within the person's brain. In fact, most brain damage is fairly diffuse, spread around large areas of the brain. However, in some cases, often the result of bullet wounds, strokes, or indeed surgery—as seen in the case of HM—the damage can be quite localized, allowing clear correlations to be drawn between the memory deficits and the brain damage. We will examine amnesia and other effects of brain damage on memory in detail in Chapter 10. (Go to study.sagepub.com/schwartz3e[7] to find links to neuropsychological research.)

CHEMICAL ENHANCEMENT OF MEMORY

From an early age, children in our society are warned of the dangers of illegal drug use. Paradoxically, over-the-counter drugs, prescription drugs, and legally available brain-altering drugs are ever present in our society. Indeed, few illegal drugs have as profound an effect on our nervous system as three legal drugs—caffeine, alcohol, and nicotine.

We take drugs when we have a cold, drugs to keep us happy, drugs to wake us up, and drugs to help us sleep. So it is not surprising that many people wonder if they can take drugs—legal or otherwise—that will help them remember new information. Unfortunately, the empirical data are mixed here. Certain drugs do improve our alertness, influence how long we can stay awake and focused, and perhaps give us more time to learn. However, to date, no drug has been shown to improve memory efficiency in normal adults. On the other hand, there is no doubt that some drugs prevent the formation of new memories. Indeed, these drugs may be considered to induce temporary amnesic symptoms. Some of these drugs—the antianxiety benzodiazepines—are widely prescribed and available. Although these drugs reduce anxiety, they may also have a profound amnesic effect on some patients (Helmes & Østbye, 2015). Thus, anyone taking drugs such as Valium (diazepam), Atavan (lorazepam), or Xanax (alprazolam) must be aware of the potential deficits in learning while taking these medications.

The only prescription drugs available to improve memory are **cholinergics** (Haense et al., 2012; McDaniel, Maier, & Einstein, 2002). Although there is no evidence that these drugs improve memory in healthy individuals, they have been shown to boost memory performance in those who suffer from memory disorders such as Alzheimer's. They do so by providing chemicals that serve as precursors to the neurotransmitter

> **Cholinergics:** Drugs prescribed to patients with Alzheimer's disease that alleviate memory loss in early phases of the disease.

acetylcholine, used by many memory circuits. The first available drug in this category was piracetam; it is now not regulated in the United States but is available with a prescription in most of Europe. Aricept (Donepezil) is now a commonly prescribed drug for patients with early Alzheimer's or other forms of cognitive dementia—it allows some temporary improvement of memory performance and speech fluency (Risacher et al., 2015).

The data on caffeine, the active drug in common products such as coffee and colas, are mixed. Some data show that caffeine improves memory, whereas others point to decrements (Lesk & Womble, 2004). In any case, the advantage that caffeine may offer to memory is allowing an individual to study longer before falling asleep rather than making the actual learning process more efficient. Indeed, some research suggests that caffeine, although it may help people study by allowing them to remain awake longer, reduces the efficiency of learning (Mednick, Cai, Kanady, & Drummond, 2008). Caffeine may hurt learning by decreasing the number of items learned per unit of time; one may be able to study more hours but learn less during each of those hours. For example, if you could learn 20 new items of information per hour without caffeine, you might only be able to learn 18 new items per hour while using caffeine. But if caffeine allows you to study for three hours instead of two, the additional time would compensate for the lower efficiency.

On the herbal side, the leaves of the ginkgo tree have been used for generations as a memory enhancer. It is marketed as such in health food stores, herbal stores, and even supermarkets. Marketers are allowed to do this because the extract from ginkgo is not considered a medicine. However, virtually no data demonstrate any positive effects of this herb on memory (Elsabagh, Hartley, Ali, Williamson, & File, 2005). Thus, it is likely that, like many "folk" remedies, ginkgo only works via the placebo effect.

In short, there does not yet exist a "memory drug"—that is, a simple pill that can increase your memory skills without affecting other aspects of your cognition or emotion. There are drugs, however, that clearly interfere with memory, causing temporary amnesia.

Benzodiazepines, such as diazepam (i.e., Valium), lorazepam (i.e., Ativan), triazolam, and midazolam, are the most commonly consumed drugs in the world because of their effects on anxiety, insomnia, and muscle relaxation (Kaplan, 2005; Risacher et al., 2015). However, they are also strong amnesia-inducing drugs, especially within the episodic memory domain.

> **Benzodiazepines:** Drugs that are used usually because of their effects on anxiety, insomnia, and muscle relaxation. They are also strong amnesia-inducing drugs, especially within the episodic memory domain.

Episodic memory refers to the memory for individual events from a person's life. Many benzodiazepines also affect semantic memory, our knowledge of the world (Bacon, Schwartz, Paire-Ficout, & Izaute, 2007). The benzodiazepines that are most commonly studied in cognitive research are diazepam, lorazepam, and midazolam. The pattern of memory impairment differs slightly from one benzodiazepine to another, but all of the benzodiazepines impair the learning of new information, creating temporary antero-grade amnesia (Danion, 1994).

OLFACTION, MEMORY, AND THE BRAIN

Olfaction is our sense of smell. Human beings have long been aware of the intimate relation between the sense of smell and memory, particularly the retrieval of highly personal autobiographical memory. Most people can describe the relation of a particular smell to some salient event from their life (Herz, 2007; Schwartz & Krantz, 2016). For example, the smell of naphthalene (mothballs) always reminds your author of visits to his grandmother's apartment as a young child. The famous writer Proust (1928) described how the scent of a French pastry called a *madeleine* transported him back to his childhood in the south of France. Many people report associations between a particular perfume or cologne with a girlfriend or boyfriend, even if the relationship ended years ago. As is clear from the examples, the connection between memory and smell also has ties to emotion. The memories elicited by odor are usually emotional memories.

The neural reason for this strong connection among our sense of smell, emotion, and memories rests in the limbic system. The limbic system is involved in both memory and emotion but is also the primary area for processing odors. Located within the limbic system is the **olfactory bulb**, the primary organ in the brain for processing odors. It receives input directly from the olfactory nerves coming from the hair cells in the nose. Only after information passes through the olfactory bulb does it go to higher areas of the brain in the cortex. But the olfactory bulb is heavily connected neurally to two important memory centers in the limbic system, the hippocampus and the amygdala. These strong connections provide the neural basis for the strong association between odors and both memory and emotion. Interestingly, it is only after these connections between the olfactory bulb and the limbic system occur that information is processed by the olfactory cortex and other areas in the prefrontal lobe. This may account for the "gut" feeling that is characteristic of these strong odor-memory-emotion associations (Herz, 2005). (For more on research on memory and olfaction, go to study.sagepub.com/schwartz3e.[8])

Olfactory bulb: The primary organ in the brain for processing odors.

MEMORY, MUSIC, AND THE BRAIN

A particular song may remind you of a long-ago dance with your high school sweetheart. Another song will rouse memories of the good old days in college. Yet another song may bring back pleasant childhood memories. Such anecdotes suggest that music may be good at eliciting strong or emotional autobiographical memories, and indeed, a connection between music and memory has been documented in the psychological laboratory. For example, Janata, Tomic, and Rakowski (2007) played segments from a large set of popular songs to participants in their experiment. The participants were asked to describe any autobiographical memories or any emotions that were elicited by the songs. More than 30% of songs elicited memories or feelings of nostalgia in each participant. In some cases, the participants reported vivid memories or strong emotions. Thus, like olfaction, music is a good inducer of autobiographical memories.

We also know that, unlike language, musical perception is processed primarily in the right hemisphere of the brain. In many professional musicians, however, hearing or playing music activates both the left and the right hemispheres equally. Many cortical areas and nearly every cortical lobe are involved in some aspect of music. Whereas the occipital lobe (vision) is mainly sidelined (except for reading music), the other three main cortical lobes all have important roles in the processing of music. The temporal lobes house the auditory cortex, the first area of the brain that processes sound, including musical sounds. The sensory cortex in the parietal lobe is essential in providing feedback when playing an instrument or dancing. And the prefrontal cortex is necessary in interpreting and appreciating music (see Levitin, 2006; Tan, Pfordresher, & Harré, 2010). Research suggests that such memory of performance is mediated by procedural memory in the cerebellum (Janata, 2001; Tan et al., 2010).

As mentioned earlier, Schaal et al. (2015) did an interesting study using tDCS, looking at the role of the right parietal cortex in the recognition of recently learned melodies. Melody refers to the main line of a song, the part of the music that we generally hum when we think of a song. In the study, participants listened to novel melodies, derived from folk songs, but otherwise never heard before. After the music had been listened to, the tDCS was applied directly to the scalp above the right parietal cortex. In a second experiment, the tDCS was also applied to the left parietal cortex to serve as a control. In addition, there was a group of participants who were set up with all the tDCS equipment, but the current was never turned on, which also served as a control. When the tDCS was being applied to the right parietal cortex, participants recognized fewer of the melodies as old in an old/new recognition test than did participants in the control condition. Thus, stimulation of the right parietal cortex interferes with memory for musical melodies. Because of this interference, one can speculate that the right parietal cortex must be an area critical in music perception or music learning. (For more on music and the brain, go to study.sagepub.com/schwartz3e.[9])

SUMMARY

The cognitive psychology of memory is increasingly influenced by the neuroscience of memory; together these areas of research form the hybrid field known as cognitive neuroscience. Cognitive neuroscience examines the relation between brain anatomy and cognitive function. Foremost in this field are the successes of neuroimaging, which have greatly contributed to our understanding of how the brain creates, represents, interprets, and retrieves memories. At the cellular level, the brain is composed of billions of neurons, which talk to each other electrically. At higher levels, several key components of the brain are involved in memory, including the amygdala, the hippocampus, the diencephalon, the medial temporal lobes, and areas in the prefrontal lobes. Damage to these areas of the brain can cause various forms of amnesia—disorders of memory. Neuroimaging studies reveal how these areas are active during memory processes. There are several common neuroscience techniques: PET scans, MRI and fMRI, MEG, EEG, TMS, tDCS, and DBS. With respect to neuroimaging, fMRI has become the state of the art in cognitive neuroscience.

The brain uses chemicals called neurotransmitters to bridge the synapses between cells. Neurotransmitter function can be influenced by drugs. Some drugs, such as benzodiazepines, interfere with memory processing. The search continues for drugs that can improve memory performance directly. A strong connection exists between some odors and certain strong auto-biographical memories by way of the limbic system and between music and memory via many areas of the brain, especially the auditory cortex in the temporal lobes, the sensory cortex in the parietal lobes, and the prefrontal cortex in the frontal lobe.

KEY TERMS

action potential

Alzheimer's disease

amnesia

amygdala

anterograde amnesia

axon

benzodiazepines

cerebral cortex

cholinergics

clinical neuropsychology

deep brain stimulation (DBS)

dendrites

diencephalon

DTI

EEG (electroencephalography)

engram

event-related potential

fMRI

frontal lobe

hippocampus

hypothalamus

limbic system

magnetoencephalography (MEG)

medial temporal lobes

MRI

multiple sclerosis

near-infrared spectroscopy (NIRS)

neuroimaging

neurons

neurotransmitters

olfactory bulb

PET

prefrontal cortex (prefrontal area)

retrograde amnesia

right hemisphere/left hemisphere

stimulation techniques

substantia nigra

synapses

temporal lobe

terminal buttons

thalamus

transcranial direct current stimulation (tDCS)

transcranial magnetic stimulation (TMS),

traumatic brain injuries

REVIEW QUESTIONS

1. What is meant by the term *engram*? What did Lashley hope to achieve by identifying it? How does the Quiroga et al. (2005) experiment relate to the concept of the engram?

2. What is a traumatic brain injury?

3. Describe the flow of information through the neuron, including how information is transmitted through the axon, dendrite, and synapse. Include the purpose of neurotransmitters.

4. What is the relation between the drugs we commonly take and the brain? By what mechanism do these drugs, such as caffeine, affect brain function?

5. Describe the functional significance of each of the following brain regions: (a) hippocampus, (b) amygdala, (c) diencephalon, (d) temporal lobe, and (e) frontal lobe.

6. How does EEG measure activity in the brain? What is EEG good for?

7. What advantages does fMRI have over EEG and PET technology?

8. What is amnesia? What is the difference between anterograde and retrograde amnesia?

9. How do benzodiazepines affect memory? How do cholinergics affect memory?

10. Why is the olfactory system so tied to emotion and memory?

ONLINE RESOURCES

1. For more on Alzheimer's disease, see http://www.alz.org.

2. For more on traumatic brain injuries, see http://www.traumaticbraininjury.com.

3. For more on neurotransmitters, go to http://faculty.washington.edu/chudler/chnt1.html or http://www.neurotransmitter.net.

4. For more on PET scans, go to http://www.radiologyinfo.org/en/info.cfm?PG = pet.

5. For the complete article on fMRI in autism, go to http://cercor.oxfordjournals.org/cgi/content/abstract/18/2/289.

6. For more information on neuropsychology, go to http://www.neuropsychologycentral.com.

7. For more on research on memory and olfaction, go to http://www.rachelherz.com.

8. For more on music and the brain, go to http://faculty.washington.edu/chudler/music.html.

Go to **study.sagepub.com/schwartz3e** for additional exercises and study resources. Select **Chapter 2, Memory and the Brain** for chapter-specific resources.

CHAPTER 3

Working Memory

Imagine you are driving your car to a friend's house. You've never been there before, so you pull off to the side of the road to speak on your cell phone with your friend. She is giving you directions: "Make a left onto Martin Luther King Boulevard, go straight for two miles, and then, when you are just past the university, make a right onto Canseco Street." Your friend gets another call, signs off, and you are on your own. Will you remember those directions? You are not sure, so you decide to repeat the directions over and over until you get to Canseco Street. What many people do is mentally rehearse those directions to keep them fresh—available, that is, in their **working memory** until they do not need them anymore. "Left on MLK, two miles, right on Canseco," might keep running through your head. The goal of rehearsing is to keep information in working memory, the active contents of our consciousness, so we can make use

> **Working memory:** The neural structures and cognitive processes that maintain the accessibility of information for short periods of time in an active conscious state.

of that information immediately. The concept of working memory is important for practical reasons; you need to remember directions, the phone number to the pizza shop, and where you just put your car keys.

Working memory systems are the neurocognitive systems that allow us to maintain information over short periods of time. Working memory used to be called short-term memory, but for a number of reasons, that term has fallen out of favor. *Short-term memory* is more often used to describe a stage in an information-processing model rather than a functional neurocognitive system (Atkinson & Shiffrin, 1968). Given current theory, *working memory* is a more appropriate term (Baddeley, 2012). However, working memory is also one of the most philosophically loaded terms in modern experimental psychology, because of its relation to conscious processing. Most cognitive psychologists today think of working memory as the active contents of consciousness (Jacobs & Silvanto, 2015). Working memory indeed can be considered consciousness itself. Whatever you are conscious of right now (hopefully this paragraph) is exactly what your working memory is representing right now. Direct your attention to the television running in the background or your roommate's game of Minecraft, and this paragraph will cease to be maintained in working memory as your attention and conscious awareness are directed elsewhere.

WHAT IS WORKING MEMORY?

Although there is still controversy about the theories used to describe what working memory is and explain how it works, almost all cognitive scientists would agree on certain basic tenets (Barrouillet & Camos, 2015). Working memory is the following: a short-term memory system. Working memory's function is to temporarily hold information over a short period of time. Estimates of this period may vary, but most run somewhere between 15 and 30 seconds (1/2 minute). If information is continually refreshed or rehearsed, it can be maintained indefinitely in working memory. However, as soon as rehearsal stops, information will be lost from working memory within that timeframe. Interestingly, the process by which information is lost from working memory has to do with interference, not time per se. In contrast, long-term memory can store information for minutes, years, and even an entire lifetime. Some researchers consider short-term memory—in the sense of a place in which information is stored—an important part of working memory (Shipstead, Lindsey, Marshall, & Engle, 2014).

- A limited capacity system. Working memory can only hold so much information. Miller (1956) identified short-term memory as maintaining about seven units of information. Research since has modified this conception of working memory; nonetheless, only a small, finite amount of information can be active at any particular point in time. In essence, working memory capacity is the amount of information that can be spoken in 1.5 seconds. This contrasts with long-term memory, which appears to have a virtually limitless capacity. Research has never been able to document the maximum amount that human long-term memory can hold.

- The current contents of working memory are thought to be equivalent to conscious awareness.

Working memory is readily contrasted with the typical conceptualization of long-term memory. Working memory maintains information for brief periods of time in an active conscious state. In contrast, long-term memory stores information for long periods before it is activated when called for. Working memory can maintain only a limited number of items in conscious awareness at any point in time. Long-term memory has seemingly limitless capacity. Indeed, most research suggests that the more someone knows, the easier it is for that person to learn more. However, the contents of long-term memory are not conscious until they are activated into working memory. Despite some popular misconceptions to the contrary, it is impossible to "fill up" one's long-term memory, as if it were a gas tank. Finally, what is in our working memory is what we are thinking about now. In long-term memory, there may be information we have not thought of for years and that may be very difficult to retrieve into an active form.

SOME TERMINOLOGICAL CLARIFICATIONS

Prior to the late 1980s (Baddeley, 1986), the term **short-term memory** was used more often to describe the phenomena covered in this chapter. Cognitive psychologists now seldom use the term *short-term memory*. First, it is associated with theory that is no longer considered to be

Short-term memory: An older term used to describe the memory system that holds information for a short period of time, up to 15 seconds.

Primary memory: A term used to mean short-term memory.

correct. Second, the term *short-term memory* is now used in everyday speech in a way that is different from its former use in psychology. As a consequence, nowadays, memory science prefers the term *working memory.* You may also see the term "primary memory" as well. **Primary memory** was the term originally used by William James to refer to working memory and has been used by some researchers since then (James, 1890; see Baddeley, 2012). This term also fell out of favor because current conceptions of working memory postulate that it is both the active area where we rehearse new information and the area that holds information after it has been retrieved from long-term memory. Thus, it is neither primary nor secondary to long-term memory. (Go to study.sagepub.com/schwartz3e[1] for more information on William James.)

Terminology is often tricky, as other subfields of psychology may use the same term to mean a different thing. Such is the case with the term *working memory*. Many animal behavior researchers are interested in animal memory systems and how they compare to each other and to human memory. Animal behavior researchers use the term *working memory,* but they use the term in a different manner. In animal memory research, the term *working memory* refers to memory of the most recent trial, regardless of the time course of that memory (see Shettleworth, 2010; also see study.sagepub.com/schwartz3e[2] for more information). This is quite different from its usage in human memory research. In keeping with current terminology, this textbook will use the term *working memory* in the manner in which it is used in the study of human memory.

SENSORY MEMORY

Although the focus of this chapter will be on working memory, it is also important to describe a memory system that functions at even shorter time spans than does working memory—that is, sensory memory. We include sensory memory here, but make sure to understand that sensory memory is thought to be a different system than working memory, though they are sometimes confused. **Sensory memory** refers to a very brief memory system that holds an exact representation of what you have seen for a fraction of a second to allow cognitive processing to occur. Unlike working memory, sensory memory occurs *prior* to conscious access. Sensory memory is thought to be composed of separate memory systems for each perceptual system. **Iconic memory** is visual sensory memory, whereas **echoic memory** is auditory sensory memory. Sensory memory is a

Sensory memory: A very brief memory system that holds literal information for a fraction of a second to allow cognitive processing.

Iconic memory: Visual sensory memory.

Echoic memory: Auditory sensory memory.

system that operates prior to consciousness and thus before working memory begins.

Sensory memory is sometimes considered a buffer system, because it holds information from our senses for a brief period of time so that we can extract more information from what we are seeing or hearing. Our eyes and ears are constantly being bombarded with information, only some of which is relevant at any particular time. In theory, sensory memory creates a buffer, which allows us to maintain sensory information—in a sensory format—long enough for cognitive mechanisms to detect and attend to relevant information.

In a now classic experiment, the cognitive psychologist George Sperling (1960) demonstrated the hypothetical existence of iconic memory or visual sensory memory. Participants were shown a matrix of 12 letters in a 4 × 3 grid for a brief period (50 msec). Participants were then asked to report letters in one of two ways, whole report and partial report. In the whole-report technique, participants were asked to retrieve all of the letters from the matrix. Under the whole-report technique, participants could only recall about five letters. In the partial-report technique, they heard a tone that indicated which line to report. A high tone indicated the top line, a medium tone indicated the middle line, and a low tone indicated the bottom line. The tones occurred just after the stimulus grid disappeared. Participants in the partial-report condition could remember three from the specified line, suggesting that nine letters were accessible visually at the time of recall rather than the 5 one might have estimated from the whole-report technique (see Figure 3.1).

Figure 3.1 Participants in Sperling's 1960 experiment would see the following grid for a very brief flash. In the partial report, they were required to report just one line. In the whole report, they were asked to recall the entire matrix.

H	J	T	E
V	Q	M	P
E	I	N	Y

SOURCE: Sperling, G. (1960).

Sperling (1960) demonstrated the existence and the function of sensory memory by comparing performance in the whole-report condition and the partial-report condition. In each condition, participants saw the 4 × 3 grid for the same amount of time, and in each condition, the interval between the offset of the stimulus and the repeating of the letters was the same. However, in the partial-report condition, participants received information about which line to report immediately after they could no longer see the stimulus. Thus, they needed to be storing a visual record of the grid mentally in order to be able to report 75% of the line that the tone told them to. The whole-report condition showed lower per-line memory, because of working memory problems. As these participants reported letters from the grid, the representation faded from sensory memory, and because of the short presentation time, few letters had entered working memory. Thus, sensory memory is a low-level system separate from working memory. Despite the success of this experiment and others, sensory memory has not been a major concern of memory researchers for some time (see Loftus, 1983).

WORKING MEMORY CAPACITY

Here's the phone number for the best pizza in the city: 555-3756. Most of us do not have a problem juggling that seven-digit number in our head. We repeat the numbers over and over until we dial the number and get our "everything but anchovies" pizza (see Figure 3.2). Now consider when you also have to remember an unfamiliar area code. Now try keeping this number in working memory, 324-555-3756. Try mentally rehearsing that number. It is likely that you will have forgotten bits of it by the time you actually get your phone out of your pocket. The task of remembering the numbers becomes much more difficult for most of us as the number of digits passes seven.

> **Capacity:** The amount of information that can be maintained in working memory.

George Miller (1956) claimed that the **capacity** of human working memory (or primary memory, to use Miller's term) is, on average, seven items of information. Capacity is the amount of information that can be maintained in working memory. Miller described the "magic number 7" as critical to working memory. It was his view that working memory could hold 7 ± 2 "items" at any point in time (we shall return to the concept of items shortly). This makes the seven-digit number relatively easy but the slightly longer 10-digit number extremely difficult. Likewise, for most people, remembering a nine-digit social security number on the first try is very difficult. The "plus or minus two" refers to individual differences in the capacity of working memory. This capacity limitation is why we need to keep glancing back at our airplane confirmation number on our ticket when we enter it into the boarding pass machine at the airport. This also works for other stimuli—it is easy to remember a bar or two of a great song you hear on the radio for the first time, but it is very difficult to sing back the entire song after listening to it once.

> **Digit span task:** A task in which a person must remember a list of digits presented by an experimenter.

One of the chief methods employed to look at the capacity of working memory is called the **digit span task**, a standard test in the memory researcher's toolkit. The digit span task is an easy but very valuable research tool. This task is similar to trying to remember the digits in the phone number for the pizza restaurant. An experimenter reads a list of numbers to a willing participant or group of participants. As soon as the list is read, the participants must repeat back the numerals in order, either by speaking the words aloud or writing them down. The experimenter can then vary the number of digits that she reads to the participants. The ability to recall the digits can be examined as a function of how long the set was. See the demonstration below and try it yourself.

Demonstration: Try your hand at the following digit sequences. Read them. Then close the book and try to repeat them.

5-digit: 9 0 3 6 7

6-digit: 4 7 6 2 9 1

7-digit: 3 7 8 5 2 6 0

8-digit: 1 9 8 7 2 0 4 6

10-digit: 1 2 0 7 3 9 6 8 2 9

12-digit: 4 1 3 5 6 7 5 8 1 8 4 6

Results in digit span experiments show that average (arithmetic mean) performance is just about seven digits, consistent with Miller's "magic" number. Given that educated and younger people tend to have longer digit spans than less educated and older people, most college students doing this demonstration will find seven digits relatively easy and succeed at the eight-digit sequence (Jones & Macken, 2015). The ten-digit sequence, however, will likely be outside their capacity.

Let's return to the concept of an "item." G. A. Miller (1956) suggested that the capacity of working memory was about seven items. For Miller, however, the word *item* was intentionally vague. Indeed, he argued that a lot of information could be packed into a single item. People can use strategies to make each item of information decomposable into several parts. For example, rather than remembering the number sequence 6-1-9 as three digits, each a unit of information, participants could simply rehearse "San Diego." Then, when it is time to retrieve the digits, the item "San Diego" could be converted into 6-1-9 because 619 is the area code for that

Figure 3.2   You will need to remember the digits of the phone number before you can have this mouth-watering pizza delivered.

© Dick Luria/Photodisc/Thinkstock

city. Using this strategy is called chunking. Miller introduced the word **chunk** to represent the basic unit of information in working memory. Each chunk in memory represents a unit of related components (Baddeley, 2012; Cowan, 2001).

Individuals can use many strategies to chunk digits in a digit span task. You can use area codes, home addresses, and even the jersey numbers of your favorite athletes. For example, another sequence, 2-3, can be encoded as "Michael Jordan" rather

Chunk: Basic unit of information in working memory. A chunk may be decomposable into more information.

than as two digits, as the basketball player was famous for that jersey number. In this way, we can extend our working memory capacity by using more and more informative chunking strategies. For example, your author can remember up to 14 digits by taking each two-digit sequence and processing it as a jersey number for a famous athlete.

In a classic demonstration of how effective chunking can be, Anders Ericsson and his colleagues trained a first-year college student in digit span tasks (Ericsson, Chase, & Faloon,

1980). At the start, the first-year college student had a normal digit span of about seven numbers. The experimenters did not suggest any methods to him. They just gave him lots of practice. However, by the end of a year of training, the young man had an 80-number digit span! That is, an experimenter could read off a list of 80 numbers, and the young man could repeat them all right back without any mistakes. How could this man with a normal digit span increase his abilities so dramatically over the course of an academic year?

First, it was his job—he spent about 10 hours a week for 40 weeks engaging in digit span tasks. That means a lot of practice and hard work. But it was not simply practice—the student used a complex mnemonic chunking strategy to build his digit span. The young man was a star runner on the university track team. He therefore chunked numbers by thinking of them in terms of times in track-and-field races. The sequence 1-9-1-9 might be encoded as "world record in 200-meter dash." The sequence 3-4-3 might be remembered as near world record pace for the mile. Because most of these sequences were already stored in his long-term memory, he was able to apply them to the new digit sequences (Ericsson et al., 1980). The complex chunking strategy combined with lots of practice made a mnemonist out of this young runner. Just to be sure there was nothing unique about this young man, Ericsson and colleagues recruited another runner from the track team the next year and gave him the same amount of practice using the same chunking strategy. This participant went from a normal seven-digit span to a 70-digit span over the course of the experiment. The implication is that anyone can use chunking strategies to boost memory performance (see Ericsson, 2003). (For more on Ericsson's work, go to study.sagepub.com/schwartz3e.[3])

MNEMONIC IMPROVEMENT TIP 3.1

If you need to keep arbitrary lists of information accessible in working memory, use chunking strategies as best you can. Try to encode multiple items of information using a common associative strategy. Use well-learned information to guide your chunking strategy. Chunking is useful in ordinary learning tasks that involve working memory, such as remembering phone numbers, keeping directions in mind, and remembering the names of new acquaintances.

Pronunciation Time

Regardless of one's ability to chunk information, most of us are still constrained by the fact that working memory usually can contain only about seven items, even if these items can be chunked. Therefore, the extraordinary digit spans of these participants do not take away from Miller's basic finding—that seven items is the average amount of information in working memory. However, factors other than the number of items in a chunk are important in determining the capacity of working memory. One such factor is phonological processing, also called pronunciation time. **Pronunciation time** refers to the amount of time it would take to say aloud the items being

Pronunciation time: The amount of time it would take to say aloud the items being rehearsed in working memory.

rehearsed in working memory. The limit on working memory is the number of words that can be pronounced, either aloud or subvocally, in about 1.5 seconds (Schweickert & Boruff, 1986). Most of us can say seven digits in American English in 1.5 seconds; hence the digit span of seven.

Because longer words require more of working memory than do shorter words, the capacity of working memory is influenced by word length. For example, you can maintain the names of European cities with one syllable (*Prague, Nice, Rome, Bruge*) more easily in working memory than the names of European cities with multiple syllables (*Amsterdam, Bratislava, Barcelona, Manchester*). For another example, consider the names of trees. Try to keep the following words rehearsed in working memory: *oak, birch, pine, palm.* Then try to keep the following words rehearsed in working memory: *eucalyptus, bottlebrush, Poinciana, sycamore.* Most of us will find it easier to maintain the short names for trees in working memory than the longer ones. This phenomenon is referred to as the **word length effect.**

> **Word length effect:** Longer words are more difficult to maintain in working memory than are shorter words.

To test the effect of word length, Ellis and Hennelly (1980) looked at digit spans in children in Great Britain. They focused their testing in the part of Great Britain called Wales. In Wales, there are still people whose first language is Welsh (a Celtic language) rather than English, although practically all Welsh do speak English. In Welsh, the words for digits take longer to pronounce than they do in English. This is largely because Welsh vowels take longer to pronounce than their English counterparts. Therefore, it takes more time to count from one to 10 in Welsh than it does in English. Ellis and Hennelly examined digit spans in Welsh English bilingual children. Consistently, the children's digit span was longer in English than it was in Welsh. Because the words mean the same thing in both languages and because most of the targeted students were more fluent in Welsh, the digit spans must be different because, at least for the names of the digits, one can say the digits faster in English than in Welsh.

A short time later, a second study confirmed this finding using different languages. Naveh-Benjamin and Ayres (1986) also made use of the fact that digits take a different amount of time to say in different languages. For example, in English, the numeral 1 is pronounced *one,* which is one syllable. In Spanish, however, the numeral 1 is pronounced *uno,* which is two syllables and takes a little more time to say than *one* does in English. Therefore, *uno* should occupy slightly more of the capacity of working memory than *one* does. Naveh-Benjamin and Ayres tested students at a university in Israel, where they were able to examine fluent speakers of four languages: English, Spanish, Hebrew, and Arabic. In terms of pronunciation time, it takes the least amount of time to count from 1 to 10 in English and the most amount of time to count from 1 to 10 in Arabic. When the digit span task was presented to speakers of each language, the digit spans reflected the pronunciation times. The digit spans were longest in English, followed by, in order, Spanish, Hebrew, and Arabic (see Figure 3.3). This decrease in digit spans is related to the increase in pronunciation time of the digits in each language. Therefore, these results support the idea that pronunciation time is relevant in evaluating the capacity of working memory.

Figure 3.3   Digit span as a function of language. The y-axis represents the number of words repeated.

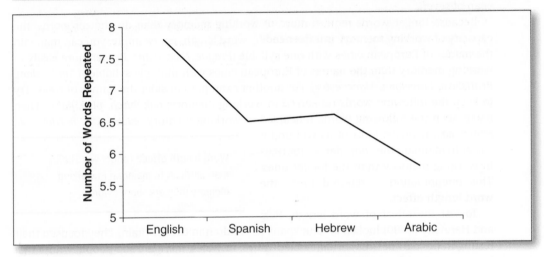

SOURCE: Based on Naveh-Benjamin and Ayres (1986).

THE DURATION OF INFORMATION IN WORKING MEMORY

Working memory holds information for only brief periods of time. Because of this, a frustrating memory experience is the rapid loss of information from working memory. Consider having just heard the phone number of your client on your answering machine. Before you can write the entire number down, you have lost the first three digits. For professors, working memory often constrains the efficiency with which we learn the names of new students. For example, I try to learn the names of many new students on the first few days of class each semester. I am well aware how insulting it can be when somebody forgets your name immediately. A student may introduce herself as "Christina Rodriguez, a sophomore, from South Miami, Florida. Majoring in psychology." I look at her face and silently repeat the name to myself. Then the next student introduces himself or herself. After a few more students, I look back at the first person, and I have no recollection of the name she just spoke mere minutes before. This is because the information pertaining to Christina Rodriguez is no longer in working memory, having been replaced by subsequent names. Because I failed to transfer her name to long-term memory, the subsequent names, faces, and other information have displaced the information in my working memory, leaving me with a complete blank on the student's name. Because the information was never encoded into long-term memory, it can no longer be recalled.

This leads us to one of the earliest issues tackled by cognitive psychologists. How long does information persist in working memory? And it also leads us to the closely related question, what causes forgetting from working memory?

To address the first question, the short answer is that it depends. And what it depends on is rehearsal, an important concept in memory science. **Rehearsal** here means actively maintaining the item in working memory by repeating it over and over (**maintenance rehearsal**) or by relating the item to some other concept (**elaborative rehearsal**). If you wish to maintain a new name in working memory, you can simply continue to mentally rehearse it. For example, as long as I am repeating the name "Christina Rodriguez" over and over, I can maintain that name in working memory. Indeed, if I continuously repeat it, I can keep that name for hours in my working memory. However, as soon as my thoughts drift off elsewhere, the new information replaces the rehearsed name in working memory.

Rehearsal: Actively maintaining the items in working memory by repeating them over and over (maintenance rehearsal) or by elaborating on the item to some other concept (elaborative rehearsal).

Maintenance rehearsal: Repeating information over and over.

Elaborative rehearsal: Processing the meaning of information in working memory.

Elaborative rehearsal means associating the item in working memory to existing long-term memory structures. So, for example, if instead of repeating the name over and over, I thought about whether Ms. Rodriguez looked like other people I know or tried to link her with other people with the same first name or same last name or even thought about whether she looks honest or not to me, I would be engaging in elaborative rehearsal. Elaborative rehearsal takes more attention but produces better encoding into long-term memory because it creates more retrieval cues that are useful for later recall.

Once you stop maintenance rehearsal, there is only a limited amount of time before information is forgotten (or replaced) in working memory. When you move on from "Christina Rodriguez" to "Sanjay Parekh," it is the new name that is now being maintained in working memory rather than the old one. Therefore, one important question is, what is the rate of forgetting once you stop rehearsing the information?

Most estimates of the duration of information unrehearsed in working memory are between 15 and 30 seconds. After that, information is lost from working memory. This has a counterintuitive implication: If you remember something *after not thinking about it* for one minute, you are retrieving that information from long-term memory, not working memory. Thus, for example, if I remember "Christina Rodriguez" just one minute after hearing her name for the first time when that minute was consumed with hearing other names, I am remembering her from long-term memory. This is an important point, because the science here diverges from popular thinking about the nature of memory. In this sense, working memory is a very short-term system, and uses of memory over the short term in our everyday lives are often subsumed by long-term memory function rather than from retrieving them from the limited duration of working memory.

What seems to be important with respect to the duration of information in working memory is whether information becomes activated that interferes with it. If we could somehow keep our minds completely blank, information might not spontaneously decay from working memory. Keeping our minds blank while awake is notoriously difficult. However, people who meditate are particularly good at keeping their minds free of interfering information, and it turns out there is a correlation between meditation and good working memory (Moss, Monti, & Newberg, 2013). But for most of us, new information is always entering working memory. This new information engages working memory, becomes part of the items being kept there, and displaces other information that is not being rehearsed.

Duration of information in working memory: The amount of time information will remain in working memory if not rehearsed.

The basis of the estimate of the **duration of information in working memory** comes from two classic sets of experiments done by John Brown (1958) in the United Kingdom and Lloyd and Margaret Peterson in the United States (1959). The two groups worked largely independently but published similar experiments within months of each other. Both researchers were interested in forgetting from working memory but also demonstrated the duration of information in working memory (or what they referred to as primary memory).

In the experimental paradigms, participants were given three words to remember (i.e., *apple, hammer, shell*). Following the presentation of the three words, the participants were given a number, such as 417, and asked to count backward by threes from that number (i.e., 417, 414, 411, 408, etc.). The counting task served as a **rehearsal prevention task**, preventing participants from repeating the words previously shown. The research teams then varied the amount of time required to count backward. In some conditions, the participant might only count backward by threes for three seconds, but in other conditions, the participant might be required to count backward for two minutes. After the rehearsal prevention period was over, the participants were asked to retrieve the three words given to them prior to rehearsal prevention. After retrieving the three words, the participants were given three new words to remember and then given a new number from which to start counting backward. In this way, the researchers could look at the effect of the amount of time spent on rehearsal prevention and the recall of the words. The method is illustrated in Figure 3.4.

Rehearsal prevention task: A task that prevents a participant from maintaining information in working memory.

The findings are illustrated graphically in Figure 3.5. More time spent in the rehearsal prevention task led to lower recall of the words presented. Indeed, much forgetting occurs after just five seconds of rehearsal prevention. L. R. Peterson and Peterson (1959) estimated that within 18 seconds, all information stored in working memory was lost, and only information that had somehow gotten into long-term memory accounted for the 20% recall. They noted that after 18 seconds, the curve had hit an asymptote (flattened out) and remained essentially the same even at much longer retention intervals.

It should be noted that typically, even at longer retention intervals, the participants remembered all three words from the very first trial. Apparently, the number counting did not produce sufficient interference to cause forgetting of the first trial, as these items were easy to encode into long-term memory. This is a common problem in studies of working memory; one always has to be careful that the retrieval is from working memory, not long-term memory, and indeed, in the Brown-Peterson task, retrieval from long-term memory can be seen on the first trial. However, on subsequent trials, memory for the words was interfered with by the combination of words from earlier trials and the rehearsal prevention task. Thus, the results shown in Figure 3.5 are a function of the average across many trials.

Both the Petersons and Brown favored an explanation based on decay—that is, information not being rehearsed naturally vanishes or decays after 20 seconds or so. However, subsequent research strongly supports an explanation based on interference. **Interference** means that new information enters working memory and displaces information already present. Because the capacity of working memory is limited, new

> **Interference:** New information enters working memory and displaces information already present.

information will necessarily displace old information. In the case of the Brown-Peterson-Peterson experiment, the numbers being spoken during the rehearsal prevention task entered working memory and displaced the words that the participant initially was asked to remember. The more time spent counting backward, the more likely those words were displaced by the interfering numbers. Thus, the best explanation for the results is that the numbers being spoken during rehearsal prevention replaced the words in working memory, thus interfering with their presence in working memory. Indeed, a few years later, Keppel and Underwood (1962) showed that part of the interference that created forgetting in working memory came not simply from the rehearsal prevention but also from previous to-be-remembered items. Keppel and Underwood showed that on the first trial, participants could remember all of words, even when the retention interval was long. However, as

Figure 3.4 Example rehearsal prevention task.

Repeat: Apple, hammer, shell
    9 seconds: 417, 414, 411 etc.
Retrieve the three words _____

Repeat: Honey, lumber, dragon
    15 seconds: 674, 671, 668, etc.
Retrieve the three words _____

Repeat: pigeon, lawyer, marker
    3 seconds: 116, 113, 110, etc.
Retrieve the three words _____

Figure 3.5   Typical results from the Brown-Peterson task. The *y*-axis represents the percentage recalled.

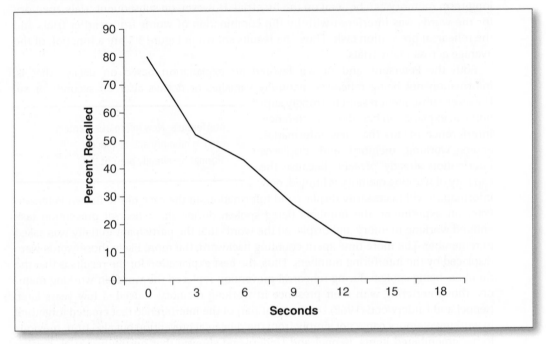

SOURCE: L. R. Peterson and Peterson (1959).

more trials occurred, it was more difficult for participants to remember digits at any retention interval because earlier items were now interfering with later items. Thus, interference played a bigger role in forgetting than did decay.

Another classic experiment demonstrated the role of interference in working memory. Waugh and Norman (1965) presented participants with a sequential list of 16 digits. After viewing all 16 digits, the participants were presented with one of the digits that they had seen in the list. Their task was to recall the digit that occurred just prior to the probe digit during the sequence. In other words, if part of the sequence was 1-5-6-2-9 and the probe digit was 6, the participant should reply with the digit 5. Waugh and Norman could then examine performance on this task as function of where in the sequence the probe digit was. If more digits occurred after the probe, then more new digits were likely to interfere with and replace the memory of the probe digit and the digit that preceded it. If the probe digit occurred toward the end of the sequence, there should have been less information to interfere with it, and therefore memory of the digit that preceded it should be better. This is exactly what Waugh and Norman found—the fewer items that followed the probe digit, the better memory was for the item that preceded it. This cemented the view that forgetting from working memory originates from interference.

THE SERIAL POSITION CURVE AND ITS IMPLICATION FOR WORKING MEMORY

In light of what we know now about the functioning of the brain and memory, it is quite clear that separate neurocognitive memory systems handle different kinds of information. For example, memory should be divided into short-term memory systems and long-term memory systems. With respect to long-term memory, most researchers agree on the distinction between semantic and episodic memory. However, 50 years ago, on the basis of the principle of parsimony (that is, opting for the simplest theory when possible), many researchers argued that the brain had just one memory system that could be used in many different ways. Thus, one of the goals of early researchers in the field of working memory was to show how it was different from long-term memory (i.e., Atkinson & Shiffrin, 1968; Baddeley & Hitch, 1974; see Baddeley, 2012). Some of the earliest evidence for the separation of working memory from long-term memory came

> **Serial position curve:** The observation that participants remember items well from the beginning and end of a list but not from the middle.

from a deceptively simple procedure, called "free recall," of single-item lists, which is typically measured by a **serial position curve**. A serial position curve plots the order of items presented and how well each of those items was recalled across participants.

In a free recall test, participants are read (or read themselves) a list of words, usually randomly chosen and with little associative structure. Immediately following the reading of the list, participants are asked to recall (usually by writing down) as many of the words as possible. As you can see, nothing could be simpler. Yet, this test is quite powerful. (For more information on serial position curves, go to study.sagepub.com/schwartz3e.[4])

After the participants can no longer recall any more words from the list, the experimenters can examine the amount recalled as a function of serial position, that is, the order in which the words appear. So the first word on the list in Figure 3.6 is *medal*. The experiments would examine the percentage of participants who successfully recalled the word *medal* at serial position 1. The experimenters then examine recall at the next serial position—that is, for the word *paintbrush* in this list. Thus, the percentage recall can be examined as a function of what serial position a word occupies in a given list. The standard result of such a test is illustrated in 3.7. (For an online demonstration, go to www.sage pub.com/schwartz3e.[5])

There are a few important aspects of the serial position curve. First, you can see that recall is very good for the first few items on the list. This effect is called the **primacy effect**. You then see a big dip in performance for items in the middle of the list. Then right at the end of the list, the words become easier to recall again. This good performance for words at the end of the list is called the **recency effect**. Primacy and recency effects can be seen under a wide range of conditions in which people must recall

> **Primacy effect:** The observation that memory is usually superior for items at the beginning of a serial position curve; thought to be caused by the encoding of those items into long-term memory.

Recency effect: The observation that memory is usually superior for items at the end of a serial position curve; thought to be caused by the maintenance of those items in working memory.

words or other items immediately. Indeed, monkeys and other primates also show primacy and recency effects in experiments that test them for serial memory (Buchanan, Gill, & Braggio, 1981; Wright, Santiago, & Sands, 1984).

Primacy effects appear to result from the encoding of information into long-term memory, even though the memory test may be administered less than a minute after the participants originally heard the words. Much research supports this point of view. In terms of people's self-reports, many participants describe trying to remember the words by constructing a story. For example, referring to the list of words in Figure 3.6, they might think of a story in which a "medal" is awarded to a person who invented a "paintbrush" key on a "typewriter," which can be used on the "sofa." The elaborative encoding necessary to create this story promotes storage in long-term memory. However, if such elaborative rehearsal is prevented, such as by presenting words at a particularly fast rate, the primacy effect can be reduced or eliminated. Reducing the amount of time per word lowers the primacy effect in free recall studies. In contrast, speeded presentation does not affect the recency portion of the serial position curve, which is based on working memory (Glanzer & Cunitz, 1966; Murdock, 1962).

Other evidence also supports the claim that the primacy effect is caused by retrieval from long-term memory. Mistakes made on early items tend to be related to their meaning, a key component of representation in long-term memory. For example, *medal* might be mistakenly recalled as *award,* whereas *paintbrush* might be remembered as *toothbrush.* The mistake here is because we encode information into long-term memory mostly in terms of what the information means. Because *medal* and *award* overlap considerably in meaning, errors of this sort tend to be thought of as resulting from long-term memory (Conrad & Hull, 1964).

Recency effects appear to be based on retrieval from working memory. As with the primacy effect, a great deal of research now supports this idea. Think about doing the task yourself. If the first few items you wrote down were the last items, you were probably likely to remember several of them. If, however, you tried to recall the list in order from start to finish, you probably did not recall the last two or three words from the list. If you ask study participants to wait 30 seconds (that is, if you introduce a retention interval) before writing down the words that they can recall, the recency effect disappears (Glanzer & Cunitz, 1966). However, this delay does not affect the primacy effect at all. This is because the participants' working memory has been engaged in other activities, causing interference with the items at the end of the list. This effect is stronger if you give participants a rehearsal prevention task so that they cannot rehearse the last few items in working memory before the test. In contrast, items recalled from the beginning of the list are in long-term memory, so the extra 30 seconds does not affect their strength in memory.

Furthermore, errors in the recency effect part of the serial position curve tend to be based on sensory errors, either visual or auditory (Conrad & Hull, 1964; Laughery, Welte, & Spector, 1973). For example, *folder* might be recalled as *bolder,* or *market* might be recalled as *markup.* This kind of mistake is characteristic of working memory, which is more dependent on sensory characteristics than is long-term memory.

Finally, participants who write down the words from the recency portion of the curve first remember more total items than those who try to retrieve the words in order. Participants who retrieve in order remember the words from early in the list based on long-term memory, but by the time they get to the end of the list, those words have already been eliminated from working memory.

For this reason, the serial position curve—the graph that shows good memory for both the beginning of the list and the end of the list—in immediate free recall tests demonstrates that working memory and long-term memory have different properties. Variables that affect the primacy effect are variables that affect long-term memory, and these variables do not influence the recency effect. By contrast, the variables that affect the recency effect are implicated in working memory and do not affect the primacy effect.

In free recall of recently presented lists, the recency effect is due to retrieval from working memory. But it turns out that the primacy and recency effects are not just restricted to free recall of lists of randomly grouped words. Both primacy and recency effects exist in other memory situations as well, including situations in which retrieval is strictly from long-term memory. For example, try writing down the names of as many U.S. presidents as you can. Take a moment away from the textbook now—so you don't see any of the names below. It turns out that recalling the names of the U.S. presidents shows a primacy effect and recency effect. Most people remember Washington, Adams, and Jefferson on the one hand and Clinton, Bush, and Obama on the other. However, few people will get Chester Alan Arthur, Millard Fillmore, or Grover Cleveland in the middle of the list. Remembering the first presidents is equivalent to the primacy effect, whereas the recall of the most recent presidents can be considered a recency effect (Roediger & Crowder, 1976; Roediger & Magdalena, 2015).

Another example comes from watching the advertisements during the Super Bowl. The advertisements have become almost as important a part of the show as the football game itself. But which advertisements are remembered the best (an important piece of information

Figure 3.6   Read aloud the following words. Immediately after reading the words, write down as many as you can. Then plot your total recall as a function of input order. However, you do not have to recall the words in order.

1. medal	8. dragon	15. mask
2. paintbrush	9. captain	16. lunch
3. typewriter	10. carbon	17. water
4. sofa	11. lawyer	18. racket
5. cushion	12. bubble	19. market
6. pasture	13. lemon	20. folder
7. clock	14. fountain	

Figure 3.7 Recall as a function of item position in a serial position curve. The y-axis represents the percentage of words recalled.

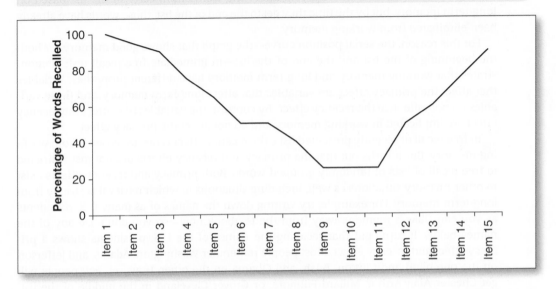

for the advertisers, who are paying a tremendous amount of money for airtime)? It turns out that the ones at the beginning and the ones at the end are recalled better than those from the middle of the game (Brunel & Nelson, 2003). Primacy and recency effects are also seen in the retention of information from academic classes. Information from the beginning of the semester and the end of the semester is remembered better than information from the middle of the semester (Conway, Cohen, & Stanhope, 1992).

SECTION SUMMARY AND QUIZ

Working memory is a short-term memory system that can hold information for a short period of time for conscious introspection. Originally, it was thought to hold about seven items, but more recent views of working memory suggest that factors such as word length and pronunciation time affect the amount that can be maintained in working memory. If unrehearsed, information will fade from working memory in approximately 15 to 30 seconds. When people learn a list of words and then have to recall them immediately after presentation, the recency effect is caused by retrieval from working memory, whereas the primacy effect is because of the early items in the list having entered long-term memory. Variables that affect working memory affect the recency portion of the serial position curve; errors here will reflect working memory processes. However, serial position curves are common in memory, and primacy and recency effects can also occur in retrieval from solely long-term memory.

Quiz

1. Which is the current term used to refer to systems of memory that hold information up to 30 seconds?
   a. Primary memory
   b. Short-term memory
   c. Working memory
   d. Unemployed memory

2. In Sperling's classic 1960 experiment on sensory memory, participants in the partial-report condition were expected to
   a. Report all of the material when they heard any tone
   b. Report only one line when cued by a particular tone
   c. Report all the vowels that they saw in the matrix
   d. Report all the consonents they saw in the matrix

3. One factor that affects the amount of information currently in working memory is
   a. The pronunciation time of the items if they were spoken aloud
   b. The ability of a person to chunk information
   c. Whether the words are long or short when spoken
   d. All of the above are factors

4. A person in a serial position curve experiment recalled the word "violin" when actually the word "violence" had been presented. Based on what you know about the serial position curve, where would you expect the word "violence" to have been presented?
   a. Right at the beginning of the list
   b. In the middle of the list
   c. As one of the last few items in the list
   d. It is impossible to tell from the information provided

1. c
2. b
3. d
4. c

THE WORKING MEMORY MODEL OF BADDELEY

Alan Baddeley is a British memory psychologist who has contributed to many areas in psychology. His most influential theory is of working memory (Baddeley, 1986, 2007, 2012; Baddeley & Hitch, 1974). Baddeley and his theory are probably most responsible for the change of terminology from *short-term memory* to *working memory*. For Baddeley, the term *working memory* more genuinely reflected what working memory is for—to work with the active contents of consciousness.

But another aspect of Baddeley's working memory theory makes it different from the theories of short-term memory that came before it—he advanced the idea that there are actual multiple working memory systems. He called these various systems "subsystems" or "slave systems." For all intents and purposes, what he proposed is that we have separate working memory systems for each major perceptual modality. He called visual working memory the **visuospatial sketchpad**, and he called auditory working memory the **phonological loop** (Baddeley, 1986). In the latest versions of the model, Baddeley introduced another system called the **episodic buffer**, which coordinates overlap between the auditory and visual systems (Baddeley, 2012). The episodic buffer is also the link between working memory and long-term memory. Coordinating the activities of these two systems is an attentional mechanism that he called the **central executive** (see Figure 3.8). We will now examine what each of these terms means and what evidence exists to support the theoretical constructs developed by Baddeley and his colleagues over the past 40 years.

Visuospatial sketchpad: Visual working memory.

Phonological loop: Auditory working memory.

Episodic buffer: Coordinates overlap between the auditory and visual systems and also interfaces working memory with long-term memory.

Central executive: The attentional mechanism of working memory.

Baddeley originally stumbled onto the concept that working memory must be composed of multiple systems while working on tasks that were designed to look at how working memory handled multiple simultaneous tasks. He and his colleagues were conducting experiments in which they asked participants to engage in two working memory tasks at the same time. All the old models predicted interference between the two tasks, leading to diminished performance in at least one, if not both, tasks. What Baddeley and Hitch (1974) discovered, in contrast, is that this is not always the case. In some instances, people can successfully do two working memory tasks at the same time without interference—that is, they can be successful at both tasks. Consider the visual working memory required to drive a car. Your visual attention must be on the road, which is why texting and driving is such a terrible combination. However, the visual attention needed for driving does not prevent you from devoting auditory working memory to listening to music or talking to a passenger (though we will discuss later in this section why even hands-free cell-phone conversations are dangerous). Similarly, in a psychological experiment, a participant can track a moving arrow on a screen and rehearse digits without a deficit in the ability to do either task.

The first published evidence to support the idea that working memory was not unitary and might consist of multiple systems goes back to a landmark study by Baddeley and Hitch (1974). In the study, participants were read aloud strings of digits to remember. These strings varied from simply one numeral to as many as eight. Participants were required to speak back the digits. This task was a standard digit span task with spans ranging from trivially easy to more difficult. However, Baddeley and Hitch also asked their participants to do a **concurrent task** (a task to be done simultaneously with the first task). In the concurrent task, the participants had to judge whether simple sentences were true or false. The participant might see the letters *JK,* and underneath would be a statement, "The *J* is before the *K*" (true), or the participant might see "The *K* is before the *J*" (false).

> **Concurrent tasks:** Tasks to be done simultaneously.

Based on the models of the time of working memory, Baddeley and Hitch (1974) expected that the concurrent task would provide an additional burden to working memory and interfere with recall in the digit span task. However, that is not what they found. Instead, there was almost no overlap between the two tasks. The retrieval of digits was just as good as it would have been without a concurrent task, and participants did as well on the concurrent task when they were rehearsing eight digits as when they rehearsed only one digit. There was no interference between the two tasks. For these two tasks, the participants really could do two things simultaneously, much as someone can drive and listen to music at the same time.

These results are interpretable when one thinks of the visuospatial sketchpad and the phonological loop as separate systems. The phonological loop handles the digit span task, whereas the visuospatial sketchpad handles the reading and processing of the simple reasoning task. Because both of these components did not need to tax the attentional mechanism (the central executive), both tasks are done at the same time without any interference. Thus, this study counts as evidence that visual and auditory working memory can function independently of each other.

In another experiment specifically designed to test the new model of working memory, Logie (1986) asked participants to learn paired associates (digit-word pairs, such as 23–typewriter or 12–candlestick). Some participants were instructed to use a visual strategy to encode the words (that is, to employ the visuospatial sketchpad by making a mental image of the association), whereas other participants were instructed to use rote encoding (to employ the phonological loop). In the concurrent task, Logie either presented pictures (visual) or required participants to listen to names (auditory). The participants had to see or hear the items—they were not required to encode them. Nonetheless, the results were striking: The visual concurrent task interfered with the learning of paired associates when the associates were learned using the visual strategy, and the auditory concurrent task interfered with learning of the paired associates when the associates were being learned using rote encoding. In contrast, cross-sensory interference was much less. Looking at pictures did not interfere with rote encoding, and hearing names did not interfere with the visual learning strategy. To restate the findings another way, when the learning task required visual imagery, viewing pictures interfered with learning, but hearing words did not. When the task required auditory processing, hearing words interfered with learning, but seeing pictures did not. This supports the idea that the visuospatial sketchpad is a different system than the phonological loop.

Now contrast the Baddeley and Hitch (1974) and Logie (1986) data with those from another experiment. L. R. Peterson and Johnson (1971) also did a digit span task with a simultaneously performed concurrent task. Peterson and Johnson asked participants to repeat simple words over and over (e.g., *the, the, the, the . . .*) while they were also supposed to be rehearsing the digits for the digit span task. Because both tasks now involved the phonological loop, this concurrent task did reduce the number of digits that could be remembered. This kind of interference is called **articulatory suppression**. You might think that silently repeating the word *the* would not interfere with processing, as it is such an easy task. But because it requires some use of the phonological loop, it does interfere with

Articulatory suppression: A concurrent task that prevents participants from engaging in rehearsal within the phonological loop.

other tasks that employ the phonological loop. In the Peterson and Johnson experiment, articulatory suppression lowered participants' digit spans.

Thus, a basic principle can be derived from these experiments. As long as the attentional demands are not too great, visual working memory (visuo-spatial sketchpad) tasks should not interfere with auditory working memory (phonological loop) tasks. By the same token, auditory working memory tasks should not interfere with visual working memory tasks. In contrast, even relatively easy tasks within the same working memory system will interfere with each other. That is, two auditory working memory tasks will interfere with each other, and two visual working memory tasks will interfere with each other.

MNEMONIC IMPROVEMENT TIP 3.2

Keeping your working memory sharp can lead to general cognitive well-being. Practicing digit spans can be considered mental exercise.

Figure 3.8 Baddeley's working memory model.

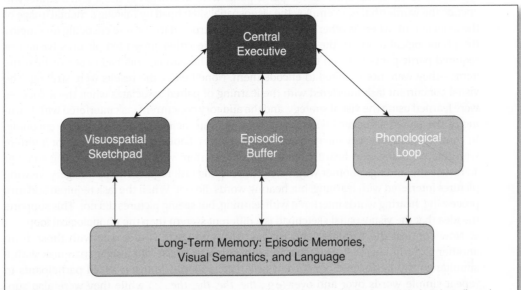

The model involves units for processing visuospatial information (visuospatial sketchpad) and auditory information (phonological loop). The central executive coordinates these units and controls the focus of attention. The episodic buffer holds episodic memories for a brief time to allow them to transfer between the working- and long-term memory systems.

SOURCE: Baddeley (2000).

WORKING MEMORY SYSTEMS

The Phonological Loop

The phonological loop is our auditory working memory system. It stores sounds, particularly language sounds, for a short period of time. It also has processes that allow us to rehearse or otherwise manipulate the information in the short-term store. In this way, it is like an "inner ear" that stores the sounds we hear in a somewhat literal format until we can process them in terms of their meaning and store them in long-term memory. Critical to the idea of the phonological loop is that it is a limited-capacity system that holds auditory information for a brief period (Baddeley, 2012).

We have already discussed the initial findings of Baddeley and Hitch (1974), which support the distinction between the phonological loop and the visuospatial sketchpad. Only a visual concurrent task interfered with the visuospatial sketchpad, and only a phonological concurrent task interfered with the phonological loop. The word length effect also supports the notion of the phonological loop. The fact that words that take longer to say are more difficult to maintain in working memory is consistent with the idea that an auditory-based working memory system is responsible for that information. Interestingly, Baddeley, Lewis, and Vallar (1984) eliminated the advantage of short words over long words when participants were simultaneously required to repeat a particular sound, such as the word "*the*" under their breath. Repeating *the* created what Baddeley et al. called articulatory suppression, which involved using the phonological loop and forcing the participants to rely on other systems, such as the sketchpad, to remember the words. In the sketchpad, the shorter words are not an advantage. Thus, the fact that articulatory suppression eliminates the word length effect also supports the idea of a separate phonological loop.

Research on articulatory suppression is critical for supporting the idea that the phonological loop is independent of other working memory systems. In an interesting variant on articulatory suppression, Otsuka and Osaka (2015) asked participants to do mentally a relatively simple arithmetic task—that is, two-digit addition. While participants were engaged in the addition task, some were asked to engage in simultaneous secondary tasks. During articulatory suppression, participants were relatively poor at arithmetic showed a greater decrease in performance than those who were more proficient in arithmetic. It is likely that the better performers used visual methods to add the numbers and may also have had less attention needed for the task, so their performance remained high despite the articulatory suppression. However, the participants who were less good at arithmetic used a more auditory strategy to add the numbers and were therefore more prone to the interference caused by the articulatory suppression.

> **Irrelevant speech effect:** The observation that the phonological loop is mildly impaired in the presence of background speech.

Other evidence that supports the existence of a phonological loop comes from the research on **irrelevant speech effect**. The irrelevant speech effect refers to the observation that the phonological loop is mildly impaired when talking is going on in the background. Irrelevant speech affects performance on phonological loop tasks but not visuospatial sketchpad tasks. For example, Salame and Baddeley (1989) asked participants to maintain information in working memory while

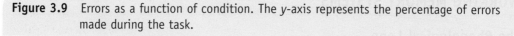

Figure 3.9   Errors as a function of condition. The *y*-axis represents the percentage of errors made during the task.

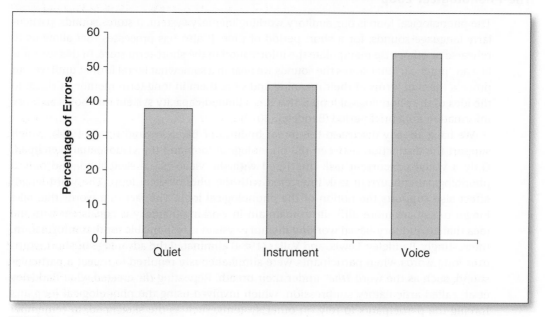

SOURCE: Based on information from Salame and Baddeley (1989).

listening to singing, music without singing, or no sounds at all (see Figure 3.9). The silent group performed the best on the working memory task, but the group that listened to music without singing outperformed the group that listened to singing. Thus, sounds of any nature, particularly meaningful sounds, interfere with our ability to maintain information in the phonological loop.

The irrelevant speech effect has implications for mnemonic improvement as well: It suggests that studying in a quiet room leads to a more efficient environment for learning, as information can be processed in the phonological loop more efficiently. This contradicts the so-called Mozart effect, which tells us that listening to Mozart can help us learn new information. The Mozart effect is a widespread myth of learning—there is no evidence that listening to Mozart can improve memory efficiency. In fact, research suggests that listening to Mozart did not have positive effects on immediate learning of spatial information (Wilson & Brown, 1997; Lilienfeld et al, 2010).

Evidence supporting the existence of the phonological loop comes from the neuropsychological domain as well. Vallar and Baddeley (1984) examined a patient with selective damage to the phonological loop. The patient tested normally in most areas of cognitive functioning. However, her working memory, as measured by digit spans, was severely impaired. Moreover, she did not show the word length effect, meaning that longer words were not more difficult to keep in working memory than shorter words. Vallar and Baddeley claimed that this occurred because whatever words she could recall were coming from the sketchpad rather than the loop. The longer words may have taken longer to pronounce, but because she was not using the phonological loop, whatever she did retain in working memory was based on visual processing. Her working memory was also unaffected by phonological similarity (that is, words that sound similar are more easy to maintain in working memory), also suggesting that only the phonological loop was affected and not the sketchpad.

Visuospatial Sketchpad

The visuospatial sketchpad stores visual and spatial information for short amounts of time in the activated contents of consciousness. It is largely independent of the phonological loop as long as attentional demands are low. Like the phonological loop, it is a short-term memory system, designed to hold visual and spatial information for short periods of time, up to about 30 seconds. Recent research suggests that it is likely that visual and spatial information may be represented in different subsystems (Baddeley, 2012), but we will treat them together here.

The visuospatial sketchpad is open to conscious introspection. For example, we experience the visuospatial sketchpad when we retrieve what a familiar person looks like. If you have a mental image of your best friend's face in your mind's eye, it is being represented in your visuospatial sketchpad. If you glance briefly at a map while driving and then try to figure out where you are supposed to get off the highway, you are using your visuospatial sketchpad to represent that information. Like the phonological loop, the visuospatial sketchpad occupies a role in cognition that brings thoughts and perceptions to our conscious awareness. Thus, whatever you are attending to visually at the moment is the contents of your visuospatial sketchpad.

A classic experiment on the nature of the visuospatial sketchpad comes from an experiment done by Lee Brooks (1968). Brooks's original purpose was to explore the nature of imagery, but his experiment provides an excellent example of the independence of the visuospatial sketchpad from the phonological loop. Brooks asked participants to imagine letters that were not actually present, such as the letter *F* (see Figure 3.10). Because participants were asked to make a visual image, we can assume that the representation of this image is being held in the visuospatial sketchpad. Keep in mind that the participants could not actually see the letter—they only had a mental image on which to base their decisions. Participants were then asked to make judgments about the letter, such as whether the angles in the letter were obtuse (greater than 180 degrees) or acute (less than 180 degrees). Look at the following *F*: Is the angle made by the line that goes straight up and the line that goes out to the right acute or obtuse? Then trying answering the same question with a *T* without actually looking at one. Participants had to rely on their image of the letter and were not allowed to draw one. Most participants found this task challenging yet possible.

Brooks's (1968) important experimental manipulation concerned how participants made their responses. Responses were made by speaking the answers aloud (phonological), tapping them out with the hands (i.e., one tap for yes; two taps for no; motor), or pointing to a field with an array of y's for yes and n's for no (visuospatial). Note that neither speaking nor tapping requires use of the visuospatial sketchpad. Thus, these response options

Figure 3.10   Imagine the letter *F*. Examine the corners where the lines making up the letter come together. Are the angles acute or not?

SOURCE: Based on Brooks (1968).

should not interfere with the imagery task. Pointing to letters on a display, however, does require visual processing, so the pointing response also employs the visuospatial sketchpad. When Brooks examined his results, he found that participants were more accurate and faster when they had to speak the answer or tap the answer than when they had to point to the array. Thus, only the visual response task interfered with the imagery task. Because of the interference across the visual domain, performance decreased in the imagery task. Thus, as we have seen throughout, interference works greater within domains. Visual interference hurts performance on tasks that use the visuospatial sketchpad, but auditory tasks interfere less with tasks that use the visuospatial sketchpad.

In the Otsuka and Osaka (2015) study, the researchers also looked at how visual tasks interfered with arithmetic performance. As described earlier, high performers in the arithmetic task were more likely to use both visual and auditory strategies to help them with mental arithmetic, whereas the low performers were more likely to use auditory strategies alone. As such, it was the higher performers whose performance was more interfered with when Otsuka and Osaka introduced a secondary visuospatial task (tapping). So again, we see that visuospatial secondary tasks interfere with the visuospatial sketchpad more than they interfere with other working memory systems.

The Episodic Buffer

The episodic buffer is a short-term memory system that holds information integrated across auditory working memory, visual-spatial working memory, and long-term memory for a brief period of time. Because it maintains information already integrated across modalities, it serves as the point of interface between working memory and long-term memory systems (see Baddeley, 2000, 2012). The episodic buffer provides needed meaning or semantic-based information to the working memory system. For example, when you retrieve information from long-term memory, such as the directions to your cousin's apartment, this information is briefly maintained in the buffer before it is converted into directions (in the phonological loop) or a visual map (in the visuospatial sketchpad). The buffer also allows new information to be integrated before it reaches long-term memory during encoding. For example, watching a ballet performance will involve dance information being processed by the visuospatial sketchpad and music information being processed by the phonological loop. The episodic buffer will integrate the dance and music with information from long-term memory related to meaning in the buffer before the experience is stored in long-term episodic memory.

Current evidence for the episodic buffer comes from amnesic patients who have very impaired encoding into long-term memory but normal working memory (Baddeley & Wilson, 2002). When encoding stories, they seem to be able maintain more than seven items of information in mind while reading the stories. The patients forget the stories later, but their "intermediate memory" extends past the usual capacity and duration of working memory. Baddeley and Wilson (2002) argued that this was because of the integrated nature of the episodic buffer. The buffer allowed for understanding even if the patient later forgot the information.

In an experimental study on healthy individuals, Langerock, Vergauwe, and Barrouillet (2014) examined the episodic buffer by asking participants to maintain in working memory associations that crossed the boundaries of working memory systems. Thus, the participants were required to maintain an association between a spoken word (phonological loop) and a location on a map (visuospatial sketchpad). They compared memory on these cross-system associations to within-system associations (e.g., word to word association). Because the within-system associations did not tax the capacity of each system, there was no within-system interference. But because the episodic buffer was necessary for the cross-system associations, some attention was needed to maintain that association, resulting in less accurate performance for the cross-system associations than for the within-system associations. Thus, drawing on the episodic buffer required more attention than if only phonological loop or the visuospatial sketchpad was required, and therefore the task that required the episodic buffer was more difficult to do.

The Central Executive

The central executive is an attentional system that supervises and coordinates the actions of the other working memory components. Baddeley (2012) argued that the central executive has three main functions: It can direct attention to a particular source of information, it can divide attention among sources of input when appropriate, and it can allow us to switch our attention among competing sources of input. In this way, the central executive determines what information will enter the phonological loop, the visuospatial sketchpad, and the episodic buffer. This makes the central executive an extremely vital aspect of cognition, as it controls what goes into and out of conscious awareness. In essence, the goal of the central executive is to allocate limited attentional resources to the working memory subsystems. Most researchers think of the central executive as part of a broader supervisory network, probably located in the prefrontal lobes, which has many other roles in cognition in addition to coordinating working memory.

One interesting study designed to probe the role of the central executive in working memory comes from the work of Teasdale et al. (1995). They asked participants to generate random numbers at a rate of one number per second. This is not as easy as it seems. You must regulate the generation of numbers to ensure that you are not making any obvious pattern. You must also do it in rhythm. If you try it yourself, you will find it does require attention—that is, a little bit of focus to make sure a clear pattern is not developing and that you are keeping up the beat. Teasdale et al. probed participants about every two minutes and asked them what they were thinking about.

When participants reported "daydreaming" (not surprising giving the repetitive nature of the random number–generation task), their patterns tended to be nonrandom (i.e., noticeable sequences, such as 1, 2, 4, 8). When they reported concentration on the task, their numbers were better approximations of randomness. Thus, when people's attention was diverted, as when they were daydreaming, insufficient attentional resources remained to devote to the number generation task. The implication is that the central executive—when directing attention to the task—allowed participants to better produce the digits in working memory.

A common way of examining the effects of the central executive on working memory performance is to vary the tasks that a person is engaging in, so that he or she has to frequently make attentional adjustments to what is being done. One way of doing this is with something called **n-back task**. In the n-back task, a participant is getting a long string of new information, such as digits. A cue will indicate to the participant that he or she must report a digit that occurred n digits before (where n will vary depending on the task requirements). This requires the central executive system to continually update what is being represented in working memory, as older items become superfluous, but new items may be needed to report.

> **n-back task:** In the n-back task, a participant is getting a long string of new information, such as digits. A cue will indicate to the participant that he or she must report a digit that occurred n digits before (where n will vary depending on the task requirements).

For example, Scharinger et al., (2015) examined the central executive using the n-back task in an interesting way. Their participants were given a 2-back test, in which the digit reported two earlier needed to be reported, a relatively difficult task. In addition, irrelevant stimuli, known as flankers, were included in the display. In order to succeed, participants needed to inhibit processing of the irrelevant flankers and continually update the digits being stored in the phonological loop. Interestingly, Scharinger et al. found that inhibiting the flankers activated the central executive, thus allowing greater attentional control, leading to better n-back performance when flankers were present than when they were absent. Thus, the central executive was able to direct attentional control to the necessary task.

The central executive also plays a role in the impairment of driving that occurs when drivers are simultaneously talking on cell phones (Sanbonmatsu et al., 2016; Strayer, Watson, & Drews, 2011). Driving can be an automated task, and Strayer et al. found little impairment of driving for cell phone users when road conditions were normal. However, when hazards suddenly presented themselves, such as swerving cars, rapidly changing lights, and other obstacles, the cell phone–using drivers took longer to respond and consequently had more crashes than those not using cell phones. Moreover, Sanbonmatsu et al. found that when people are talking on cell phones, they are less aware of their driving skills than when they are not using phones. Thus, ironically, even though driving performance is impaired, drivers will continue to think they are driving well, despite mistakes they may make, because they are not be monitoring these mistakes. Thus, even accidents will be attributed to factors other than their cell phone use.

In the event of a dangerous situation, it is likely that the central executive must disengage attention from the cell phone conversation, switch it to the current situation, and then allow for a response. The extra time involved in switching attention from one task to another can be detrimental and dangerous in driving because of the high speeds involved. Strayer et al. (2011) also showed that conversations with passengers in the car do not require as much attention and thus do not result in more accidents. This is likely because there is some degree of joint attention. If the passenger sees a dangerous situation, he or she may disengage in the conversation, giving the driver more time to react. Because under normal driving circumstances, cell phone use does not interfere with driving, most drivers ignore data such as those from the Strayer et al. study. However, the results suggest that, due to demands on the central executive, using a cell phone slows one's responses when one needs to respond most quickly.

SECTION SUMMARY AND QUIZ

The working memory model proposed by Baddeley (2012) states that working memory is actually composed of a number of systems bound together by an attentional mechanism. The phonological loop is our auditory working memory system, responsible for maintaining auditory and speech as conscious content to allow us to process that information. The visuospatial sketchpad has the same function for visual and spatial information. And episodic buffer links the two systems together and is activated when meaning needs to be extracted from the phonological loop and the visuospatial sketchpad. A central executive system maintains attentional control across these systems, allowing some systems to be activated while others need to be inhibited. Much of the data presented in this section are dissociations between these systems, presented to convince the reader of the reality of these separate systems within working memory.

Quiz

1. If a person is doing two rather easy concurrent tasks, one requiring the person to monitor sounds and the other requiring the person to follow a moving cursor, one would expect
   a. Massive interference from the central executive
   b. Only the visuospatial sketchpad requires use of the episodic buffer
   c. Little to no interference, because the two tasks tap into different systems
   d. Interference will only occur with the visuospatial sketchpad

2. Articulatory suppression occurs when
   a. Rehearsal is prevented, because the phonological loop is occupied by a concurrent task
   b. The visuospatial sketchpad is forced into handling phonological information
   c. The episodic buffer is inhibited
   d. All of the above

3. In Brook's (1968) imagery task, people were asked to imagine an image of a letter. They were then required to make a decision about that letter. Brooks found that
    a. Performance was worse when the test task required participants to use the visuospatial sketchpad
    b. Performance was better when the test task required participants to use the visuospatial sketchpad
    c. Performance was worse when the test task required participants to use the phonological loop
    d. Performance was better when the test task required participants to use the phonological loop

4. One reason why talking on cell phones decreases one's driving ability is that
    a. Attention must be disengaged in the conversation before it can be reengaged on the hazards of driving
    b. The cell phone conversation uses the phonological loop, which is critical for driving
    c. The cell phone conversation causes peturbations in working memory, which are hard for the attentional system to allocate elsewhere
    d. All of the above are true

1. c
2. a
3. a
4. a

WORKING MEMORY AND THE BRAIN

Working memory has also become the intense focus of cognitive neuroscientists recently, with the central executive being of particular interest and importance. Baddeley's (2012) multiple-component model has found great support in brain-based studies. Indeed, the phonological loop, the visuospatial sketchpad, and the central executive appear not to be based on fine distinctions in areas of adjacent cortex but seemingly housed in different lobes of the cerebral cortex! So let's start looking at the correlations between behavioral measures of working memory and the brain. We will start with a neuropsychological study and then consider the more recent neuroimaging research.

Warrington and Shallice (1969) studied a young man with brain damage identified in their paper by the initials KF. KF's brain was injured as the result of a motorcycle accident in England. KF's long-term memory was unaffected, both in terms of new learning and retrieving prior knowledge. However, his working memory was severely impaired. On a digit span task, he could not recall spans longer than two digits when tested auditorily. Think about this—if you read out the numbers 5-8-9 to him, he would not be able to repeat them back to you. His visual working memory, however, was somewhat better though still impaired. This pattern suggests that the problem was more with the phonological loop than with the visuospatial sketchpad. Subsequent examination of his brain confirmed this pattern—KF's damage was in the left temporal lobe, in areas typically associated with speech comprehension.

Jonides (1995), in one of the earliest positron emission tomography (PET) studies to look at memory phenomena, tested Baddeley's model. Jonides examined the brains of participants engaged in tasks designed to measure the phonological loop or the visuo-spatial sketchpad. In the task designed to examine the phonological loop, participants watched a sequence of letters at a rate of one letter every three seconds. If a given letter was the same as one two spaces back (i.e., six seconds ago), the participant indicated this by saying yes. If not, the participant said no (this is the *n*-back task again). Most people will do this task by mentally rehearsing the digits as they appear. Thus, even though the presentation is visual, it is sensible to consider this a task for the phonological loop. To occupy the visuospatial sketchpad, participants saw three dots presented in different locations for a 200-msec interval. The dots then disappeared, and three seconds later, a circle appeared. The participants indicated whether this circle marked a spot where one of the dots had been just prior.

The PET data showed that the two tasks led to different patterns of activation in the cerebral cortex. The phonological loop task was associated with activity in Broca's area of the left frontal lobe (known as an important area in speech) as well as areas in the left parietal lobe. In contrast, the visuospatial sketchpad task led to activation in the right occipital lobe (visual processing) as well as the right parietal and right prefrontal lobes. Thus, the distinction between the visuospatial sketchpad and the phonological loop is supported by PET studies, which show different activation patterns for each task (see Jonides, Lacey, & Nee, 2005; Jonides et al., 2008). Indeed, these data suggest that the basis of the phonological loop may be in the left hemisphere, but the basis for the visuospatial sketchpad may be in the right hemisphere. So, the early neuroimaging data suggest strong differences between the neural bases of these two systems.

Neuroimaging data from fMRI confirm that the central executive is an important component of working memory. Areas of the prefrontal cortex that are known to be involved in other attentional or monitoring tasks also appear to be active during working memory tasks, including digit span and other verbal working memory tasks. For example, PET studies and functional magnetic resonance imaging (fMRI) studies agree that verbal working memory tasks activate the right dorsolateral prefrontal cortex (Chen et al, 2015; Ruchkin, Grafman, Cameron, & Berndt, 2003; Rypma & D'Esposito, 2003) as well as the anterior cingulate (Otsuka & Osaka, 2005, 2015). The anterior cingulate is located toward the back of the prefrontal regions of the brain. Both of these brain regions (right dorsolateral prefrontal cortex and anterior cingulate) are important in self-regulation, attention, and cognitive monitoring as well as verbal working memory. In an interesting study of the neural correlates of the central executive, Chen et al. (2015) required participants to scan visual arrays or auditory lists for "oddball" items—that is, items that did not fit into a pattern being presented. The oddball items for visual tasks could be a green dot presented among red dots. The oddball item for an auditory task could be a note of higher pitch presented among other notes all of the same lower pitch. Finally, in a multisensory task, the participant had to detect when both the color and pitch were oddballs. In this study, the anterior cingulate (prefrontal) showed a crucial role in detecting the oddball item and more so when the task became more difficult, as in the multisensory condition. Thus, this study confirms the importance of prefrontal regions to the control exerted by the central executive.

Thus, the pattern of activity that emerges from the neuroimaging studies is the following. The phonological loop is mainly housed in the language-related areas of the brain, particularly in areas associated with the production of speech. The visuospatial sketchpad appears to be located in areas of the right hemisphere associated with vision and spatial skills, including the occipital lobe, which is the visual lobe of the brain. Finally, the central executive is centered in prefrontal regions of the brain, which are also active in planning, monitoring, and other executive cognitive functions.

APPLICATIONS OF WORKING MEMORY

Reading Fluency

When we read, we use our working memory. In fact, your working memory—at this very moment—is holding the words (phonological loop) and ideas (episodic buffer) in this sentence so that you can understand this sentence. Consider how difficult it must have been for the patient KF to read, given he could only keep two words in his working memory at any particular time. It is likely that his reading was slow and laborious. Given how important working memory is to reading, it is likely that there may be some connection between working memory capacity and reading ability. Indeed, in children just becoming fully fluent readers (age 12 and under), there is a clear correlation between the capacity of working memory and **reading fluency** (Daneman & Carpenter, 1980). If the child can maintain more information in his or her working memory, he or she can understand the material quicker with less "looking back." Stated another way, the better a child's working memory is, the better his or her reading ability is.

> **Reading fluency:** The ability to read at speeds sufficient to process and understand written material.

Daneman and Carpenter (1980) asked young participants to read sentences and process them for meaning. They were then asked questions about the meaning of the passage and asked to retrieve as many words as they could from the end of the last sentence. They found that participants who could retrieve more of the last few words also scored higher on comprehension. This supports the idea that there is a relation between good working memory ability and reading ability. This advantage continues into college. Daneman and Hannon (2001) found that young adults with high working memory capacity did better on their SAT tests than those with lower working memory capacity. Shipstead, Harrison, and Engle (2015) also found correlations between measures of working memory, both visual and auditory, and fluid intelligence. They argue that part of this advantage comes from the central-executive component. When one is better able to direct attention, one will have more working space to devote to problem-solving. On the other hand, this group has also shown that training working memory to be better does not necessarily result in better abilities on other tasks (Shipstead, Redick, & Engle, 2012). Although with practice, we can improve our ability to remember digit spans and do better on serial position curve tests and other measures of working memory, improving on these tasks does not automatically translate to better reading comprehension, verbal fluency, or multitasking.

Verbal Fluency

Engle (2002) argued that working memory capacity was also related to **verbal fluency**—that is, the ability to speak fluently without pausing. In other words, those of us who intrude frequent "uhs" or "hmms" in our speech are likely to have less efficient working memory than those who are less likely to make these errors. Engle argued that those with larger working memory capacities were also those who spoke with fewer pauses. To test this, Engle and his colleagues divided students into groups with high working memory scores and those with lower working memory scores. The students with the higher working memory scores were able to generate more examples in a given category (e.g., tools) during a particular time period than those with lower working memory scores.

> **Verbal fluency:** The ability to talk without pausing or stopping.

Attention-Deficit/Hyperactivity Disorder

Some studies have shown that children with attention deficit disorders have weaker working memory capacity than normal controls (Klingberg, Forssberg, & Westerberg, 2002). However, this is reversible. Children with attention-deficit/hyperactivity disorder (ADHD) who receive training and practice in working memory tasks can improve their working memory capacity. Interestingly, recent research has focused on the relation of the hyperactive movement typically seen in children with ADHD and their attentional deficits. Sarver et al. (2015) examined whether the two symptoms co-varied or whether there was no relation between them. Instead, they found that the more movement a child engaged in, the better their working memory performance was, suggesting that the excess movement actually helps ADHD children concentrate rather than hurting them.

Alzheimer's Disease

Alzheimer's disease is often hard to diagnose. Its early symptoms are difficult to distinguish from other forms of amnesia. However, unlike amnesia that results directly from damage to the medial temporal lobe, in which there is no deficit in working memory, Alzheimer's disease is accompanied by a deficit in working memory (Caza & Belleville, 2008). Therefore, Alzheimer's can be distinguished during its early phases from other organic deficits by examining working memory performance.

SUMMARY

Working memory refers to the neural structures and cognitive processes that maintain the accessibility of information for short periods of time in an active conscious state. Working memory holds a small amount of information at any one time, which can be maintained by rehearsal. Rehearsal is the active repetition of information in conscious awareness. *Working memory is* the current term for this kind of memory, while previous generations referred to it by the name *short-term memory*. Working memory capacity can be measured by the digit span task or by the recency effect in serial position curves. Most estimates of the capacity of working memory indicate that we can maintain about seven items. However, this is modulated by the length of the words we are maintaining in working memory. Words that take less time to pronounce are easier to maintain in working memory. In free recall of serial lists, the primacy effect is associated with long-term memory, whereas the recency effect is associated with working memory. Most recently, working memory is thought to consist of several subsystems, including the visuospatial sketchpad, the phonological loop, the episodic buffer, and the central executive. Each subsystem is responsible for one aspect of the working memory process, with the central executive coordinating among them. Areas in the prefrontal and medial temporal lobes appear to be the neural regions mediating working memory. Working memory is linked to reading fluency and verbal fluency. It is impaired in children with ADHD and in older adults with Alzheimer's disease (see also study.sagepub.com/schwartz3e[5,6]).

KEY TERMS

articulatory suppression	iconic memory	recency effect
capacity	interference	rehearsal
central executive	irrelevant speech effect	rehearsal prevention task
chunking	maintenance rehearsal	sensory memory
concurrent tasks	*n*-back task	serial position curve
digit span task	phonological loop	short-term memory
duration of information in working memory	primacy effect	verbal fluency
	primary memory	visuospatial sketchpad
echoic memory	pronunciation time	word length effect
elaborative rehearsal	reading fluency	working memory
episodic buffer		

REVIEW QUESTIONS

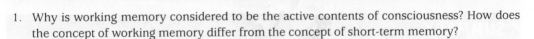

1. Why is working memory considered to be the active contents of consciousness? How does the concept of working memory differ from the concept of short-term memory?

2. Describe three main differences between working memory and long-term memory.

3. How does the digit span task measure working memory? How is it modified by the pronunciation time effect?

4. How did Naveh-Benjamin and his colleagues demonstrate the importance of pronunciation time on the capacity of working memory?

5. How is the serial position curve measured?

6. Describe one variable that affects the primacy portion of the curve and one variable that affects the recency portion of the curve.

7. What evidence supports the idea that the visuospatial sketchpad and the phonological loop are separate subsystems in working memory?

8. What is the role of the central executive in working memory?

9. What neuropsychological evidence exists to support the notion that working memory is a distinct memory system separate from long-term memory?

10. How is working memory related to reading ability?

ONLINE RESOURCES

1. For information on William James, go to http://plato.stanford.edu/entries/james/.

2. For animal working memory, see http://www.psych.utoronto.ca/users/shettle/sararsch.html.

3. For more on K. Anders Ericsson's work, go to http://www.psy.fsu.edu/faculty/ericsson/ericsson.hp.html.

4. For a demonstration of serial position, go to http://cat.xula.edu/thinker/memory/working/serial/.

5. For information on Alan Baddeley, go to http://www.gocognitive.net/interviews/alan-baddeley-working-memory/.

6. For a nice overview of working memory, go to http://cat.xula.edu/thinker/memory/working/.

Go to **study.sagepub.com/schwartz3e** for additional exercises and study resources. Select **Chapter 3, Working Memory** for chapter-specific resources.

CHAPTER 4

Episodic Memory

Remember some of the important and significant events from your life. Think about your high school graduation ceremony or when you and your partner agreed to get married. Also think of more mundane information—have you brushed your teeth yet today? Was your professor drinking Coca-Cola or Pepsi this morning? Did you go to the gym, and what exercises did you do there? Each of these represents the memory of a specific event from your life. In some cases, they happened years ago and are very important, whereas in other cases, they happened recently and are much less important. But each event happened in the past and only happened once, yet we can relive and feel again what we felt then. This is the hallmark of episodic memory—our long-term memory for the personal events from our lives.

Many memory theorists today think that long-term memory is also divided into systems—each designed to handle different kinds of information. Starting with the work of Endel Tulving (discussed in Chapter 1), many memory researchers think we have a unique neurocognitive system, known as episodic memory, designed to encode, store, and retrieve the unique events of our lives (Tulving, 2002; Perrin & Rousset, 2014). Memory systems have to be able to encode new information, represent it, and then later provide the person with access to that information when remembering is called for. Unlike working memory, which stores only a small amount of information, long-term memory systems, such as episodic memory, must be able to store a tremendous amount of information and for much longer periods of time. For any particular event, one must remember when the event took place, where it took place, what was involved in the event, and who was present. It may also be important to remember what our emotions were and what the outcome was. We need to store this information for all of the thousands and thousands of events that we participate in over the course of our lives. Thus, finding a way to store or represent all this information is crucial for episodic and other long-term memory systems. Moreover, we must be able to retrieve this information accurately and quickly when we need it.

Tulving hypothesized an important difference between two functional aspects of memory: knowledge of the world (semantic memory) and memory of personal events (episodic memory). (See Table 4.1.) According to Tulving, episodic memory is our personal memory for the events from our lives. For example, the memory of your high school graduation ceremony is stored in your episodic memory, as is the memory of using the stair-climbing machine this morning at the gym. On the other hand, semantic memory encompasses our knowledge of the world. For example, your knowledge that George Washington was the first president of the United States is stored in semantic memory, as is your knowledge that Ottawa is the capital of Canada. Episodic and semantic memory, therefore, differ in the *content* of what is represented, in their personal meaning to the individual and in the emotions they inspire.

Tulving's assertion was that we have different neurocognitive systems for episodic and semantic memory. Tulving claimed that our brains have different systems that operate according to different principles for these two types of memory. When Tulving first proposed this point of view in the early 1970s, it was met with great skepticism. However, a considerable amount of evidence now supports both the cognitive and neural basis for this hypothesis.

Let's start with semantic memory. Semantic memory is the neurocognitive memory system that encodes, stores, and retrieves information concerning knowledge of the world. The contents of semantic memory are the facts, stories, and associations we make as we learn about our world. Semantic memory is

> **Semantic memory:** The neurocognitive memory system that encodes, stores, and retrieves information concerning knowledge of the world.

impersonal in that many of the facts that we store in it are detached from our actual experience, and we may not remember when and where we learned these facts. Moreover, we are more likely to express semantic memory by saying "I know" rather than "I remember." Each individual person stores thousands upon thousands of semantic memories. For example, that the role of Sherlock Holmes is played by the actor Benedict Cumberbatch is an example of knowledge about the world. "Angela Merkel was chancellor of Germany in 2016," is also stored in semantic memory. So are facts such as "Pittsburgh is east of Miami," "Vegans do not eat eggs," and "Casey Kasem was the original voice of Shaggy on *Scooby Doo*." In addition, we may also have semantic memory that does reference ourselves. Thus, you can say, "I went to South Valley Elementary School," without actually thinking about any particular experience in elementary school. Most of us also know our birthday, even though we do not remember being born. We will continue our discussion of semantic memory in Chapter 5. For now, it is presented just to contrast with episodic memory.

Episodic memory is the neurocognitive memory system that encodes, stores, and retrieves memories of our personal individual experiences. Episodic memory is the system responsible for encoding the *what, when,* and *where* of an event and representing the pastness of the event. This means we are sure the event is past and not occurring at present. Moreover, the memory pertains to the past rather than the present. For example, you may remember shaking President

> **Episodic memory:** The neurocognitive memory system that encodes, stores, and retrieves memories of our personal individual experiences.

Obama's hand at a campaign rally. You attribute this to the past and will continue to do so. In addition, you are likely to remember the where (on your college campus) and the when (while he was running for reelection) as well as the what (shaking hands with the president). For most of us, meeting the president is an exciting event that we are not likely to forget. Thus, many episodic memories are maintained for our entire lifetimes.

Episodic memories are usually characterized by feelings of "remembering" rather than knowing. For it to be an episodic memory, it must be directly based on personal experiences that you have had. For example, remembering the time I saw an iguana fall out of a tree and land directly in front of me is an example of episodic memory. So is the memory of the time I drove a rented convertible Ford Mustang from the airport to my hotel in San Francisco. Episodic memories can be big events from one's life (remembering the moment when you say "I do" in a wedding ceremony) to small events from your life (remembering the act of pouring cereal during this morning's breakfast). Episodic memory even includes **flashbulb memories**, those highly salient memories people have of their own circumstances during major public events. Anyone who was older than age six on September 11, 2001, probably remembers what they were doing and where they were when they heard the news of the terrorist attacks

Flashbulb memories: Highly confident personal memories of surprising events. In order to study them, researchers have focused on the memory of public tragedies.

that day. Some of us may also have more recent flashbulb memories of learning of Michael Jackson's death, the death of Osama bin Laden, or the resignation of the pope, to name a few that have been studied recently (Demiray & Freund, 2015).

Note some of the functional differences between the episodic and semantic memory. Again, semantic memory need not be personal. Indeed, we can have semantic memories concerning events that occurred long before we were born. For example, you probably know that George Washington was the first president of the United States, even though it happened hundreds of years before your birth. On the other hand, episodic memories are always *personal experiences*. Thus, you remember your visit to the Washington Monument in which your umbrella was blown out by the wind while you ran to your car in a thunderstorm. Furthermore, semantic memories are usually not emotionally tinged. You may know that an earthquake in Turkey killed tens of thousands of people, but that fact alone may not elicit emotion. It is only when you retrieve your own episodic memory of seeing television news coverage of the tragedy that emotion becomes involved. Emotion is, however, an essential component of many episodic memories. Anguish, anger, and grief are all vital components of most of our flashbulb memories of 9/11. On the positive side, happiness is (usually) a key component of memories of wedding ceremonies.

Another difference between episodic memory and semantic memory, however subtle, is that episodic memories necessarily are concerned about the past, whereas semantic memories usually concern the present. So the knowledge (semantic memory) that seitan is used as a meat substitute by vegans is usually retrieved when somebody wants information about what to expect at a vegan restaurant now. Likewise, we might retrieve "Dr. Hughes's office is on the fourth floor of Silsby Hall," because we want to direct someone to Dr. Hughes right now. Because semantic memory serves our present purposes, it is important to update semantic memory. If Dr. Hughes moves his office from the fourth floor of Silsby Hall to the third floor of Moore Hall, I have to update my memory to direct people to the right office.

In contrast, episodic memory truly concerns the past. We want people to know not that vegan restaurants exist but that we ate at The Green Bowl last week and had a delicious dinner and a fun time with friends. You retrieve your day of snorkeling off the coast of Cozumel, Mexico, and you want to reexperience the peacefulness and beauty of the event.

In this way, episodic memory emphasizes the past rather than the present (Tulving & Lepage, 2000). Indeed, Tulving has called episodic memory "mental time travel." Episodic memory is also a highly social phenomenon. We want to share our episodic memories with our friends and family. Indeed, we all know someone who shares his or episodic memories too often. Think of your reaction when your uncle tells you for the fifth time about his giant meal on the cruise ship: you cannot wait to get away. In a more positive vein, when you meet old friends whom you may not have seen or spoken with in some time, you are likely to start reminiscing about old times—that is, sharing your common memories of the exciting, fun, and embarrassing experiences that you shared. All of these aspects of social experience involve being able to recall and share episodic memories.

The term *autobiographical memory* means the memories we have of our own lives. Autobiographical memory is not associated with any individual particular neurocognitive system in the way that episodic and semantic memory are. In fact, autobiographical memory is a combination of episodic memory and self-referential semantic memories. Our total memory of our lives is composed of our memory for both events from our lives and the facts of our lives; some of the latter may not be based on the memory of individual experiences. For example, you may know the details concerning your birth—such as what city you were born in, what hospital, and your actual birthday—as well as similar details for a sibling born a year or two after you. These memories are semantic in nature, as you were too young to encode them yourself episodically. Your knowledge of them is semantic knowledge, not episodic memory. Similarly, you may have information about your personality—that you are kind and generous—even when you are not thinking about a particular event in which you acted kindly or generously. In semantic memory, we may form categories concerning our lives, such as "when I was in high school," which do not necessitate any episodic memories of being in high school, although the semantic category may facilitate the retrieval of related episodic memories. For these reasons, be careful not to confuse the term *autobiographical memory* with the term *episodic memory*. Bear in mind that all episodic memories are autobiographical, but not all autobiographical memories are episodic. We will focus on autobiographical memory in Chapter 7.

Table 4.1 Differences Between Episodic and Semantic Memory

Characteristics	Episodic Memory	Semantic Memory
Type of information stored	Personally experienced events	General facts
Unit of information	Events or episodes	Facts, ideas, concepts
Mental experience	"Mental time travel"/remembering	"Knowledge of facts"/knowing
Neural regions/retrieval: frontal lobe	Right prefrontal	Left prefrontal
Neural regions: temporal lobe	Medial temporal lobes	Medial temporal lobes

SOURCE: Adapted from Tulving (1983).

EVIDENCE FOR THE EPISODIC/SEMANTIC DISTINCTION

When Tulving first proposed the distinction between episodic and semantic memory, it was a largely unsubstantiated hypothesis (Tulving, 1972, 1983). It made some intuitive sense, but there was little evidence to demonstrate that semantic and episodic memory form distinct systems. Today, a large body of evidence supports the reality of this distinction, some of it coming from cognitive psychology and much of it coming from the neuropsychological and neuroimaging domain (Kwok, Shallice, & Macaluso, 2012).

Behavioral Evidence

We have already pointed out that many of us prefer the expression "I know" to describe a semantic memory but "I remember" to describe an episodic memory. Tulving (1983) thought this distinction was important and that the feeling of knowing versus remembering captures some underlying difference between the two mental states. Indeed, most languages make a distinction between *know* and *remember* (e.g., *savoir* and *souvenir* in French). It is also the case that the boundaries between "I know" and "I remember" are flexible. No one would look at you oddly if you said, "I *know* where and whom I was with when I saw Michael Phelps get his eight gold medals in the Olympics." However, it connotes something different if you say, "I *remember* where and whom I was with when I saw Michael Phelps get his eight gold medals in the Olympics." The latter is clearly more personal and "episodic."

Tulving (1985) devised a test in which people were asked if they "remembered" information or if they "knew" information, and then examined whether different experimental variables affected the two subjective states in different ways. In these studies, "remembered" meant that the participants could retrieve the personal context in which they encountered the information. Remembering also meant an experience of "mental time travel"—that is, that the participant was aware of the past. In contrast, "know" judgments were simply declarations that the information was accessible in memory. "Know" judgments are about what the person knows now, not about the past per se. Tulving found that people reliably make the distinction between "remember" and "know" judgments. Moreover, the judgments are correlated with other behavioral traits. For example, "remember" judgments are more likely than "know" judgments to be accompanied by contextual details—that is, what participants were thinking of when they encoded the items. However, "remember" and "know" judgments do not differ with respect to how well they correlate with correct recognition. So the difference is not one of memory strength but rather the subjective experience that accompanies the retrieval. Here is a thought experiment for you: If you learn a list of unrelated words (e.g., *dog, fork, pasture, compass,* etc.), when you see one of the words later, what factors will cause you to experience that you "know" that the word was on the list versus that you "remember" that the word was on the list?

Consider an experiment in which you study some words by focusing on what the words mean. We shall see shortly that this leads to good recall of those words. In another condition, however, you study some words by focusing on what color the word is printed in. Later, you are asked to recognize the words from among distractors and also asked to distinguish whether you "remember" (henceforth *R judgments*) or "know" (henceforth *K judgments*) the words. Research shows that K judgments occur equally often when you study for meaning and when you study for visual characteristics. However, R judgments are much more common for meaning-based learning than for visual-based learning (Gardiner, 2002). In contrast, studying words versus nonwords (strings of letters that look like words but are not, such as *bloon*) does not affect the number of R judgments, but non-words are much more likely to receive K judgments than words. Rimmele, Davachi, and Phelps (2012) looked at complex memory for events that happened in particular places at particular times. They found that R judgments were more likely to be accompanied by memories of the time and place of the event than were K judgments. Rimmele et al.'s findings are also consistent with the idea of episodic memory referring to past events in time (when) and space (where). To summarize, these and other experimental variables show that R judgments and K judgments are influenced by different factors.

These data led Tulving and many other researchers to conclude that **remember judgments** are more likely to accompany episodic events, whereas **know judgments** (sometimes pronounced "kih-no," to differentiate them from "no" or don't-remember judgments) are more likely to

> **Remember/know judgments:** Tasks in which participants determine the feeling of memories by assigning them categories of "remember" or "know."

accompany semantic knowledge. These subjective variables are correlated with many objective variables—that is, how participants behave in experiments as measured by their recall or recognition.

Neuropsychological Evidence

Neuropsychology refers to the relation between brain damage and memory and cognitive deficits. Research in this area now shows that damage to the brain can impair both episodic memory and semantic memory and that there can be impairment to one form of memory but not to the other. Memory impairment occurs much more often for episodic memory. Semantic memory amnesia is, in fact, quite rare. Moreover, even when both episodic memory and semantic memory are affected by brain damage, memory impairment is usually much greater for episodic memory than for semantic memory. In these cases, amnesic patients can lose much of the access to their episodic memories without substantial impairment of retrieval from semantic memory, although they may have impaired encoding into semantic memory.

Consider the case of the amnesic patient KC (Rosenbaum et al., 2005). KC suffered extensive brain damage following a terrible motorcycle accident. During testing, KC could retrieve information from semantic memory essentially normally. He was able to list all the teams that had won the Stanley Cup in hockey over the previous 10 years, for example. He could also tell you how a car engine worked and how to repair one. However, retrieval from episodic memory was severely impaired. He could not remember any details of his life at all: none of the individual times he had fixed cars, none of his previous motorcycle crashes, or even the details concerning the tragic death of his brother. Nor could he form new episodic memories. Thus, with KC, we see that both encoding and retrieval from episodic memory can occur without damage to semantic memory. These patients point to an important neurological difference between semantic and episodic memory. (To see KC for yourself, find the link to a YouTube video here: study.sagepub.com/schwartz3e.[1])

Developmental amnesia: A congenital memory deficit, usually restrictive to episodic memory.

Dissociation: Brain damage that affects one cognitive system but leaves another one intact.

Vargha-Khadem et al. (1997) studied patients who have **developmental amnesia**. Unlike HM (see Chapter 2) or KC, these patients did not have traumatic brain injuries, at least none that they or their doctors were aware of. Nonetheless, they appeared to be impaired at encoding new episodic events and retrieving events from their lives. Nonetheless, they learned new facts about the world—that is, they learned semantic information—normally. Thus, their deficits seemed to be solely in the episodic memory system. Therefore, based on patterns of deficits seen in neuropsychological patients, there is a **dissociation** between episodic and semantic memory (Rosenbaum, Casidy, & Herdman, 2015). Dissociation means that brain damage can affect one cognitive system but leave another one intact. (For more information on developmental amnesia, go to www.sage pub.com/schwartz3e.[2])

Evidence From Neuroimaging

The *neuro* in the term *neurocognitive systems of memory* was given a giant boost when people began looking at differences between episodic and semantic memory using neuroimaging techniques. Although there is some overlap in the engagement of neural regions during both kinds of memory tasks, there are also great differences. It is these differences that are now the best support to the claim that episodic and semantic memory are different neurocognitive systems.

Prince, Tsukiura, and Cabeza (2007) were interested in the neural underpinnings of episodic and semantic memory. In particular, they were interested in what brain regions are responsible for each memory system. They were able to look for such differences using fMRI technology. In their study, they asked participants to study word pairs while being monitored by a scanner. Pairs with a stronger semantic connection (e.g., safety-welfare) were considered to tap semantic memory encoding, whereas pairs without an obvious association (e.g., donor-sequel) were considered to tap episodic memory. Later, participants were required to recall the target pair while also in the scanner. This allowed them to compare both episodic encoding to semantic encoding and episodic retrieval to semantic retrieval. One of their concerns was the similarity between episodic encoding and semantic retrieval. In their view, these two processes are similar, because both involve getting to the associations made between cues and targets. Thus, one way of examining differences in the two memory systems is to compare the two.

Consistent with the view that episodic and semantic memory represent different systems, Prince et al. (2007) found distinct areas of the brain that were active during the retrieval from the different systems (also see Habib, Nyberg, Tulving, 2003; Shimamura, 2014). With respect to episodic encoding, Prince et al. found that the hippocampus was involved, but a posterior region of the temporal cortex was more associated with semantic retrieval. Moreover, there were differences between episodic encoding and semantic retrieval in the frontal lobe as well. The activity stimulated by semantic retrieval was more in the back (posterior) of the left prefrontal lobe, but for episodic encoding, it was more towards the front (anterior) of the left prefrontal lobe. Thus, this study suggests differences between episodic and semantic memory.

An interesting follow-up examined memory for taste (Okamoto et al., 2011). In this study, participants sampled new tastes, via sipping on a straw, and were scanned as they compared tastes to see which taste matched an earlier one (a form of recognition test). Okamoto et al. found that during retrieval, there was greater activity in the right prefrontal lobe than in the left prefrontal lobe, supporting the idea that retrieval from episodic memory employs a network that uses the right prefrontal lobe more than the left prefrontal lobe. More recent accounts of episodic memory show more left hemisphere involvement in many aspects of episodic memory (Benoit & Schacter, 2015). Nonetheless, researchers continue to find differences between the neural systems underlying episodic and semantic memory (Bergström et al., 2015).

Thus, although semantic and episodic memory may share many features, they have different underlying neural networks in the brain. To summarize, the neuroimaging data are consistent with the behavioral data; episodic memory and semantic memory are likely the products of different neurocognitive systems.

Section Summary and Quiz

1. Dwayne is a college senior who remembers the moment in time he won the spelling bee when he was in 8th grade and how happy he felt. Dwayne is recalling from
   a. Semantic memory
   b. Episodic memory
   c. Avuncular memory
   d. Working memory

2. In the remember/know distinction, the evidence suggests that, when people make "remember" judgments, they are using primarily_____, but when they make "know" judgments, they are using primarily _____.
   a. Semantic memory; episodic memory
   b. Episodic memory; semantic memory
   c. Working memory; episodic memory
   d. Episodic memory; working memory

3. In developmental amnesia, one of the key symptoms is
   a. Lowered general intelligence
   b. A gradual decline in semantic memory performance as a child approaches adulthood
   c. A decrement in episodic memory only
   d. All of the above

4. The experience of mental time travel is associated with which form of memory?
   a. Episodic memory
   b. Reprisodic memory
   c. Autobiographical memory
   d. Maniacal memory

Answers
1. b
2. b
3. c
4. a

MEMORY PROCESSES: ENCODING, REPRESENTATION, AND RETRIEVAL (PART I)

Encoding: The learning process—that is, how information is learned.

Representation: The storage of information in memory when that information is not in use.

Retrieval: The process of how we activate information from long-term memory and access it when we need it.

Both episodic and semantic memory can be divided into three important processes that are necessary for any memory system: encoding, representation, and retrieval. **Encoding** refers to the learning process—that is, how information is initially learned. **Representation** is how we store information when it is not currently in use. **Retrieval** is the process of how we activate information from long-term memory and access it when we need it. There is strong overlap in how semantic memory and episodic memory accomplish these goals on a cognitive level. In this chapter, we focus on episodic memory, but the processes of encoding follow similar rules in semantic memory. Representation and semantic memory will be discussed in Chapter 5.

Encoding in Episodic Memory

Encoding is the process by which we learn—that is, we perceive the world and process that information into memory. Encoding can also occur when we commit something we are imagining to memory. Thus, when someone you have just met tells you her name, you encode that name so that you can remember her later. When you go skydiving for the first time, you encode the exciting experiences you have so that you can relive them later. In semantic memory, encoding is usually a very deliberate process—you want to encode the translations of words into Spanish for your Spanish class, and you want to learn the directions to locations on campus. However, in episodic memory, encoding is usually not the goal—we want to thoroughly enjoy the experience of the skydiving trip. That we form a strong encoding of it is secondary. Because encoding is the first step in the memory process, we will consider it first.

Levels of Processing

The concept of **levels of processing** refers to the fact that more meaning-based handling of information leads to better encoding of that information. That processing for meaning leads to better encoding of information is one of the widely applicable principles in

> **Levels of processing:** More meaningful handling of information leads to better encoding of that information.

modern cognitive psychology. In all but a few rare exceptions, if we think about meaning as we learn new information, we will retain it better (Fisher & Craik, 1977). It is also relevant to point out that levels of processing applies to encoding into both episodic memory and to semantic memory.

Two University of Toronto memory researchers, Fergus Craik and Robert Lockhart, developed the theory of levels of processing in the early 1970s (Craik & Lockhart, 1972). Although they originally presented it as a theory that would allow for short-term memory and long-term memory to be considered two different processes of the same system, nowadays levels-of-processing theory has broader application, providing the basis of much of what we know about encoding. (For an alternate view of levels of processing, go to www.sagepub.com/schwartz3e.[3]). Although Craik and Lockhart were interested in levels of processing from a theoretical point of view, the application of the logic of levels of processing can be useful to students wishing to improve the efficiency of their learning.

Craik and Lockhart (1972) were interested in incidental learning more than in intentional learning. **Incidental learning** occurs when people encode information not by actively trying to remember but rather as a by-product of perceiving and understanding the world. In incidental learning, the individual's goal is not to encode information but to understand speech, interact with others, find where one needs to go, and so forth. For example, you don't study the names of people at your party—they are your friends. In the course of achieving these goals, one also learns information. Thus, if asked later who was at your party, you are able to identify the names of your friends at the party. **Intentional learning** takes place when people actively engage in learning information, because they know that

> **Incidental learning:** People encode information not through active efforts to remember but rather as a by-product of perceiving and understanding the world.

> **Intentional learning:** People actively engage in learning information, because they know that their memories may be tested.

their memories may be tested. In intentional learning, we intend to remember something and work hard to do so (see Figure 4.1). Thus, intentional learning maps onto what you typically do in a college class—your goal is to learn the material specified on the syllabus.

Figure 4.1 Most learning is incidental, in contrast to the intentional learning necessary in school situations, in which students make great efforts to master large amounts of material.

Thinkstock/Jupiter Images/Brand X Pictures

Craik and Lockhart (1972) considered incidental learning to be an important aspect of cognition. They argued that much of our learning in ordinary life is, in fact, incidental learning. In this view, most of our knowledge and memory is based not on explicit memorization but just on processing the events and information we need. For example, we don't normally say to ourselves, "I have to remember how to get to Johnny's house," or "I have to remember how to chop the onions just right," or even, "I have to remember the plot of that great new movie we just saw." Yet in each case, you encode something, such as the directions, the recipe, or the plot, even though you are not specifically studying this information as you might do for a test in a college class. Another example is when a friend is coming over for dinner. You try to remember what that person likes to eat and perhaps what you served the last time that he or she was at your house for dinner. You probably never sat down with a notebook and recorded your friend's dining preferences, but if that person is a good friend, you have incidentally learned his or her favorite foods. Thus, incidental learning is important to our lives. To simulate such learning in their experiments, Craik and Lockhart decided to use incidental learning.

Craik and Lockhart (1972) argued that our attentional resources are limited, so we can focus on only some aspects of any particular stimulus. However, people can control on what aspects of the stimulus they focus. For example, when reading a novel, we can focus on the quality of the writing, the excitement of the plot, and the development of the characters. But it is usually difficult to concentrate on all of these aspects of reading a novel at once. This is where the idea of levels of processing fits in: The manner in which information is first encountered and rehearsed leads to a different depth of processing. **Elaborative rehearsal** leads to deeper processing, and **maintenance rehearsal** leads to shallow processing. Thus, when reading a novel, if you only pay attention to the size of the type, whether the book is old or new, or what designs are on the cover, you are engaged in **shallow processing**. If you are trying to connect the plot to ideas about the world, consider the book's applications to your life, and gauge whether the book is enjoyable or not, this is considered **deep processing**. If you are listening to someone speak, deep processing means attending to the message of the speaker, whereas shallow processing would include attending to the speaker's accent, his or her raspy voice, or how he or she pronounced the letter *r*. In real life, we normally are expected to pay attention to meaning, but in rare circumstances lower-level processing may be more important.

Elaborative rehearsal: Processing the meaning of information in working memory.

Maintenance rehearsal: Repeating information over and over.

Shallow processing: Processing information by using maintenance rehearsal or processing for sensory characteristics to produce less remembering than deep processing.

Deep processing: Processing information by using elaborative or meaningful processing to produce more remembering than shallow processing.

Craik and Lockhart (1972) then derived the following hypothesis: When we process more deeply—that is, using elaborative or meaningful processing—we will be more likely to remember the information processed; when we process more shallowly—that is, using maintenance rehearsal or processing for sensory characteristics—we will remember less of the information processed. In retrospect nearly 40 years later, these ideas appear relatively straightforward. But at the time, they offered a new way of looking at memory. They also have clear implications for memory improvement: Process more deeply, and you will remember more of what you are studying.

To test this hypothesis, Craik teamed up with Endel Tulving to create what is now considered a landmark study (Craik & Tulving, 1975). In a series of experiments, Craik and Tulving employed a number of new methods, which became standard in much of the research that would follow ever since in memory research. First, they wanted their participants to encode the information through incidental learning, because this approximates many real-life situations. Therefore, they did not tell the participants that their memory would be tested later. Second, they wanted the participants to encode some ideas through shallow or sensory-level processing and other items through deep or meaning-based processing. To accomplish both of these objectives, Craik and Tulving employed **orienting tasks**. An orienting task directs the participant's attention to some aspect of the stimuli—either deep or shallow—but does not alert the participant to the potential of a later memory test. Participants were later given a surprise test of recognition or recall for the words on which they had worked. In the orienting task, participants thought that they were being tested on the speed at which they could perform simple tasks involving words but were not told that their memory for

> **Orienting tasks:** Direct the participant's attention to some aspect of the stimuli—either deep or shallow—but do not alert the participant to the potential of a later memory test.

these words would be tested later. For example, the participant might see the word *beetle* and have to decide whether it is written in all capital letters or not. This would qualify as a shallow or sensory task. A deep or meaning-based task involved asking something about the meaning. Therefore, deciding whether a "beetle" is an example of an animal is a meaning-based task. It is easy—but it requires the participants to think about the meaning of the word.

In the experiments, participants were first asked a question (the orienting task). They were then presented visually with a word and asked to answer the question with a yes or no. Some of the questions concerned physical characteristics of the printed word (visual-shallow), some of the questions concerned what the word sounded like (auditory-shallow), and others were concerned with the meaning of the word (meaning based-deep).

For example, if the word was *chip*

Visual-shallow: Does the word have any capital letters?   NO

Auditory-shallow: Does the word rhyme with "skip"?   YES

Meaningful: Does it fit in the following sentence:

"The boys were only allowed to eat one potato ___ each"?   YES

The experimental hypothesis was that deeper processing should lead to better retention of the words than shallow processing. In terms of the experiment, this means that the meaningful orienting task would produce better recall or recognition performance than the shallow processing, even though the participants were not trying to remember in any condition. And indeed, this is precisely what Craik and Tulving (1975) found in their experiment (see Figure 4.2). When the participants were given a surprise recognition test or a surprise recall test, the items that had been encoded with meaningful or deep processing were remembered better than those items that had been encoded with shallow processing.

The idea of levels of processing has many implications and applications. First of all, it implies that simply using deep or meaning-based encoding strategies can improve memory without any additional investment of time and effort. This can be very useful for students who must master large amounts of material in relatively short periods of

Figure 4.2   Percentage of words correctly recognized on a subsequent test as a function of levels of processing. *Y*-axis represents the percent recognized.

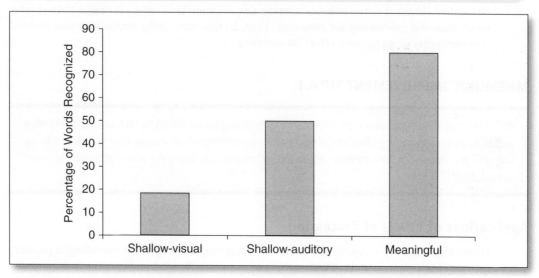

SOURCE: Based on Craik and Tulving (1975).

time. Many literature students have to read many books in a very short period of time and then remember many details from them. Consider preparing for a quiz on a novel. Concentrating on the ideas in the novel (probably what your literature professor is after anyway) will help you remember the details about the book that you also need to know for the quiz. It's a win-win. The ultimate goal is to understand the novel, the author's intentions, and how they play out in the plot and the characters. When you focus on the big picture, details follow.

Deep levels of processing can also improve memory in areas in which you might not think it would help, namely memory for visual information. For example, the levels-of-processing framework predicts how well people can remember faces. Deeper levels of processing lead to better memory for faces, even though the test itself requires one to recognize visual images of faces. Sporer (1991) showed that people were better at recognizing faces if they had first processed them in terms of whether or not the face looked "honest" than if they had processed them in terms of whether or not the person had a wide nose. Judging for honesty is similar to the meaning-based processing we have been discussing, whereas judging the physical characteristics of the face is clearly shallow processing. Although most of us would agree we should not judge a person's honesty by how they look, doing so allowed the participants to remember those faces later.

The levels-of-processing approach has had its critics as well. One major criticism is that the theory is circular—that is, anything that produces good memory performance is thought to be deep processing. In this view, deep processing is not defined separately from good memory performance. Aware of this possibility, Fisher and Craik (1977) showed that under some conditions, deep processing produced worse memory performance than did shallow processing. The key was in the test. If the test required the participant to recall perceptual details (i.e., the color of a written word), then processing for color led to better recall than did processing for meaning. Thus, in this case, deep processing was defined independently of its positive effect on memory.

MNEMONIC IMPROVEMENT TIP 4.1

When learning new information, use elaborative or meaning-based encoding techniques. Elaborative encoding or deep encoding leads to stronger memory representations. Elaborative encoding can be idiosyncratic, but one of the best meaning-based techniques is to relate the information to one's own personal life.

Applications of Levels of Processing

Levels of processing is a powerful tool in investigating differences in encoding. It predicts memory performance under a wide variety of situations. Indeed, any variable that increases the meaning-based processing of a to-be-learned item will also increase that item's memorability in most situations. Thus, when learning a new language, placing a new vocabulary term in a sentence produces better learning than simply repeating the word and its definition over and over. We will now discuss a number of extensions of levels of processing: the self-reference effect, survival processing, the generation effect, organization, and distinctiveness. All of these effects work because they produce deeper or more meaningful processing. Some critics of levels of processing point out that researchers call "meaningful" whichever processing leads to good memory recall. See if you can apply this criticism to each of the applications and decide whether or not the criticism holds up. Whether it does or not, thinking about the material in this way will foster deep processing, which will allow you to remember the information better!

The Self-Reference Effect

Self-reference effect: The observation that linking to-be-learned information to personally relevant information about oneself creates strong encoding.

The **self-reference effect** refers to the observation that linking to-be-learned information to personally relevant information about oneself creates strong encoding. To demonstrate the self-reference effect, Rogers, Kuiper, and Kirker (1977) found that relating information to oneself was particularly useful in creating strongly encoding memory traces. In another study, Kelley et al. (2002) showed that words that referred to personality traits were more likely to be recalled if the person applied that trait to himself or herself than if he or she did not. Kelley et al. also found that when people applied these traits to themselves during encoding, there was increased activity in the prefrontal cortex, including the anterior cingulate, relative to when they did not apply the traits to themselves, as measured by functional magnetic resonance imaging (fMRI). The anterior cingulate is an area in the prefrontal lobe associated with novelty, surprise, and cognitive conflict (Botvinick, 2007). Activating this area makes a stimulus particularly distinctive. Leshikar et al. (2015) found that self-referencing was equally effective for older adults as it is for younger adults, suggesting that relating materials to oneself is a good way to offset natural age-related declines in memory. Klein (2012b) argued that although it is difficult to psychologically define a unitary self, there are several independent self-reference effects, all of which contribute to increasing encoding power for those items that are processed relative to the self.

Survival Processing

Imagine you are lost in the desert without food or water or a compass to guide you back to civilization. You must survive on your own, using the plants and animals you find along the way. You must avoid predators, such as lions and leopards, which may be hiding behind every boulder. What would be useful to you under such circumstances? A radio? Opium? A priest? Nairne (2010) argued that evaluating information in terms of its relevance to survival increases our ability to encode and retrieve that information. Indeed, this type of encoding may be a particularly deep and self-relevant encoding strategy, one that may have served our long-ago ancestors well.

To test this idea, Nairne, Thompson, and Pandeirada (2007) asked participants to rate a group of unrelated words in terms of how relevant they were to surviving on the grasslands of a foreign land. Nairne et al. defined this type of processing as **survival processing**. They compared subsequent memory for these words with words that had been learned using a variety of other orienting tasks, including rating the words for pleasantness, usually considered a deep level of processing because it focuses participants on the meaning of words. Interestingly, the survival scenario led to 10% better recall than did the pleasantness judgments or judgments about surviving in a city (see Figure 4.3). This result has now been replicated numerous times (see Klein, 2012b; Kazanas & Altarriba, 2015). Nairne (2010) argued that a memory system that operated this way would be selected over evolutionary time, and it may be that factors such as meaningful processing reflect these ancestral concerns. Klein (2012a) argued that the need to accumulate social information and predict the future can account for the evolution of modern episodic memory. Either way, the next time you have to study for a test, imagine you are studying on the African savannah surrounded by hungry lions. You just may do better on that test than you would have, and it may be fun as well.

Bell, Röer, and Buchner (2015) were interested in the proximate causes of the survival processing effect—that is, what memory mechanisms lead to the advantages we see

> **Survival processing:** Processing information in terms of its value to surviving in the wild is a surprisingly effective manner in which to encode information.

when people are using survival processing to help them learn information. They considered two possible mechanisms. The first is that survival processing activates threat mechanisms—that is, we think about the dangers lurking in wild situations, which causes us to focus more on the material present. The second possible mechanism is that survival processing causes us to focus on the potential function of the objects or ideas the words represents, in other words, deep levels of processing. When they asked participants to focus on threat and dangers, however, there was actually a decrease in performance, ruling this theory out as an explanation for survival processing. However, when participants were specifically asked to focus on the function of objects that the words represent, a strong survival processing effect was demonstrated. Bell et al. argue that function is therefore important in explaining survival processing. But this functional view is also compatible with a levels-of-processing explanation (see Kazanas & Altarriba, 2015, for a thorough review of this topic).

In terms of our current concerns, survival processing can be considered almost the "ultimate" deep-level processing. It instantly focuses you on the meaning of the words. For what possible purpose or function could a "priest" help me survive in the desert? Well, he could perform last rites if I cannot find enough water. Opium? It might be useful if I have to walk a long distance in the intense discomfort caused by the heat and lack of water. What about a radio? Now, that's useful—I could find out the direction to the nearest town, where help would be waiting. Thus, processing for survival rivets our attention on the meaning of words and therefore promotes deep processing in a way few other tasks can match. However, it remains to be seen whether survival processing generalizes beyond the learning of unrelated lists, as some studies have shown that survival processing is not useful when learning stories and when tested by cued recall (Seamon et al., 2012).

The Generation Effect

According to the levels-of-processing framework, anything we do to increase elaborative or meaning-based processing will strengthen an item in long-term memory. The generation effect refers to the fact that memory is better when we generate associations ourselves than when we simply read them (MacLeod, Pottruff, Forrin, & Masson, 2012; McCabe, 2015a). Slamecka and Graf (1978) demonstrated this effect in a particularly clever way. They controlled the material so that generating items would be trivially easy, as easy as it was to simply read the materials. If memory performance was better for the generated items, it would not be the result of the extra effort used to generate the items but because the person generated the items himself or herself. Here is how they did it.

Generation effect: Memory is better when we generate associations ourselves than when we simply read them.

Participants in this experiment knew that their memory for associations would be tested, so the task was intentional learning, not incidental learning. The participants also knew that they would see the left-hand cue of a paired associate and have to remember the right-hand target. Encoding the items was done in one of two ways. In the read

Figure 4.3 The advantage of processing for survival. *Y*-axis represents amount recalled.

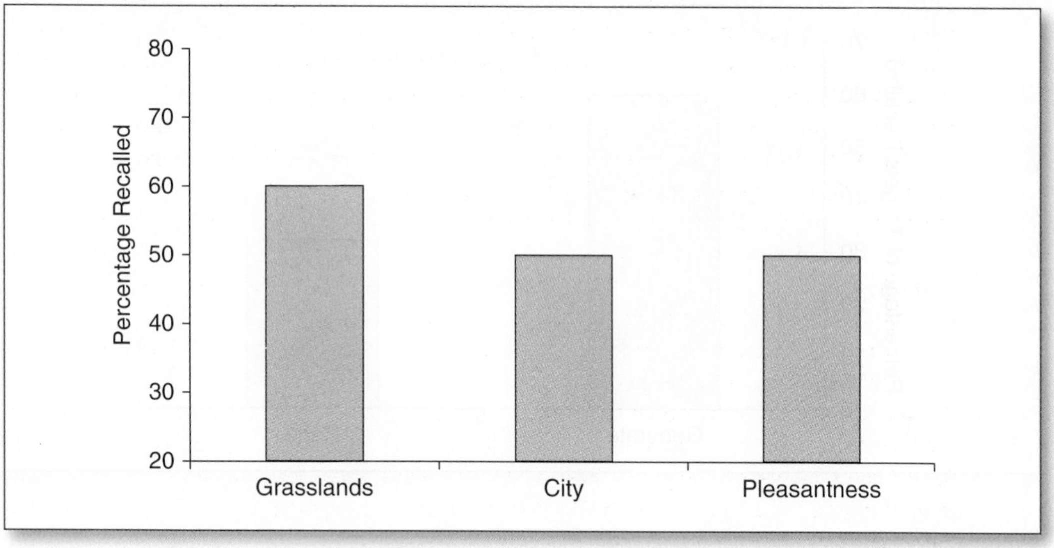

SOURCE: Based on Nairne, Thompson, and Pandeirada (2007).

condition, participants simply read the pair of items, but in the generate condition, they followed a rule that allowed them to generate the same target item as was provided in the read condition.

Read condition: rose–hose

Generate condition: mash–cr____ (rhyme)

The generate condition is rather easy. Almost all participants successfully generated the expected target without error. As you can see, it takes little mental effort to generate the word *crash*. Yet the effect on memory performance was profound. Recall of the target words was 28 % better in the generate condition (see Figure 4.4).

This effect is not limited to paired associates in the laboratory. It also works in real-world settings. For example, Butler and Roediger (2007) tested it in a simulated classroom setting. Participants viewed three lectures on different topics over three consecutive days. After each lecture, some "students" received a lecture summary (equivalent to the read condition), whereas other "students" received short-answer tests (equivalent to the generate condition) with feedback given to the participants on half of their answers. In the short-answer tests, the participants retrieved or generated the same item that was provided to participants in the read/summary condition. A final control group of participants did not get a summary or receive a short-answer test. One month later, the participants returned and took a test on the materials covered in the lectures. The group that performed the

Figure 4.4 Generation effect. *Y*-axis represents number of targets recalled.

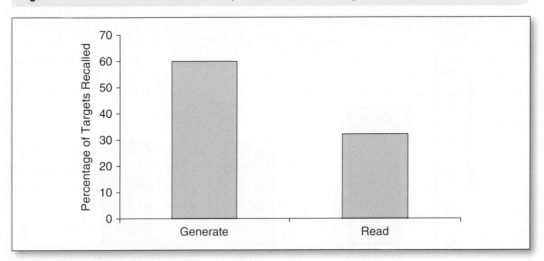

best on this final test was the group that had been given a short-answer test—that is, the group that had to generate the answers. Thus, in real-world learning situations, generating items can lead to the best memory performance as well as in typical laboratory conditions. Although Butler and Roediger called their effect a "testing effect" rather than a generation effect, the reasoning is similar. Producing the answer oneself leads to a stronger memory trace than reading the answer already printed.

In an applied example of this principle, McCabe (2015a) looked at real classroom material, in particular the section on neuroscience in an Introductory Psychology textbook. Some students were asked to generate ways of remembering the material whereas other students read experimenter-provided summaries of the material. Consistent with the generation effect, the students who self-generated means of studying performed better later on an evaluation of the material than those who read the experimenter-provided summaries.

A related effect is called the **enactment effect**. According to the enactment effect, performed tasks are remembered better than those that are simply read about (Helstrup, 2004). That is, actually bending a paperclip is better than reading "bending a paperclip" for remembering this activity at a subsequent time period. In Helstrup's study, participants were asked either to perform the task or to read about the task. Later, they were given a recognition test. Participants were better at recognizing activities they had actually done than those they had read. Interestingly, this effect appears to be mediated by the parietal lobe rather than the normal areas of the brain involved in memory, the prefrontal and temporal lobes (Russ, Mack, Grama, Lanfermann, & Knoff, 2003).

Enactment effect: Performed tasks are remembered better than those that are simply read about.

MNEMONIC IMPROVEMENT TIP 4.2

The generation effect: Generating answers is a more powerful memory aid than simply reading answers. This can be a very effective studying tool. Rather than simply reading and rereading the material, writing it down and generating the answer leads to stronger memory traces and better long-term performance.

Organization

Organization means imposing a meaningful structure on to-be-learned material. Applying organization to new learning causes the learner to focus on the meaning of the material and thus increases the depth of processing. Thus, organizing what we learn into categories and meaning-based connections is also an effective way to improve encoding. For example, imagine that you are doing a memory experiment. If you encounter a random list of words in a memory experiment, divide them into categories and try to use the categories to help you remember the words. If you have to study for a history test on the French Revolution, you could divide the material into "before the overthrow of the king" and "after the overthrow," or you could separate historical figures into "those who supported the monarchy" and "those who favored the republic." Tulving (1962) pointed out that the best organizational strategies are the ones that rely on the person's own subjective experience.

> **Organization:** Imposing a meaningful structure on to-be-learned material.

MNEMONIC IMPROVEMENT TIP 4.3

Another potent memory aid is organization. You can use both standard and subjective strategies to organize information. Organization leads to deeper processing, which leads to more strongly encoded memories.

Distinctiveness

Another feature that causes learners to focus on the meaning is to focus on the unique distinctive meaning of each item. In contrast to organization, in which we group items together based on meaning, **distinctiveness** implies that we search for the unique meaning for each item. Thus, even though organization and distinctiveness are opposites (one focuses on uniqueness of a

> **Distinctiveness:** Searching for the unique meaning for each item. Focusing on distinctive aspects of a stimulus causes good memory performance relative to items for which we do not seek distinctiveness.

stimulus, whereas the other focuses on commonalities among stimuli), they both focus the learner on meaning and therefore increase the depth of processing. Deeper processing leads to better encoding.

The study of the effect of distinctiveness on memory has an interesting history. Hedwig von Restorff, in 1933, published an important paper on the effects of distinctiveness in memory encoding. Von Restorff was German and continued her work on distinctiveness until the Nazis interfered with her lab and forced the university she worked for to fire her (Hunt, 1995). However, because of her seminal research, the advantage in memory that distinctive items have over less distinctive items is known as the **von Restorff effect**. Consider the following list of words: *jump, hop, fly, swim, crawl, putter, VOMIT, run, skip, skate, flip*. It is likely that the word *vomit* will stand out. Why? Well, all the other words are neutral or pleasant words, but

> **von Restorff effect:** Advantage in memory that distinctive items have over less distinctive items.

vomit is a decidedly unpleasant word. In addition, all of the other words convey a manner of motion, quite different from the motion involved in the word *vomit* (grossed you out yet?). All the other words do not normally evoke strong emotions, whereas the word *vomit* can evoke strong emotions. Finally, the word *vomit,* unlike the other words in the list, is in bold and all caps, which further enhance its distinctiveness. Indeed, although you may consider this to be a crude example, it has virtually guaranteed that you will never forget the von Restorff effect. The goal here is to make one item in the list undeniably distinctive from the rest. Von Restorff showed that the distinctive item was remembered better than a category-consistent word placed in the same serial position (see Hunt, 1995).

Let's consider the von Restorff effect (also known by the term *isolation effect*) in more depth as well as the general variable of distinctiveness. In the von Restorff effect, participants are given a list of words to commit to memory. The words on the list are homogeneous along one dimension, except for one word, which differs from the rest in terms of category, color, size, and so on. For example, participants might study the names of 11 birds (e.g., *sparrow, pigeon, owl, jay,* etc.) but also see the name of one boat (e.g., *kayak*). The typical finding is that the isolated word or distinctive word is recalled much better than a within-category word in the same serial position. This occurs regardless of the dimension on which the word differs from the others (Singer, Fazaluddin, & Andrew, 2011)

However, we do not have to rely on distinctiveness being provided for us. When we study, we can focus on distinctive aspects of material that we need to remember. Consider learning the people in your new study group. Look for distinctive aspects of a person's name or face. For example, if a person has a unibrow (hair connecting the eyebrows to each other), try to use that distinct feature as a way of remembering that person and his (hopefully) name. Also, if the person has an unusual name (e.g., Dweezel), that helps, but if this person doesn't (e.g., Christina), find a way to make it distinctive ("Christina the ballerina"). Thus, focusing on some unique aspect of a person will allow you to remember that person better, just as focusing on unique features of to-be-learned information allows you to encode it more quickly. As do the other variables that influence encoding, distinctiveness works by accentuating an aspect of meaning in the distinctive stimuli. This in turn increases the depth of processing, leading to better encoding of that item.

MNEMONIC IMPROVEMENT TIP 4.4

Distinctiveness provides another variable that can improve memory. Focusing on distinctive aspects of to-be-remembered items improves memory greatly. This is applicable to learning school information, faces, and names of people.

SECTION SUMMARY AND QUIZ

Episodic memory is a form of "mental time travel." This differentiates it from semantic memory, the representations we have of "facts." A generation of research now shows that episodic memory is a distinct neurocognitive system. This research includes behavioral evidence, neuroimaging, and neuropsychology. Encoding into long-term memory is based on meaningful processing. The levels-of-processing framework shows that deeper processing leads to better encoding into long-term episodic memory. Many factors that increase meaningful processing also lead to better encoding. These include the self-reference effect, survival processing, the generation effect, organization, and distinctiveness. We have seen that one of the key elements of encoding is meaning-based processing. What we learn from a particular experience is its meaning. This is what is generally relevant to us later, so adaptive memory focuses on meaning.

Quiz

1. Randolf is studying for his Economics midterm. In terms of memory theory, Randolf is engaged in
   a. Incidental learning
   b. Intentional learning
   c. Episodic reframing
   d. An orienting task

2. Craik and Lockhart developed the levels of processing framework. Levels of processing means that
   a. More meaningful information will be remembered better than less meaningful information
   b. Episodic memory is superior to semantic memory
   c. Retrieval actually occurs before encoding
   d. Most learning is intentional and very rarely does incidental learning occur

3. Survival processing refers to
   a. The observation that memory is better when we generate associations than when they are given to us by others
   b. The memories that survive are those that are strongest
   c. People with superior memories are more likely to live longer lives
   d. Processing information in terms of its value to survival leads to effective learning

4. Participants are presented a list of words, such as "cucumbers, asparagus, onions, pepper, canoe, kale, corn, potatoes." Which of the following is expected to occur?
    a. Participants will use organizational strategies to help them remember the list
    b. The word "canoe" will be well recalled because it is a distinctive item on the list
    c. Processing the words in terms of their survival value may aid memory
    d. All of the above are true

Answers
1. b
2. a
3. d
4. d

MEMORY PROCESSES: ENCODING, REPRESENTATION, AND RETRIEVAL (PART II)

Retrieval From Episodic Memory

Retrieval is the process by which information is recovered from memory. In episodic memory, we retrieve events—that is, specific individual happenings from our lives. An event can include memories of what people said or did, it can include visual images, and it can include our emotions about the event. Information about an event can include when it occurred, how long ago, where it took place, and its significance to the person doing the remembering. We have many memories stored in episodic memory, which leads to a core question in episodic memory research: How do we access them?

Think of your computer. Inside it, many millions of bits of information are stored, including the paper you are writing for your Memory class. The paper is no good to you when the computer is turned off and stowed away. You can't say to your professor, "I have the paper—it is on my computer, but you can't see it." For that computer file to be of any use, you and your computer must be able to access it and then print it, upload it to your professor's website, or email it to her. All of these activities are acts of *retrieval*. Memory is only as good as the retrieval system that allows us to draw information from it. Episodic memory is no exception.

Retrieval is the process whereby information is recovered and brought to consciousness in working memory. An important feature of retrieval is that it must be accurate. From all the information stored in memory, we must get exactly the memory sought. If you are asked about your dietary restrictions, and you respond with "walnuts" when it is "peanuts" that you are allergic to, this can have important and negative consequences. If you are asked, by a classmate, to describe your high school graduation and instead you retrieve the memory of your sister's graduation, you might not be able to help your classmate learn about the event that he or she may have missed. Similarly, when a parent accidentally calls one child by the name of another child in the family, that parent probably insults both children. Last, if you need to retrieve the name of your current significant other and you instead call that person by the name of your last boyfriend or girlfriend, you may have a new ex. Sometimes accurate retrieval is really important! Therefore, we need a memory system that is as precise as possible in retrieving the correct memory.

Not only must retrieval be accurate, but it must also be fast. The waiter is busy and has other tables to get to and cannot wait forever for you to say that you are allergic to peanuts. Moreover, if you want your classmate to be interested in your story from high school graduation, you must be able to tell the story without too many pauses. To further illustrate the need for speed in retrieval, consider a time when you were sure you knew someone's name but you could not think of it at the moment. When the person leaves later, you remember the name. The embarrassment of not knowing your acquaintance's name is the cost of a too-slow retrieval system. So we need a retrieval system that, like the Karate Kid, has both speed and accuracy.

One of the ways in which we achieve both speed and accuracy is to keep memories that we are likely to retrieve more accessible to recall than others we are less likely to need to remember. Thus, you may be more likely to need to remember where the local grocery store is than a grocery store you went to on vacation last summer. It is likely that we will need to retrieve information that we have retrieved recently and information that is stored strongly in memory (Bjork & Bjork, 1992). This leads us to an important theoretical distinction: the difference between availability and accessibility.

Availability refers to all information present in the memory system—that is, everything that you have ever learned and is currently stored in your episodic memory! Availability can never be directly measured, because although all of this information may be stored in memory, we can never retrieve it all at any particular time. In contrast, **accessibility** refers to that part of our stored memories that we can retrieve under the present conditions. At any given time,

> **Availability:** All information present in the memory system.

> **Accessibility:** That part of our stored memories that we can retrieve under the present conditions.

we may be able to access only some of our memories but not all of them. Thus, availability and accessibility are very different concepts. As it turns out, the key to ensuring that a memory is accessible is having the right retrieval cue. Consider the following anecdote.

Consider the case of a retired civil engineer, whom we will call Mr. Rojas (not his real name). Mr. Rojas had come from Cuba to attend college in the United States in the late 1950s. When the Cuban revolution catapulted Fidel Castro to power, Mr. Rojas was unable to return safely to Cuba. He continued with graduate school and became a very successful engineer in the United Sates. Fifty years later, his brother died. His brother had remained behind in Cuba and had become a prominent government official in Castro's regime. Because Mr. Rojas opposed the communists, he and his brother had seldom spoken or seen each other in all those years. Yet Mr. Rojas returned to Cuba for the first time in nearly 50 years to attend the funeral of his brother. Upon arriving in his home country, Mr. Rojas experienced an incredible wave of memories. Many events, which he had not thought of in years—or indeed he thought he would not have recalled under any circumstances—came flooding back to him. There was the place where his father had taught him how to ride a bicycle. There was the place where he and his girlfriend had snuck off to so they could be alone. For Mr. Rojas, returning to the land of his childhood provided the cues to remember events that he doubted he would ever have thought of in his adult world back in the United States.

Most of us will fortunately never be in the position of Mr. Rojas, but to experience what he did, all you need to do is to return to your high school (assuming you have not visited since starting college). You too will likely remember many things you have not thought of in a long time. Other readers may have moved from one town to another when they were quite young. A trip back to the early town will bring back a flood of memories of events not thought of in years.

This is the essence of the concept of **retrieval cues**. We use information present in our current environment—that is, retrieval cues—to trigger our memories of past events. Therefore, it is the presence of the right retrieval cues that activates or makes accessible a particular memory. As we will discuss shortly, geographic location may serve as a retrieval cue. Remove Mr. Rojas from his hometown, and he will not remember his bicycle lesson. Place him back in it, and he vividly remembers his father helping him balance on two wheels all those years ago.

Retrieval cues: Information present in our current environment that we use to trigger our memories of past events.

In terms of practical issues of memory, nothing could be more important than this principle. Retrieval cues matter! If you want to remember something important, structure your environment such that ample cues are around to trigger this memory (or technically, to make this memory accessible). This is the basis of many memory strategies, such as tying a string around your finger to remind you to feed your neighbor's cat. Very little in your house, apartment, or car may exist to remind you of Fluffy next door. However, remembering to feed her is important because (a) you don't want the cat to starve and (b) you don't want to disappoint your neighbor. So you tie the string around your finger to serve as a retrieval cue; every time you glance at your finger, you remember you need to go next door and open a can of tuna for Fluffy. The timer on the microwave serves a similar function for your own feeding. When the timer goes off, the sound reminds you that it is time to take the popcorn out and let the last few kernels pop before ripping open the bag.

Because retrieval cues are so important to memory, it is critical to understand some of the factors that lead to good retrieval cues. The assertion here is that good cues are items, information, and events present in the environment that are highly linked, associated, or connected to the event or idea you need to remember. A mistake I frequently make while learning names of new students every semester is focusing on learning first name–last name associations. I may know that "Isabel" goes with "Sanchez," but I fail to make the connection between the name and the face or physical appearance. And it is this association that I must learn if I want to call Isabel by name the next time I see her. A number of factors make retrieval cues effective. Many of them are grouped under the heading of the encoding specificity principle.

MNEMONIC IMPROVEMENT TIP 4.5

Retrieval cues are the single most important feature of remembering. If you need to remember something important, structure your environment such that many cues are accessible to help trigger your memory.

Encoding Specificity

Encoding specificity means that retrieval of information from memory will be maximized when the conditions at retrieval match the conditions at encoding. That is, recall or recognition of information will be easier, faster, and greater in amount when there is overlap between conditions of

> **Encoding specificity:** Retrieval of information from memory is maximized when the conditions at retrieval match the conditions at encoding.

retrieval and encoding (Thompson & Tulving, 1970). The term *condition* can mean the physical location of the person and her mental state, emotional state, or even physiological state. For example, if we study for a test when we are feeling angry, we will actually do better on the test if we are also angry when we take it. If we have a conversation with a friend in the bookstore café, we will better remember that conversation if we try to recall it while in the same café. The encoding specificity principle is observable across a great many different circumstances. Let's take a look at some of the circumstances under which the encoding specificity can be observed.

Research on the encoding specificity principle takes the following form. Participants encode information under one of two conditions. Then, after a retention interval, the participants return to either the same condition or the opposite condition and attempt to retrieve the information that they encoded. The typical pattern is that people recall better when they encode and retrieve under the same conditions.

Our first example of this form of experiment is a now-classic study done by two British researchers, Godden and Baddeley (1975), who studied British naval divers. The participants were all trained scuba divers who were quite comfortable working underwater in scuba gear. Godden and Baddeley asked half of the divers to learn a list of words on a waterproof whiteboard anchored 15 feet underwater. The other half of the participants studied the same list of words on land. This is called the encoding manipulation—that is, the researchers established two contexts at the time of encoding, land and water.

Each encoding group was divided into two groups, a group that retrieved the words on land and a group that retrieved the words underwater by writing the list of words on the underwater whiteboard. This was the retrieval manipulation with two conditions, retrieving underwater and retrieving on land. Therefore, there were four conditions in total: encoding on land/retrieving on land, encoding on land/retrieving underwater, encoding underwater/retrieving underwater, and encoding underwater/retrieving on land. The results can be seen in Figure 4.5.

Figure 4.5   Encoding specificity. *Y*-axis represents amount of words recalled.

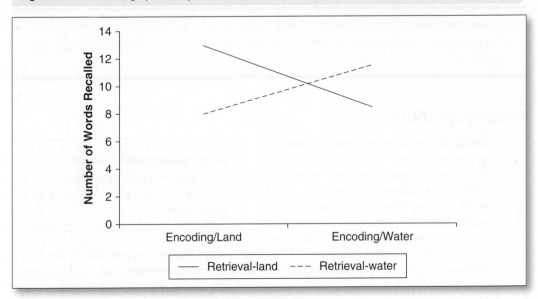

SOURCE: Based on Godden and Baddeley (1975).

As you can see in Figure 4.5, the divers recalled more words when the conditions at test (retrieval) matched the conditions at learning (encoding). When participants studied and retrieved only on land or only underwater, recall was better than when the conditions mismatched. This is the essence of the encoding specificity principle. The closer you are to your physical and mental state when you try to retrieve something, the more likely you will succeed.

Scuba diving is now a vastly popular recreational activity, despite its inherent dangers. Many people find it extremely relaxing, particularly if they are diving on beautiful coral reefs (see Figure 4.6). A frequent comment heard on dive boats is that all one's troubles and stressors seem to melt away once one submerges beneath the ocean's waves. It is possible that encoding specificity has something to do with this. When you are in an environment completely surrounded by corals, sponges, angelfish, and parrotfish, it is likely more difficult than normal to remember your grades, student loans, parking tickets, arguments with boy- or girlfriends, and—if you are bit older—mortgages, health insurance premiums, and car payments.

State-dependent memory: When encoding specificity is applied to internal human states such as drug states or mood states.

When encoding specificity is applied to internal human states, such as drug state or mood states, it is also referred to as **state-dependent memory**. In one of the more daring demonstrations of state-dependent learning and the encoding specificity principle, Eich, Weingartner, Stillman, and Gillian (1975) examined the influence of marijuana on

Figure 4.6 Scuba diving is a very relaxing activity for many people. Could it be that people find it relaxing because it is difficult to retrieve normal stressful events while in such a different environment?

Thinkstock/Comstock

people's memory. In an ad in the University of British Columbia newspaper, they recruited smokers to participate in this study. On Day 1, the participants were given either a marijuana cigarette or a tobacco cigarette. The researchers then waited about an hour for the drugs (THC and nicotine, respectively) from each of the cigarettes to enter the participant's bloodstream. Then the participants were given a list of unrelated words to study. The participants were dismissed and asked to refrain from smoking for the ensuing 48 hours. This was important to ensure that the drugs would be eliminated from the participants' bloodstream when they returned for the recall test. When the participants returned, they were again given a cigarette to smoke. Of the participants who had originally smoked marijuana, half again smoked marijuana, and half smoked tobacco. Likewise, of the participants who had originally smoked a tobacco cigarette, half again smoked tobacco and half smoked marijuana.

The results were strikingly similar to those from Godden and Baddeley (1975). The conditions in which encoding and retrieval were matched led to the best recall (see Figure 4.7). In this case, the two conditions that led to the best recall were when the

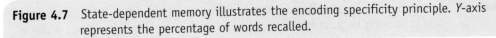

Figure 4.7 State-dependent memory illustrates the encoding specificity principle. *Y*-axis represents the percentage of words recalled.

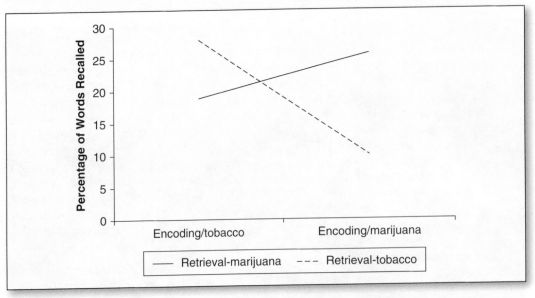

SOURCE: Based on Eich, Weingartner, Stillman, and Gillian (1975).

participants had smoked the same drug at both encoding and retrieval, the marijuana/marijuana condition and the tobacco/tobacco condition. The mismatched conditions in which the people smoked different drugs at different times led to relatively poor recall. Eich (2008) has also found similar results for alcohol (also see Goodwin, Powell, Bremer, Hoine, & Stern, 1969). Thus, encoding specificity also holds for drug-induced cognitive-emotional conditions.

I will note here that tobacco, marijuana, and alcohol are very unhealthy. Indeed, long-term use of marijuana has been shown to cause deficits in memory performance. Smoking cigarettes increases your likelihood of dying of lung cancer 400 times. It also causes heart disease, asthma, emphysema, and glaucoma and increases the likelihood of strokes. So I do not recommend starting with any of these drugs. However, if you smoke when you study for a test, you should probably smoke just before you go into a test.

So far, we have seen place-dependent memory in the navy diver experiment and drug-dependent memory in the Eich studies. Encoding specificity also applies to mood-dependent memory.

Eich and Metcalfe (1989) examined whether mood states were subject to the encoding specificity principle. Like the earlier studies, they had two encoding conditions crossed with two retrieval conditions. In their study, they tested Canadian college students by inducing them into either happy or sad moods by having them listen to either happy or sad music. The experimenters instructed the students to think about pleasant or unpleasant incidents while listening to the music. This was sufficient to induce most of the students into a happy or sad mood, depending on which condition they were in. Eich and Metcalfe waited until students reached a predetermined level of mood and then asked them to learn a list of paired associates (e.g., *silver–gold*). The students returned to the lab two days later and were again induced into either a happy or sad mood. Half of the participants who had studied while sad studied again while sad, whereas half of the participants who had studied while happy studied again while happy; half of the participants who had studied while sad studied after being made happy, whereas half of the participants who had studied while happy studied again while sad. Again, consistent with the earlier data, cued recall was better when the participants were in the same mood as when they learned the paired associates. Thus, if the participants had been sad at encoding, they recalled more when they were also sad at test, and if the participants had been happy at retrieval, they recalled more when they were also happy at test. Eich and Metcalfe called this pattern mood dependence, but you can see that it is practically identical to the other encoding specificity effects. Figure 4.8 demonstrates this.

A related phenomenon to mood dependence is called mood-congruent memory. **Mood congruence** means that you are more likely to remember events or information that are positive when you are in a positive mood and more likely to remember events or information that are negative when you are in a negative mood. For example, if you have just had an argument with your boyfriend or girlfriend, you are likely to remember negative things about that person, perhaps all the reasons you might want to go looking for a new intimate friend. On the other hand, while you are walking down the beach in the moonlight, you may be more

> **Mood congruence:** People are more likely to remember events or information that are positive when they are in a positive mood and more likely to remember events or information that are negative when they are in a negative mood.

likely to think of all the reasons you love that person. Many studies support the idea that we remember mood-congruent information more than mood-incongruent information (Blaney, 1986). Note the difference between mood congruence and mood dependence. Mood congruence refers to the kind of information we retrieve—positive or negative—whereas mood dependence refers to the match between our state at learning and our state at remembering.

A concept closely related to encoding specificity is the idea of **transfer-appropriate processing**. Transfer-appropriate processing is a more general term than encoding specificity, as it applies to cognitive processes other than memory (MacLeod et al., 2012). In the context of memory, it means that retrieval will be stronger when the cognitive processes present at the time of retrieval are most similar to the ones that were present at the time of encoding. Thus, a word like *jam* will be retrieved better when *grape* is given as a retrieval cue if the word was originally encoded with *strawberry* than with *traffic*.

> **Transfer-appropriate processing:** Retrieval will be stronger when the cognitive processes present at the time of retrieval are most similar to the ones that were present at the time of encoding.

MNEMONIC IMPROVEMENT TIP 4.6

Make use of the encoding specificity principle. If you know you are going to be tested on to-be-learned material, such as preparing for an exam, you can aid your preparation by looking for ways to make your study conditions actually match your test conditions. If you are usually nervous when you take exams, review your notes when you are feeling nervous about something else. Make sure to study during the same mood/chemical condition as when you take the test. Spend a few minutes studying in the room in which you are going to take the test. All of these activities will allow encoding specificity to work for you: Your test conditions will be similar to your learning conditions.

Inhibition in Episodic Memory

Consider the following situation. You are visiting all the universities that have accepted you to medical school (congratulations!). This is something you always wanted to achieve, so choosing the right medical school is a very important decision. So you embark on a tour to visit all the potential schools. On each of the next several days, you will be staying in a different hotel in a different city adjacent to a different university. When visiting Harvard Medical School, you check into the Tipton Hotel in Boston and are assigned room number 653. When you leave to visit the medical school admissions office, remembering your hotel room number is vital if you want a good night's sleep.

Figure 4.8   Mood-dependent memory illustrates the encoding specificity principle. *Y*-axis represents the percentage recalled.

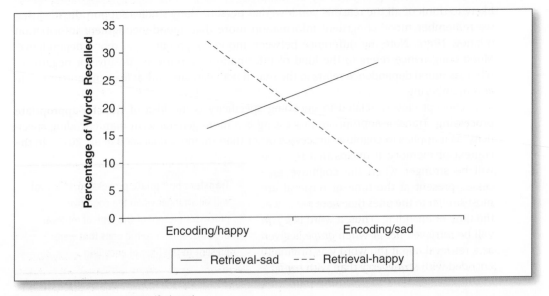

SOURCE: Based on Eich and Metcalfe (1989).

However, once you leave Boston on your way to the Big Blue Bug Motel in Providence, Rhode Island, the number 653 is no longer important. What becomes important is your new room number, suite 54, at the Big Blue Bug. When you return from your visit to Alpert Medical School at Brown University, you don't want to mistakenly remember the room number from the Tipton; you need your suite number at the Big Blue Bug. Therefore, it is actually adaptive to forget your room number from the Tipton as soon as you check out so that it will not interfere with your retrieval of the room number at the Big Blue Bug. And indeed, our memory systems have such an inhibitory mechanism.

Turning now to a more serious example, consider the situation of a veteran returning home from the battlefields of Afghanistan or some other recent war. He or she may wish to return to normal life and not be reminded of the horrors witnessed during war. Blocking out these painful memories is an important part of normal adjustment to civilian life. Indeed, one of the major symptoms of posttraumatic stress disorder (PTSD) is the constant recurrence of unbidden memories. This symptom of PTSD is really a failure of the inhibitory mechanism to prevent the retrieval of unwanted memories. Thus, in situations both relatively trivial (remembering your hotel number) and life altering (memories of wartime battles), inhibiting the retrieval of information can be just as crucial as retrieval itself. Therefore, an effective inhibition system is important to proper memory functioning (Anderson, 2007; Anderson & Huddleston, 2012; Catarino et al., 2015).

The importance of inhibition to memory function is currently drawing support from cognitive neuroscience. Specific areas of the brain appear to be devoted to inhibiting unwanted memories. Charest, Kriegeskorte, and Anderson (2015) using fMRI technology, showed that areas of the prefrontal lobe were particularly active when participants were actively trying to block out unwanted memories—that is, when suppressing unwanted memories. This suggests that the failure to inhibit painful memories, seen in PTSD, may be the result of improper functioning of the prefrontal lobe. As we will see throughout our discussion of memory, the prefrontal lobes are involved in many aspects of memory that have to do with, control of memory, monitoring of memory, and inhibition of responses (Thompson-Schill, Ramscar, & Chrysikou, 2009). In this way, the prefrontal lobes are said to have a supervisory role in memory.

Inhibition is a mechanism that actively interferes with and reduces the likelihood of recall of particular information. What allows us to inhibit information that we don't want to remember? For many of us, it seems that as soon as we decide we don't want to think of something (that catchy jingle from the McDonald's commercial, for example), it turns out we can't think of anything else. Thus, a reasonable question is, what processes allow us to inhibit information we want to forget? It turns out the act of retrieving some information can inhibit the

> **Inhibition:** The mechanism that actively interferes with and reduces the likelihood of recall of particular information.

> **Retrieval-induced inhibition:** When recently retrieved information interferes with the retrieval of other related information.

retrieval of other, related information (Anderson & Huddleston, 2012; Charest et al., 2015). In this way, constantly recalling your current suite number at the Big Blue Bug will inhibit retrieval of your room number at the Tipton. Consider the following experiment demonstrating what Anderson, Bjork, and Bjork (1994) called **retrieval-induced inhibition.**

Retrieval-Induced Inhibition

Anderson et al. (1994) gave participants word lists within a particular category to study and asked them to engage in extended retrieval practice (see Figure 4.9). For example, if the category was vegetables, the participants might initially study *squash, carrots, cucumbers,* and *broccoli.* Later, the participant engages in retrieval practice. Retrieval practice involves repeated retrieval of certain items. Thus, a participant saw *vegetables: car___* and *vegetables: broc____* and had to retrieve the words *carrot* and *broccoli.* In contrast, a participant also had unpracticed items in the category, such as *squash* and *cucumber.* Thus, within the category of "vegetables," the participant sees practiced items (*carrot, broccoli*), but also has unpracticed items (*squash, cucumber*). The unpracticed items were seen in the original phase of the experiment but not in the retrieval practice phase. Anderson et al. also had categories for which participants engaged in no retrieval practice on any items. They read through the category once but then did not engage in retrieval practice. Thus, there are three basic conditions: There are practiced items (RP+) and unpracticed items (RP-), and then there are the unpracticed categories (NRP).

The question asked by Anderson et al. (1994) was whether or not the repeated retrieval of some items would inhibit the later retrieval of related items for which retrieval practice had not taken place. Thus, after the retrieval practice sessions, the participants were asked to free-recall the examples from each category, both practiced and unpracticed. Consider this example. Anderson et al. presented the participants with long lists of category examples from several categories (Fish—*trout, herring, barracuda,* etc.). Participants were then given practice retrieving some examples from that category (e.g., Fish—*trout*) but not others from that category (Fish—*herring*). Other categories (e.g., Trees—*hemlock, oak, palm, pine*) did not receive any practice. Participants retrieved these examples up to three times from the practiced categories before the final test was given. The final test was a free-recall test in which participants were asked to recall all of the originally studied examples from each category.

The methods seem complex, but a brief inspection of Figure 4.9 shows that the results are quite straightforward. Consider first the practiced category (e.g., Fish). There are two types of words in a practiced category: examples that have been practiced (labeled RP +) and examples that have not been practiced (labeled RP–). Participants also engaged in final recall for the unpracticed category (Trees, labeled NRP).

RP+ = target items from practiced category that were practiced

RP– = target items from practiced category that were unpracticed

NRP = target items from the nonpracticed category

The prediction is that RP+ items will be remembered the best—this is not surprising. However, the interesting comparison is between the RP– and the NRP items. The prediction from retrieval inhibition is that the RP– items will be inhibited by the constant retrieval of the RP+ items. Therefore, the RP– items are inhibited, their recall will be worse than the baseline control condition provided by the NRP items. Thus, if retrieval inhibition is real, the NRP items should be better remembered than the RP– items.

Figure 4.9 Retrieval inhibition. *Y*-axis represents the percentage of words recalled.

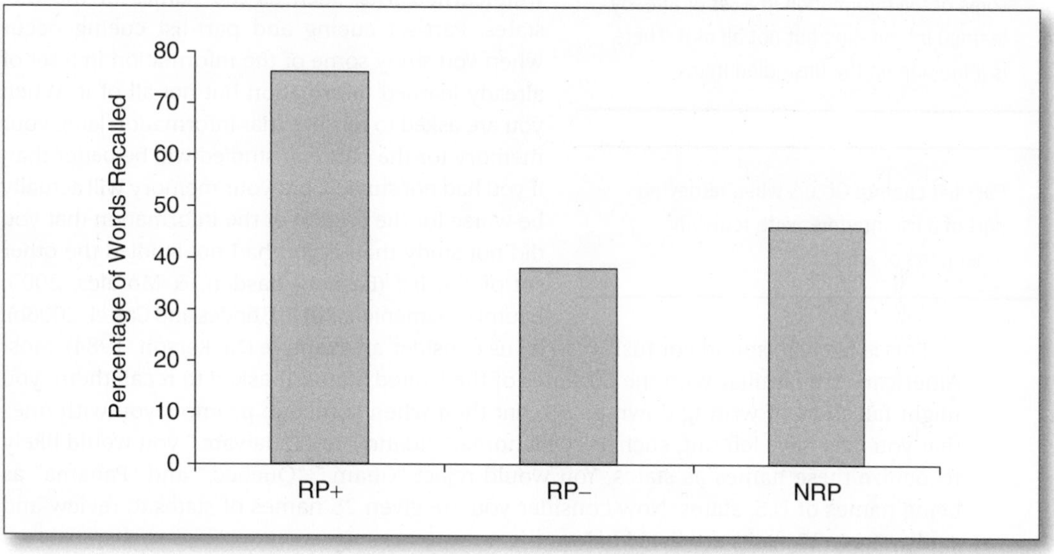

SOURCE: Based on Anderson, Bjork, and Bjork (1994).

Inspection of Figure 4.9 reveals this pattern. The best recall was for the RP+ items, but the NRP items were recalled better than the RP– items. Thus, repeated retrieving of RP+ items was making it more difficult to retrieve the related but nonpracticed items, which functioned as a control. This retrieval-induced forgetting demonstrates inhibition. What causes the inhibition? Well, the RP+ items are remembered well, better than items in the other two conditions. So it is the act of retrieving RP+ items that drives down memory of RP– items, thus demonstrating that the act of retrieval is causing the inhibition.

What is the implication of inhibition for real-world memory? It supports the idea that refreshing the memory of your current hotel room number will make it less likely that you will accidentally go to the room number of last night's hotel. It is also potentially useful in treating patients with PTSD. Therapy that encourages patients to recall related but nontraumatic wartime memories may work to inhibit the unbidden retrieval of the traumatic ones. Indeed, Catarino et al. (2015) compared patients with PTSD to control participants with respect to their ability to inhibit selected memories in a laboratory task. The PTSD patients had a harder time inhibiting retrieval of laboratory-generated memories than did the control patients, thus lending support to the view that part of what happens in PTSD is the inability to inhibit the retrieval of unwanted memories.

Part-Set Cueing

Inhibition can be seen in other experimental paradigms as well. Consider part-set cueing. **Part-set cueing** refers to the phenomenon in which cueing part of a list of items interferes with

Part-set cueing: Occurs when people study some of the information in a set of already learned information but not all of it. There is inhibition on the unstudied items.

Part-list cueing: Occurs when retrieving part of a list interferes with retrieving other parts of a list.

retrieving the rest of the list items. **Part-list cueing** is a related phenomenon that relies on the recall of well-learned lists, such as the names of the U.S. states. Part-set cueing and part-list cueing occur when you study some of the information in a set of already learned information but not all of it. When you are asked to retrieve that information later, your memory for the part you studied will be better than if you had not studied, but your memory will actually be worse for the section of the information that you did not study than if you had not studied the other set of the list (Basden, Basden, & Morales, 2003; Bäuml & Samenieh, 2012; Rhodes and Castel, 2008b).

This is likely to sound confusing, so let us consider an example (Nickerson, 1984). Most Americans are familiar with the 50 states of the United States. If asked to recall them, you might fall short of writing down all 50, but then when someone prompts you with ones that you may have left out, such as "Oklahoma," "Idaho," or "Delaware," you would likely recognize these names as states. You would reject "Guam," "Quebec," and "Panama" as being names of U.S. states. Now consider you are given 25 names of states to review and study. These 25 states are listed below.

1. Washington
2. Florida
3. New Hampshire
4. Minnesota
5. Oklahoma
6. North Dakota
7. Alabama
8. Idaho
9. Connecticut
10. Arizona
11. Missouri
12. Virginia
13. South Dakota
14. Delaware
15. Michigan
16. New Jersey

17. Indiana

18. Kentucky

19. West Virginia

20. Wisconsin

21. New York

22. Georgia

23. New Mexico

24. Kansas

25. Illinois

Now find a separate piece of paper and try to write down all 50 states of the United States. You will find that you will remember the above 25 rather well but will remember the 25 states not listed less well than you would have if you had not studied the above list. In fact, if you compare your retrieval of the 25 not on the above list to that of people who did not study at all, your performance will be, on average, worse than theirs for your unpracticed items. Nickerson (1984) did a version of this experiment. He compared a baseline condition in which people who had not reviewed any of the states attempted to recall all the states with a part-list condition, in which participants had previously reviewed half of the states. The part-list participants recalled more of the reviewed states than did the baseline control, but in keeping with the part-set cueing effect, they recalled fewer of the nonreviewed states than did the baseline control.

DIRECTED FORGETTING

What happens when someone—your boyfriend/girlfriend, brother or sister, parent, teacher, or boss—tells you to forget something? "Just forget I dented the car, Dad. I'll get it fixed, and you don't have to worry about it." "Forget how much money I spent on your birthday present—just enjoy it." "Forget that the Yankees just lost and come help me with the laundry." "Forget the scary parts of the movie and just focus on the happy ending." Most of us would consider these requests futile. No matter how much your father may want to forget that you dented his car, he is not going to forget. Next time, you'll have to take the 10-year-old station wagon instead of the brand-new convertible sports car. However, research does demonstrate that, under the right conditions, it is possible to forget the material that you want to forget. This form of forgetting is called **directed forgetting**.

Interesting, specific instructions to forget information can inhibit the retrieval of that information (see Bjork, 1992; Bjork &

> **Directed forgetting:** The inhibition in memory that occurs when people are asked to forget some information but not other information.

Bjork, 1992). In a typical directed-forgetting paradigm, participants are given a list of words to remember. Then, the experimenter feigns that she has made a mistake, instructs the participant to forget that list, and then gives the participant a new list to remember. In the control condition, a participant is given one list to remember, some incidental instructions, and then a new list to study but is not told to forget the first list. The final test is for the first list for each group. The question is, is there a difference between the group that was explicitly told to forget the first list and the group that was not?

Results have shown that groups given instructions to forget experience poorer recall performance than do groups not given instructions to forget. The effect is not large but has been demonstrated at a statistically significant level in many experiments (see Abel & Bäuml, 2015; Bäuml & Samenieh, 2012). Simply giving people instructions to forget material does result in less complete recall. Interestingly, though, this does not mean the material is entirely forgotten. If you switch from a recall test to a recognition test, the performance of the "forget" group and the control group is the same, suggesting the information is made less accessible but not less available in the directed-forgetting conditions. Therefore, it is likely that this inhibition is at least partially under conscious control. (For more information on the Bjorks's research on directed forgetting, go to www.sagepub .com/schwartz3e.[4])

PROSPECTIVE MEMORY

Memory does not only concern remembering the past. Remembering what lies in the future is also important. To be successful on any given day, students must remember what classes they will have that day and when and where they will meet. Parents must remember to pick up their children from school. Airline pilots must remember to turn off the autopilot at the right time and manually land the plane. Patients must remember when to take their medications. All of these tasks involve remembering actions or intentions that will take place in the future. This is the domain of prospective memory. **Prospective memory** is memory for the things we need to do in the future. Prospective memory is, in some ways, the flip side of episodic memory. In episodic memory, the goal is to retrieve past events, whereas in prospective memory, the goal is to retrieve future events. Episodic memories usually concern what happened at a particular point in the past, whereas prospective memory usually concerns what will happen at a particular point in the future.

> **Prospective memory:** Memory for the things we need to do in the future.

Prospective memory can be studied using both laboratory methods and field methods. In the lab, participants are asked to remember to do something during the experiment, and then they are kept busy doing other activities. The experimenter can then observe if the participant remembers to do the task at the appointed time. In one early experiment on prospective memory, Harris and Wilkens (1982) invited participants to watch a two-hour movie, which most participants reported enjoying. However, they were supposed to pick up cards and display them to a camera at specified intervals throughout the movie. The clock was obscured by other objects, so participants needed to turn their heads in order to check the clock, a behavior clearly visible to the experimenters. Harris and Wilkens found participants increased their rate of checking the clock just before it was the right time to show the cards. In some cases, they checked the clock a few minutes before they were supposed to show a card, but then forgot to show the card anyway! Another early experiment on the topic involved baking cupcakes (Ceci & Bronfenbrenner, 1985). Children needed to remember when to take cupcakes out of the oven. Successful children checked the time at decreasing intervals in advance while the cupcakes were in the oven. The closer the cupcakes were to being fully baked, the more often the children checked on them. This repeated checking allowed them to monitor the task so as to remember to take the cupcakes out at the right time.

In essence, a prospective memory task consists of the following: Participants are given a designated target task, such as remembering to remove cupcakes from an oven. Then, participants may be kept occupied with other tasks, so they cannot use rote rehearsal to know when to complete the prospective-memory task. The alternate task is intended to remove the designated target task from working memory. This also simulates real-world conditions in which intentions to do things, such as remove cooking food from the oven, must be remembered even as you engage in other activities, which may include tasks as different as setting the table and checking your phone for incoming texts. Finally, in experiments, performance is measured by looking at how often participants actually perform the actual target task (see McDaniel & Einstein, 2007, for a book-length description of the research on prospective memory).

Some prospective memory tasks are event based—that is, they require participants to perform an action when a particular event occurs. In event-based prospective memory, a particular cue—not a specific time—lets you know when to perform the remembered task. Thus, you might have to relay a phone message to your mother when she gets home. Your task—giving the message—is based on a specific event—your mother getting home. Other prospective memory tasks are time based. In these tasks, you must remember to do a particular activity at a particular time. Thus, you might be required to put the cookies in the oven at exactly 5:00 p.m. (Hicks, Marsh, & Cook, 2005; McDaniel et al., in press).

When people have little else to do, they are usually good at prospective memory tasks. If you need to pick up a file at work at 10:00 a.m. and you have nothing else to do that day at work, your likelihood of remembering the future task is high. However, in the presence of competing attentional demands, prospective memory performance can decline rapidly (Marsh & Hicks, 1998). If you have a busy morning of other tasks, it is easier to forget to leave for the file room and pick up the specified file at just the right time. It is likely that the explanation for this phenomenon has to do with the interaction of prospective memory and working memory. Acting on prospective memory appears to draw on working memory's central executive. When the central executive is absorbed in other tasks, participants are less able to recall when they have to perform a particular event (Marsh, Hicks, & Cook, 2006; McDaniel et al., in press).

Recent research suggests that, in some cases, the problems people have with prospective memory is not that they forget to do an intended action but that they forget that they did the action already and repeat it (Scullin & Bugg, 2012). This has potentially dangerous consequences if someone forgets that they have just taken their medicine and retakes it too soon. Scullin and Bugg showed that 25 % of errors that people made during a prospective memory task were such redoing errors, in which participants re-performed a task that they had already done. This suggests that we do not immediately forget completed intentions and need to be mindful of not repeating already-performed tasks.

Because of the importance of attention and the central executive in prospective memory, neuroscience has focused on the role of the prefrontal cortex in prospective memory. Indeed, converging evidence supports the hypothesis that the prefrontal lobe is critical in performing prospective memory tasks (McDaniel et al., in press; Momennejad & Haynes, 2012). For example, Simons, Schölvinck, Gilbert, Frith, and Burgess (2006) used fMRI technology to examine the brain during prospective memory tasks. They compared brain activity during a control task with brain activity when participants had to maintain a future intention using prospective memory. Under these conditions, there was more activity in both the left and right prefrontal lobes for the task involving prospective memory relative to the one with no prospective memory. Momennejad and Haynes examined a time-based prospective memory task. They found that during the delay between forming the intention and activating the intention, certain areas of the prefrontal lobe showed higher activity than during control tasks that did not require a person to maintain an intention. A different area of the prefrontal cortex became active just before the activity was to be executed. Momennejad and Haynes argued that the first area maintained the "what" of the prospective area, whereas the second area in the prefrontal cortex maintained the "when" of the task. These fMRI studies are consistent with neuropsychological studies, which show that patients with damage to the prefrontal lobe may have deficits in prospective memory (McDaniel & Einstein, 2007).

In everyday life, prospective memory is important. Each day, most of us have many future actions planned. Failure to retrieve them may result in costly mistakes. Think of a doctor who forgets her intention to remove a surgical clip from a patient. The failure to remember this task may imperil the patient's health. A patient who forgets his intention to take needed medications may also be endangering his health. An air traffic controller who forgets her intention to warn a pilot about incoming weather endangers many more lives. Thus, developing ways of studying and ultimately improving prospective memory is an important task for memory science.

SUMMARY

Episodic memory is a system of memory that encodes, stores, and retrieves individual events from our personal lives. It contrasts with semantic memory, which is knowledge of the world. Substantial evidence now exists to support the idea that these two forms of memory are subserved by separate neurocognitive systems. Encoding into episodic memory is aided by principles that lead to deeper encoding. The levels-of-processing framework specifies that any factor that leads to deeper or more meaning-based encoding will lead to better retention of that event or information. Relating the information to oneself, organizing it, or recognizing distinct aspects of the to-be-remembered event leads to better encoding.

On the retrieval side, memory is dependent on retrieval cues, the environmental triggers that allow us to access stored information. With respect to retrieval, encoding specificity means that when the psychological and physical conditions at retrieval match those of encoding, there will be more retrieval cues around, and hence memory performance will improve. This includes external physical landscapes, internal drug states, and internal mood states.

Inhibition revolves around the idea that sometimes it is adaptive to forget. Retrieval-induced inhibition shows that when we frequently retrieve some information, it actually inhibits the retrieval of related information. Part-set cueing demonstrates that studying part of a list may actually make it more difficult to recall the rest of the list. Directed-forgetting studies show that explicit directions to forget some material actually cause recall performance to decline. Prospective memory refers to our memory for future intentions rather than events from the past. Prospective memory appears to be directed by mechanisms in the frontal lobes. When attention is distracted from the intended task, prospective memory can suffer.

KEY TERMS

accessibility	generation effect	representation
availability	incidental learning	retrieval
deep processing	inhibition	retrieval cues
developmental amnesia	intentional learning	retrieval-induced inhibition
directed forgetting	levels of processing	self-reference effect
dissociation	maintenance rehearsal	shallow processing
distinctiveness	mood congruence	semantic memory
elaborative rehearsal	organization	state-dependent memory
enactment effect	orienting tasks	survival processing
encoding	part-list cueing	transfer-appropriate processing
encoding specificity	part-set cueing	von Restorff effect
episodic memory	prospective memory	
flashbulb memories	remember/know judgments	

REVIEW QUESTIONS

1. What are the differences between episodic and semantic memory? What kinds of memory does each refer to?

2. List three reasons why episodic memory and semantic memory are considered separate neurocognitive systems.

3. What is meant by the term *levels of processing*? Describe an experiment that supports the hypotheses put forth by levels of processing.

4. What is incidental learning? How does it differ from intentional learning?

5. What is survival processing? What experiment was done to demonstrate it?

6. What is the generation effect? How does it improve memory?

7. What is the von Restorff effect? How is it linked to distinctiveness?

8. What is the theoretical difference between availability and accessibility?

9. What is encoding specificity? Describe an experiment that supports its contentions.

10. What is retrieval-induced inhibition? How has it been tested in experiments?

ONLINE RESOURCES

1. To see KC the amnesic patient, go to the following YouTube site: http://www.youtube.com/watch?v = tXHk0a3RvLc.

2. For more information on developmental amnesia, go to http://www.bbc.co.uk/radio4/memory/programmes/me_and_my_memory2.shtml.

3. For an alternate view of levels of processing, go to http://www.uark.edu/misc/lampinen/LOP.html.

4. For more on the work of the Bjorks, go to http://bjorklab.psych.ucla.edu.

Go to **study.sagepub.com/schwartz3e** for additional exercises and study resources. Select **Chapter 4, Episodic Memory** for chapter-specific resources.

CHAPTER 5

Semantic Memory

Think of the many things that you have learned in school. In economics, you learned that prices are determined by supply and demand. In physics, you learned that electricity and magnetism are related. In literature, you learned that T. S. Elliot was an important poet of the 20th century. In music history, you learned that Debussy was an impressionist composer. Also think of the things you know that you have learned elsewhere. You have learned the function of your car's carburetor; you have learned that in double knitting, two or more yarns are alternated; and you have learned that hybrid cars use less gasoline and emit less greenhouse gases than normal cars. You also learned that Democrat Barack Obama won the U.S. presidential election in 2012 and that Republican Donald Trump won it in 2016, and you may know the name of the current prime minister of Great Britain (Theresa May, in late 2016). You may also know who is dating Taylor Swift, and that Christie Brinkley posed for bikini photographs at age 61. These facts about the world are not things that you are born knowing. We learn them as we go and need a memory system to store them until we need them.

Our memory for knowledge of the world—from knitting to literature to politics to gossip—is called semantic memory. **Semantic memory** is broadly defined as general knowledge of the world. Semantic memory includes our knowledge of history, sports, ideas, geography, pop culture, and even music. As such, it covers a broad range of topics, only some of which we will be able to address here. What unites these topics is that the memory involved is stored in a common representational system. Semantic memory is thought of as sup-

> **Semantic memory:** The neurocognitive memory system that encodes, stores, and retrieves information concerning knowledge of the world.

ported by a separate neurocognitive system than is episodic memory, which we discussed in the last chapter. Recall that episodic memory has a temporal dynamic—we attribute retrieval from episodic memory to the past. In semantic memory, we attribute retrieval of information to truth about the world. In this chapter, we will consider how people represent information into semantic memory as well as issues of encoding and retrieval.

Lexical memory (also known as the **lexicon**) is our mental dictionary, a representational system for the words of our language. Lexical memory is also considered a separate neurocognitive system from semantic (and episodic memory). There is much overlap between what is meant by semantic memory and what is meant by lexical memory.

Lexical memory (lexicon): Our mental dictionary; a representational system for the words of our language.

However, semantic memory is usually studied by researchers interested in memory, and lexical memory is usually studied by researchers interested in language.

Psycholinguists are interested in the structure of the representational system involved in lexical memory for a number of reasons. Lexical memory must maintain a huge number of items (words and rules of grammar). Access to these items must be extremely fast in order to support normal speech and normal speech comprehension. Given that human beings start life knowing no words at all but children acquire vocabulary at astonishing rates, the encoding of words into lexical memory is also of great interest. We will consider lexical memory alongside semantic memory, but note that there are important differences.

ASSOCIATIVE STRUCTURES IN SEMANTIC MEMORY

Each of us knows countless facts about the world. One goal for memory researchers is to try to model how all this information is represented by one's cognitive systems (not to mention how it is physically stored by the brain). To achieve this goal, most theorists have focused on associative models of semantic memory. An **associative model** means that we represent information in semantic memory in terms of connections among units of information (see Figure 5.1). A node is the unit of memory, which is then connected to other nodes. For example, you might have a node for the 18th-century British philosopher George Berkeley, who championed the ideas of associationism. The node for the memory of this philosopher might be linked to the node for John Locke (another associationist philosopher), to the node for the University of California at Berkely, and to the node for Charles Barkley, the star basketball player for the Philadelphia 76ers in the 1980s and 1990s. Nodes may be strongly connected, as in the Berkeley-Locke connection, or less strongly connected, as in the Berkeley-UC-Berkeley connection and the Berkeley-Barkley connection. Eventually, as the activation spreads to multiple nodes, it fades, and we can no longer see the trail of activation. Thus, in association models of semantic memory, our memory is a web of interconnected ideas and facts. (For more on the life of George Berkeley, go to study.sagepub.com/schwartz3e.[1])

Associative model: We represent information in semantic memory in terms of connections among units of information. A node is the unit of memory, which is then connected to other nodes.

Semantic network models posit that retrieval takes place when one node is activated based on the input from a cue. Once a node is activated, this activation will spread to existing associated nodes (Collins & Loftus, 1975). The term **spreading activation** refers to the transfer of activation from one node to an associated node. For example, if you are asked, "Who was the British philosopher most noted for his theories of associationism and his theory that the mind starts as a blank slate?" this should activate the node in memory for "John Locke." Activating

Spreading activation: Refers to the transfer of activation from one node to an associated node.

the node for John Locke can lead to the spoken response "Of course, I know that one, it's that bloke from Somerset, England—John Locke." The current thinking in cognitive psychology is that activation spreads—that is, as soon as the node for John Locke is activated, some, but a lesser amount of activation, spreads to the node for George Berkeley because the nodes for Berkeley and Locke are connected. In turn, some activation spreads to the node for Charles Barkley. Thus, activation spreads from one node to the next when one node is activated. However, an important component of these models is that activation weakens as it spreads from node to node. Thus, "Charles Barkley" will be less activated than "George Berkeley." It is also likely that the activation will not spread further than "Barkley" (e.g., failing to activate any other basketball knowledge).

Collins and Loftus (1975) spreading activation model focuses on the idea of a web of connections among nodes (or concepts) within the model. Activation spreads along this web, even when the web is not necessarily logical or organized. Thus, for example the connection between the philosopher Berkeley and the basketball player Barkley is circumstantial. There is no

Hierarchical network model: A model in which semantic memory is organized by levels or hierarchies in which particular nodes are associated with characteristics associated with that level, but not with higher or lower levels.

other reason to group these two people together other than the similarity in their names. To some extent, the Collins and Loftus (1975) model was an elaboration (and a criticism) of an earlier model, the **hierarchical network model** developed by Collins and Quillian (1969) some years earlier (see Figure 2).

Figure 5.1   An associative network in semantic memory. Arrows show spreading activation. Actual associations are bidirectional.

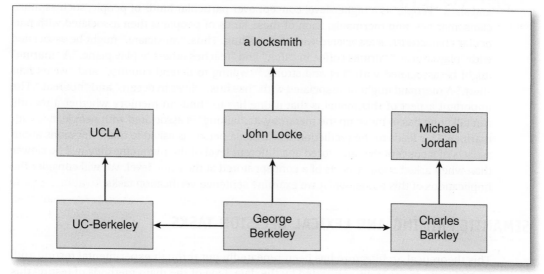

SOURCE: Based on theory by Collins and Loftus (1975).

Figure 5.2   Collins and Qullian's (1969) model of semantic memory: the hierarchical network.

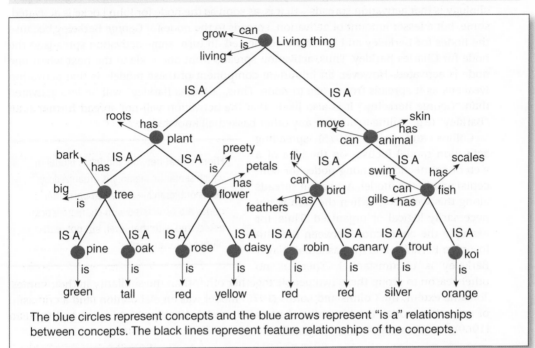

The blue circles represent concepts and the blue arrows represent "is a" relationships between concepts. The black lines represent feature relationships of the concepts.

In the hierarchical network model, semantic memory is organized hierarchically. Thus, if we take the concept "people," you would find that concept associated with general characteristics of people—that is, they have faces, they talk, and they come in all different ages and sizes. "People" is a higher-level concept over particular kinds of people, such as musicians, marines, and mermaids. Each of these kinds of people is then associated with particular characteristics associated with their calling. Thus, "musicians" might be associated with "plays music," "drinks coffee in cafes," and "teaches others to play piano." A "marine" might be associated with "big and strong," "willing to defend country," and "wears hair short." A mermaid might be associated with "has fins," "lives in ocean," and "not real." The important aspect of this model is that if one has to "find" in memory whether a marine can talk, one has to move up the hierarchy, as "talking" is associated with people, not with marines. This leads to the prediction that when a person is asked to make decisions about aspects of a concept that are stored at a different level of the hierarchy, they will be slower than when asked about aspects of a concept stored at the same level. We will consider the implications of this model when we examine sentence-verification tasks.

SEMANTIC PRIMING AND LEXICAL DECISION TASKS

This theoretical architecture has been repeatedly put through experimental testing and, by and large, is generally supported by the data. One of the main methods of testing this model is **semantic priming**. The basic idea of semantic priming is as follows. When a particular node is activated (e.g., by hearing "John Locke"), that activation will spread to associated nodes, including the one for George Berkeley. Similarly, if one reads the word *tiger,* activation should spread to related nodes for concepts such as "striped" and "lion." Activation of these additional nodes should make it easier for the person

> **Semantic priming:** The effect of one word or idea on the processing of a related word or idea. A related word will activate a target item and allow it to be processed more quickly.

to process the associated items. Thus, we should respond faster to the name George Berkeley if we have just heard the name John Locke, and we should respond faster to the word *lion* if we have just heard the word *tiger.* Thus, priming refers to the effect of the first presented word or name on the response to the later word or name. Priming will generally work better when the two items are also presented closely in time.

In experimental situations, semantic priming is typically measured by use of a **lexical decision task**. In a lexical decision task, participants must judge as quickly as

> **Lexical decision task:** A cognitive task in which participants judge whether a string of letters is a word as quickly as they can.

they can whether a string of letters is a word or not (Meyer & Schvaneveldt, 1976). For example, the words *doctor* and *cranberry* should elicit a response of yes, but the nonsense string *xffxere* should elicit a response of no. Possible words that are not used in English, such as *pluckban* or *scrawps,* should also elicit a response of no. Participants are asked to make such judgments as quickly as they can so that reaction times can be measured. Typically, a young adult in college can make these decisions in under half a second. In most experiments, nonsense strings (e.g., xffxere) are easier and therefore quicker to reject than possible, but not employed non-words (e.g., scrawps). More common words (e.g., doctor) are easier and therefore quicker to verify than obscure words (e.g., jejeune).

Semantic priming can then be added to the lexical decision task. Participants still have to judge if a string of letters is a word, but now that string is preceded by a prime, which is also usually a word but may be a picture as well. Primes may be related or unrelated to the to-be-judged words. For example, if the target word is *doctor,* a related prime is *nurse,* and an unrelated prime is *gumball.* Research consistently shows that related primes produce faster and easier processing of the target word. This translates into faster reaction times in the lexical decision task for words preceded by related primes than those preceded by unrelated primes (McNamara, 2005; Meyer & Schvaneveldt, 1971). Semantic priming occurs because the participant processes the prime and the prime enters semantic memory, and activation from the prime spreads to adjacent nodes in memory. Thus, *nurse* activates nearby concepts, such as *doctor,* and this activation allows one to respond faster to whether or not *doctor* is a word. Indeed, the closer the prime is connected to the target word, the greater the semantic priming effect (Moldovan, Ferré, Demestre, & Sánchez-Casas, 2015). There will be a bigger semantic priming effect if *nurse* primes *doctor* than if *heart* primes *doctor.*

Moreover, this priming can cross languages. Poort, Warren, and Rodd (2016) showed that priming with sentences in one language (Dutch) was sufficient to prime words in a lexical decision task in English. In another recent experiment, Schröter & Schroeder (2016) found that beginning readers in third grade showed robust semantic priming effects. Thus, shortly after one becomes a competent reader, semantic priming effects are apparent.

Semantic priming can also occur when the participant is not consciously aware of the prime, as in subliminal priming (Marcel, 1983). Subliminal priming may be sufficient to activate the network and allow that activation to spread.

Semantic priming can also serve as a marker of certain neurological impairments (Howells & Cardell, 2015). For example, anomic aphasia is a condition in which patients have difficulties finding the correct word in a given context. Their speech is characterized by pauses and attempts to compensate for their inability to recall a word clearly in their lexical memory. Howells and Cardell compared patients with anomic aphasia to control patients on a semantic priming task. Interestingly, despite their word retrieval problems, patients with anomic aphasia showed strong semantic priming effects, even if their overall reaction times were slower than the control patients. Thus, even though they have difficulty retrieving words, the nodes exist within their semantic memory, and priming existing nodes will spread to related nodes, allowing these patients with anomic aphasia to respond faster during semantic priming.

Spreading activation states that activation will move from one node to the next. Thus, *nurse* will prime *doctor,* which is associated with the word *lawyer.* Thus, the associative model predicts that a word like *nurse* will also show some small priming effect on a second-order association. The smaller amount of priming occurs because activation spreads and dissipates. Anticipating how much priming occurs is important for developing quantitative (mathematical) models of how priming occurs. This kind of priming is called *mediated priming.* Mediated priming occurs when the prime word is related to a word, which is also related to the target word. For example, if the target word is *lion,* then the word *stripes* will prime it. The reason is that *stripes* is associated with *tiger,* and *tiger* is associated with *lion.* Therefore, preceding *lion* with *stripes* allows for faster processing (McNamara & Altarriba, 1988; Jones, 2012). In an interesting study on mediated priming, Duñabeitia, Carreiras, and Perea (2008) showed that mediated priming could also cross over from semantic characteristics to phonological characteristics. The first link in priming is semantic (*lion* to *tiger*), but the second link is phonological—that is, sound related (*tiger* to *Geiger*). In a similar way, *John Locke* can prime *Charles Barkley* through *George Berkeley.* Duñabeitia's stimuli were in Spanish, but their example is that *cup* is semantically related to *coffee,* but cup also primes *toffee,* which is related to *coffee* in sound as well as the visual appearance of the letters but does not have the same meaning overlap.

SENTENCE VERIFICATION TASKS

Another manner in which spreading activation of association and the hierarchical model have been experimentally tested is by looking at sentence verification tasks. In a **sentence verification task**, participants are asked to decide as quickly as possible if a sentence is true or false. Thus, a sentence such as "All men are mortal," should be judged to be true, whereas a sentence such as "Hawaii is located in the Atlantic Ocean," should be judged to be false. According to the

Sentence verification task: Participants are asked to decide as quickly as possible if a sentence is true or false.

model of spreading activation, sentences reflecting closely linked nodes will be verified faster than sentences reflecting distantly linked nodes. This is likely because activation can spread from one node to a nearby node faster than it can spread to a more distant node. For example, the sentence "Tigers have stripes," should be verified faster than an equally true sentence that reflects a more distant association, such as "Tigers have lungs." Collins and Quillian (1969) reasoned that characteristics that are unique to a particular item will be closely linked in associative space, whereas characteristics that are shared with other items will be more distantly linked. *Stripes* will be stored closely to *tiger,* but *lungs* will be linked through a common link to "land animals." Thus, Collins and Quillian had participants judge the truth value of sentences, and participants were instructed to do so as quickly as possible. Returning to our example from earlier, sentences like "Marines wear their hair short" were verified as being true faster than sentences like "Marines have faces." Both sentences are true, but "short hair" is closely linked to the concept of a marine. In their experiment, this prediction turned out to be correct; closer associations led to faster verification times.

Neuroimaging work employing sentence-verification tasks supports the basic ideas that associative networks exist. In one study, Raposo, Mendes, and Marques (2012) looked at semantic verification tasks while participants were being scanned by fMRI technology. They found that areas of the left prefrontal lobe and areas of the left medial temporal lobe were particularly active during sentence verification. However, left temporal lobe activity was equally high regardless of the associative distance between the subject clause and verb clause of the sentences used in sentence verification, whereas greater frontal lobe activity was needed to do sentence verification when the associative distance between the subject clause and verb clause was greater. Thus, for example, "Limes are sour," requires less frontal involvement than an equally true statement such as "Limes are fruit." This supports the notion of spreading activation because the closer associates (lime-sour) require less recruitment of brain regions than the more distant association, though equally true (lime-fruit).

Therefore, it is a reasonable conclusion that semantic memory is organized into an associative network. In this associative network, information is linked with varying strengths and at varying distances. Strong connective links or close links lead to much shared activation, whereas weaker links or more distant links lead to less shared activation. When a particular node is activated, that activation spreads to other, adjacent links. In the next section, we will expand on the notion of associative structure in semantic memory and discuss how items in semantic memory are bound together into categories and concepts and how the mind creates these.

BILINGUAL REPRESENTATION

Lexical memory is a close cousin of semantic memory but focuses on how language is represented in memory. As with semantic memory, huge stores of information must be stored so as to be easily accessed when that knowledge is called for. A debated issue is whether bilingual or multilingual people have independent representation of concepts in semantic/lexical memory (which we call simply semantic memory here) for all the languages that they speak or each language has its own lexical memory system within the cognitive architecture of that individual (Cai, Pickering, Yan, & Branigan, 2011). One view is called the **single-store view of bilingual representation**. This view argues that there is a common semantic level of representation—that is, meaning is shared. The shared semantic representational system then connects to a system that produces the right way of saying that concept in each language. The alternate view is the **dual-store view (or separate store) of bilingual representation**, which postulates that meaning is represented separately for each language. Much of the recent research on the topic supports the single-store view (Cai et al., 2011; Gianico & Altarriba, 2008; Kroll, Bobb, Misra, & Guo, 2008). (For more information on this topic, go to study.sagepub.com/schwartz3e.[5])

Single-store view of bilingual representation: There is a common semantic level of representation in bilinguals.

Dual-store view (or separate store) of bilingual representation: Meaning is represented separately for each language in the lexical memory of a bilingual.

Think of a person you know who is bilingual. This person has two phonological forms that may represent any particular concept, one in one language and one in the other. Thus, an English-Spanish bilingual will know both the English word *clock* and the Spanish word *el reloj*. Obviously, these words will have different phonological (sound) representations, given that there is no overlap in sound. However, is the semantic representation stored jointly, or is there a separate representation for the meaning in each language? The single-store view states that each concept is stored in a single system and is linked to the separate phonology in each language. The dual-store view states that your friend has two separate semantic stores, one for each language (Gianico & Altarriba, 2008; Wang & Forster, 2015).

The view that semantic representations are shared across a multilingual's languages is supported by **cross-language semantic priming**. Cross-language semantic priming is similar to the semantic priming discussed earlier, except that the prime and the target word are in different languages. Consider a lexical decision task in which a participant has to determine whether a string of letters is a word. The prime word is presented in Spanish (e.g., *el libro*, meaning "book"). Shortly thereafter, the target word

Cross-language semantic priming: The effect of priming a word in one language has on a related word in another language in bilinguals or multilinguals.

appears in English (e.g., *magazine*). The single-store view of lexical memory predicts that *el libro* should prime *magazine*. However, the dual-store view argues that meaning is represented separately for both languages and therefore, the Spanish word should not prime the English word. Studies with cross-language semantic priming typically show that cross-language priming occurs, supporting the single-store view (Guasch, Sánchez-Casas, Ferré, & Garcia-Albea, 2011). Poort et al. (2016) found that presenting sentences in one language (Dutch) primed participants on a lexical decision task even when there was nearly twenty minutes between the prime and the target, suggesting that some forms of spreading activation can last much more than fleeting seconds.

Semantic memory is our memory for knowledge. Lexical memory is our knowledge of the words in the languages we speak. Given the size that each memory system must be in any human being, memory science has focused on how all this information is represented. For semantic memory, the representational system is thought of as a system of interlocking nodes. Activation spreads from node to node when a cue is given to elicit retrieval. We can test this spread of activation by doing semantic priming experiments on lexical decision tasks. Semantic priming means the effect of one word or idea on the processing of a related word or idea. A related word will activate a target item and allow it to be processed more quickly, thus allowing faster response times in a lexical decision task. A lexical decision task is a cognitive task in which participants judge whether a string of letters is a word as quickly as they can. Semantic verification tasks assess how participants are asked to decide as quickly as possible if a sentence is true or false. Results show some evidence for hierarchical organization. Closely associated information is verified faster than more distant information. Cross-language semantic priming also supports the single-store view of bilingual representation. The single-store view of bilingual representation states that there is a common semantic level of representation in bilinguals.

Section Summary and Quiz

1. Mediated priming means that
   a. The priming only occurs in the presence of a masking stimuli
   b. Episodic representations are primed so that people can make semantic responses
   c. An intermediate associative link is present between the prime word and the target word
   d. In some instances, spreading activation does not apply to lexical decision tasks

2. In a sentence verification task, the participant is required to
   a. Determine as quickly as possible whether a group of words is a grammatical sentence
   b. Decide as quickly as possible if the content of the sentence is true or false
   c. Determine as quickly as possible if the sentence possesses words that were given earlier in the priming phase
   d. All of the above

3. The single-store view of bilingual representation means that
   a. A bilingual represents meaning in one representational system across his or her two languages
   b. A bilingual represents meaning in a representational system for each language
   c. Bilinguals will respond faster in a lexical decision task because of multiple association routes
   d. Bilingual memory storage is organized substantially different from monolinguals

4. Which finding is best explained by the hierarchical network model?
   a. That we are faster to verify that "sharks have big teeth," than "sharks have blood"
   b. That *nurse* primes *doctor*
   c. That *gato* (Spanish for *cat*) primes *cat*
   d. That we are faster to verify sentences presented in our native language

Answers

1. c
2. b
3. a
4. a

CONCEPTS AND CATEGORIES

Concepts and *categories* are two terms borrowed from everyday usage, but their definitions within cognitive psychology are quite specific. A **concept** is a mental construct that contains information associated with a specific idea. A concept is a mental representation of an idea. Concepts can be representations of concrete objects such as "automobiles" and "chili peppers," and they can also be abstract, such as the representation of "peace" and "prosperity." A **category** is a mental construct referring to a set of objects or ideas that are grouped together or are associated with each other. That is, a category usually refers to things that are similar in some respect. Categories include items that are like each other in some way, for example, "tools," "furniture," "flowering plants," "forms of government," and "Mexican-Americans." Note the flexibility of a category. A hammer has little in common with a pressure cleaner, except that they are both used to maintain order in a household. The category "Mexican-American" means all people in the United States who share a common origin in Mexico. It says nothing about how old they are, what they look like, what language they speak, where they live, their socioeconomic status, or which political parties they prefer.

Concept: Mental construct that contains information associated with a specific idea.

Category: Mental construct referring to a set of objects or ideas that are grouped together or are associated with each other.

Concepts can refer to our mental representations of categories. For example, the concept of a "tool" is our mental representation of the characteristics that tools share. However, *concept* is a broader term than *category*. For example, concepts such as truth, love, and literacy are abstract ideas not easily translated into categories. Categories tend to be more concrete, such as "things that are true," "the reasons we love," and "literacy rates among Western countries." It is your semantic memory system that stores concepts and categories and allows you to access them when you need to. It is important for cognitive systems to be able to categorize material so that we can organize information and understand it.

Because of the complexity of concepts and the need for spreading activation networks to account for them, cognitive neuroscientists expected that representation of concepts would be widely distributed throughout the brain. In fact, activating a concept may draw on a great many different brain regions. Kuchinke, van der Meer, and Krueger (2009) examined decisions made about whether two objects belonged to the same category while monitoring participants using functional magnetic resonance imaging (fMRI). They found a wide distribution of brain areas became active, including areas in the frontal lobes and in the temporal lobes. Because they were dealing with linguistic concepts, there was a decided emphasis on the left hemisphere, but areas in the right hemisphere were activated as well.

Categories Are Fuzzy

At first, a category seems like a concrete entity. "Tools," "furniture," "literacy rates," and "Mexican-Americans" all seem like fairly straightforward categories. But each category has fuzzy boundaries. Consider the category of "tools." Clearly, hammers and pressure cleaners are tools, despite differences in what they are used for and how they operate. But is a pickle jar a tool? Looking up the word *tool* in a dictionary might yield something like this: a device that helps us accomplish a task. Using this definition, a pickle jar certainly is a tool. It is a human-made object whose function is to store pickles, something that would be much more difficult to do without a pickle jar. Yet to most of us, a pickle jar does not quite fit into our mental category of "tools." It is too passive—it just sits there holding pickles. Tools need to be wielded. Tools are entities like axes, hammers, and blowtorches, and a pickle jar is not quite one of them.

Consider the category of "Mexican-American." More straightforward? Clearly, someone whose parents were born in Guadalajara, grew up speaking Spanish, and has a last name of Garcia fits into our category of "Mexican-American." But others may be a bit more confusing. What about Californians whose ancestors lived in California while it was still part of Mexico (until 1847) but whose ancestors have been American for over 150 years? What about former Republican presidential candidate Mitt Romney, whose father was born in Mexico to American parents temporarily living there? Is he "Mexican-American"?

There are other ways of looking at boundary conditions as well. For example, function is an important defining feature of many concepts. Thus, for tools, function—that they aid humans in tasks—is at the heart of what a tool is (see Figure 5.3). What happens when an object is no longer able to serve that function? What about broken tools? Is a pressure cleaner that is out of gas a tool? Is a broken hammer a tool? They cannot serve the function of being a tool even though they still resemble tools. Which is more important for the definition of a tool—its function or its appearance? Consider the concept "bachelor," which refers to an unmarried adult male. Certainly, an unmarried sexually active heterosexual male at the age of 40 who lives alone is a bachelor. But there are unmarried heterosexual adult males who would not be considered bachelors—Catholic priests, for example. One might choose to revise the definition of "bachelor" to mean heterosexual unmarried adult men who have not taken vows of celibacy. But then there are widowers and divorcees. Do they revert to bachelorhood? Without belaboring this example, suffice it so say that boundary conditions are important in defining categories.

Because of these boundary conditions, researchers think of categories as complex and related to each other in multiple ways. The complexity of categories seems to be clear in the way memory is organized for categories. An important variable that has psychological reality is called **levels of categorization**—that is, categories are nested structures in which

Figure 5.3 All these implements are a part of a common category, tools. What does an object have to be in order to be considered a tool? Is an aspirin a tool? Is a computer a tool?

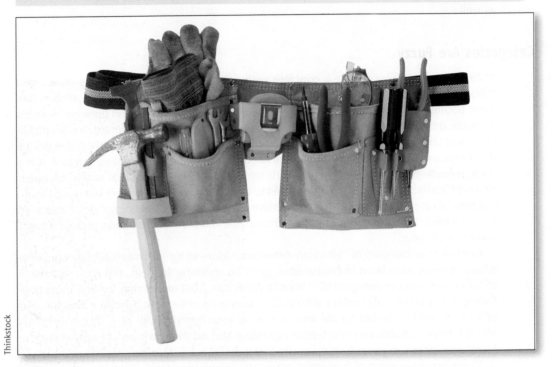

Thinkstock

Levels of categorization: Categories are nested structures in which the level of organization is important in defining the category. There are three such levels: basic, subordinate, and superordinate.

the level of organization is important in defining the category. There are three such levels: basic, subordinate, and superordinate (Rosch & Mervis, 1975). The basic level is the one we are most likely to invoke. For example, "tools" is a basic-level category for most people. The subordinate level allows for more specific or specialized categories to be formed (e.g., "power tools"). Superordinate categories are higher-order categories that include general information and include many more common categories (e.g., "human implements").

Levels of categorization are fluid, depending on a person's expertise. For example, for most of us, "cat" is the basic-level category and "Scottish fold" is the subordinate category. But for a cat fancier who takes her cats to shows across the country, "cat" might assume a superordinate classification, as the person endlessly discusses the variants among various types of purebred cats. For the cat fancier, "Scottish fold" takes on the basic-level classification, and the differences between American short-hair Scottish folds and European piebald Scottish folds become the subordinate category (see Figure 5.4).

Levels of categorization have a psychological reality. Research has demonstrated that basic-level information is retrieved faster than subordinate or superordinate information (T. T. Rogers & McClelland, 2004; Rosch, Mervis, Gray, Johnson, & Boyes-Braem, 1976). Indeed, when we see an object, we tend to use the basic level first. For example, we call the object on your desk generally a "computer," not a "MacBook Air laptop computer." Furthermore, different levels of categorization are associated with different areas of the brain. Kosslyn, Alpert, and Thompson (1995) used positron emission tomography (PET) technology to examine categorization. They did so by asking participants to match pictures to words. Thus, a picture of a dog was accompanied by three words: *animal* (superordinate), *dog* (basic), and *miniature poodle* (subordinate). They showed that superordinate levels were more likely to activate the prefrontal cortex than basic-level categories. In contrast, when people chose subordinate categories, there was more activity in the parietal lobe of the brain. It is possible that superordinate categories cause people to reason about the category or have to remember more features, taxing the prefrontal lobe, whereas it is likely that the subordinate level draws on more sensory representations, thus drawing on the parietal lobe.

Figure 5.4 A Scottish fold. At a basic level, we call this animal a "cat." For most of us, "Scottish fold" is a subordinate category, and "feline" is a superordinate category.

Thinkstock

Family Resemblance

We've seen that categories are ambiguous, depending on the viewpoint of the person conceptualizing them. Moreover, nearly every natural category will defy a definition and will have members that differ from the mainstream. Think of the category "Mexican-American." A U.S. citizen living in San Diego, named Garcia, and fluent in Spanish is a typical Mexican-American. However, the grandson of a German immigrant who lived briefly in Mexico before moving to the United States is a less typical Mexican American. **Family resemblance** means that membership in a category may be defined by each item's general similarity to other members in the category rather than by a specific list of features (Rosch & Mervis, 1975; Johansen, Savage, Fouquet, & Shanks, 2015). Family resemblance takes into account

Family resemblance: Membership in a category may be defined by each item's general similarity to other members in the category rather than by a specific list of features.

that many categories are multimodal, with many characteristics that may apply. For example, think of the category "bird." When we consider birds from a purely zoological understanding, both penguins and ostriches are every bit as much of a bird as is a sparrow, a robin, or an eagle. Yet because penguins and ostriches vary from most birds in many respects (most notably, flying), they are often considered less central members of the category.

Because of the complexity of categories and their fuzzy boundary conditions, cognitive psychologists have found it necessary to create models to account for how concepts and categories are represented in semantic memory. The following sections describe the major models that have been advanced.

Exemplar Theory and Feature Comparison Theory

Exemplar Theory. According to **exemplar theory**, categories are classified by maintaining a large number of specific instances of a category that are associated with each other in semantic memory (Smith & Ell, 2015). When we encounter a new item, we compare it to each and every exemplar in that category to determine whether it matches or not. The individual items that are stored in semantic memory as evidence of a particular category are called exemplars. As we will see, this contrasts with prototype theory in that prototype theory suggests that we draw an average of all the instances of a category and use that as a comparison. Exemplar theory contends that the category is all of the associated items (Medin & Rips, 2005).

Exemplar theory: Categories are classified by maintaining a large number of specific instances of a category (exemplars) that are associated with each other in semantic memory.

Exemplar theory is successful in accounting for the multidimensional nature of a category. Consider the category "tools." It is difficult to imagine what an average or prototypical tool would look like. Consider the difference between hand tools and power tools. Thus, prototype theory is challenged here. However, if each and every exemplar is represented in an associated structure in semantic memory, any new item can be compared against the appropriate match.

What evidence exists for the reality of the exemplar theory? It turns out that priming can be specific to the particular aspect of the exemplar that is being primed (Gagné & Shoben, 2002). If the prime focuses on one aspect of the category (e.g., color), it will better prime those members of the category for which that aspect is salient. Thus, it will be easier to verify what the term *television show* means if it is preceded by *reality show* than if it is preceded by *trade show*, because both *television show* and *reality show* share a common meaning of the word *show*.

Some have criticized the exemplar approach because it necessitates a large memory system that can store hundreds, if not thousands, of exemplars for each and every different category. However, the capacity of long-term memory to store information is seemingly limitless, so large demands on capacity alone are not enough to disqualify the theory. It is also possible that both exemplars and prototypes may be used in the formation of categories and in comparing new instances to existing categories.

Feature Comparison Theory. Another theory as to how categories are represented in semantic memory is the feature comparison theory. **Feature comparison theory** states that we maintain a list of features for each category. According to this view, each category is represented by an associated list of the kinds of characteristics that make up the category. Thus, for example, the category of "books" might include the following: (a) contains written material; (b) is intended to be read; (c) contains a set number of pages, usually enclosed in covers of paper or cardboard; and (d) is intended to last a long time.

> **Feature comparison theory:** We define our categories by maintaining a list of features for any particular category.

New objects are compared neither to a constructed prototype nor to a set of exemplars. Rather, new objects are matched to the list of features. Thus, when one encounters a magazine, it fails to fit into the category of "books," because it does not fulfill Feature 4 of the category "books." Your textbook, however, does fulfill the features and would be classified as a "book."

Smith, Shoben, and Rips (1974) distinguished between defining features and characteristic features. **Defining features** are required for any example of a particular category. For example, the defining feature of a book is that it stores words. **Characteristic features** generally accompany an instance of the category but are not required. Characteristic features of books include that they are meant to be read, have covers, are made of paper, and have an author. Most of us would still classify books-on-tape as books, because they store words, which can transmit meaning even if they are not printed, not made of paper, and not meant to be read.

> **Defining features:** According to feature comparison theory, defining features are required for any example of a particular category.

Feature comparison theory is essentially flawed because so few categories have clear defining features. Consider the example of the category "books." The defining feature of a book is that it stores

> **Characteristic features:** According to feature comparison theory, characteristic features generally accompany an instance of the category but are not required.

words. But is the defining feature really accurate? What about a children's book that only has pictures but not words? What does that leave as a defining feature of the category "books" when it includes picture books, audiobooks, electronic books, and so on? The category "books" becomes multidimensional, and a single set of features no longer defines it. Another example of this problem is to think of what the defining feature is of the category "cat." Is it that it is a living thing, that it meows, and that it has cat genes? What about a dead cat, a mute cat, and a stuffed animal cat? All of these exceptions propelled theorists to consider the prototype as being better able to explain the structure of semantic memory.

Prototype Theory

> **Prototype theory:** States that prototypes form the central characteristic in our representation of categories. A prototype is defined as the most typical member of a particular category.

A prototype is defined as the most typical member of a particular category. **Prototype theory** states that prototypes form the central characteristics in our representation of categories. In prototype theory, we compare examples that we encounter in the real world to a constructed mental prototype. If the example matches the prototype, we decide it is an example of the category. If it does not match, we reject the category label for that item. For example, we compare an example of a tool to our prototype of a tool. The prototype itself need not be a real member of the category. In fact, it is likely to be an averaged mental representation of the concept (Rosch, 1975). Thus, the prototype may not exist at all in the real world; it is an abstraction. Consider your prototype of a bird. If you live in the Northeast of the United States, your prototype may look something like a robin, but without the specific coloring. If you live farther south or closer to the ocean, your "bird" may obtain longer legs and a longer beak but is not yet an egret. If you live in a big city, your prototype may resemble a pigeon. When you encounter a new animal, you match the animal to your prototype of a bird. If it is a close enough match, you assign it to the category "bird." If it fails to match, you dismiss that example as a bird.

What evidence is there that we represent categories in terms of prototypes? We will consider two main lines of research. The first demonstrates that prototypes are rapidly remembered and named when a category is supplied. The second shows the effects of semantic priming on prototypical members of a category and nonprototypical members of a category. Each of these points to a strong role for prototypes in our semantic memory.

- *Prototypes are easily named.* In studies done by Eleanor Rosch and her colleagues, participants were asked to judge how prototypical a given instance was of a particular category. For example, "raccoon" might be judged highly prototypical of the category "mammal," but "platypus" might be judged less prototypical. Similarly, "carrot" may be judged more prototypical of the category "vegetable" than "kale." A second group of participants was then asked to generate the names of examples from categories, such as "mammal" and "vegetable." The researchers found that the items named first and more frequently by the participants were the ones that were usually judged as more prototypical (Mervis, Catlin, & Rosch, 1976). Thus, the first and most common vegetables generated included prototypical vegetables like carrots and peas and only later, if at all, did the participants produce items like kale and bok choy.

- *Prototypes and semantic priming.* The more prototypical an example is, the more likely it is to be judged more quickly after semantic priming. Semantic priming works better if the target words are prototypical rather than nonprototypical. For example, the prime word *feathers* will create faster response speed if it precedes *robin* than if it precedes *cormorant*. Thus, prototypical examples are more locked into the associative structure that creates categories. For example, using subliminal priming, in which participants did not consciously see the prime word, Miles and Minda (2012) found that priming led to faster judgments for category members and also led to more errors in which non–category members were judged as being a member of the category.

Situated Simulation Theory

The **situated simulation theory** states that the representation of a particular concept varies as a function of the situation or context (Barsalou, 2003). In this view, the context in which a category is encountered calls upon different aspects of its representation. For example, we think about the concept of "hydrogen" very differently when we encounter it in the context of hydrogen-cell batteries than when we encounter it in the context of theories of the early universe. Similarly, we draw on different aspects of

> **Situated Simulation Theory:** The situated simulation theory states that the representation of a particular concept varies as a function of the situation or context.

the concept "pumpkin" when we are thinking of preparing soup and when we are thinking of preparing for a Halloween party. This idea makes intuitive sense, but are there data that support the situated simulation model?

Wu and Barsalou (2009) examined the situated simulation theory by asking participants to regard specific concepts from different perspectives. The experimenters gave participants a phrase, such as "split coconut" or "chipped coconut" and asked participants to generate as many properties as possible for each phrase. Though both stimuli call one's attention to the concept of a coconut, the adjective served as context, and people focused on different aspects of the concept depending on that context. Thus, a "split coconut" elicited phrases relating to the opening of a coconut, whereas "chipped coconut" elicited phrases related to the drinking of coconut milk. In this way, Wu and Barsalou demonstrated that context is important when considering our semantic memory for concepts.

A concept is a mental construct that contains information associated with a specific idea. A concept is a mental representation of an idea. A category is a mental construct referring to a set of objects or ideas that are grouped together or are associated with each other. A number of models seek to account for how we represent concepts categories in our semantic memory. These include the feature comparison, exemplar, prototype, and the situated simulation model. The most successful theory is prototype theory. Prototype theory successfully predicts that prototypes will be more easily named than other examples of the category. Prototypical examples also show greater semantic priming effects than less prototypical examples.

Section Summary and Quiz

1. A mental construct referring to a set of objects or ideas that are grouped together or are associated with each other is known as a
   a. Lemma
   b. Prototype

    c.   Exemplar
    d.   Category

2. In prototype theory, our mental representation of a particular concept is
    a.   A very specific example that we use to compare other instances of that category to
    b.   A hierarchical model in which category confusion is limited through semantic priming
    c.   Represented by a series of exemplars
    d.   A generalized or average idea of that category

3. In which theory of concept representation do we define our categories by maintaining a list of features for any particular category?
    a.   Feature comparison theory
    b.   Prototype theory
    c.   Exemplar theory
    d.   Situated simulation theory

4. That membership in a category may be defined by each item's general similarity to other members in the category rather than by a specific list of features is associated with which aspect of concept representation?
    a.   Family resemblance
    b.   Situated cognition
    c.   Exemplar specification
    d.   Prototype priming

Answers
1. d
2. d
3. a
4. a

SCHEMAS AND SCRIPTS

To this point, our discussion of semantic memory has concerned the topic of concepts, categories, and the connections among them. Semantic memory also includes more general aspects of memory—that is, units of memory that are more complex, which are commonly called schemas or scripts. For example, think of the concept of "parking"—that is, the idea that a car can be turned off and left for a while in a safe location where you can return to it later. In U.S. society, parking one's car is a well-learned ritual. The script for parking a car involves (a) arriving at the parking lot, (b) searching for a spot—get there early or the spots will be all taken, and (c) choosing to swing around the lot an extra time in the hope that someone with a really good spot is just leaving and you can take that one. (d) Once you have your spot, position your car so that other cars cannot sneak in front of you, (e) place your car in the spot—and maximize the difference from nearby cars so as to avoid "door dings," and (f) note the location of your car so you can return to it later. Many of us follow this script many times a week. The point is—we all have this script memorized already. We know what to expect when we enter the parking lot. The script of "how to park your car" is another form of information stored in semantic memory.

Fundamental to this area is the idea of a schema. A **schema** is generalized knowledge about an event, a person, or a situation (the plural of *schema* can be either *schemas* or *schemata*). Schemas are patterns of connected information about a particular topic. We have schemas, for example, as to what you find in a car. We expect seats, beverage holders, controls, and transparent windows. Imagine your surprise if you entered your friend's car and there were no seats, but there was a sink. Think of a car in which all the windows were rendered completely opaque. These cars would violate your schema of a car (and be quite dangerous). We also have schemas about what to expect during college exams. This particular schema may be all too familiar to college students. But imagine coming to an exam to find your professor dancing and playing loud disco music from the 1970s on a phonograph player while you were trying to take the test. This would violate our schema, as included in our schema of taking an exam is that the professor will be quiet. From the point of view of memory representation, schemas and scripts are well-learned patterns that guide our behavior and organize information in memory (Abelson, 1981).

> **Schema:** Generalized knowledge about an event, a person, or a situation.

Scripts refer to a particular kind of schema. **Scripts** are well-learned sequences of events associated with common activities. For example, we have scripts for such common activities as "going to a restaurant." Without having to recall specific instances of restaurant-going, you can describe the common process. A person shows you to a table and gives you menus. You spend several minutes deciding what to eat. Then a waiter comes by, and you give him your order (politely, hopefully). Several minutes later, the waiter returns bearing your meal. You eat your meal. And so on and so forth. Our memories abound in such scripts—waiting to board an airplane, checking out at the grocery store, and your morning "getting ready" ritual are just a few of the many scripts you have stored in your semantic memory. Violations of scripts often turn out to be memorable events. Consider an airplane flight in which the flight attendants decided to forgo boarding by seat numbers. The ensuing crush to board the airplane may prompt you to avoid that airline in the future. Consider a restaurant without menus. This puts a maximal demand on the waiter, who must tell you all of the options for the day's meal. It also puts memory demands on the patron, as she must remember all of these options. However, you may also consider a restaurant without menus an interesting novelty and recommend the restaurant to friends.

> **Scripts:** Well-learned sequences of events associated with common activities.

Consider a schema for a dentist's office. There is a waiting room with relatively comfortable chairs. Magazines are available for patients while they wait. These magazines usually include *Time, Sports Illustrated,* and *National Geographic.* A few children's toys lie unused under a television showing *Oprah.* A woman sits behind a glass panel and checks you in. The office is decorated with hokey signs ("A bright smile shines on everyone's day"). An anthropomorphic tooth, encouraging kids to brush, stands to one side. Beyond a door is a maze of rooms with dental chairs, X-ray machines, and occasionally an actual dentist. These are items we come to expect after a lifetime of visiting dentist's offices. However, consider when an event or item is inconsistent with the schema. Consider sitting down in the waiting room and finding pornographic magazines instead of the expected *National Geographic.* Consider coming to a waiting room that had yoga mats instead of chairs. Consider a dentist's office covered in Marxist slogans ("Viva Castro") instead of the usual platitudes. Such variations from the dentist schema would not go unnoticed. Indeed, many of us would find these deviations from the schema sufficient reason to find a new dentist.

A classic study by Brewer and Treyens (1981) illustrates points about schemas and our expectations very nicely. Participants arrived for an experiment and were asked to wait in a lab room (Figure 5.5). The participants waited in the room a short time and then entered another room for testing. To their surprise, the participants were then asked to recall all of the objects that they could remember from the waiting room.

Participants remembered many items from the office that were consistent with the concept of a waiting room. For example, people remembered the desk, the chair, and the typewriter (this was 1981 after all). Some people even falsely remembered schema-consistent items not present in the room (e.g., books). However, several items in the room are generally not found in offices but did not strongly violate the schema for a waiting room. For example, wine bottles and picnic baskets are seldom found in offices but their presence here should not have been particularly surprising, and very few participants remembered these items. However, items that violate the office schema were well recalled; most participants recalled the skull, even though this is seldom found in academic offices. Thus, we can conclude that schemas help us recall items and events that are consistent with the schema and help us remember violations of the schema. However, items irrelevant to the schema may go unnoticed. To summarize Brewer and Treyens's (1981) results: Schema-consistent items were well remembered, schema-violating items were also well remembered, but schema-irrelevant items were less well remembered.

The reconstructive nature of maintaining schemas also has a dark side. Stereotypes function as schemas for our semantic memory representations of people (Jackson & Rose, 2013). If you think about stereotypes, they are bodies of knowledge (however false) that make generalizations about specific groups of people. Thus, like our schema for the dentist office, a stereotype provides us with a roadmap about what to expect from a particular kind of person. Regardless of whether the stereotype is benevolent or malign, it promotes the encoding of stereotype-consistent information and the ignoring of stereotype-inconsistent information. It can also lead us to falsely remember something that is stereotype-consistent but not actually true about the specific individual.

Figure 5.5   What can you remember from this room?

SOURCE: Brewers and Treyens (1981).

In normal circumstances, however, once a schema is formed, it is useful in encoding new information. The schema forms the backbone upon which new information can be associated. For example, Bransford and Johnson (1972) presented participants with confusing passages to read, such as the one shown in Box 5.1. Some participants were given schematic information to assist them in understanding the passage. For example, in the passage below, some participants had the title "Washing Clothes" to aid their understanding. Those provided with the title recalled more information from the passage than those who had not read the title.

As you can see, the text is written in an ambiguous way. Once you know, however, that it is about washing clothes, most of the ambiguous words should make sense. Therefore, having a schema in mind (in this case, for washing clothes) can help an individual encode new information into memory.

BOX 5.1 WASHING CLOTHES

The procedure is actually quite simple. First arrange items into different groups. Of course one pile may be sufficient depending on how much there is to do. If you have to go somewhere else due to lack of facilities, that is the next step; otherwise, you are pretty well set. It is important not to overdo things. That is, it is better to do too few things at once than too many. In the short run this may not seem important, but complications can easily arise. A mistake can be expensive as well. At first, the whole procedure will seem complicated. Soon, however, it will become just another facet of life. It is difficult to foresee any end to necessity for this task in the immediate future, but then, one can never tell. After the procedure is completed one arranges the material into different groups again. Then they can be put into their appropriate places. Eventually they will be used once more and the whole cycle will then have to be repeated. However, that is part of life.

SOURCE: Bransford and Johnson (1972).

In some situations, using schemas may be counterproductive to learning new information. Think about the typical clothing shop at the mall—after a few minutes of browsing, a nosy salesperson will engage you and try to get you to buy the most expensive clothes. Having a schema for this form of shopping may not help you when you shop at the Salvation Army store. Thus, it will not help you to invoke the mall schema when trying to remember your trip to buy clothes for charity. Indeed, if the goal it to learn new episodic information, using schema information will lead to the kind of errors we just saw in the Brewer and Treyens (1981) experiment in which participants often recalled items from the room that were consistent with the schema but not actually present in the room. Badham and Maylor (2016) asked participants to learn weakly related word pairs, such as "barbell-saucepan." In one condition, participants were given a schema that helped them organize the items ("metal," in the example), whereas in other conditions they relied on their own idiosyncratic encoding techniques. Interestingly, in this experiment, providing the schema did not improve memory performance for younger adults and hurt performance in older adults. Presumably, in this case, providing schema-type information led participants to use less than optimal encoding techniques, thereby lowering the performance in the schema condition relative to the control.

Reconstruction of Events

Schemas are also useful in providing structure for retrieving longer events and information, such as stories. Consider describing a recent trip to a restaurant. The distinctive feature about this lunch was getting together with an old friend whom you had not seen in a long time, and you dined at a restaurant with food you are not accustomed to, perhaps a Middle Eastern restaurant. Thus, what you remember is catching up with your friend, on one hand, and the interesting tastes, on the other—such as hummus and baba ghanoush.

Now consider describing the event. Do you really remember the maitre d' bringing you to the table? Do you remember whether the maitre d' or the waiter brought you the menus? Did the same waiter who took your order bring you your food? In many cases, we may use the schema to help us fill in this information. In telling the story of your visit to the restaurant, what is important is communicating to your listener the gist of the story: the good food and the good friendship. The listener is not expecting you to get the details of the service accurate, but it may be necessary to insert such information to maintain the narrative flow. For example, you might say, "By the time the waiter came to take our order, we were already drinking the most interesting tea," when in fact, you ordered before the waiter brought the tea.

Indeed, a classic experiment concerns the use of schemas in storytelling. Bartlett (1932) asked his British college students to play a "telephone game." In the experiment, he asked one student to read a story derived from a Native American folktale from the Pacific Northwest. The story was called "War of the Ghosts" and is shown in Box 5.2. Sometime after hearing the story, the student was asked to tell another student the story, who then had to tell the story to yet another person. After several such retellings, Bartlett had the final student write down the story. He found that changes in the story from the original had to do with making it more consistent with the schema for a story from someone from British culture. For example, "hunting seals" became "going fishing," and often an explanation for the sudden and unexplained death at the end of the story was included. In short, the British participants transformed the story according to their own schemas. In another experiment, Bartlett had students read the story, and then each student wrote it down four months later. As in the telephone game, the errors that students intruded into the story made the story more consistent with British story schemas. (For more information on Bartlett himself, go to study.sagepub.com/schwartz3e.[2])

BOX 5.2 THE WAR OF THE GHOSTS

One night two young men from Egulac went down to the river to hunt seals, and while they were there it became foggy and calm. Then they heard war-cries, and they thought: "Maybe this is a war party." They escaped to the shore and hid behind a log. Now canoes came up, and they heard the noise of paddles, and saw one canoe coming up to them. There were five men in the canoe, and they said:

"What do you think? We wish to take you along. We are going up the river to make war on the people."

One of the young men said, "I have no arrows."

"Arrows are in the canoe," they said.

"I will not go along. I might be killed. My relatives do not know where I have gone. But you," he said turning to the other, "may go with them."

(Continued)

(Continued)

So one of the young men went, but the other returned home.

And the warriors went up the river to a town on the other side of Kalama. The people came down to the water, and they began to fight, and many were killed. But presently the young man heard one of the warriors say: "Quick, let us go home: that Indian has been hit." Now he thought: "Oh, they are ghosts." He did not feel sick, but they said he had been shot.

So the canoes went back to Egulac, and the young man went ashore to his house, and made a fire. And he told everybody and said: "Behold I accompanied the ghosts, and we went to fight. Many of our fellows were killed, and many of those who attacked us were killed. They said I was hit, but I did not feel sick."

He told it all, and then he became quiet. When the sun rose he fell down. Something black came out of his mouth. His face became contorted. The people jumped up and cried.

He was dead.

SOURCE: Bartlett (1932).

SEMANTIC MEMORY AND MUSIC

Most of us have many songs and melodies stored in our memory. You may know the lyrics and music to Bob Dylan's "The Times They Are a-Changin'," Carly Rae Jepsen's "Call Me Maybe," and Beethoven's "Ode to Joy." In most cases, it is semantic memory that is responsible for this store of musical information. Although some songs may have powerful associations with certain episodic memories (e.g., the song you danced to with your future spouse the first time you met), much of what we store in memory is semantic memory in nature. A professional musician may have thousands of songs accessible in semantic memory. Recently, for example, I attended a concert and watched a young pianist play a complex Rachmaninoff piano concerto. The young man never looked at a sheet of music, having memorized thousands of notes and complex rhythms. Indeed, entrance to most top music conservatories requires young musicians to play long pieces of music from memory.

Sherman and Kennerley (2014) looked at semantic memory for music in an interesting way. They were interested in how schemas help us organize our knowledge of music in semantic memory. They reasoned that—like other forms of semantic memory—semantic memory for music would use schemas to help the individual represent information. Thus, when thinking about a particular form of music or a particular artist, we will use both prototypes to help us represent the style of music and schemas as to what to expect from that genre or artist. Thus, consider the Beatles, the 1960s British rock band. Consistent with our schema for this group would be to hear "Hard Day's Night" or "Octopus's Garden." Hearing them sing arias from a Wagner opera would violate your schema for the Beatles.

Sherman and Kennerley (2014) simulated these expectations in the lab. They played five clips of music from currently popular artists (e.g., Robbie Williams). However, they did not present each artist's biggest hit. The participants listened to the clips and then engaged in a distractor task. When they were asked to recall the names of the songs that they listened to for each artist, they often recalled the absent hit song. Sherman and Kennerley reasoned that the participants used their schema for that artist to help them recall songs. Unfortunately, in this case, using the schema led to false memories, in particular of the artist's top hit. For our purposes here, however, what Sherman and Kennerley do is illustrate that schemas are important in representing our musical knowledge.

It has been argued that the function of music itself is mnemonic (Racette & Peretz, 2007)—that is, the rhythms and cadences of music allow for easier encoding of verbal material such as stories. Indeed, we teach our children to learn the alphabet with a song, and many companies sell their products by having us associate their product with a catchy jingle. Schulkind (2004) emphasized that for most forms of semantic memory, it is meaning that is critical, but that for music semantic memory, it is melodic structure that is crucial.

LANGUAGE, LEXICAL MEMORY, AND SEMANTIC MEMORY

Although often treated as separate topics in separate courses, language and memory are closely intertwined. Language is heavily dependent on the proper functioning of the memory systems that serve it. We need to remember tens of thousands of words, thousands of aspects of grammar, and the way in which to pronounce certain words, and in languages such as English, we also need to memorize the spelling of thousands of irregular words. In other languages, such as French and Spanish, every noun has a gender, and we must memorize that *la mesa* (the table) is feminine but *el corazon* (the heart) is masculine. For this reason, we introduce the concept of lexical memory. Lexical memory is closely related to the concept of semantic memory, but lexical memory is specific to the representation of the words that we use to express ideas—and the use of words involves language. Thus, in the section, we are not interested in psycholinguistics per se, but rather the memory representations that make language possible.

Lexical Memory. Episodic memory refers to our memory for individual events from our lives, and semantic memory refers to our knowledge of the world. Both of these memory systems are considered **declarative memory**, because we can verbalize the contents of each kind of memory. It is possible to talk about your past experiences and what you know about the world. Thus, both

> **Declarative memory:** Any memory that can be verbalized; includes both episodic and semantic memory.

> **Lexicon:** Our mental dictionary.

of these memory systems are based on our ability to manipulate and use words. However, to use words, we must have those words represented in memory and easy to access. Lexical memory refers to the memory system that stores words and other linguistic entities in memory. It is also called the **lexicon**.

In theory, lexical memory is a representational system that stores words. But words are not that simple. Words have multiple meanings and many associations in different contexts. They may be pronounced in different ways depending on the context (e.g., "You say *tomato*, and I say *tomahto*"). In bilinguals, it is important to address the relation in memory between translation equivalents (e.g., *tomato/tomate* or *book/libro* in English and Spanish).

What makes models of lexical memory even more complicated is the speed of access with which speakers must be able to access words. First, consider how fast most of us speak: We usually produce three to four words per second. In order to speak, we must be able to rapidly access our lexical memory. We must also be able to rapidly choose the right word from as many as 100,000 words in our lexicon. In addition, there must be representation space that stores our basic knowledge of the grammatical rules of our language. (For more on research on the mental substrates of words and grammar, go to www.sagepub.com/schwartz3e.[4])

Most models of lexical memory focus on three levels of representation—one at the level of meaning, one at the level of syntax (that is, grammar), and a third at the level that contains information about the phonology (that is, sound) of the word (see Levelt, 1989; Marelli, Aggujaro, Molteni, & Luzzatti, 2012; see Figure 5.6). The assumption in these models is that a network of semantic associations carries meanings and relating concepts from one association to another—in essence, a semantic memory system. In this conceptual system, the meaning of *tiger* may be represented as an image of a big cat (associated with other concepts such as "lion," "leopard," etc.), an image of a baseball player from Detroit and its associations (e.g., "the baseball team," "the Detroit Tigers"), and any other secondary meanings of the word *tiger* (e.g., "a sexually charged person"). This conceptual-level representation informs a level of representation known as the lemma. A **lemma** is a hypothetical entity containing only meaning-based and syntactical information without any information concerning the phonology of the word (Chang et al., 2015). But unlike the conceptual level, the lemma is lexical in nature in that it contains information about language usage, such as the part of speech (noun, verb, etc.), how to make it plural, its grammatical gender (in many languages other than English), and other grammatical features. The lemma informs the next highest level, known as the lexeme. The **lexeme** is the level of representation that stores the phonology of a word—that is, how the word sounds. When the lexeme is retrieved, the word can then be sent to the motor system (Caramazza & Miozzo, 1997; Levelt, 1989).

Lemma: A hypothetical entity containing only semantic and syntactical information without any information concerning the phonology of the word.

Lexeme: The level of representation that stores the phonology of a word—that is, how the word sounds.

Let's see how this hypothetical system works. Say a person asks you a question, "What is the word that means 'second to last item on any list?'" The question starts by inducing the lexical retrieval process in the person who must answer the question. According to the model outlined above, first the respondent must access information at the semantic level—information such as "toward the end," "part of a list," "fancy word for showing off your vocabulary," and so on. This initial response results in the retrieval of the lemma,

Figure 5.6 A model of lexical memory.

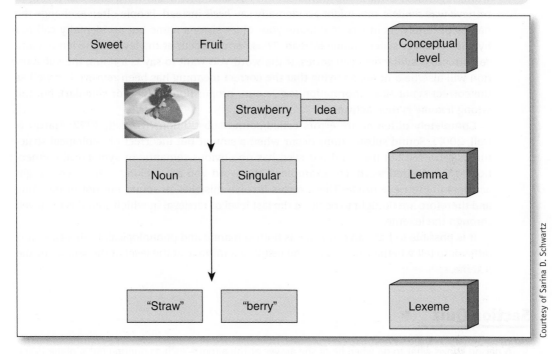

Courtesy of Sarina D. Schwartz

which contains both semantic and syntactical information. Here, grammar information might be added—noun or adjective, derived from Latin—as well as the semantic information from the previous level. However, the lemma does not contain any phonological information about how to say the word.

Once the lemma representation has been retrieved, the next stage begins: the retrieval of the lexeme representation. In retrieving at the lexeme level, the person retrieves the phonological information for the word *penultimate*. The lexeme is still an abstract representation, but it is a representation of sound. The phonological entry *penultimate* is then sent to the motor system so that the person can articulate the answer. Thus, according to this view, every time we retrieve a word (even in normal speech), it passes through these three stages of representation: semantics, lemma, and lexeme. Most researchers in psycholinguistics agree on this general model, although, of course, they argue over the specifics (see Harley, 2008; Levelt, 1989; Marelli et al., 2012).

Much of the research that supports this model comes from errors in ordinary speech called **speech errors** (Garrett, 1992; Warker & Dell, 2015). Research focuses on two kinds of speech errors. The first are called word exchange errors. Word

Speech errors: Errors in ordinary speech, including speech errors and sound substitutions.

exchange errors occur when we substitute a word with a similar meaning for another word, regardless of how the words sound. For example, if the word one was trying to retrieve was *sandals,* one might accidentally say *heels* instead. People often exchange the names of family members. You know your older sister's name but accidentally call her by your younger sister's name instead. These errors occur at the level of the lemma and seldom cross syntactical categories. If the word you want to say is a noun, the substitution will also be a noun, showing that the correct meaning has been retrieved as well as the correct syntactical information (e.g., noun, proper noun, plural or singular), but the wrong lexeme is then activated.

Completely different are errors called sound substitutions (Garrett, 1992; Martin & Dell, 2007). Sound substitutions occur when a similar but incorrect phonological structure is retrieved but the word retrieved has no obvious semantic or syntactical connection to the desired word. For example, if the word you are seeking is *tiger,* you might accidentally retrieve *tirade.* These errors involve mistakes in sound but not in meaning and therefore are thought to occur at the last level of retrieval in which sound is retrieved through the lexeme.

It is possible to have an error that is both semantic and phonological. In this case, it is difficult to tell whether the error is the result of a mistake at the level of the lemma or the lexeme.

Section Quiz

1. A person knows what to do when he or she arrives at the airport—such as printing out a plane ticket, presenting it the agent, taking off his or her shoes before going through the security screening. The knowledge of this procedure can be classified as
   a. The defining features of a category
   b. A script
   c. A lemma
   d. A syntactical procedure

2. In the representation of words in language, the representation at the level of sound is called the
   a. Lemma
   b. Schema
   c. Lexeme
   d. Lexicon

3. Brewer and Treyens (1981) asked participants to recall the waiting room they had just been in. This experiment showed that
   a. People have outstanding visual memories
   b. Lemmas are necessary for the retrieval of speech errors
      ___mas guide our recall, even if that leads to an occasional schema-based error
         ie above are true

4. Bartlett's (1932) experiment on the "War of the Ghosts" showed that
   a. Cultural schemas are important in memory
   b. Scripts have no effect on memory when narrative recall is required
   c. All scripts are schemas, but not all schemas are scripts
   d. None of the above are true

1. b
2. c
3. c
4. a

SUMMARY

Schemas and scripts are higher-order semantic memory representations. Schemas are general-ized knowledge about an event, person, or situation, whereas scripts are well-learned sequences of events associated with common activities. In a classic experiment, Brewer and Treyens (1981) showed how important schemas are to the organization of semantic memory. In another clas-sic experiment, Barlett showed that culture has an important role in schemas. We also reviewed evidence of the importance of semantic memory in music. Language is also dependent on memory. Lemmas are hypothetical entities containing only meaning and grammatical informa-tion, whereas lexemes are the level of representation that stores the sounds of words. Studies on speech errors show the theoretical advantage of both the concept of the lemma and the lexeme.

KEY TERMS

associative model

category

characteristic features

concept

cross-language semantic priming

declarative memory

defining features

dual-store view (or separate store) of bilingual representation

exemplar theory

family resemblance

feature comparison theory

hierarchical network model

lemma

levels of categorization

lexeme

lexical decision task

lexical memory (lexicon)

prototype theory

schema

scripts

semantic memory

semantic priming

sentence verification task

single-store view of bilingual representation

situated simulation theory

speech errors

spreading activation

REVIEW QUESTIONS

1. What is semantic memory? How does it differ from episodic memory and lexical memory?

2. What is meant by the term *spreading activation*? How do experiments on semantic priming support the idea of spreading activation?

3. What is meant by the term *levels of categorization*? What empirical evidence suggests that human memory is organized according to these levels?

4. What is meant by the term *family resemblance for categories*? How does it relate to the idea that categories have fuzzy boundaries?

5. What are the differences among prototype theory, exemplar theory, and feature comparison theory?

6. What were the results of Brewer and Treyen's classic experiment on students' memory for a waiting room? What do these results tell us about schemas?

7. What is situated simulation theory? How does it explain how concepts are represented in semantic memory?

8. What is the difference between the single-store and dual-store view of a bilingual's lexical memory? Which view do the data on cross-language priming support?

9. When does relying on schemas lead to errors in retrieval from memory? Can you give an example of this from the discussion of music and memory?

10. What is the difference between a lemma and lexeme? How do speech errors support this conceptual difference?

ONLINE RESOURCES

1. For more on the life of George Berkeley, go to http://www.iep.utm.edu/b/berkeley.htm.

2. For more information on Frederic Bartlett, go to http://www.bartlett.psychol.cam.ac.uk.

3. For a different view of language in nonhuman primates, go to the following website: http://www .iowaprimatelearning.org.

4. For more information on bilingual representation, go to http://www.albany.edu/coglanlab/.

Go to **study.sagepub.com/schwartz3e** for additional exercises and study resources. Select **Chapter 5, Semantic and Lexical Memory** for chapter-specific resources.

CHAPTER 6

Visual Memory

Most of the first five chapters have concerned memory for words, stories, narratives—in essence, verbal materials. However, we remember much more than just words. We remember images, sounds, smells, and emotions, to name a few. This chapter will focus on visual memory, our ability to learn and retrieve visual images. Visual memory has many similarities to memory for words but also significant differences, which will be explored here. We will also discuss how we represent or store images in memory. Memory consists of representational processes as well as encoding and retrieval processes. Of great importance in this area is how we store or represent visual information. But before we can do that, it is necessary to discuss a little bit about how imagery feels—what is often called the phenomenology (i.e., the experience) of visual memory.

Consider the following exercise. Retrieve from memory an image of the face of President Trump, elected in November of 2016 without consulting a photograph (see Figure 6.1). Once you have President Trump's face accessible in your mind's "eye," answer the following questions.

Figure 6.1 Can you fill in the president's appearance with your mind's eye?

iStock.com/Bastiaan Slabbers

1. Does he have more gray hair than blond hair?

2. Does he have any freckles?

3. Is he wearing a blue suit?

Chances are that you have never intentionally encoded any of these features of President Trump. Yet you are likely to see him wearing a suit, as he usually dresses formally. Based on your mental image, you

Figure 6.2   The Parthenon—did you correctly count the number of columns in your mind's eye?

can make a decision about the first two questions, even though these may not have been aspects of his appearance that you have ever paid attention to, as they are not relevant to the job of being president. But there are other iconic images that we may think we know but really do not. A classic (in two ways) example of this is to try to answer the question "How many columns does the Parthenon in Athens, Greece, have?" Most of us can form a visual image of the famous ancient building, still standing on a hillside in Athens. However, actually counting the columns in our mind's eye view is much more difficult than counting the columns from a photograph or from the real thing (see Figure 6.2). If our images are really pictures, this should not be the case. If you are not familiar with the Parthenon in Athens, think of a landmark you do know, perhaps the Empire State Building. Can you count the number of floors in your visual image of the building? Probably not. Thus, visual imagery differs from visual perception in important ways. One of the sections in this chapter will address differences between visual perception and visual imagery.

VISUAL MEMORY: RECOGNITION AND RECALL

Our eyes are open continuously during our waking hours. We visually perceive the world about 16 hours a day, day in and day out. We are therefore bombarded with a tremendous amount of visual stimulation, not all of which we can attend to at any one time. How much of what you see do you actually remember?

Unlike word memory, in which recall can be measured by asking the participant to speak a word or write a word, visual memory presents several difficult methodological issues. First, how do you get someone to report a visual image? Do you have him or her describe the image verbally or draw it, or is some kind of recognition test preferable? Each one presents problems. A verbal description brings the researcher back into the domain of words. And our verbal descriptions may often be inadequate. Asking for drawing is simply not possible with many people who lack the requisite skill. In fact, even experienced talented sketch artists draw only rough approximations based on a witness's description. Therefore, both drawing and giving verbal descriptions are problematic, because we "feel" as if neither format conveys the information that we think is in our visual memory. Thus, most researchers will opt for the recognition test when assessing visual memory, which is problematic because most verbal memory studies can also use recall.

Recognition is usually the measure that researchers use when examining long-term visual memory. In particular, old–new recognition tests are used. A picture is presented, and the participant is asked whether he or she has seen this exact picture before. If new pictures are interspersed with old pictures, this method can tell us something about visual memory. When recognition measures are used, demonstrating the power of visual memory is straightforward. Standing (1973), for example, presented participants with 10,000 pictures over a five-day period. At the end of the presentation period, a recognition test ensued. During the test, Standing presented some of the original pictures mixed in with pictures that had not been presented. Thus, on half of the trials, the correct answer was "old," whereas on the other half of trials, the correct answer was "new." Participants correctly identified about two-thirds of the pictures, which they had only seen once before. In fact, even when people are doing a concurrent task (that is, another cognitive task in addition to looking at pictures), they are still able to recognize pictures that they saw earlier (Wolfe, Horowitz, & Michod, 2007). Thus, we do have strong visual memories and visual images. Fine recognition distinctions between old and new pictures demonstrate that we are attending to the details in visual images.

An important question is: How does our mind-brain system store visual images? One of the oldest debates in visual imagery is about exactly how, at both cognitive and neural levels, we code the images we store and remember. The next section on representation of visual images is one of the more difficult ones in the text. Keep in mind that the goal of the research is to infer—from people's performance—what the exact nature of the representational code is. This representational code is not the visual image itself that we call up in visual working memory. Rather, the code is the manner in which that image is stored when not in use—that is, when it is being stored for future use. With that in mind, we will jump into this topic.

REPRESENTATION AND IMAGERY

> **Representation:** The storage of information in memory when that information is not in use.

Representation means the storage of information in long-term memory when that information is not in use. When we need to retrieve information, we activate it from this long-term representational system. In the case of visual imagery, activating that information means creating a visual image. Once the image is activated, we can inspect it and make decisions about it. For example, at one point in your life, you may have visited your local fire department's station. You may not have thought of this event in a long time, but chances are that you have some visual memories of the living quarters for the firefighters on duty and perhaps the bay where they keep the big trucks. Representation means the format in which we maintain these visual images between the time we perceived them and the time we remember them, forming a mental image. When we retrieve these representations, we then experience mental imagery.

The problem of studying representation is that scientists cannot directly examine mental images or their stored representations. We cannot pull them out of a person's head and inspect them. They exist only in mental space. Therefore, cognitive psychologists must devise experiments so as to infer what mental representations are like based on visible behaviors or reports of the person doing the imaging. This restriction presented some serious challenges to cognitive psychologists when they first began to investigate visual imagery.

There are two main classes of theories as to how we represent visual information in memory. The first is called **analog representation**, and the second is called **propositional representation**. Analog representation means we store visual images in a manner a lot like pictures. When we retrieve a representation of President Trump, we retrieve the neural equivalent of a photograph. Propositional representation means that we store visual images in terms of a language-like code. When we retrieve an image of the president, what we get is equivalent to a list of features—visual descriptions of the president. Our imagery system then recreates an image in visual working memory (i.e., the visuo-spatial sketchpad).

> **Analog representation:** The theory that we store visual images in a manner similar to actual pictures.

> **Propositional representation:** The theory that we store visual images in terms of a language-like code.

Note that the propositional view does not deny that our images appear to us as pictures. However, the propositional view states that we do not store images in a pictorial format. Our representation is in an abstract code. At the time of retrieval, we reconstruct a visual image based on that representation.

To put this issue in perspective, when researchers first began debating issues of image representation in the 1960s, most researchers thought that the propositional view would turn out to be correct. One reason for this view was that these researchers argued that analog visual memory would take up huge amounts of memory within the brain. Just a few pictures stored in analog fashion, they argued, would eat up the brain's entire memory capacity. This reasoning emanated from the realization that in computers, text requires much less memory storage space than visual images, and back then computers had much less overall memory storage. Storing information in a descriptive text-like representation requires much less memory on your computer and presumably would require much less memory in your brain. However, just as modern personal computers are more than able to handle many digital pictures, it turns out that the brain too has a lot more capacity for storing pictures than had been originally thought. The propositional view, however, does allow more information to be stored in a less-demanding format, a model that still appeals to some theorists today (see Pylyshyn, 2003).

However, most researchers today are convinced by the vast amount of empirical data that support the analog view (Provost & Heathcote, 2015). It may be memory intensive, but the brain appears to be able to handle the load. Studies using behavioral

> **Shepard and Metzler's (1971) mental rotation experiment:** An experiment on visual imagery that showed that representation is analog.

and neuroscientific methodologies all support the analog view. One of the earliest studies to support the analog view is also one of the most famous studies in psychology. It is **Shepard and Metzler's (1971) mental rotation experiment**.

Shepard and Metzler's Mental Rotation Experiment

Shepard and Metzler (1971) set out to show that, at least in some circumstances, **imagery** was best explained by the analog view. To demonstrate this, Shepard and Metzler wanted to show that mental images behave like real pictures, at least in some ways. They thought that mental images ought to respond to experimental manipulations in the same

> **Imagery:** The experience of retrieving a memory that is mostly visual or experienced primarily as a sensory experience. Imagery can also refer to the representation of those memories.

or similar way as actual perception of those objects would. If inspecting a visual image is like inspecting a real picture, then we might be able to answer at least some novel questions about it. If, however, inspecting images is not like inspecting a real picture, then, as was commonly believed in 1970, the propositional view is the default position. Thus, the goal of Shepard and Metzler was to determine whether we can use mental images as we would real images. To test this notion, participants were asked to mentally rotate objects that were shown to them in pictures (see Figure 6.3). The task was relatively simple—decide whether two figures were geometrically the same or different as quickly as possible.

Consider the participants' task: For each trial, participants saw a pair of objects displayed in pictorial format. Half of the pictures were identical, and half were not. One of the objects was rotated to be in a different orientation than its partner. Participants were asked to determine whether the two objects were identical or different. For participants to determine whether the two figures were identical, they needed to mentally rotate one of the figures to see if it matched its pair. If, in a participant's mind's eye, the figures matched up, he or she was expected to say "same." If they did not, he or she was expected to say "different." Most people who do this task describe imagining one of the figures and "moving" it in their mind's eye to see whether, when rotated, it fits perfectly onto the other figure.

The empirical question asked in this experiment was whether the participants take longer to mentally rotate a figure more. Shepard and Metzler (1971) reasoned that if images were stored in an analog manner, then it would take a finite amount of time for the participant to rotate one figure to match the other. If one figure was rotated only a small amount to the left or right, it should take less time to mentally rotate it than if it had been rotated closer to 180 degrees. This is analogous to how we would do this task if we were given toy-size objects and asked if the objects were the same shape or different. We would rotate one until it matched the other. If it did, we would say they were identical. If we could not rotate them until they matched, we would say different. Shepard and Metzler's goal was to see if our imagery systems function in the same way. Shepard and Metzler varied the extent to which the two figures were rotated relative to each other. In some cases, one was rotated just 15 degrees to the left or right of its partner. In other cases, one figure was rotated as much as 180 degrees to the left or right of its partner. This was true for both pairs that were identical and pairs that were different. The extent to which the two figures were rotated relative to each other was the main independent variable.

Therefore, Shepard and Metzler (1971) measured the amount of time it took participants to come to a decision of same versus different as a function of the degrees of difference between the two figures in a pair. They found that the more the two figures were rotated away from each other, the more time it took participants to make their decisions. In fact, there was a clear linear relation between the degrees of difference between the two figures in a pair and how long the decision took, as can be seen in Figure 6.4. It took—on average—just about two seconds to determine that the images were the same or different when the two figures were rotated 20 degrees off each other but nearly five seconds when the figures were 160 degrees different. The Shepard and Metzler data support the analog view; people's imagery systems appeared to be actually manipulating images or pictures and not abstract, code-like representations.

To review, here is a short summary of the points to keep in mind both to understand the experiment and its importance. Keep in mind that the participants only see two images per trial—that is, they do not see the figures actually move. They must rotate them mentally—that is, to align them, they must use visual imagery. Because it takes more time to mentally rotate a greater degree than a smaller degree, there must be something similar between mental rotation and actual physical rotation. Because of this, we conclude that the visual images are being used in an analog vision-like representation (but see Liesefeld & Zimmer, 2013), for a different view). (For an illustration of this experiment and to participate yourself, go to study.sagepub.com/schwartz3e.[1])

Shepard and Metzler (1971) were not the first to demonstrate the nature of imagery as being a vision-like analog system. One demonstration came shortly before from the work of Lee Brooks (reviewed in Chapter 3, because of its relevance to the visuospatial sketchpad). In Brooks's (1968) experiment, participants retrieved a mental letter—that is, they imagined a letter, such as *T*, in their mind's eye. Then they were asked to make decisions about the angles in that letter. Brooks found that responding by pointing was more difficult than responding by speaking. The visual aspects of pointing apparently interfered with the vision-like processes going on during imagery. Thus, this experiment also supports the analog view. If imagery were propositional, it would not require an overlap between real visual tasks and imagery tasks.

Many other researchers subsequently became intrigued by the notion that they could study the nature of imagery. One such prominent researcher was Stephen Kosslyn, who invented many creative ways of studying imagery (Kosslyn, 2010). Like Shepard, he was restricted to measuring behavior, but also like Shepard, he came up with ingenious ways of inferring how the imagery representation system worked from seemingly ordinary behaviors. In Kosslyn's studies, people were asked to make simple judgments on images but to make them as fast as possible. Participants studied a picture and later had to make decisions based on the image they remembered from the picture. In other studies, people were simply asked to make images of familiar objects. In one such study, it took participants less time to verify that a rabbit has soft fur when they imagined the rabbit next to a fly than when they imagined the rabbit next to an elephant (see Figure 6.5). Kosslyn (1975) argued that this occurs because the image of the rabbit is likely to be bigger and more detailed in our imagery system when we contrast it to something smaller, like a fly, than when we contrast it to something bigger, like an elephant. Therefore, details such as the quality of the fur will be more salient in the mentally bigger image than in the mentally smaller one. This only matters if we are using a picture-like representation of each of the animals.

In another study, Kosslyn, Ball, and Reiser (1978) showed participants a map of an imaginary island (see Figure 6.6). The participants were given ample time to memorize the features of the map. When the participants were satisfied that they had memorized the map, the map was removed. They were then asked to imagine the map and make several decisions based on their mental map. They were asked to imagine a dot moving around the island from various locations to various locations. Kosslyn et al. (1978) found that response time for getting the imaginary dot from Place A to Place B was longer if the two locations were further away on the map; the response times were faster if the two locations were closer together. Thus, as in the Shepard and Metzler (1971) experiment, mental imagery followed the same principles as the real world does—longer distances take longer amounts of time to travel. This suggests that the mental image people made of the island had visual and spatial properties, much as a real picture does (Kosslyn, 2010).

Theorists who argue for the propositional view have criticized much of the data presented here (Pylyshyn, 2003). They argue that we do not need analog visual imagery and that mental propositions or sentences can account for much of the data. For example, when you are asked about the map of the island, you may experience a visual image of the map, but according to the propositional view, that experience is not causal. Rather, that image is a by-product of the proposition that stores the information.

To explain this view in a bit more depth, in Pylyshyn's version of the propositional view, images are not represented as pictures. Rather, they are abstract, language-like descriptions. As such, what we retrieve when we access a visual memory is this description. Therefore, it is at retrieval that we reconstruct the image that we "see" in our mind's eye. According to this model, the visual image is a by-product of a retrieval process and not the result of encoding and storage. As such, the image does not have a direct causal role in our behavior, because the image does not become accessible until after all the internal decisions are made on the language-like description. To explain Kosslyn's data, Pylyshyn argued that we slow our response time because we think it must take longer to get from one point on the island to the other but that the actual image of the island is not being used to determine that distance.

Figure 6.3 Objects to be mentally rotated.

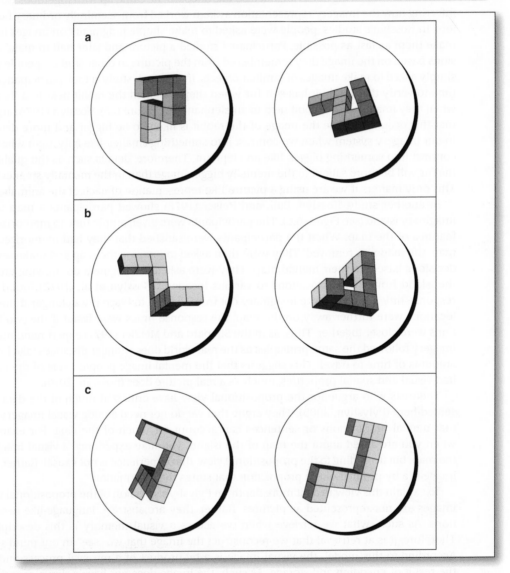

SOURCE: From Shepard, R. N., & Metzler, J. (1971). Mental rotation of thee-dimensional objects. *Science, 171,* 701–703. Reprinted with permission from AAAS.

Figure 6.4 Results of mental rotation experiment.

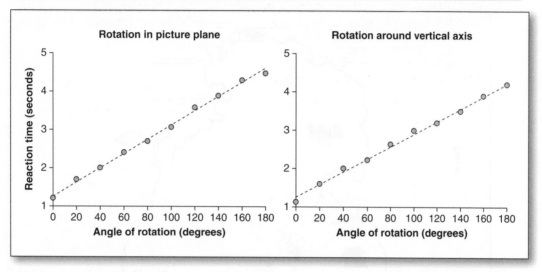

SOURCE: From Shepard, R. N., & Metzler, J. (1971). Mental rotation of thee-dimensional objects. *Science, 171,* 701–703. Reprinted with permission from AAAS.

Figure 6.5 Picture of big rabbit/small rabbit.

SOURCE: Kosslyn, S. M. (1975). Information representation in visual images. *Cognitive Psychology, 7,* 341–370. Published by Elsevier, Ltd.

Figure 6.6   Briefly look at this map. Then look away and see if you can make an image.

SOURCE: Kosslyn, S. M., Ball, T. M., & Reiser, B. J. (1978). Visual images preserve metric spatial information: Evidence from studies of mental scanning. *Journal of Experimental Psychology: Human Perception and Performance, 4,* 47–60. Published by the American Psychological Association

Neuroimaging and the Analog View

With neuroimaging, we can look at the neural correlates of imagery in the brain directly while people are engaged in imagery tasks without having to measure a behavior. With the aid of neuroimaging, a number of researchers have been able to determine the regions of the brain involved in mental imagery. These neuroimaging studies support the view that imagery is analog (Kosslyn, 2005; Slotnick, Thomson, & Kosslyn, 2012). Kosslyn and his colleagues have found that areas of the visual cortex are excited while people are engaged in visual imagery tasks. In many cases, this activation extends to the primary visual cortex.

The primary areas of vision are located in the back of the brain in the occipital lobe. The **primary visual cortex** (also known as striate cortex, V1, or Area 17) is the first area in the cerebral cortex that receives input from the retina of the eye (see Figure 6.7). Countless studies have shown it

Primary visual cortex: The first area in the occipital cortex that processes visual images.

to be involved in basic visual processing. Indeed, damage to the primary visual cortex results in blindness. Surrounding the primary visual cortex are other areas in the occipital lobe that process visual information (named V2, V3, etc.). All of these areas become activated when people engage in visual imagery (Kosslyn, Ganis, & Thompson, 2006; Slotnick, Thompson, & Kosslyn 2012). In fact, the more similar the imagery task is to an actual visual task, the more activation is seen in visual areas of the brain. Finally, those individuals who do better in imagery tasks also show more activity in the primary visual cortex than those who are less good at imagery tasks (Kosslyn, 2005). Thus, it is clear that imagery is housed in many of the same areas of the brain that house visual perception.

To demonstrate the importance of visual regions of the brain in visual imagery, consider the patient studied by Boucard et al. (2016). At the time of the study, SH was a 70-year old woman. At the age of 23, both of her eyes were severely damaged in an auto accident, and she lost sight in both eyes. Despite the 47 years of blindness, patient SH still reports strong visual imagery. Boucard and her colleagues asked SH to engage in visual imagery while her brain was being monitored by fMRI. The brain scans revealed strong activity in V1 when SH was engaged in visual imagery, consistent with that of sighted controls. Thus, visual areas of the brain, such as V1, appear to be involved in visual imagery as well as visual perception, in this case, even after years of not being able to actually see.

However, V1 is not essential for visual imagery. Other areas of the visual cortex seem to be sufficient to support visual imagery. Another recent study looked at visual imagery in a blind patient, but a blind patient's whose etiology is very different from SH (de Gelder, Tamieto, Pegna, & Van den Stock, 2015). Patient TN became blind following two successive strokes that completely destroyed the V1 regions on both the left and right side of his occipital lobe. Thus, his blindness is caused not by damage to the eyes, but by damage to the primary visual cortex. TN also claims to have visual imagery, and his visual imagery is associated with other regions of the occipital cortex (and activation in other regions of the brain). Thus, V1 activation may cause greater and more intense visual imagery, but other areas of the occipital lobe can support it as well.

In another striking demonstration of visual imagery and brain injury, Bisiach and Luzzatti (1978) studied a patient with **hemifield neglect** (also known as **unilateral neglect**). Hemifield neglect describes a condition in which patients ignore one half of the visual world. When forced to, they will report that they see what is in that half of the visual world but simply pay it no heed. For example, male hemifield patients will not shave half of their face, because they ignore it in the mirror. Hemifield neglect is caused by damage to the parietal lobe, usually on the right side of the brain. Luckily, the severe effects of hemifield neglect often wear off relatively quickly after the brain damage, leaving the patient with a mild tendency to ignore information in that half of the visual world. (For more on hemifield neglect, go to www .sagepub.com/schwartz3e.[2])

> **Hemifield neglect (unilateral neglect):** A condition in which patients ignore one half of the visual world. It occurs because of damage to the right parietal lobe.

The patient studied by Bisiach and Luzzatti (1978) had suffered from a stroke, which resulted in hemifield neglect. The neglect wore off to the point that the patient, a prominent

Figure 6.7 The occipital lobe is in the back of the brain.

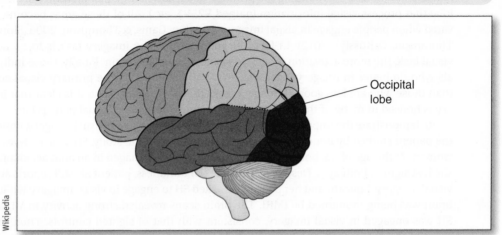

Occipital
lobe

Wikipedia

newspaper editor, could return to his professional duties. The researchers had him return to the lab periodically. In the study, they tested his visual imagery, which showed evidence of imagery-based hemifield neglect. Asked to imagine himself walking down the main square from north to south in his native city in Italy, the patient described the monuments and buildings only on the west side (his right). When asked to imagine himself walking up the main square from south to north, the patient described the sites only on the east side (now on his right). Thus, there was nothing wrong with his visual memory. He successfully retrieved the buildings on either side of the main square during one of the tests. However, he always ignored the left side of the square. Thus, the imagery deficit mirrored the perceptual deficit. Both neuroimaging and neuropsychology point to the role of visual areas of the brain as being critical to visual imagery.

Returning to the issue of representation of imagery, neuroscience data support the analog view. Remember that the analog view advances the idea that images are stored as "pictures" rather than descriptions. Pictures are most logically stored in the visual areas of the brain, which is, in fact, activated during visual imagery. If representations were more like descriptions, one might expect to see the representation of them in verbal areas of the brain, which does not occur. Thus, the neuroimaging and neuropsychological data are consistent with the analog position.

SECTION SUMMARY AND QUIZ

One of the major issues in visual imagery is the nature of representation. Analog representation essentially means we store visual images like pictures. Propositional representation essentially means that we store visual images in terms of a language-like code. Much of the early cognitive research on this topic was done to differentiate these two views. At present, almost all data strongly support the analog view. Shepard and Metzler (1971) conducted an experiment on mental rotation in which participants who mentally rotated objects took longer to match objects that were at greater angles relative to each other, thereby supporting the analog view. Kosslyn's (2005) research has also shown that it takes longer to obtain information from small images than from large images, consistent with the analog view. It has been found through neuroimaging studies that visual areas of the brain are active during visual imagery. Even in neuropsychological patients, there is evidence that imagery is analog; a patient suffering from hemifield neglect has deficits in both visual attention and attention in visual imagery.

Section Quiz

1. In cognitive science, representation means
   a. The storage of information in neurocognitive systems
   b. Interpolation between analog and proposititional imagery
   c. The encoding of visual information
   d. The transformation of visual rotation

2. In Shepard and Metzler's (1971) experiment, the participants were asked to
   a. Rotate objects until they matched the visual image stored in their memory
   b. Compare two presented pictures to determine if their shape was the same
   c. Rotate mental objects to determine the depth of their visual imagery
   d. Recall the number of locations marked on a map seen earlier

3. In Shepard and Metzler's (1971) experiment, the researchers found that
   a. Visual imagery is propositional
   b. If you ask participants to rotate visual objects, they will
   c. The greater the angle of rotation, the more time it took to determine if two figures were the same
   d. When participants were given mental rotation instructions, they rotated the objects faster than when they were not given these instructions

4. Boucard et al. (2016) tested a patient who had been blinded as an adult. Their study showed that
   a. The blinded patient also lost her ability to do visual imagery
   b. Area V1 of the brain was active when this patient engaged in visual imagery
   c. Only non-occipital regions of the brain were active when the patient was given imagery instructions
   d. None of the above are true

Answers
1. a
2. b
3. c
4. b

OTHER TOPICS IN VISUAL MEMORY

The issue of how imagery is represented in the neurocognitive system has been a dominant topic over the past four decades. However, many other aspects of visual memory are also important and perhaps more practically valuable to the nonscientist. In the next few sections, we will consider several of these varied topics. We will consider the issue of photographic (or eidetic) memory, cognitive maps, memory for faces, and applications of visual memory to mnemonics. Another major topic in visual memory is eyewitness memory. In eyewitness memory, typically, a person must describe what he or she *saw* at the scene of a crime. Eyewitness memory is clearly an important topic in visual memory, and it will be discussed again in Chapter 8 in the context of false memories. But here we address basic issues of face recognition and its application to eyewitness memory.

PHOTOGRAPHIC MEMORY: REALITY OR FANTASY?

As a professor who teaches courses in memory, I frequently hear from students about someone they know who possesses **photographic memory**. Belief in photographic memory is quite common in our society. The questioner usually wants to know how that person acquired this photographic-like memory and whether the skill is learnable. It is often thought that a photographic memory provides a huge advantage in the academic world, as it allows the person with it to memorize vast amounts of materials without effort. I usually reply that self-professed "photographic memory" may be correlated with a good visual imagery system but is not photographic in the sense that it creates a literal representation of what the person saw. I also add that although photographic memory may seem to help that person, it is no substitute for hard work and understanding. In some sense, this section here is an attempt to debunk the myth of "photographic memory."

> **Photographic memory:** Very strong visual memories that have a strong feeling of being images.

It is likely that those who claim to possess "photographic memory" (or eidetic imagery, in technical terms) do have extraordinarily good visual imagery systems that allow them to form strong visual images of the material that they learn. However, these images are not truly photographs. This can be demonstrated empirically. It has been shown that people who have "photographic" memories do remember visual information better than those who do not make this claim. However, they still make errors in memory, and even when they claim to be "reading" off their photograph, their errors tend to be related to meaning, as in normal long-term memory, rather than pictorial (Crowder, 1992).

Surprisingly, little research has been conducted on people who claim to have photographic memory (but see Bywaters, Andrade, & Turpin, 2004). Some has been directed at eidetikers. These are people who are able to maintain an image in visual working memory for anywhere from 30 seconds to five minutes. It apparently is more common among young children, many of whom lose this ability as they learn to read. But even here, the research suggests that eidetic imagery is not purely visual, as errors based on meaning

Figure 6.8 Which is the real penny?

SOURCE: Nickerson, R. S., and Adams, J. J. (1979). Long-term memory for a common object. *Cognitive Psychology, 11,* 287–307. Published by Elsevier, Ltd.

creep in (Crowder, 1992). Based on the persistence of claims of eidetic imagery and the number of questions about it, it may well be an important area to examine again. (For more on photographic memory and eidetic memory, go to study.sagepub.com/schwartz3e[3].)

That normal human memory is not photographic is easy to demonstrate empirically. Consider an experiment conducted by Nickerson and Adams (1979). They asked people to recognize the "real" penny (that is, how an actual penny appears) from a number of close distractors (see Figure 6.8). They found that, despite familiarity with pennies, the participants were surprisingly poor at picking out the real penny from the distractors. Try it for yourself in the demonstration. You may have to find a penny in your change jar to be sure of the answer. (See this demonstration also at study.sagepub.com/schwartz3e[4]).

In a similar, but perhaps more contemporary version of this idea, Blake, Nazarian, and Castel (2015) looked at people's memory for the Apple logo, another image that most people may see on a daily basis (see Figure 6.9). When people had to pick out the real Apple logo from a number of similar images, only half of the participants could pick out the correct image from the distractors, despite high confidence in their ability to do so. Indeed, when people were asked to draw the Apple logo, only one out of 85 participants got the bite and the stem in the correct direction (see Figure 6.9). In another study, Vendetti, Castel, and Holyoak (2013) showed that long-time workers in an office building could not

Figure 6.9 Which is the real Apple logo?

SOURCE: Blake, A. B., Nazarian, M., & Castel, A. D. (2015). The Apple of the mind's eye: Everyday attention, metamemory, and reconstructive memory for the Apple logo. *The Quarterly Journal of Experimental Psychology*, 68, 858–865.

accurately recognize elevator panels that they saw several times a day, in some cases, for years. These studies demonstrate that we typically extract meaning from images rather than their literal visual representation.

Thus, contrary to popular belief, even those who claim to have photographic memory employ meaning-based representations as well as visual ones. Indeed, this is adaptive, as in most situations, it is meaning that is relevant rather than literal visual representation. The "penny" and the "apple logo" study are illustrative examples of this—despite our frequent exposure to the stimuli in these experiments, our literal representation of a penny or the apple logo is likely to be inaccurate.

COGNITIVE MAPS

Cognitive maps: Mental representations of the external world. Based on our spatial representation of the world.

An important feature of visual memory is that it allows us to learn and remember our physical landscape. We all have "cognitive maps" stored in our visual memory. **Cognitive maps** are mental representations of the external world (Tversky, 2000). These cognitive maps usually refer to the familiar environments we inhabit. We may have a cognitive map of our own homes, our neighborhood, our dorm complex, the campus, and perhaps familiar towns and cities. We may have cognitive maps of roads that we use frequently. After returning from a visit abroad, you may have many new cognitive maps, which you learned as you travelled in a new country. We may also have cognitive maps based on drawn maps. You may never have been to India, for example, but you may be able to create a mental image of a map of India.

Consider the following example. You are asked to give directions to the student center just as you leave your class in the business school. You might consult your cognitive map and then give the following directions: "Go over the bridge on the pond. Then continue on the path past the library. Then make a right, and you'll be at the student center. It should take you about 10 minutes at most." To provide these directions, you must have some mental representation of what the campus looks like, the relative distances between buildings, and how long it takes to walk these distances. You may also have more specific information, such as the fact that the student center is due east of the business school, but providing this information would probably be of little use to a stranger on campus.

Our cognitive maps are heavily influenced by the distinctiveness of landmarks in our environment. This is why, when giving directions, we often refer to landmarks ("the egg-like sculpture") instead of streets (SW 10th Street). However, when street names are distinctive, they too can be helpful in remembering directions (you'll never forget your drive down Ha-Ha Road). Indeed, Tom and Tversky (2012) showed that remembering directions was better when there were distinctive streets and landmarks than when there were neither, and distinctive street names were the most helpful in remembering a route from one place to another. Such information may be useful both when giving and trying to learn directions.

Unlike ordinary maps, our cognitive maps are affected by **semantic categories**. For example, consider the borders between towns, states, and countries. In some cases, such borders may be physical boundaries as well as semantic ones, as rivers or coastlines may define such borders. But in almost all cases, such borders are semantic in nature—that is, it defines the human-defined differences between two states. We judge places on our cognitive maps that are grouped together to be closer than places that are not grouped together, even though the items in different categories may be closer (Friedman, Montello, & Burte, 2012; Huttenlocher, Hedges, & Duncan, 1991). For example, most Americans would likely judge that the city of Wayne, Michigan, is closer to Detroit, Michigan, than Windsor, Ontario is. However, in reality, Windsor and Detroit are separated by a thin river and are much closer than are Detroit and Wayne. Semantic categories also affect our judgments of cardinal directions. Our semantic category "the United States" is placed south of our semantic category for "Canada." Thus, most of us would judge Windsor to be north of Detroit. Not so! Detroit—in the United States—is north of Windsor, in Canada. One of the most famous examples of this derives from our semantic categories of the "Atlantic Ocean" and the "Pacific Ocean." Think of your cognitive map. It is pretty easy to determine from that map that the Atlantic Ocean is east relative to the Pacific Ocean. Thus, most people would judge the Atlantic/Caribbean entrance to the Panama Canal as being east of the Pacific entrance to the Panama Canal. Close inspection of a real map reveals the surprising fact that the Pacific entrance is further east than the Atlantic entrance. The point here is that we use categories,

> **Semantic categories:** Meaning affects our cognitive maps. For example, people tend to think of borders between countries as being straighter than they often are.

such as the general locations of the Pacific and Atlantic Oceans, to create cognitive maps, and these may lead to inaccuracies.

To illustrate this concept, Friedman et al. (2012) had American and Canadian college students examine maps of California and Alberta. The maps were either marked with only dots and not with city names or marked with dots and the corresponding city names. Participants were directed to attend to the maps. A short time after seeing the map, participants were asked to judge the distance between various dots based on their cognitive maps formed by viewing the physical maps. Friedman et al. were interested in how the inclusion of city names would influence these judgments, given that the city names provided semantic information. In the condition in which the names were supplied, estimates of distance between dots were heavily influenced by perceived proximity to nearby cities. That is, the semantic information influenced the judgments. Thus, cities perceived as related, such as Los Angeles and Long Beach, were often judged to be closer than they actually are, whereas cities perceived to be unrelated, such as Los Angeles and Bakersfield, were judged to be further apart than they actually are. Indeed, the distance estimates were more accurate for those participants who had not had the names supplied originally. This experiment, therefore, supports the idea that category information is used when making cognitive maps.

MEMORY FOR FACES

Humans live in a social world. We interact with other people daily. Being able to identify other people is crucial. Therefore, being able to recognize faces of other people is an important practical skill. Indeed, many researchers argue that we have evolutionarily designed facial recognition mechanisms. Because being able to recognize friend from foe was so important to our early ancestors, it is likely that face recognition was shaped by natural selection. Thus, it is likely that face memory is especially good when compared to other stimuli.

How many times have you had the following experience? You are walking across campus and you see someone you know. However, when you greet that person, you cannot remember the person's name or how you know the person. Did you attend a class together? Did you meet at a concert? However, you recognize his or her face. Recognizing faces but failing to retrieve a name is a common experience (Buján, Galdo-Álvarez, Lindin, & Díaz, 2012). However, despite occasional failures, recognition of familiar faces is a strong skill in human cognition (Bruce, Burton, & Hancock, 2007; Russell, Duchaine, and Nakayama, 2009). Indeed, some of the most important visual stimuli to remember are the faces of the people we come to know in our lives. Imagine arriving at work and not recognizing anyone there. Remember the first day of college before you knew anyone? Not recognizing any familiar faces can be an intimidating experience. Learning new faces and remembering old ones is a critical skill in almost all walks of life.

In some cases, remembering a face correctly can be a matter of life and death. Giving testimony after witnessing a crime (known as **eyewitness memory**) is one such case. Juries often consider recognizing a face the strongest piece of testimony (Loftus, 1979). However, in many cases, eyewitness identification may be inaccurate, with often terrible consequences. We have all heard of cases in which, unfortunately, the witness misremembered a face and as a consequence, someone was erroneously sent to prison.

> **Eyewitness memory:** Memory for the events that transpire in a single event, usually a crime.

Thus, finding ways that minimize misidentification but maximize correct recognition is an important topic in face memory. In this section, we will address some research that has been directed at just that goal.

SIMULTANEOUS AND SEQUENTIAL LINEUPS IN EYEWITNESS MEMORY

We discussed earlier how it is difficult to demonstrate recall from visual memory. For example, you may be able to imagine your father's face but have no skill at drawing. Thus, if asked about your father's appearance, you must resort to words—somehow convert that visual image into a verbal description. In many situations, we are asked to describe what someone looks like. Asked to describe your father, you might describe him as having "an older but healthy face. Not fat, but not skinny. Balding on top, with hair a mix of gray and black. Green eyes. Clean-shaven." As most of you have never seen this man, you now have a rough description of what he looks like. But how many other 50-year-old men also fit that description? It is likely that many do; therefore, at some level, this verbal description is inadequate. Note that we have already indicated that people are not good at drawing their visual memories. Here we are also saying that verbal descriptions do not reflect people's good memory for faces. As a consequence of most people's inability to draw faces and the inadequacy of verbal description to capture what a person looks like, most researchers use recognition tests to measure face memory.

Now consider a situation in which you see someone briefly. For example, if you witness a crime, you just have a minute or less to actually see the thief. In this case, you might also be asked to do a face-recognition test. However, this is not an experiment without obvious consequences—this is a police procedure to help identify the criminal. Thus, face memory has immediate applications in eyewitness identification. Indeed, much research has been directed at how best we can test the face memory of eyewitnesses and what methods lead to the most successful identifications of actual perpetrators (Wells, Steblay, & Dysart, 2012).

Eyewitness identification research focuses on two kinds of recognition tests, simultaneous and sequential lineups. In a **simultaneous lineup,** (also known simply as a **lineup**), a participant must choose one face from a series of faces, based on the match between the participant's memory and the match to the faces provided (see Figure 6.10). This test is equivalent to a multiple-choice recognition test. The second form of test is a **sequential lineup** (also known as a

> **Simultaneous lineup (lineup):** A multiple-choice form of a face recognition test in which the participant sees several faces, including the one seen earlier.

Sequential lineup (show-up): An old-new form of a face recognition test in which the participant sees only one face and must decide if that face is one seen earlier.

show-up), in which the participant sees only one face and must decide whether he or she has seen that face earlier. This test is equivalent to an old-new recognition test. In legal contexts, the choice of a simultaneous lineup or a sequential lineup has implications for the likelihood of a witness choosing the correct suspect or the wrong suspect.

Unfortunately, there is still a great deal of controversy over whether simultaneous lineups or sequential lineups lead to better identification of guilty suspects and greater rejection of innocents (Amendola & Wixted, 2015; Wells, Dysart, & Steblay, 2015). However, most of the data now suggest that simultaneous lineups are better than sequential lineups (Neuschatz et al., in press). However, in earlier versions of this textbook, I concluded the opposite, but I now think the data clearly show the advantages of simultaneous lineups (but see Dekle, 2006). We invite students to learn more about this controversy by reading the papers by Wixted and Wells, respectively at sagepub.com.

In a simultaneous lineup, the face that you saw earlier will be presented along with several similar faces. The faces are usually matched on such features as gender, age, race, height and weight, the presence or absence of facial hair, and so on. Under these circumstances, participants have to match their memory of the face that they saw to each of the presented faces and then determine which is the closest match. Some have argued that this leads to a **relative judgment**—that is, choosing the face that yields the closest match to the target (Dekle, 2006). By contrast, in a sequential lineup, the witness matches the particular face to his or her memory of the face seen and decides whether this particular face matches the memory. This is called an **absolute judgment**. The nature of these judgments will be relevant when we talk about the effects of verbal overshadowing in just a moment.

Relative judgment: In a simultaneous lineup, participants may choose the face that most closely matches their memory of the target face.

Absolute judgment: In a sequential line up (show-up), the witness matches the face to his or her memory of the face seen and decides if this particular face matches the memory.

Neuschatz et al. (in press) argued that simultaneous lineups are better than sequential lineups for identifying suspects and rejecting distractors for several reasons. First, the presence of distractors may cause participants to assume a higher criterion for identification. Because the alternates look similar to the person they saw at the crime, they demand of themselves more internal proof and confidence that the suspect they are choosing is actually the criminal. Neuschatz et al. also argued that simultaneous lineups are better than sequential lineups, because the simultaneous lineups participants can better identify traits of a face that are not consistent with the person they saw at the crime. Thus, with the ability to compare across faces, it is easier for participants to reject faces that they did not see.

These ideas have now been tested empirically repeatedly in several labs (Neuschatz et al., in press). In the lab, participants witness a videotaped crime, such as a robbery at a convenience store. Later, the participants are shown either simultaneous lineups or sequential lineups. The lineups are equated in terms of how many total suspects the participant sees and how often the suspect is actually present among the presented faces. In most research, the simultaneous lineups show better accuracy both in terms of suspects identified and innocent people rejected. Thus, based on this reasoning and their assessment of the data, Neuschatz et al. (in press) concluded that sequential lineups put innocent people at greater risk of being falsely identified by witnesses.

Returning to practical considerations and leading to our discussion of the effects of verbalization on eyewitness memory—consider the witness to a crime. He or she will most likely give a verbal description of the perpetrator many times before actually seeing any kind of lineup, possibly describing the perpetrator not only to police investigators but also to friends, family, and coworkers. Therefore, by the time the witness is asked for an identification, he or she may have given or heard from other witnesses many verbal descriptions of the perpetrator. One question that can be asked is whether making verbal descriptions of the perpetrator can affect a person's ability to identify a suspect.

Meissner et al. (2008) investigated what happens when a witness/participant gives a verbal description of a suspect's face after the initial encounter with the suspect. They were interested in whether giving a verbal description would help or hurt the identification of a suspect when the recognition test was a simultaneous lineup. Following a verbal description, the participant is then shown a simultaneous lineup of faces and asked which of the possible faces was the one he or she had seen. With simultaneous lineups, giving a prior description interfered with one's ability to discriminate among the faces, and people's memory for those faces declined—that is, the participant was less likely to identify the correct face. This is called the **verbal overshadowing** effect and likely occurs because the verbal description is similar to more than one of the faces in a lineup (Hatano et al., 2015). Because the lineup encourages a relative judgment, the description can bias the participant toward the face that best matches the description, even if that face is not the one of the actual perpetrator.

> **Verbal overshadowing:** Hearing or giving a verbal description of a face makes remembering visual features more difficult.

> **Verbal facilitation:** Hearing or giving a verbal description of a face makes remembering visual features easier.

Sequential lineups are affected differently by verbal descriptions (C. Brown & Lloyd-Jones, 2005; Nakabayashi, Lloyd-Jones, Butcher, & Liu, 2012; Steblay, Dysart, & Wells, 2011). Again, in a sequential lineup, the task is to match the presented face with the memory of the previously seen face. Under these circumstances, having given a verbal description of the to-be-remembered face actually improves people's ability to recognize the face. This is called **verbal facilitation.**

Thus, depending on test format (simultaneous vs. sequential), making a verbal description of a face will either facilitate or hurt (overshadow) later memory performance. The theoretical explanation lies in what kinds of processes the test situation calls for. The verbalization of a description itself creates a strong memory. Given the limits of verbalization of facial features, most of the distractors in a simultaneous lineup match the verbalization as well as the actual target, if the target is even present; as a consequence,

Figure 6.10 Who done it? A lineup. Faces have been chosen because they are similar in age, gender, hair color, approximate size, and skin color.

Courtesy of Bennett Schwartz

memory suffers, as it is now harder to discriminate among the faces. On the other hand, if you are just deciding whether the face is one that you have seen before or one that is novel, the verbal description gives you a second way of recognizing the face. Therefore, verbalization increases memory performance in sequential lineups, though seemingly not sufficiently to overcome the overall advantages of simultaneous lineups in general (Mickes & Wixted, 2015).

This creates a paradox for investigators, such as police interviewing an eyewitness to a crime. They need to get the witness to describe the criminal, as the suspect may be nearby and dangerous and both police and civilians must be on the lookout for people who resemble the suspect. On the other hand, gathering that description will make it more difficult for that witness to correctly identify the suspect in a typical police lineup. Thus, investigators might choose not to ask the witness to describe the criminal if the suspect is already being followed or in custody, as the verbal description may hurt the witness's ability to identify the culprit later in a lineup. However, if the suspect is at large and dangerous, the public need for safety may outweigh subtleties of later prosecution.

Own-Race Bias

One well-studied phenomenon is that people are, by and large, better at recognizing faces from their own "race" than from other racial groups (see DeLozier & Rhodes, 2015; Marcon, Susa, & Meissner, 2009; Nakabayashi et al., 2012). This has been called the **own-race bias** effect (go to study.sagepub.com/schwartz3e[5]). When European Americans are asked to study faces of both other European Americans as well as African Americans, the European Americans are more accurate in identifying European American faces than African American faces. Interestingly, African Americans perform as accurately on

> **Own-race bias:** People are, by and large, better at recognizing faces from their own "race" than from other racial groups.

European American faces as do the European Americans. African Americans also do better than European Americans at accurately recognizing African American faces, but both African Americans and European Americans do relatively worse than Hispanic Americans when asked to remember Hispanic faces. These data suggest that nothing about the physical features of any particular ethnic group makes them more or less memorable, nor does one group have a better memory than another. So what then causes the own-race bias in facial memory?

One hypothesis centers on familiarity. In this view, we need experience with different ethnic groups in order to identify the characteristics that distinguish faces in that ethnic group. As such, we are better at recognizing features of racial groups with whom we are familiar. In general, in the United Sates, most African Americans have more contact with European American culture than vice versa. Therefore, African Americans do better at recognizing European American faces than European Americans do at recognizing African American faces. But this is a contingency of U.S. culture. In other cultures, which ethnic groups are in the majority or minority may be different, causing different patterns of own-race bias in face recognition. The idea that this has to do with familiarity is bolstered by Chiroro, Tredoux, Radaelli, and Meissner's (2008) finding that White South Africans performed equivalently to Black South Africans in the identification of Black faces. Because people of European ancestry are in the minority in South Africa, they should have more experience with Black faces than European Americans do with African Americans. Therefore, their face recognition for Black faces should be better. This is exactly what was found. White South Africans were as accurate as Black South Africans at identifying faces of Black South Africans, but the Black South Africans showed lower accuracy than White South Africans at identifying the faces of White South Africans. Thus, the own-race bias seems to be a function of cross-cultural familiarity, with whatever group is the majority showing a deficit in facial recognition of minority faces.

Interestingly, own-race bias extends from natural facial features to socially constructed external facial features, including hats, scarves, and jewelry. Megreya, Memon, and Havard (2012) showed that Egyptian participants were more accurate at identifying female faces when those women were wearing headscarves, but that British participants were more accurate at identifying female faces when the women did not have their hair covered. As with own-race bias, Megreya et al. (2012) suggested that Egyptian participants were more experienced with seeing unfamiliar women with heads covered and therefore attended more to internal facial features, whereas the British participants were more familiar with seeing women with their hair visible. In this case as well, cultural familiarity affects which group we are better at recognizing.

Can own-race bias be overcome? Can a European American improve his or her recognition of African American faces (or can a Black South African improve his or her recognition of White faces)? One recent study suggests that this is possible. DeLozier and Rhodes (2015) presented faces during encoding with values attached to each one. The values indicated which faces were more important to encode. Participants were also given control over their study time, meaning that they could spend more time to study on some faces than on other faces. European Americans spent more time studying high-value African American faces than low-value ones and as a consequence, improved their recognition score for those faces. This suggests that motivation to learn may help eliminate the own-race bias.

The own-race bias effect does have some practical implications, especially in eyewitness situations. If the witness comes from the majority group in a culture, he or she will be more accurate at identifying a suspect if the suspect is also from the majority racial or cultural group than if the suspect is from a minority cultural group. In American terms, European American witnesses will be less accurate than African American witnesses in correctly identifying African American suspects. Thus, in practical terms, although our justice system is predicated on equal treatment for all, police investigations may proceed better if they know which witnesses may be more accurate than others.

The Neuroscience of Face Memory

Certain areas in the temporal lobe of the brain specialize in face recognition. In particular, the **fusiform face area (FFA)** in the inferior-temporal cortex appears to specialize in face recognition (Harvey & Burgund, 2012; Hasinki & Sederberg, 2016; Kanwisher, 2004). This area of the brain is selectively activated when people are looking at unfamiliar faces and when they are recognizing familiar faces (Hasinki & Sederberg, 2016). The specialized areas of the brain appear to be evolutionarily determined areas for face recognition; equivalent areas in monkeys are also maximally responsive to monkey faces. In addition to the FFA, an area of the occipital lobe has also been identified as crucial to face recognition. This area in the occipital lobe is known, aptly, as the **occipital face area (OFA)** (Large, Cavina-Pratesi, Vilis, & Culham, 2008). Both of these areas are activated during face recognition tasks in functional magnetic

Fusiform face area (FFA): A part of the brain in the inferior-temporal cortex that appears to specialize in face recognition.

resonance imaging (fMRI) studies (Grill-Spector, Knouf, & Kanwisher, 2004), and damage to these areas are associated with deficits in face recognition.

Damage to the FFA results in a neuropsychological condition called **prosopagnosia**. Prosopagnosia, also called face blindness, is defined as an acquired deficit in recognizing familiar faces (see Duchaine & Yovel, 2015; Shlomo, DeGutis, D'Esposito, & Robertson, 2007). It usually results from damage to the FFA and surrounding areas in the temporal lobe, typically as the result

Occipital face area (OFA): An area of the occipital lobe that has been identified as crucial to face recognition.

Prosopagnosia: An acquired deficit in face recognition and face identification caused by brain damage. Developmental prosopagnosia is a congenital deficit in face recognition.

of a stroke or another event that prevents oxygen from reaching these areas of the brain. People suffering from prosopagnosia lose the ability to recognize familiar faces. They know that faces are faces but can no longer distinguish faces of people that they know. This includes recognizing the faces of people they have known for a long time and learning to recognize the faces of new individuals. Most people can recognize a face regardless of context. You can recognize your father's face, regardless of whether you see it in the newspaper, on the "fan-cam" at a sporting event, or in a family photo album. A patient with prosopagnosia cannot do this. If the damage is restricted to the FFA, the patient is still able to recognize familiar people by their voices, their particular way of walking, or other clues. For example, if the patient's spouse always wears a trademark hat, recognition can occur by noting the hat. Also, patients with prosopagnosia can recognize objects other than faces.

There is also a rare condition called developmental prosopagnosia. Developmental prosopagnosia is a congenital deficit in face recognition. Developmental prosopagnosia appears early in life and is not associated with any particular brain trauma (Dalrymple, Elison, & Duchaine, in press; Duchaine & Yovel, 2015). Patients with developmental prosopagnosia show normal vision and normal visual perception in all areas other than face recognition (Dalyrimple et al., in press). Typically, patients with developmental prosopagnosia can recognize some faces, particularly those of close family and friends. However, they are slower to recognize familiar faces and slower to learn new faces than a comparison sample of people without developmental prosopagnosia. Because developmental prosopagnosia is limited to face recognition, people who suffer from it can compensate by focusing on auditory features of a person in order to recognize that person. They can also rely on other visual processes to help them with face recognition. Bennetts et al. (2015) showed that patients with developmental prosopagnosia showed better face recognition when those faces were moving than when they were stationary. This suggests that developmental prosopagnosia is not as debilitating as one might think, if patients learn compensatory strategies.

In summary, face memory seems to be an integrated process involving both areas in the occipital lobe, which we know are involved with the perception of faces, and areas in the temporal lobe, which we know are involved in recognizing complex objects and memory for those objects. Damage to these areas results in prosopagnosia, which is a selective deficit at recognizing and remembering human faces. Developmental prosopagnosia when people have this deficit seemingly from birth. Most of us, however, are constantly using these regions of the brain as we negotiate the sea of human faces that surround us.

SECTION SUMMARY AND QUIZ

By and large, photographic memory is a myth. Even people with very strong visual memories make errors that are based on meaning. Studies such as the "penny" study and the "Apple logo" study show how meaning typically trumps visual realism in representation. Cognitive maps are visual representations of space that guide our navigation through the world. As with most issues in this chapter, cognitive maps are also heavily influenced by meaning, in this case, categories such as countries, states, towns, and borders. Face memory research is critical in a number of areas, including eyewitness memory. Studies show that simultaneous lineups result in more accurate identification than do sequential lineups. Verbal facilitation occurs when giving a description of the face results in better visual recognition, as in sequential lineups, but verbal overshadowing occurs when giving a verbal description impairs visual recognition, as in simultaneous lineups. The own-race bias describes the phenomenon in which people from the cultural majority group have a harder time recognizing minority faces than they do faces from the majority group. Minority groups do not show this effect. That we are good at recognizing familiar faces seems to have a neural basis. In particular, the FFA (fusiform face area) in the temporal lobe and OFA (occipital face area) in the occipital lobe are areas of the brain associated with face recognition. Prosopagnosia is an acquired condition in which brain damage to the FFA results in poor face recognition. Developmental prosopagnosia occurs when people have a congenital deficit in face recognition.

Section Quiz

1. In a study in which people were asked to recognize the pattern of floors on the panel of an elevator, the researchers showed that
    a. Recall of the pattern was at floor (0%), but recognition approached ceiling (100%)
    b. Even for people who had worked in the building for many years, recognition was still quite low
    c. Participants preferred the penny study and the Apple-logo study to the elevator study
    d. Participants refused to enter the elevator, as the weight load had been exceeded

2. Research on cognitive maps shows that
    a. People use meaningful landmarks to shape their cognitive maps
    b. People with eidetic imagery use more semantic organization in their cognitive maps
    c. People judge distances to be closer if they cross meaningful boundaries
    d. None of the above are true

3. Verbal facilitation occurs when
   a. Giving a spoken description helps recognition of visually presented faces
   b. Sketching out a picture as best one cans helps people describe faces
   c. Giving a spoken description impairs recognition of visually presented faces
   d. All of the above are true

4. Bennetts et al. (2015) showed that patients with developmental prosopagnosia
   a. Eventually overcome their developmental prosopagnosia
   b. Also show a deficit in the recognition of animal faces
   c. Will show better recognition of faces when those faces are moving than when they are static
   d. Have damage to the OFA rather than the FFA

1. b
2. a
3. a
4. c

APPLICATION OF VISUAL IMAGERY TO MNEMONICS

One of the oldest techniques to aid memory is the use of visual imagery. The use of imagery techniques to improve encoding and memory performance goes back all the way to the ancient Greeks, approximately 2,500 years ago. Indeed, in 477 BCE, the Greek poet Simonides introduced a mnemonic method still used today. According to the legend, Simonides gave a speech at a banquet sponsored by a nobleman named Scopas. Scopas expected Simonides to praise him, but instead Simonides praised the gods Castor and Pollux. Scopas was upset at the speech and paid Simonides only half of the agreed upon amount. The gods then sent a messenger to the banquet and called Simonides away. While Simonides, who had shown his respect to the gods, was out of the room, the gods destroyed the banquet hall, killing all the guests except Simonides. When family members came to collect their loved one's remains, Simonides was able to direct each person to his or her family member's body, as he had memorized where every guest had been seated that night using the strategy that has come

Method of loci: The learner uses visual imagery to associate a list of new items with a series of well-known physical locations.

to be known as the **method of loci** (Yates, 1966). It is not clear why all of the guests had to die because Scopas had an inflated ego, but that is the way stories ended back in ancient times. Although this story may seem a bit violent and gruesome for a textbook on memory, it is generally considered the first recorded description of imagery-based learning.

If you visit your college bookstore or any bookstore of any size, you will find many books on memory improvement. A quick check of the Internet will reveal many sites that claim to have found ways in which people can vastly improve their ability to remember information (e.g., go to study.sagepub.com/schwartz3e[6]). In the popular press on memory improvement, visual mnemonic techniques are often overemphasized at the expense of many of the other mnemonic "hints" that I have provided throughout this book (e.g., Hagwood, 2007; Lorayne & Lucas, 1974; White, 2013). In fact, visual mnemonics are limited in their usefulness, as will become apparent in the discussion below.

In imagery-based learning, the goal is often not to actually remember visual information. Rather, we capitalize on our good visual memory to aid us in learning more difficult, usually verbal information. The basic strategy is to associate the difficult to-be-learned information with existing well-known visual memories. Once we do this, we form a strong association between the two, and the new information will be better encoded. Let's look at the oldest method, Simonides's method of loci, and see how it works.

Method of Loci

In the method of loci, the learner uses visual imagery to associate a list of new to-be-learned items with a series of well-known physical locations. To use this technique, you must be very familiar with a particular landscape. This might be your house and yard, the central square of your college campus, or perhaps a favorite trail through the woods. You designate a series of landmarks as the memory loci and then associate the new items with each location. The new to-be-learned items can really be anything, but the technique is particularly useful for remembering lists of unrelated items, such as grocery lists. Medical students may find it useful to successfully remember the names of the bones or nerves of the body.

When you get the items on the list, you associate each one with a well-known location in your mental landscape. Thus, if your loci are located in the front yard of your house, you might place the "loaf of bread" in the mailbox, the "butter" in front of the petunias growing under the window, the "salad dressing" right under the doorknob (don't trip on it), the "toilet paper" hung in the tree by the front window, and so on. When you get to the grocery store, you recreate the mental landscape and walk through it in your imagination. You visit each of the landmarks and "find" the item you need to buy for your family. Each landmark should remind you of what you need to purchase, and as you walk through the order of landmarks, you should be able to retrieve your entire list.

What is particularly useful about this list is its portability. When you use it the next time, you may still remember the previous items "left" in each landmark. In your mind's eye, simply remove the loaf of bread left in the mailbox and replace it with the new item ("tomato sauce"). In this way, the same landmarks can be used over and over again for different lists. The method of loci also helps you preserve order information. Because each item is associated with a spot on your mental walk, which you go through the same way every time, you can also remember where in a list an item is, if this information is important. Some people construct multiple "memory palaces" in which they can store vast amount of unrelated information (McCabe, 2015b).

There is not a lot of recent research on the method of loci (see Engvig et al., 2010; McCabe, 2015b; Verhaeghen & Marcoen, 1996), because this is such an old and well-established technique. But older studies support the idea that the method of loci is useful for memory. For example, Groninger (1971) instructed college students to imagine a sequence of 25 spatial locations on their college campus. He then gave them a list of 25 unrelated words to learn using the method of loci. He compared them to students who were not given instruction in how to use the method of loci. Students who used the method of loci outperformed those who did not on recalling the unrelated words. McCabe (2015b) replicated this and showed that participants remembered more information after learning the method of loci than they had in a similar task prior to learning the technique. Kondo et al. (2005) showed that the method of loci improved memory. This improvement was correlated with increased activity in a variety of areas in the right prefrontal lobe. Engvig et al. (2010) showed that training older adults with the method of loci led to better memory performance and structural changes in the brain.

MNEMONIC IMPROVEMENT TIP 6.1

The method of loci: For learning arbitrary lists of unrelated items, the method of loci can be very effective. Mentally associate each of the to-be-learned items with a well-known physical location in a well-known landscape. When it is time to retrieve, imagine again the physical location and mentally walk through it. Look for the to-be-learned item in each location.

Keyword Technique

The **keyword technique** (also marketed as Linkword) is a common mnemonic technique that also employs visual imagery. It is particularly useful for learning new vocabulary words, especially for foreign-language vocabulary (Bellezza, 1996). More generally speaking, the keyword technique is useful for paired-associate learning. We use paired-associate learning when we learn new vocabulary or vocabulary in another language. The technique involves creating an image that links two items in memory. With respect to language learn-

> **Keyword technique:** Involves creating an image that links two items in memory. With respect to language learning, it means creating an image that links a word in the language you know to a word in the new language.

ing, it means creating an image that links the word in the language you know to the word in the language you are learning. For example, if you are learning words in Spanish, you will have to study many English-Spanish pairs to master a sufficient Spanish vocabulary. Consider studying the Spanish word *arbol,* meaning "tree." From the word *arbol,* you might think of the English word *arbor* (meaning a grove of trees—both words come from the same Latin root). And *arbor*, of course, conjures up images of trees. It also works for items that do not necessarily have the same roots. For example, if you are learning the Tagalog word *salamin,* meaning eyeglasses, you might imagine a fish (a *salmon*) wearing eyeglasses. (Tagalog is a widely spoken language in the Philippines.) Think of this image, and you will always know at least one word in Tagalog (see Wang & Thomas, 1995, for this example). The keyword technique can also be used to learn other kinds of paired-associate information. For example, at some point, you might need to memorize the capitals of all the countries of Europe. When learning that Tallinn is the capital of Estonia, you might imagine a cat with its "tail" stuck "in" a refrigerator (because it is so cold in Estonia). Asked to learn the capital of Estonia's neighbor, Finland, you might visualize a "sink on fire" to help you remember that Hel*sink*i is the capital of Finland.

According to Wang and Thomas (1995), the keyword technique is particularly useful for the initial encoding of new language vocabulary—that is, for the first time you encounter the new words. However, they contend that subsequent study should use meaning-based study. After the initial study session, you should use elaborative encoding or some other deep level of processing to help you remember the vocabulary. Wang and Thomas reasoned that the keyword technique is good at forming initial connections between disparate items (for example, arbitrary associations such as *Estonia–Tallinn* or *salamin–eyeglasses*). But they also noticed that most studies examining the keyword mnemonic employed relatively short retention intervals. Earlier studies in their own lab suggested that with time, forgetting occurred just as rapidly with the keyword technique as with other methods, and Wang and Thomas were concerned about the educational implications of this finding.

This is a clear concern, because most of us want to remember information that we learn not just for a few minutes but for much longer. For language learning, our ultimate goal is to be able to use the words we are learning when we visit a country that speaks that language. For example, you may choose to study a little Tagalog for a half hour a day for weeks before an anticipated trip to the Philippines. Remembering the words in Tagalog is only useful if you can use them much later, when you find yourself in the Philippines with someone who speaks only that language. So we usually want to use mnemonic techniques that produce long-term retention, not just provide a temporary boost. Even if our only goal is to do well on a vocabulary test, using techniques that promote long-term retention are superior to those that do not.

Wang and Thomas (1995) noted that the keyword technique runs contrary to the principles of levels of processing. This troubled them, because as memory scientists, they were aware of how important meaning-based processing is. And yet, here were all these memory experts promoting the keyword technique. Using a linking keyword to relate the appearance of a word to a similar-looking word in English is classified as shallow processing in the levels-of-processing framework. Therefore, the levels-of-processing framework suggests that the keyword technique may not produce good representation in long-term memory, because it emphasizes sensory overlap (either visual or auditory) between the words in the two languages. Thus, although the keyword technique may produce a temporary boost in memory performance, it does not promote the kinds of processes that lead to strong memory representations. For this reason, Wang and Thomas decided to do some experimental work to resolve these issues.

Wang and Thomas (1995) conducted an experiment comparing the keyword technique to standard semantic context encoding. In the experiment, participants were taught words in Tagalog along with their English translation (as in *salamin–eyeglasses*). Half of the participants were given instructions in how to use the keyword technique and were given an intermediary word to help them form a visual image (*salamin–salmon–eyeglasses*). In the semantic context, the participants saw an English-language sentence with the Tagalog word substituted in the place in which its language equivalent would appear ("The woman returned from the optometrist with a new pair of reading salamin"). Wang and Thomas gave their participants two tests: one five minutes after learning, the next two days later. The tests consisted of giving the Tagalog word and asking the participants to supply the English equivalent.

The results are seen in Figure 6.11. Wang and Thomas (1995) found that at the five-minute delay, more items were recalled if they had been encoded via the keyword method than via semantic context. However, after a two-day delay, many of these items had been forgotten, whereas there was comparatively less forgetting from the semantic context condition. Recall was better at the two-day delay overall in the semantic context condition than it was in the keyword condition. These results suggest that the keyword technique may not be all that it is cracked up to be. After all, in most cases, we want to remember the words in a new language for longer than five minutes—perhaps when our travels bring us to the Philippines.

Figure 6.11   Semantic encoding is better than keyword encoding at longer retention intervals. *Y*-axis represents the number of words recalled.

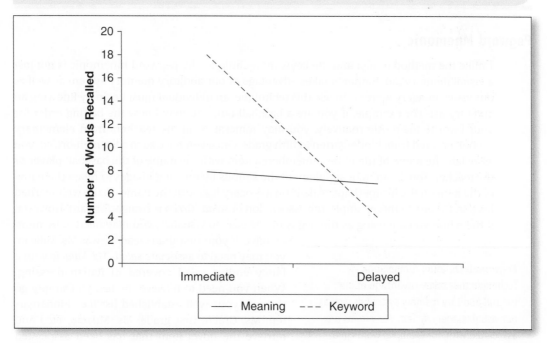

SOURCE: Based on Wang and Thomas (1995).

Wang and Thomas (1995) took a more optimistic view of their data, however. They suggested that the keyword technique leads to good initial encoding, as indicated by the good performance in the five-minute condition seen in Figure 6.10. They therefore suggested that the keyword technique is a good way to initially encode items. However, after one or two study sessions using the keyword technique, it is advisable to switch to deeper levels of processing, as exemplified by the semantic encoding in this experiment. This way, the student can capitalize on the long-term advantages provided by the semantic encoding. Because most students will study any particular item several times before they are actually tested on it, the keyword method can create good initial learning, and the semantic encoding can cement that knowledge. (For more information on the keyword technique, go to study.sagepub.com/schwartz3e.[7])

MNEMONIC IMPROVEMENT TIP 6.2

Keyword technique: An especially strong way to encode paired associates, such as new language vocabulary, is to use the keyword technique. This method provides good initial encoding but should be followed by deeper processing. The keyword technique involves finding a visual image that bridges one word to the other. For example, if you are studying the English French pair *pen–stylo*, you might imagine a fancy pen in the latest styles. This will provide a vivid visual image that will emphasize the sound of the word *stylo*.

Pegword Mnemonic

Unlike the method of loci and the keyword technique, the pegword mnemonic is not just a visual memory aid. Rather, it takes advantage of our auditory memory system as well as our visual imagery system. To use this technique, an individual must begin by knowing an auditory list. For example, if you are a baseball fan, you may know the batting order for your favorite team. Alternatively, you may remember all the teachers from elementary school, ordered from kindergarten to fifth grade. Once you have such a list memorized, you associate the name of the to-be-remembered item with the name of the baseball player or the teacher. You could then supplement the sounds by forming images to relate the name of the item on the list (perhaps "salad" on a grocery list) with the name on the well-learned list (Ms. Green). In this example, the association of *salad–Green* is straightforward. However, if the name you are using as the peg is not as easy to visualize, you may need to be more

Pegword technique: A mnemonic technique that takes advantage of our natural auditory memory system as well as our visual imagery system. New items are associated with, for example, words in a known rhyme scheme.

creative. If your first-grade teacher was Ms. Milacio, you may need to associate *salad–Ms. Milacio* with a fancy endive salad covered in Italian dressing. When you need to retrieve the list, you simply go through your well-established list (i.e., kindergarten, Ms. Green; first grade, Ms. Milacio; etc.) and retrieve the novel item that has been associated with each teacher. Empirical research has demonstrated that the **pegword technique** is helpful in memory (Paivio, 1969). However, like the keyword technique, the pegword helps with initial encoding, but subsequent memorization is better done by a more meaning-driven encoding (Carney & Levin, 2011; the following website nicely illustrates this method: www .sagepub .com/schwartz3e[8]).

MNEMONIC IMPROVEMENT TIP 6.3

Pegword technique: This technique combines visual and auditory memory into a powerful memory mnemonic for remembering ordered lists. First, you need a well-established word list. Then associate, using visual imagery, the new to-be-learned item with an item from the well-established list. At the time of test, go through your well-established list, and the associated items should be retrieved.

Interactive Versus Bizarre Imagery

Although not considered a formal mnemonic as the above three are, **bizarre imagery** can be a memory aid as well. Using this technique, we construct an image that, rather than conforming to our general way of thinking, is strange in some way. Essentially, we create a visual von Restorff effect and simul-

> **Bizarre imagery:** Forming strange visual images based on to-be-learned information to achieve strong memory for that information.

taneously take advantage of both the power of visual imagery and the power of distinctiveness to improve our memory. Make the images interact, and you can boost memory strength even more.

For example, Wollen, Weber, and Lowry (1972) asked participants to use bizarre interactive imagery in learning new paired associates, such as *piano–cigar*. They found that the interacting images, even if not bizarre, led to the best memory recall relative to noninteracting images or rote encoding. Thus, they suggested that interactive images are better than bizarre ones at producing good memory (see Figure 6.12). Interestingly, N. E. Kroll, Schepeler, and Angin (1986) replicated this finding but found that people thought they had done better on the bizarre items than they actually did. Therefore, when using this technique, it is good to test yourself (as when using any mnemonics) to ensure that you have mastered the material.

In this section, we have discussed a number of visual-based mnemonics to add to the growing list of study suggestions, tricks, strategies, and aids that can help each of us become more efficient at remembering information. Keep in mind, of course, that even these visual mnemonics require work and that they are useful in some circumstances but not in others. I repeat the warning that there is no memory pill or magic bullet that will ensure you remember everything all the time (nor would this be desirable—as we've seen, inhibiting some memories can be important to making new ones). Nonetheless, visual mnemonic techniques are useful for learning the kinds of arbitrary lists of items that we have been discussing here.

Figure 6.12 Bizarre imagery.

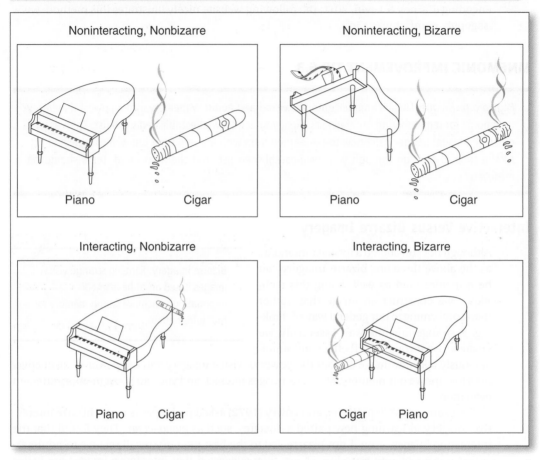

Noninteracting, Nonbizarre

Piano   Cigar

Noninteracting, Bizarre

Piano   Cigar

Interacting, Nonbizarre

Piano   Cigar

Interacting, Bizarre

Cigar   Piano

SOURCE: Wollen, K. A., Weber, A., & Lowry, D. (1972). Bizarreness versus interaction of mental images as determinants of learning. *Cognitive Psychology, 3,* 518–523. Published by Elsevier, Ltd.

SUMMARY

Finally, we discussed the advantages and disadvantages of the classic visual mnemonics, including the method of loci, the keyword technique, and the pegword mnemonic. These techniques use visual imagery to promote memory but should be supplemented with meaning-based techniques.

KEY TERMS

absolute judgment

analog representation

bizarre imagery

cognitive maps

eyewitness memory

fusiform face area (FFA)

hemifield neglect
(unilateral neglect)

imagery

keyword technique

method of loci

occipital face area (OFA)

own-race bias

pegword technique

photographic memory

primary visual cortex

propositional representation

prosopagnosia

relative judgment

representation

sequential line-up (show-up)

semantic categories

Shepard and Metzler's (1971)
mental rotation experiment

simultaneous lineup (lineup)

verbal facilitation

verbal overshadowing

REVIEW QUESTIONS

1. What is meant by the term *visual memory*? Why are recall measures hard to test when assessing visual memory?

2. What are the theoretical differences between a visual memory system that uses analog representation and one that uses propositional representation?

3. Describe the Shepard-Metzler experiment. What was their hypothesis? How was the experiment conducted? What results did they get? And how were these results interpreted?

4. Why does the finding that engaging in visual imagery activates the primary visual cortex support the analog view of imagery representation?

5. What is meant by verbal overshadowing in face memory? How does it occur? When does the opposite (verbal facilitation) occur?

6. What is own-race bias? Why do minorities have better ability to recognize own-race faces than majority groups?

7. What is prosopagnosia? With what areas of the brain is it associated?

8. What is the method of loci? How is it used, and what kinds of materials is it good for?

9. What is the keyword technique? How is it used? Why do Wang and Thomas only recommend it for initial studying?

10. What is the pegword mnemonic? How does it differ from the method of loci and the keyword technique?

ONLINE RESOURCES

1. For an illustration of the mental rotation experiment and to participate yourself, go to https://www.psytoolkit.org/experiment-library/mentalrotation.html

2. For information on hemifield neglect, go to http://psych.ucalgary.ca/PACE/VA-Lab/Visual%20 Agnosias/hemi-neglect.htm.

3. For more on photographic memory and eidetic memory, go to http://www.straightdope.com/columns/read/2350/is-there-such-a-thing-as-photographic-memory/.

4. For a demonstration of Nickerson and Adams (1979), go to http://www.indiana.edu/~p1013447/dictionary/penny.htm

5. For more on the own-race bias effect, go to http://works.bepress.com/christian_meissner/.

6. For memory improvement resources based on imagery, go to http://www.mindtools.com/memory.html.

7. For information on the keyword technique, go to http://www.memory-key.com/improving/strategies/advanced/mnemonics/using-keyword-method-learn-vocabulary/.

8. The following website nicely illustrates this pegword method: http://www.psychologistworld.com/memory/mnemonics_pegword.php.

Go to **study.sagepub.com/schwartz3e** for additional exercises and study resources. Select **Chapter 6, Visual Memory** for chapter-specific resources.

CHAPTER 7

Autobiographical Memory

I was driving my car, my old Honda Civic, from my home to my university on a hot sunny Tuesday morning, typical of mid-September in Miami. As I usually do, I was listening to the news on NPR. I was just passing Miami International Airport when the newscaster announced that a plane had crashed into the World Trade Center. NPR did not have much more news, but when I arrived at the university, the department secretary was in tears. Someone found a portable television, and we started monitoring the news. That is my recollection of my personal whereabouts the morning of September 11, 2001.

Most people who were old enough on 9/11 can vividly remember the personal details of how they heard the news, where they were, and what they were doing during the attacks on the United States. This is true for people who, like myself, had nothing directly to do with the attacks. I was in Miami, a thousand miles away, safe in my car and, later, in my office. My whereabouts had no impact on the tragedy unfolding that day or the courageous efforts ongoing to rescue survivors. I made no decisions about how to respond and whether or not to scramble fighter jets. This same situation is true for most people that day, who nonetheless remember their whereabouts as well. (For more thoughts on memories of 9/11, go to study.sagepub.com/schwartz3e.[1]) If you are not old enough to remember 9/11, you may remember the death of Michael Jackson, the death of Osama bin Laden, the surprise resignation of the pope, or the surprise election of Donald Trump." You may remember your personal circumstances when you heard the news, but it is unlikely that your personal circumstances were part of the news.

The kind of memory just discussed is called a **flashbulb memory** (Demiray & Freund, 2015). Most people are certain that their flashbulb memories, which are detailed, are accurate. Try telling someone that he or she misremembers, and you will be met with surprise and concern. Earlier generations of Americans have equally strong flashbulb memories of the assassination of John F. Kennedy or the attack on Pearl Harbor, which launched the United States into World War II. British people may have flashbulb memories of the auto accident that killed Princess Diana. Spaniards may have flashbulb memories of hearing the news of the Madrid train bombings. Israelis may have flashbulb memories of the assassination of

> **Flashbulb memories:** Highly confident personal memories of surprising events. To study them, researchers have focused on public tragedies.

Prime Minister Rabin. Turks may have flashbulb memories of the devastating earthquake that struck in Izmit, Turkey, in 1999 or the 2016 failed coup attempt. Catholics (and others) may have flashbulb memories of the surprise resignation of Pope Benedict XVI in 2013. And music fans may have flashbulb memories for the deaths of musical icons, such as Michael Jackson or David Bowie. In general, flashbulb memories are studied by examining these public tragedies, because these events tend to be unexpected and surprising. We also have flashbulb memories of personal events, but public events have several advantages for researchers, most notably that large numbers of people experience the same unexpected event. You might have noticed that most of the events mentioned here are negative events, such as deaths or bombings. People may also have flashbulb memories for positive events, but good public events tend to be less surprising. We usually have a good idea who is going to win an election or win a sports game before the event actually takes place. Thus, the typical study looks at surprising and bad public news.

Not all autobiographical memories need be so traumatic and weighty as those studied in flashbulb memory studies. Autobiographical memories include the memory of your first day of first grade, your first romantic kiss, your first day at a new job, or the recital of your wedding vows. They may also include more mundane events, such as what you ate for breakfast this morning, what movie you watched on television last night, what old friend sent you an unexpected text message, and where you left your keys when you got home the previous night.

The retrieval of autobiographical memories may also seem capricious, as the events that others recall, you may not recall, and vice versa. Moreover, we may strive to remember one event, but another surfaces instead. In some cases, it may not be clear why we recall some events but not others. Some of you may remember your first day at college, whereas others may not, even though the importance of college may be equal for you and others. Other memories may arise without having any particular importance. It may surprise us in that we remember some events at all, such as seeing a skinny raccoon on a vacation in Everglades National Park 25 years ago. People often wonder why such memories are still accessible so many years later, when their meaning is seemingly so inconsequential. The contention here is that we stitch together a series of episodic memories with semantic memory to create a life narrative that defines who we are as individuals (Conway & Loveday, 2015).

Autobiographical memory refers to our specific memories (episodic memory) and self-knowledge (semantic memory). In this sense, autobiographical memory does not define a system of memory, but rather a function of memory: representing our individual lives in memory. Thus, autobiographical memory combines information from episodic events ("falling out of a tree at Aunt Beulah's when I was 10 years old") and semantic knowledge ("I was born in the small town of Ottauquechee, Vermont"). On the episodic side, it includes important events, such as one's memory of high school graduation, and less important events, such as replacing a flat tire. On the semantic side, it may include highly self-relevant knowledge, such as the medicines you take and the allergies you have, and knowledge about yourself that you only know indirectly, such as where you were born. However, both episodic memories and semantic memories can be about our individual life story, so both are relevant to the topic of autobiographical memory.

In this chapter, we cover the major theory that organizes research on autobiographical memory—namely, the hierarchical model of autobiographical memory and the working self, advanced by Martin Conway and his colleagues (Conway, 2005; Conway & Loveday, 2015). We will then consider a number of important phenomena in autobiographical memory, including infant or childhood amnesia, flashbulb memories, diary studies, the reminiscence bump, shared memories, perspective in autobiographical memory, the interaction between odor and autobiographical memory, and the neuroimaging of autobiographical memory.

CONWAY'S THEORY OF REPRESENTATION IN AUTOBIOGRAPHICAL MEMORY

Martin Conway is a prominent British memory researcher who has been interested in the nature of autobiographical memory for many years (see Figure 7.1). His theory concerns the representation of autobiographical memory—that is, how our memories are stored and organized for retrieval. Conway's theory starts with three levels of representation that correspond to specific episodic memories, generalized and repeated events, and lifetime themes. To examine how his theory fits into ordinary memory, consider the following mini story: "When I was in graduate school, I often played basketball with friends at lunchtime. At one basketball game, a professional basketball player joined us."

This serves as a good example of some of the ideas Conway brings to our attention with respect to autobiographical memory. First, the memory is of a specific event—that is, it is an episodic memory of a particular event (playing basketball with the professional) at a particular time ("at one . . . game"). Second, there is a "general event" script that can be used to fill in details—that is, the storyteller often played basketball at lunchtime. Third, Conway talks about our use of lifetime periods to organize our memory (in this case, "when I was in graduate school"). Thus, Conway's organizational schema can neatly catch the nature of how we discuss autobiographical memory. (You can hear Dr. Conway talk about his research at study.sagepub.com/schwartz3e.[2])

We now examine the formal model of autobiographical memory described by Martin Conway and his colleagues. The model focuses on how autobiographical memories are represented at the cognitive level. Paramount to this model is the idea that representation of autobiographical memory correspond to (a) **event-specific memories**, (b) **general events**, and (c) **lifetime periods**. These representational levels create an interacting but hierarchical representation structure in our memory system (Conway & Pleydell-Pearce, 2000; see Figure 7.2). Specific events are organized

Event-specific memories: Individual events stored in episodic memory.

General events: Include the combined, averaged, and cumulative memory of highly similar events. General events also include extended events, which are long sequences of connected episodic events.

Figure 7.1   Noted memory theorist Martin Conway.

© Martin Conway

Lifetime periods: The idiosyncratic, personal ways in which we organize our autobiographical past. These lifetime periods are usually organized by a common theme and may overlap in the time periods that they cover.

into general events, which in turn are organized into cohesive units as lifetime periods. When people retrieve from this representational system, they can access a lifetime period (e.g., "when I was in graduate school"), which should unlock a host of general events and specific events associated with that lifetime period.

Any particular memory should be able to fit this schema. For example, a memory of "playing volleyball by the dorm" might be activated by the lifetime period of when you were in "your first year of college." This is a general event, synthesizing many such late afternoons during that year when you played volleyball on the lawn with friends. Or it could activate a specific volleyball event, such as when you dived for the volleyball and suffered a deep gash in your elbow. Another person might have a lifetime period of "when I was training hard for the marathon." This lifetime period will activate general events—that is, the combined and synthesized memory of many days spent in uneventful and monotonous running. Furthermore, specific events might be activated, such as the time the runner almost got hit by a car, the time the runner twisted an ankle and had to hitchhike home, or the exact moment when this runner passed the finish line at the New York Marathon in 2017. Let's look at each component of Conway's model in more detail.

Event-Specific Memories

In Conway's scheme, part of the representational system of autobiographical memory is the vast reservoir of episodic memories that we accumulate over our lifetimes (Conway & Loveday, 2015). Events are the fundamental units of cognitive memory. Thus, an event can be the briefest moment in time, such as the instant you sat down on your aunt's glass coffee table and shattered it or the time your cat knocked over the groceries and got her claws stuck in the bread. Or an event can be extended in time, such as your first date with your spouse or the time you drove on the California freeway in a convertible. Both the instant events and the extended events refer to particular and unique events; they simply differ in the extent to which they last.

Some researchers find that the term *episode* is too vague, as it can either mean an isolated instant or an extended event. Linton (1986), for example, suggested that any particular event can be broken down into elements called *details*. Details refer to precise moments in time, whereas events refer to extended but continuous memories. For example, think of the episodic memory of seeing a hammerhead shark while scuba diving. The detail is the exact moment when the dangerous fish flashed by. It lasted only a second, and the shark was gone. However, the event includes the subsequent adrenaline rush in your body, the concern about air supply, and the relaxation induced by subsequently watching a peaceful angelfish. Despite this critique, the concept of an episodic memory referring to both a detail and an event has become accepted within this field. Future research should sort out how people demarcate the boundaries between details and between events.

General Events

For Conway, general events include two different forms of representation. First, general events include the *combined, averaged, and cumulative memory of similar events*. This means that similar repetitive events may be mixed together to form a generic representation of that kind of event (Rubin & Umanath, 2015). For example, you may go grocery shopping once a week. Normally, grocery shopping is unexciting, but it is also an important, if repetitive, event. Over time, the specific visits blend into one schema-driven representation. Indeed, when you attempt to retrieve such an event, it may be impossible to recall any specific visit to the grocery store, but that is not to say that you have forgotten that you ever do it. Rather, the specific events combine in memory into a general event of what you do when you go grocery shopping. This contrasts with the event-specific memory, which might be the time you saw your old gym teacher shopping at your grocery store. This one-time event remains memorable above and beyond the general event. Our lives are filled with such repeating cycles of work, school, exercise, bedtime rituals, and so on. The ability to form such representations requires that the individual be able to integrate and interpret across individual events, an important skill for creating an autobiography

Figure 7.2   Conway's model.

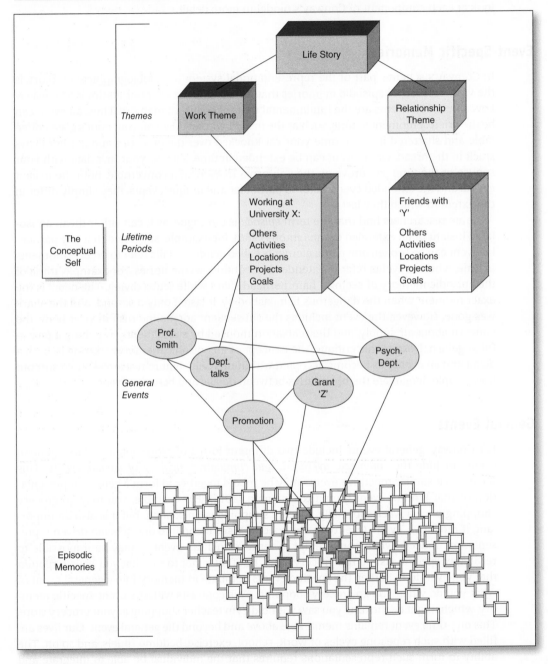

SOURCE: Conway (2005).

The second form of "general" event, according to Conway, is an *extended event*. An extended event is a representation of a long sequence of connected episodic events. An extended event represents memory over continuous time in the past. It is different from the averaged memory in that it is the memory of a single sequence of events that occurred only once. However, it is similar in that it requires integrative processes to join the units into a coherent schema. For example, a two-week vacation might be remembered in terms of a "general event." It is composed of individual episodes, such as skinning your knee on the steps of the Lincoln Memorial; getting stuck in traffic on the Beltway; sweating in the hot, sticky weather while waiting to get into the Smithsonian; or waiting in a long line to visit the White House. Each of these is a unique event, but they are joined to form the memory of your wonderful vacation in the nation's capital. As do memories of the other form of general event, these extended memories require integrating individual events into the general memory (see Burt, Kemp, & Conway, 2003). Robinson (1992) studied a pattern of general memories called "mini-histories," which are the integrated sequence for activities with a straightforward goal and timeline, such as "learning to drive a car" or "my first romantic relationship" (see Figure 7.3).

Lifetime Periods

We use lifetime periods to organize the representation of autobiographical memories (both event-specific and general events). Lifetime periods are the idiosyncratic, personal ways in which we organize our autobiographical past. Lifetime periods are usually organized by a common theme and may overlap in the actual physical time periods that they cover. For example, such lifetime periods might be "when I was in college," "being a child in Cincinnati, Ohio," "before I got married," or "when I went to tennis camp." Retrieving these labels tend to activate a common set of memories associated with each theme. Thus, when the lifetime period "when I was in college" is evoked, retrieved memories occur of long nights of studying, fraternity parties, college football games, and so on. "Before I got married" might evoke memories of the joys and frustrations of dating. "When I lived in Cincinnati, Ohio," might evoke memories of attending baseball games with your father or going to Girl Scout camp with your troop.

Lifetime periods need not be linear; they can overlap. For example, it is possible that the lifetime period "when I was in college" coincides with "before I got married," but each is associated with a different set of general and specific event memories. Similarly, "when I went to tennis camp" may overlap with "when I lived in Cincinnati," but each lifetime period evokes different sets of specific and general events. Lifetime periods can provide direction and a sense of goals and accomplishments for some. These lifetime periods can also serve as good cues to retrieve general events or episodic events. When lifetime periods are used as cues, people retrieve autobiographical memories faster (Conway & Pleydell-Pearce, 2000; Conway and Loveday, 2015).

The Working Self

The final component of autobiographical memory is the **working self**. The working self is not a level of representation. Rather, it is a monitoring function that controls the

Figure 7.3   Do you remember the very first time you drove a car on your own? Despite the many thousands of times they may have driven since, most people remember this coming-of-age act.

Thinkstock/Comstock

retrieval of information from the levels of representation. The working self serves as a gateway that allows some memories to be retrieved and others to stay unretrieved. It promotes the retrieval of memories needed in a situation—in particular, memories that will be helpful to the person given their current situation. In this way, the working self is analogous to the central executive in working memory. The working self allows for the intelligent curation of memory. Thus, the working self includes the goals and self-images that make up our view of ourselves. For example, you may think of yourself as being a light sleeper, setting high goals, but sometimes being lazy when you should work hard. This "working self" is the function of your aspirations and expectations, combined with your actual memory. Many nights of being woken by the slightest sound has formed a general event in your memory of being a light sleeper. Many evenings spent watching television shows when you thought you should be studying contributes to your working self-perspective that you are lazy.

> **Working self:** The monitoring function that controls the retrieval of information from the levels of representation. The working self includes the goals and self-images that make up our view of ourselves.

With respect to autobiographical memory, the working self functions to keep two features of memory intact, **coherence** and **correspondence** (Conway & Loveday, 2015). *Coherence* means the processes that yield autobiographical memories that are consistent with the working self. For example, if one's working self includes the image of oneself as an animal lover, the working self will work to yield coherent autobiographical memories of instances in which one was kind to animals. When this aspect of yourself is invoked, you will recall the time when you stopped to help a turtle cross the road and not the time you accidentally ran over a wild rabbit. *Correspondence*, by contrast, means the requirement that retrieved memories match actual past events. For example, even if one thinks of oneself as a good baseball player, it is important to accurately remember that it was you who struck out with the bases loaded to end your team's opportunity to advance to the playoffs. Thus, correspondence is necessary for a person's memory to be accurate reflections of their personal past, whereas coherence is necessary for a person's retrieval to be consistent with their own self-image.

> **Coherence:** The processes that yield autobiographical memories that are consistent with the working self.

> **Correspondence:** The match between the retrieved memory and the actual past event.

As the above examples may indicate, conflicts between coherence and correspondence may arise in circumstances in which these processes work at cross-purposes. For example, you may want to remember your vacations as relaxed and enjoyable events. On one vacation, however, you may have spent a long, unpleasant wait in a crowded, hot bus station. The working self integrates these two conflicting aspects of the vacation into the construction of autobiographical memory. Although we have not elaborated on the data that support Conway's model of autobiographical memory, it is a worthwhile framework to keep in mind while evaluating the research in the topics to be covered in this chapter.

SECTION SUMMARY AND QUIZ

Autobiographical memory refers to the memories we have of ourselves, both of individual events from our lives and the facts of our lives. Autobiographical memory is a functional term—it describes a class of memories that have to do with the individual self, which include both episodic and semantic memory. An important theory developed by Martin Conway and his colleagues examines the representation of autobiographical memory. In this theory, there are three overlapping levels of organization in the representation of autobiographical memory—event-specific memories, general events, and lifetime periods—and this is a working self that monitors these levels. Event-specific memories are the individual episodic details of unique events. General events are the average of repeated events or longer events, extended in time. Lifetime periods are organizational frameworks that help us organize our autobiographical memory. The working self maintains coherence and correspondence of the memories we retrieve from autobiographical memory.

Section Quiz

1. Toni remembers the exact moment she kicked the ball to win her high school soccer championships. This memory would be considered
   a. A life-time period
   b. A general event
   c. A projection of the working self
   d. An event-specific memory

2. Conway's theory of autobiographical memory emphasizes
   a. How episodic events are encoded
   b. Why false memories are so common for general events
   c. The relation of working memory to the working self
   d. The nature of representation in autobiographical memory

3. Which of the following would be considered a general event?
   a. Hortensia describes the usual things she does when she drives to school
   b. Hung-tao describes how he heard the news of the pope's resignation
   c. Karwan describes his feelings when he first arrived in the United States
   d. Elijah remembers being brought into the hospital room to see his little sister for the first time

4. The process that yields autobiographical memories that are consistent with the working self is known as
   a. Correspondence
   b. Coherence
   c. Coinvestigation
   d. Colinear

Answers
1. d
2. d
3. a
4. b

CHILDHOOD AMNESIA

Childhood amnesia refers to our poor to non-existent memory of early childhood (poor) and infancy (non-existent; Bauer, 2015; Jack & Hayne, 2010; Madsen & Kim, 2016). It is important to point out that young children and infants are not amnesic. It is adults who are amnesic for events that occurred when they were young children. The amnesia covers the first two years of life, and then, depending on the individual, we start to have memories of episodes from our life, sometimes as early as age two but more often at age three or four. These earliest memories tend to be fragments, bits and pieces of memory largely unconnected to the narratives that form later memories (Nelson, 1989). Usually, we have more and more detailed memories of our lives from age six or seven. Figure 7.4 shows the childhood amnesia phenomenon and its offset by five or six years of age. It is also at this age that adults remember childhood events in terms of the structure in Conway's framework. Indeed, early memories tend to be disjointed—not connected with anything—whereas memories from the early elementary school years often feel as though they are of events that happened to us—our current selves. Think about your own earliest memories. What are they about? How do they differ from memories from later in childhood or of recent events? Do they feel somehow different or fragmented?

Childhood amnesia has been a topic of interest to psychologists from a number of perspectives. Early psychoanalysts thought that childhood amnesia reflected the turbulent nature of the unconscious mind. Henri and Henri (1898) were the first to describe childhood amnesia in the scientific literature. Freud (1905/1953) described the phenomenon and noted its relevance to topics such as repression. Freud thought the first few years of life were so inherently traumatic that adults had to repress memories from those years. The psychiatrist Ernest Schachtel (1947/2000) also noted its importance in unraveling theories of the unconscious mind. Nowadays, the psychoanalytic view of childhood amnesia is usually dismissed, as there is little empirical evidence to support it. (For a website on childhood amnesia, go to study.sagepub.com/schwartz3e.[3])

> **Childhood amnesia:** Also known as infantile amnesia, refers to the observation that adults have almost no episodic memories from the first three to five years of their lives.

> **Childhood amnesia—psychodynamic view:** The view that childhood amnesia is caused by active repression.

> **Childhood amnesia—age-related changes in self-concept:** The view that childhood amnesia is caused by the lack of development of a coherent psychological self.

> **Childhood amnesia—neurological transitions in memory systems:** The view that childhood amnesia is caused by changes in the brain as it matures.

> **Childhood amnesia—influence of language on memory development:** The view that childhood amnesia is caused by the growth of language ability in the young child. Language provides the structure and narrative schemas necessary to support episodic memories.

Some people do report memories from earlier ages. However, it is likely that many of these memories are not truly episodic memories. Rather, it is likely that they are stories people have heard about themselves that later became illusory self-memories, or they may be memories of pictures people saw when they were somewhat older. They may also be false memories, the topic of the next chapter. In fact, although it is hard to test the reliability of such memories, most researchers studying the area would agree that any memories from the first two years of life are not true episodic memories, regardless of whether they reflect an event that happened or not.

In many cases, having a clear life boundary around the age of two and a half can prompt the first memory of early childhood (Eacott & Crawley, 1998; Usher & Neisser, 1993)—that is, some obvious transition or big event at that age can leave a lasting episodic memory. For example, moving to a new house or a different city, the birth of a younger sibling, or some other big change can prompt the first memory. For example, one student described moving from San Antonio to Miami when she was two and a half years old. They drove the whole way—but all she remembers from the drive was seeing a shiny 18-wheeler truck with a picture of a baby on it. She has no idea why this image has stuck in her mind but feels certain that it occurred while they were on the road, moving to a new city. Another student described being just over two years old, waiting for his little sister to be born, but then being sent to his grandfather's house because his mother went into labor just as Hurricane Andrew was approaching Miami. Most of the storm he does not remember, but he does remember listening to records at his grandfather's house while the storm raged outside. These anecdotes are consistent with the data in this area. According to Eacott and Crawley, adults who are 2.1 years or older than their younger sibling tend to remember the younger child's birth. Those younger have no conscious memory of their life before their sibling arrived or the event of their sibling's birth. Eacott and Crawley find, however, that most people do remember the birth of a sibling if the younger sibling is more than three years younger than they, and some do report it during that third year of life.

Childhood amnesia is a difficult topic to investigate from an experimental point of view. First, researchers can rarely verify the accuracy of the memories. In some cases, parents or teachers can be contacted to verify that the event described really did occur, but in most studies, that is simply impossible. Indeed, new research on false memories suggests it is not difficult to induce a false memory of an early childhood experience (Strange, Wade, & Hayne, 2008). Second, even if the event is verified, the researcher must rely on the subjective judgment by the participant that the memory is a real episodic memory and not the memory of a story told by someone else. Third, in some cases, these early memories may be associated with trauma or abuse. Therefore, the researcher needs to advise participants of the risks involved in the studies. Fourth, participants may have trouble dating an early memory. In some cases, such as the birth of a sibling, the information is datable by knowledge of the sibling's birthday and history, but other memories (e.g., a bad dream, a trip to the beach, an angry babysitter) may be much harder to place in time. Thus, even with a memory that can be considered true, it may sometimes be difficult to place it in, for example, the third, fourth, or fifth year of life. Fifth, it also appears that cultural factors influence the offset of childhood amnesia. Some cultural groups emphasize remembering events from childhood, and these cultures tend to have earlier offsets (Wang, 2006). For example, conversations about past events between parents and children are most common among Americans relative to other cultures, and this is correlated with an earlier offset of childhood amnesia among American participants than those from other cultures (Artioli, Cicogna, Occhionero, & Reese, 2012).

Luckily, researchers have identified a number of methods for examining the offset of childhood amnesia (Jack & Hayne, 2007). The simplest method is, of course, to ask people about their earliest memory. Across a number of studies, this procedure produces an average of about 3.1 years of age for the first reported memory by adults. This estimate of 3.1 comes from the participants themselves, not from objective sources that might be able to verify the memory. A second and more involved way of examining the offset of childhood amnesia is to target particular memories, such as the birth of a younger sibling, an illness, or a move to a new home or city. This method will only work for the subset of people who have such clear transitions, and it is not always clear whether these people differ from those who do not have such transitions. Nonetheless, targeting transition memories actually yields a slightly younger estimate than the more open method, as most adults remember the birth of a sibling even if they were just 2.5 years older than that sibling. A third method involves asking for exhaustive searches of memory. In this technique, the participant must remember as many memories as possible from the earliest date forward. As adults retrieve childhood events, one sees a steady increase in the number of memories produced as they recall from age three and older (Jack & Hayne, 2007). Usually, there is just a smattering of memories from the earliest childhood years, but from around seven years old or so, the memories increase greatly. Fourth, some researchers have used the cue-word method. A particular word (e.g., *church, river, raccoon*) is provided, and the adult must remember the earliest memory associated with the particular word. Like the other methods, this method has a bottom limit of two years of age. In addition, the cue-word technique yields only a smattering of early childhood memories, although it is often quite successful at producing memories from later childhood and adolescence.

Why do adults fail to recall events from their earliest years, and what changes allow them to start remembering events from age three and more events from older years? A number of explanations have been offered with varying degrees of success at explaining the phenomena (Bauer, 2015). These include but are not limited to the following:

1. Psychodynamic view

2. Age-related changes in self-concept

3. Neurological transitions in memory systems

4. Influence of language on memory development

5. Multiple-factor theory

We consider each here.

Psychodynamic View

Starting with Freud (1905/1953), some theorists considered that memories of early childhood were repressed. For Freud, this repression was important to personal development, because he thought that young children went through a period of sexual thinking and wishing with respect to their parents. (In light of what we know now about development, Freud's view on this was, of course, ridiculous.) As we grow older, however, we learn the rules and norms of our society, which make such wish fulfillment disgusting, vulgar, and inappropriate. Rather than acknowledge such incestuous thoughts, our subconscious blocks out all access to the first five or six years of our lives. In the Freudian

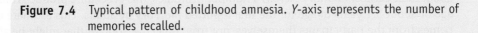

Figure 7.4 Typical pattern of childhood amnesia. *Y*-axis represents the number of memories recalled.

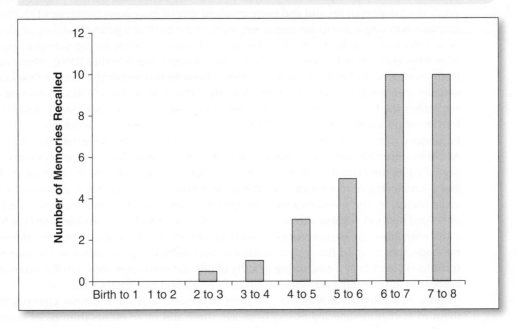

view, psychoanalysis can unlock these early childhood memories, even for the youngest of ages. Thus, these memories are not completely lost; they are only lost to those who have not gone through psychoanalysis. No scientific memory researcher takes any of this seriously anymore, because absolutely no empirical data support it. This view is acknowledged here, because it has had such a big influence outside of memory science and for historical completeness. Freudian thinking is surprisingly still influential outside of academic psychology, but most memory researchers focus on the remaining explanations for childhood amnesia.

Age-Related Changes in Self-Concept

In this view, infants lack a coherent view of the self as differentiated from their surrounding environment. Therefore, there is no working self around which to associate episodic memories (Conway, 2005). It is for this reason, perhaps, that our earliest memories often feel so fragmented. Around the age of 1.5, infants start to develop a sense of self, which continues to mature as the child starts his or her third and fourth year. For example, only at 18 months do infants start responding to their mirror image as if they are looking at themselves (Rochat, 2003). Before then, it is unclear what infants perceive when they look in the mirror. In this view, as the sense of self develops, the individual can begin to code his or her memories into this developing sense of coherent personhood, and these episodic memories can be stored in such a way as to be retrieved later in life (Bauer, 2015; Howe & Courage, 1993).

Neurological Transitions in Memory Systems

Until recently, this view was the leading contender among serious memory researchers. Recently, however, it has fallen into disfavor, as evidence suggests that some neurological changes necessary for episodic memory occur much earlier than the offset of childhood amnesia and others appear not to be online until after the offset of childhood amnesia. The neurological view argues that the relevant neural structures for forming episodic and hence autobiographical memories are not fully mature until a child reaches about age three. Therefore, long-term episodic memories cannot be maintained for the simple reason that the neural machinery is not yet in place (Madsen & Kim, 2016). Two areas of the brain have become the focus of this explanation. First, the learning area of the limbic system, the hippocampus, continues to mature in infants until the age of three. However, memory studies often yield ages of offset of childhood amnesia before then. We also know that the prefrontal lobes are still maturing well into childhood, perhaps still changing and growing in adolescence. However, this growth cannot account for the offset of childhood amnesia, which occurs much earlier. Thus, because the changes in the brain do no correspond to the landmark points in childhood amnesia, the neurological account has been largely rejected (Madsen & Kim, 2016).

Influence of Language on Memory Development

In this view, the growth of language ability in the young child provides the structure and narrative schemas necessary to support episodic memories. An ability to describe an event is necessary to remember that event. As such, the forms in which we do encode information at an early age are nonlinguistic and without narrative form, leaving whatever memory traces are established very difficult to retrieve when the person is older. Then, as our ability to speak and communicate grows, we are able to start encoding episodic memories in narrative form that will be retrievable when we are adults. As adults, we do not have access to the earliest forms of memory that were established pre-linguistically, but we do have access to our linguistic representations.

Although this explanation is not as intuitively straightforward as some of the others, considerable data support this view (see Jack, Simcock, & Hayne, 2012). First, women tend to have an earlier offset of childhood amnesia than do men, and women develop linguistically earlier than men do. Second, studies on memory in children show that, regardless of gender, those with stronger linguistic abilities at three or four years of age are more likely to recall events from that age later in childhood (Simcock & Hayne, 2002). Third, information that is encoded in nonverbal forms in early childhood tends to stay that way and is not later converted into a verbal format in later childhood (Hayne, 2004).

An interesting experiment conducted with young children supports the importance of language development to childhood amnesia. Simcock and Hayne (2002) presented two-, three-, and four-year-old children with a demonstration of an "incredible shrinking machine" (see Figure 7.5). An object, such as a beach ball, is placed at the top of the machine. It drops in, and the machine makes a lot of noise. After a minute of noise making, a smaller beach ball emerges from the bottom of the machine. Simcock and Hayne "shrunk" a number of objects for the children, who watched the machine with rapt attention. Simcock and Hayne then tested the verbal abilities of the children to see if they knew all of the words that described the shrunken objects. And in case you were worried, they did not shrink any heads for the children.

Simcock and Hayne (2002) then tracked down the children a year later. Many of the children still remembered the "magic shrinking machine" and described the event from a year earlier. This is consistent with other research that suggests that young children do not immediately forget complex events—it is only later, as adults, that these events are forgotten. However, the children only remembered those objects for which they possessed the vocabulary when they had witnessed the event. If they knew the word *beach ball* when they were two, they would often recall seeing a beach ball being shrunk a year later. However, if they did not know the word *beach ball* at age two, they would not recall that object being shrunk a year later. Simcock and Hayne found no exceptions to this pattern—if the child did not know the word at the time of seeing the event, he or she did not recall that object a year later. This supports the idea that language is critical to the offset of childhood amnesia.

Jack et al. (2012) tracked down the children who had participated in the "magic shrinking machine" experiment six years later when the children were ages eight to 10. They found that 20% of the children still remembered the event and could recall details. There appeared to be no correlation between age at the time of the event and whether or not the event was remembered six years later. Although two of the children seemingly mentioned aspects of the event for which they did not have words in their vocabulary during the witnessing of the event, by and large, the older children continued to recall only what they had words for as younger children. More important, the fact that memory of the shrinking machine could persist in so many children past the cutoff of childhood amnesia and into later childhood suggests that the researchers were producing an event that adequately captures the kind of events for which adults will have childhood memories. Thus, the follow-up study, like the initial study supports the idea that being able to create a narrative memory with language aids in the remembering of events from early in development.

Childhood Amnesia May Result From Multiple Causes

Another view of childhood amnesia posits that there is no one specific reason for this phenomenon, but rather childhood amnesia is the result of a number of converging factors (Bauer, 2015). In this view, childhood amnesia results from relatively poor encoding processes in episodic memory during early childhood. Moreover, in early childhood, individuals have not yet learned the strategies that keep autobiographical memories retrievable later. This second reason is actually more about why events from later in life are more easy to recall than why early events are so inaccessible. Nonetheless, Bauer argues that these two processes can account for childhood amnesia. To support this view, Bauer points to a number of studies in which young children do less well at encoding information than do

Figure 7.5   The magic shrinking machine.

SOURCE: Simcock, G., & Hayne, H. (2002). Breaking the barrier? Children fail to translate their preverbal memories into language. *Psychological Science, 13,* 225–231. Published by Wiley-Blackwell.

older children and adults, and that the narrative description of autobiographical events in young children is also inferior to those older than them. However, they do encode events, and thus, childhood amnesia cannot be dismissed exclusively as an encoding problem in infancy (Cleveland and Reese, 2008). To support the second half of the view, Bauer points to studies in which forgetting occurs more rapidly in young children than it does in older children and adults (Bauer and Larkina, 2014). Bauer and Larkina tested children in mid-childhood (ages 7 to 11) and college-aged adults. Participants were asked to remember autobiographical events. The growth of memories across age was much greater for the young children than for the young adults, suggesting that younger children are more likely to forget autobiographical events.

Bauer (2015) does not address the issue of how young children's inability to create episodic memory interacts with the development of narrative and language ability. Thus, one potential area for further research is to determine how weaker encoding and quicker forgetting in early childhood are related to language development. Does less developed language explain, for example, why young children are weaker at encoding, or are these two separate phenomena? It is likely that the language view will need to be integrated into the multiple-cause view in order to come up with a more complete handle on childhood amnesia.

FLASHBULB MEMORIES

For many Americans, the shocking news of the attack on Pearl Harbor in 1941; the assassinations of John F. Kennedy, Robert Kennedy, and Martin Luther King Jr. in the 1960s; or the attack on the World Trade Center in 2001 are indelibly marked on their memory. Some of us may have flashbulb memories about hearing the news of the Boston Marathon bombing in 2013 or the attack on the Pulse nightclub in Orlando in 2016. In other cultures, similar events may leave these indelible marks on people's memory. For example, Catholics the world over may remember hearing the news of the surprise resignation of Pope Benedict XVI also in 2013 (Curci et al., 2015). These momentous events in the history of our culture provide people of certain ages with strong memories of where they were and what they were doing during these events, even if they had nothing to do with them directly. These memories are called flashbulb memories, the term chosen to capture the subjective feeling that the memory will always be maintained. Other cultures have had their share of events creating flashbulb memories, from tsunamis to earthquakes to assassinations, many of which have become the subject of memory research.

As noted above, flashbulb memories have typically been studied by looking at public events. This has the advantage that researchers can gather information from many people about the same event. Nonetheless, people may also have flashbulb memories for other surprising events that are more personal. These may include getting a letter of acceptance to a first-choice college (a positive event) or getting the news that a close family member had suddenly died (negative event). Because not everyone gets accepted to the same first-choice college at the same time, public events provide a useful benchmark to study flashbulb memories. (For the neuroimaging of flashbulb memories, go to www.sagepub .com/schwartz3e.[4])

The first empirical study of flashbulb memories concerned Americans' memories for the spate of dreadful assassinations in the 1960s (Brown & Kulik, 1977). This first study was done several years after the murders, so there was no possible way to verify the memory reports of individuals. Thus, this study cannot address the accuracy of the reported memories. However, some interesting facts emerged. First, despite the passage of time, people claimed to have vivid, confident, and detailed flashbulb memories of some of the events. Second, the older memories (the death of President John F. Kennedy) were just as strong as later ones (the death of civil rights leader Martin Luther King Jr.). Third, the more relevant the event was to an individual, the more likely the person was to have a flashbulb memory of the event. Thus, for example, African Americans were more likely to have a flashbulb memory of the assassination of Martin Luther King Jr. than were White Americans. For these reasons, Brown and Kulik (1977) argued that the term *flashbulb* "fit." It was as if people recorded the event and hit the "now, print" button in their memory. Evidence suggests that it is not necessary for the news to be surprising. Indeed, many French citizens have flashbulb memories of the death of their former president, François Mitterand, even though his death did not come as a surprise (Curci & Luminet, 2009).

In a large, multicity study, William Hirst and his colleagues examined flashbulb memories for the terrorist attacks of 9/11 (Hirst et al., 2009). In initial reports collected in the days after the attack, participants reported strong negative emotions. However, one year later and four years later, when participants were re-contacted and asked about the event, they remembered where and when they heard the news but tended to forget their strong emotional reactions. Most of this forgetting was apparent one year after the event. After that, the memories stabilized. A subsequent study showed that 10 years later, people were still very confident in their memories about the where and what of their memories for 9/11 (Hirst et al., 2015). Thus, although a strong emotional impact appears to be a prerequisite for a flashbulb memory to form, remembering the emotional response itself seems to be less important than remembering the details that people speak about (where and when you heard the news).

Accuracy of Flashbulb Memories

As in many areas of autobiographical memory, there is an issue of correspondence—that is, the relation between the event and the memory. This means how close to the actual event that we experienced is the memory we have for that event. How do flashbulb memories correspond to the actual situation in which people "heard the news"? Think about your own flashbulb memories. You are likely to have strong feelings about these memories. You remember the events vividly, and you feel strongly that your memories are accurate. However, a series of studies suggests that, as vivid as our flashbulb memories are and as confident as we are that they are real, they are subject to the same distortions and inaccuracies as normal memories. We will consider a few of the studies that address this issue.

Weaver (1993) conducted a study comparing an ordinary memory and a flashbulb memory, which now serves as an excellent test of whether or not flashbulb memories are accurate. Weaver was teaching a class on cognitive psychology and wanted to do a demonstration of autobiographical memory. He asked each of his students to write down the details of an ordinary interaction with a college roommate or friend. He made this request in class on January 16, 1991. That evening, the U.S. Air Force began bombing Baghdad, Iraq, to start the Gulf War of 1991 in an effort to liberate Kuwait from occupying Iraqi forces. Many Americans who were adults at the time formed flashbulb memories of that evening and can still remember where they were when they heard the news of the start of that war. Though the war was brief, and the United States won quickly, at the very start of the war many people were worried, surprised, and alarmed. Two days later (January 18, 1991), Weaver's students wrote down as many details as they could remember from the ordinary interaction with their roommate and their memory of hearing the news of the war.

At the end of the semester (three months later), Weaver asked the students to describe the contents of each memory. The students answered questions concerning the events and indicated their confidence in the accuracy of their memories. Eight months after that (or nearly a year after the original events), some students were contacted again and asked to describe their memories yet again, allowing Weaver to compare the accuracy of the memories over time. By assuming that the report given the day after the event was the benchmark against which to measure memory accuracy, he could compare what people reported three months and 11 months after the event with the initial report and determine the correspondence.

Weaver (1993) found more similarities between the regular memory and the flashbulb memory than he did differences. The amount and detail in the memory reports declined over time at about the same rate. Moreover, the students remembered about the same number of details from each event. Accuracy of the two memories was equivalent, meaning that discrepancies between the original description and later descriptions were about the same for both the roommate memory and the flashbulb memory. Notice here that Weaver found that flashbulb memories contained errors. They were not indelibly inscribed into people's memory as Brown and Kulik (1977) had originally thought. This accuracy rate of flashbulb memories has now been replicated many times (Hirst et al., 2015; Lanciano & Curci, 2012).

The lack of correspondence between the initial report and the later report could be either small discrepancies or in some cases, completely different versions of the event. Small discrepancies included originally reporting that the event happened just before dinner, then later reporting it happened just after dinner. Larger discrepancies included reporting first hearing the news from a professor and then later remembering hearing it on the television news.

One might think that flashbulb memories would be immune to such discrepancies, but in fact, Weaver's (1993) study and many studies have demonstrated that errors do creep into flashbulb memories at about the same rate as they occur in normal memories. For example, in a study of flashbulb memories for the acquittal of O. J. Simpson, errors in flashbulb memories were clear as well (Schmolck, Buffalo, & Squire, 2000). Even in studies of memory for 9/11, errors are detectable (Talarico & Rubin, 2007). Indeed, Hirst et al. (2015) showed that errors were apparent one year after 9/11 in people's recall of the events, but then stabilized, so that 10 years later, the memories were similar to one year after the event, even if this was inconsistent with what people had reported in the immediate aftermath of the attack. Thus, despite our beliefs that our flashbulb memories are potent and strong, evidence suggests that they are not more accurate than normal memories. Indeed, it is likely that the studies overestimate accuracy, because the studies require participants to make original reports of the event. Participants may, therefore, recall making the original report rather than the event itself.

One critical difference does exist between regular memories and flashbulb memories. Confidence remains high for our flashbulb memories relative to our ordinary memories. In the Weaver (1993) study, the confidence that the memory was accurate remained high in flashbulb memories 11 months after the event. Confidence in flashbulb memories did decline over time but not nearly as much as the confidence in the roommate event (similar results were found in Hirst et al., 2015 for the 9/11 attacks). Thus, Weaver argued that the true hallmark of a flashbulb memory is not how accurate it is but rather the confidence with which we assert that our memories are accurate. In other words, something about the flashbulb experience and talking about it later forms a subjectively strong memory, even when that memory does not correspond to the actual event (see Figure 7.6).

In fact, some researchers have begun to think that the aspects of flashbulb memories that make them unique are not only the confidence that we feel in them but the vividness with which we remember them (Lanciano & Curci, 2012; Talarico & Rubin, 2007). Talarico and Rubin, for example, compared memories of people's personal whereabouts when they heard the news of 9/11 and an ordinary event around the same time. As had Weaver, they found that the flashbulb memories were no more accurate than the ordinary memories, but vividness ratings, confidence ratings, and other subjective ratings were all higher for the flashbulb memories than for the normal memories. Thus, vividness of the memory experience also appears to be important in a flashbulb memory.

However, there appears to be more to the story of accuracy than originally thought. Tekcan and his colleagues made the distinction between memory for the news event itself and memory for the inception—the personal what, where, and when of hearing the news—that they claim is sometimes confounded in other flashbulb memory experiments (Tekcan, Ece, Gülgöz, & Er, 2003). In their studies, they make a distinction between the news event and the personal reception event. Thus, in their study, the news event was the 9/11 attack, but the personal reception event was how students some distance from New York (indeed, Istanbul, Turkey) heard of the news. For another example, you might remember that you were on vacation in the mountains when you heard about the attack on the Pulse nightclub, but you can also remember many details about the attack as well. The memory of your own situation is considered the memory for personal context. Tekcan et al. argue that this is an important difference and that accuracy for personal context is actually quite high, even though memory for the actual event is subject to changes equivalent to normal memories (Kızılöz & Tekcan, 2013).

To examine this idea, Tekcan and his colleagues examined how people recalled hearing the news of a terrible earthquake that struck western Turkey, not far from Istanbul, in 1999 with a force of 7.6 on the Richter scale. Er (2003) found that participants had high recall and low inaccuracy in their later report when only personal context was considered (Er, 2003). Furthermore, flashbulb memories of 9/11 have also been shown to be highly accurate when only personal context information is considered (Tekcan, Ece, Gülgöz, & Er, 2003). In this latter study, participants' memory for the actual events of 9/11 shifted from the original report, but there were almost no deviations in their reports of personal whereabouts. Thus, it is possible that in the earlier studies, context memory remained accurate, but the researchers did not differentiate between the two types of information.

An additional consideration is what kinds of events evoke flashbulb memories. They must be surprising and important. This may vary by proximity and relevance. Therefore, it is likely that more Americans have flashbulb memories for when and where they were when the levies broke in New Orleans, flooding the city during Hurricane Katrina, than they do for the Christmas tsunami that destroyed many areas in southeast Asia. Conversely, it is likely that more people from Indonesia and Thailand have flashbulb memories of the tsunami than they do of Hurricane Katrina. Consistent with this view, Conway et al. (1994) found high consistency across time in the flashbulb memories of British citizens of the sudden resignation of Prime Minister Margaret Thatcher. On the other hand, Danish and American participants showed much fewer flashbulb reports and much less consistency and more error in their memories of the event. More recently, Lanciano and Curci (2012) found that Catholics were more likely to have flashbulb memories concerning the death of Pope John Paul II than were non-Catholics. Catholics also have more flashbulb memories of the resignation of Pope Benedict XVI than do non-Catholics (Curci et al., 2015).

Another largely unresolved question is whether flashbulb memory for negative events differs from flashbulb memory for positive events in domains other than the valence of the emotion experienced. Some have argued that it is harder to create a flashbulb memory for a positive event than a negative event (Kraha, Talarico, & Boals, 2014). Kraha et al. found that very few Americans formed a flashbulb memory concerning the killing of Osama bin Laden, even though most Americans viewed this event as both important and positive. With respect to the differences between positive and negative events, an interesting study on flashbulb memories concerns that of sports fans. What is victory for one team is defeat for another. Thus, sports events allow one to examine the same event from the perspective of different fans. Kensinger and Schacter (2006) examined memories of baseball fans in New York and Boston for the surprise Game 7 victory of the Boston Red Sox over the New York Yankees in the American League Championship of 2004. This is an interesting study because the event was extremely positive for fans of the Boston team but very negative for the fans of the New York team. Thus, using the same event, Kensinger and Schacter were able to examine the effect of emotional valence (that is, positive or negative feelings about the event) on flashbulb memories. To ensure that the New York fans and Boston fans did not differ in other ways with respect to their memories, Kensinger and Schacter also tested their memory for a personal event and for their memory of the 2004 presidential debates, which had taken place during the same month as the baseball game. The fans of both teams did not differ with respect to their memories of the personal event and the presidential debate. However, when it came to the game, differences did emerge. For the New York fans, there was decidedly more consistency between an initial report and a later report than for the Boston fans. Ironically, the Boston fans showed considerable overconfidence in the accuracy of their memories, which the New York fans did not. While baseball may not be important to everyone, there are fans of both of these teams for whom baseball is everything, so these events may have been as critical to some participants as the other public events discussed here. Kensinger and Schacter suggested that their data support the idea that positive events lead to more distortion and overconfidence, whereas negative events lead to less overconfidence and more accuracy. In terms of flashbulb memories, it suggests that studies of assassinations, terrorist attacks, death of public leaders, and so forth may underestimate the inconsistency in flashbulb memories, as many of us may also have flashbulb memories of private and positive events (e.g., a marriage proposal or a college acceptance).

Theories of Flashbulb Memory Formation

Special Mechanism Approach

In this view, a unique and special mechanism is responsible for flashbulb memories only. Originally called the "now, print" mechanism by Brown and Kulik (1977), it stipulates that flashbulb memories are virtually literal representations of the what, how, and where of the original event. When an event of great emotional impact and importance occurs, the system immediately encodes in real time with great detail and vividness. The implication of this model is that flashbulb memories will be subjectively strong. As we have seen, this is true. But the other implication of the model is that flashbulb memories will be accurate. The majority of the research supports the idea that errors do enter our flashbulb memories and these memories are not always veridical (but see Lanciano & Curci, 2012, for a new look at this hypothesis).

Figure 7.6 Flashbulb memories. Flashbulb memories are no more accurate than ordinary memories. However, our confidence in them is much greater

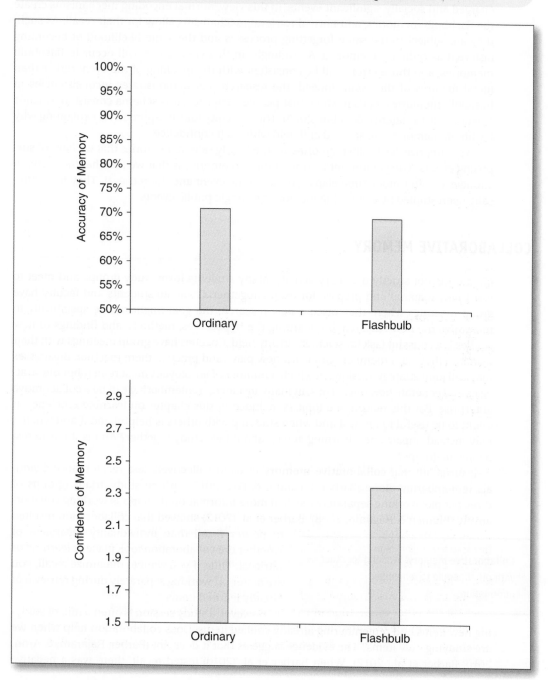

Ordinary Mechanism Approach

This view claims that flashbulb memories are simply normal memories but of emotionally charged and socially significant events. In this view, normal encoding mechanisms create the flashbulb memories, and normal retrieval mechanisms allow for their recall. As such, they are subject to the same forgetting processes and the same likelihood of becoming distorted as ordinary memories. Accordingly, in this view, errors will occur in flashbulb memories, and those errors will be consistent with the meaning of the event rather than literal features of the event. Indeed, the research that demonstrates inconsistencies in flashbulb memories tends to show that people's later recall is schema consistent (Kızılöz & Tekcan, 2013; Talarico & Rubin, 2003). The difficulty for this approach is explaining why flashbulb memories are so vivid and held with such confidence.

To summarize, flashbulb memories are the highly salient memories that we have of surprising events. The paramount feature of these memories is that we feel that they remain strong even after much time elapses between the event and the retrieval. They have typically been studied by examining memories of tragic public events.

COLLABORATIVE MEMORY

Memory is not strictly a solitary activity. Many students form study groups and meet to learn new material and prepare for exams together. Graduate students and faculty have group meetings where they discuss new research; the goal might not be specifically to memorize the new research, but learning the hypotheses, methods, and findings of new studies is a constant task for scientists in any field. Coaches have group meetings with their teams so that team members can learn new plays and practice them together. Businesses may call joint strategy sessions in which a number of employees must remember old strategies and generate new ones. Thus, in many instances, remembering can be a collaborative enterprise. For this reason, the topic is included in this chapter on learning efficiency. It ought to be useful to know if and when studying with others is helpful and if and when it may instead impair one's learning ability. Should we study together? And is it fair to test people in groups?

It turns out that **collaborative memory** leads to collectively less recall than individuals remembering alone (Barber, Rajaram, & Fox, 2012). In one study, triads (groups of three people) working separately recalled more information than triads working collaboratively (Blumen & Rajaram, 2008). Barber et al. (2012) showed that collaboration resulted in poorer recall than individuality regardless of whether the collaboration took place at learning or retrieval. Thus, if you want to maximize recall, you are better off working separately during retrieval of already learned items.

Collaborative memory: Working together with other people to remember information.

However, a study session is often a mix of studying new items and remembering already studied items. Does collaboration help when we are studying new items? The evidence suggests that it does not (Barber, Rajaram, & Aron, 2010; Barber et al., 2012). When Barber et al. (2010) tested recall, there was a negative effect of collaborative study relative to individual study. Barber et al. (2012) also showed that individual study led to better recall later. Thus, the tentative evidence suggests that one is better off studying alone than in a group.

SECTION SUMMARY AND QUIZ

Childhood amnesia refers to the observation that adults remember little to nothing from birth to about age four. A number of theories have been advanced to account for amnesia for early childhood. Flashbulb memory refers to our vivid personal recollection of surprising and emotional public and private events. In general, people have a great level of confidence in their flashbulb memories, but the memories are no more or less accurate than memories of ordinary events. Collaborative memory occurs when people are working together with other people to remember information.

Section Quiz

1. Childhood amnesia refers to
   a. The poor episodic retrieval of young children
   b. The inability of children to accurately predict the future based on past events
   c. The poor ability of adults to remember autobiographical events from their early childhood
   d. All of the above are false

2. In an experiment by Simcock and Haynes, children were shown a "magic shrinking box." The research found that
   a. The younger children remembered nothing of an event that took place a year earlier
   b. The younger children remembered more of the event because it was more meaningful to them
   c. Young children only remembered a year later objects about which they had a vocabulary term for the previous year
   d. Even the youngest children had already entered the period of childhood amnesia

3. The general finding in research on flashbulb memories is that
   a. Confidence remains very high in the accuracy of one's flashbulb memories
   b. Flashbulb memories are more likely to occur for negative events than positive events
   c. The accuracy of the memories is higher for personal context than it is for the public aspects of the event
   d. All of the above are true

4. In a study on people's memory of the baseball American league championships, it was found that
   a. Fans of the losing team remembered the event with less overconfidence
   b. Fans of the losing team showed strong evidence of conscious repression of the event
   c. There were no differences between the memories of fans of the winning and losing teams
   d. The game was misreported—the Yankees won after all

1. c
2. c
3. d
4. a

DIARY STUDIES AND AUTOBIOGRAPHICAL MEMORY

Go into a bookstore or a stationery store, and you can find dozens of different kinds of notebook diaries. Some have austere black binders, whereas others have kittens, hearts, or superheroes on them. You can usually find more notebook diaries in a typical Barnes and Noble bookstore than you can find books about science. This suggests that, at one time or another, many people keep diaries, which essentially are written-down memories and records of their life. Some people use the diaries to schedule their days, whereas others choose to write down their feelings. In memory research, we can use diaries to keep a near-veridical record of a person's life so that we can test his or her autobiographical memory later.

Diaries provide a written record by which memories can be compared. As such, diaries are extremely useful tools in the study of autobiographical memory. A memory diary is a bit different from the diary in which you record your feelings. In a memory diary, the participant must record facts, events, and perhaps numerical ratings of feelings. An entry in the diary will include information about the what, where, when, and who of an event. This record is then turned in to an experimenter, who can later devise questions based on each record for the participant to answer.

For example, on a particular day, let's say September 19, 2016, the participant will have to record one event from that day. Here's what the entry might look like:

Date: September 19, 2016

What: Had a tire with a leak. I went the gas station and put air in the tire after dropping my daughter at school.

Where: In the car, near home.

When: In the morning, after taking my daughter to school.

Who: After filling my own tires, I helped a woman fill her car's tires with air, as she was dressed in fancy work clothes and did not want to get dirty.

Pleasantness: Mildly unpleasant.

Emotion: Low; just a tire low on air.

Importance: Minor.

In some **diary studies** aimed at autobiographical memory, the experimenters themselves recorded events from their own lives and kept track of events over long periods of time. In one study, a researcher went back and tested his memory 20 years after the original events (White, 2002). Other studies ask volunteers to keep diaries. These studies, typically with student populations, tend to be of shorter duration (e.g., five months), because of the difficulty of contacting people after a longer period of time (Larsen &

> **Diary studies:** The experimenters or participants record events from their own lives to keep track of events over long periods of time. Later, their memory for these events can be tested.

Thompson, 1995; Thomsen, Olesen, Schnieber, Jensen, & Tønnesvang, 2012). However, Thomsen et al. (2015) had people retrieve memories from diaries made 3.5 years earlier. Diary studies have the advantage of measuring memory for events that really happened in a person's life and that are recorded that day in a veridical format.

In one landmark diary study, Willem Wagenaar, a Dutch psychologist, recorded over 2,400 events over the course of six years (Wagenaar, 1986). Each event was recorded in terms of four major features: what happened, where it happened, when it happened, and who was present. In addition, each memory was coded in terms of pleasantness, emotion, and importance. After each entry was made, it was turned over to a colleague who did not allow Wagenaar to see the entry during the "retention interval." Six years later, Wagenaar's colleague used different features of this record as cues for recalling the memory. For example, if "what" was the cue, his colleague would present him with "saw the famous painting *The Scream,*" and Wagenaar would attempt to remember with whom he went to the art museum, when he made the visit, and in this case, where the art museum was. If one cue was not sufficient to trigger recall, the experimenter gave him additional cues. For other items, Wagenaar's colleague would tell him where an event occurred, and Wagenaar would start with that as the cue to remember the event. For yet other items, the "who" was used, and for other items, the "when" was used as the cue.

Wagenaar found that he could, given enough cues, recall 80% of the events he had recorded. However, in some cases, it took him multiple cues to do so. And not all cues were equally successful at prompting the memory of the event. "What," "where," and "who" were all equally good cues to retrieving an event, but "when" was much worse than the other three classes of cues. In addition, highly emotional and pleasant events were remembered better than less emotional and less pleasant events.

One problem with this diary study (and others that followed) is that it tested only one person's memory. In particular, this study examined the memory of a professional memory researcher. Although being a memory researcher does not immediately imply that the person has an exceptional memory, it is likely that a deep interest in the processes of memory might affect the keeping of a memory diary. However, most of the results seem to hold up when non-specialists are asked to keep diaries (Burt, Kemp, & Conway, 2001; Larsen & Thompson, 1995). In these studies, the researchers recruited college undergraduates to keep memory diaries, and the college students' abilities to recall events differed little from those of Professor Wagenaar. The astonishing observation from these studies is that people can recall so many of the events.

Thomsen et al. (2012) asked first-year college students to keep structured diaries over the first semester of their first year at college. They recorded two events per day, about which they were later tested. Thomsen et al. addressed one aspect of Conway's (2005) model of autobiographical memory, the importance of lifetime periods. Memories that were scored as relevant to the person's "life story" were recalled better than those that were not. Thus, both the retrieval cue and the meaning of the memory are critical in the retrieval of real-world autobiographical memories. When these students reached the end of their college experience, Thomsen et al. (2015) contacted a set of the students who had initially kept diaries. Again, there was a correlation between what was remembered and whether those events were consistent with the life. Moreover, like Wagenaar's (1986) study, participants remembered about 60% of the events that had occurred 3.5 years earlier.

One of the themes of this text is to emphasize the many ways in which we can improve our own memory abilities. From this perspective, diaries are useful memory devices. They do not help us learn material for school, but they do provide powerful cues to help us retrieve events from our lives. Without them, we are left to the whims of the retrieval cues we can generate or are present around us. Thus, for people who value their own autobiographical memories, diaries can be useful memory aids. Many people complain that they can no longer remember vacations, fancy dinners, and the like. Keeping a memory diary in which one records the what, where, and who of such an event provides strong retrieval cues to unlock the memory of that event. For example, if someone is trying to remember who was at your 20th birthday party and asks you (after all, it was your party), you might be hard-pressed to remember all the people there. But you can check your diary. In today's world, this might also be accomplished online by keeping a memory blog.

MNEMONIC IMPROVEMENT TIP 7.1

Keep a memory diary or memory blog. Maintaining such a record allows you to later return to it and cue your memory. The diary itself serves as an external memory aid, storing the events of your life. But more significantly, the memory diary triggers your own episodic memory of particular events.

THE CUE-WORD TECHNIQUE FOR ELICITING AUTOBIOGRAPHICAL MEMORIES AND THE REMINISCENCE BUMP

The **cue-word technique** is a common tool for investigating autobiographical memory. An ordinary word is provided to participants, and they are asked to provide an autobiographical memory that the word elicits. As noted above, the cue-word technique has been used, by directing the participant to report memories from early life, to explore childhood amnesia. But the person can also be free to choose memories from any point in his life. Consider the following words and the memories that they elicit for you:

Cue-word technique: An ordinary word is provided to participants, and they are asked to provide the first memory that the word elicits.

- bird

- whisper

- wrinkle

- lazy

- saddle

Chances are that each word quickly elicited an event from your life. Perhaps you thought about the time you fed the pigeons at a park with your partner or the time a crazy swan attacked you. Perhaps you remember whispering to your friend about a party during memory class last week. In some cases, the memories may be strong and painful, such as the time you slid out of your saddle and broke your leg. Some may be important, but others may be unimportant, such as the memory of discovering that the dry cleaner had failed to get a spot out of your shirt. Most memories are relatively recent, like the recent evening when you felt lazy and ordered out for food instead of cooking yourself. Most people can report events pretty quickly after being given a cue word, although occasionally a particular word will fail to elicit any memory at all.

When this cue-word technique is used on older people, an interesting phenomenon occurs. The memories that people describe are not evenly spaced over their lifetime (see Figure 7.7). First, there is the period of childhood amnesia from which no events are reported. Then reported memories increase through later childhood. Reported memories peak between ages 16 and 25. There is then a decline, and memories after 25 are not as likely to be retrieved in response to cues as those before 25. Finally, there is a recency effect, reflecting a preponderance of memories that are recalled from the past two years or so. The **reminiscence bump** refers to a spike in recalled memories from late adolescence to early adulthood.

In some studies, participants are given sets of cues relating to specific topics, such as words that are only about music, films, book, or public events. The reminiscence bump is found for the retrieval of personal events from one's individual life and public events, such as those discussed in the section on flashbulb memories (Koppel & Bernsten, 2016). Regardless of the type of stimuli, a robust reminiscence effect is still seen (see Conway, 2005). The effect is also robust across cultures. Despite the differences among American, British, Chinese, Bangladeshi, and Japanese cultures all show reminiscence bumps in the same age range (Conway, Wang, Hanyu, & Haque, 2005).

There are several explanations for why the reminiscence bump occurs, although no single view is without problems. The views can be divided into memory-fluency views, neurological fluency views, and sociocultural views. Let's consider each in turn.

Reminiscence bump: The spike in recalled memories corresponding to late adolescence to early adulthood or roughly the ages of 16 to 25.

Memory-Fluency

This view is based on the idea that the time between ages 16 and 25 is a period with many "first experiences"—that is, events that are unique and novel. Many studies show that

Figure 7.7 The reminiscence bump. Percent of memories recalled as a function of how old the person was when he or she experienced the events. In older adults, both a recency effect and a reminiscence bump are seen. *Y*-axis represents the percent of memories recalled.

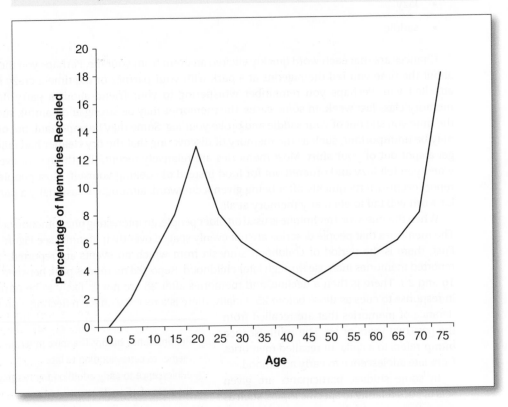

unique and novel events tend to be better remembered. These include but are not limited to first romantic encounters, first jobs, the first time away from home, and the first day of college. In this view, these years are a time of rapid change, which render the events that take place during this period highly memorable (Conway, 2005). In support of this view, Dickson, Pillemer, and Bruehl (2011) found a reminiscence bump for events that were surprising and therefore not part of the person's lifetime period or cultural scripts as well as for positive and script-relevant events. Moreover, Koppel and Bernsten (2016) showed that there is a reminiscence bump for public events, such as the elections of presidents, sports events, and celebrity scandals. In response to cues, people will come up with more public events that correspond to the 16- to 25-year-old period of life, though Koppel and Bernsten find that most of the public events were from the older side of the age bracket. The problem with the fluency view is that we find it in cultures where many of these events typically happen on the earlier side of the 16- to 25-year age range regardless of whether there are big changes in place of residency and occupation. Moreover, the reasoning itself is a bit circular. We already know from the data that memory during this time period is more accessible. Accounting for that by arguing that memories from this time are more memorable is just deferring an explanation.

Neurological Views

This view centers on the idea that young adults have the most efficient encoding system based on optimal maturation of the brain mechanisms of memory before the inevitable decline in memory abilities associated with age. Conway (2005) speculated that the 16- to 25-year age range represents the maximal maturity of the fronto-hippocampal circuitry, which maximally encodes information. Conway also pointed out that this view is supported by the cultural universality of the phenomenon. We all have the same brains, even if different cultures emphasize different time courses for dating, sex, and marriage on one hand and learning an occupation on the other.

Sociocultural Views

In this view, the 16- to 25-year age range is associated with changes in identity formation of the individual. The particular decisions people make about who they are as individuals may vary from culture to culture, but the time period of these decisions is the same. The fluency, therefore, espoused in the first view is merely a symptom of the changes occurring in a person's life. This view suggests that the reminiscence bump should consist of many memories that are consistent with a culture's particular set of transitions. Indeed, this turns out to be the case. Thomsen and Berntsen (2008) found that, among Danish elders, the bump was particularly noticeable for the memory of events that were consistent with cultural life scripts, such as first jobs, dating, and leaving home, whereas it was less noticeable for less socially marked memories, such as travel, memorable meals, or political events. The older adults showed a bigger reminiscence bump for their memories of culturally consistent events than for their memories of culturally inconsistent events. Thomsen and Berntsen argued that these scripts themselves, culturally defined, provide the set of cues to rehearsal and experience, forming the bulwark of autobiographical memory. One culture may emphasize educational landmarks and another culture may emphasize family milestones, but for both, life scripts emphasize the importance of young adulthood. In keeping with this view, Zaragoza Scherman, Salgado, Shao, and Bernsten (2015) found that there was a reminiscence bump across several cultures, including Chinese, Danish, Greenlandic, and Mexican. All showed similar patterns of age distributions, though the content of positive and negative memories varied by culture.

To summarize, the reminiscence bump refers to the large number of memories from late adolescence to early adulthood remembered by adults (40 +) when they are given cue words and asked to remember events from any point in their lives. Scholars have varied in their interpretation of this phenomenon, but its existence seems to be not limited to those from Western cultures (Berntsen & Rubin, 2004; Zaragoza, Scherman et al., 2015). The explanation for this phenomenon remains elusive, but the most recent theories focus on how events from this life period fit into a particular culture's view of how lives are defined.

ASPECTS OF AUTOBIOGRAPHICAL MEMORY

Field and Observer Memories

Recall an event from early childhood. Imagine the event in your mind. Write down what you are experiencing before you continue with this section. Did you have an image in your mind's eye (that is, activate a visual memory in working memory)? What do you see? Where are you in the memory? Are you seeing the event as if through your own eyes, or are you looking at the "memory" from another vantage point—that is, seeing yourself in the memory?

Many people report "observer memories" from early childhood (Nigro & Neisser, 1983). **Observer memories** are memories in which we take the vantage point of an outside observer and see ourselves as actors in our visual memory. In contrast, when reporting later childhood and more recent adult memories, most people describe "field memories." **Field memories** are autobiographical and visual memories in which we see the memory as if we were looking at the event through our own eyes.

Observer memories: Autobiographical memories in which we take the vantage point of an outside observer and see ourselves as actors in our visual memory.

Field memories: Autobiographical and visual memories in which we see the memory as if we were looking at the event through our own eyes.

It turns out that these points of view in memory are flexible. Once alerted to this difference, people can move back and forth between field and observer memories as they think about an event from the past (Robinson & Swanson, 1993). Initially, however, a larger proportion of memories from early childhood take the observer form than the field memory form. Interestingly, observer memories are also associated with less emotional content and reduced sensory vividness of the memory. When participants consciously shift from field to observer memories, their ratings of emotionality decrease relative to the original emotional rating for the field memory (Berntsen & Rubin, 2006).

The relation between field and observer memories is an important one. People suffering from posttraumatic stress disorder (PTSD) are often bothered by recurrent memories of the traumatic event that haunts them. McIsaac and Eich (2004) found that when patients suffering from PTSD retrieved memories as field memories, their emotional response was more negative and more intense. However, retrieving from an observer perspective lowered the negative emotional response. It is possible that switching to the observer perspective puts some emotional distance between one's sense of self and the memory. McIsaac and Eich argued that this is potentially useful in the treatment of PTSD. Training participants to recall their traumatic memories in observer mode will allow them to think about and cope with their past without that memory eliciting the full weight of its associated negative emotions.

Involuntary Memories

Even though you are on a date with your new girlfriend or boyfriend, you hear a song on the radio that reminds you of your old flame. You try to push it out of your mind because you want to be in the moment with the new person. Mace, Bernas, and Clevinger (2015) asked participants to keep memory diaries, in which people were asked to record instances of involuntary memories. When participants were later given cues to remember their involuntary memories, more concrete cues were better at re-prompting those memories than more abstract cues, consistent with the experience of people who are reminded of something from their past by an everyday cue. Involuntary memories can also be a problem for many, as negative involuntary memories are a major source of distress in PTSD. For example, a soldier returning from war may want very much to not be reminded of his or her war experiences. However, environmental cues may still trigger an unpleasant and involuntary memory. We all experience involuntary memories, but only in PTSD do we get overwhelmed by them. In addition to involuntary memories, people may also have involuntary thoughts about what is going to happen in the future, which luckily tend to be more about positive events than negative ones (Finnbogadóttir & Berntsen, 2013). Studying involuntary memory is a bit more difficult because researchers cannot give direct cues—as they would lead to voluntary memories. But researchers increasingly are coming up with effective ways of examining this issue.

Berntsen, Staugaard, and Sörensen (2012) were interested in the underlying mechanisms of involuntary memory. To investigate this issue, participants were asked to engage in a sound-location task that involved determining whether two sounds were being played to the same ear or one to each ear. During this task, participants were also expected to note any involuntary memories. Some of the sounds had been played earlier in the experiment, whereas others were novel. Berntsen et al. found that novel sounds were more likely to elicit involuntary memories. They argued that this likely occurred because the novel sounds were harder to localize and thus required more attention. As more attention was directed to this task, the participants had less cognitive control, resulting in more involuntary memories. In another condition, in which participants were required to retrieve specific memories, this did not occur. Thus, interestingly, when our attention is focused elsewhere, we are more likely to find ourselves having involuntary memories.

Disputed Memories

Does our autobiographical memory only come from our own life? Consider the following anecdote. Joe relates that he had a clear memory of being bitten by a mean dog that lived in the house behind his when he was a child. Yet Joe's parents claim that it was his older brother who was actually bitten by this dog when Joe was about six and his brother was about eight. Somewhere along the line, Joe misattributed his memory of having seen and later heard about his brother's injury as his own. The older brother has the scar to prove that the bite was really on his hand, not Joe's. Joe's recollection is what is known as a **disputed memory**.

> **Disputed memories:** When we feel a memory is our own when it actually corresponds to an event in another's past.

It turns out that "disputed memories" are more common among twins than among others. Only 8% of siblings have memories such as the one I described above, but the percentage rises to about 70% among twins (Sheen, Kemp, & Rubin, 2001). Among identical twins, the percentages are even higher (Küntay, Gülgöz, & Tekcan, 2004). Like the memory above, for twins, these borrowed events tend to come from early in childhood.

Music and Autobiographical Memory

A common experience for most people is hearing an old song on the radio that elicits a memory, perhaps of dancing with your date at the prom or "your song" with an old boyfriend or girlfriend. The song seems to transport us back in time, and we relive the happy moment. This issue was investigated experimentally by Janata et al. (2007). They collected a large selection of music from the popular literature by downloading songs from the iTunes top 100 songs from the previous few years. They then played 30-second excerpts from these songs to students and asked the students to report any autobiographical memories cued by each song. More than 30% of the songs elicited autobiographical memories from the participants. Most of these memories were emotional memories, with a majority being positive in affect. The researchers found that most memories were of event-specific memories, but some songs elicited general events or lifetime periods. Many of the songs also elicited feelings of nostalgia (a longing for an earlier, better time). This study confirms the idea that music, particularly popular songs, can be a powerful retrieval cue for autobiographical memories.

Sense of Smell and Autobiographical Memory

The writer Marcel Proust wrote several famous novels that describe how one's memory affects one's sense of self. In one of his most vivid and well-known passages, the main character (named Marcel) describes how the smell and taste of a small French pastry called a madeleine evokes a memory of his peaceful childhood (Proust, 1928). This description captures the strong connections between odor and memory. Indeed, as we discussed in Chapter 2, odors can be powerful cues to retrieve events from our lives. On a neural level, the strong connections between the olfactory bulb and the limbic system may drive this phenomenon. (For Proust's description of this experience, go to study.sagepub.com/schwartz3e.[5])

Take a moment and visit your spice cabinet. Pick a jar at random and don't look at the name on the jar or at the contents. Just open it and hold it under your nose. Does it elicit a memory? From what time period in your life? Does it bring back any emotions? If the first jar you select does not work, try another one. Sooner or later as you go through a well-stocked spice shelf, you, like Proust, may be transported back to your grandmother's kitchen and have a powerful emotional memory in the process. Hopefully, at any rate, you will be transported back to your grandmother's kitchen and not, say, to your elementary school cafeteria, with probably less warm and emotionally satisfying feelings. Let's turn now to the empirical studies done on this topic.

This strong sense of longing for the past that is often elicited by odors is called nostalgia. Nostalgia is the longing for the past as well as its recollection. Reid, Green, Wildschut, and Sedikides (2015) examined this experience of nostalgia after participants sniffed a variety of odors. Reid et al. found that odors frequently invoked this sense of nostalgia and that such odor-induced nostalgia was correlated with a sense of well-being, positive emotion, and optimism. Thus, similar to Proust's experience, that of everyday people is also one of being uplifted by the recollections of the past that occur when experiencing an odor.

Willander and Larsson (2007) conducted a fascinating study on the role odors play in autobiographical memory, finding that odors can create powerful memory effects. They tested three conditions. In one condition, they presented odors alone and asked participants to report the first autobiographical memory that they experienced. In the second condition, they presented the names of the odors (as words) without the smell accompanying them. In the third condition, they presented the names of the odors and the actual odors. As expected, the name-only condition produced the fewest and the least emotional autobiographical memories. However, the odor-alone condition actually produced more, older, and more emotional autobiographical memories than did the odor-and-name condition. Not only did odors elicit more autobiographical memories than the odor names did, but including the names along with the odors actually interfered with the retrieval of memories.

Odors also seem to create different patterns in autobiographical memories than do cue words. As discussed earlier, the cue-word technique produces the reminiscence bump, the characteristic increase in memories for late childhood to early adulthood. Presenting odors, however, has a different effect on memory. Willander and Larsson (2006) found that presenting odors and asking for the first memory that came to mind produced mostly memories from earlier in childhood, with most of the memories clustering before the age of 10. In another study, Herz (2004) showed that autobiographical memories produced by odor cues were given higher emotion ratings than were autobiographical memories elicited by either visual cues or auditory cues. Interestingly, these effects are typically bigger in women than in men; Zucco, Aiello, Turuani, and Koster (2012) found that odors were more likely to elicit autobiographical memories in women than in men. Thus, the bottom line is this: It is true—odors elicit old and emotional memories.

THE NEUROSCIENCE OF AUTOBIOGRAPHICAL MEMORY

Autobiographical memory is a complex process. Imagine, for example, you are a participant in an autobiographical memory study. Even though you have been given specific instructions to retrieve the first event that comes to mind given a particular cue, most of us might edit even this. Suppose the cue word is *school,* and what comes to mind is sneaking out to smoke marijuana in the schoolyard with your friends while in high school. It is likely that (a) you may think this is not a good memory to have in response to the word *school* and (b) you may not want to share this memory with an authoritative stranger—that is, the researcher. So you may quickly shift your memory to a more socially acceptable memory of, say, attending a school assembly. In Chapter 4, we discussed the importance of inhibition in memory. In this example, the socially undesirable memory is inhibited, and a more socially acceptable memory is retrieved and described. Therefore, we should expect to see the neural correlates of autobiographical memory to be complex as well, as the unacceptable memory is retrieved, then not reported, and a new memory is generated. Indeed, during the course of retrieving an autobiographical memory, many areas of the brain become active. As a consequence, neuroscientists have become interested in not only which areas are active but the sequence of activity in the brain as an autobiographical memory is being recalled.

For example, Donna Addis and her colleagues (Addis, Knapp, Roberts, & Schacter, 2012) conducted a study in which they examined the relation between regions within the brain and retrieval of autobiographical events (see also Conway, Pleydell-Pearce, Whitecross, & Sharpe, 2003). Think about an event that happened recently to you, such as visiting the zoo. What areas of the brain become active as you contemplate your memory of the trip? This is what Addis and her colleagues were interested in.

Addis et al. (2012) studied this phenomenon by asking people to remember particular events while imaging equipment was monitoring their brains. More specifically, the participants thought of the first personal memory that a particular word evoked. The cue word was provided to the participants by the researchers. Thus, in response to the word *rock,* an individual might remember his recent visit to the local rock-climbing gym and his satisfaction at completing a particularly difficult route. In response to the word *church,* a participant might remember her sister's wedding ceremony and how beautiful the church looked that day. Using a neuroimaging technique called fMRI (functional magnetic resonance imagery), Addis et al. followed the path of memory retrieval as it played out in the brain.

Addis et al. (2012) found that immediately after the presentation of the word, areas in the prefrontal cortex (the very front of the brain, just under your forehead) became active. This has been interpreted to indicate that the brain is going into "retrieval mode." At just about the point people indicated that they "had the memory," areas in the occipital lobe (in the back of the brain, associated with vision) became active (Conway et al., 2003). The visual imagery associated with a particular memory becomes apparent on the brain scans. At the same time, areas in the hippocampus (associated with memory encoding and retrieval) also became active. Thus, Addis et al. were able to map out in both time and space the pattern of retrieval in the brain and correlate it with how people remember autobiographical events. In their view, the left hippocampus is particularly involved in generating the memory, whereas the medial prefrontal region is involved in starting the search and then screening out inappropriate answers. In another fMRI study, Kalenzaga et al. (2015) came to similar conclusions.

In another study using fMRI, Daselaar et al. (2008) used a standard cue-word technique in which participants heard a word and were asked to think of the first autobiographical memory that came to mind. They pressed a button when they felt that they had the memory in mind. Exactly 24 seconds after the participants heard the word, they were asked to rate the emotion that went along with the memory and the extent to which they felt they were "reliving" the memory as they recalled it. During retrieval, the participants' brains were monitored via fMRI (see Figure 7.8).

Daselaar et al. (2008) started tracking at the time when the cue word was presented. By 1.5 seconds after presentation of the word, there was activity in three known memory areas of the brain: the medial temporal lobe, the hippocampus, and right prefrontal cortex, as was the case in the Addis, Knapp, et al. (2012) experiment in the general cue condition. The right prefrontal cortex is associated with going into "retrieval mode"—that is, initiating the memory search. The hippocampus and the medial temporal lobe are associated with activating the memory itself. This initial activity was brief. By about three seconds after the presentation of the word, activity in all of these areas was decreasing.

At three seconds after the cue word, Daselaar et al. (2008) found that activity in the occipital cortex (visual cortex) and the left prefrontal cortex starts occurring, and this activity increases until about 12 seconds before leveling off. The occipital cortex is associated with the visual imagery that usually accompanies autobiographical memories, and the left prefrontal activity is probably related to verbal aspects of the memory, including

Figure 7.8 Brain regions active during autobiographical memory retrieval.

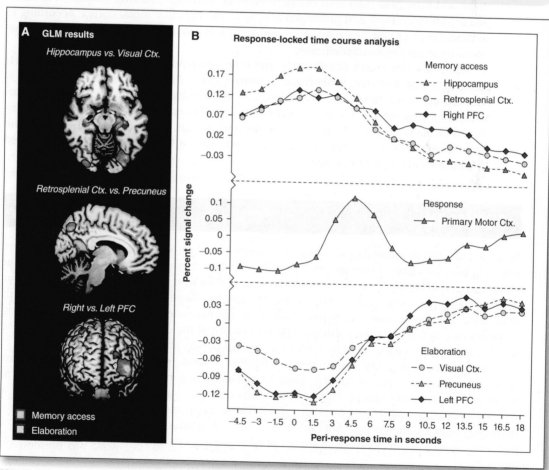

SOURCE: Daselaar et al. (2008).

any elaboration or interpretation of the memory. The activity in this area remains high as long as the person is still thinking about the memory.

What about the neural correlates of emotion? Those memories that were given high judgments of emotionality were correlated with greater activity in the hippocampus and the amygdala in the limbic system. Both of these areas were active early on, even before the person indicated that he had retrieved the memory. Thus, it is likely that the feeling of emotion associated with the memory occurs before the memory itself is experienced. An area in the prefrontal lobe, called the frontopolar cortex, was also more activated in high-emotion memories than in low-emotion memories.

The neural correlates of "reliving" the memory were seen later in the time course of remembering. Starting around 12 seconds after presentation of the cue, memories with strong "reliving" scores showed greater activity in the visual cortex, especially areas in the occipital lobe next to areas involved in primary visual processing. In addition to showing increased activity in the visual cortex, memories with high "reliving" scores were correlated with heightened and prolonged activity in the right prefrontal cortex. According to Daselaar et al. (2008), this right prefrontal activity is probably correlated with attentional focus on these particular memories.

Thus, Daselaar et al.'s (2008) study and others (see Addis, Roberts, & Schacter, 2011; Conway, Pleydell-Pearce, Whitecross, & Sharpe, 2003; Kalenzaga et al., 2015; Rabin & Rosenbaum, 2012, for similar studies with similar results) show the complexity of autobiographical memory. They also show the detailed relation of memory areas with memory function. Many areas of the brain are active, and there is a flow of information from the front of the brain to the back of the brain and then, at least for emotional and relived memories, back to the front again.

SUMMARY

As adults, we tend to remember our earliest memories in observer mode—that is, as if we were watching ourselves from a vantage point outside ourselves. Memories of our adult life and later childhood tend to be remembered as field memories, as if we were watching the event through our own eyes. Memories, especially among twins, can also be "disputed." A number of studies with twins show that many falsely "remember" an event that happened to their sibling as happening to themselves. In diary studies, participants keep a record of the events of their lives. Later, these diaries can be used as a source of material to query that person about his or her personal past.

Autobiographical memory is examined in a number of ways. In one well-used technique, participants are given ordinary words (e.g., *cupcake*) and asked to generate the first autobiographical memory that they can think of. Studies with adults older than age 35 reveal a pattern called a reminiscence bump. Memories from late childhood to early adulthood are remembered more frequently than are memories from earlier in childhood or later in adulthood. Early adulthood memories show a bump in almost all studies of adult populations. Recent memories are also well remembered.

Finally, neuroscientific study of autobiographical memory is becoming possible. Recent fMRI studies of autobiographical memory show that early in retrieval, areas in the hippocampus and right prefrontal cortex are active. As we retrieve the memory, activity spreads to the visual areas of the brain and left prefrontal cortex.

Section Quiz

1. In Wagenaar's (1986) diary study of memory, he found that
   a. He remembered less than 10% of the events that he had recorded
   b. Using "when" cues was less effective than "what," "where," and "who" cues
   c. Many of his participants discontinued use of their diaries
   d. His own memory differed greatly than those tested in Thomsen et al. (2012) study

2. Which of the following statements about the reminiscence bump is true?
   a. It seems to occur in all cultures.
   b. When given cues, participants retrieve more events from early adulthood and late adolescence than they do from other time periods, except the very recent past.
   c. When looking at a curve of the reminiscence bump effect, one can detect the childhood amnesia phenomenon as well.
   d. All of the above statements are true

3. In a study by Reid et al. (2015), the experimenters looked at the nostalgia that occurs when
   a. The participant is smelling various odors
   b. The brain of the participant is being stimulated by TMS
   c. The participant is watching old films
   d. The participant is listening to music that corresponds to the music listened to when the person was in early adulthood

4. Which brain regions are associated with autobiographical memory?
   a. The hippocampus and medial prefrontal regions
   b. The pulvinar and the M5 region of the occipital lobe
   c. The limbic system and the brain stem
   d. The distal posterior frontal lobe and the temporal lobe pole

1. b
2. d
3. a
4. a

KEY TERMS

childhood amnesia

childhood amnesia—age-
   related changes in
   self-concept

childhood amnesia—influence
   of language on memory
   development

childhood amnesia—
   multiple-factor theory

childhood amnesia—
   neurological transitions in
   memory systems

childhood amnesia—
   psychodynamic view

coherence

collaborative memory

correspondence

cue-word technique

diary studies

disputed memories

event-specific memories

field memories

flashbulb memories

general events

lifetime periods

nostaglia

observer memories

reminiscence bump

working self

REVIEW QUESTIONS

1. What are the three levels of Conway's theory of autobiographical memory representation? How do the levels interact?

2. What does Conway mean by an extended event? How does it differ from an episodic memory?

3. What is childhood amnesia? What are the four explanations for it? Which explanation works best?

4. What is a flashbulb memory? How do these memories differ from ordinary memories? How are they similar to ordinary memories?

5. Why does keeping a diary help you remember important events from your life?

6. What is the cue-word technique? How can it be used to study autobiographical memory?

7. What is the reminiscence bump? What three explanations have been put forward to explain it?

8. What is the difference between a field memory and an observer memory?

9. What are involuntary memories? What factors increase their retrieval?

10. What area of the brain is associated with visual imagery in autobiographical memory? What area of the brain is associated with emotion in autobiographical memory?

ONLINE RESOURCES

1. For more thoughts on memories of 9/11, go to http://scienceblogs.com/cognitivedaily/2005/04/18/is-memory-better-for-shocking/.

2. You can hear Dr. Conway talk about his research at http://www.bbc.co.uk/sn/tvradio/programmes/horizon/broadband/tx/memory/senses/.

3. For more on childhood amnesia, go to http://www.apa.org/science/about/psa/2008/03/wang.aspx.

4. For more information about the neuroimaging of flashbulb memories, go to http://affective brain.com/wp-content/uploads/2014/09/How-personal-experience-modulates-the-neural-circuitry-of-memories-of-September-11.pdf

5. For Proust's description of this experience, go to http://www.haverford.edu/psych/ddavis/p109g/proust.html.

Go to **study.sagepub.com/schwartz3e** for additional exercises and study resources. Select **Chapter 7, Autobiographical Memory** for chapter-specific resources.

CHAPTER 8

False Memory

Donald Thomson is a prominent memory researcher from Australia. He has been studying applications of memory research to eyewitness memory and legal proceedings for years. He worked with Endel Tulving for his dissertation at the University of Toronto and then returned to Australia to become a university professor in his homeland. He frequently testifies as an expert witness in many cases that have to do with eyewitness memory.

In 1975, when he was a young researcher, Dr. Thomson appeared on live television, discussing issues of eyewitness memory on a talk show. Also on the talk show was the chief of police of a major city in Australia. Dr. Thomson explained to the television audience how, in some cases, eyewitnesses can be mistaken in their identifications. Shortly after he returned home, police arrived at his door and brought him to the station for questioning. A rape victim had identified him as the culprit. After what must have been a terrifying evening for all involved, Thomson was released. After all, he had a foolproof alibi. At the time of the crime, he had been on live television and could not possibly have committed this terrible act. Subsequent questioning of the victim revealed that she had been watching the program that Dr. Thomson was appearing on just before the crime. Apparently, the woman had confused the face of the rapist with the face she was seeing at the same time or just prior on television—that is, Dr. Thomson. Dr. Thomson was released, but the real criminal was never brought to justice. This woman had been through a horrible ordeal, made worse by the strange memory error that led to the false accusation of an innocent man and may have allowed a guilty one to get away. (For more on this strange misidentification, go to study.sagepub.com/schwartz3e.[1])

In another case, the U.S. government deported a man named John Demjanjuk to Israel to stand trial for Nazi war crimes. The Israeli government accused Demjanjuk of being "Ivan the Terrible," a bloodthirsty Nazi executioner during World War II, personally responsible for perhaps hundreds of thousands of murders. Five Holocaust survivors came forward and swore that they remembered Demjanjuk's face from 40 years earlier and confirmed that he was "Ivan." Demjanjuk claimed to be innocent, but the Israeli court went with the compelling testimony of the survivors. Demjanjuk was convicted and sentenced to death for genocide and murder. However, shortly before his scheduled execution, the Russian government found documents that proved—without a shadow of doubt—that Demjanjuk was not "Ivan." The Israeli Supreme Court overturned the verdict and eventually allowed Demjanjuk to return to his home in the United States. How had this happened? Presumably, the witnesses were claiming in good faith that they recognized the criminal, yet this turned out to be another case of mistaken eyewitness identification (Loftus & Ketcham, 1991). Demjanjuk was subsequently deported to Germany and convicted of other crimes associated with his Nazi past. Though evidence wound up pointing him out as a war criminal, he was not the war criminal he had originally been accused of being.

In both cases, people who had been horribly violated by the worst of criminals came forward to identify their assailants. Despite their fundamental honesty and desire to do right, these witnesses identified the wrong person. How can people form these erroneous memories of what happened? And how do people come to believe that their memories are accurate when they are not? These are two of the topics of this chapter.

In the cases described above, real crimes were committed, and the victims involved remember them. Their problem was that they did not identify the correct person as the criminal. In other cases, entire fictional events are made up and then later remembered as if they were truth. Consider the strange phenomenon involved in the memory of alien induction, studied by Susan Clancy and explored in her 2005 book. Clancy described the memories of abductees, whom she thinks of as normal people who come to believe that their memories of being taken aboard alien spaceships are actually true.

Abductees are people who believe they have been kidnapped by aliens from outer space. Abductees tell similar stories about being removed from their beds in the middle of the night, taken to a spaceship, and then experimented on. The experiments usually involve sexual abuse. Clancy chose to study abductees because she thought that there would be general agreement in the scientific community that their memories are false. And thus, these abductees could be used as a model of false memory in general. Indeed, Clancy (2005) reported that these abductees had similar psychological profiles as normal controls and that they did not have a higher rate of psychiatric illness than did a control population. Yet abductees insisted that their memories were true. Thus, Clancy investigated how these false memories were formed and what allowed otherwise normal people to believe them.

Clancy (2005) inferred that the false memories arise when people with vivid visual imaginations who believe in alien visits experience sleep paralysis. Sleep paralysis occurs when the brain emerges from REM sleep but the body is still paralyzed—this happens in all of us so we do not act out our dreams. During sleep paralysis, the mind is conscious but dream imagery may persist, lending a very real-world sensation to the dreams. This experience can be very distressing for some people. However, either on their own or with the help of therapy, many of the abductees come to believe that these sleep-paralysis dreams were not dreams but reality, and thus they come to really believe that they were abducted by aliens. For Clancy's research, the abductees constituted a sample of individuals who had come to believe their strong false memories. Indeed, in a battery of tests assessing false memory, Clancy found her abductees were more likely to show memory illusions, some of which will be described shortly. Thus, individual differences in susceptibility to false memories exist, and the abductees fell on the extreme of this scale. (For the transcript of an interview with Dr. Clancy, go to study.sagepub.com/schwartz3e.[2])

False memories are memories that do not correspond to events as they actually happened. First, to be a false memory, it has to be something that feels like a memory—that is, a person has a recollective experience of an event that took place in the past. Lies

False memories: Memories that people have that do not correspond to events as they actually happened.

Correspondence: A match between a retrieved memory and an actual event from the past.

and made-up stories do not count as false memories. Secondly, to be a false memory, the memory must deviate from the event as it actually occurred. **Correspondence** is an important part of the definition. A true memory is one in which the recollective experience corresponds to an event that actually occurred in the past, whereas a false memory is one in which the recollective experience does not correspond to an actual event.

Historically, the study of false memories has come in two waves. In the 1970s, a memory scientist then at the University of Washington named Elizabeth Loftus introduced a paradigm known as the "misinformation effect" into the memory literature (see Figure 8.1). This effect refers to false memories created by post event misinformation. Participants witness an event and then later receive false information about what occurred during that event. If they later remember the false information, a "misinformation" effect is said to have occurred. Loftus used these data to demonstrate the unreliability of eyewitness memory, and indeed, throughout her career, Loftus has emphasized the role that memory science has played in the field of eyewitness testimony.

In the 1990s, memory scientists turned their attention to another battle being waged in the courtrooms, clinics, and newspapers of the time: the reality of recovered memories of repressed childhood abuse. On one side were people claiming that they had "recovered" memories of abuse after having forgotten for many years. On the other side were people claiming that the recovered memories were false and were a function of leading and misleading therapeutic techniques. Elizabeth Loftus took up the cause of those who thought recovered memories were false memories and was soon developing experimental methodologies to study the issue. This battle raged through much of the 1990s, although a middle ground based on solid science was eventually recognized (Belli, 2012).

The plan for this chapter is first to provide some basic background memory science on the issue of false memory. Then we will look at the issue of how false memories are formed and contrast this with how repressed memories are recovered. We will also outline how false or distorted memory has been examined in the context of legal applications. We will also discuss landmark work on the misinformation effect. Memory researchers have designed protocols that help investigators limit false memories and that promote accurate memory; this "cognitive interview" will also be discussed.

Figure 8.1   Dr. Elizabeth Loftus.

Courtesy of Elizabeth Loftus

CORRESPONDENCE, ACCURACY, AND AMOUNT

In some situations, what matters is the amount of information a person remembers. In semantic memory, the sheer bulk of memory is often important. How many names for the bones of the body can you remember? How many kings and queens of Great Britain do you know? However, in autobiographical memory, correspondence is more important—that is, the relation between the memory of the event and the actual event. For example, consider that you went on a walk through the park and saw five swans, three ducks, two squirrels, and seven bicycle riders. Later you report that you saw a bunch of birds and some people on bicycles; your memory is accurate (corresponds to the event), even if you do not recall a lot of details. However, if your memory report includes a description of the pigeons, deer, and ATVs that you saw, then you are showing poor correspondence, resulting in false memories. In legal settings, correspondence is paramount, as false memories can lead to wrongful convictions. Of course, the best testimony is both accurate and complete. But completeness only matters if there is a high degree of correspondence between the witness's testimony and the events that unfolded (Goldsmith & Koriat, 2008; Wixted et al., 2015).

One of the most powerful contributors to poor correspondence is suggestibility. **Suggestibility** is the tendency to incorporate suggestions or postevent information into one's memory of an event. All people may wind up with false memories as a function of suggestibility, but some, such as the "alien abductees," are more suggest-

> **Suggestibility:** The tendency to incorporate information from sources other than the original witnessed event, such as other people, written materials, or pictures, which may be misleading.

ible. Thus, understanding suggestibility is an important issue in false memory research (Belli, 2012). However, first, we turn our attention to source monitoring.

SOURCE MONITORING

A critical feature of retrieval is determining where your memory comes from. How do we know what we are remembering is, in fact, true? Try to remember what you had for breakfast this morning. Are you sure that is what you had for breakfast, or are you remembering what you had for breakfast yesterday? Or are you remembering what you wished you had for breakfast? We have to make decisions about the source and veracity of our memories quickly. Now think about the memory you have of your younger sibling being born. Do you remember this story from your own experience at his or her birth? Or do you know it because you have heard it throughout your life from others? In this case, a source-monitoring decision involves determining whether your memory is of your own experience or is based on stories from your parents.

Attributing a memory to the wrong source can have potentially negative consequences. You may remember that your friend Betty just broke up with her boyfriend. But before you send her flowers, you might consider how you heard of the breakup. If you heard it from an unreliable gossip, you might make certain first by asking Betty herself. If she confirms it, you get the flowers and take her out for lunch. If you heard it directly from Betty originally, then you will go ahead and order those flowers without calling her about it. Thus, when we retrieve the fact "Betty and her boyfriend broke up," we automatically make a judgment about the source—reliable or unreliable—and act accordingly. The ability to distinguish between reliable and unreliable sources in memory is called **source monitoring**.

> **Source monitoring:** Our ability to distinguish among the sources of our retrieved memories, in both the external and internal world.

Failures in source monitoring can lead to false memories. Some researchers have argued that many false memories are the result of failures of source monitoring (Lindner & Henkel, 2015; Meissner, Brigham, & Kelley, 2001). Imagine someone who fails to source monitor effectively and thinks a memory of being a professional basketball player is real and not a function of wishful thinking. By forgetting that the source of this "memory" is a personal fantasy, this person has generated a false memory.

How do we successfully source monitor? The current theory is that source monitoring occurs at the time of retrieval. When a memory is brought to mind, source-monitoring processes unconsciously examine the memory for clues to its origin. Memories with lots of sensory details are usually judged to be real, as are those with strong emotional associations (Johnson, Hashtroudi, & Lindsay, 1993). Note, however, that a strongly imagined and plausible memory (say, shooting the winning basket in a basketball game) may pass this source-monitoring test and be retrieved as a memory of a real event. **Reality monitoring** (source monitoring between real and imagined sources) has been implicated in false memories concerning both childhood abuse and failures in eyewitness memory.

> **Reality monitoring:** Our ability to distinguish whether our memory is of a real event or an imagined event.

METHODS OF STUDYING FALSE MEMORY

Deese-Roediger-McDermott Procedure (DRM)

Before you read the rest of this paragraph, test yourself on the demonstration in Figure 8.2. Look at the words you wrote down. You probably remembered most of the words on the list. Now check to see if you wrote down any words that were not on the original list. About 55% of people who recall the words from this list will falsely recall the word *sleep*. The word *sleep* is not on the page in your textbook. Thus, if you wrote down *sleep* on your list, you have made at least one false memory in your life. You may even have felt certain it was on the list. You are not alone; the word's presence is strongly implied by the associations of the words on the list, and as a consequence, it is likely to be falsely recalled (Arndt, 2012, 2015). Almost every individual will make what is called a **critical intrusion** if given enough of

> **Critical intrusion:** The false memory created by a list in which all of the words are related or associated with the absent but suggested word.

these lists—that is, a false memory created by a list in which all of the words are related or associated with the absent but suggested word. Roediger and McDermott (1995) devised a number of lists with a similar theme in mind (based on earlier work by Deese, 1959; hence the **Deese-Roediger-McDermott or DRM procedure**). (Go to study.sagepub.com/schwartz3e[3] and copy some of the lists—then try this experiment on some of your friends.)

The Deese-Roediger-McDermott (DRM) procedure rapidly induces a false memory (Arndt, 2012, 2015). Many people recall the word *sleep,* ascribe it to a source, and describe its retrieval as a "recollective experience." Thus, the DRM procedure provides an excellent experimental window on false memories (Roediger & McDermott, 1995). It is quick and easy to do, reliably produces false memories, involves no misinformation and no questionable ethical procedures, and can lend itself to a great number of experimental manipulations.

> **Deese-Roediger-McDermott (DRM) procedure:** Used to induce false memories for items on word lists. Associates to an unpresented word are given, and the unpresented word is often recalled.

There are two standard explanations of the false memories produced via the DRM procedure. One explanation focuses on the nature of the contextual associations. Contextual **association's** arise from all of the presented words being linked to or associated with the critical intrusion in some way. In the example, all of the words are related to the critical intrusion, *sleep.* The context allows for the associations between sleep and all of the presented words to strongly activate the word *sleep* in the person's memory. Thus, at the time of recall, the word *sleep* is highly activated. This activation is then mistakenly confused with episodic memory. Many experiments support this particular point of view (Barnhardt, Choi, Gerkens, & Smith, 2006; Corson, Mahé, Verrier, Columbel, & Jagot, 2011; Huff, Bodner, & Fawcett, 2015; Jou, 2008).

> **Contextual associations:** An explanation for the retrieval of critical intrusions in the DRM. All of the presented words are linked to or associated with the critical intrusion.

When the list is relatively small (e.g., *nurse, sick, lawyer, medicine*), the critical intrusion (*doctor*) is less likely to be recalled than if the list is relatively long (e.g., *nurse, sick, lawyer, medicine, health, hospital, dentist, physician, ill, patient, office, stethoscope, surgeon, clinic, cure*; Roediger, Watson, McDermott, & Gallo, 2001). Longer lists result in a greater likelihood of remembering the critical intrusion as a word on the list. This is likely because the greater number of associations is more likely to strongly activate the absent but associated word. Huff et al. (2015) showed that when people engage in distinctive processing on each item rather than contextual processing to relate the items, the number of critical intrusions is reduced, though not eliminated. Often, when learning lists for free recall, participants will try to make a story linking the items—this increases contextual processing. Focusing on what makes an item unique captures the idea of distinctiveness processing. Huff et al.'s results mean that when people focus more on what makes each item in a list unique rather than how they can relate the items, false memories decrease. These data are consistent with the contextual association view, because not attending to context decreases the likelihood of a false memory.

An alternate explanation of false memories in the DRM procedure focuses on the idea that memory representation is not exact. This has been labelled **fuzzy-trace theory** (Brainerd, Wright, Reyna, & Mojardin, 2001; Bland, Howe, & Knott, in press; Marche & Brainerd, 2012). I prefer the term *gist of the list,* as what is encoded refers to the primary meaning of the list rather than its individual examples. In this view, when items are encoded, they are not encoded literally but rather in terms of their meaning, a reasonable hypothesis given what we know about long-term memory. Thus, when a person encodes words such as *physician, dentist,* and *surgeon,* these words may be transformed into the word *doctor* at encoding, as the correct meaning is extracted rather than the literal words. This theory explains why participants are good at recognizing the actual words that were on the list, as they are consistent with the gist of the fuzzy trace. However, when participants are asked to recall items, the critical intrusion is likely to be recalled, as it is the word most strongly encoded by the meaning or gist of the list (Marche & Brainerd, 2012). To test this view, Lampinen et al. (2006) asked both children and adults to study DRM lists that were either mixed together, so that it was more difficult to detect the gist of mixed-up lists, or listed one after the other, such that it was much easier to detect the gist of each list. After all items had been presented, the participants were asked to free recall the lists. Lampinen et al. found that there were more critical intrusions—for both children and adults—when the lists were presented one after the other, allowing the gist to be extracted more easily. When it was harder to detect the gist, critical intrusions went down, consistent with fuzzy-trace theory.

> **Fuzzy-trace theory:** An explanation for the retrieval of critical intrusions in the DRM. When items are encoded, they are not encoded literally but rather in terms of their meaning.

The DRM is a good experimental paradigm for looking at false memories induced by associative structures. However, there is some concern as to whether it serves as a model for real-world false memories. The issue of ecological validity has been raised. Many think that a large gap exists between false memories for words and the kinds of false memories that disrupt people's lives. Although individuals clearly have different propensities to

Figure 8.2 Read the following words aloud at a rate of one word every three seconds. After you have read all the words, close your book, take out a piece of paper, and write down as many of these words as you can.

Bed	Dream	Slumber
Drowsy	Awake	Snore
Rest	Tired	Wake
Yawn	Doze	Snooze
Peace	Nap	Blanket

SOURCE: Roediger and McDermott (1995).

produce critical intrusions, it is unclear how DRM predicts false memories in real-world situations (Watson, Bunting, Poole, & Conway, 2005). However, some research shows some interesting patterns that are predictive of real-world phenomena. Leding (2011) showed that people who have a greater "need for cognition"—that is, value the time they spend on cognitive tasks—show more false memories in the DRM than those with a lesser "need for cognition." Baugerud et al. (2016) compared maltreated children and non-maltreated children concerning the likelihood of generating critical intrusions in the DRM procedure. Maltreated children showed a higher rate of critical intrusions for lists that had emotional content that those that were neutral, suggesting that maltreated children may be more prone to memory illusions. In another study, Wilson et al. (2015) found that meditation actually increased false memory rates in the DRM, suggesting a note of caution for meditating before testifying in court. In short, much of the recent focus on the DRM has been on showing on how it is applicable to everyday situations.

Visual False Memory Procedure

The visual false memory procedure is closely related to the DRM procedure. In this procedure, people are presented with a series of closely related pictures, such as pictures of fruit or pictures of people engaged in sports. Later, participants will examine a series of pictures, some of which are new, some of which are new but related to earlier pictures, and some of which are old pictures. Participants must decide if the picture was seen earlier. False memory can be measured when participants endorse new pictures, and the analog to critical intrusions is when they recognize related but new pictures as being old (Olszewska et al., 2015). The visual false memory procedure creates bigger false memory effects than does the DRM (Hege & Dodson, 2004). Moradi et al. (2015) looked at visual false memories in combat veterans who had post-traumatic stress disorder and those that did not. The post-traumatic stress disorder veterans were more susceptible to critical intrusions than the un-traumatized veterans, suggesting that exposure to trauma may increase the likelihood that people develop false memories.

> **Visual false memory procedure:** Used to induce false memories for pictures. Unpresented pictures similar to presented pictures are more likely to be recognized as seen than dissimilar pictures.

False Memory Induction Procedure

Elizabeth Loftus and her colleagues invented another way of examining false memories in experimental participants. In this technique, Loftus was able to better model the kinds of false memories that are of concern outside the laboratory. This method is called the **false memory induction procedure** (Loftus, Coan, & Pickrell, 1996). In this method, false memories of events are induced in participants. Of course, for ethical reasons, abuse memories are avoided, but Loftus and her team have been able to show that ordinary college students will generate false

> **False memory induction procedure:** False memories of events are induced in participants by repeatedly asking them about events they never experienced.

memories of episodic events when put in this procedure. (For an article on this topic by Elizabeth Loftus, go to study.sagepub.com/schwartz3e.[4])

Before discussion of the false memory induction procedure, we need to look briefly at the controversy over recovery of repressed memories. There are some psychologists who argue that all recovered repressed memories are necessarily false, and there are some psychologists who accept the veracity of all recovered memories. Here we will try to present the best scientific evidence on this issue. However, the debate is not between cognitive psychology and evidence-based clinical psychology. Rather, the debate arises from different views of memory between cognitive psychology and schools of psychotherapy still largely grounded in Freudian theory, which has never had much scientific support within clinical psychology. Cognitive-based memory researchers argue that many of these recovered memories may, in fact, be false memories brought about by the processes described in this chapter. Freudian psychotherapy argues that these recovered repressed memories are almost always true. In order to address this issue, a reasonable model of repressed memories must be presented. The false-memory induction procedure attempts to provide a model for how psychotherapy can actually produced false memories.

Loftus and Davis (2006) described several controversial psychotherapy techniques that some therapists have used to promote the recovery of repressed memories of childhood abuse, usually sexual abuse. The **recovery of repressed memories** is the retrieval of previously forgotten events. Loftus and Davis contended that many of these techniques are also powerful at inducing false memories. These techniques include hypnosis, guided imagery (that is, imagining oneself in an abuse situation to see if it is real), writing in journals, and more strange activities such as "trance writing." Laboratory studies show that each of these techniques can lead to false memories. **Hypnosis**, for example, leads to a strong increase in the number of reported false memories with a small, if any, increase in the number of reported true memories. With respect to "guided imagery," some therapists believe that it will help clients remember abusive events from their childhood. However, empirical research also links it with false memories. Thus, Loftus and Davis argued that rather than help clients confront what is really causing them psychological distress—the reason they seek psychotherapy in the first place—these techniques simply instill false memories in them. Thus, for Loftus and Davis, these techniques are a double-edged sword. They induce false memories, which may have negative repercussions in a person's life, and they distract attention from the root causes of the person's problems (see Lynn et al., 2015).

Recovery of repressed memories: The ability to recover previously forgotten memories.

Hypnosis: Increases the number of false memories without increasing the number of accurate memories.

The false memory induction procedure is modeled on these psychotherapy techniques, except that the goal is not to provide insight and relief to people suffering from psychological distress. Rather, the goal is to determine whether these techniques induce false memories in healthy normal adults.

In the false memory induction procedure, experimenters ask participants about particular events from their childhood that, in fact, never happened. Researchers tell participants that they have spoken to a parent or an older sibling and received information about the childhood event, and that they want to see how much the individual can remember about the event. In fact, the experimenters do contact a family member but just to confirm that a similar event did *not* happen to the participant. Participants might be asked about the time, as a young child, they spilled punch on the bride's wedding dress at a family wedding. They might be asked about the time they took a ride in a hot air balloon while on vacation. They might be asked about the time that they got lost at the mall. They might be asked about the time a school nurse took a skin sample. Because the events never took place, almost all participants initially deny remembering the event. However, in the false memory induction procedure, the experimenters will repeatedly and leadingly question the participants about such memories. In some cases, people do start to remember details of events that never took place.

For example, Loftus and Pickrell (1995) recruited 24 parents who tried to convince their children that they had been lost in the mall as a child when, in fact, they had not. Participants were repeatedly questioned about this event as if it had taken place and were also asked to imagine themselves back in the mall. Although most of the participants never generated false memories of being lost in the mall, 25% did. Six of the 24 participants "remembered" partial or complete details of the never-experienced event. Hyman, Husband, and Billings (1995) found a similar percentage of people generated false memories in a similar paradigm.

Repeated questioning combined with the authority of a close family member leads some participants to create false memories. The rate of false memory induction is relatively low. At best, it reaches rates of about 50% for memories that are ordinary and not traumatic (i.e., taking a ride in a hot air balloon). For some items, it remains at 0% (being treated with an enema at the doctor's office; see Pezdek, Finger, & Hodge, 1997). In most cases, it takes the form of accepting the wisdom of the parent or sibling—that is, the belief that the event must be true if Mom says it is true, without any recollective experience. However, in some cases, the participants wind up not just believing that the event occurred but elaborating on the event, providing details that were not presented to them by the researchers. In these cases, the participant truly has an autobiographical episodic memory that just happens to not correspond to a real event. Hyman and Pentland (1996) found that 25% of participants wound up elaborating on and describing new details concerning events that never happened.

We can conclude from the above data that human memory is susceptible to false memory. Not all the time, not for all events, and perhaps not even for everybody, but by and large, false memories can and do occur. A question remains: Can false memories of truly traumatic memories occur? Is it possible to induce these false memories in unsuspecting participants?

All memory researchers have considered it unethical to attempt to falsely induce memories of childhood abuse, but some memory researchers have pushed the limits of ethically acceptable false memory induction to demonstrate the power of false memory induction. For example, Heaps and Nash (2001) induced false memories of childhood near-drowning events. Porter, Yuille, and Lehman (1999) induced false memories of vicious animal attacks in childhood. In both cases, false memories were produced at rates similar to those of other studies with less traumatic memories. Shaw and Porter (2015) used repeated suggestive questioning and guided imagery in order to examine if they could induce memories of having committed a crime. After three sessions of intense questioning, they found that the majority of participants produced false memories of having committed crimes, such as theft or assault. This particular study has applications to harsh interrogation techniques, which have often been blamed for false confessions. In fact, Kaplan et al. (2016) argue that highly emotional conditions, such as those involved in being asked about a crime one committed, lead to higher false memory rates than less emotional situations. I will hasten to add that in these studies, participants went through rigorous debriefing sessions. However, even after being told that the memories were induced, many participants continue to maintain vivid memories that they know are false (Clark, Nash, Fincham, & Mazzoni, 2012). So it is likely that these kinds of false memories demonstrate that at least some recovered memories of traumatic events are really just false memories.

The false memory induction procedure has also led to some other interesting findings. In particular, the induction of false memories can lead to changes in patterns of food preferences. Bernstein and Loftus (2009) described experiments in which participants were induced to have false memories of getting sick from eating particular foods, such as egg salad. Later, participants expressed an aversion to egg salad that they had not had before. In contrast, Laney, Morris, Bernstein, Wakefield, and Loftus (2008) induced false memories of food preferences. They induced participants to remember how much they enjoyed eating asparagus as children. Later, these participants demonstrated increased desire and liking of asparagus. These researchers suggested that inducing false memories may be a way of getting people to eat a healthier diet.

Imagination Inflation

Imagine that, when you were a six-year-old child, your parents took you on a trip in a hot air balloon while on vacation. It was a warm and sunny day in Napa Valley, California. You were a little bit scared, but once you were aloft, the flight was kind of boring. You could not see out over the basket, and when you tried, your father pulled you back, fearing you would fall out. So you just counted the number of people in the balloon who were wearing "Crocs" (a kind of sandal popular in the early 2000s). Afterward, you told your parents the hot air balloon ride was boring, and they scolded you, explaining they had spent a lot of money so that you could have that experience. You decided it was better not to talk about the balloon ride after that because all you could remember of it anyway was being pulled away from the side and the blue Crocs the tall, weird-looking man with the mustache was wearing (see Figure 8.3).

Sound plausible? I am not saying this really happened to you, just that you should imagine it. Try to imagine it vividly—try to see the excitement of the morning; the giant, colorful balloon; the disappointment at not being able to see anything; and the image of the blue sandals. Amazingly, research shows that imagining a scenario such as this increases the likelihood that you will later falsely remember an event of that type.

In **imagination inflation**, researchers induce false memories by simply having the participant

Imagination inflation: Researchers induce false memories by simply having the participant imagine an event.

imagine the event. False memories can be induced without any deception on the part of the researcher. The researcher simply asks the participant to imagine an event, such as taking a hot air balloon ride. The simple act of imagining it influences the rate at which those participants later report whether they have ever experienced that event (Bays, Zabrucky, & Foley, 2015; Leding, 2012).

Mazzoni and Memon (2003) asked people to rate the likelihood that each of several events had happened to them. Some of the events were plausible, such as finding money in the back of a taxicab or having a tooth removed by a dentist, and others were impossible, such as having a skin sample taken by a school nurse (something not done in Great Britain, where the experiment took place). Participants were asked the likelihood that each of these events had taken place before they were six years old. One week later, the participants returned and imagined the plausible event or the impossible event. As a control, they read a brief description of the other event. For the memory test, participants returned a week after that. Here, they were asked to judge whether various events had happened to them, including both the plausible and impossible event. Participants' recall was rated on a scale that ranged from "no memory of the event" to "vivid memory of the event with details."

Mazzoni and Memon (2003) did not attempt to convince the person that the event had actually occurred. The researchers only asked for the participant to imagine an event. Nonetheless, this procedure can and does induce false memories. More participants believed that they had a skin sample taken from them as children than if they had not imagined the event. Furthermore, more participants now reported new details of their

Figure 8.3 Is that you in the hot air balloon? See text for explanation.

Thinkstock/Getty Images/Photos.com

memory of the event, convinced that it was real, than if they had not imagined the event. Thus, simply imagining an event can increase the likelihood that we have a false memory for that event.

Bays et al. (2015) used a similar procedure to the Mazzoni and Memon (2003) procedure, but Bays et al. also varied the kind of imagery that participants used during the imagination procedure. In one condition, participants were prompted to imagine events that may or may not have occurred, but in a second condition, the experimenters used guided imagery, in which they led participants through the imagery procedure. Bays et al. found this guided imagery procedure led to the belief that more of the events had actually happened to participants than the prompted imagery, especially for negative events.

One of the questionable psychotherapeutic techniques criticized by Loftus and her colleagues is guided imagery. In guided imagery, a therapist who suspects a client might have been abused as a child may ask the client to imagine such an event and see if it "feels real." This is what is happening in the imagination inflation paradigm, except that the experimenter does not give implicit suggestions that the memory is real. This research suggests that therapists must be careful about what they suggest that their clients imagine because their more suggestible clients might develop false memories. Furthermore, these false memories might have devastating consequences for the client and his or her relationship to other people. Consider the following study. Scoboria, Mazzoni, and Jarry (2008) suggested to participants that they had gotten sick eating peach yogurt as a child. One week later, the participants returned for what they thought was a different experiment on food preferences. Compared to control participants, those who thought that they had gotten sick on spoiled yogurt rated their preferences for yogurt lower and were less likely to choose yogurt than crackers when offered food. Thus, a false memory of a food reaction can create an aversion to that food. (To find out more about imagination inflation, go to www.sagepub .com/schwartz3e.[5])

Fabricated or Altered Evidence

Consider looking at a photograph of yourself in a hot air balloon. There you are, six years old, smiling from above the railing of the balloon. There's the proof—you may not remember it now—but you definitely were in the balloon. Recent studies have used programs like Photoshop to alter photographs to provide false evidence that events took place. The question is whether these doctored photographs and videos can induce false memories in the people who view them. The answer is a resounding yes. Doctored photos and videos are very strong inducers of false memories (Nash, Wade, & Lindsay, 2009).

Nash et al. (2009) asked participants to engage in simple acts, such as rolling dice and browsing through books. The participants were filmed while they were doing these acts. In a second session, participants were simply asked to imagine doing similar actions. Two weeks, later the participants returned for the test phase. In the meantime, Nash et al. had altered some of the videos to create videos of the people doing actions that they had only imagined during the second session. At the time of test, Nash et al. showed the altered videotapes to participants. Compared to participants who had not seen altered videotapes, those who had seen the altered videotapes had far more false memories. The effect of doctored videos was increased when those participants were also asked to imagine the false events as well. Moreover, Wade, Green, and Nash (2010) showed that after having viewed fabricated videotapes, participants were more likely to sign documents claiming they had witnessed a behavior (cheating) that they actually did not see. Thus, fabricated visual evidence can also induce false memories and potentially lead to inaccurate testimony.

In an interesting variant on this theme, Patihis and Loftus (2016) found that people could have false memories of video presentations when none actually exists. Patihis used both a computer survey and an in-person interview to ask whether participants could remember the video coverage of the plane that crashed in Pennsylvania on 9/11, which occurred when most of the participants were young children. In fact, there never was any video of that plane, though there was of the other planes that were brought down by terrorists that day. In both the computer survey format and the in-person interview, some participants reported false memories of seeing the video and generated details about that memory. As in other studies, not all participants generated false memories, with 33% of individuals in the computer survey generating false memories and only 13% of people in the in-person interview generating false memories. Nonetheless, these are false memories that occur even in the absence of presented altered imagery.

SECTION SUMMARY AND QUIZ

False memory refers to the observation that people do misremember events. The cognitive study of false memory attempts to determine the how and the why of false memory. Psychologists who study false memory are interested in the correspondence between the actual event and the person's memory of it. One mechanism that produces false memory is the failure to source monitor. If you remember something but attribute it to the wrong source, it may wind up as a false memory. False memories have been investigated with a number of techniques, including the Deese-Roediger-McDermott (DRM) procedure, visual false memory procedure, the false memory induction procedure, imagination inflation, and fabricated or altered evidence.

Section Quiz

1. Clancy (2005) studied memory processes in people who believed that they were abducted by space aliens:
   a. Because all scientists would agree that memories of being abducted by space aliens were false, this would provide a good model of false memory
   b. Because people who believe that they have been abducted by space aliens represent a population vastly different from normal individuals
   c. Because people who believe they have been abducted by space aliens are less prone to false memories in the DRM procedure
   d. Because she was interested in the characteristics of space aliens

2. In the context of research on human memory and false memory, correspondence means
   a. The amount of information a person can recall about an event
   b. The match between a person's memory and the event as it actually happened in the past
   c. The dialogue between memory researchers and their experimental participants
   d. All of the above

3. In the DRM procedure, false memories are thought to occur because
   a. The experimenters introduce implicit false information
   b. Most participants are highly suggestible
   c. The participants extract the gist or meaning from a list, which is associated with a non-presented but related item
   d. Demand characteristics of the study create the expectation that people should misremember

4. In studies using altered video of earlier events, the researchers find that
   a. Doctored photos and videos are very strong inducers of false memories
   b. Not all people, but some, will be induced to have false memories
   c. Participants were more likely to sign documents claiming they had witnessed a behavior (cheating) that they actually did not see
   d. All of the above

1. a
2. b
3. c
4. d

HYPNOSIS AND MEMORY

Research suggests that hypnosis does not increase the number of true memories produced. Indeed, to the contrary, it increases the possibility of succumbing to false memories. More information is retrieved during hypnosis than when the witness is in his or her normal state, but most of the additional information is false. In some instances, a new and true memory can be produced by hypnosis. However, the increase in memories produced by hypnosis is dominated by false memories (Kirsch, Mazzoni, & Montgomery, 2007; Lynn, Laurence, & Kirsch, 2015).

Hypnosis itself is a real phenomenon. In hypnosis, an individual is placed in an altered state of consciousness in which he or she is more likely to incorporate suggestions into his or her behaviors, beliefs, and memories (Hunter & Eimer, 2012). People tend to vary in the extent to which they can be hypnotized. Some people are highly suggestible and easily hypnotized. Others are highly resistant and are practically impossible to hypnotize. Suggestibility is another method whereby people can incorporate false information into autobiographical memory. Thus, hypnosis is not a good option when trying to elicit more information from a confused witness.

This is not to say suggestibility is always a bad thing. In some circumstances, being suggestible has its advantages, and hypnosis does have practical value (see Hunter & Eimer, 2012). Suggestions can be made to people under hypnosis to help them overcome medical conditions, especially with respect to pain tolerance (e.g., Otani, 1992). A highly suggestible person can be hypnotized and made to feel less pain, while the less suggestible person has to bear the more intense pain. But for memory, the contention here is simply that hypnosis is another means of suggestibility and thus increases the possibility that false memories will be created (Mazzoni & Lynn, 2007; Mazzoni, Laurence, & Heap, 2014).

RECOVERED MEMORIES: THE REALITY OF REPRESSION

False memories are a real phenomenon. They are relatively straightforward to demonstrate in the lab, and we have evidence that they exist in the real world. It is almost *certain* that some recovered memories of childhood abuse are the result of false memories induced by shaky therapeutic procedures. This has led some to conclude that all recovered memories of repressed events are essentially false memories (Loftus & Ketcham, 1994). Is it possible to show that forgotten memories of childhood trauma can later be retrieved? Nowadays, the consensus is that there is evidence that some childhood trauma is forgotten, only to be remembered much later. This implies that not all recovered memories are therapy-induced false memories. First, the data that suggest that repression and recovery are possible will be discussed. Second, two explanations for this phenomenon will be offered, and experiments that support these explanations will be discussed.

In a landmark study, Williams (1995) tracked down 129 women who had been abused as children and as children, sent to the hospital for treatment. Thus, these were cases in which the abuse was documented shortly after it occurred. Williams used this sample to satisfy potential critics who might question whether abuse had occurred: It would be hard to argue that recovered memories of abuse in this sample were completely false, given that the women had, as children, been admitted to a hospital for treatment for abuse. The age at the time of the abuse ranged from less than one year to 12 years old. Williams contacted the participants after they had reached adulthood.

Williams (1995) found that 12% of the women did not remember the abuse. Some of these women were younger than age five at the time of abuse, and for those, the forgetting may have been normal childhood amnesia. But for the women who were older at the time of the abuse, the explanation for forgetting cannot be attributed to childhood amnesia. Thus, strange as it may seem, it is possible to forget being the victim of awful crimes that required hospitalization. Possible reasons for forgetting such traumatic events will be discussed shortly. Furthermore, 16% of women reported that there was a time when they had forgotten about the abuse even though they remembered it at the time of the interview. Indeed, they reported that an external cue triggered their memory of the abuse. Other studies have also shown that some well-documented abuse victims lost their memory of the event and later recovered it (Shobe & Schooler, 2001).

Critics have argued that the Williams (1995) data are open to alternate explanations because of flaws in the study's methodology and data analysis. Yes, these women have a documented history of abuse, but that does not preclude the possibility that the memory of that abuse is false—that is, not a true episodic memory, but a secondary memory based on learning of the events later. Indeed, the memory may have been a function of reconstructive processes and stories that the woman heard rather than a true episodic memory. Thus, some memory theorists, like Loftus and Davis (2006), remain skeptical of Williams's study.

Can we do better? Can we distinguish between a recovered memory that is a real episodic memory and a recovered episodic memory that is false (even if it captures a historically true event)? The key here is in looking at features that typically appear in false memories and in true memories. For example, research suggests that memories that are *gradually* recovered during suggestive therapy share many properties with false memories. They tend to be vague, have more to do with thought processes, are less emotional, and have fewer sensory details. Memories that arise during therapy and have these characteristics may, in fact, be false memories. On the other hand, some recovered memories of childhood abuse are spontaneous and happen all at once. These spontaneous, sudden memories are more likely to be correlated with documented histories of abuse (Geraerts, Raymaekers, & Merckelbach, 2008). These spontaneous, sudden memories are also more likely to be highly charged emotionally and have more sensory detail. Thus, it appears that the hallmark of the true recovered memory is its spontaneous nature, usually brought on by a seemingly random retrieval cue. Memories recovered by the leading nature of a therapist's inquiry are more likely to be false.

In Freudian psychology, it is important for the patient to become aware of the childhood trauma that is now causing psychological distress in adulthood. For this reason, many psychotherapists probe for hidden memories of abuse. However, some research in modern clinical psychology tells us that preventing traumatic memory from entering our conscious awareness can have positive benefits (Philippot, Baeyens, Douilliez, & Francart, 2004), directly contradicting the Freudian view. So for some clinical psychologists, recovering repressed memories may not be a desirable outcome for their clients. But whichever clinical school one adheres to, it is relevant to find out the mechanism whereby repression and recovery take place.

For cognitive psychologists, emotional memories are generally thought to be better remembered than less emotional memories, under normal circumstances (Reisberg & Heuer, 2004). Thus, situations that produce repressed but recoverable memories may result from complex processes operating on those memories. From the point of view of memory science, the questions of why some memories are repressed and why some are later recovered are equally important. Lately, some intriguing experimental paradigms have been developed to explore this issue.

Mechanisms of Repression and Recovery

What does it mean to repress an event? Repression is usually thought of as the blocking out of traumatic memories of childhood trauma, particularly trauma associated with sexual abuse. This view of repression dates back to the work of Freud. **Repression** is defined here as forgetting highly emotional memories, usually from childhood. But what cognitive mechanisms can account for repression? For memory scientists, it is necessary to examine these mechanisms, especially given that in most circumstances, highly distinctive and emotional events tend to be well remembered and not forgotten.

Recent theory has focused on two potential mechanisms. The first is the **failure-to-rehearse** explanation. Because memories of childhood trauma are highly negative, often private, and potentially embarrassing, they are not likely to be rehearsed often. We often reflect on positive events, but for some negative events, we may not do so. Then if we do not rehearse the event, the normal processes of updating and elaboration will not be invoked, leading to a poor and less accessible memory trace. So simply failing to rehearse a memory can have a passive effect that leads to that memory becoming

> **Repression:** The active forgetting of highly emotional memories, usually from childhood.

> **Failure to rehearse:** A theory that explains repression. Because memories of childhood trauma are highly negative, often private, and potentially embarrassing, they are not likely to be rehearsed often.

> **Active suppression:** A theory that explains repression. People may deliberately force themselves to not remember the event.

inaccessible. Second, **active suppression** may account for repression. Active suppression here means that people may deliberately force themselves not to remember the item. Every time the memory is activated, people will distract themselves or force themselves to think about something else. Although this sounds paradoxical at first, research suggests that people can inhibit particular memories from growing stronger. We will consider the data for both of these ideas.

Failure to Rehearse

Smith and Moynan (2008) conducted a study that examined the failure-to-rehearse hypothesis. They wanted to demonstrate that rehearsal failure could account for some initial forgetting and then later recovery of memory. They did the experiment in a lab setting with the goal of demonstrating powerful forgetting and equally strong recovery with simple word stimuli. Using this methodology, they planned to develop an experimental analog to the kinds of memories that people may repress outside of the lab. The experiment served as a basis for speculating about the nature of repression and recovery.

First, participants viewed a long series of categorized lists. For each list, the participants saw the category label (e.g., "fish") and many exemplars (e.g., *salmon, halibut, trout, snapper*). Participants wrote down each word and made a judgment as to the fit of each word to the category. Thus, *trout* would be a good fit to the category of "fish," but perhaps *seahorse* might be less so. Three of these lists were called critical lists, in which forgetting was to be induced, whereas the rest were filler lists. The three critical lists were composed of two word lists designed to elicit emotional responses (e.g., "curse words," "deadly diseases") and one neutral list (e.g., "tools"). The fillers were all neutral categories (e.g., "fish"). Participants were not told about any future memory tests, thus mirroring the incidental learning that would initially occur in any real-world event that induced repression (see Figure 8.4).

Following the category judgments, participants were given one of two intervening tasks. In one intervening task, the control group was given nonverbal problems to solve, such as math problems. In the other filler task, the "forget" group was given semantic tasks with the filler categories. They were asked to make judgments of the pleasantness of the items on the list, the size of the items on the list, or the number of syllables in each word on the list. What is important here is that these additional tasks were done with the filler categories—that is, not the critical lists. The idea was that retrieval practice with the filler categories would make the critical categories less accessible later. Important to note here is that in the "forget" group, the task involved making judgments about items within the categories, which would promote thinking about these categories and prevent rehearsing items in the critical categories. This was important later, as the memory tests would include both recall of the categories and recall of items within a category.

This procedure induced **retrieval bias**. Retrieval bias occurs when a procedure is employed that makes some information easier to recall than other information. Retrieval

---

Retrieval bias: The result of employing a procedure that makes some information easier to recall than other information.

---

bias can be induced by requiring a participant to retrieve certain information, such as examples of "fish," a filler category. This makes the fish information easier to retrieve, while making it more difficult to retrieve other categories that were not rehearsed, such as "diseases." Put another way, the filler categories are rendered more accessible and thus are more likely to be retrieved; the critical lists are not rehearsed, become less accessible, and therefore, are less likely to be retrieved.

Retrieval bias is relevant to the situation of repressing memories of childhood abuse. These memories are painful, confusing, and embarrassing both to a child and to an adult. It is likely that some people will spend much more time thinking of other things and as little time as possible focusing on the memory of the abuse. Eventually, as the events that are rehearsed continue to grow in accessibility, the memory of the abuse, through lack of retrieval, is rendered inaccessible and hence repressed. Smith and Moynan (2008) described a situation in which a long continuous event or set of events occurred (i.e., summer camp), filled mostly with positive recurring events (soccer, campfires), which are described and retold many times (that is, rehearsed), and a single isolated negative event (the abuse), which occurred once and then was never spoken about (i.e., failure to rehearse).

Think of the experimental conditions in Smith and Moynan's (2008) experiment. First, we have the critical, emotion-inducing lists and non-emotional control lists. Second, we have a variable in which one group does a nonverbal distractor task and a second group does a verbal task with the filler lists, designed to induce retrieval bias. To mirror the repression situation, Smith and Moynan followed these experimental variables with two memory tests. In the first test, participants were asked to free-recall the names of the *categories* presented during the initial phase. The experimenter asked the person to recall as many categories as possible without providing any clues, cues, or hints. In this test, the participants were expected to recall the category names, not the exemplars

Figure 8.4   Methodology for Smith and Moynan (2008).

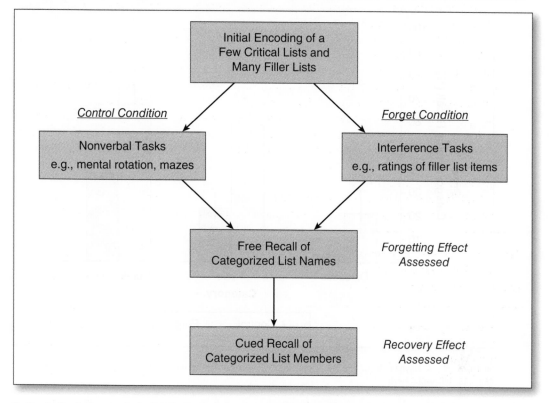

Smith, S. M., & Moynan, S. C. (2008). Forgetting and recovering the unforgettable. *Psychological Science, 19,* 462–468. Wiley-Blackwell.

within a category. Second, following the free recall of categories, the category names were given as cues to remember the exemplars from each list. In the category-cued list, participants were expected to recall the exemplars from each category, including the critical lists (see Figure 8.4).

The results reveal some interesting features about the critical lists. First, consider the recall of category names. In the "forget" condition (verbal filler task), participants were *less* likely to recall the category names of the critical emotional items than they were in the control condition (that is, the nonverbal task; see Figure 8.5). Indeed, for the category "diseases," the level of category recall fell from over 20% in the control condition to just about 2% in the "forget" condition. Only 2% of participants recalled the category name "disease" when they had engaged in semantic practice with items from the filler lists.

However, in the category-cued retrieval of list exemplars, there was no difference in recall between the control and "forget" conditions in the number of exemplars recalled from the critical categories ("disease," "curse words," "tools"). Thus, once the category had been activated, then it was possible to retrieve the words that had been presented in that

Figure 8.5   Results from Smith and Moynan (2008).

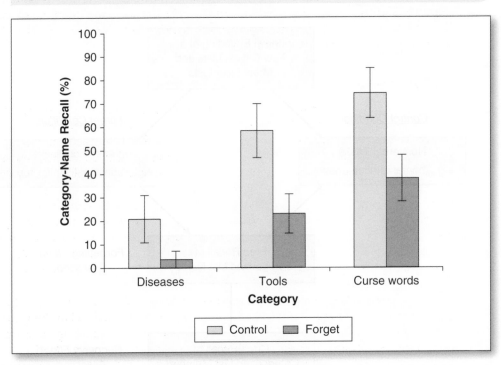

Smith, S. M., & Moynan, S. C. (2008). Forgetting and recovering the unforgettable. *Psychological Science, 19,* 462–468. Wiley-Blackwell.

category. Smith and Moynan (2008) pointed out that the participants were not generating words that fit the category. Participants rarely included intrusions—that is, words from the same category that were not on the list (only about 1 % did so). To restate the experiment's results: The forget condition led to decreased free recall of critical category names, but it did not lead to any changes in the cued recall of category exemplars.

Let's see how closely these results fit the pattern of repression and recovery of abuse. First, amid a large number of neutral categories, two categories were emotional and negative in nature ("diseases," "curse words"). This is like a normal childhood (neutral categories, such as campfires and soccer games) shattered occasionally by an abusive event (the negative emotional categories, such as the abuse). Then, in the "forget" condition, the neutral categories are rehearsed (as we tell stories of the positive events of childhood), but the emotional critical categories are not rehearsed (as some individuals and families may steadfastly refuse to discuss the abuse and its consequences). When people are asked to recall the categories (or remember the important events of their lives), they are good at remembering the practiced categories but often fail to remember the critical categories (i.e., the abuse). However, when given the appropriate retrieval cue (in this case, the category name, such as "curse words"), the participants have no difficulty retrieving the items from that list (just as, once the right cue is given, abuse victims spontaneously recall the abuse). This method potentially explains why repressed memories may be recovered in therapy, as therapy may provide just the right retrieval cues. The Smith and Moynan (2008) experiment, with its complexity, may serve as a good model of the significance of rehearsal or lack of it in repressing and then recovering memories.

Retrieval Suppression

Another mechanism whereby repression might occur is active suppression of the retrieval of unwanted memories. People may actively work to push an unpleasant memory out of consciousness, eventually leading to the event being completely forgotten, at least until the appropriate retrieval cue is given (Anderson & Huddleston, 2012). Think about something really terrible—the horrors of the Holocaust, the images of the Twin Towers collapsing, or perhaps even the fact that you, like all people, will eventually die. Most people prefer not to think about these events and quickly focus their attention and working memory elsewhere. Thus, even non-abused people often attempt to suppress unpleasant thoughts or memories. In the case of 9/11, the public images and discussions in schools, news programs, and other venues will always remind you that this event did take place. But a personal tragedy may not receive the same public attention. Thus, actively working to avoid remembering a personal tragedy might just succeed.

A landmark study on this topic was conducted by Anderson and Green (2001). They were specifically interested in whether repression could be simulated in the laboratory and modeled on active suppression. First, they trained participants on simple word pairs (they used the example of *ordeal–roach*). When the participants had mastered a list of 40 word pairs (i.e., improved to the point where they could recall all the target words when given the cue word), Anderson and Green moved on to the next phase of the experiment.

Anderson and Green (2001) employed what they called a "think/no think" procedure (see Figure 8.6). On some trials, participants were given "think" instructions. When the cue word (*ordeal*) was presented, participants were supposed to recall the target word that went with it and say it aloud. On other trials, they received "no think" instructions, which meant they were meant to actively avoid thinking about the target word. Saying it aloud, as in the think condition, led to a loud buzzing sound. In some cases, items in the no-think condition occurred as many as 16 times—that is, people were asked to suppress the target on 16 different occasions. Note that, unlike in the Smith and Moynan (2008) study, participants were actively suppressing the retrieval of these items instead of simply not having opportunities to rehearse.

The retrieval suppression worked! When Anderson and Green (2001) gave a final recall test after all of the suppression and practice trials were over, they found that the suppressed items were recalled much worse than control items that were neither practiced nor suppressed, and recall of suppressed items was also worse than that for the practiced items. Moreover, the more suppression per item (16 times vs. fewer), the worse recall was. Anderson and Green were afraid that expectations might inhibit some people from reporting recall for some of the suppressed items, so they paid participants 25 cents for each item recalled. Nonetheless, that incentive failed to increase the number of recalled targets in the suppressed conditions.

Benoit, Hulbert, et al. (2015) employed the same basic procedure while participants were being monitored by fMRI (also see Anderson et al., 2004). Benoit et al. asked participants to either suppress or rehearse more real-world stimuli, such as pictures of faces and physical locations. Moreover, after engaging in suppression or rehearsal, they indicated their success at doing just that. Benoit et al. found that the dorsolateral region of the prefrontal cortex was a key region in suppression and this region became most active when the act of suppressing the memory proved difficult. Suppression was associated with a decrease in activity in the hippocampus, a key memory-encoding region of the brain. The dorsolateral regions prefrontal cortex was apparently driving the conscious suppression of the no-think item and working to inhibit the hippocampus from making memory connections. Moreover, people whose problem is recalling too much rather than too little—that is, those with post-traumatic stress disorder, show a decided deficit in the think/no-think procedure (Catarino et al., 2015). Thus, the neuroscience and clinical science also supports their view—people are actively attending to the action, and the action is inhibiting memory.

What does this mean? Well, at least in a laboratory simulation, people can actively suppress retrieval items, and this active suppression later makes those items more difficult to recall (Anderson & Huddleston, 2012). Is this similar to what happens in repression of traumatic events? It is not clear. The material used in this experiment is a far cry from memories of traumatic events in childhood. Nonetheless, people who have suffered from a traumatic event may actively work to not retrieve that event. This experiment shows that such active suppression can work.

Figure 8.6   Experimental paradigm from Anderson and Green (2001).

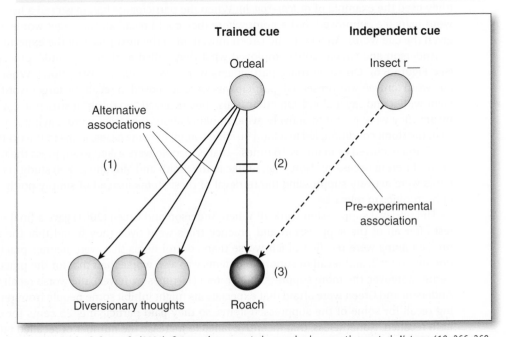

Anderson, M. C., & Green, C. (2001). Suppressing unwanted memories by executive control. *Nature, 410,* 366–369. Reprinted by permission from Macmillan Publishers Ltd.

FALSE MEMORIES AND LEGAL PSYCHOLOGY

Psychology is contributing to many aspects of how we view the law and our legal system. Think about how many aspects of the legal system reflect important psychological processes. Witnesses to crimes must rely on memory to help police with their investigations. Police detectives themselves must engage in any number of problem-solving skills to solve crimes and catch suspected criminals. How we interrogate criminal suspects also depends heavily on psychological research. In the courtroom, attorneys must influence jury decision-making, and judges must decide what juries should or should not know about the case. During deliberation, jury members must convince each other of the logic and correctness of their views on a particular trial. All of these aspects of legal behavior are now under investigation by one team of psychological researchers or another.

Psychologists are studying the cognitive and social processes involved in these activities and offering their expertise to propose ways in which the system can be improved. Scholars are studying how juries make decisions, how jurors interpret evidence that they are told to discard, how juries and judges interpret scientific evidence, how police can maximize the evidence they can obtain from an honest witness, how police can detect dishonest testimony, how police conduct lineups, how children differ from adults when giving testimony, and of course, the unreliability of eyewitness memory. In this chapter, we will consider eyewitness memory and what processes can lead eyewitnesses to incorrectly remember aspects of a crime.

EYEWITNESS TESTIMONY

Many years ago, on a cold winter New Hampshire day, a friend offered to drive me home. It was freezing and snowing, and my boots were already soaked through, so I was not looking forward to my usually relaxing mile walk home. We pulled out of my friend's parking spot and were just about to make a right turn, when, out of nowhere, a large truck with a snowplow smashed into my friend's car. Surprisingly, neither my friend nor I was hurt, and there was little damage to either the car or the truck. The snowplow driver, a large man, stepped out of his truck, checked his truck for damage (there was none), and started belligerently swearing at my friend and me. He then got back into his truck and drove off without exchanging insurance information or waiting for the police. I quickly wrote down his license plate number. My friend and I then drove to the police station to report the incident. After my friend described what happened, a police officer pulled me aside and politely asked me to describe the snowplow driver. "He was tall, almost your height," I responded. But then I was silent. I couldn't describe one more thing about him. The best the police officer could put down on his report was "a tall white man between the ages of 30 and 50," which probably fit the description of every snowplow driver in the state of New Hampshire at the time. I could not recall one detail about his face. Did he have a big nose? Was his hair light or dark? I could not even recall if he had facial hair. Now this was a minor accident, and my friend had insurance, so a massive manhunt was not ordered for this crime. But what if it had been? Was I worthless as a witness? Would I have been

272   MEMORY: FOUNDATIONS AND APPLICATIONS

able to pick him out of a lineup? I seriously doubted it. I was a graduate student studying memory and well versed in the literature on eyewitness memory. But it did me no good. I failed as a witness.

I started off this chapter with two cases in which eyewitnesses identified a person as a criminal and later evidence exonerated that person. Here is another. In 1985, Kirk Bloodsworth was convicted and sentenced to death for the brutal rape and murder of a young child. Much of the evidence of his guilt was testimony from an eyewitness who claimed she saw him with the girl just before the crime. Almost immediately, his lawyers started working on the testimony of the witness, which changed considerably from her first encounter with police investigators to the time she testified in court. But her firm assertion that she saw Bloodsworth with the girl convinced the jury. Eight years later, Bloodsworth was pardoned and released after DNA evidence demonstrated he could not possibly have been the killer. An honest eyewitness who was trying to help solve a brutal crime actually made things worse by identifying the wrong man and helping the actual criminal to remain free. (For more on this case, go to study.sagepub.com/schwartz3e.[6])

What leads people to misremember such important information? It turns out that one of the flaws of human memory is suggestibility—that our memories readily incorporate information from other sources into our original memory of an event. Think of the witness who may have misidentified the man that she saw with the doomed girl. The witness wants to help bring the guilty to justice, and the police thought they had the right man. The police, even if trying their best to be fair and impartial, may have said things that led the witness to imagine Bloodsworth's face in place of the man that she really saw. She may have found out that other witnesses had already identified Bloodsworth. These factors may lead to a subtle but steady altering of the memory. By the time the witness reaches the courtroom many weeks after witnessing the event, she is convinced that her memory was of the indicted suspect. Let's start examining some of the psychological research on this topic.

Effects of Wording on Memory of an Accident

Suggestibility includes incorporating information from leading questions. People assume that there is certain "given" information in questions, particularly when the questions come from authority figures, such as police officers or lawyers. This information contained in the questions then subtly influences the nature of the witness's memory. Loftus and Palmer (1974) demonstrated this in what is considered a classic experiment on eyewitness memory (see Figure 8.7). They asked participants to watch a short film depicting a motor vehicle accident. After the film, the participants were asked one of five questions:

1. How fast were the cars going when they *smashed* into each other?
2. How fast were the cars going when they *collided* with each other?
3. How fast were the cars going when they *bumped* each other?
4. How fast were the cars going when they *hit* each other?
5. How fast were the cars going when they *contacted* each other?

They found that the estimates of speed given by participants were different depending on which question they were asked. Using the term *smashed* led to estimates nearly 10 miles per hour faster than when the word *contacted* was used. Everyone had seen the same crash, but the way in which the question was asked affected the estimate of speed. Thus, a subtle difference in wording affected people's memory enough to bias their report of the accident (see Table 8.1).

Table 8.1 Speed Estimates From Loftus and Palmer (1974).

Verb Used	Estimated Speed
Smashed	41
Collided	39
Bumped	38
Hit	34
Contacted	32

Sometimes a single word can influence people's memory. Indeed, Loftus and Zanni (1975) found that the subtle difference between the words *the* and *a* can have a strong effect on memory. In their study, participants viewed a film of an automobile accident. Later, they answered a series of questions about the accident. Half of the participants received the following question: "Did you see *a* broken headlight?" The other half of the participants received this question: "Did you see *the* broken headlight?" In fact, the film did not depict an accident with a broken headlight. In these questions, "*the* broken headlight" implies that there was a broken headlight and inquires whether the person noticed it, whereas "*a* broken headlight" implies that it is not known whether the headlight was broken and asks the witness whether it was or not. Only 7% erroneously reported a broken headlight when the word *a* was used. However, 18% reported that they had seen a broken headlight when the word *the* was used. Thus, changing from an indefinite article to a definite article raised the rate of false memory from 7% to 18%.

Figure 8.7 Stimulus for Loftus and Palmer (1974).

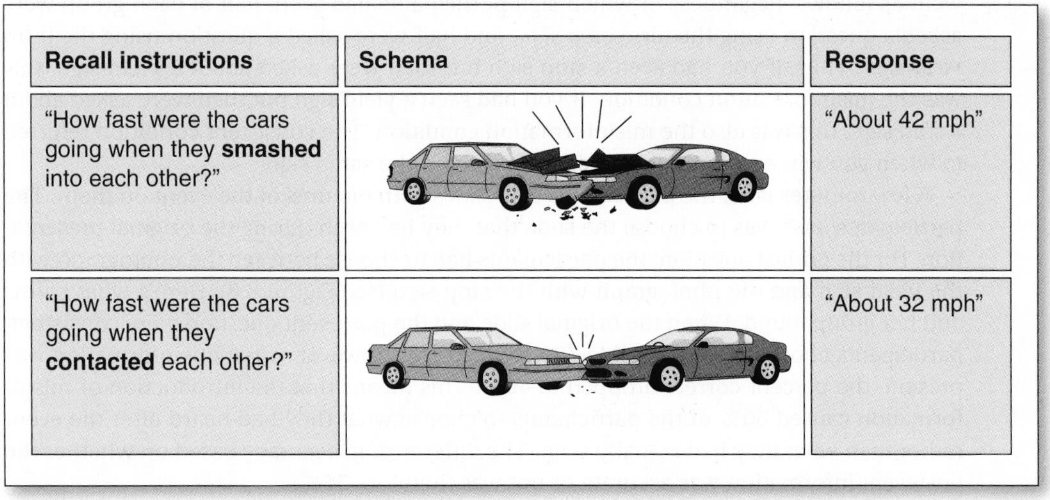
Recall instructions
Schema
Response
"How fast were the cars going when they **smashed** into each other?"
"About 42 mph"
"How fast were the cars going when they **contacted** each other?"
"About 32 mph"

Reprinted from *Journal of Verbal Learning and Verbal Behavior, 13*, Loftus. E. F., & Palmer, J. C. Reconstruction of automobile destruction: an example of the interaction between language and memory, 585–589. Copyright (1974), with permission from Elsevier.

THE MISINFORMATION EFFECT

One of the most influential experimental paradigms ever in memory science is the **misinformation effect** technique developed by Elizabeth Loftus (see Loftus, 1979; Kaplan et al., 2016). It has changed the way memory researchers think about memory and the way the legal system handles witnesses. The basic methodology of the misinformation effect is as follows. Participants witness an event, usually a crime, usually by watching a film of a simulated crime. Following the event, participants receive written information about it, either implied through questions (Did you see the criminal's gang tattoos?) or by reading a description (The thief had a tattoo of the Skull gang). Loftus embedded in these descriptions some factual information (consistent with actual event) and some misleading information (contradictory to the actual event). For example, the misleading information might be that the criminal did not have a tattoo. The critical independent variable is the presence or absence of misleading information for any particular detail of the crime. Thus, some witnesses receive misinformation about a tattoo, whereas others receive accurate information about the tattoo. The third stage is a memory test, usually recognition but sometimes recall. The critical dependent measure is the performance of participants on questions referring to the misleading information compared to control conditions. The results consistently show that providing misleading information leads to worse memory performance (see Table 8.2).

> **Misinformation effect:** Result of presenting postevent misinformation about a witnessed event that can obscure, change, or degrade the memory of the original event.

Consider the following experiment from Loftus's work (Loftus, Miller, & Burns, 1978). Participants saw a slide show of a small red sports car moving toward an accident with another car. One group of participants saw a slide showing a yield sign, whereas the other group saw a stop sign. Immediately after seeing the slides, the two groups were asked to answer questions about what they had seen. The important misinformation manipulation went as follows: Regardless of which sign participants had seen, half of each group were asked a question using the term *stop sign,* and half were asked a question using the term *yield sign.* Thus, if you had seen a stop sign but then were asked about a yield sign, this was the misinformation condition. If you had seen a yield sign but then were asked about a stop sign, this was also the misinformation condition. The consistent condition referred to when you witnessed and then were asked about the same sign.

A few minutes later, the participants saw slides with pictures of the event on them. The participants' task was to choose the slide that they had seen during the original presentation. For the critical question, the participants had to choose between the photograph with the yield sign and the photograph with the stop sign (see Figure 8.8). Here's what Loftus and her group found. When the original slide and the postevent question were consistent, participants chose the correct slide 75% of the time. However, when misinformation was present, the percent correct dropped to 40%. This means that the introduction of misinformation caused 60% of the participants to choose what they had heard after the event rather than what they had actually seen. The difference in accuracy based on whether the postevent information was accurate or not was therefore 35%.

Cochran et al. (2016) combined the misinformation paradigm with a version of the altered memory paradigm. Cochran et al. asked participants to watch a slide show depicting

Table 8.2   Misinformation Procedure

1. Witnesses view crime film.
2. Receive Condition 1 (some factual information) and Condition 2 (some misleading information).
3. Take memory test.
4. Performance on Condition 2 is worse than on Condition 1.

a crime. Some participants then wrote descriptions of what they had witnessed immediately after the slide show. The researchers then altered these descriptions to include
misinformation. Fifteen minutes later, the participants viewed their own—albeit altered—
descriptions of the events. Two findings from this study are relevant. First, the majority
of participants failed to detect the alteration in their own reports. And second, consistent
with the misinformation effect, many participants incorporated the misinformation into
their memory report in a final memory test. Thus, the misinformation effect occurs even
when people's own reports are changed to include misinformation.

The misinformation effect is a robust finding. It is easily found and easily replicated. It
can work on people's memory of people or objects in an event. It can work on central or
peripheral details of an event. It works with details that arouse emotion (such as the presence of a gun) and with details that do not (whether the victim was eating potato chips or
cookies; Tiwari, 2012). It can work at short- and long-retention intervals. It works when people have already engaged in retrieval of the event before the misinformation is introduced
(Rindal, DeFranco, Rich, & Zaragoza, 2016). It works with sober and intoxicated individuals
(Schreiber Compo, Evans, Carol, Villalba, & Ham, 2012). It works when recall is the final test
and when recognition is the final test (Loftus, 1979; Paz-Alonso & Goodman, 2008).

Explanations for the Misinformation Effect

The data from misinformation effects experiments show that people's memories are influenced by the misinformation, leading them to falsely report what they witnessed during
the crime scene. One question concerning the explanation for this phenomenon is, What
happens to the representation of the event in memory. Is the memory representation
altered by the misinformation? Or does the postevent information set up a second memory
representation, and the participant does not know which one to report? On one hand, it is
possible that the person retrieves the mem-
ory of the event and then inserts the misinformation into the original record of the
event. On the other hand, the person may
form a second memory—that is, a memory
of hearing the postevent information.

Loftus (1992) argued that the original

> **Trace impairment view:** A theory that
> explains the misinformation effect. The
> original memory is altered by the
> misinformation.

memory is altered by the misinformation. This view is known as the **trace impairment view**.
The trace impairment view states that the misinformation distorts or alters the memory

Coexistence hypothesis: A theory that explains the misinformation effect. Participants form one memory about the original event and then form a second memory of reading questions or a summary after the event.

for the original event. It has also been called the "blending" view, because the new memory is a blending of the original event and the memory of the later information, including the misinformation. In contrast, McCloskey and Zaragoza (1985) presented the **coexistence hypothesis**. This is the view that participants form one memory about the original event and then form a second memory of reading the questions or summary after the event. The second memory is composed of both retrieved information from the first event and any new information derived from the postevent questions. In this view, each retrieval attempt generates its own new memory. Moreover, it is the retrieval of these later memories that leads to the misinformation effect.

To test these two theories, McCloskey and Zaragoza (1985) designed an experiment with a simple variation of the misinformation paradigm. The variation was to examine the effect of the kind of incorrect distractors used on the recognition test. In one condition, McCloskey and Zaragoza presented two choices, an object seen in the original event (i.e., a Coca-Cola can) and the object suggested in the misinformation (i.e., a Budweiser can). This is identical to how Loftus originally measured the misinformation effect. However, in the second condition, McCloskey and Zaragoza presented the object from the original event (i.e., the Coke can) with a new distractor—that is, one that was not part of the misinformation (i.e., a 7-Up can). Thus, the comparison is between the number of times participants are incorrect when the suggested but wrong item is present and the number of times participants are incorrect when the suggested but wrong item has been replaced by a novel object.

If the trace impairment view is correct, then the misinformation should alter and distort the original memory representation. During the presentation of misinformation, the original memory is retrieved, and the misinformation then causes our memory system to replace or alter the representation, thus changing the representation to include the misinformation. In the example, in the person's memory of the crime, the "can" becomes a visual image of the Budweiser can instead of the originally seen Coca-Cola can. If this is true, performance on the recognition test should be worse in the misinformation condition regardless of the type of test used, because the memory is altered. The alternatives now—that is, the original "Coke" and novel "7-Up"—are equally at odds with the "Budweiser" in the person's memory. Thus, the item presented as a distractor at the time of the recognition test should not matter, because the memory trace is altered and therefore, recognition performance should be impaired even when the distractor is a totally novel item.

In contrast, if the coexistence hypothesis is correct, two memories are formed, one for the original event and one for the misinformation. There are two memories side-by-side. At the time of the test, when the recognition test is a choice between the original item and a novel item, there is no cue to induce retrieval of the second memory. Thus, under these circumstances, the coexistence view argues that the misinformation effect should disappear. This is exactly what McCloskey and Zaragoza (1985) found. In the

Figure 8.8   Stimuli used to examine the misinformation effect.

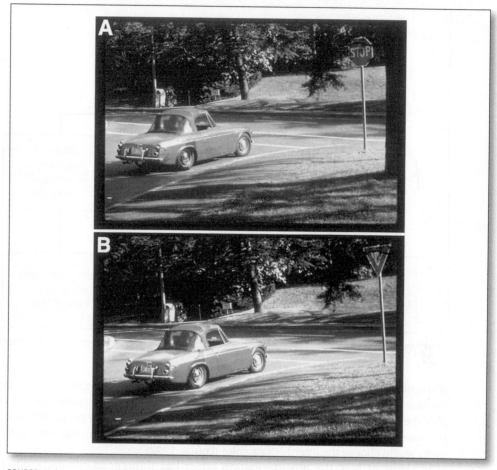

SOURCE: Loftus, Miller, and Burns (1978).

recognition test in which there was a novel distractor, there was no misinformation effect (see Figure 8.9). The McCloskey and Zaragoza (1985) study supports the coexistence hypothesis. This means that when we choose the misinformation item during the recognition test, it is because we are recalling the misinformation from the time of its presentation rather than from a distorted view of the original event.

However, there are also data that support the trace impairment view (Belli, Windschitl, McCarthy, & Winfrey, 1992). Evidence for the trace impairment view comes from research on blending. For example, in one study, participants saw a blue car during a short film of an accident. Later, it was erroneously suggested that the car was green. At the time of test, the participants had to choose the color of the car. Participants tended to choose a blue-green

Figure 8.9   McCloskey and Zaragoza's (1985) design.

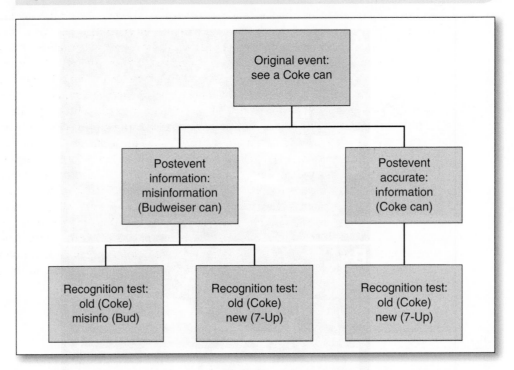

when given a palette of colors. The blue-green represented something intermediate between the blue that they saw and the green that was suggested. If the coexistence view is correct, then the participants would have chosen either blue or green but not the intermediate color. However, if trace impairment is correct, then the colors might mix in memory, and participants would choose the intermediate color (Loftus, 1992).

In terms of how the misinformation effect has influenced our understanding of suggestibility and false memory, the contrast between these two theories is minor. Nonetheless, as you know from other sections in this book, the issue of representation is critical to understanding how memory works. Moreover, whether the representation is altered or whether the person has two separable memory traces does have practical implications. For example, Rindal et al. (in press) challenged the idea that retrieving the witnessed memory led a person to be in a vulnerable state for memory distortion. Using the modified recognition test, Rindal et al. showed that the original memory is strong when the distractor is not the misinformation introduced at the time of the initial retrieval. This suggests that—as long as concerned people can shield witnesses from misinformation—repeated retrieval does not necessarily lead to a degraded representation of the original event, a finding with encouraging implications for eyewitness memory.

SECTION SUMMARY AND QUIZ

One of the debates in the area concerns the nature of the recovery of repressed memories. Are such recovered memories real or false? Although the data suggest that many are false, new research attempts to explore the cognitive mechanisms that could produce both initial repression and subsequent recovery. Smith and Moynan (2008) investigated the hypothesis that repression occurs because of failures to rehearse, and Anderson and colleagues (2004) have conducted experiments on retrieval suppression. Witnessing a crime is a rare and emotionally laden event. Memory for that event is often important in helping police solve the crime and for the court system to prosecute an accused criminal. However, research on eyewitness memory tells us that such memories are not always accurate. Like other memories, they may be false. In particular, memory researchers have looked at the effect of suggestibility on eyewitness memory. First, subtle differences in words can affect people's memory reports. Second, the introduction of misinformation can also distort or alter people's memory for a crime. Elizabeth Loftus introduced a procedure, called the misinformation effect, to measure suggestibility in eyewitness memory. In the procedure, a person witnesses an event but then sees misinformation about it later. The misinformation impairs memory relative to appropriate controls. It is likely that this decrement in performance is caused by a change to the original memory as a result of its interaction with the misinformation.

Section Quiz

1. The "failure to rehearse" hypothesis explains which phenomenon?
   a. The misinformation effect
   b. Repression
   c. Change blindness
   d. The coexistence view of representation

2. Benoit et al. asked participants to either suppress or rehearse more real-world stimuli, such as pictures of faces and physical locations. They found
   a. The dorsolateral region of the prefrontal cortex was a key region in suppression, and this region became most active when the act of suppressing the memory proved difficult
   b. The medial prefrontal region was the key region in inhibiting suppression
   c. Unlike lab stimuli, suppression was not possible with faces and physical locations
   d. All of the above are false

3. Research on suggestibility shows that
   a. Only a small minority of people can be influenced by misinformation
   b. Only patients with brain damage show suggestibility effects
   c. Even the change of a single word can sometimes influence people's memory reports
   d. Suggestibility is the likely cause of false memories in the DRM procedure

4. The coexistence theory of the misinformation effect states that
   a. Misinformation alters the original memory
   b. Misinformation blends with the original memory
   c. The presentation of misinformation creates a second memory, which then can be confused for the original memory
   d. All of the above are true

1. b
2. a
3. c
4. c

THE COGNITIVE INTERVIEW: MORE INFORMATION WITHOUT SUGGESTION

We know that all of us may have false memories from time to time. We also know that we all may fall prey to suggestion, even in sensitive legal proceedings. Is there anything we can do about it? When the witness confidently proclaims, "I'll never forget that day—it was that man over there who committed the crime," can we ever put confidence in that statement?

Cognitive interview: A protocol designed to help police investigators obtain the maximum amount of information from witnesses with the least likelihood of inducing false memories.

Amount of information: The quantity of information retrieved while recalling an episodic event.

Open-ended questions: Retrieval questions that contain very few cues that allow the participant to describe her memory without suggestions. These limit the possibility of introducing inadvertent misinformation.

Should we ever trust such a statement? Are there ways of gathering information from witnesses that do not run the risk of inadvertently providing misinformation?

Ron Fisher and Ed Geiselman devised something they called the **cognitive interview** (Fisher & Geiselman, 1992; see Gabbert et al., 2016). The cognitive interview is a protocol designed to help police investigators obtain the maximum **amount of information** from witnesses with the least likelihood of inducing false memories. The cognitive interview is based on several principles of memory retrieval that we have discussed earlier in this book. It has also been tested empirically to substantiate its claim to boost memory without increasing the rate of false memory. The cognitive interview passes these tests (Fisher & Schreiber, 2007). Let's see how the cognitive interview works.

First, the police officer or other initial investigator is instructed to ask **open-ended questions**. Open-ended questions limit the possibility of introducing inadvertent misinformation. For example, an open-ended question is simply "What did you see?" rather than "Did you see the man who pulled out a gun?" It is possible that it was a woman who pulled out a gun, two men who had guns, and or there was no gun at all. So unless the investigator actually saw the crime, there is the possibility of introducing misinformation with the directed question, however plausible it may seem. Open-ended questions provide no opportunity for the introduction of misinformation. However, police officers actually conducting witness interviews have difficulty following these instructions. In a study of police officers trying to follow guidelines that encourage open-ended questions, many officers interrupted and asked more directed questions (Schreiber Compo, Gregory, & Fisher, 2012). Nonetheless, the use of open-ended questions is advisable in maximizing recall and minimizing false memories.

The cognitive interview uses three retrieval-enhancing principles. First, witnesses are encouraged to think about the physical context of the witnessed event (context reinstatement). Witnesses are asked to imagine themselves at the scene of the crime and to report what they see. However, the interviewer avoids directed questions that might mislead the witness. Context reinstatement has been shown to increase the amount remembered (Fisher & Geiselman, 1992). Second, the witness is encouraged to remember the event from different time sequences—first most recent to most distant, then from the beginning of the event to the end of the event (different temporal patterns). Third, witnesses are asked to mentally visualize the crime scene from a variety of perspectives—from their own and from that of someone looking from the outside. The hope is that different perspectives will provide different retrieval cues and more information will be provided. Again, it is especially important to avoid giving any suggestions, especially as participants will be imagining themselves at the scene of the crime. Indeed, research shows that the cognitive interview can boost the report of recalled information by 30% compared to a standard police interview without raising the percentage of information that is inaccurate (Fisher & Schreiber, 2007). Indeed, in one study in which the witnesses were children, correct recall was increased significantly and misremembering was decreased significantly (El Asam & Samara, 2015). It is worth noting that the cognitive interview is designed to work with cooperative witnesses without mental disabilities. Studies with autistic individuals show that context reinstatement does not work in improving their memories (Maras & Bowler, 2012). Also, suspects are certainly not cooperative witnesses and may lie under any interview technique. However, a 30% increase in information from well-meaning witnesses without mental disabilities may be very beneficial.

Ron Fisher, Ed Geiselman, and others who have developed the cognitive interview have worked with police departments all over the world, including in Miami, Los Angeles, Sydney, and London. As a consequence, the cognitive interview has been tested and used successfully in real-world settings (Gabbert et al. 2016). Some police investigators now swear by it. It is also possible that the cognitive interview will be useful for other kinds of investigations. For example, doctors could use it to maximize the amount of information that they get from their patients. Laguna-Camacho and Booth (2015) showed that the cognitive interview was helpful in getting people to remember instances in which they had not adhered to a prescribed diet. The technique could also be used by historians trying to investigate a historical event by probing the details of remaining witnesses. If you are interested in more information on the cognitive interview, a recent edited book contains many chapters on the cognitive interview (Oxburgh, Myklebust, Grant, & Milne, 2016). (And for a transcript of an interview with Ron Fisher, go to www.sage pub.com/schwartz3e.[7])

One study on eyewitness memory suggests a simple but potent means of increasing the ability of eyewitnesses to accurately recall an event: Close your eyes while you remember the event. Perfect et al. (2008) showed that simply closing one's eyes allowed witnesses to remember more information about a crime with no increase in false memories. Because it led to an increase in the recollection of many visual details, the researchers suspected that the improved memory likely occurs because closing one's eyes removes an important part of memory interference—namely, the currently visible world and its impingement on working memory. Perfect and his colleagues suggested that eye closure ought to be incorporated into the cognitive interview.

MNEMONIC IMPROVEMENT TIP 8.1

The cognitive interview: When trying to recall details of a particular event, use the three principles of the cognitive interview: (1) context reinstatement, (2) different temporal patterns, and (3) different spatial patterns. Recall as much as possible and sort out what is relevant later.

MNEMONIC IMPROVEMENT TIP 8.2

Close your eyes when trying to remember episodic events, such as an eyewitness memory. Closing your eyes may allow you to recall more details without a cost in false memories.

SUMMARY

False memories are the relatively small amounts of information that we recall that do not correspond to reality. Accuracy measures correspondence or the extent to which retrieved memories correspond to the factual past. False memories have been highly controversial and well studied in two domains, the recovery of repressed memories of childhood abuse and eyewitness memory. Because of the controversies surrounding these two areas, cognitive psychologists have devised a number of ways to study false memory in the laboratory. These methods include the Deese-Roediger-McDermott (DRM) procedure, the visual false memory procedure, the false memory induction procedure, imagination inflation, and the misinformation effect. Explanations for false memories vary, but some center on source monitoring, remembering the gist instead of specific details, and suggestibility. Hypnosis can also lead to an increase in false memories. New research suggests, however, that repressed memories may occur under some circumstances. Two mechanisms for repression may be failure to rehearse the information and active suppression. In the legal context, eyewitness memory is fallible, and the dangers of misinformation are well documented. The cognitive interview provides a way for witnesses to recall lots of details from a crime scene without increasing the risk of false memories.

KEY TERMS

active suppression

amount of
   information

coexistence hypothesis

cognitive interview

contextual associations

correspondence

critical intrusion

Deese-Roediger-McDermott
   procedure

failure to rehearse

false memories

false memory induction
   procedure

fuzzy-trace theory

hypnosis

imagination inflation

misinformation
   effect

open-ended questions

reality monitoring

recovery of repressed
   memories

repression

retrieval bias

source monitoring

suggestibility

trace impairment view

visual false memory
   procedure

REVIEW QUESTIONS

1. What are false memories? Do they only happen to people who have been traumatized, or are they a more general phenomenon?

2. What does *correspondence* mean? Why is reporting the amount that people recall not enough to fully describe memory ability?

3. What is the Deese-Roediger-McDermott (DRM) procedure? What does it measure, and how does it do so?

4. What is the false memory induction procedure? What does it measure, and how does it do so?

5. What is hypnosis? Why is it not considered advisable to help eyewitnesses remember more information from a crime scene?

6. What evidence exists to show that repression is a real phenomenon? Why would cognitive scientists have doubted repression in the first place?

7. What cognitive mechanisms have been postulated to explain repression? What experimental data support that these cognitive mechanisms are real?

8. What is suggestibility? What evidence exists to show how it influences eyewitness memory?

9. What are the two explanations for the misinformation effect? What evidence supports each one?

10. What is the cognitive interview? How is it used to prevent false memories but still produce good recall?

ONLINE RESOURCES

1. For more on Dr. Thompson's ordeal, go to http://www.spring.org.uk/2008/02/how-memories-are-distorted-and-invented.php

2. For the transcript of an interview with Dr. Clancy, go to http://www.nuforc.org/npr.html.

3. For more on the Roediger-McDermott illusion, go to http://gocognitive.net/demo/memory-lists-roediger-mcdermott-1995

4. For an article on this topic by Elizabeth Loftus, go to http://faculty.washington.edu/eloftus/Articles/sciam.htm.

5. To find out more about imagination inflation, go to http://faculty.washington.edu/eloftus/Articles/Imagine.htm.

6. Visit the website of the Innocence Project for other cases in which people have been wrongly convicted: http://www.innocenceproject.org.

7. For the transcript of an interview with Ron Fisher, go to http://www.au.af.mil/au/awc/awcgate/gov/ntsb_cognitive_interview.pdf.

Go to **study.sagepub.com/schwartz3e** for additional exercises and study resources. Select **Chapter 8, False Memory** for chapter-specific resources.

CHAPTER 9

Metamemory

Many of you have probably seen the popular game show *Who Wants to Be a Millionaire?* On the show, contestants are asked trivia questions. For example, they might be asked "What expression is both a brand of ham and a type of cake?" Contestants see the question with four possible answers, one of which is the correct answer (Black Forest). It is the contestants' job to select the correct answer from among the four possibilities. With each trivia question they answer correctly, they win more money. If they answer a question incorrectly, however, they lose half or more of their money, and their "15 minutes" of fame comes to an end. Interestingly, the rules of the game allow a contestant several options if he or she does not know the answer or is unsure of the answer to a particular question. All of these options rely on the use of metamemory, our ability to introspect on our own memory system. For example, a contestant may choose another question instead of the one originally presented. The contestant must recognize that he or she does not know the answer to the first question before opting for a new question. If this question is also beyond the contestant, he or she can choose to not answer at all and keep all the money he or she has won. The contestant must rely on his or her confidence in knowing the answer to make these financially relevant decisions.

Most of us will never be on a game show, but the show described above is similar to situations a student is in when taking an exam. Metamemory has a role in the ordinary studying that every college student must engage in. Imagine a student studying for two exams, both scheduled for the following day. She has an exam in social psychology, her favorite class in her intended major. The second exam is in statistics, which this student finds difficult and not very interesting. What should she study? The answer is, "It depends." It depends on a host of factors that the student must actively consider. How important is it for her to get a really good grade in social psychology? Perhaps she wants to work on an honors thesis with the professor. If so, it may be worth putting all of the study time into social psychology, even if that means doing poorly on the statistics test. But statistics is an important class for graduate school. Should that class get more study time because of the consequences of having a bad grade in that class for likely admission to graduate school? Also, if the student has, by and large, mastered the social psychology content, should she instead focus her study on the harder statistics class? On the other hand, her yoga instructor suggested that on the night before the exams, she should simply relax, take a bath, get a good night's sleep, and trust that she knows the material well. These real-life dilemmas are the domain of metamemory.

Metacognition: Our knowledge and awareness of our own cognitive processes.

Metamemory: Our knowledge and awareness of our own memory processes.

Metacognition is our knowledge and awareness of our own cognitive processes. Research suggests that based on our metacognitive awareness, we often make sophisticated decisions about how to go about learning, remembering, and finding our way when lost. The area of metacognition that deals with memory is called metamemory, the subject of this chapter. **Metamemory** means our knowledge and awareness of our own memory processes.

Metamemory includes the ability to both monitor one's own memory abilities and control them. It allows human beings to reflect on their own memory processes and to actively and expertly self-regulate their memory. It may be that some animals have rudimentary metamemory processes (Kornell, 2009; Washburn, Beran, & Smith, 2016), but by and large, metamemory abilities are unique to humans. Metamemory allows us to reflect on what we know and what we do not know. For example, if you state, "I know the names of every person who has been president of the United States but just a handful of the people who have been prime minister of Great Britain," you are making a metamemory statement—the knowledge of what is or is not in your memory. When you state that you are certain you know the directions to the restaurant, your certainty is a metacognitive experience—it is the feeling that you know something and therefore the domain of metamemory. We can also apply this metamemory thinking to our learning and remembering. We can focus our study on what we are unsure of and avoid what we are confident is beyond our abilities. Metamemory allows us to focus on the most difficult items, if those are what we need to focus on. It also informs us we have studied enough and can take that warm bath.

WHAT IS METAMEMORY?

Like most of the topics we have been considering, metamemory is of interest because of both its theoretical importance in understanding the science of human memory and its practical importance for understanding human learning and memory improvement. It is for this reason that, in the 21st century, metamemory has become one of the hot topics in memory research (Beran, Brandl, Perner, & Proust, 2012; Dunlosky & Tauber, 2016). (For information on active research on metamemory, go to study.sagepub.com/schwartz3e.[1])

Here are the important terms and definitions and brief descriptions of a few critical ideas concerning metamemory.

Monitoring: Our ability to reflect on and become aware of what we know and do not know.

Monitoring occurs whenever we take measure of our own mental states. When we judge whether or not we think we can remember something, when we feel more or less confident that we know something, and when we feel more or less confident that we have understood something, we are engaging in monitoring. For example, if you state that you are confident that you will remember the vocabulary you just studied when you take your French test tomorrow, you are demonstrating metamemory monitoring. You are confident that you know the words. Similarly, when you are sure you will not recall something, that is also metamemory monitoring. Thus, one is monitoring one's metamemory when one is certain that one cannot recall the name of the president of Kazakhstan. Monitoring is important in many applied settings, such as educational ones. If you are accurately monitoring your learning, you will know what to expect when you take an exam (or as we will see, what you need to do to do better).

Nelson and Narens (1990) likened monitoring to a thermometer: A thermometer tells us the ambient temperature, and metamemory tells us the state of our personal memories. Both are measuring some quantity by one means or another. Both the thermometer and your metamemory provide information, which may be quite useful. A low reading on the thermometer lets you know to grab a coat, and a low rating on a metamemory scale lets you know you have not learned the material well enough for a test. What is essential to monitoring is that the person becomes consciously aware of whether or not the information is accessible in memory. Monitoring can be as simple as noting, "I am not going to remember that phone number." Alternatively, if I am experiencing a tip-of-the-tongue state for the name of the cellist who played at President Obama's first inauguration, I have become aware that I may remember that fact soon. If monitoring did not occur, I would not know that I knew the name of the famous cellist. Similarly, if you hear a sentence spoken in a strange language, such as Mongolian, you are certain you do not understand it.

Monitoring accuracy means that when you think you know something, you do know it, and when you think you do not know something, you indeed do not know it. If you think you can remember something, then fail to do so, your monitoring has failed you as well as your memory. And if you think you cannot remember something but then do so, your monitoring has also failed. The importance for metamemory is not necessarily that you know a fact, but that you know if you know it or not. Thus, it is the correspondence between your actual state of knowledge and your metamemory that matters. If that sounds confusing, just keep in mind that accuracy here refers to whether or not monitoring correctly reflects our internal state. In our thermometer metaphor, if you have a thermometer that measures cold temperatures as too hot and hot temperatures as too cold, it is not useful. Thus, monitoring is only helpful if it accurately reflects what we do or do not have represented in our memory system. Think of the game show participant. If, after announcing that he is taking the money and leaving an unanswered question on the board, he realizes that he does know the answer, it is too late. He has already given his "final answer." The money is lost, and the participant must pack his bags and go home. By contrast, if I have a tip-of-the-tongue state for the famous cello player and then recall the name (Yo-Yo Ma), then my monitoring is accurate. Of course, being able to monitor our internal state is only useful if we can do something about it. Thus, monitoring must be able to feed into actual behaviors that can control our learning. We call this self-regulation or metacognitive control.

Self-regulation is important in many aspects of human behavior. When self-regulation is directed at memory, we call it **metacognitive control**. These processes use the output

Metacognitive control: Self-regulation directed at memory.

of monitoring to inform decisions we make about learning and remembering. For example, if a person is experiencing a tip-of-the-tongue, he or she may decide to spend more time trying to come up with the answer without looking it up. In Nelson and Narens's (1990) analogy, the control device is the thermostat. Based on the temperature reading of the thermometer (monitoring), the thermostat device will either start the heat, if the room has gotten too cold, or trigger the air-conditioning, if the room is too warm. Thus, the "control" here is the implementation of cooling or warming. Control processes are only as good as the accuracy of the monitoring that allows for appropriate adjustment of behavior. A thermostat that turned on the heat when it reached 80 degrees inside or turned on the air-conditioning when it cooled to 55 degrees inside would require an immediate call to the technician. Thus, our control processes must be tuned to a monitoring process that is accurate.

Control (in metamemory): Our ability to regulate our learning or retrieval based upon our own monitoring.

Ease-of-learning judgments: Estimates made before studying an item of how likely it will be remembered and how difficult it will be to learn.

Judgments of learning: Determinations made during study of whether the item has been learned already.

Feeling-of-knowing judgments: Estimations of the likelihood that an unrecalled item will be recognized.

Control involves the behaviors we engage in to ensure learning. For example, when the student studying for two exams elects to focus her attention and study time on the social psychology class, she is engaged in control. Based on her monitoring, she may come to realize that statistics is hopeless—so she better do well in social psychology. As a result, she spends all of her study time on that class. For another example, think of cooking a special dinner. If you are confident you have the recipe memorized (monitoring), you will start gathering the ingredients and turning on the oven (control). However, if you are uncertain that you remember the recipe (monitoring), you will look for the cookbook on your bookshelf (control).

Nelson and Narens (1990) divided metamemory judgments at various stages of memory processing. As you can see in Figure 9.1, just as memory is divided into encoding, representation, and retrieval, metamemory can be divided along similar lines. During encoding or learning, people can make two kinds of metamemory judgments. **Ease-of-learning judgments** are estimates in advance of studying an item of how likely it will be remembered and how difficult it will be to learn. **Judgments of learning**, made during study, are determinations of whether the item has been learned already. During retrieval, people can make **feeling-of-knowing judgments** on unrecalled items; these judgments are estimations of the likelihood that an unrecalled item will be recognized. **Tip-of-the-tongue states (TOTs)** are feelings that an unrecalled item will be recalled soon. After an item has been retrieved, the person can make a variety of metamemory judgments, including **retrospective confidence judgments** (also known as the confidence in retrieved answers), which are estimations that the retrieved answer is indeed correct. As discussed in Chapter 8, source-monitoring judgments are awareness of the likely sources of the information.

Tip-of-the-tongue states (TOTs): Feelings that an unrecalled item will be recalled soon.

Retrospective confidence judgments: Estimations that a retrieved answer is indeed correct.

Figure 9.1 A model of metamemory.

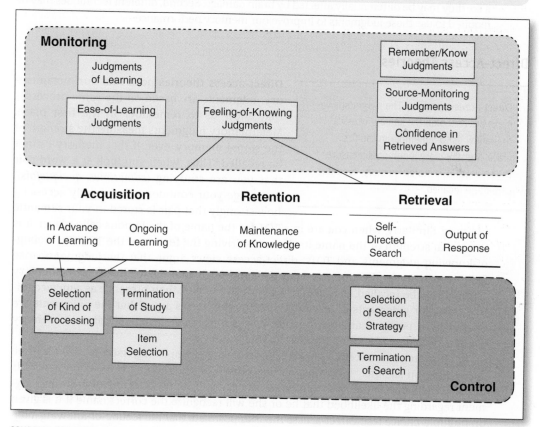

SOURCES: Adapted from Dunlosky, J., Serra, M., & Baker, J. M. C. (2007). Metamemory applied. In F. Durso et al. (Eds.) *Handbook of Applied Cognition* (2nd ed., pp. 137–159) New York: John Wiley & Sons.

THEORIES OF METAMEMORY

Metamemory concerns our awareness of memory processes. But it is also a cognitive process itself and therefore, can be studied with the same tools that are applied to other areas of memory research. In this section, we will examine the classes of theories that researchers have advanced to account for metamemory. What cognitive processes allow us to monitor our memory, and what cognitive processes are involved in controlling our memory? We will see that each kind of judgment is unique—it draws upon different internal processes based upon different neural mechanisms. As such, the accuracy of monitoring and the ability to effectively control memory will vary across judgments. Feeling-of-knowing judgments are very much influenced by the cues or questions provided, but judgments of learning are more influenced by the fluency with which one retrieves an answer (Souchay & Isingrini, 2012; Thomas, Lee, & Hughes, 2016). The different mechanisms that underlie judgments of learning and feeling-of-knowing judgments have a number of important implications. First, they may have different neural substrates, and if so, they may be differentially affected by brain damage. Second, different techniques may be required to use these judgments to improve our memory performance.

Direct-Access Theories

Direct-access theories: The judgments we make are based on the same processes that allow us to remember in the first place. Metamemory judgments measure the strength of a stored memory, even if it cannot be recalled.

Direct-access theories posit that our metamemory judgments are based on the same processes that allow us to remember in the first place. Metamemory judgments measure the strength of the stored memory, even if that memory cannot be recalled. Thus, when you look at a word pair that you are studying (*sometimes–quelquefois*), you judge your confidence by directly accessing how strongly that pair is stored in your semantic memory. Similarly, when you are in a TOT for the name of the famous cello player, it is the actual strength of the name itself that is driving the feeling of the TOT. For feeling-of-knowing judgments and TOTs, direct-access views argue that the judgments arise from sensitivity to the unretrieved target. Although items have insufficient memory "strength" to be recalled, they are strong enough to signal their presence as a metacognitive state. For judgments of learning, direct-access views argue that the judgments are caused by a person's ability to gauge how strong an item has become in memory (Dunlosky & Metcalfe, 2009; Rhodes, 2016).

To illustrate this concept, consider the following example. A person is asked a game show question such as "Who was the first person on the moon?" If the contestant fails to recall the name of the astronaut, he or she can still supply a feeling-of-knowing judgment regarding the likelihood that he or she will recognize the correct name if it is given on multiple-choice test. Direct-access theories postulate that the feeling-of-knowing judgment is driven by unconscious activation of the unrecalled target name (*Neil Armstrong*). The memory (the knowledge that Neil Armstrong was the first man on the moon) and the metamemory ("I will recognize the name") are a function of the same cognitive process.

Indirect or Inferential Theories

Indirect or inferential theories are based on the idea that we use a variety of clues, cues, tricks, and heuristics to estimate the strength of an item in memory, which we cannot measure directly. Imagine estimating the temperature on a cold day by seeing whether your breath is visible. You are not directly measuring temperature (as a thermometer might), but you can get reliable information about the temperature through this indirect means. If you can see your breath, you may know the temperature is below 45°F. If your nostrils start to freeze, then you know it is below 0°F. Your physiological characteristics serve as a proxy for temperature. Many scuba divers can estimate the temperature of the ocean within 1°F just by feeling the water. With respect to metamemory, a host of other cognitive processes estimate how well we have learned or how likely we are to remember information. This information may include the retrieval of related information, knowledge that you have studied or remembered

> **Indirect or inferential theories:** We use a variety of clues, cues, tricks, and heuristics to estimate the strength of an item in memory, which we cannot measure directly.

> **Cue familiarity:** Stored information about the cue or the degree to which we recognize that the cue influences our metamemory judgment about the to-be-remembered target.

> **Retrieval of related information:** We retrieve information related to a target that can influence our metamemory judgment about learning or remembering the target.

the information earlier, or general familiarity with the topic in question. If these clues point to success, we give strong metamemory judgments; if they point to failure, we give low metamemory judgments. Applied to feeling-of-knowing judgments, for example, this theory tells us that we may use information about the general topic, **cue familiarity, retrieval of related information** to the target, and partial information about the target (Rhodes, 2016; Thomas et al., 2016). It is not the exact memory that drives the feeling of knowing. Instead, it is other kinds of information that correlate with the likelihood that we do have that memory.

SECTION SUMMARY AND QUIZ

Metamemory is our knowledge and awareness of our own memory processes. In a broader sense, metacognition refers to our knowledge and awareness of our cognitive processes. Monitoring is our ability to reflect on our own memory processes, whereas control is our ability to direct our memory processes in advantageous ways. Two main theories have organized research on the mechanism of metamemory. According to direct-access theory, we make metamemory judgments via a mechanism that directly measures the strength of a memory. According to inferential theory, people make metamemory judgments by measuring a host of accessible information that is correlated with the strength of the memory.

Section Quiz

1. Our ability to reflect on and become aware of what we know and do not know is known as
   a. Monitoring
   b. Control
   c. Syncopation
   d. Cue familiarity

2. Which is an example of metacognitive control?
   a. A person decides to study more for a test because she thinks she has not studied enough
   b. A person realizes that she has not yet mastered the material
   c. A person experiences a tip-of-the-tongue state for a celebrity's name
   d. A person designs an experiment to examine accuracy of feeling-of-knowing judgments

3. Retrospective confidence judgments are
   a. Assessments of whether one should study an item or not
   b. Assessments of whether one will forget an item that one just learned
   c. Judgments about whether or not an answer just retrieved is correct or not
   d. Judgments about whether a feeling of knowing has occurred

4. Inferential theories of metacognition center around the idea that
   a. We intuitively know if we know or not
   b. We have direct access to unretrieved information
   c. We use a variety of clues and heuristics to estimate the strength of an item in memory
   d. All of the above are false

1. a
2. a
3. c
4. c

TYPES OF JUDGMENTS

Tip-of-the-Tongue States

The tip-of-the-tongue state (to be abbreviated as TOT) is defined as the feeling of temporary inaccessibility. *Inaccessibility* here means that an item is stored (available) in memory but cannot be retrieved at present. **Availability** means all the information that is stored in memory, whereas **accessibility** refers to the information that is currently retrievable (see Bjork & Bjork, 1992; Tulving & Pearlstone, 1966). In a TOT, we feel as if an item is inaccessible but eventually recoverable (Brown & McNeill, 1966; Schwartz & Metcalfe, 2011). Note that a TOT has two components. First, the feeling—it is a subjective state—the TOT experience can feel quite strong. And second, that feeling has a reference—namely, that a particular item is in our memory. It is the feeling of the TOT that concerns metamemory. (For an interesting overview on tip-of-the-tongue states from science writer Jonah Lehrer, go to www.sagepub .com/schwartz3e.[2])

Availability: All information present in our memory.

Accessibility: That part of our stored memories that we can retrieve under present conditions.

Researchers have examined TOTs by prospecting for them (Brown, 1991, 2012; Schwartz & Brown, 2014). Researchers present participants with a series of general-information questions. If the participant knows the answer, he or she moves on. If the participant cannot recall the answer, however, he or she may be in a TOT for that item. If so, the experimenter can then probe for different variables that may arise during TOTs. Consider the following questions. Do any of them elicit a TOT in you?

1. What is the largest planet in the solar system?
2. Which precious gem is red?
3. What is the capital of Jamaica?
4. What is the capital of Chile?
5. What is the name for the legendary one-eyed giants in Greek mythology?
6. What is the last name of the author of the James Bond novels?
7. What is the last name of the author who wrote under the pseudonym of Mark Twain?
8. What is the city in Italy that is known for its canals?
9. What is the last name of the composer who wrote the opera *Don Giovanni?*
10. What is the last name of the author of *Little Women?*

Did you experience a TOT? What happens when you are in a TOT? Do you feel frustrated that you cannot recall the answer? Do you feel like you are about to get the answer, or do you think it will come later? Do you have the first letter of the missing word and just can't seem to fill it out? All of these are common experiences during TOTs. The answers to each trivia question are presented below and upside down.

When a participant reports a TOT in an experiment, the researcher can then make a number of inquiries into the mental state of the participant and the knowledge possessed during the TOT. In many cases, the participant may know the word for the item in another language (Gollan & Brown, 2006); if the TOT is for a person's name, whether or not that person has a middle name (Hanley & Chapman, 2008); the first letter and how many syllables are in the word (Brown, 1991; Koriat & Lieblich, 1974); words that sound similar to the target and words that mean something similar to the target (Kornell & Metcalfe,

2006; Smith, 1994); whether the word has been retrieved before or not (D'Angelo and Humphreys, 2015); and many other aspects of the word other than the actual word itself (Brown, 2012; Schwartz, & Metcalfe, 2011). Indeed, it is likely that the accessibility of this related information feeds back and makes the TOT all the more frustrating.

After this information has been gleaned from the participant, usually the researchers present a final recognition test. The likelihood of recognition can be compared for TOTs and for items the participant simply does not know. By and large, TOTs are highly accurate at predicting subsequent recognition. If the participant is in a TOT, the person will be more likely to recognize the correct answer than if the person was not in a TOT (Schwartz & Brown, 2014).

There are a number of other closely related phenomena (see Schwartz & Cleary, 2016). For example, Chinese speakers experience "tip-of-the-pen" states when they are writing. This occurs when they know how to say a word but do not remember the written character that represents that word. This largely unstudied phenomenon exists in Chinese, because that writing system mostly goes directly from a visual symbol to the meaning of an item, without visual coding for sound, as we do in alphabetic languages. Thus, a person can see the symbol and know what it means, but not be able to recall how to say it. Sign language speakers experience "tip-of-the-finger" states in which they are certain they know a manual word but cannot recall how to form the sign. Exactly analogous to a TOT, tip-of-the-finger states are usually accompanied by partial and related information to the missing target word, including partial information about the shape of the hand used to make the sign (Thompson, Emmorey, & Gollan, 2005). Moreover, many people will experience the tip-of-the-nose phenomenon, in which a smell is recognized as being familiar, but one cannot recall the name of that odor (Schwartz & Cleary, 2016). It is likely that tip-of-the-nose states, tip-of-the-finger states, and tip-of-the-pen states closely resemble TOTs, but psychological scientists have only briefly studied these.

The research supports the idea that TOTs are caused by inferential or indirect processes (see Schwartz & Metcalfe, 2011). The clues and cues that we recognize and retrieve allow us unconsciously to infer that an item is likely to be remembered. This unconscious inference is experienced as a TOT. Research has suggested that both cue familiarity and the partial retrieval of related information play a role in this inference. For example, when a person can retrieve more related information, such as what the object the word represents looks like or whether it has been retrieved previously, more TOTs will occur. In contrast, variables that increase the likelihood of recalling an item do not always affect TOT rates (Schwartz & Cleary, 2016).

| 1. Jupiter | 2. Ruby | 3. Kingston | 4. Santiago | 5. Cyclops |
| 6. Fleming | 7. Clemens | 8. Venice | 9. Mozart | 10. Alcott |

Brain Mechanisms

Circuits in the prefrontal lobes of the cerebral cortex appear to be important for metamemory (Do Lam et al., 2012; Metcalfe & Schwartz, 2016). Monitoring is linked to areas of the prefrontal cortex known as the dorsomedial prefrontal cortex, whereas control is linked to the dorsolateral prefrontal cortex. Both of these areas appear to be activated during TOTs. That these areas are clearly activated is evidence that TOTs should be considered metamemory and not simply an issue of word retrieval. Much of the data have come from the work of Anat Maril, then at Harvard University. She and her colleagues have shown that there are areas of the brain unique to TOTs in the prefrontal lobe (see Figure 9.2). In particular, the anterior cingulate (considered part of the dorsomedial prefrontal cortex) is activated during TOTs (Maril, Simons, Weaver, & Schacter, 2005). This area is associated with a number of experiential components associated with surprise and novelty as well as cognitive monitoring (Metcalfe & Schwartz, 2016), of which the TOT is one kind. In addition to the anterior cingulate, the dorsolateral cortex is also activated during TOTs. This area has been associated with metacognitive control and perhaps is responsible for guiding the behaviors that people engage in to resolve TOTs when they occur.

Feeling of Knowing

Feeling-of-knowing judgments, like TOTs, are predictions of the future retrievability of a particular item. Thus, if one cannot recall the name of the artist who recorded the song "My House," one may be able to recognize his name among a list of other artists (it is Flo Rida). People can make a feeling-of-knowing judgment to assess this possibility. Unlike TOTs, feeling-of-knowing judgments can be made without the feeling that the person will recall the answer. This is a subtle difference but easily explained. For example, a person may be reasonably sure that she will not recall her seventh-grade science teacher's name but may be confident that she could *recognize* it in a multiple-choice format. In a TOT, on the other hand, she feels sure that she will be able to *recall* it.

The feeling of knowing has been studied in two ways. One is similar to the prospecting technique with TOTs. With feeling-of-knowing judgments, though, it is called the recall-judgment-recognition procedure (RJR). It was first used by Joseph Hart (1965) to initiate the formal study of metamemory. The participant tries to recall the answer to general-information questions or the target of a cue-target pair. If unsuccessful, the participant provides a feeling-of-knowing judgment for recognition of that item. A recognition test then is given to measure accuracy.

Another way of examining feeling of knowing is the "game show" paradigm developed by Lynne Reder and her colleagues in the 1980s (Reder, 1987; Reder & Ritter, 1992). In the game show paradigm, the participant is given a question and as fast as possible, must either indicate the answer or simply that he knows the answer. For example, if the question is "What was the name of the first person on the moon?" some participants would have to say "Armstrong" as fast as possible, whereas others would simply have to say "know it" as fast as possible. Reder and her colleagues discovered that people could make the "know it" response faster than they could retrieve the name. This suggests that we have an initial and rapid feeling of knowing that we can act on even before we recall the target word. The fact that we can determine that we know an answer faster than we can actually recall the answer also strongly supports the view that our metamemory judgments are heuristic and based on clues to the correct answer rather than nonconscious access to that answer.

Figure 9.2 Functional magnetic resonance imaging results from Maril, Simons, Weaver, and Schacter (2005). Inspection of Graph b shows that, during TOTs, the anterior cingulate is very active, but during successful retrieval, it does not exhibit more than normal activation. In contrast, other areas of the brain (in Graphs a, c, and d) do not show this contrast.

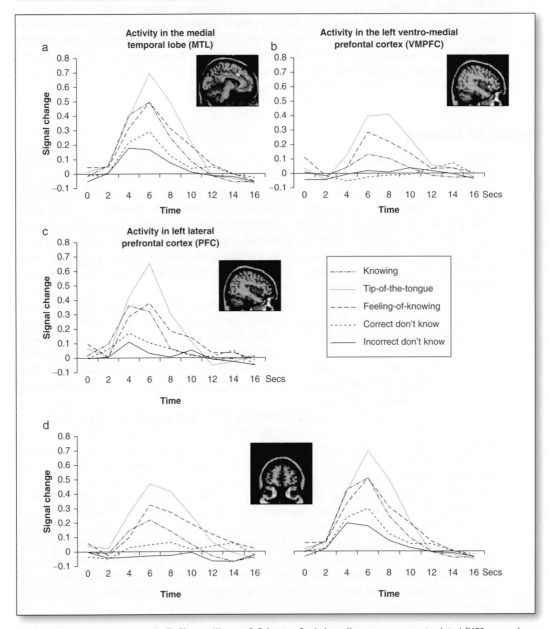

Reprinted from *NeuroImage, 24*, Maril, Simons, Weaver, & Schacter, Graded recall success: an event-related fMRI comparison of tip of the tongue and feeling of knowing, 1130–1138. Copyright (2005), with permission from Elsevier.

Mechanisms of Feeling of Knowing

One of the inferential mechanisms thought to be responsible for metamemory is cue familiarity (Thomas et al., 2016). Cue familiarity means that if we recognize or are familiar with a general-information question or if the cue in a cue-target pair elicits a sense of familiarity, we will experience a stronger feeling of knowing that we can recognize the answer. For example, at this point, the man-on-the-moon question should be quite familiar to you. The feeling of familiarity that the question now evokes will drive your feeling of knowing higher. Indeed, studies have shown that when the cue of a cue-target pair is made arbitrarily more familiar, the feeling-of-knowing judgments are higher for that item (Koriat & Levy-Sadot, 2001).

Another mechanism that may contribute to the feeling of knowing, like with the TOT, is the retrieval of related and partial information about the target. If this view is correct, factors that influence memory of the target itself will also influence feeling-of-knowing judgments. For example, if the question is "What is the name of the ancient warrior who was dipped in the river Styx?" even if we do not know the answer (Achilles), if we can remember other aspects of the story, such as how his heel was left unprotected and he was a hero in the Trojan war, then this related information informs our feeling of knowing. Thus, any factor that increased our specific knowledge about a particular target will influence feeling-of-knowing judgments.

Consider an experiment by Boduroglu, Pehlivanoglu, Tekcan, and Kapucu (2015). They were interested in the effect of relating to-be-learned information to the person remembering, the self-reference effect, on feeling-of-knowing judgments. The self-reference effect refers to the observation that encoding is superior when people relate the to-be-learned information to themselves rather than to a variety of control encoding conditions. Thus, when people are asked to evaluate words for traits that are either relevant or not to oneself, performance is better later than if people are asked to evaluate words for traits that are positive or negative (Yang, Truong, Fuss, and Bislimovic, 2012).

In the Boduroglu et al. (2015) study, participants studied related word-word cue-target pairs (e.g., "silver–gold") and unrelated pairs (e.g., "kitchen–police") with the expectation of a future cued-recall test. For half of the items, participants were asked if the cue and target words meant something they would be interested in buying together (the self-reference condition). For the other half of items, participants were asked if the cue and target word were likely to appear equally often in books. Later, when people were given the cue and had to respond with the target word, Boduroglu et al. collected feeling-of-knowing judgments. The question was whether feeling-of-knowing judgments would be higher in the condition that produced better memory—that is, the self-reference condition—consistent with the view that related and partial information influence feeling-of-knowing judgments. Indeed, this is exactly what they found. Across the related and the unrelated items, feeling-of-knowing judgments were higher for the self-reference items than they were for the control condition. Moreover, accuracy of those feeling-of-knowing judgments was higher in the self-reference condition. Thus, the strength of encoding, like cue familiarity, influences feeling-of-knowing judgments.

What does this study mean? Feeling-of-knowing judgments were higher in the self-reference condition, consistent with the view that retrieved information is relevant to these judgments. This is a good thing, because retrieval of partial information is correlated with later performance on recognition test. So, in addition to examining the cognitive mechanism underlying feeling-of-knowing judgments, this study also demonstrates that such mechanisms are helpful in allowing us to accurately monitor the state of our retrieval.

Brain Mechanisms of Feeling of Knowing

You might expect that the areas of the brain responsible for feeling of knowing would be similar to those in TOTs. The answer is both yes and no. Both TOTs and feeling-of-knowing judgments appear to be produced in the prefrontal lobe, but they appear to be a function of different areas within the prefrontal lobe. Feeling-of-knowing judgments also appear to activate areas in the parietal lobe. Whereas TOTs are more concentrated in the right hemisphere, feeling-of-knowing judgments are more concentrated in the left hemisphere. Maril, Simons, Mitchell, Schwartz, and Schacter (2003) showed that the inferior frontal gyrus was activated when participants reported feeling-of-knowing judgments, an area not activated during TOTs. Nonetheless, only a few neuroimaging studies have been done, so research may yet indicate some more direct overlap between the two.

Neuropsychology and Feeling of Knowing

Feeling-of-knowing judgments have also been examined in amnesic patients. Amnesic patients are people who suffer problems with memory as a function of brain damage. Not all amnesic patients, however, have the same symptoms. Shimamura and Squire (1986) compared the ability of temporal lobe amnesiacs (i.e., patients with damage to their temporal lobe) to patients with Korsakoff's syndrome (who have damage to the diencephalon as well as damage in frontal areas of the brain). Both groups of amnesic patients scored very low on the learning of new information. However, the temporal lobe amnesiacs were no different from controls in the accuracy of their feeling-of-knowing judgments. For them, the feeling-of-knowing task was easy. They knew that they would not remember. In patients with Korsakoff's syndrome, on the other hand, feeling-of-knowing judgments were essentially random, with no relation between their feeling-of-knowing judgments and which items they would recognize. As a result, their accuracy was much lower than that of controls. Given that patients with Korsakoff's syndrome have damage to the frontal lobe and temporal lobe amnesiacs do not, these data also support the idea that metamemory is housed in the frontal lobes (also see Schnyer et al., 2004).

Judgments of Learning

Judgments of learning are made during study and are predictions of future memory performance (see Arbuckle & Cuddy, 1969, for the origins of this research area). For example, while learning a cue-target word pair, such as *cat–fork*, you might make a judgment as to whether you will recall *fork* when given the word *cat* in a subsequent test. Judgments of learning are important both to understanding the theory of metamemory and as a practical concern. Students can use judgments of learning to help them decide which of the items they are studying are likely to be remembered later and which items they will not remember. The judgments can also be directed at which items will be forgotten and which will not be forgotten (Finn, 2008).

Judgments of learning are important for a number of reasons. First, they are the main judgments that researchers use to study metacognition during the encoding process. Second, for experimentalists, judgments of learning offer an advantage over feeling-of-knowing judgments and TOTs—namely, that judgments of learning can be made on all items, not just the subset that remains unrecalled. This allows more precise experimental control of which items receive judgments. Third, it is likely that many people implicitly make judgments of learning that directly affect their choices when they sit down and decide how they are going to learn or prepare for an exam. Fourth, if people naturally use judgments of learning to guide their study, it is important to know whether they are accurate and whether that accuracy can be improved.

Consider the role of judgments of learning in normal studying. We can imagine a student studying for a vocabulary test in French class. During the quiz, the student will be given words in French and will have to provide the meaning in English. Presumably, anyone who is reading this book for a college course has had to take such a quiz (if not in French, then in some other language) at some point. Imagine that the following items are on the to-be-studied list.

Le mur–the wall

La tache–the stain

Le chant–the song

Le porte-voix–the megaphone

Le singe–the monkey

As we study each pair, we make an implicit judgment of learning. For example, you might judge *le chant–the song* as an easy one, because the word *chant* in English has some overlap with its meaning in French. However, *le porte-voix–the megaphone* may be judged to be difficult, as it is unlikely that most English-speaking students have seen this French word before. Also, the compound nature of the word suggests that it may be more difficult to remember.

When experimenters elicit judgments of learning, they can do so in one of two ways. **Cue-target judgments of learning** involve presenting the participant with both the cue and the target and asking the participant to predict whether he or she will recall that item later when presented with only the cue. This would look something like this:

Cue-target judgments of learning: Upon seeing a target word and cue word, the participant judges the likelihood of later being able to recall the target when presented with its cue.

How likely are you to remember the English meaning of the French word when presented with only the French word on tomorrow's test?

Le singe—the monkey

0	20	40	60	80	100

In contrast, **cue-only judgments of learning** involve presenting the participant with only the cue and asking the participant to predict whether that item will be recalled later when presented with only the cue. This would look something like this:

How likely are you to remember the English meaning of the French word when presented with only the French word on tomorrow's test?

La tache—?

0	20	40	60	80	100

Cue-only judgments of learning: Upon seeing only a cue word, the participant judges the likelihood of later being able to recall the target when presented with its cue.

The accuracy of judgments of learning refers to the relation between the judgment of learning and whether or not the answer was correct or not. Thus, if a person gives a high judgment of learning (100) and then gets the answer correct, that person has made an accurate judgment of learning. In addition, if a person gives a low judgment of learning (0) and then does not get the correct answer, that judgment of learning is also accurate. Inaccuracy occurs when high judgments of learning are given to items later not recalled, and low judgments of learning are given to those that are recalled. This aspect of metacognitive accuracy is important to keep in mind when considering results of judgment-of-learning experiments.

Research by John Dunlosky and his colleagues (e.g., Dunlosky & Nelson, 1994) has demonstrated that cue-only judgments of learning are more accurate at predicting future test performance if there is a delay between the initial study of the pair (*la tache–the stain*) and the judgment of learning (*la tache—?*). Just a few minutes of delay can raise the accuracy of the judgment of learning to very high levels (correlations of above .9). This is called the delayed judgment of learning effect (Dunlosky & Nelson, 1992, 1994). It has been studied extensively both because of its theoretical interest and because it is of some practical import (Rhodes, 2016), which we will get to shortly. The question is, why does taking away information (the target) lead to more accurate monitoring?

Dunlosky and Bjork (2008) summarized the explanations for the increase in accuracy in delayed judgments of learning. Dunlosky and his group have argued that accuracy increases because if participants retrieve the target at the time of making the judgment, then they are also likely to retrieve the target at the time of test. Conversely, if you cannot recall the target at the time of judgment, you are unlikely to get it later. So the judgment of learning serves as a dry run for the final test. However, if the judgment of learning is not delayed, the target will be retrieved from working memory, and the judgment of learn-ing will not be as diagnostic of later recall as would a delayed judgment. This is called the monitoring dual-memories hypothesis. This dry run cannot occur with the cue-target judgment of learning, because the target is already provided to you, so you must rely on other, perhaps inferential mechanisms to predict your test performance.

Bjork's view arises from the observation that self-testing leads to stronger encoding of a particular item. Thus, Spellman, Bloomfield, and Bjork (2008) argued that whenever we engage in a judgment of learning, we are implicitly testing ourselves. If we recall the target dur-ing the judgment of learning, we are giving that item a huge boost in memory strength, which will carry over to the test. This is similar to the testing effect (a testing trial produces better learning than a study trial), which will be discussed in Chapter 13. Thus, those items that are successfully retrieved during the judgment of learning process are then stronger in memory than they otherwise would be, and this ensures the accuracy of the judgment of learning itself. However, recent research suggests that judgment of learning improves later recall, but not as much as actual self-testing (Akdoğan, Izaute, Danion, Vidailhet, & Bacon, 2016).

Dunlosky's view and Bjork's view are not exclusive; indeed, both could contribute to the increase in accuracy for delayed judgments of learning. Rhodes and Tauber (2011) in a metaanalysis of the literature found that the monitoring dual-memories hypothesis accounts for a greater percentage of the delayed judgments of learning effect than does boost-in-memory strength mechanism. Either mechanism, however, points to the pos-sibility that the strategic use of judgments of learning can be advantageous for efficient learning and memory improvement.

MNEMONIC IMPROVEMENT TIP 9.1

Use judgments of learning to help you study. After you've studied an item, make an index card with a question on one side and an answer on the other. Ten to 30 minutes later, pick up the card with the question on it and make a judgment of learning. If your judgment of learning is high, say the answer and then check to make sure you are correct. Put these in one pile, as you will not need to restudy them now. If your judgment of learning is low, check the answer, and put the low judgments-of-learning cards in a separate pile for later study.

Factors That Influence Judgments of Learning

There are two important aspects of any metamemory judgment: what causes it to be accu-rate and what causes it to be strong. Accuracy means whether or not the judgment predicts later memory performance, and strength means the level of confidence a person expresses in that judgment. A person may be highly confident but have low accuracy, whereas another person may be less confident (and give lower overall judgments) but be more accu-rate. As we discussed in the last section, it is likely that a delayed judgment of learning is accurate, because successful retrieval now predicts successful retrieval later. But what causes judgments of learning to be strong?

One factor that influences judgments of learning is the fluency and speed of encoding (Rhodes, 2016). Think of learning an easy item, such as *song* in response to *le chant*. It is likely that *song* is retrieved quickly and effortlessly when the French word is given as a cue. Moreover, an impossible item (perhaps because it has never been studied) may generate a very quick "don't know" response. Thus, in response to "greatcoat," a person may quickly generate a low judgment of learning (the French word is *houppelande*). However, in response to the studied word *le porte-voix*, the word *megaphone* may take a bit longer and require more thought but eventually be recalled. Son and Metcalfe (2005) showed that judgments of learning were affected by these factors. High and low judgments of learning were made fluently and quickly. Intermediate judgments of learning—on items that might be hard but possible to retrieve—received the longest response times. Metcalfe and Finn (2008) found that when cue-only judgments of learning were made under speeded conditions, the judgments were influenced by cue familiarity (that is, how easy it was to recognize the cue word), but when participants were not timed, the factors that influenced the memorability of the target also influenced the judgments of learning. Rhodes and Castel (2008a) found that when word pairs were given in a larger font, they received higher judgments of learning than when given in a smaller font. The authors argued that result is likely because the words in larger fonts are easier to read and thus are more fluently processed than words in smaller fonts. In another study, Koriat (2008) demonstrated that "easily learned" is "easily remembered." Items that we learn more quickly are objectively easy and as a consequence, are more likely to be remembered. People's judgments of learning appear to be sensitive to this feature and are related to the speed at which particular items are acquired during study. A considerable number of studies show that fluent processing increases judgments of learning.

Thus, it appears that a number of factors combine to determine people's judgments of learning; some factors are related to the properties of what is studied, and some are related to the properties of the learners' memory systems. Because of the importance of judgments of learning to study, it is important to understand the factors that can affect them. In particular, it is important to understand those factors that can create artificially high judgments of learning, as these illusory feelings may affect study and ultimately, performance.

Another factor that influences people's judgments of learning is their beliefs about how memory works (Rhodes, 2016). If a person has an expectation that some items will be easier than others (say, learning Spanish translations compared to Russian translations), then judgments of learning will be higher for those believed to be less difficult. Thus, for example, Mueller, Dunlosky, and Tauber (2016) showed that people gave higher judgments of learning to identity pairs (e.g., *knife-knife—when both words are the same*) than related pairs (e.g., *fork-knife*). Because fluency variables could not account for this effect, Mueller et al. argue that people believe such identity pairs are easy, and therefore give them high judgments of learning. In another study, Li, Jia, Li, and Li (2016) asked participants to make judgments of learning on items that were animate-stimuli pairs (e.g., *rabbit-squirrel*) and inanimate stimuli pairs (e.g., *fork-candle*). Li et al. found that judgments of learning were higher for the animate pairs, even when a number of fluency factors were controlled for. However, people believed that animate pairs would be easier to recall, and this seemed to dictate their judgments of learning. Thus, beliefs about learning also play a role in judgments of learning in addition to fluency.

Figure 9.3   Functional magnetic resonance imaging results from Kao, Davis, and Gabrieli (2005). Figures a and b show areas of the brain that are activated during recall, whereas c and d show areas of the brain that are activated during judgments of learning.

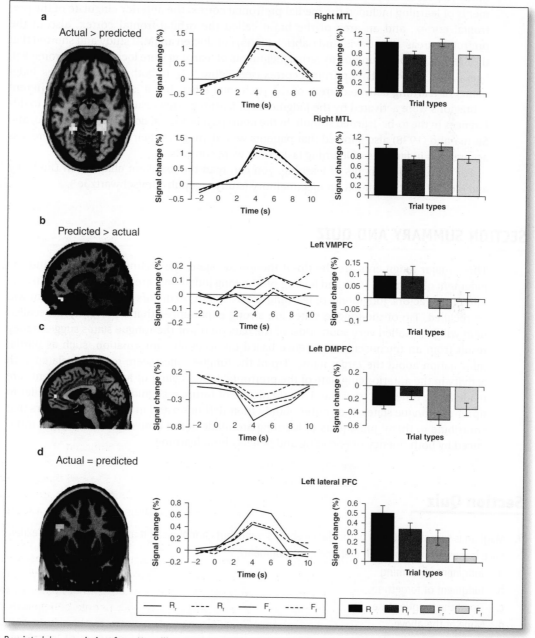

Reprinted by permission from Macmillan Publishers LTD: *Nature Neuroscience.* Neural correlates of actual and predicted memory formation by Kao, Davis, and Gabrieli, copyright 2005.

Brain Mechanisms for Judgments of Learning

As in feeling of knowing and TOTs, the areas of the brain that are activated during judgments of learning reside in the prefrontal lobe of the cerebral cortex. Do Lam et al. (2012) had people make judgments of learning on face-name pairs while being scanned with fMRI. The researchers found that the areas of the brain uniquely activated during judgments of learning included the medial prefrontal cortex; the anterior cingulate of the prefrontal cortex; and an area of the brain called the orbital-frontal cortex, also in the prefrontal areas. Kao, Davis, and Gabrieli (2005) conducted an fMRI study and showed that the areas of the brain unique to verbal judgments of learning were located in ventromedial, lateral, and dorsomedial prefrontal cortex (see Figure 9.3). In both of these studies, judgments of learning activated areas of the prefrontal lobes, but it is unclear why different subregions were activated by the judgments of learning. This result may be related to differences in the to-be-learned stimuli. In the neuropsychological domain, Vilkki, Servo, and Surma-aho (1998) also showed that patients with damage to their frontal lobes were less accurate on judgments of learning tasks than were controls.

For more on judgments of learning, you can read the excellent chapters in Dunlosky and Metcalfe's (2009) book on metamemory (study.sagepub.com/schwartz3e[3]).

SECTION SUMMARY AND QUIZ

Three major judgments are the tip-of-the-tongue state, the feeling of knowing, and the judgment of learning. TOTs and feeling-of-knowing judgments are particularly sensitive to inferential factors. Judgments of learning are excellent predictors of whether an item will be recalled. Tip-of-the-tongue states are strong experiences that a currently unrecalled item will be recalled very soon. Most of the data on tip-of-the-tongue states suggests they result from an unconscious inference based on accessible information, such as partial information about the target name. Tip-of-the-tongue states seem to be correlated with activity in the anterior cingulate of the prefrontal lobe. Feeling-of-knowing judgments are made at the time of retrieval and are predictors of future recognition. Although similar to tip-of-the-tongue states, they differ both in their definition and in some of the factors that contribute to them. Judgments of learning are made at the time of study; they are influenced by both fluency of encoding and beliefs about learning.

Section Quiz

1. Meghan is sure she knows a particular celebrity's name but cannot recall it at the moment. Her experience is most similar to which metamemory judgment?
   a. Judgment of learning
   b. Judgment of forgetting
   c. Tip-of-the-tongue state
   d. None of the above

2. Boduroglu et al. (2015) found that self-referencing led to
   a. An increase in both feeling-of-knowing strength and feeling-of-knowing accuracy
   b. A decrease in feeling-of-knowing strength but an increase in actual recall
   c. An increase in the feeling-of-knowing judgments but a decrease in judgments of learning
   d. More tip-of-the-tongue states but less actual recall

3. Delayed cue-only judgments of learning are expected to show
   a. Very high accuracy relative to other judgments
   b. Interactions with feeling-of-knowing judgments that render both unnecessary
   c. A positive correlation with the animacy effect
   d. All of the above

4. Which factors are thought to contribute to the strength of judgments of learning?
   a. Fluency of encoding
   b. The idea that easily learned is easily remembered
   c. Beliefs about learning
   d. All of the above

1. c
2. a
3. a
4. d

CONTROL PROCESSES IN METAMEMORY

Metamemory has two important components. Monitoring allows us to become aware of what items we will and will not remember and what our mnemonic strengths and weaknesses are. Control processes involve the decisions and behaviors that we engage in to improve or alter or memory processes. Control processes include asking someone to repeat a name because we are not sure that we heard that person correctly. For students, engaging in an "all-nighter" to prepare for an exam in the morning is an example of how metacognition can control our behaviors. The student knows that he has not tried to learn the information and may be aware of how little he knows; therefore, the student decides to study all night long. Even doing an Internet search on the name of a movie character because you cannot remember the actor's name is an act of metacognitive control. Indeed, any behavior one engages in that is a consequence of cognitive uncertainty can be thought of in terms of metacognitive control. In this section, the relation of monitoring and control will be discussed, as will the topic of how successful metamemory control can be.

Consider again the student studying for two exams, one in social psychology and the other in statistics. She must decide which exam to study first. Following this, she must decide how much to time to allocate to each course. Both of these are metamemory control decisions. Metamemory control exists at numerous levels—the decisions as to which class to study for exist at a more global level, but she also must make decisions at a more local level. For example, during study for each class, she must allocate study time among the various concepts, definitions, and examples provided by her professor in that topic. For instance, does she know the definition of *cognitive dissonance* well enough to answer the likely test questions without mistakes? Should she devote her study time to the difficult statistical concept of multivariate analysis, or should she make sure that she has *t*-tests down pat? Researchers study **allocation of study time** because it lends itself to careful experimentation.

> **Allocation of study time:** The decisions participants make about which items to study during an experiment.

Metamemory control can also take place at the time of retrieval. Consider the student taking a standardized exam like the SAT. In many tests like this, if the student answers incorrectly, more points are deducted than if the student leaves that question blank. Thus, a student who can assess her feeling of knowing for a difficult question has an advantage. If the student has a feeling of knowing, she might be tempted to guess at the most appealing answer. However, if the student is sure that the answer would be a pure guess (that is, a strong feeling of *not* knowing), then it is better strategically to leave it blank. Therefore, metamemory control means either making the strategic decision to guess, if one can eliminate a few of the multiple-choice answers as wrong, or leaving the question blank and not risking the penalty. Another example of metacognitive control at the time of retrieval is a decision to self-cue during a TOT state. Many people report mentally running through the alphabet to cue themselves to the forgotten name when they are in a TOT (Brown, 2012). If they did not feel the TOT, they might not choose to self-cue. We will now consider the experimental literature on this topic.

Labor-in-Vain Effect

One of the major questions concerning allocation of study time is how judgments of learning and allocation of study time relate to each other. The first questions that we can ask about this relation are whether students allocate their study time based on the judgments of learning they give to items and whether this allocation improves performance. In one of the earliest empirical papers on the topic, Nelson and Leonesio (1988) found a correlation between judgments of learning and the allocation of study time. The lower the judgments of learning given to an item, the more time the person spent studying it. This negative correlation suggests that participants might have been using their judgments of learning as a metric to determine how long to study individual items. Note the negative correlation— lower judgments of learning means that the person does not think that the item has been learned, and this leads to longer study time.

Here's the basic methodology. Nelson and Leonesio (1988) asked participants to study words paired with nonsense syllables (e.g., *monkey–DAX*). Participants made judgments of learning in an initial stage. Then, when given a chance to study the items again, each participant could choose the amount of time to study for each item. A participant could choose to study one items for a long time, such as 60 seconds, whereas another item for only a few seconds. Finally, in a cued-recall test, participants were given the English word and asked to recall the nonsense syllable.

Nelson and Leonesio (1988) made two important discoveries. First, in this experiment, the relation between judgments of learning and study time was negative. The items that were given the lowest judgments of learning (i.e., the most difficult items) received the most study. In other words, the participants focused on learning the most difficult items and gave them the most attention. The second finding was equally revealing. When the participants were tested on the vocabulary at the end of the experiment, participants still remembered more of the items for which they had given high judgments of learning. Even though they spent most of their time studying the difficult items, they were still better at remembering the easy ones. For this reason, Nelson and Leonesio labeled the effect **labor in vain**, because their experiment showed that participants were unable to compensate for the difficulty of those items.

> **Labor in vain:** When extra study does not result in mastery of difficult items.

Nelson and Leonesio (1988) found that people chose to study the most difficult items. This may make sense, because the easier items are already learned and therefore do not require subsequent study. But think about how you study: Do you always choose the hardest items to study? Imagine you are preparing for a particularly difficult test that you need to pass to keep your scholarship. At some point, completely mastering the material no longer becomes the goal—you just want to pass the test! Under these circumstances, many students will opt to forgo the most difficult material and instead concentrate on what they think they can master in the shortest time period. This intuition led Lisa Son and Janet Metcalfe (2000) to challenge the notion that there will always be a negative correlation between judgments of learning and study time. They thought that in some circumstances, people choose to study the easy items (high judgments of learning) if the material is particularly difficult or they are constrained for time. So Son and Metcalfe set out to do an experiment on this topic.

Son and Metcalfe (2000) conducted an important study that challenged the ideas of Nelson and Leonesio (1988) concerning allocation of study time. The key variable for Son and Metcalfe was the norm of study. The norm of study here refers to how much time a person has to prepare for a test, and how that affects a person's choice of what to study. If time is limited or the goal of mastery is limited, a student may choose to concentrate on the easier items, guaranteeing his success even if *success* is defined as simply getting a C (at least you pass!). If time is not an issue or the goal is complete mastery, then a student will choose more difficult items to study (allowing that student to "go for the A").

In the Son and Metcalfe (2000) study, participants were given several short passages of text to study and told to master all of them. The topics varied—some were about the use of bacteria in making beer, whereas others were about Shakespeare's difficulties getting his first plays produced. Among other judgments, the participants gave judgments of learning to assess the degree of learning on an initial run-through for each passage. After the participants had read all of the passages, some were told that they would have 30 minutes to study the passages for an upcoming test, whereas others were told that they would have 60 minutes to study the passages. Both groups of participants were told that, in general, students required 60 minutes to master this material. Each group was free to divide the 30 or 60 minutes among the passages as they saw fit, spending more or less time on difficult or easy passages. The question was whether the norm of study, as indexed by the amount of time each group had, would dictate study patterns.

Son and Metcalfe (2000) found that the students who had 60 minutes to study for the test chose the hardest passages to review more often than easier passages. For them, as in the Nelson and Leonesio (1988) experiment, there was a negative correlation between judgments of learning and study time. However, for the students who only had 30 minutes to study for the test, the pattern reversed. For these students, there was a positive correlation between judgments of learning and study time (see Figure 9.4). These participants were more likely to choose easy items to restudy. Therefore, the norm of study is important. When time is short, we focus on consolidating what we already know. When we have more time, we can focus on the edge of our learning, the most difficult items.

Region of Proximal Learning

Region of proximal learning: A theory of metamemory that an adaptive strategy is to study the easiest items among those that have not yet been learned.

Metcalfe (2002, 2011) described the idea of the **region of proximal learning**, which states that an adaptive strategy is to study those items that have not yet been learned but are not too difficult. This view suggests that we choose first to study items of intermediate difficulty—under ordinary circumstances. However, when we have lots of time to study, we can then move on to study the difficult items after the intermediate items, and if more time is available, review the easy ones as well. In contrast, as in Son and Metcalfe (2000), when time is limited, we study the easiest ones that we already know first. But usually, we are somewhat but not completely time limited. Under normal studying conditions, our studying is optimal if we devote our time to the easiest items that we have not yet learned.

Think about this in terms of your own studying. You may have a big test coming up tomorrow, but because of various other obligations, you only have two hours the evening before the exam to study for it. What do you study from amongst all the information you know you need to prepare? You may not worry about the easy stuff, and you may decide to leave some of the most difficult material for the end, if you have the time. So you strategically focus on the "region of proximal" learning, the band of information that you have not yet mastered but is most likely to be mastered. Metcalfe's (2011) work on the region of proximal learning suggests that this strategy is often used and quite successful.

Using this strategy, participants should allocate study time not to easy items that they have already mastered or to the extraordinarily difficult items, but to learnable items. In an experiment in which participants made multiple judgments of learning and had multiple opportunities to study items, participants consistently followed this strategy, choosing the items judged least difficult that had not yet been committed to memory (Metcalfe, 2002). Thus, the items that were given high judgments of learning were not studied, nor were the items given the lowest judgments of learning. In another experiment, Metcalfe (2011) showed that both college students and middle-school students used this strategy. She also showed that using this strategy is preferable to a number of alternative strategies for people of both age groups. There are also added benefits to using the region of proximal learning approach to studying. Xu and Metcalfe (2016) found that people reported less mind-wandering when they were engaged in items for which they perceived to be relatively easy but had not yet learned than when they were focusing on only easy items or only difficult items.

Therefore, if you are not employing this technique already in your study, you can improve your learning efficiency by studying at the "leading edge of difficulty." (For more on Janet Metcalfe's research, go to www .sagepub.com/schwartz3e.[4])

An alternative view has been proposed by John Dunlosky and his colleagues (see Dunlosky & Ariel, 2011). This view is called the **agenda-based regulation**. Agenda-based regulation means that participants initially develop a plan of study that takes into account both their study goals and their study constraints. This also accounts for both negative and positive correlations between study time and judgment of learning, as when participants are under different time constraints and face items of varying difficulty, their plan will be different. Agenda-based regulation also accounts for situations in which a rigid adherence to proximal learning would be inappropriate, such as when time is extremely limited and it might be worth reviewing what you know rather than trying to learn anything new. Dunlosky and Ariel were also concerned about habitual learning, in which people follow simple rules

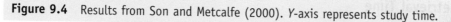

Agenda-based regulation: Participants develop a plan of study that takes into account both study goals and study constraints.

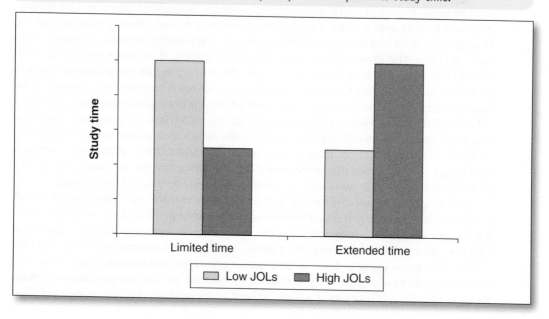

Figure 9.4 Results from Son and Metcalfe (2000). *Y*-axis represents study time.

that are not necessarily predictive of performance. For example, they found that participants often studied the leftmost item first rather than the easiest item not yet learned, simply because their participants read from left to right. Dunlosky and Ariel pointed out that replacing such habitual strategies with planning would produce more efficient learning.

MNEMONIC IMPROVEMENT TIP 9.2

As you study, make judgments of learning on the items you need to remember for your test (or job). When you have completed your initial review, start with the easiest ones you don't yet know and start working your way to the harder items. Once you have mastered all the items, then you can go back and review the easier ones.

Control Processes at Retrieval

Conscious control over our memory system allows us to tailor our memory to our needs at any particular time. We have just seen how judgments of learning can be used as a guide to what to study. What about retrieval? Sometimes it feels as if we have no control over our retrieval. When we are stymied in a TOT, we are frustrated, because the item is seemingly blocked. However, it turns out that we can use our metamemory judgments to affect control at the time of retrieval.

TOTs and Retrieval Time

Most often, we experience TOTs as frustrating. We know the person's name, and yet we cannot recall it. TOTs appear to be a quirky, annoying error in our memory systems. But the experience of TOTs also serves an important monitoring function. It makes us aware of the retrieval failure. This allows us to exert metacognitive control. If we are experiencing a TOT, then we should be able to recall the actual word. Thus, one possible metacognitive function of the TOT is to cause one to search longer for an item that is currently inaccessible. To be more specific, the TOT tells us that the unrecalled word is both in memory store and likely to be recalled, so we devote more time in our attempt to retrieve the item. One study that tested this idea examined the relation of TOTs to the time it took people to retrieve answers or decide that they could not retrieve the answers (Schwartz, 2001). TOTs were associated with longer retrieval times than were non-TOTs, suggesting that the TOT state indicated to participants that the item was likely in memory and that they should keep looking.

Interestingly, TOTs have also been linked to motivation to learn. Ryan, Petty, and Wenzlaff (1982) and Schwartz (2008) found that when people were in TOTs, their performance on other tasks was slowed, suggesting that the motivation to recall the TOT item interfered with the other tasks. In another study, Litman, Hutchins, and Russon (2005) showed that people were more likely to look up in a dictionary or an encyclopedia those items for which they had experienced TOTs. Therefore, at retrieval, we can use metamemory judgments to help us. A TOT serves as a warning light—we can recall this item eventually if we keep working at it. A person not experiencing a TOT is more likely to give up. Thus, despite the sense of frustration that accompanies TOTs, they do serve a vital control function.

A Note on Accuracy

In this chapter, we have focused on the mechanisms that produce judgments of metamemory and on how these judgments direct our behavior, particularly study behavior. Equally important from the point of view of both research and practical considerations is that our metamemory judgments accurately predict our learning and performance. Accurate metamemory means two things: that we know what we will learn or remember and that we know what we will not learn or remember. Typically, this accuracy is measured by correlating the metamemory judgments with performance on some later test (Benjamin & Diaz, 2008; Nelson, 1984). Accurate metamemory judgments best serve our needs to control and direct our behavior. Imagine if our metamemory was perversely inaccurate, for example, if what we thought we had learned was what we had actually forgotten and what we thought we would not learn was what we actually could learn. This system would lead to poor control of memory. Thus, it is important to know which kinds of judgments are accurate, as these are the ones that are best used to drive our learning behavior. Luckily, almost all studies on metamemory show that such judgments are accurate at predicting future behavior.

OTHER KINDS OF METAMEMORY

Retrospective Confidence

Retrospective confidence refers to the metacognitive judgment one makes to indicate how certain one feels that a retrieved answer is correct. Strong retrospective confidence means that you think the answer that you have recalled is correct, while weak retrospective confidence means that you think the answer that you have recalled is incorrect. Have you ever recalled something only to doubt that what you have recalled is accurate? For example, if you are asked which actor played the title character in the movie *Wonder Woman* (2017), Lynda Carter may come to mind, but you may realize that this is incorrect. You may search for the information on the Internet and learn that it was actually Gal Gadot. This is an example of weak retrospective confidence at work (Koriat & Goldsmith, 1996).

It is important to note that retrieval can be covert. You can retrieve the name Lynda Carter but then opt not to report it or say it aloud, if you are unsure you have recalled the correct actor's name. Or you may retrieve the name that you think goes with a person you think you should know, but you may want to spare yourself embarrassment if you are wrong and forgo saying the person's name.

Koriat and Goldsmith (1996) were interested in the issue of whether one should say what one thinks. They investigated this by looking at retrospective confidence judgments. They thought that control mechanisms exist at the time of retrieval that screen out unlikely answers that pop into our mind. For example, given a question such as "Who is the only man who died on the moon?" the name Tommy Lee Jones might be retrieved, as his character in the movie *Space Cowboys* (2000) dies on the moon. However, as this answer pops out, we are able to screen it out as being fictional, not fact, and so we answer, "Nobody—all the astronauts returned safely from the moon." There are also social situations in which we might think better than to express an answer. The honors student in high school may know the answer to the teacher's question but answers "I don't know," so as not to get teased by his or her classmates. Thus, output monitoring is important in a number of situations. Koriat and Goldsmith examined these post-retrieval decisions about whether or not to report a retrieved item by asking people trivia or general-information questions.

In Koriat and Goldsmith's (1996) study, some participants were told that they always had to report an answer (the forced-recall condition), whereas other participants were allowed to report only those answers that they were confident were the correct answers (free-recall condition). This allowed Koriat and Goldsmith to look at two aspects of the students' performance: both the quantity of their output (that is, how many items they remembered in total) and the quality of their output (that is, what percentage of their answers were indeed correct). As expected, the participants in the forced-recall condition reported more items, but the free-recall condition participants showed a better accuracy rate. As obvious as this may seem, the difference is important. It means that when participants have control over their output, not all retrieved answers will be reported. In other words, participants can and do screen their own answers for accuracy and discard information considered inaccurate. This provides another example of the use of metamemory in the control of memory performance.

Retrospective confidence is important in eyewitness situations. First of all, we expect witnesses to give testimony only if they are highly confident that they are correct. The costs of misremembering are high, so we want witnesses to screen answers for accuracy. Second, if a witness is highly confident that his or her memory is correct, this confidence is given substantial weight by juries (Cutler, Penrod, & Dexter, 1990). Fortunately, research shows that most of what we retrieve is correct. Incorrectly retrieved information represents only about 10% of responses (Dunning & Stern, 1992). However, legal psychologists have struggled to demonstrate a relation between retrospective confidence and the accuracy of eyewitness identification. This is in part because juries must frequently distinguish between two witnesses, one who expresses strong confidence ("I'll never forget that face!") and another who may not speak as demonstratively ("I think it was him"). Most of us would be more likely to believe the witness who expresses strong confidence, but the data do not show that more confident witnesses are more accurate witnesses. However, if one looks at confidence within each witness—that is, the confidence that some of his or her memories are more likely to be accurate than others—then retrospective confidence predicts performance quite well (Perfect, 2002).

Students often emerge from an exam feeling that they did well, only to find out that their performance was less than they expected. Why does this occur, given the general high accuracy of individual retrospective confidence judgments? It turns out that, although retrospective confidence judgments discriminate well between correct and incorrect answers, we also have a tendency to be overconfident (Miller & Geraci, 2011). Thus, if we rate a number of answers as likely to be 90% correct, it is likely that only 80% will be correct. This general **overconfidence** leads to the illusion that we did better than we actually did; we will return to the topic of overconfidence in Chapter 13 and discuss ways to compensate for it.

> **Overconfidence:** Overestimating the likelihood that a to-be-learned item or set of items will be remembered.

The Déjà Vu Experience

A **déjà vu experience** is the feeling that a new situation has been experienced before. Although it occurs rarely, most individuals can describe a situation in which they had a déjà vu experience. The person may be absolutely certain that he or she has never

> **Déjà vu experience:** The feeling that a new situation has been experienced before.

been to a certain place before yet have an odd feeling of familiarity. For example, a person may find herself in Trafalgar Square in London for the first time. She knows that this is her first trip to London but is beset by déjà vu when she walks through the square. Another person may stop to pet a cat while walking to work, and the rubbing of the cat against his leg may trigger a déjà vu experience. A déjà vu experience is a metamemory experience, because it concerns the feeling that an event has been experienced before (even though the person knows objectively it has not). In this sense, déjà vu experiences are unique among metamemory judgments, because they cannot be classified as either accurate or inaccurate (Schwartz & Cleary, 2016).

Anne Cleary and her colleagues (2012) have been pursuing objective research on the déjà vu experience. They developed an ingenious way to induce déjà vu experiences in people under laboratory conditions. In their experiments, participants move through virtual 3-D environments using virtual reality glasses. Thus, a participant negotiates a virtual bowling alley, airport, junkyard, or other scenes throughout the experiment. This immersive environment recreates the experience one might get when actually visiting a new location.

Cleary et al. (2012) suspected that one potential cause of the déjà vu experience is misplaced familiarity. A scene looks familiar, because of its similarity to another scene that is in memory but that fails to be recalled. They were able to test this hypothesis in their virtual-reality experiment. At Time 1, participants were placed into a particular scene, such as a bowling alley. After spending time in the virtual bowling alley, they moved on to other scenes. At Time 2, they were placed in new scenes. However, some of the new scenes had identical geometry to earlier scenes. Thus, a trip through a cathedral might be a completely different experience than being in a bowling alley, but in Cleary et al.'s experiment, the scenes were configurally identical. Thus, Cleary et al. could find out whether déjà vu experiences were more common in scenes that had identical geometry to earlier scenes or in those that did not share geometry with an earlier scene (see Figure 9.5).

When viewing the second set of scenes, participants were asked to report any déjà vu experiences as well as a number of other judgments, such as simply whether or not the scene was familiar and whether the scene triggered recall of any particular earlier scene. Déjà vu experiences were not frequent, but they were common enough to allow Cleary et al. (2012)

to do statistical analyses. They found that there were more déjà vu experiences for those scenes that were configurally similar to other earlier scenes than for scenes that were not. Similarly, familiarity was higher for the scenes that were configurally similar to other earlier scenes. Thus, perceptual familiarity—the similarity in geometry between the earlier and later scenes—was causing déjà vu experiences. In this way, Cleary et al. showed that déjà vu experiences can be examined in the lab and that scene familiarity can account for them.

In the real world, familiarity might easily be generated in one domain, causing déjà vu in another domain. For example, the average person may see Trafalgar Square in many movies (*Skyfall, The Core, 101 Dalmations*, just to name a few). Thus, most first-time visitors

Figure 9.5   Sample screenshots of study scenes (left) and configurally similar novel scenes (right).

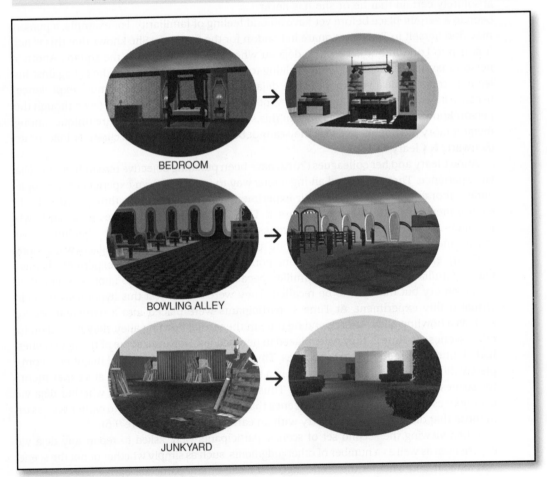

SOURCE: Cleary et. al. (2012).

to London have seen Trafalgar Square before they ever get there. However, when visiting, they might not successfully attribute the familiarity to one of these movies. The unattributable familiarity is then experienced as déjà vu.

Déjà vu experiences are compelling when they occur. They have inspired people to think of spiritual origins (Brown, 2004). But a straightforward psychological experiment has yielded interpretable data (Cleary et al., 2012). In this way, memory science can bring scientific understanding to some of the most perplexing puzzles of human memory.

Section Quiz

1. When a person continues to study difficult items but then still cannot recall them on the test, this is called the
   a. Labor-in-vain effect
   b. Region of proximal learning
   c. Retrospective-confidence effect
   d. A judgment of forgetting

2. The region of proximal learning refers to
   a. The observation that difficult items are easiest to learn, under some circumstances
   b. The idea that it is adaptive to study the easiest items that have not yet been learned
   c. The idea that it is adaptive to study the most difficult items first
   d. None of the above are true

3. Which is an example of retrospective confidence?
   a. Charlie makes a judgment of learning that he will remember a translation pair later on a test
   b. Veronica has a tip-of-the-tongue state for the name of a famous actress
   c. Natasha is certain that she has correctly recalled the name of the 11th president of the United States
   d. Rajiv has a déjà vu experience when visiting San Francisco for the first time

4. In Cleary et al. (2012) study on déjà vu experiences, familiarity was manipulated by
   a. Directly stimulating the temporal lobe of patients about to undergo epilepsy surgery
   b. Presenting scenes initially that had identical geometry to scenes presented later—at test
   c. Changing certain subtle details in faces presented at both study and test
   d. Presenting subliminal hints about the nature of the test stimuli

1. a
2. b
3. c
4. b

SUMMARY

Metacognitive control refers to the ability of people to direct their learning or other behaviors as a function of metacognitive monitoring. Thus, a decision to study more based on the feeling that learning has not occurred is an example of metacognitive control. Unfortunately, even when people know that they do not know, they often do not study sufficiently to compensate for that, a phenomenon known as the labor-in-vain effect. The region of proximal learning refers to an adaptive strategy, often employed by people in which we study the easiest items that have not yet been mastered. As we master those items, we can move on to more difficult items. Agenda-based regulation means that participants initially develop a plan of study that takes into account both their study goals and their study constraints. This also accounts for both negative and positive correlations between study time and judgment of learning, as when participants are under different time constraints and face items of varying difficulty, their plan will be different. Metacognitive control also occurs at the time of test. We can use our tip-of-the-tongue states for example to make adaptive retrieval decisions. Retrospective confidence refers to the metacognitive judgment one makes to indicate how certain one feels that a retrieved answer is correct. Strong retrospective confidence means that you think the answer that you have recalled is correct, while weak retrospective confidence means that you think the answer that you have recalled is incorrect. A déjà vu experience is the feeling that a new situation has been experienced before. Research suggests that it is based on misplaced familiarity.

KEY TERMS

accessibility
agenda-based regulation
allocation of study time
availability
control
cue familiarity
cue-only judgments of learning
cue-target judgments of learning

déjà vu experience
direct-access theories
ease-of-learning judgments
feeling-of-knowing judgments
indirect or inferential theories
judgments of learning
labor in vain
metacognition
metacognitive control

metamemory
monitoring
overconfidence
region of proximal learning
retrieval of related information
retrospective confidence judgments
tip-of-the-tongue states

REVIEW QUESTIONS

1. What is metamemory, and how does it differ from memory?

2. What are monitoring and control? How do they work together to form an efficient metamemory system?

3. What do each of the following judgments measure?
   a. Ease of learning
   b. Judgments of learning
   c. Feeling of knowing
   d. Tip of the tongue (TOT)
   e. Retrospective confidence

4. How do direct-access theory and inferential theory explain metamemory judgment differently?

5. What is a TOT? How is it best explained?

6. How does the cue-familiarity hypothesis explain feeling-of-knowing judgments?

7. How can individuals use delayed judgments of learning to improve their learning?

8. What is allocation of study time? How can it be used to make learning more efficient?

9. What is the region of proximal learning?

10. What is the déjà vu experience? Why is it considered metacognition?

ONLINE RESOURCES

1. For information on active research on metamemory, go to the website of the International Association for Metacognition at http://iametacognition.wixsite.com/metacognition

2. For an interesting article in the popular press on the tip-of-the-tongue phenomenon, go to http://www.boston.com/bostonglobe/ideas/articles/2008/06/01/whats_that_name/.

3. For more on judgments of learning, you can read the excellent chapters in Dunlosky and Metcalfe's (2009) book on metamemory at http://www.sagepub.com/booksProdDesc.nav?prodId=Book229322#tabview=google.

4. For more on Janet Metcalfe's research, go to http://www.columbia.edu/cu/psychology/metcalfe/People.html

Go to **study.sagepub.com/schwartz3e** for additional exercises and study resources. Select **Chapter 9, Metamemory** for chapter-specific resources.

CHAPTER 10

Memory Disorders

$\mathbf{I}$n movies, amnesia varies from a source of humor to a minor inconvenience to a life-altering experience. In the children's movie *Finding Nemo* (2003), a good-natured but amnesic fish named Dory helps a father save his son. Her frequent forgetting of names provides the bulk of the laughs in the movie. In the Adam Sandler movie *50 First Dates* (2004), the character played by Drew Barrymore suffers a dense, albeit unrealistic, amnesia. She forgets all post-accident information when she goes to sleep each night, although she remembers the events of the day throughout the day (a literature search revealed no real cases of amnesia following this pattern). Nonetheless, for Drew Barrymore's character, these symptoms present only minor problems for her in finding love and ultimately traveling the world aboard a yacht with her husband and child. Indeed, that her husband, played by Adam Sandler, must woo and win her each new day is portrayed as romantic. Real-life amnesia is far from romantic. In *Memento* (2000), an amnesic widower is bent on getting revenge for the murder of his wife, which he believes is unsolved. Because his dense amnesia prevents him from learning anything new, he must tattoo himself with the evidence he discovers, lest he miss an important clue. Unlike the first two movies, *Memento* is realistic in its portrayal of anterograde amnesia (if not in how to investigate a crime). Indeed, to emphasize the disorder of time in amnesia, *Memento* starts in the middle and then goes both forward and backward in time. Nonetheless, the main character, "Leonard," despite his amnesia, "gets things done." Thus, in each movie, amnesia does not prevent the character from fulfilling an important mission. In reality, amnesia can be extremely debilitating. (See the following video to get a sense of this: study.sagepub.com/schwartz3e.[1])

As an example, I will describe a case of amnesia within my own family. This account is not unique. Many families can describe similar stories of amnesic symptoms. About twenty-five years ago, I visited my then 80-year-old grandmother in the assisted-living facility she had just moved to. My grandmother had spent most of her adult life as a music teacher and had only retired a few years earlier. Unfortunately, by the age of 80, she had suffered from a series of small, undiagnosed strokes and was no longer able to work or live on her own. I told her that I had just finished my PhD and would be moving to Florida soon to start a job as an assistant professor. "Mazel tov," she replied (*Mazel tov* is Yiddish for "congratulations"), and I told her about how excited I was to be moving to Miami. I then told her my younger brother had just gotten engaged, and we talked about that for a while. She was excited about hearing of my brother's engagement and the eventual prospect of great-grandchildren. She then said, "Enough about your brother—I want to hear about you. When are you going to finish at that school of yours?" I told her that I had just finished my PhD and would be moving to Florida soon to start a job as an assistant professor. "Mazel tov," she replied, completely unaware that we had just had this conversation not more than 15 minutes earlier. Like some other older adults, my grandmother had suffered a stroke (cerebral infarct) that had left her with strong antero-grade amnesia, leaving her with a deficit in encoding new information. Notice that, at this point, my grandmother had lost only episodic memory. She forgot the specifics of the conversation, but her lexical memory was intact—that is, her ability to talk and com-municate was not affected. In addition, her semantic memory was unaffected; she knew what a PhD was, for example, and was able to talk intelligently about my job opportunity. Anterograde amnesia, restricted to episodic memory, is a quite common result of strokes and also one of the first symptoms seen in Alzheimer's disease, which also disproportion-ately affects older adults.

Memory disorders are devastating, both for the person who has lost his or her mem-ory and for that person's family. The most common form of amnesia is associated with Alzheimer's disease. Approximately 360,000 new cases are diagnosed every year (Brookmeyer et al., 2007). Amnesia also frequently results from brain damage that occurs in strokes or motor vehicle accidents. Memory impairment can result from tumors, near-drowning experiences (apoxia), brain surgery, bullet wounds, and other damage to the brain. Although we focus here on amnesia brought about by neurological injuries, psycho-logical conditions can cause memory deficits as well. In this chapter, we will consider psy-chogenic amnesia (specific amnesias caused by psychological trauma) but not memory deficits that occur in other psychological disorders, such as schizophrenia. We will sort out the various forms of amnesia and define what they are and whom they affect, and we will discuss the areas of the brain affected and the behavioral deficits that result.

WHAT IS AMNESIA?

Amnesia is any impairment of memory abilities beyond normal forgetting. In most cases, the term *amnesia* refers to an acquired condition brought about by trauma to the brain. A whole host of different disorders can be classified as amnesia. What these disorders have in common is memory loss. In most, the major deficit is in encoding new infor-mation into episodic memory, but some

> **Amnesia:** Memory deficits acquired through brain damage.

amnesias affect retrieval from episodic memory, access to semantic memory, access to working memory, and executive control of memory. We will mostly focus on neurological amnesias—that is, amnesias that result from physical destruction of different regions of the brain. We will touch on psychogenic amnesias, much heralded by Hollywood but quite uncommon in the real world; these amnesias do not result directly from brain damage but seem to be elicited by psychological trauma.

CASE STUDIES OF AMNESIA

Patient HM

In Chapter 2, we introduced the patient HM. The study of HM's memory initiated the modern study of amnesia. In 1953, neurosurgeon William Scoville removed HM's hippocampi as a treatment for epilepsy. Much of the surrounding medial temporal tissue was excised as well. The surgery was, in one sense, successful, as HM's seizures decreased. His measured IQ remained stable before and after surgery. Indeed, it appeared to rise from a normal 101 to an above-average 112. He continued to enjoy crossword puzzles. His working memory was normal. His ability to speak, understand, read, and write was not impaired. He was also able to remember much of his life from before the surgery. His stored episodic memories were still accessible. However, the effect on his ability to encode new information was devastating. For the next 55 years of his life, HM never learned anything new in a direct and conscious manner. For example, if he was given a list of words to recall, he could read them and tell you what they meant. However, five minutes later, he would have forgotten both the words on the list and the experience of reading them. This anterograde amnesia—that is, the inability to encode new information into episodic memory—extended to events in his life. He was unable to remember events he participated in, such as a game of miniature golf, a few minutes after he had completed the game. Despite his inability to encode information episodically, he was able to learn some information, but only after countless repetitions. For example, he eventually learned that family members (such as his parents) had died. HM died in December 2008 at the age of 82. (Go here to read HM's obituary: study.sagepub.com/schwartz3e.[2])

HM represents an extreme case of anterograde amnesia. Interestingly, as in many patients with amnesic syndrome (to be discussed shortly), HM's memory deficits were largely restricted to the encoding of events. For example, his implicit memory was largely intact. Moreover, his procedural memory was intact. For example, he learned various skills, including mirror writing (that is, writing that can only be read by looking at the text in a mirror). Nonetheless, when asked to write in mirror style, he would often report that he could not do so. Furthermore, he could not remember any episode of writing mirror style, even though he had learned to do it since his surgery. Thus, he found it a surprise when he could successfully mirror-write. When shown a word list, he remembered none of the items later in an episodic memory test but did show implicit memory when tested via priming techniques later. Because of his symptoms, anterograde amnesia was originally attributed to deficits in the hippocampus and surrounding temporal lobe areas. However, more recent MRI on HM also showed damage to other areas of the brain, including the amygdala (Corkin, Amaral, González, Johnson, & Hyman, 1997). It is likely that the widespread bilateral damage to HM's memory areas in his brain was responsible for the very strong anterograde amnesia with which he was stricken.

Clive Wearing

Clive Wearing was born in 1938 in England and went on to have a successful musical career as a singer, piano player, conductor, and composer. Indeed, he composed and conducted the music played at the wedding of Princess Diana and Prince Charles. However, in 1985,

Wearing contracted viral encephalitis. Viral encephalitis is a rare but dangerous disease that causes massive swelling of the brain. In Wearing's case, it was associated with an earlier herpes infection. It caused massive damage to his brain, including to his medial temporal lobes and prefrontal lobes. Wearing has severe anterograde amnesia; in the roughly 30 years since his illness, he has not learned a single new thing about the world. He also has severe retrograde amnesia; he cannot remember a single event from his past. As such, he lives in a perpetual present. In fact, he writes over and over in his "diary" that he has just returned to consciousness after a long illness. He has written this entry several times a day for many years. His wife estimated that if his attention is distracted, his working memory maintains information for about 10 seconds, and then that experience is lost forever. Indeed, his wife can leave the room for 30 seconds and return, at which point Wearing will greet her joyously and emotionally as if he has not seen her for years. Unlike HM, Wearing cannot remember events from before his illness. Ask him about a concert or some other important event, and he cannot retrieve it, despite his former illustrious career.

Like HM, Wearing has profound amnesia in the episodic domain. Also, like HM, the problem seems restricted to memory. His amnesia does not extend to lexical memory; he is still articulate and has full command of spoken language. Nor does it extend to procedural memory; he is still an accomplished piano player. Nonetheless, he does not remember a single event from his life, and he has learned nothing new in over 30 years (see B. A. Wilson & Wearing, 1995, for a complete description of this case). (To observe his symptoms yourself, go to study.sagepub.com/schwartz3e.[3])

These two individuals are cases of extreme amnesia. More typical amnesiacs have less severe anterograde amnesia and less severe retrograde amnesia. Campbell and Conway (1995) provided poignant descriptions in their book of the problems faced by people with less severe amnesia. Often they must find extraordinary ways to remember to turn off the stove, remember what needs to be purchased at the store, and remember when to pick up the children from their soccer game.

ANTEROGRADE AMNESIA

Anterograde amnesia refers to an inability to form new memories following brain damage. It varies from mild impairment, in which a person simply requires more time to encode information than normal individuals do, to the severe impairment seen in patients like HM, in which the person may remember little of anything new. Such severe impairment essentially leaves the person frozen in time and in need of round-the-clock supervision—patients may forget where they live if they have moved since their accident or injury. In almost all cases, severe impairment also means the person cannot continue to work. In contrast, mild amnesiacs may be able to compensate for their deficit; return home; and in some cases, even resume their careers. What is unifying in anterograde amnesia is the difficulty in learning new information, whether that information is episodic or semantic in nature.

> **Anterograde amnesia:** An inability to form new memories following brain damage.

Hippocampus: An area of the brain associated with learning and memory. Damage can cause anterograde amnesia.

Medial temporal lobes: A cortical area of the brain in the temporal lobes associated with learning and memory. Damage can cause anterograde amnesia.

Mammillary bodies: A subcortical region of the brain associated with learning. Damage can cause anterograde amnesia.

Amnesic syndrome: Specific impairment of encoding new information into both episodic and semantic memory while most other cognitive functions remain intact.

In many cases, the deficit can be quite specific—that is, the person is impaired in the learning of new information and the encoding of episodic events, but other aspects of memory are intact—that is, people may have access to already-encoded past memories and have no other cognitive deficits. Anterograde amnesiacs can remember information that they learned from before their accident, have no deficits in speech or intelligence, and have no deficits in working memory. Damage in the brain tends to be in the **hippocampus** and **medial temporal lobes**. A second locus in the brain also causes the amnesic syndrome—namely, the **mammillary bodies** of the diencephalon. Damage to the adjacent fornix can also induce anterograde amnesia (Aggleton, 2008). Differences in symptoms from damage to the different loci is observable in some but not all cases.

Damage to these areas of the brain produces the **amnesic syndrome**, so called because many patients suffer a common set of problems (and spared abilities) regardless of whether the amnesia was induced by stroke, auto accident, head injury, brain tumor, viral infection, or neurosurgery (see Table 10.1). A characteristic of the amnesic syndrome is a specific impairment of encoding new information into both episodic and semantic memory, while most other cognitive functions remain intact.

If patients with the amnesic syndrome are given a list of words to recall, they will remember few, if any, of the words after more than a 30-second delay. This is also the case if the test is recognition. Indeed, any test that calls on the patient to consciously remember new information from episodic memory will result in poor performance. By contrast, patients can recount events from their pre-injury life in a normal manner.

Table 10.1 Symptoms of the Amnesic Syndrome

1. Anterograde amnesia for both episodic and semantic memory

2. Intact working memory

3. Intact language and intelligence

4. Intact implicit memory

5. Damage to hippocampus and surrounding medial temporal lobe

One hint of a difference between patients with hippocampal damage and patients with damage to the diencephalon is differing performance on recall tests versus recognition tests. Patients with damage to the hippocampus and to the surrounding medial temporal lobes will show deficits on both recall and recognition tests. Patients with damage to areas of the diencephalon will show relatively preserved performance on tests of recognition. Thus, if the test asks patients to distinguish between new words and old words, the hippocampus patients will show an amnesic pattern, but the diencephalon patients will not (Tsivilis et al., 2008).

Implicit Memory in the Amnesic Syndrome

Implicit **memory** refers to the preserved ability to perform tasks that are influenced by a past event, without being aware of the event experience. For example, after hearing and then forgetting a sentence, such as the "The grizzly bear scared the campers," you will still be more likely to spell the word

> **Implicit memory:** The preserved ability to perform tasks that are influenced by a past event without being aware of the event experience.

bear/bare as bear than if you had not heard the sentence. It turns out that amnesic patients may sometimes show the influence of earlier events, even when they do not recall those events. What happens here is that amnesic patients process this information, and it influences their thinking even when they do not remember the event later. Because it is not registered by the episodic memory system, the amnesiac does not return a conscious memory. Implicit memory is the result of the influence of processing on areas of the brain that are not directly involved in the episodic-memory circuits (Slotnick & Schacter, 2006). For example, remembering spatial routes may be spared even when episodic events are not encoded (Oudman et al., 2016).

Here's how implicit memory is tested in amnesic patients. Consider an experiment in which an amnesic individual is given a list of words to recall. Immediately following the presentation of the list, the amnesiac is asked to recall as many words as possible from the list. Given that the patient is amnesic, he or she may recall very few, if any at all, and certainly far fewer than a non-amnesic control. In cases like that of Clive Wearing, the patient may promptly forget that he or she had even been given a list of words.

Now, the patient is given an implicit test of memory. In implicit memory tests, participants are not required to retrieve an answer from memory but instead can use general cognitive reasoning skills, which are often preserved in anterograde amnesia. For example, one classic test of implicit memory is **word fragment completion**. In this task, a participant is given some letters of a word but not all of them and must

> **Word fragment completion:** A participant is given some letters of a word but not all of them and must figure out the word.

figure out the word. For example, "s_h_l _r" is a word fragment. The task can be completed without any reference to the past (that is, the episodic past). The participant can simply determine what letters are needed to make the fragment an acceptable word.

> **Repetition priming:** The effect of presenting a stimulus on the later processing of that same stimulus. Amnesiacs show repetition priming even if they do not consciously recall the target.

Indeed, amnesiacs may be just as good as normal individuals in completing this task.

However, **repetition priming** studies show that a relatively recent prior experience with the word *scholar* makes solving the word fragment easier. Normal participants will be more likely to solve "s_h_l _r" if they saw *scholar* in another context, sometimes as much as a year earlier. Because participants are not always aware of the connection between their earlier experience and the present task, researchers have called the effects of repetition priming *implicit memory*. Certainly, this term applies to amnesiacs who do not consciously remember the words from the list but benefit, as do normal individuals, from the earlier experience when they are tested with an implicit test. What is relevant here is that even when amnesiacs do not recall the word they just saw (e.g., *scholar*), they show normal repetition priming effects in word-fragment completion. Even though the word does not register in their episodic memory, it was processed at some level, as their behavior in the implicit memory test is later affected by that experience. Many studies have documented this preserved implicit memory in amnesic patients (Tulving & Schacter, 1990; Vaidya et al., 1995).

Awareness in the Amnesic Syndrome

Do amnesic patients know that they are amnesic? The answer to this question is, it depends. It depends on the form of amnesia they have acquired. You may know someone with Alzheimer's disease. In early stages, patients with Alzheimer's may be acutely aware of their memory loss, but as the disease progresses, this awareness is lost. In the amnesic syndrome, patients tend to be keenly aware of their deficits. They are aware of how amnesia has changed their lives and struggle to overcome it. In some ways, this is an important feature, as it gives clinical neuropsychology a manner in which to help these patients, by focusing them on ways to compensate for their memory loss. Diaries, index cards, sticky notes, portable computers, smartphones, and tablet computers can all be kept close by to record events and appointments. In this way, neuropsychological interventions can help patients with mild to moderate anterograde amnesia. Although external memory aids can be used to compensate for some aspects of amnesia, being amnesic can be frustrating for both the amnesiac and her family. For example, consider the pride and satisfaction you may have had today after having successfully climbed a new route on the rock-climbing wall at the gym. You worked on it for weeks and finally mastered the moves. An amnesiac would feel just as much pride at having succeeded at the task but a few minutes later, would have completely forgotten not just the accomplishment but also the ensuing feeling of pride. Similarly, think back to your last summer vacation. Perhaps the highlight was going waterskiing, something you had never done before. Remembering that event may bolster your mood and remind you that all the hard work you do pays off, as it allows you to afford your vacations. An amnesiac may thoroughly enjoy the waterskiing trip but will not remember it later or be able to mentally time travel to that event to relive the fun.

Medved (2007) interviewed a number of patients with anterograde amnesia with the goal of understanding what it was like to be amnesic. The patients had suffered brain damage from a variety of causes about a year prior to the interview. Medved was interested in the coping strategies that amnesiacs use to discuss past events with others, when their ability to retrieve such events is impaired. More specifically, Medved's goal was to understand how these people approached **memory conversations**. Memory conversation refers to the discussions we have with others about the past. Normal individuals frequently have memory conversations. For

> **Memory conversations:** The discussions we have with others about the past.

example, think of a woman coming home from work and sharing the aggravations of the day with her spouse. Or think of a man happily describing bowling a perfect game in his neighborhood league. These routine discussions all involve a common understanding that we can recall recent events that occurred in our lives. The amnesic, however, does not have this access to the recent past, and therefore Medved was interested in what skills such patients use to adapt in these situations.

Medved (2007) found that amnesiacs used three major coping strategies when discussing memories in their everyday lives. First, many used **memory importation**. This means that amnesiacs described a memory from before their injury as if it had happened after the injury. One patient interviewed by Medved described having a job interview—even though he was no longer able to work at his old job. After more questioning, he realized that this event was from his pre-injury past, not his post-injury present. In many conversations, however, describing such older pre-injury memories may allow the amnesiac to participate in memory conversations. Second, amnesiacs may use **memory appropriation**, which means describing semantic knowledge as if it were a specific episodic memory. Because semantic memory is almost always less severely affected than episodic memory, in many cases, a person may be able to retrieve an event based on someone else's repeated retelling of the event. Finally, amnesiacs engage in **memory compensation**, in which rather than trying to answer a question about the past, they talk instead about the issues that they are having with their amnesic syndrome. Conversationally, this may convey to the listener that they would like to talk about

> **Memory importation:** An amnesiac describes a memory from before the injury as if it had happened after.

> **Memory appropriation:** An amnesiac retrieves an event based on someone else's repeated retelling of the event.

> **Memory compensation:** Rather than trying to answer a question about the past, an amnesiac talks about the issues that have arisen from amnesic syndrome.

their memories, but the memories are simply lacking. According to Medved, these three strategies help amnesiacs fit in with their families and in other conversational situations.

Patients with the amnesic syndrome are usually aware that they have memory deficits. This awareness can make the suffering more profound, as is clear in the cases above, but it also provides an avenue for people to find ways of compensating. Patients are encouraged to maintain memory books, in which they write down the events of each day. They can also use electronic devices, such as cell phones or laptop computers, to record events from their life and to plan events for the future. In this way, even if they cannot recall them episodically, they can always consult their book or phone to determine what they did on a particular day. Patients can also structure their lives in ways that are helpful. Common objects (keys, kitchen utensils, etc.) can always be returned to the same location for easy finding. People can place sticky notes or program their cell phone to beep when they have to remember to do something. Patients can stay close to home, so they do not get lost. Some patients can return to a job, provided the job calls upon well-learned skills from the past or involves simple skills that can be learned. Amnesiacs are particularly good at doing repetitive tasks that might bore others. The amnesiac forgets the previous repetitions, so he or she can do the task the next time with more attention than the ordinary person might (Campbell & Conway, 1995; Wilson, 2009).

Specific programs have been designed to help patients with the amnesic syndrome cope with their condition. These patients can learn through classical and operational conditioning, and as we have shown, they also have intact implicit memory. A number of remediation programs take advantage of these skills to help patients resume normal functions. Schacter (1996) described a technique he called the **method of vanishing cues** to train an amnesic woman to perform a simple but new computer task required by her employer. This technique uses the spared implicit memory of amnesiacs to help them learn new skills (Kessels & de Haan, 2003).

> **Method of vanishing cues:** Technique that uses the spared implicit memory of amnesiacs to help them learn new skills.

Schacter presented the woman with the definitions of tasks she would be required to carry out along with their name. Thus, "Run the antivirus program: Norton," might be her first trial of learning. Schacter would then slowly remove letters from "Norton." After many trials, the participant might be able to generate the word *Norton* from simply "Run the antivirus program: No . . ." Eventually, Schacter could remove all cues. Even though the patient did not remember learning about Norton antivirus software, she would know to apply it when the topic came up. This and other intervention strategies help people suffering from amnesia learn new skills and allow them to continue to be productive members of society.

Simulated Anterograde Amnesia

There are forms of amnesia that are temporary, some of which can be induced by particular drugs. Certain drugs temporarily mimic the symptoms of anterograde amnesia. In particular, a class of drugs called **benzodiazepines**, which are frequently prescribed by doctors as sedatives, have strong amnesic effects on memory. Benzodiazepines, such as diazepam (Valium), lorazepam, triazolam, and midazolam, are given for their effects on anxiety, insomnia, and muscle relaxation (Kaplan, 2005). These drugs can produce a temporary condition that resembles the amnesic syndrome (Tannenbaum, Paquette, Hilmer, Holroyd-Leduc, & Carnahan, 2012). While people are under the influence of these medications, they can converse normally and

> **Benzodiazepines:** Drugs that are used usually to relieve anxiety, insomnia, and muscle tension. They are also strong amnesia-inducing drugs, especially within the episodic memory domain.

retrieve well-learned information, but they cannot encode new information well, particularly into episodic memory.

Benzodiazepines have achieved notoriety with respect to their amnesic effect. Attackers, particularly in date-rape situations, give benzodiazepines, especially flunitrazepam (i.e., "roofies,") to potential victims (Juhascik et al., 2007). When combined with alcohol, the benzodiazepines leave the victims more vulnerable to attack and amnesia for the event later. Given the prevalence of benzodiazepines as legally prescribed drugs, people make sure their drinks are not tampered with, particularly at raucous parties. (To read about a heroic waiter who saved a woman from a potential benzodiazepine-linked date rape, go to study.sagepub.com/schwartz3e.[4])

All benzodiazepines impair episodic memory, but their effects on short-term memory and semantic memory are mixed, depending on the specific drug and the specific task (Bacon, Schwartz, Paire-Ficout, & Izaute, 2007; Izaute & Bacon, 2006). In experiments, when volunteers take benzodiazepines, they have poor memory of word lists, paired associates, and other materials when tested later. Once the drug wears off, the amnesic effects do so also. However, information seen or heard while the drug was in the patient's bloodstream will not be recovered.

Observations indicate that patients who develop a transient amnesia following administration of benzodiazepine are unaware of their episodic memory deficit. This condition is called **anosognosia**, the failure to become aware of a cognitive deficit. This distinguishes them from the amnesic syndrome, which is characterized by awareness of the amnesia. Benzodiazepine-linked temporary amnesia is not a long-term problem, as both the amnesia and the anosognosia wears off. Nonetheless, patients will overestimate the likelihood that they will remember studied material while under the influence of the benzodiazepine (Weingartner et al., 1993).

> **Anosognosia:** The failure to become aware of a cognitive deficit.

SECTION SUMMARY AND QUIZ

Amnesia refers to memory deficits, usually brought about by damage to the brain. Anterograde amnesia is a deficit in learning new information, whereas retrograde amnesia is a deficit in retrieving already learned information. The amnesic syndrome, a common form of amnesia, is brought about by damage to the hippocampus and other areas in the surrounding temporal lobe. Even though conscious learning is impaired in the amnesic syndrome, there still is evidence that amnesiacs show normal implicit memory. Implicit memory is the preserved ability to perform tasks that can be influenced by a past event without the person being aware of the event. It is often tested by a word-fragment completion task. Repetition priming is the effect of presenting a stimulus on the later processing of that same stimulus. Amnesiacs show repetition priming, even if they do not consciously recall the target. Simulated amnesia can be induced in normal people by giving them benzodiazipines, a class of drugs usually used for anxiety relief. However, these drugs also induce a temporary anterograde amnesia.

Section Quiz

1. Patient HM and Clive Wearing are most associated with which form of amnesia?
    a. Anterograde amnesia
    b. Retrograde amnesia
    c. Transient amnesia
    d. All of the above

2. Which of the following is impaired in the amnesic syndrome?
    a. Retrieval of distal events
    b. The ability to fluently retrieve words
    c. The encoding of new information
    d. Implicit access to memory

3. Memory compensation means that
    a. Amnesic patients receive financial rewards when they correctly remember details of an event
    b. Rather than trying to answer a question about the past, an amnesiac will talk about the issues related to the amnesia itself
    c. Patients will make up stories that are not true in order to compensate for the memory loss
    d. None of the above

4. A class of drugs called benzodiazepines are known for
    a. Their effects on anxiety, insomnia, and muscle relaxation, but also for their propensity to induce amnesia
    b. Their ability to counteract the effects of amnesia-inducing illness, such as Alzheimer's disease
    c. Their ability to counteract the effect of drugs that induce temporary amnesia
    d. Their ability to induce a permanent state of global amnesia

1. a
2. c
3. b
4. a

RETROGRADE AMNESIA

Retrograde amnesia occurs when patients lose the ability to retrieve memories of events prior to brain damage. This means that the patient cannot remember experiences or events that happened before the brain damage. Retrograde amnesia is not necessarily accompanied by anterograde amnesia. In most cases of retrograde amnesia, the inability to retrieve from memory is limited to episodic memory. The person may not be able to recall an event from twenty years ago, but otherwise knowledge is intact. Recalling facts about the world is not impaired as often. Typically, the retrograde amnesia is not complete. Rather, it extends back in time from the injury to a particular point in the past. People with retrograde amnesia will have periods of their lives from which they cannot recall any specific events.

> **Retrograde amnesia:** When patients lose the ability to retrieve memories of events prior to brain damage.

When given autobiographical cueing, all of their reported memories (if any) will come from a different period of their life than the one for which they have retrograde amnesia.

Keep in mind that for most patients, the retrograde amnesia is not total. Instead, events cannot be recalled from memory for a period starting just before the brain damage and extending backward to some point in time. This period may be small and the consequences relatively inconsequential, or it may stretch back for many years. Or as we saw with Clive Wearing, the retrograde period may stretch back across an entire lifetime.

A well-known case of a relatively short window of retrograde amnesia is Trevor Rees-Jones, the only survivor of the tragic car crash in 1997 that killed Princess Diana of Britain; her boyfriend, billionaire Dodi Fayed; and their driver, Henri Paul. Mr. Rees-Jones, who was Mr. Fayed's bodyguard, suffered severe injuries, including a blow to his head. Rees-Jones eventually made a full recovery from the auto accident, with no long-term deficits in his physical or cognitive abilities. The head injury did create a window of retrograde amnesia from the time of the accident to several hours before. Despite repeated questioning, Mr. Rees-Jones never remembered any of the events of the evening leading up to the crash, although he can remember events from earlier that day. In this case, the retrograde amnesia was unfortunate, as his testimony would have been useful in piecing together the events that led to the fatal crash. As a complete aside, it is worth noting that Mr. Rees-Jones, the only survivor of the car rash, was also the only one in the car wearing a seat belt.

In almost all cases of retrograde amnesia, the loss of memory occurs for events closest to the point of brain damage. Older memories are more difficult to dislodge from memory in patients with retrograde amnesia. This observation has been called **Ribot's law**: Newer memories will be more affected by retrograde amnesia than older memories. This has led some researchers to argue that a neurological process called **consolidation** is disrupted in retrograde amnesia. In consolidation, memory traces are made permanent in a person's long-term memory (Kopelman & Bright, 2012). Many memories may be held in a temporary state (in long-term memory) and only preserved if they turn out to have significance for the

> **Ribot's law:** Newer memories will be more affected by retrograde amnesia than older memories.

> **Consolidation:** A neurological process whereby memory traces are made permanent in a person's long-term memory.

individual. For example, the many hours you spend working on a paper for your English class are typically lost to memory once the paper has been handed in. The goal is to produce the paper; the memory of drinking coffee and eating pizza while you spent hours in front of your computer is generally forgotten, as the coffee and pizza are seldom relevant.

However, if your computer crashes and you lose all your work, you are more likely to remember all that now-wasted time. Although consolidation cannot explain retrograde amnesia over periods of years, it can account for the retrograde amnesia seen in cases like Trevor Rees-Jones.

In relatively minor injuries, such as concussion, the period of retrograde amnesia can be quite short, often just a few minutes before the injury. Lynch and Yarnell (1973), for example, found that football players who suffered from concussions during games could no longer remember the play in which they had gotten injured, although most remembered the rest of the game prior to their injury. In some cases, the retrograde period will initially be somewhat longer, perhaps several days or even a month, but as the person recovers from the head trauma, provided there is no permanent damage to the brain, the retrograde period will shrink. Older memories return first, followed by more recent memories. In most cases, however, a small window of time, anywhere from five to 60 minutes, will remain permanently lost to the accident victim. It is worth noting that brain damage from concussions is cumulative. Each concussion brings a greater and greater risk of permanent brain damage (Tushima, Geling, & Arnold, 2016). For this reason, many neurologists advise athletes to retire from such sports as football, soccer, and boxing if they have had too many concussions.

With permanent damage to the brain, the retrograde period can remain lengthy and unchanged for the rest of the person's life. Consider the case of KC (Rosenbaum et al., 2005). KC was a college-educated man living near the city of Toronto in Ontario, Canada, who died in 2014 at the age of 62. Before his injury, he worked as a foreperson in a factory. He was also a motorcycle enthusiast who spent most weekends riding around in the countryside outside of Toronto. He was not a newcomer to injury, having had a head injury as a child and a fractured leg in a major motorcycle accident. However, in 1981 at the age of 30, he suffered a major head trauma in a single-vehicle motorcycle crash. The injury destroyed large amounts of brain tissue in his frontal and temporal lobes, inflicting extensive damage to his left hippocampus. As a result of these injuries, KC was left with profound anterograde and retrograde amnesia. Like Clive Wearing, KC remembered no events from his life at all. He had no episodic memory, as he could neither recall any events from his life nor encode any new events. However, the amnesia only affected his episodic memory. His lexical memory and semantic memory were largely intact. Because of these spared skills, KC, after recovering from his physical injuries, spent the next 30 years living with his family at home and working at the local library, filing and reselling books. (For a series of interviews with KC by the prominent memory researcher Endel Tulving, go to study.sagepub.com/schwartz3e.[5])

Rosenbaum et al. (2005) and other researchers who studied KC found that his retrograde amnesia for episodic memory was complete. He did not remember any of his motorcycle crashes and did not remember attending hockey games or going out with friends. He did not remember holiday dinners with family, any of the times when he changed a flat tire, or having played a game of chess with Endel Tulving. Even more monumental events escaped his memory, including having been evacuated when a train derailed, spilling toxic chemicals in his neighborhood, and the tragic drowning death of his brother. However, he did not lose pre-accident semantic memory, which was largely intact. For example, KC could have told you how to change a tire, which team won the Stanley Cup every year up until 1981, and the address where he grew up. Moreover, he maintained his sense of personal identity, and his verbal abilities and his intelligence remained intact as well.

The exact locus in the brain that causes retrograde amnesia is elusive. Retrograde amnesia is seen in cases of amnesia related to damage to the diencephalon (as in Korsakoff's disease, to be discussed shortly), damage to the frontal lobes, and damage to the medial temporal lobes. There is some debate as to the role of the hippocampus in retrograde amnesia. Some argue that damage to the hippocampus results in a restricted time-limited retrograde amnesia, similar to that seen in concussions (although anterograde amnesia may be extensive). Others argue that the retrograde amnesia in these cases is because of the damage to the surrounding medial temporal lobe (Cole et al., 2016; Lah & Miller, 2008).

A less severe form of retrograde amnesia can be seen in patients with temporal lobe epilepsy. Epilepsy is a disease in which damaged brain tissue (usually as the result of brain trauma) results in abnormal neuronal discharging, resulting in seizures. In most cases, epilepsy can be controlled by medications, but in some cases, it requires surgery. The focal point of the brain damage that causes epilepsy is often the temporal lobe, which is critical to memory processes. Epilepsy patients will often demonstrate retrograde amnesia for a seizure and some time before the seizure. Greater retrograde amnesia correlates with more frequent seizures (Bergen, Thompson, Baxendale, Fish, & Shorvon, 2000).

Just a note to students concerned about their own memory: All of us forget events from our past, including the recent past. There is nothing abnormal about that. The retrograde-amnesia patients we are discussing have suffered extensive damage to their brains. If you are concerned about your own memory and perhaps have had had a recent auto accident, a trip to the neuropsychologist can be illuminating. Clinical neuropsychologists will run you through a battery of tests to examine your cognitive and emotional skills. If you score poorly on tests of remote memory (memory for the past) relative to your other tests, the neuropsychologist may diagnose a memory problem. However, in most cases, people's concerns about their own memory are unfounded.

Electroconvulsive Therapy

Electroconvulsive shock may bring up images of torture or barbaric medical practices of the past. Indeed, its use has been quite controversial in psychiatry for many years. Most psychiatrists no longer think it is appropriate for schizophrenia, bipolar disorder, or a host of other psychiatric disorders. However, most clinical psychologists agree that the evidence shows it is actually beneficial for patients with clinical depression. For clinically depressed patients, usually those with suicidal thoughts, a last course of treatment may involve **electroconvulsive therapy (ECT)**. A strong electric shock is delivered

> **Electroconvulsive therapy (ECT):** An effective treatment for depression that involves delivering a strong electric shock to the head of a patient. It creates periods of retrograde amnesia.

to the patient's head. Drugs are administered to prevent convulsions and injury during the treatment. As strange as it sounds, a repeated course of ECT actually successfully works to heighten mood and reduce suicidal tendencies among the clinically depressed (O'Conner et al., 2008).

One of the side effects of ECT is that it induces retrograde amnesia (Semkovska, Noone, Carton, & McLoughlin, 2012). This retrograde period is not trivial—it may extend to up to one year or more before the shock, mostly for episodic events but often for semantic memories as well. However, recent improvements in ECT technology have reduced the amount of retrograde amnesia (Rasmussen et al., 2016). In most cases, it wears off once the sessions are complete but usually remains intact for the ECT procedure itself and a short period before it. Some have even speculated that the memory loss itself creates the improved mood—patients can no longer recall what is depressing them so much. However, ECT appears not to cause anterograde amnesia (O'Conner et al., 2008; Semkovska et al., 2012). Patients can encode new information soon after their ECT treatment. Despite its negative impact on remote memory, ECT continues to be used because of its beneficial effects on alleviating depression.

Korsakoff's Disease

One of the most life-shattering forms of amnesia is Korsakoff's disease. Named after the Russian physician who first categorized the disease, **Korsakoff's disease** mostly affects older adults with a history of chronic alcohol abuse. As such, the etiology of Korsakoff's disease differs from other forms of amnesia. It is not the result of stroke or a sudden accident but a disease that results from alcohol abuse (Kril & Harper, 2012; Oudman et al., 2015).

> **Korsakoff's disease:** A severe form of amnesia brought on by long-term alcoholism. Characterized by anterograde amnesia, retrograde amnesia, anosognosia, and confabulation.

Korsakoff's disease begins with a vitamin B1 (thiamine) deficiency, almost always a result of the long-term, chronic alcohol abuse. Most Americans have little difficulty acquiring enough vitamin B1 in their diets and so are not at risk of developing Korsakoff's disease. However, alcohol interferes with the synthesis of vitamin B1, so alcoholics may develop B1 deficiencies. In rare cases, Korsakoff's disease can also develop because the patient has a genetic deficit that prevents the synthesis of vitamin B1. Long-term deficiencies in vitamin B1 can damage parts of the brain, including the diencephalon (mammillary bodies and thalamus); the basal forebrain; and sometimes, connections to the frontal lobes (see Figure 10.1).

Despite the gradual accumulation of the brain damage, the onset of the symptoms in Korsakoff's disease is sudden, usually occurring after a period of illness that includes delirium tremens. In some cases, immediate reintroduction of thiamine into the bloodstream can alleviate symptoms. If thiamine is not given immediately, the effects are devastating. In most cases, the damage is irreversible, and there is often very little a neuropsychologist can do to foster improvement in a patient with Korsakoff's disease (Wijnia, van de Wetering, Zwart, Nieuwehuis, & Goossensen, 2012).

> **Diencephalon:** The part of the brain that includes the thalamus and hypothalamus. It serves as an important relay point in the human memory circuit.

The **diencephalon** (i.e., thalamus) is a major relay center connecting different areas in the brain. In particular, it gathers information from the hippocampus and medial temporal lobes and sends it to the prefrontal lobe. Korsakoff's disease is characterized by deficits associated with damage to both the temporal lobes and to the frontal lobes and the resulting difficulty that the brain has in communicating internally.

Korsakoff's patients generally present both anterograde and retrograde amnesia. Their anterograde amnesia can often be as dense as that of a patient with damage to the medial temporal lobes. However, they perform differently on different kinds of memory tests. Both Korsakoff's patients and medial temporal lobe patients do equally poorly on recall tests, but Korsakoff's patients may do better on recognition tests, consistent with the idea that they can encode information but have difficulties processing and retrieving it (Hirst et al., 1986; Kril & Harper, 2012; Oudman et al., 2015).

Korsakoff's patients may also have severe retrograde amnesia, sometimes dating back to some significant event in their life, in many cases years prior to the onset of Korsakoff's disease (Race & Verfaellie, 2012). The retrograde amnesia is similar to that discussed earlier, except that it is combined with the other deficits seen in Korsakoff's disease. Sacks (1985) described a Korsakoff's patient who had retrograde amnesia extending back to his return from military service in World War II. The patient, "Jimmy" (not his real name), was a career naval sailor who was hospitalized in 1975, 30 years after the end of the war. Jimmy's retrograde amnesia period was complete for that 30-year period, although he remembered information prior to 1945 with a great degree of accuracy. Sacks's eloquent description of a Korsakoff's amnesia patient is as poignant as it is revealing. The following interview took place in 1975, when Jimmy was 49 years old (Sacks, pp. 24–26):

[Jimmy] was a genial soul, very ready to talk and to answer any questions I asked him. He told me his name and birth date, and the name of the little Connecticut town where he was born. He described it in affectionate detail, even drew me a map. . . . He remembered the names of the various submarines on which he had served [during World War II], their missions, where they had been stationed, the names of his shipmates. He remembered Morse code, and was still fluent in Morse-tapping and touch-typing.

"What year is this, Mr. G.?" I asked, concealing my perplexity under a casual manner.

"Forty-five, man. What do you mean?"

He went on, "We've won the war, FDR's dead. Truman's at the helm. There's great times ahead."

"And you, Jimmy, how old would you be?"

Oddly, uncertainly he hesitated a moment, as if engaged in calculation.

"Why, I guess I'm nineteen, Doc. I'll be twenty next birthday."

"Okay," I said. "I'll tell you a story. A man went to his doctor complaining of memory lapses. The doctor asked him some routine questions, and then said, 'These lapses. What about them?'

'What lapses?'" the patient replied.

"So that's my problem," Jimmy laughed. "I kind of thought it was. I do find myself forgetting things, once in a while, things that have just happened. The past is clear, though."

(Sacks, pp. 24–26)

This is not the comment of a person deeply troubled by having lost the memory of the past 30 years of his life. The patient, Jimmy, is clearly without any awareness of the severity of his memory loss. The retrograde amnesia is obvious from his words. "Jimmy" believes he is 19, not 49, and he does not know that 30 years have passed without his having any memory for them. However, unlike patients with simple retrograde amnesia, "Jimmy" and many patients with Korsakoff's disease have an additional problem: They have anosognosia, meaning a lack of awareness of their own memory deficits. At best, Korsakoff's patients have only a dim awareness of their memory problems. Indeed, their lack of insight into their own condition makes treatment and intervention extremely difficult. Often, when patients are confronted with their poor memory performance or inconsistencies in their story, they make countless excuses, blaming the situation or the tester. This contrasts with the behavior of medial temporal lobe amnesiacs, who are often aware of their own memory deficits.

Another identifying characteristic of Korsakoff's is confabulation. **Confabulation** is defined as honest lying. This paradoxical definition is not an oxymoron; rather, it reflects both the falsehood of the stories and the patients' belief that the stories they tell are true. Confabulation means that the person will make up stories and identify them as personal memories (Moscovitch, 1989). Korsakoff's patients believe these false memories while they are generating them, even if they forget them moments later and confabulate entirely new ones.

> **Confabulation:** When amnesic patients lie about their past. They do not know they are not telling the truth because of deficits in source monitoring.

Confabulated memories appear to be the function of confusion between imagination and memory, which allows patients with Korsakoff's disease to fill in inconsistencies in their life narrative. In this sense, confabulation is considered a failure of source monitoring. Moscovitch (1989) argued that confabulation also arises from an inability to order events in memory—that is, temporal sequencing. Combined with the failure to screen out false memories, many memory reports from Korsakoff's patients will appear extremely odd to friends, family, and doctors, not to mention students. Consider this conversation between Morris Moscovitch and a patient (HW) who suffered from Korsakoff's (taken from Moscovitch, 1989, pp. 136–137). MM stands for Morris Moscovitch.

HW: I'm 40, 42, pardon me, 62.

MM: Are you married or single?

HW: Married.

MM: How long have you been married?

HW: About four months.

MM: What's your wife's name?

HW: Martha.

MM: How many children do you have?

HW: Four. (He laughs). Not bad for four months.

MM: How old are your children?

HW: The eldest is 32; his name is Bob; and the youngest is 22; his name is Joe.

MM: (He laughs again.) How did you get these children in four months?

HW: They're adopted.

MM: Who adopted them?

HW: Martha and I.

MM: Immediately after you got married you wanted to adopt these older children?

HW: Before we were married we adopted one of them, two of them. The eldest girl, Brenda, and Bob, and Joe and Dina since we were married.

In this conversation, you can see a vivid example of confabulation, as the patient has to square the knowledge of his four adult children with the confabulated memory of being a newlywed. This kind of confabulation is relatively common among Korsakoff's patients. Sacks (1985) described a patient who thought he was still running his butcher shop from his hospital bed. Also apparent in the conversation with HW is that the Korsakoff's patient has no insight into his memory deficit. The incongruities between the stories they tell and the reality around them does not seem to bother these patients. (For more on Dr. Moscovitch's research, go to study.sagepub.com/schwartz3e.[6])

Another interesting feature of Korsakoff's patients is their poor metamemory, consistent with their general anosognosia. For example, when asked to do feeling-of-knowing judgments on both episodic and semantic memories, Korsakoff's patients show impaired accuracy relative to controls. Shimamura and Squire (1986) showed that the metamemory accuracy of patients with Korsakoff's disease was not above what would be expected from random guessing, meaning that the patients did not know what they did know and they did not know what they did not know. In contrast, temporal lobe amnesiacs (amnesic syndrome patients) were accurate in this task. The Korsakoff's patients were also highly overconfident, thinking they would remember many items that they could not.

Eric Oudman and his colleagues have argued that Korsakoff's patients do have preserved implicit or procedural memory and that this aspect of cognition can be used to help them adjust (Oudman et al., 2015). Remember that implicit memory occurs without the patient being consciously aware of remembering. Oudman has used implicit memory to help Korsakoff's patients learn novel tasks. In addition, when attention demands are extremely low, Korsakoff's patients can pay attention to salient cues to help them remember. In a prospective memory task, Altgassen et al. (2016) found that Korsakoff's patients could remember to do a future task when cues were made very salient, and there was no competing task. Despite this progress, rehabilitation with Korsakoff's patients is extremely difficult, given their anosagnosia.

To summarize, Korsakoff's disease is a devastating illness. Korsakoff's patients suffer from both anterograde amnesia and retrograde amnesia. They may also confabulate

Figure 10.1   Illustration of the location of the diencephalon.

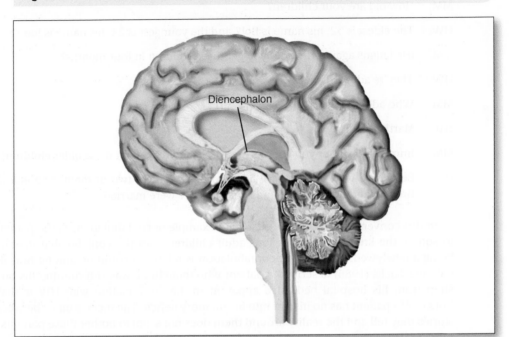

SOURCE: B. Garrett (2009).

and lack awareness of their amnesia. Korsakoff's disease is caused by damage to the diencephalon (in particular, the thalamus), the part of the brain that connects the temporal lobes to the frontal lobes, usually the result of chronic, long-term alcohol abuse (Oudman et al., 2015).

FRONTAL SYNDROME

Frontal syndrome is characterized by damage to the frontal lobes and behavioral symptoms that include retrograde amnesia, anosognosia, and confabulation (Shingaki, Park, Ueda, Murai, & Tsukiura, 2016). Many of the symptoms of frontal lobe damage are similar to those seen in Korsakoff's amnesia. For example, both anosognosia and confabulation are typical of both forms of brain damage. On the other hand, unlike in Korsakoff's disease, anterograde amnesia is usually only a minor issue in frontal lobe injuries. Retrograde amnesia is also a frequent symptom of damage to the frontal lobes (see Kopelman, 2002).

> **Frontal syndrome:** People often show retrograde amnesia and may show anterograde amnesia, although the latter tends to be much less severe than in other patients. They may also show anosognosia and confabulation.

The frontal lobes are enormous areas in the human brain, encompassing regions responsible for many cognitive, emotional, motor, and behavioral functions. The areas of the frontal lobe that are correlated with memory deficits are the areas most anterior (that is, to the front) of the human brain, known collectively as the prefrontal cortex. Prefrontal areas in both the left and right hemispheres are associated with memory functions. Within the prefrontal cortex, the specific areas associated with memory deficits include the dorsolateral, ventrolateral, anterior, and anterior cingulate (Shimamura, 2008).

Behavioral Issues in Frontal Patients

Frontal patients may show some evidence of anterograde amnesia, although it tends to be less severe than in amnesic syndrome patients or Korsakoff's disease patients. As in the Korsakoff's disease patients, anterograde amnesia in frontal patients appears related to difficulties in processing and accessing information rather than with its initial encoding. Thus, when tested on recognition, frontal lobe patients will show relatively small deficits relative to control patients, although they will show more evidence of anterograde amnesia when tested in free recall. Frontal lobe patients will also show a high rate of false alarms (responding "old" to new items) in recognition (Parkin, Bindschaedler, Harsent, & Metzler, 1996). This suggests that frontal lobe patients are likely to accept false information as self-experienced episodic memory. However, other research shows that frontal patients do not show higher rates of false memories on the Deese-Roediger-McDermott (DRM) paradigm than other amnesics (Shingaki et al., 2016).

Frontal syndrome patients may also confabulate in a manner similar to that of Korsakoff's patients. Like their high false alarm rates, confabulation appears to be a function of the inability of frontal lobe patients to screen or monitor the contents of their retrieval. When an image comes to mind, most of us make a nearly automatic judgment as to its source. If we conclude it comes from imagination, we immediately discount it as a memory. For example, if an image arises of you having a drink with Pharrell Williams (or some other pop star), you may discredit it as not being a real memory. In frontal lobe patients, like Korsakoff's patients, this reality-monitoring process is lacking, leading to confabulation and false memories.

This monitoring deficit extends to source information as well. Frontal lobe patients have deficits in correctly attributing the source of a memory; these deficits are sometimes known as **source amnesia**. The frontal lobe patients can acquire new information but forget where they heard the information at rates much greater than those of control patients. Thus, an event the person read about might be misremembered as an event the patient actually witnessed. In experiments, participants might hear a list of words in which two narrators alternate the reciting of each word. Then at test, participants must remember the words from the list and

> **Source amnesia:** Deficits in correctly attributing the source of a memory.

who said each one. Relative to controls, the frontal lobe patients will make many more errors in source monitoring, even when their recall of words is roughly equivalent to that of normal participants. Note that normal people make source memory errors as well, but they are much more common among frontal lobe patients (Shimamura, 2008).

Table 10.2 Symptoms of Frontal Syndrome

1. Damage to prefrontal areas of cortex

2. Anosognosia (lack of awareness of deficits)

3. Confabulation

4. Frequent false memories

5. Deficits in source monitoring

6. Deficits in temporal ordering

Frontal lobe patients have selective difficulties with temporal order information (Shingaki et al., 2016). This means they have relative difficulty in organizing past events into the correct order. This deficit includes both semantic and autobiographical information. For example, a frontal lobe patient might have difficulty reporting whether her visit to the hospital came before or after her weekly golf match. She might also forget whether she had taken her medicines already for the day or had not taken them since the previous evening. In some cases, temporal order may also play into source confusions. Therefore, a patient may complain that visits to the hospital took place before the accident that injured his brain. In addition, frontal patients have difficulties with ordering semantic memory. Thus, they might report that Barak Obama was president prior to George W. Bush. Normal individuals also forget the order of information about events but not to the extent to which frontal lobe patients do.

Damage to the prefrontal lobe can create other cognitive deficits besides problems with memory. Frontal lobe patients may have deficits with planning, problem-solving, language, and emotion. Damage to the orbital frontal area in the frontal cortex can also change personality. The orbital frontal cortex appears to be a part of the brain that inhibits impulsive behavior. Damage to this area can, depending on the damage and the situation, make someone more impulsive or in other cases, extremely passive. Thus, typically, the memory deficits in frontal lobe patients are accompanied by a number of other cognitive and behavioral problems (see Table 10.2).

TRANSIENT GLOBAL AMNESIA

Transient global amnesia (TGA) is a rare form of amnesia in which the amnesic effects are short lived, usually on the order of hours (Brown, 1998; Hunter, 2011). TGA often does not recur in the individual who gets it, but there have now been documented cases of people who have had repeated attacks of TGA (Moon, Moon, & Han, in press). TGA can put quite a jolt of fear through the victim and his family. In TGA, the amnesic effects are extremely strong but last a short time and then, by and large, vanish. Apparently, there is also no long-term damage to any part of the brain, though recent work suggests that white-matter fibers may be affect (Moon et al., in press).

Transient global amnesia: A rare form of amnesia in which the amnesic effects are short-lived, usually on the order of hours.

TGA is characterized by a dense, anterograde amnesia—new information is simply not encoded during the TGA episode (Hainselin et al., 2012). A person may repeatedly ask the same questions, such as "Where am I?" "Who drove me to the hospital?" or "When did I put on these clothes?" Because the person does not remember the answers to these questions, he may ask them just a few minutes later and then continue to repeat them. Because the onset of TGA is so unexpected and the offset so fast, there are few comparative studies of the extent of the anterograde amnesia in TGA relative to other neuropsychological syndromes and to normal controls, but reports from patients and their doctors point to a strong anterograde amnesia. TGA is also characterized by retrograde amnesia. The TGA patient may suffer a retrograde period from a few hours into the past to several years into the past during the TGA episode (Moon et al., in press). Hainselin et al. (2012) also showed that although TGA patients are aware that there is a problem, they are not aware of the extent of their amnesia. Once the TGA episode is over, almost all of the retrograde amnesia disappears, except a small window just before the onset and often concerning the TGA episode itself.

TGA onset is sudden; there is usually no warning or physical cues that an attack of TGA is about to occur. Despite the robustness of both the anterograde and retrograde amnesia, there is typically no loss of personal identity, and other aspects of cognition appear unimpaired. Language, reading, attention, and problem-solving all appear unimpaired. Working memory also appears unimpaired (Brown, 1998).

TGA attacks tend to occur in people from middle age to early old age (roughly ages 50 to 70) and then decreases among older adults. For younger people, a history of migraines is associated with TGA attacks. Neither men nor women are more or less likely to have TGA attacks. The onset is often triggered by rigorous exercise or physical stress. This can include physical exertion, sexual intercourse, and a hot bath after being cold or immersion in cold water after being hot, as well as psychological stress, such as an argument with a spouse or bad news at work. This covers a lot of ground, but all of these activities are associated with an increased heart rate.

The etiology of TGA is less than clear. Once hospitalized, a patient will undergo screening for stroke, seizure, and head injury, but none of these are associated with TGA. Hunter (2011) suggested that the most likely explanation for TGA is temporary disruption of blood flow within the brain, technically known as an ischemia. Compression of veins preventing the proper flow of blood from the brain back to heart has also been suggested as a potential cause (Brown, 1998). However, it is not clear which explanation is better or whether both contribute to TGA.

The good news with TGA is that it wears off. By the next day, the patient is feeling fine and is left with only a small retrograde amnesia period just prior to the attack. There is no residual anterograde amnesia; by the next day, the person is learning and remembering normally. Most people who get a TGA attack will never get another.

SHORT-TERM MEMORY AMNESIA

In each form of amnesia so far discussed, the deficit has been in long-term memory. These forms of amnesia are much more common than deficits in short-term memory. Nonetheless, short-term/working memory can be impaired while long-term memory is left relatively intact. In this form of amnesia, people have deficits keeping larger amounts of information stored or rehearsed in working memory. Thus, a patient might have difficulty remembering a phone number long enough to dial. In the lab, the patient would have difficulties with digit spans, being able to hold far fewer digits in working memory than a control patient.

> **Short-term memory amnesia:** Deficits in the capacity of working memory.

Short-term memory amnesia was first studied by Shallice and Warrington (1970), who worked with a patient known by the initials KF. KF was a young man who injured his head in a motorcycle accident. He suffered from a selective impairment of short-term memory, even though he experienced neither anterograde nor retrograde amnesia in the long-term memory domain. He learned paired associates just as rapidly as did control participants. However, on digit span tasks, KF was severely impaired. Whereas normal adults can recall seven digits, KF was unable to maintain more than two digits when tested in the auditory modality and four when tested with visual presentation.

KF suffered extensive damage to the frontal lobe of the left hemisphere. Localization of the lesion revealed that it was close to the Sylvan fissure, which separates the frontal lobes from the temporal lobes. This is an area of the brain closely associated with language formation and processing. For this reason, KF's deficit might have been limited to the phonological loop or auditory working memory with less damage to visual working memory.

A similar patient was studied some years later by Vallar and Baddeley (1984). This patient, PV, seemed to have selective damage to the phonological loop. PV was intellectually normal in most areas and showed no evidence of impaired long-term memory. However, she showed impairments on all tests that made use of the phonological loop. PV showed deficits in digit span tasks—but only when the items were presented in an auditory format. Her visual working memory appeared unimpaired. She also showed deficits remembering lists of words that were presented to her in the auditory modality. When the same stimuli were presented to her visually, she showed no differences from normal control patients.

PV had damage not to the frontal lobes but to an area of the brain in the parietal lobe in the left hemisphere, near the back of the frontal lobes. Belleville, Caza, and Peretz (2003) have also documented a case of a patient with selective deficits to the phonological loop with damage in this area of the brain. So it remains to be seen if it is the parietal lobe, the frontal lobe, or both that are the culprit in short-term memory amnesia.

REDUPLICATIVE PARAMNESIA AND CAPGRAS SYNDROME

Two rare but bizarre forms of amnesia are the result of organic damage to the brain but resemble psychiatric illnesses. **Reduplicative paramnesia** is a condition in which patients believe that places or locations have been duplicated and that the two locations exist simultaneously. Its closely related cousin is **Capgras syndrome**, in which patients come to believe that other people have been duplicated and that sets of identical people may exist

(Wise, 2016). In some cases, the two syndromes may coexist, but they may also exist independently (Ramachandran, 2011).

Reading the above definitions of reduplicative paramnesia and Capgras syndrome might leave you confused. What's going on here? The best way to illustrate these conditions is with examples. Let's start with reduplicative paramnesia. In one case of reduplicative paramnesia, a patient agreed that his hospital room looked just like ones found in the hospital in the local city. Moreover, the patient agreed that the view out the window revealed a view of a town

> **Reduplicative paramnesia:** A condition caused by brain damage in which patients believe that places or locations have been duplicated and that the two locations exist simultaneously.

> **Capgras syndrome:** A condition caused by brain damage in which patients believe that other people have been duplicated and that two identical people may exist.

just like the small city near his home. But the patient insisted that the hospital was a different one and the city, although a lookalike of the patient's home city, was actually a fake (Benson, Gardner, & Meadows, 1976). Thus, although the patient recognized the surroundings, they lacked a feeling of familiarity for the patient. To explain this lack of familiarity, the patient thought the world around him was a fake, made to look like the world he knew. Thus, he recognized the surroundings but also found them unfamiliar. These symptoms appear delusional, and indeed they are. But reduplicative paramnesia occurs after traumatic brain damage, not from schizophrenia or other psychiatric disorders.

Consider another reported case of reduplicative paramnesia. Hinkebein, Callahan, and Gelber (2001) described a case of reduplicative paramnesia in a 67-year-old man who had recently undergone brain surgery to repair a damaged artery. The man had no history of psychiatric disorder, was a high school graduate, and had owned a small business most of his adult life. He was hospitalized in a small hospital in southern Illinois. He insisted, however, that he was in a hospital in Southern California that was an exact duplicate of the hospital located in Illinois. He believed that his visitors were commuting from Illinois to California. He often wondered aloud why "they" were trying to trick him into thinking he was in Illinois, when he "knew" that he was in California. Therapists subtly and repeatedly tried to convince the patient that he really was in Illinois, to no avail. He was eventually released to a rehabilitation center, because he was normal in all respects except for his paramnesia. Nine months after the brain injury, his reduplicative paramnesia seemed to have passed, and he reliably reported that he was, in fact, at home in Illinois. Although he rationally agreed that he must have been hospitalized near home, he continued to report that it *felt to him* like he had been in California. A similar case was reported in Japan. Yamada, Murai, and Ohigashi (2003) reported a case of a 73-year-old woman with the same basic set of symptoms. This woman needed two years of treatment to dispel the paramnesia symptoms.

Hinkebein et al. (2001) argued that two neurological deficits combine to create the symptoms seen in reduplicative paramnesia. First, damage to areas in the right parietal lobe creates impaired visual perception and visual memory. This damage creates the feeling that well-known places are no longer familiar. It may also induce the experience that familiar places have something peculiar or different about them (that is, they are in California instead of Illinois). Second, bilateral damage in the prefrontal lobes prevents the individual from experiencing familiarity or dismissing its lack as an illusion. Lee, Shinbo, Kanai, and Nagumo (2011), however, examined a patient who had reduplicative paramnesia after only damage to his right prefrontal lobe. Thus, reduplicative paramnesia may not require the parietal damage. Nonetheless, Lee et al.'s patient also had visual impairments, likely brought about from connections between his damaged right prefrontal lobe and areas in the visual cortex. Thus, the research points to an impairment of visual familiarity brought about by neurological changes to the prefrontal lobes.

Capgras syndrome involves the delusional belief that people have been duplicated. In general, it occurs when the patient believes that his or her family members and close friends have been duplicated and replaced by imposters or robots (Young, 2008; Wise, 2016). It must be kept in mind that Capgras syndrome, like the equally bizarre reduplicative paramnesia, is brought about by neurological injury. A striking case was described by Hermanowicz (2002). The patient was a 73-year-old man suffering from retinitis pigmentosa, which left him nearly blind, and Parkinson's disease. He had begun to suffer from visual hallucinations at age 71, usually of strange people approaching his wife. He came to believe that his wife was variously replaced by a series of men and women who dressed up to impersonate her. He believed he could always tell the difference between his wife and the imposters. As such, he frequently angrily turned away from his wife, believing she was a male imposter. Various changes to his medications were made with no success. Brain scans revealed minor scattered damage in his frontal lobes but nothing major. Unfortunately, in this case, the symptoms persisted despite therapy and medication.

Ryan and Caplan (2016) describe another interesting case of Capgras syndrome. Their 71-year-old had prefrontal damage from a potential variety of causes, including earlier brain trauma, psychiatric illness, and heavy alcohol use. Thus, the Capgras syndrome in question may have arisen from any of these causes. He was brought in for treatment after several years of seemingly paranoid behavior. But what caught Ryan and Caplan's attention is that this patient had Capgras syndrome for his pet cat. He recognized that his pet cat looked just as it should, but claimed that it had been replaced by an imposter that was part of a conspiracy against him. Tongue-in-cheek, the authors called this "cat-gras" syndrome. Luckily, the patient's symptoms eased with medication.

Relative to reduplicative paramnesia, Capgras syndrome is more associated with psychiatric conditions, such as schizophrenia, than it is with traumatic brain injuries. Indeed, most cases of Capgras syndrome occur in schizophrenics (Ramachandran, 2011). In cases where it does occur because of brain damage, it often occurs in conjunction with deficits in face recognition (prosopagnosia). Ramachandran and Blakeslee (1998) have argued that Capgras syndrome arises from a breakdown in the connections between the temporal lobe areas involved in face recognition and the limbic system involved in emotion. Thus, the patient will see a familiar face but not feel any of the associated sense of familiarity and emotion that seeing one's spouse, parents, or children might evoke. Left without an explanation for this, the brain presupposes duplication (see Ramachandran, 2011). In some advanced cases, the patient no longer recognizes himself or herself in the mirror and may ask who has altered the mirror to portray someone else (Diard-Detoeuf et al., 2016). In this case, there is a complete breakdown of connections between the areas responsible for face recognition and the production of familiarity.

SECTION SUMMARY AND QUIZ

Retrograde amnesia can be induced by electroconvulsive shock, which is nonetheless considered a worthwhile treatment for depression that has not responded to other treatments. A debilitating form of amnesia is Korsakoff's disease, which is usually brought on by chronic alcohol abuse. Korsakoff's patients have anterograde amnesia, retrograde amnesia, and anosognosia or a deficit in recognizing their own deficits. Korsakoff's patients also have a tendency to confabulate—that is, to tell lies without knowing they are doing so. Frontal lobe patients also have demonstrated confabulation and have deficits in source monitoring and temporal order information. Short-term memory amnesia occurs when long-term encoding is not affected, but patients cannot maintain normal spans in working memory. Transient global amnesia occurs when a profound but temporary amnesia occurs, probably the result of a temporary disruption of blood flow in the brain. Reduplicative paramnesia is a condition in which patients believe that places or locations have been duplicated and that the two locations exist simultaneously. Its closely related cousin is Capgras syndrome, in which patients come to believe that other people have been duplicated and that sets of identical people may exist.

Section Quiz

1. Confabulation refers to
   a. The process of changing a memory from a temporary representation to a permanent representation
   b. The process by which a person undergoing electroconvulsive shock recovers lost memories
   c. Reporting made-up stories or lies in lieu of actual recall
   d. None of the above

2. Which of these symptoms commonly occurs in Korsakoff's disease?
   a. Confabulation
   b. Retrograde amnesia
   c. Anosoagnosia
   d. All of the above

3. Patient DJT shows a tendency to make up stories instead of recalling actual events. He also has difficulties remembering the recent past. He is totally unaware of his deficits. He has no history with alcohol abuse. Your diagnosis?
   a. Frontal syndrome
   b. Repuduplicative paramnesia
   c. Capgras syndrome
   d. Transient global amnesia

4. Capgras syndrome is thought to arise from
   a. Profound damage to the hippocampus
   b. A breakdown in the connections between the temporal lobe areas involved in face recognition and the limbic system involved in emotion
   c. An excess of benzodiazepine in the limbic system that interferes with recognition performance
   d. A neurological block between the areas in the frontal lobe involved in source monitoring and those in the occipital lobe involved in visual processing

1. c
2. d
3. a
4. b

PSYCHOGENIC AMNESIA

Psychogenic amnesia is a broad term that covers all forms of amnesia that are not directly linked to disruption or injury to the brain. Psychogenic amnesias are caused by psychological disorders or psychological trauma rather than physical insult to the brain (Thomas-Antérion, 2012). Because of this, psychogenic amnesia is much more difficult to classify and also exceedingly rare. However, it is often symptoms of psychogenic amnesia that capture the public attention, reflected in how amnesia is portrayed in movies. In particular, in psychogenic amnesia, we occasionally see a loss of personal identity. This means that, although patients are verbal, responsive to surroundings, and socially aware, they do not know their name or very much about themselves. They are unable to recall any events from their life (Thomas-Antérion, 2012). This loss of identity may occur without anterograde amnesia. The patient may be learning new information, including autobiographical, information starting from the time of the onset of the amnesia. This puzzling condition is often dramatized in movies (e.g., Goldie Hawn's character in *Overboard* [1987]). We start with a well-reported and well-documented real case of psychogenic amnesia.

Schacter (1996) described the fascinating story of the patient Lumberjack. Lumberjack (an alias chosen by Schacter) was admitted to a hospital in Toronto, Canada, in 1980. He had been discovered by a police officer roaming the streets of Toronto in midwinter. Lumberjack was not wearing a coat and looked freezing, so the police officer questioned him. When the officer was unable to obtain information from him, Lumberjack was brought to the hospital for testing. Lumberjack was suffering from a dense and complete psychogenic amnesia. His amnesia was so dense that he did not know his own name or where he lived. Indeed, Lumberjack could remember nothing from his personal past, except for the events just prior and subsequent to his interaction with the police officer. Local newspapers printed his photograph in a vain effort to locate relatives who could identify him. During the next few days, Lumberjack remained in a dense amnesic state. Then, while watching television at the hospital, some images from a movie he was watching triggered his memory. The specific image that triggered his memory was the depiction of a funeral in the miniseries *Shogun* (1980). This caused him to remember the funeral of his own grandfather, which was the traumatic event that had triggered the amnesic episode. Within a matter of hours, he had recalled not just his name and home address, but complete autobiographical memory returned as well.

In another documented cases, the patient JH actually spent six years in a state of psychogenic amnesia in which he could remember nothing of the first 53 years of his life (Rathbone, Ellis, Baker, & Butler, 2015). JH was brought to a hospital in 2005 after initially being reported missing by his family. Unlike Lumberjack, JH never lost his personal identity. He displayed strong anterograde and retrograde amnesia, but showed no brain abnormalities. During the ensuing years, he did his best to cope with is intense retrograde amnesia and persistent anterograde amnesia. Despite this, he was able to return to his family and to his job. However, at the age 60, a variety of psychotherapy approaches allowed JH to regain the missing past. Because of the extended period of JH's psychogenic amnesia, he was also extensively tested. Rathbone documented severe deficits in self-knowledge as well as an ability to plan for the future while JH was amnesic. These returned to a more normal level, once the fugue finally wore off. That such a profound amnesia could be allayed by psychotherapy is fortunate.

This form of amnesia is called psychogenic amnesia. **Psychogenic amnesia** is caused by psychological problems rather than neurological problems. In most cases, a traumatic event of one kind or another causes a strong block, preventing access to episodic and autobiographical memories, in some cases even facts of self-identity. In the case of Lumberjack, the funeral of his grandfather triggered his psychogenic amnesia. His

> **Psychogenic amnesia:** All forms of amnesia that are not directly linked to disruption or injury to the brain.

grandfather had raised Lumberjack and was his only committed relative. The shock of his grandfather's death apparently was sufficiently traumatic to induce the amnesia. In JH, personal problems such as financial difficulties may have contributed to his development of psychogenic amnesia. Some argue that the amnesia is one way in which the person copes with the trauma (Thomas-Antérion, 2012).

Psychiatrists rather than neurologists and neuropsychologists are the ones who typically study psychogenic amnesias. They have identified a number of different forms of psychogenic amnesia. Although psychogenic amnesias have a psychological cause, Schacter (1996) pointed out that a large proportion of documented cases of psychogenic amnesia are in people who have a history of brain injury, as indeed was the case with Lumberjack. But because of the rareness of this state, little empirical data exist on this topic.

Dissociative Amnesia

Dissociative amnesia is a condition in which only the traumatic event or events closely related to that trauma are not remembered. For example, a veteran may have selective amnesia for the event in which he or she lost a limb in combat. **Dissociative amnesia** is a retrograde amnesia, as it refers to the inability to remember a specific past event or events.

Dissociative amnesia: A condition in which only the traumatic event or events closely related to that trauma are not remembered.

Most patients suffering from dissociative amnesia have equivalent semantic knowledge of the traumatic event but have lost episodic access to the trauma. This distinguishes dissociative amnesia from "repression," in which both episodic and semantic access is lost. Because dissociative amnesia is a psychological amnesia, there can be a great deal of variation from patient to patient. Some will experience amnesia only for the event, whereas others will also be amnesic for events that surround the trauma in time or that are related to the trauma (Kihlstrom & Schacter, 1995).

Dissociative Fugue

Dissociative fugue is a psychogenic amnesia in which the patient forgets his or her personal identity in addition to access to his or her autobiographical past. The case of Lumberjack involved a dissociative fugue state. **Dissociative fugue** is therefore also a retrograde amnesia. Characteristic of dissociative fugue is forgetting one's name, occupation, place and date of birth, and where one currently lives. In most documented cases of dissociative fugue, the fugue state wears off in a matter of days. But there are some reports of dissociative fugues lasting years. In some cases, something—often either a word or an image—serves as a cue or trigger for the person in a fugue to remember his or her past. With that one cue, the person's entire past seems to return in a flood of memories. However, in one recently documented case, much retrograde amnesia remained even after the fugue state had worn off and the patient regained his identity (Hennig-Fast et al., 2008). Thus, not all dissociative fugue states end in a flood of memories from the past. Future research will be required to determine whether these two types of recovery from dissociative fugue differ as a function of the psychological and neurological origins of the amnesic state.

Dissociative fugue: A psychogenic amnesia in which the patient forgets his or her personal identity in addition to access to his or her autobiographical past.

Post-Traumatic Stress Disorder

Memory deficits in **post-traumatic stress disorder** (PTSD) differ greatly from memory deficits in other neurological or psychological disorders. This is mainly because the deficit in PTSD is not with having amnesia but in not being able to inhibit the retrieval of unwanted memories. In PTSD, harmless events can cue the retrieval of traumatic events, such as of being a victim of a violent crime or a wartime tragedy. For example, a veteran might be reminded of a violent explosion on the battlefield when his or her shopping cart accidentally bumps into a cart of another shopper. Treatment usually involves trying to desensitize these cues (Wilson, 2009).

Post-traumatic stress disorder: A psychological disorder that includes the inability to inhibit unwanted memories because of exposure to extremely dangerous or stressful situations.

Repression

The standard view of **repression** is that psychological mechanisms (defense mechanisms) act to block out access to memory of traumatic events. In this sense, repression can be defined as a psychogenic retrograde amnesia for selective events. This view of repression is generally associated with Freudian theory. Much debate concerns whether this condition exists at all. However, to the extent that it does, it should be classified as a psychogenic amnesia.

> **Repression:** The active forgetting of highly emotional memories, usually from childhood.

In general, psychogenic amnesia is exceedingly rare. It occurs because of psychological trauma instead of organic damage to the brain. It is seldom confused with organic brain damage because the symptoms are usually quite different. In the final section of this chapter, we will tackle the biggest producer of amnesic patients, Alzheimer's disease.

ALZHEIMER'S DISEASE

Alzheimer's disease is a frighteningly common condition that attacks mainly older adults. As medical technology has improved and people live longer, more people are suffering from Alzheimer's disease. With increasing age, a person's likelihood of being diagnosed with Alzheimer's disease increases. However, it is important to note that not all older adults will get Alzheimer's disease (Bermejo-Pareja, Benito-León, Vega, Medrano, & Román, 2008). Nonetheless, there are approximately 5.4 million people with Alzheimer's in the United States today. However, the simple fact is that many older adults *do not* get Alzheimer's disease. (For more information and statistics on Alzheimer's disease, go to study.sagepub.com/schwartz3e.[7])

> **Alzheimer's disease:** One of many dementia-type illnesses that are more common in older adults than in younger adults. Memory is the first deficit detected in this disease.

Alzheimer's disease is a terminal illness. At present, medical science has various ways of slowing the progress of the disease and at least during the early phase of the illness, slowing the development of symptoms (Demirtas-Tatlidede, Vahabzadeh-Hagh, & Pascual-Leone, 2013). Unfortunately, a cure for the disease is still not in our reach, and Alzheimer's disease is inevitably fatal.

Although each individual may follow a unique course of decline, once the person has been diagnosed with Alzheimer's disease, a pattern of deterioration is typically seen in most patients (Brandt & Rich, 1995). With almost all victims of Alzheimer's disease, memory decline is the first symptom noticed by the patient and his or her family. Memory deficits are followed by more general cognitive problems, requiring the person to have help to perform even simple tasks. As the disease progresses, more and more cognitive systems fail, and then in the latest stages, physical systems decline rapidly as well, requiring nursing home care until the disease finally results in death.

In the earliest stage of the disease, the patient will recognize that his or her memory is "not what it used to be." Complaints include misplacing items, forgetting people's names, and requiring more time to learn new information. In the earliest states, such memory deficits may be difficult to distinguish behaviorally from normal age-related declines in memory. However, neuropsychological tests can often distinguish between the two. Alzheimer's patients will show deficits in working memory performance relative to age-matched controls. Although digit spans may be normal, Alzheimer's disease patients do not show normal recency effect on free-recall tasks (Germano, Kinsella, Storey, Ong, & Ames, 2008). Usually, by the end of the early phase, an individual will have sought medical attention and have a diagnosis of Alzheimer's disease. We will turn later to the steps that can be taken to alleviate the progress of the disease. For now, we will continue to discuss its natural progression.

In the intermediate stages, cognitive deficits mount. The anterograde amnesia grows stronger, and retrograde amnesia may also occur, although usually for only relatively recent events. The patient may begin to experience difficulties in naming familiar people. Problem-solving and decision-making may also be impaired. Language problems may surface. These tend to be a decreasing vocabulary and a lower word fluency—that is, the person's speech may be characterized by frequent word-finding difficulties, similar to tip-of-the-tongue experiences. At this point, the patient may also begin to experience motor deficits (called apraxias). These are deficits in implementing complex motor patterns, such as dressing, writing, threading a needle, or loading a dishwasher. At first, these tasks may just become difficult, and the person will appear clumsy to others, but eventually the patient will need help with these tasks.

As Alzheimer's disease progresses, there is more and more retrograde amnesia. There is usually a temporal gradient to the retrograde amnesia, with more recent information being lost before older information. With the progression of Alzheimer's disease, the failures of retrograde amnesia stretch farther back in time. By the later stages of Alzheimer's disease, the patient may remember little of his or her past.

In the late stages of Alzheimer's disease, the patient is completely dependent on caregivers, as even basic motor movement may be difficult. Muscle mass declines as the person neither is capable nor wants to exercise. Memory declines to the point that the patient no longer appears to recognize even close family members, such as a spouse, children, or

Table 10.3 Stages of Alzheimer's Disease

Initial stage: Forgetfulness; may last for several years before diagnosis

Early stage: Deficits in episodic memory; mild anterograde amnesia; lexical retrieval difficulties

Intermediate stages: Deficits begin in reasoning and problem-solving; deficits in understanding speech; help often needed with daily living skills, including feeding, dressing, and bathing

Late state: Loss of language skills; failure to recognize close family members; loss of personal identity; round-the-clock care necessary

siblings. In many cases, the patient will no longer respond to hearing his or her own name. In late stages of Alzheimer's diseases, the patient may also lose all access to language and be unable to either speak or understand others. Death is usually the result of external factors, such as pneumonia, rather than the Alzheimer's disease itself (see Table 10.3).

Causes of Alzheimer's Disease

The cause of Alzheimer's disease is still largely unknown, although what happens inside the brains of people with Alzheimer's is relatively well understood. At present, a tremendous amount of research is investigating the cause of Alzheimer's. Perhaps within a decade, we will know the causes of the disease, which might allow us to prevent or cure it.

It is known that Alzheimer's disease has a genetic component. If you have a close relative with Alzheimer's disease, for example, your likelihood of someday getting it is greater than that of someone without a close relative with Alzheimer's disease. However, its cause is not entirely genetic. Indeed, even for a person who has an identical twin who has already developed the disease, the risk of developing Alzheimer's disease is 50%. This is a high correlation, but given that identical twins are 100% genetically identical, it argues against the idea that Alzheimer's disease is completely genetic.

The brains of Alzheimer's disease patients come under incredible stress. Neurons and synapses between the neurons start to degenerate and die. This neuronal degeneration begins in the cerebral cortex, including the temporal lobes, frontal lobes, and parietal lobes. In later stages of the disease, it spreads to subcortical areas as well. Furthermore, dense **amyloid plaques** form throughout the cortex. These plaques are gooey masses of unnecessary proteins that interfere with normal brain function. They twist around the neurons, causing **neurofibrillary tangles**, which lead to more neuron death by interfering with the function of the axons (Wenk, 2003). Thus, one clear goal of medical science is to determine how and why amyloid plaques form and how their formation can be prevented.

> **Amyloid plaques:** Masses of unnecessary proteins that interfere with normal brain function.

> **Neurofibrillary tangles:** The twisting of amyloid plaques around neurons, which causes destruction of those neurons.

Furthermore, there appear to be changes to the brain's cholinergic system. Specifically, the brain appears to have difficulty producing the neurotransmitter acetylcholine. Acetylcholine is used by the brain in many of its learning and memory circuits (Wenk, 2003). Thus, as the amyloid plaques and neurofibrillary tangles grow and cholinergic production declines, the brain shuts down more and more function, leading to the progressive loss of cognitive function seen in Alzheimer's disease patients.

Treatment of Alzheimer's Disease

At present, there is no way to prevent the development of Alzheimer's disease, nor is there any way to cure it once someone develops it. However, a number of factors reduce the likelihood that someone will develop Alzheimer's disease, and a number of treatments are available to ease or delay some of the symptoms in the earlier stages of the disease. This section will briefly review each of these considerations.

Prevention. First of all, there is no 100% guaranteed manner in which to prevent Alzheimer's disease. Any individual may engage in all of the behaviors that lower the rate of the illness and still develop it. However, a number of factors are associated with lower rates of Alzheimer's disease. First, lifelong involvement in intellectually challenging activities lowers the risk of Alzheimer's disease. These activities can vary from crossword puzzles to playing musical instruments to engaging in quantum physics research. An active social life is also associated with a lower risk of developing Alzheimer's disease (Bennett, Schneider, Tang, Arnold, & Wilson, 2006). It is thought that these activities spur the growth of synapses in the brain, which may act to reduce the development of plaques. Diet also plays a role in Alzheimer's disease prevention. Healthy, low-cholesterol diets are correlated with lower rates of the disease. A variety of other conditions such as hypertension, high cholesterol, diabetes, and smoking are all correlated with higher rates of Alzheimer's disease.

Treatment. A number of drugs are now available in the United States and other countries to combat symptoms in early Alzheimer's disease. These drugs work by reducing the rate at which acetylcholine is broken down (destroyed) in the brain. Because acetylcholine production is decreased in Alzheimer's disease, lowering its rate of destruction will lead to temporary improvements in memory and cognitive processes. However, in the long run, these drugs do not slow the progress of the disease, because they do not interfere with the processes that lead to neuron death. Current research is directed at finding drugs that will inhibit, reverse, or prevent the forming of the amyloid plaques (Ait-Ghezala et al., 2005). Other research shows that mild magnetic stimulation of the brain can cause temporary improvements of cognitive function in Alzheimer's patients (Demirtas-Tatlidede et al., 2013).

MEMORY REHABILITATION

Memory rehabilitation is the domain of the burgeoning field of clinical neuropsychology. Neuropsychologists are tasked with the job of helping the many people who suffer memory loss from stroke, accidents, warfare, and disease. For many patients, memory recovery will come either spontaneously or not at all, but for some, rigorous intervention by neuropsychologists is crucial in regaining memory skills (Wilson, 2009). Some patients, like Korsakoff's disease patients, seldom regain memory function, but memory rehabilitation can benefit those in the early stages of Alzheimer's disease and those with the amnesic syndrome.

Memory rehabilitation: The interventions that clinical neuropsychologists use to promote improved memory performance in memory-impaired individuals.

Memory rehabilitation focuses on compensation. For example, amnesic syndrome patients will be taught to make use of external memory aids. These can include clock alarms, cell phones, and keeping a notebook handy. Patients also can be taught mnemonic strategies, including many of the hints listed throughout this book. In addition, intact skills can be used to transfer function from episodic memory to surviving memory systems. For example, many patients can learn new skills by capitalizing on their intact implicit memory system (Wilson, 2009).

One of the most important neuropsychological interventions is called errorless learning. **Errorless learning** is a technique that trains a patient to learn a particular fact or skill while preventing that person from making errors during training. Because much of learning in amnesic patients requires the use of implicit and procedural memory, it is important for the patient to avoid developing bad habits. If he is guided such that mistakes are avoided, bad habits

> **Errorless learning:** A technique that trains a patient to learn a particular fact or skill while preventing that person from making errors during training.

will not develop. In practice, this means providing immediate and constant feedback, lots of cues, and lots of repetitions. For example, if a patient must learn "red pill, green pill, white pill," he will start off by repeating these phrases over and over. Then the patient will have to complete exercises in which more and more cues are removed. At first, he will see "red pi__, green pi__, white pi___." Then more and more parts of the phrase will be removed as the patient successfully learns the phrase. After training, the patient will know the sequence of medications that he must take. Clare, Wilson, Carter, and Hodges (2003) have shown that errorless learning leads to better retention of sentences in patients with early stage Alzheimer's disease, and Evans et al. (2000) found it to be successful with other amnesic patients. For more on this topic, please see Barbara Wilson's (2009) book, *Memory Rehabilitation*.

SUMMARY

Psychogenic amnesia refers to all forms of amnesia that are not directly linked to disruption or injury to the brain. This includes dissociative amnesia, dissociative fugue, post-traumatic stress disorder, and repression. Dissociative fugue is associated with the loss of personal identity as well as retrograde and anterograde amnesia. Alzheimer's disease is a degenerative and terminal illness whose first noticeable symptom is memory deficits. There is no known cure for Alzheimer's disease, but there are various behaviors that people can do to lower their risk of getting Alzheimer's disease. Alzheimer's disease is caused by amyloid plaques, which are masses of unnecessary proteins that interfere with normal brain function and neurofibrillary tangles, which cause destruction of neurons. Memory rehabilitation is the interventions that neuropsychologists use to help patients improve memory performance.

Section Quiz

1. In psychogenic amnesia, we see
   a. Patients really don't have amnesia, they just think they do
   b. There is no obvious neural cause of the amnesia
   c. Only anterograde amnesia is seen, but never retrograde amnesia
   d. That it is usually caused by damage to the hippocampus

2. A psychological disorder that includes the inability to inhibit unwanted memories because of exposure to extremely dangerous or stressful situations is known as
   a. Psychogenic fugue
   b. Post-traumatic stress disorder
   c. Pre-traumatic stress disorder
   d. Al of the above

3. Neurofibrillary tangles are associated with
   a. Alzheimer's disease
   b. Parkinson's disease
   c. Korsakoff's disease
   d. Schwartz's disease

4. Errorless learning is
   a. Impossible
   b. A technique that trains a patient to learn a particular fact or skill while preventing that person from making errors during training
   c. A technique that trains a patient to learn skills while they sleep, so that it does not matter if they are amnesic
   d. A technique that trains a patient to learn skills by allowing them to use anterograde learning instead of retrograde learning

1. b
2. b
3. a
4. b

KEY TERMS

Alzheimer's disease   amnesic syndrome   anosognosia

amnesia   amyloid plaques   anterograde amnesia

benzodiazepines

capgras syndrome

confabulation

consolidation

diencephalon

dissociative amnesia

dissociative fugue

electroconvulsive therapy (ECT)

errorless learning

frontal syndrome

hippocampus

implicit memory

Korsakoff's disease

mammillary bodies

medial temporal lobes

memory appropriation

memory compensation

memory conversations

memory importation

memory rehabilitation

method of vanishing cues

neurofibrillary tangles

post-traumatic stress disorder

psychogenic amnesia

reduplicative paramnesia

repetition priming

repression

retrograde amnesia

Ribot's law

short-term memory amnesia

source amnesia

transient global amnesia

word fragment completion

REVIEW QUESTIONS

1. What is amnesia? What is the main difference between anterograde and retrograde amnesia?

2. Describe the amnesic symptoms of HM and Clive Wearing. Describe at least two differences in their memory profile following the onset of their amnesia.

3. What is the amnesic syndrome? What cognitive functions are preserved? What cognitive functions are impaired? What parts of the brain are typically impaired?

4. What is implicit memory? How is it studied in amnesic patients? What outcomes are typically seen with anterograde amnesiacs?

5. What is Ribot's law? How does it apply to cases of retrograde amnesia?

6. What causes Korsakoff's disease? What are the primary symptoms of Korsakoff's disease? How does it differ from the amnesic syndrome?

7. What is anosognosia? How does it affect the outcome of neuropsychological treatment? In what forms of amnesia is there evidence of anosognosia?

8. What is confabulation? Why does confabulation occur in both Korsakoff's disease patients and in frontal lobe patients?

9. What are the causes of psychogenic amnesia? What symptoms differ from organic amnesia caused by brain injury?

10. What are the stages of Alzheimer's disease? How is memory affected during each stage?

ONLINE RESOURCES

1. For an overview of amnesia, go to http://www.medicalnewstoday.com/articles/9673.php

2. For an article about HM, go to http://www.nytimes.com/2008/12/05/us/05hm.html.

3. For more on Clive Wearing, go to http://www.youtube.com/watch?v = Vwigmktix2Y.

4. Go to the following website to read about a heroic waiter who saved a woman from a potential benzodiazepine-linked date rape, go to http://www.cbsnews.com/stories/2008/02/21/earlyshow/main3855974.shtml.

5. For a series of interviews with KC by the prominent memory researcher Endel Tulving, go to http://www.youtube.com/watch?v = tXHk0a3RvLc or go to http://video.healthhaven.com/Tulving.htm.

6. For more on Dr. Moscovitch's research, go to http://psych.utoronto.ca/Neuropsychologylab/morris2.html.

7. For more information and statistics on Alzheimer's disease, go to http://www.alz.org.

SAGE VIDEOS

What is amnesia?

http://sk.sagepub.com/video/cognitive-neuropsychology-memory-and-amnesia?seq = 1

And related videos (39 in total)

Interviews with patient KC by Endel Tulving

https://www.youtube.com/watch?v = tXHk0a3RvLc

https://www.youtube.com/watch?v = Ai2Ir1HpO0Y

https://www.youtube.com/watch?v = mvWjahGfONk

https://www.youtube.com/watch?v = 2bzNio8LiZk

https://www.youtube.com/watch?v = Z0P03rxVIZ4

https://www.youtube.com/watch?v = 2TBr5EC3PmY

Patient HM

https://www.youtube.com/watch?v = IKP6tBhM2T4

Clive Wearing

https://www.youtube.com/watch?v = Vwigmktix2Y

https://www.youtube.com/watch?v = k_P7Y0-wgos

https://www.youtube.com/watch?v = 5ObnErfTblY

Korsakoff's Disease

https://www.youtube.com/watch?v = xpE5iUkCETo

Capgras Syndrome

https://www.youtube.com/watch?v = JQsQgoPQ24s

Go to **study.sagepub.com/schwartz3e** for additional exercises and study resources. Select **Chapter 10, Memory Disorders** for chapter-specific resources.

CHAPTER 11

Memory in Childhood

In this chapter, we consider the development of memory in infants and young children. As we have seen, the term *memory* covers a great many different kinds of systems and processes. However, there are some parallels among the development of memory systems in early life. Early childhood is a time of rapid cognitive growth, although some systems grow more quickly than others. Indeed, the differential growth of different systems, such as episodic and semantic memory, is one way we know that the systems are different. When examining the development of memory in infants and young children, we learn by examining the differences in how separate memory processes develop and change. For example, by the end of the first year of life, infants are rapidly adding words to their memory for language (lexical memory). Some evidence, however, suggests that there is little to no representation of autobiographical events at this point in a person's life. Thus, by studying development, we gain insight into the memory processes of children and gain some understanding of the nature of memory systems.

We will not cover procedural learning in this chapter. Procedural learning is the acquisition of complex motor tasks. Almost all infants, for example, learn to walk during the first 18 months of life. This takes practice and learning—and of course, that learning involves memory. But in this book, we have, by and large, avoided procedural learning and its representation. This chapter instead focuses on the development of declarative memory systems—that is, those memory systems, such as episodic, semantic, and lexical memory, that can eventually be reported on verbally once an infant has started to acquire language. We will also discuss, albeit briefly, how language is learned in infants.

MEMORY IN INFANCY

Human infants are born in a precocious state. This means that for several months after birth, human infants are completely dependent on caregivers and have little motor control. Compare that motor control with that of a horse, which must be up on its feet moments after birth and able to run on the day of its birth. This lack of motor control in humans presents a problem for memory researchers, as researchers must be able to observe a behavior to document memory. Moreover, human infants cannot make any verbal responses until they are about one year old. Thus, without an obvious set of behaviors that psychologists can observe and with limited means of communication, the study of infant memory has had to rely on clever innovations. We review the methods that researchers use to ask what infants remember of what they experience (see Figure 11.1).

Visual Recognition

Although newborns are restricted in their ability to move their limbs, they can move their eyes. Indeed, they spend a lot of time looking around their worlds with seeming curiosity. This allows researchers to observe **visual recognition** behavior in young infants. We can use gaze direction as a proxy for memory. Consider a colorful mobile placed over an infant's crib. The mobile may grab the infant's attention, and he or she may direct his or her gaze toward it. Eventually, the novelty wears off, and the

> **Visual recognition:** Infants look selectively at novel stimuli over familiar stimuli.

> **Novelty preference:** Bias to look at things that are new. Researchers can tell when an infant remembers something, because the novelty preference will not be present.

infant's attention is directed elsewhere. The mobile is removed and stored out of the infant's view. Later, the mobile is again placed above the infant's crib. If the infant now does not attend to it or spends less time attending to it, this may be evidence of memory. Because the infant has already examined it, it does not appear novel. This could only occur if at some level, the infant recognizes the mobile (Hayne, 2004; Luo, Baillargeon, Brueckner, & Munakata, 2003). Similarly, one can track the beginnings of semantic memory with this technique. Four-month-old children look longer at upright faces than they do at upside-down faces, indicating some familiarity with the correct orientation of the face (Konishi et al., 2012). This recognition is again evidence that there is some memory of the earlier experience. (For more on eye tracking in infants, go to study.sagepub.com/schwartz3e.[1])

As suggested, infants show a novelty preference. Infants prefer to look at new things. Thus, if they do not show a preference for something they have seen earlier, it indicates that the have some form of memory for that earlier object. However, if the novelty preference persists, then a memory may not have formed. Thus, continuing novelty preference for old objects indicates that something is interfering with learning. For example, de Barbero, Clackson, and Wass (2016) examined infant novelty preferences in response to external stressors. Because the participants were infants, de Barbero could not tell them they were losing their jobs or their grades were poor. Rather, the infants were stressed by videos of other infants crying. In most of their infants, heart rate increased, suggesting stress. Relative to infants watching less-stressful stimuli, the infants who watched other crying infants showed a longer novelty preference to stimuli, indicating that their learning was slower. Thus, even in babies, stress can interfere with learning.

Newborns are equipped with a functioning auditory system. This allows researchers to examine auditory recognition as well as visual recognition. Studies have shown that

Figure 11.1   Infants learn rapidly.

Thinkstock/Jupiterimages;

Nonnutritive sucking: Infants suck a pacifier differentially in the presence of a novel stimulus compared to a familiar stimulus.

---

newborns already can discriminate their mother's voice from that of other women. In contrast to the visual recognition studies, infants will look more toward the source of the mother's voice than to that of a control woman. In this regard, the infants show a familiarity preference rather than a novelty preference. Note that as long as the infants are showing either a novelty preference or a familiarity preference, they are demonstrating memory. If they look at each stimuli the same amount of time, then we cannot be sure if learning has occurred.

The functioning auditory system appears to support recognition of the mother's voice, even before birth. In a startling study, Kisilevsky et al. (2003) showed that fetuses one to two weeks before birth recognized their mother's voice. Heart rate monitoring showed an increase in the fetus's heart rate when a tape recording of the mother's voice reading a story was played, as compared to when a tape recording of another woman reading the story was played. This finding has now been replicated many times, suggesting that auditory recognition begins before birth (Kisilevsky & Brown, 2016).

Nonnutritive Sucking

Another behavior that young infants, almost from birth, do naturally is sucking. This is a natural reflexive behavior that is biologically necessary for obtaining milk. Infants can suck on pacifiers, which have no nutritive value, and this **nonnutritive sucking** can be monitored by sensitive electronic equipment, which can measure how fast or slow the infants are sucking. Their rate of sucking may increase or decrease depending on what they see or hear in the environment around them. Memory researchers can measure the increase or decrease in sucking in response to presented stimuli. A novel stimulus will usually elicit an increase in sucking, most likely because the stimulus is new and exciting. Familiar stimuli will either not affect the rate of sucking or decrease it (Eimas, Siqueland, Jusczyk, & Vigorito, 1971). Thus, the infant can tell us something about what is novel or what is familiar by adjusting his or her sucking rate. Because we cannot tell the infant to suck faster when he or she sees something novel, researchers must measure baseline sucking rates in response to different stimuli so that any difference in sucking rates can be attributed to a function of memory.

Conjugate Reinforcement Technique

The **conjugate reinforcement technique** is useful to study memory in infants approximately age two months to about six months. In the technique, an infant lies on his or her back in a crib, usually the baby's home crib. A ribbon is attached to the infant's foot, which will eventually be attached to a mobile placed overhead. At first, however, the ribbon is not attached to the mobile. During this phase, a

> **Conjugate reinforcement technique:** A ribbon is attached to the infant's foot and eventually will be attached to a mobile placed overhead. Kicking behavior is observed to measure learning and memory.

baseline measure of kicking is made—that is, how often does the infant make kicking movements with the foot that has the ribbon attached to it? The ribbon is then attached to the mobile. In this way, whenever the infant moves or kicks his or her foot, it will make the mobile move and jiggle. This is very exciting and entertaining for the infant. Within a few minutes, most infants will be shaking their feet and kicking repeatedly to get the mobile to move. The researchers measure how long it takes for the infant to learn that moving the foot results in the reinforcing display of the moving mobile. In behavioral terms, the response behavior is the kicking, and the movement of the mobile is the reinforcement (Rovee-Collier & Cuevas, 2009).

To test memory, researchers impose a retention interval of a few minutes or several weeks. During this retention interval, the infant does not have access to the ribbon or the attached mobile. This allows the possibility that the learned response may be forgotten. At the end of the retention interval, the ribbon is again attached to both the infant's foot and to the mobile. Given the intrinsically rewarding nature of the moving mobile, an infant who remembers the game will begin kicking immediately. However, an infant who has forgotten the relation between the ribbon and the mobile will have to relearn it again, and this may take several minutes. Thus, memory can be measured by counting the number of kicks or by recording the time until above-baseline kicking begins.

Rovee-Collier and her colleagues showed that babies as young as three months will remember the relation between kicking and reinforcement up to one week later. As infants get older, the amount of time that they will retain such information increases. For instance, a six-month-old infant will remember the relation two weeks later. Researchers have used this technique to look at a number of memory variables. For instance, they have demonstrated a spacing effect. Two practice trials close in time to each other will not be as effective at producing good remembering as two practice trials more effectively spaced in time (Bearce & Rovee-Collier, 2006). In another experiment, Rovee-Collier demonstrated a "misinformation" effect. Exposure to a second mobile reduced the likelihood that the infant would remember the first mobile (Rovee-Collier & Cuevas, 2009). Thus, there are parallels between early memory in infants and later memory in adults.

By the time infants are seven months old, they are no longer interested in the mobiles or in kicking them to make them move. As a consequence, Rovee-Collier developed a parallel technique to work with older infants. Hartshorn and Rovee-Collier (1997) found that older infants learned the relation between pressing a lever and following a toy train move around a track with their eyes. The infants remembered to press the lever even several weeks after they last saw the relation between the train and the lever.

Imitation

> **Imitation:** Mimicking the actions of another.

Although most adults see **imitation** as a simple process not requiring much thought, the ability to imitate can be used as a marker of memory in infants, because imitation requires learning. Indeed, studies with nonhuman primates demonstrate that imitation is more complex than most of us might think. To be able to duplicate the motor patterns of another, one must be able to perceive those patterns, remember those patterns, and then translate them into self-governed actions. As such, imitation is more similar to recall than to recognition. Thus, demonstrating that infants can imitate behavior suggests complex memory abilities. Bauer (2002) has examined the ability of infants (usually closer to age one year than birth) to imitate actions of experimenters up to one month later. Most infants can duplicate simple actions by an adult experimenter by the age of nine months (Hayne, 2004).

These methods have allowed memory development researchers to examine a host of issues with nonverbal infants. Using these methods, researchers have been able to explore the origins of many of the memory systems that will come to dominate cognition in older children and adults. Perhaps no memory system develops sooner and faster than does lexical memory, the system that allows infants to speak their first word and leave infancy behind. We will address lexical memory first.

Memory for Language in Infancy

One of the most monumental achievements of each and every infant is success in breaking the code of language. Think of a one-year-old infant. Although he or she may have just learned to walk, this infant cannot use keys to open a door, cannot tie shoes, and certainly cannot balance a checkbook. Yet this infant is well on the way to producing speech and likely understands some speech already. We know that infants are learning and storing language-related information early in development. Indeed, a massive amount of language-related information is learned by a baby's first birthday, even if that infant is not actually talking yet.

Infants home in on the phonemes (sounds) of their native language very early, within the first few months. Eimas et al. (1971) showed that babies as young as one month habituated to a particular phoneme—that is, their sucking rate decreased after hearing the phoneme over and over. When a new phoneme was played, their sucking rate increased again. By six months of age, infants are distinguishing between phonemes of their native language and similar sounds that are not present in their native language (Werker & Tees, 1999). Some of these distinctions can be quite subtle (think of the minor difference between the "p" sound in English and the "p" sound in Spanish), yet infants are able to distinguish the sounds.

Infants are also learning the symbolic meanings of words by the end of the first year. As most parents know, one-year-old infants recognize many common words, such as *mommy, daddy, cookie, milk, doggie,* and so on. Tincoff and Jusczyk (1999) demonstrated this empirically in a clever way. They placed two videotapes side by side in front of six-month-old infants. One video depicted their mothers, and the other video depicted their fathers. After hearing the word *mommy,* infants looked longer at the video of their mothers, whereas after hearing the word *daddy,* the infants looked longer at the video of their fathers. They did not show this preference when the adults depicted were strangers. Thus, even six-month-old infants have learned a few important linguistic concepts.

Semantic Memory

Semantic memory develops rapidly during the first year of life. Research suggests that by age three to four months, infants are starting to understand categorization and to group objects together into specific concepts, such as by making the cat/dog distinction (Eimas & Quinn, 1994). Early semantic memory appears limited. For example, infants cannot acquire superordinate categories, but semantic memory, perhaps in association with lexical memory, appears to develop early in infancy.

Episodic Memory

Performance in the conjugate reinforcement tasks suggests that infants can learn based on a single event and maintain that knowledge across a long-term memory retention interval. Similarly, infants can imitate behavior even when the model is no longer engaging in the behavior after seeing that behavior only once. Therefore, infants satisfy one of the conditions whereby memory is considered to be episodic. They can learn based on unique single events. However, given their lack of verbal abilities, it is difficult to determine whether infants are aware of the past event when they begin kicking at the sight of the mobile or engaging in the imitation behavior. It is possible that these memories are mediated by conditioning and not by a cognitive mechanism of episodic memory. Given that young children are unable to remember events from their first year of life (as are adults), it is likely that most learning that takes place during the first year of life is not episodic in nature. Thus, it is likely that true episodic memory is not online until at least the second year of a person's life.

SECTION SUMMARY AND QUIZ

Infancy and early childhood are times of rapid cognitive growth. Memory develops rapidly during this time. Studying infant memory is fraught with difficulties, because infants cannot yet use language. To study memory in infancy, researchers use visual recognition, non-nutritive sucking, conjugate reinforcement technique, and imitation. Novelty preference is a bias to look at things that are new in a visual recognition task. Visual recognition tasks are when infants look selectively at novel stimuli over familiar stimuli. Researchers can tell when an infant remembers something, because the novelty preference will not be present. The conjugate reinforcement technique uses a ribbon attached to the infant's foot, which will be attached to a mobile placed overhead. Kicking behavior is observed to measure learning and memory. Imitation is defined as the mimicking the actions of another. Language learning takes place quickly, and by age one year, most infants are starting to understand language.

Section Quiz

1. De Barbaro, Clackson, and Wass (2016) examined infant novelty preferences in response to external stressors. They found that
   a. Stressed infants showed longer novelty preferences
   b. Stressed infants showed shorter novelty preferences
   c. Stressed infants were more affected by attentional manipulations
   d. All of the above are true

2. In the conjugate reinforcement technique, memory is measured by
   a. Seeing if the infant kicks the mobile when it is placed again in the crib
   b. Seeing if the infant imitates the action of the experimenter
   c. Seeing if the infant has novelty preferences for familiar faces
   d. Seeing if the infant has familiarity preferences for novel faces

3. Infants as young as six months seem to show an ability to
   a. Distinguish phonemes from the language their parents speak from similar phonemes of other languages
   b. Look preferentially at a video of their father rather than a video of another man
   c. Remember a particular mobile in the conjugate-reinforcement task up to two weeks later
   d. All of the above are true

4. Which is a reason why episodic memory is difficult to test in infants less than one-years old?
   a. They lack the motor coordination to show episodic memory
   b. Their imitation skills are not yet developed
   c. Infants less than one year do not yet show novelty preferences
   d. Infants less than one year are nonverbal; they cannot talk about their memories

1. a
2. a
3. d
4. d

MEMORY IN EARLY CHILDHOOD

By the time children are two years old, most have entered the world of language and can both understand and produce speech. This makes the task of the memory research easier, as experimenters can use verbal commands and children can produce verbal reports. This allows many more aspects of memory to be examined than during the first year of life. In particular, verbal abilities allow researchers to explore the origins of the declarative memory systems—semantic memory and episodic memory. Nonetheless, it is often a challenge to examine memory in young children, as they may not understand instructions that older children or adults will understand, and children younger than five years of age cannot use any written instructions or written responses. In this section, we will consider a few topics in the development of memory in early childhood.

Why Does Memory Improve During Early Childhood?

It is probably not surprising that research shows that five-year-old children are better at a variety of memory tasks than are two-year-old children (Flavell, Miller, & Miller, 1993). They have a greater capacity in working memory, learn more quickly when learning semantic memory materials, and begin to show clear evidence of functioning episodic memory systems. A two-year-old has little knowledge or understanding of the greater world around him or her; a five-year-old is ready to begin formal schooling. What changes during this critical period that allows children to start learning the material that they will need to master in school? As cognitive psychologists, memory researchers want to explore how these developmental changes occur. That memory improves during this period of development is not surprising, but how it does so is an important question.

There are two basic theories as to how and why memory improves during this period. According to the **memory efficiency view**, memory improves because the processes of memory themselves improve as a child grows. Working memory capacity increases, learning processes become faster and more efficient, and episodic memory processes start functioning. Hence, better memory systems allow young children to learn more rapidly. In contrast, the **memory strategies view** argues that as children grow, they learn strategic behaviors (e.g., elaboration, rehearsal, organization) that allow them to use their memory better. Thus, it is their knowledge of the tools they have available to them that leads to faster learning in young children (see Flavell et al., 1993). As with many contrasting views, the reality of human memory development is that both are important features. Because an earlier generation assumed that the improvement was because of greater memory efficiency as children grow, much of the research has concentrated on the extent to which young children learn and use memory strategies.

> **Memory efficiency view:** Memory improves in young children because of increases in speed and efficiency in learning new information and storing it in long-term memory.

> **Memory strategies view:** Memory improves in young children because of the development of conscious activities a child engages in to assist the remembering of information.

Memory Strategies View

We first consider how young children develop memory strategies—that is, the conscious activities a person engages in to assist the remembering of information. Memory strategies include reminding oneself of things that need to be remembered, rehearsing unlearned information, allocating cognitive resources, and using retrieval strategies (Schneider & Ornstein, 2015).

Memory strategies start to develop early, perhaps as early as around two years of age. For example, in one study, children as young as 18 months verbally rehearsed the location of a toy more often when it was hidden than when it was in open view. This may seem obvious to a reader, but it indicates that a young child is aware that forgetting may occur when the object is out of view. In the study, DeLoache, Cassidy, and Brown (1985) asked children between the ages of 18 and 24 months to watch as an experimenter hid a desirable stuffed animal (Big Bird) somewhere in the room. The experimenter told the children to remember where Big Bird was so that they could play with him later. Despite the availability of other toys, children frequently verbally reminded themselves of the hidden location of Big Bird, thus lowering the likelihood of forgetting the location. In control conditions, in which Big Bird was visible during the retention interval, the children did not engage in verbal reminders. Thus, in this study, children as young as 1.5 years are showing evidence of using memory strategies (see Figure 11.2). (For more information on Judy DeLoache's research, go to study.sagepub.com/schwartz3e.[2])

Elaboration means connecting the new to-be-learned material to well-learned material, by looking for meaningful connections between the two. The question can be posed: At what age do young children learn to use elaborative encoding? We know that younger children do not spontaneously use elaboration. When children are asked to encode paired

Figure 11.2   Young children use strategies. The *Y*-axis is the number of items remembered.

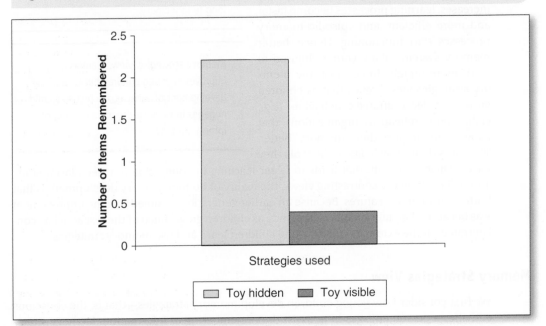

SOURCE: Based on DeLoache, Cassidy, and Brown (1985).

associates, younger children (ages 3–6) do not use elaborative encoding, although their performance benefits when researchers provide elaboration for them. For example, if asking children to remember "flower–dog," researchers might then give the sentence "The flower fell on the dog's back," to help them encode the pair. If so, memory performance will improve, but they do not use such strategies spontaneously. However, at age seven or eight, children are using and benefiting from elaborative strategies (Beuhring & Kee, 1987). Similar patterns are seen in the use of organizational strategies—they do not seem to be used by children until third grade (Pressley & Hilden, 2006).

Imagery can also be a powerful tool to assist in the learning of new information. With training, adults can use imagery to remember long lists of unrelated items. Many adults spontaneously use imagery to assist their memory. Young children do not spontaneously use imagery to boost their memory. Nonetheless, when children are trained to use imagery, they too can benefit from it (Howe, 2006). For example, de Graaff, Verhoeven, Bosman, and Hasselman (2007) showed that kindergarten-age children who were taught visual mnemonics to help them learn the letters of the alphabet had quicker acquisition of those letters.

To summarize, children do start using strategies at an early age. However, some of the most sophisticated memory strategies, such as the use of imagery, elaborative encoding, and organization skills, do not develop until much later in childhood. Although children can be trained to use these techniques at early ages, they do not spontaneously use them until they are around seven to eight years old (Schneider & Ornstein, 2015).

Memory Efficiency View

According to the memory efficiency view, memory improves during development, because memory capacity, the speed of learning, and the ability to retain information in long-term memory increase. Memory efficiency could be a function of more efficient cognitive processes or more mature neurological mechanisms (Schneider & Ornstein, 2015). In this section, we will consider the evidence that supports the view that memory capacity increases during early childhood. *Memory capacity* is defined here as the amount of information that can be stored in working memory.

Improved working memory capacity means that older children have a larger buffer in which to store information than do younger children. To demonstrate this, Kail (1991) compared digit spans of younger children (age 2) and older children (age 9). The digit spans of the younger children were only two items, whereas the older children had digit spans of six, not much different from those of adults. Improved working memory capacity is important for children as they mature, as countless studies have correlated working memory capacity with reading ability. Indeed, children who perform well on tasks that tap into the phonological loop also score high on tests of reading and writing (Alloway et al., 2005).

Working memory efficiency is related to the ability to screen out irrelevant information. For example, if you want to be able to use the full capacity of your working memory on digit spans, you need to be able to inhibit other thoughts or ideas from entering working memory and "crowding" out the digits. Research shows that older children are better able than younger children to inhibit irrelevant information in working memory. Harnishfeger and Pope (1996) tested school-age children on a directed forgetting task.

In directed forgetting, participants are told to inhibit or ignore items that they have already studied—that is, to forget them. After they are instructed to forget certain materials, they are then asked to learn new materials. To maximize performance on the new material, you must inhibit the to-be-forgotten information, as it may interfere with the new learning. Adults in directed forgetting will show poor recall for items that they were directed to forget. Harnishfeger and Pope found that older children (age 10) were better at directed forgetting than the younger participants (age 6). Howe, Toth, and Cicchetti (2011) also found that children could use directed forgetting to inhibit items that they were not supposed to remember. Interestingly, this study found that the children were better able to inhibit emotional items than neutral items, which has implications for the memory of traumatic events, to be discussed later.

Long-term memory also improves in efficiency in early childhood, although it is usually quite difficult to tease apart the changes that derive from improved strategic use of memory and the changes that derive from efficiency. But there are studies that show that, given an equal amount of study time, older children will retain more information than younger children. For example, Myers and Perlmutter (1978) examined the ability of children to remember objects shown to them. The four-year-olds remembered twice as many objects as did the two-year-olds (40% to 20%). We know that four-year-olds already use somewhat complex memory strategies, but the test in this experiment was a recognition test. Recognition tests are less sensitive to the use of memory strategies than are recall tests, so it is likely that some of the improvement of the older children is because they use better strategies to encode information.

Episodic Memory

Episodic memory is the memory of individual events from our lives. Adults remember no events from the first three years of life (by and large) and few from the next two years. This is the phenomenon of childhood amnesia (or infantile amnesia) discussed in Chapter 7. It has led some researchers to speculate that episodic memory does not develop until a child is around three years of age. However, as any parent will tell you, young children do discuss the past. Many three-year-olds will discuss events that may have happened to them as much as a year earlier. These events will be forgotten when the children become adults but are retained for long periods of time in the young children (Ornstein, Haden, & Elischberger, 2006). Thus, young children have something very similar or identical to episodic memory at quite young ages. The explanation for childhood amnesia lies elsewhere. (For more on the relation of early childhood memory and later childhood amnesia, go to study.sagepub.com/schwartz3e.[3])

In an important study, Tessler and Nelson (1994) examined the memory of three-and-a-half-year-old children who visited a museum. Mothers and children attended a visit to a museum in New York City. One week later, Tessler and Nelson asked the children to describe the event. Seven days later, the children remembered the event in some detail, clearly demonstrating episodic remembering (even though they will not remember this event later as adults). However, some interesting features distinguished the children's memory reports from memory reports of adults. For example, the manner in which the mothers interacted with their children influenced the amount and accuracy of their recall. The more the mother discussed the event with the child, the more the child was able to recall. We will see shortly that young children's episodic memory is highly prone to distortion. In this case, the mothers were probably not distorting information, but their talk influenced the children's reports. The point here is that the young children remembered a specific event one week later, demonstrating the beginnings of episodic memory.

Other research points to the hypothesis that young children can retain autobiographical events over intervals of years rather than simply days. Sutcliffe Cleveland and Reese (2008) showed that young children (age 5) recalled events that happened to them before the age of two. They asked children about events that they also had reports on from the parents. Thus, the researchers had a manner in which to corroborate the narratives of the children. In the study, the children were given an actual event, such as "Remember the time you went on a hayride in the country," and children were given the opportunity to describe the event. Sutcliffe Cleveland and Reese showed that some five-and-a-half-year-olds reported remembering events from before age two. Although some of the children's reports were verified by the parents, there was also a high degree of inaccuracy in their reports. When asked to recall events from two years earlier, five-and-a-half-year-olds accurately recalled more events from age three-and-a-half and older than from age two. In another study, Van Abbema and Bauer (2005) were able to get children to visit the lab at age three and then again between ages seven and nine. In their first visit, the three-year-olds described six events that had recently happened to them. Approximately five years later, the children returned to the lab and were asked again about those events. The researchers also found that the older children were able to remember some (about 50%) of the original events and did so in an accurate manner.

Thus, this research suggests that, at least early on, children can reach across the "childhood amnesia" barrier and remember events from before they reached three years of age that they certainly would not be able to remember later, as adults. This suggests that childhood amnesia may be an issue of retrieval from episodic memory in adults rather than encoding into episodic memory in young children.

Memory Conversations and Episodic Memory

What influences the kinds of episodic events young children will remember? To many parents, what their children remember is often a mystery. The salient events that adults remember may not be the salient events that young children remember. For example, a parent may ask a child about an event that the parent thought would be very salient, such as a visit to a theme park, only to find that the child does not recall the event at all. Then later, the child asks about an event—perhaps stopping the car to help a turtle cross the road safely—that the parent has long since forgotten. Parents might be tempted to argue that they have little influence on what their children remember from childhood. But in fact, research suggests that parents do have a strong influence on their children's episodic memory development. This conclusion comes from studies on parent-child **memory conversations.**

Memory conversations are the verbal exchanges that typically go back and forth between a parent and a child concerning past events. Most research suggests that parents

Memory conversations: Talk between a parent and a child concerning past events. Discussions we have with others about the past.

often dictate the kinds of recollections that children have and direct recall in particular directions. However, not all parents employ the same style while discussing past events with their young children. Some parents spend more time talking about past events with their children than do other parents. And among the parents who do speak of the past with their young children, some encourage their children to elaborate on the past events and what they mean and encourage their children to participate in much of the memory talk. Other parents correct their young children when they make a mistake and provide much of the details of the earlier event themselves. Indeed, such memory conversations also appear to vary across culture (Sahin-Acar & Leichtman, 2015). Some cultures, like American and Western Turkish culture, emphasize description and elaboration, whereas others, including Eastern Turkish and Chinese, emphasize repetition and learning (Alea & Wang, 2015; Sahin-Acar & Leichtman, 2015). These parental styles have been correlated with the amount and accuracy of children's recollection—the more open-ended and elaborative the conversation between parent and child, the more the child will remember later (Peterson, McDermott Sales, Rees, & Fivush, 2007). Parents' style affects the recall of young children in both formal and informal settings.

For example, Tessler and Nelson (1994) varied the kinds of interactions the parents had when discussing the museum visit with their children. In the study, some parents were directed to discuss the events at a museum in a more interactive, participatory style, and other parents were instructed not to discuss the events at all. The children of the parents who discussed the event together remembered more of the event. These findings show that not only do children *report* more information if their parents adopt the more interactive style of memory conversation, but they actually *remember* more. This result has been corroborated by a number of recent studies. In the Peterson et al. (2007) study, the researchers examined memories of a hospital emergency visit. They showed that open-ended and elaborative styles even helped young children (ages 2–5) remember more from this stressful event. Children recalled more of a hospital emergency visit if they later discussed the events in an elaborative style with their parents. Thus, elaborative discussions, in general, lead to children with better autobiographical memory. They also work in specific cases; an open-ended elaborative memory conversation increases recall of a particular event.

Some research suggests that not all cultures equally emphasize the role of autobiographical memory. Wang and Fivush (2005) point out that parent-child interactions in the United States are much more likely to be discussions of past events than are parent-child interactions in China. Chinese families are much more likely to stress moral precepts and family standards, whereas U.S. families revel in sharing past experiences. Therefore, U.S. families have more memory conversations in general and more memory conversations that are elaborative and open-ended. This suggests that U.S. children might show better recall of episodic events than do Chinese children. Indeed, Wang and her colleagues have shown in a number of different contexts that young U.S. children are more likely to remember recent events than are young Chinese children. Wang also speculates that this may account for why U.S. adults remember events from earlier in childhood better than do Chinese adults. A number of studies demonstrate that the offset of childhood amnesia is earlier for Americans than it is for Chinese (see Wang, Peterson, & Hou, 2010). (For more on Qi Wang's research, go to study.sagepub.com/schwartz3e.[4])

MNEMONIC IMPROVEMENT TIP 11.2

Memory conversations increase recall from episodic memory with young children and in adults, although they can induce false memories in the latter.

CHILDREN'S EYEWITNESS MEMORY

In many legal proceedings, children may be the victim of a crime or the only witness to a crime. Therefore, some court cases are dependent on the accuracy of a young child's memory of a stressful event, such as many crimes are likely to be. In our society, we consider crimes against children as most despicable, and we reserve our harshest criminal sentences for those who commit crimes against children. Thus, we place great weight on convicting the perpetrators of violence against children. However, research has determined that young children are highly suggestible and therefore prone to false memories (Melnyk, Crossman, & Scullin, 2007; Sellers & Bjorklund, 2014). This can often make it quite difficult to prosecute people accused of harming children.

Back in the 1980s, several high-profile criminal trials that relied heavily on testimony from young children thrust the issue of children's eyewitness memory into the spotlight. For example, in one high-profile case, a woman who ran a childcare center was accused of sexually molesting numerous children (see study.sagepub.com/schwartz3e[5]). In this case, repeated and suggestive questioning led to what were surely many instances of false memory in the child witnesses. Some children claimed that the accused could fly, whereas others reported that famous actors had participated in the abuse. Because of the confused and clearly false memories on the part of the children who had been through the questioning procedures, much of the evidence against the accused was suspect and eventually dismissed. What actually happened is anyone's guess, as suggestive questioning rendered the children's testimony invalid, and the accused was not required to testify. Because of this preschool abuse case and a few other similar cases, police are now much more careful about leading questions when questioning child witnesses. In the wake of this trial and others, developmental psychologists rushed in to examine the nature of the child as a witness.

In a classic study on this topic, Leichtman and Ceci (1995) investigated the suggestibility of child witnesses. They used children ages three to six years as participants. In the study, a man—a confederate of the researchers—named "Sam Stone" came to visit the children's preschool class. Sam Stone wandered around the classroom for a couple of minutes, made a couple of innocent comments, and then left. Three conditions, however, defined what happened just before or after Sam Stone's visit. In a control condition, nothing else happened either before or after. In the stereotype condition, another research assistant visited the class several times starting three weeks before Sam Stone's visit. The research assistant described repeatedly to the children how Sam Stone was a nice man but clumsy. In the suggestibility condition, children were interviewed after his visit. The interviewer incorrectly mentioned that Sam Stone had spilled a drink and ripped a book while visiting the classroom. Leichtman and Ceci were curious to know what the effect of the biasing information would be, whether it occurred before Sam Stone's visit, as in the stereotype condition, or after Sam Stone's visit, as in the suggestibility condition.

About 10 weeks later, a new interviewer came to class. This interviewer asked a number of things about Sam Stone's visit, including whether the children had seen Sam Stone spill his drink or had seen Sam Stone rip up a book. In the control condition, children's recall was quite accurate. That is, few children reported seeing Sam Stone spill or rip anything. Among the five- and six-year-old kids, there were no inaccuracies in their reports and only a marginal number of inaccuracies for the three- and four-year-olds. The false memory rate in the control condition was practically zero (see Figure 11.3). However, in the stereotype condition in which children had been told that Sam Stone was clumsy, the false memory rate increased to about 20% for the younger children and about 10% for the older children. In the suggestibility condition, in which the children had been told that Sam Stone ripped a book and spilled a drink, the false memory rate was even higher. That is, about 40% of the younger kids and 10% of the older kids reported *seeing* Sam Stone do these things, even though he had not (Leichtman & Ceci, 1995).

To repeat, in this study, 40% of the three- and four-year-olds reported seeing Sam Stone rip a book apart, something the actual Sam Stone had not done. Given the large number of false memories based on a simple suggestion spoken only once, it is likely that it is easy to induce false memories in young children. This effect has now been documented in a great many studies (for reviews, see Melnyk et al., 2007; Otgaar, Howe, Brackmann, & Smeets, 2016; Peterson, 2012). Certainly 40% is beyond any conceivable definition of "beyond a shadow of a doubt." Therefore, unless the prosecution in court cases can document that no misleading procedures have been introduced in the interviewing of child witnesses, courts should use extreme caution in evaluating the testimony of very young children. (For the transcript of an interview with Dr. Ceci, go to study.sagepub.com/schwartz3e.[6])

Memory and Stress in Children's Episodic Memory

Any person—especially a young child—may be stressed and anxious while witnessing a crime. Thus, it is important to understand how stress affects memory, especially in the context of eyewitness memory. In the Leichtman and Ceci (1995) study, there was no attempt to duplicate the real stress a child might experience in a situation that would later lead that child to testify in court. Even the alleged "crimes" that Sam Stone was accused of—spilling a drink and ripping a book—are not uncommon events in a preschool classroom.

The problem, of course, is that intentionally putting children into a stressful situation is unethical. Nor would many parents sign a consent form to put their child in a stressful situation or one in which he or she witnesses a simulated crime. However, a number of studies

Figure 11.3   Younger children are more suggestible. The *Y*-axis represents percent false recall.

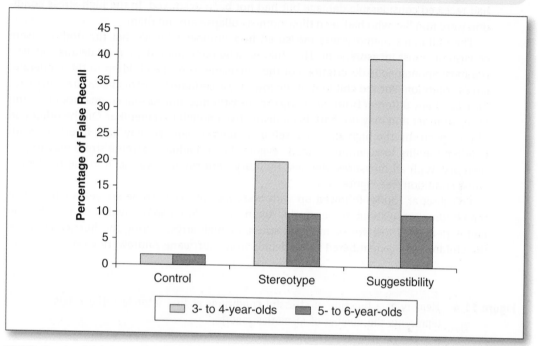

SOURCE: Based on Leichtman and Ceci (1995).

have used naturalistic settings—that is, researchers have examined memory for real-life trauma. Studies can include tests for memory of painful but necessary medical procedures, of natural disasters, and of witnessing a real crime. The problem with these studies is that it is difficult to control the stress level, as it depends on the procedure or event. It is also difficult to compare across studies. Thus, the only solid evidence to come from these studies is that young children can recall events even if the events are highly stressful, but how stress affects memory is not clear (Peterson, 2012; Price & Connolly, 2008). However, one study was able to examine children's memory under three levels of stress, allowing a comparison of low and high stress to a middle condition. We will consider this study in detail.

Fivush, McDermott Sales, Goldberg, Bahrick, and Parker (2004) examined the memories of children who had experienced Hurricane Andrew in 1992. Hurricane Andrew was a Category 5 storm that ripped through Miami, Florida, on August 24, 1992, destroying homes and knocking out power across the city. Shortly after the storm, the researchers interviewed over one hundred three- to four-year-old children about their experiences in the storm. In the first interview, the sample was divided into children who had experienced low, medium, and high stress, as indicated by the amount of damage sustained to the child's home. In the low-stress condition were families whose homes had received no damage or minor damage. In the medium-stress condition were families whose homes had received considerable damage but had not been destroyed. In the high-stress condition were families who had seen their homes collapse around them.

The children's memory was measured in a number of ways, but the findings were consistent across measurement. The children who remembered the most details and gave the most spontaneous descriptions of the hurricane were the children in the moderate-stress condition. For the children in the low-stress condition, Hurricane Andrew may not have been any different from the many ordinary thunderstorms that come through Miami every summer and may not have been distinctive enough to remember. On the other end of the spectrum, the high stress caused by extensive damage may have interfered with children's ability to accurately encode events. As with adults, extreme stress may impair memory. With all measures, the best memory performance was seen in the moderate-stress condition (see Figure 11.4).

Fivush et al. (2004) followed up with a second interview some six years later, when the children were about 10 years old. Again, the children were divided into those who had experienced low stress, medium stress, or high stress during the hurricane. All of the children still remembered some details from Hurricane Andrew. However, the effect

Figure 11.4 Memory as a function of stressful conditions at first interview. The *Y*-axis represents the number of memories reported.

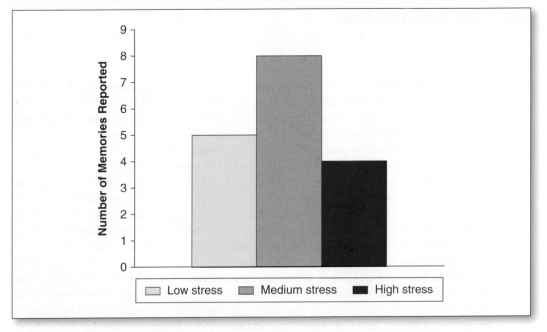

SOURCE: Based on information from Fivush, McDermott Sales, Goldberg, Bahrick, and Parker (2004).

of initial stress was no longer obvious. The high-stress children recalled as much as the lower-stress children. The high-stress children were also more accurate in their recall than the lower-stress children.

Based on this analysis, it is clear that stress can influence children's memory. In the young children who experienced the hurricane, high stress led to worse memory than medium stress. This is similar to patterns of memory observed with adults under stress. Why the high-stress children's memory caught up to that of the lower-stress kids when tested six years later is less easily interpreted. It is possible that in families that sustained extensive damage to the family home, there was more continued focus on remembering the storm and the consequences of the storm for that family.

Many studies have attempted to examine the effects of stress, especially those associated with being a witness to or victim of a crime (Quas et al., 2016). Within this area are those who argue that children's memory is reliable and can be trusted in cases of great import and those who argue that stress increases the likelihood of memory distortion and false memory. However, the bulk of the data support the view that (a) children are at greater risk of false memories than adults and (b) high-stress situations can increase that risk while lowering the amount of veridical recall (Price & Connolly, 2008). Thus, criminal investigators must proceed with caution when interviewing a child who has experienced a stressful event.

SECTION SUMMARY AND QUIZ

Two theories have been advanced to explain the growth of memory in early childhood. In the memory efficiency view, memory improves because the processes of memory themselves improve as a child grows. In contrast, the memory strategies view argues that as children grow, they learn strategic behaviors that allow them to use their memory better. Episodic memory starts to develop in early childhood, particularly in the context of memory conversations between parent and child. Cultures that spend more time engaged in memory conversations have children who form autobiographical representations earlier.

Preschool years are marked by the beginnings of episodic memory. Although many researchers have thought that episodic memory did not begin to develop until the school years, ample data suggest that young children can learn and retain event information. In the preschool years, we see the continued growth of working memory and the beginnings of the use of memory strategies. As children begin formal schooling, their memory processes are becoming faster and more efficient, and they are learning to use memory strategies and developing their metamemory skills. Events are encoded into episodic memory in such a manner as they can be retrieved later when the child becomes an adult. As children enter adolescence, their memories are more guided by the use of meaning-based strategies at encoding. This further strengthens their ability to encode and retain information. However, it also leads older children to experience more meaning-based false memories. Research shows that children, especially younger children, are highly prone to suggestion. This has led to the claim that young children should not be treated as reliable witnesses.

Section Quiz

1. As children grow, they learn strategic behaviors (e.g., elaboration, rehearsal, organization) that allow them to use their memory better is known as the
   a. Memory strategies view
   b. Memory efficiency view
   c. Developmental trend methodology
   d. Memory development view

2. In a study, Tessler and Nelson (1994) examined the memory of three-and-a-half-year-old children who visited a museum. They found that
   a. Ten years later, children could not remember the event
   b. Children did not encode the event and therefore could not remember it six months later
   c. Memory for the museum was actually better in children who did not visit the museum
   d. The more a mother discussed the event with a child, the more the child was able to recall of the event

3. Memory conversations refer to
   a. A rare phenomenon in children who remember events from before birth
   b. The talk between a parent and a child concerning past events
   c. When memory is converted from one form to another
   d. All of the above

4. Leichtman and Ceci (1995) investigated the suggestibility of child witnesses. They found that
   a. Younger children were paradoxically better at recalling accurately
   b. Younger children showed little evidence of false memories, even in the suggestibility condition
   c. False memories were very high for all children in the control condition
   d. False memory rates reached 40% in the suggestibility condition for the younger children

1. a
2. d
3. b
4. d

MEMORY IN OLDER CHILDREN

The previous section focused on children as they make the transition from preschool (age 3) to elementary school (ages 6–7). This section will address changes in the human memory system that occur later in childhood. This transition to middle childhood begins around the age of seven and ends as the teenage mind becomes essentially adult-like, at least with respect to memory, around the age of 14 or 15. We find that changes in memory generally focus on the integration of meaning into episodic memory and the emergence of adult features in working memory.

Consider working memory. Younger children are not able to maintain more than two or three digits in the phonological loop. However, by the age of nine, most children average around six digits, just a little less than the adult average of seven, which is in place by age 12 (Dempster, 1981). As we discussed earlier, data suggest this improvement is both a function of improved strategic regulation of memory and improved fluency of memory processing. For example, older children are both more likely to report using chunking strategies—that is, strategic regulation—and respond faster in reaction time experiments—that is, fluency (Hale, 1990).

Episodic memory also changes as it matures during this period. Many studies indicate that older children can remember more information and in greater detail than can younger children. One of the key contributors to this improvement is that older children elaborate on the to-be-learned information or tie new events to already existing knowledge structures. Thus, starting around the age of seven, the meaning of an event becomes increasingly important. By the age of 13, meaning is the central aspect in a memory. Think about your own memory for a moment. Think of an event that happened to you before the age of six or so. What strikes us about these memories is that they are often of complete trivia—a random snapshot out of our childhoods. Now think about your memory for events after the age of eight. Most of these memories seem to fit into the thematic constraints of our lives—that is, we remember that which is personally meaningful.

There is, however, a paradoxical effect of the transition from literal memory to meaning-based memory in this time period (Otgaar, Verschuere, Meijer, & Van Oorsouw, 2012). Several studies have shown that older children are more susceptible to a number of memory illusions than are younger children, because they are now encoding for meaning, whereas the younger children are not. For example, consider the Deese-Roediger-McDermott procedure (DRM procedure; see Chapter 8). As a reminder, in the DRM procedure, participants are given a list of related words. The critical word, however, which relates all the other words to each other, is missing. At recall, many participants will include this critical intrusion when they recall the list from memory. Holliday, Reyna, and Brainerd (2008) examined the DRM effect in children ages seven to 13. They found that the older the children were, the better they did on the recall test. That should not come as a surprise—the overwhelming majority of developmental studies find that older children perform better than younger children in tests of recall. However, older children also made more critical intrusions than did younger children. The younger children were more accurate and less likely to include a false memory in their memory report. Metzger et al. (2008) also found that older children recalled more correct information but recalled more critical intrusions than did younger children. Metzger et al. found that by age 11 the children's pattern of responses was essentially the same as that of college students. Similarly, Baugerud et al. (2016) found more false memories in the DRM in older children than younger children. This study included a group of children who had a documented record of abuse and among this group, there were also more critical intrusions among older children (Baugerud et al., 2016). The explanation here is that, because older children are more likely to encode for meaning, they are more likely to produce meaning-based critical intrusions when they recall the list. (For more on this topic and its relation to eye-witness memory, go to study.sagepub.com/schwartz3e.[7])

Other studies show similar age-inverted effects with respect to false memory. Fazio and Marsh (2006) looked at memory for false facts embedded in stories given to children from ages five to seven. Even though the age range was relatively narrow, Fazio and Marsh found that the older children remembered more in total from the stories than did the younger children. However, the older children were also more likely to make mistakes on a general-information test based on the errors they had heard in the story. Again, the increasing attention to meaning drives the increase in false memories. Ceci, Papierno, and Kulkofsky (2007) found a similar pattern with a greater range of ages. Comparing children from ages four to nine, they found that older children were more likely to have story-based false memories, again pointing to the importance of meaning in memory as children move from early childhood into middle childhood.

These data do not mean that older children are always more susceptible to false memories. It simply shows that older children have more meaning-based memory errors. Thus, when meaning helps to disambiguate truth from falsehood, older children will have *fewer* false memories than younger children. Strange et al. (2006) conducted an interesting study on autobiographical memory. They compared memories of six-year-olds and 10-year-olds for events from their lives. Most of the events were real events gathered from interviews with parents. However, the researchers doctored some photographs to show the children participating events that they had never experienced. Some of these false events were plausible (going on a hot air balloon ride at a fair), and others were less plausible (having tea with the Queen of England). False memories occurred for both types of events with both ages of children, but in this paradigm, the older children were much less susceptible to false memories. In this study, we see the effects of suggestibility in younger children outweighing the meaning-based errors in older children. Thus, whether more or fewer false memories occur in older children is not a characteristic of being older but a function of their increased focus on meaning.

This pattern was confirmed by an interesting study examining memory in children ages seven to 12. In this study, Otgaar, Candel, Merckelbach, and Wade (2009) found that many children ages seven to eight developed false memories of having been abducted by a UFO when it was suggested that this had actually happened to them. In fact, a *majority* of children in this age range developed false memories when it was also suggested that UFO abductions were common. In contrast, the 11- to 12-year-old children were much less likely (although some still did) to develop false memories of UFO abduction. Moreover, the suggestion that UFO abductions were common did not increase the rate of false memories. Therefore, in this case, more knowledge and greater coding for meaning meant fewer, not more, false memories for the older children.

In another study, Otgaar, Smeets, and Peters (2012) repeatedly asked children ages seven to nine about a true event (their first day of school) and a false event (a visit to a burn treatment center). In one condition, the children were given script knowledge about each of these events, and in a control condition, they were not given such generalized information. The question was whether or not providing such information would affect false memory rates. As these children are already processing for meaning, giving more of such information in the form of semantic memory scripts increased the likelihood of false memories, thereby confirming the role of meaning in children's memory. (For more on Dr. Otgaar's research, go to study.sagepub.com/schwartz3e.[8])

Can this change in memory processes be tracked by neuroimaging? In an interesting study that found a neural basis for the change from literal-based memory to meaning-based memory in children, Chiu, Schmithorst, Brown, Holland, and Dunn (2006) examined memory in children while scanning those children using fMRI. Children were given two incidental memory tasks. In one task, they generated verbs in response to nouns. The second task involved story comprehension. Later, a recognition memory test was given. There were no differences in brain activation for the verb-generation task between eight- and 10-year-old children. However, in the story-comprehension task, activation in the left prefrontal lobe was associated with correct recognition in the older children but not in the younger children. The left prefrontal lobe is associated with the extraction of meaning. Thus, this study provides a neural correlate of increased meaning-based processing in older children.

METAMEMORY IN CHILDREN

Metamemory is our knowledge and awareness of our own memory processes. We discussed this topic at length in Chapter 9 with a focus on metamemory in adults, but it is also of interest to know how and when it develops in children. Indeed, the study of metacognition got its start in developmental psychology rather than cognitive psychology, because some researchers thought that metacognition was the key to understanding the development of memory. For example, Flavell et al. (1993) argued that metacognition was the basis of improvement in memory during early childhood. It turns out that metacognition develops earlier than was originally thought but does play a role in memory improvement in young children.

> **Metamemory:** Our knowledge and awareness of our own memory processes.

How early in a person's life can we see evidence of metamemory processes? At least one study suggests that children are experiencing tip-of-the-tongue (TOT) states during their third year of life. Elbers (1985) recorded conversations with her two-and-a-half-year-old son concerning a difficult retrieval in Dutch, their native language. On the previous day, Elbers and her son had visited the aquarium, where the child saw some dolphins. The next day, when trying to retrieve the word for dolphins, the boy could not do so. Elbers suggested that her son was in a genuine TOT state—that he was aware of failed retrieval and was trying to recall the word anyway. If this anecdote is true, then metamemory develops early. This is consistent with the idea that other memory strategies start appearing early in childhood. Before we discuss metamemory in children, however, it is important to understand the development of an important cognitive process called theory of mind, because metamemory development and the development of a theory of mind have often been linked conceptually.

Theory of mind: The awareness that other individuals have separate states of awareness different from that of our own.

Theory of mind refers to the awareness that other individuals have separate states of awareness different from that of our own. A person with theory of mind can contemplate that another may know (or not know) information that he or she does not know. For example, when you order at a restaurant, you are aware that the waiter does not know what you want to eat. Looking up blankly at the waiter won't get you the result you want! As simple and obvious as it is, you must tell the waiter what you want to eat in order for the waiter to know. Therefore, the simple interaction of ordering food at a restaurant involves theory of mind. (Waiters will tell you, however, that their customers seldom have theory of mind and instead expect all kinds of miracles from their servers.) The waiter must have theory of mind, too. She must understand that she does not know what you want in order to fulfill her job and so must ask you what you want. Think about any human interaction you might have: Almost all interactions involve knowing that you do not know something about another person or knowing that person does not know something about you. Of course, to adults, theory of mind seems self-evident. But developmental psychology suggests that children are not fully equipped with theory of mind until about the age of four (Gopnik & Wellman, 2012; Perner, 2000).

Theory of mind is tested in young children with the **false-belief test**. The false-belief test capitalizes on the simple fact that you may know something another person does not

False-belief test: A child learns something that another person does not have the opportunity to learn. The child must decide whether the other person knows what he or she knows.

know (Perner & Roessler, 2012). For example, you may have hidden your grandmother's cigarettes in the cookie jar. When your grandmother goes to look for her lung cancer–causing cigarettes, she looks in her cigarette box, because she does not know that they are actually in the cookie jar. Because she does not know what you know, she cannot do further damage to her body, at least for the time being. Now, you know that by hiding the cigarettes, your grandmother will not know their location. But a young child who has not yet developed theory of mind will think that because he knows where the cigarettes are, so too will his grandmother. Children under the age of four assume that other people have access to the same knowledge that they do, even when objectively they do not.

In the false-belief test (see Figure 11.5), a child learns something that another person does not have the opportunity to learn. The child must then decide if the other person knows what he or she knows. Consider the following experiment by Wimmer and Perner (1983). Children ages three, four, and five served as participants. The children were shown a bag of M&M's. While a child was watching, the M&Ms were poured out of the M&M bag and into a bag marked "crayons." Both boxes were then sealed up so that no one could see what was inside. At this time, a research assistant entered the room, and the child was asked where the new person thinks the M&Ms are. Because the research assistant did not see the M&M's placed in the crayon box, the child should indicate that the research assistant thinks that they are in the M&M bag. However, all of the three-year-olds and some of the four-year-olds incorrectly answered that the research assistant knew that the M&M's were in the crayon box. Why? Because these children knew the correct location of the M&M's, and they could not conceive, therefore, that another would be missing knowledge that they had. Most of the five-year-olds were correct and realized that because the research assistant had not seen the switch, he would not know the actual location of the M&M's. Thus, at the age of three, children cannot separate what they know from what others know. This ability to do so, which develops in the four to five age range, is called theory of mind. The five-year-old child is now aware that mental states of others differ from his or her own. In keeping with this knowledge, deception begins around this age as well. Behavioral variants of this test have been done on nonhuman animals, and at present, no experiment has shown that even chimpanzees can "pass" the false-belief test. Like three-year-olds, chimpanzees assume that others know what they know.

In understanding false belief, the child realizes that other minds have content different than his or her own mind has and that others may not have access to the same information that the child does. Thus, theory of mind refers to our knowledge of *other* minds (Perner & Roessler, 2012). Metacognition refers to our understanding of *our own* minds. The rudiments of metacognition appear to develop around the same time in development as does theory of mind. This applies to both metamemory knowledge (explicit information about how memory works) and metamemory experience (the subjective feelings that accompany memory, such as confidence).

With respect to metamemory knowledge, consider a few of the "mnemonic hints" included in this textbook. Many of them are rather self-evident to an experienced college student. For example, it is obvious to most college students that related items are easier to remember together than unrelated items. This leads to the hint that students seek out relations among the material they are studying, because this elaboration improves memory. A fair developmental question is "At what age do children become aware of the advantage of related information over unrelated information?" Another fair question might be "At what age do children become aware that elaborative encoding leads to better memory performance than rote encoding?" Research suggests that children younger than seven years old have little awareness of these seemingly obvious memory strategies but that by the second or third grade, most children have incorporated an accurate theory of memory (Schneider & Pressley, 1997). Moreover, recent research suggests that first-grade teachers who emphasize the development of metamemory skills wind up with students who learn faster by the end of first grade (Coffman, Ornstein, McCall, & Curran, 2008).

Children start to show the ability to monitor and control their memory based on metacognitive judgments in the early school-age years. By the time most children are in second grade, they know which material is easy or difficult for them. It is also around this age that metacognitive experiences can be channeled into explicit judgments, such as judgments of learning. As we discussed in the chapter on metamemory, judgments of learning are predictions that people make as to the likelihood that they will remember an item when asked to do so on a later test. Judgments of learning are usually studied in the context of paired-associate learning. A person is given a pair of items (e.g., *leaf–city*) and later will have to remember the second word (*city*) when provided with the first word (*leaf*).

Research shows that children are able to make accurate judgments of learning by the time they are in kindergarten, although older children tend to be more accurate. Remember here that *accuracy* means the relation between the magnitude of the judgment (high or low) and the correctness of the answer. A high-magnitude judgment followed by a correct answer is accurate, as is a low-magnitude judgment followed by an incorrect answer. Let's consider a representative study.

Schneider, Visé, Lockl, and Nelson (2000) examined the ability of kindergartners, second graders, and fourth graders to make judgments of learning. The children studied paired associates (pictures instead of words). The children made immediate judgments of learning for half of the picture pairs and delayed judgments of learning for the other half. Following study and judgments of learning on all items, the children were given a cued-recall test. Interestingly, all three groups of children showed the delayed judgment of learning effect—that is, their accuracy for the delayed judgments of learning was greater than it was for immediate judgments of learning. Also of interest and perhaps surprisingly, there were no differences in accuracy among the age groups. All groups were above chance in predicting performance, but the kindergartners were as good as the older children. Other studies have, however, found developmental trends in the accuracy of judgments of learning. Koriat and Shitzer-Reichert (2002) found that fourth-grade children gave more accurate judgments of learning than did second-grade children. The conclusion that can be drawn from these studies is that judgments of learning are accurate by the early elementary years and probably improve in accuracy as children move from first grade through fourth grade. But because this accuracy increase is in dispute, it is likely that accuracy improvements are, at best, small and that judgments of learning are "online" by the time a child is in second grade.

Metacognitive control is the ability to use metacognitive knowledge or experience to influence learning behaviors. Thus, a college student who does not feel that she has sufficiently mastered the material for an exam will choose to spend more time studying the material before the test. Data were just presented that show that young children can accurately monitor their learning. But can they also use that monitoring to successfully control their learning? Indeed, even elementary school–age children show evidence of metacognitive control. They use the output of their monitoring to control their study behavior. Children in the second grade will spend more time studying items to which they gave low judgments of learning (i.e., judged to be more difficult) than items to which they gave high judgments of learning (i.e., judged to be easier items). In one study, children were given the opportunity to allocate study time after initially making judgments of learning. Both second- and fourth-grade children chose the more difficult items to restudy (Schneider & Löffler, 2016).

Overconfidence in Judgments

Overconfidence in judgments: People's overestimating the likelihood that they will remember a to-be-learned item or set of items.

Overconfidence in judgments occurs when people overestimate the likelihood that they will remember a to-be-learned item or set of items. The judgment can be whether a person will answer a

Figure 11.5 An illustration of the false-belief test.

This is Mary.

This is Alice.

Mary has a basket.

Alice has a box.

Mary has a ball. She puts the ball into her basket.

Mary goes out for a walk.

Alice takes the ball out of the basket and puts it into the box.

Now Mary comes back.

She wants to play with her ball.

Where will Mary look for her ball?

SOURCE: Created by Jack L. Frazier. © Jack L. Frazier.

particular question correctly or about how well that person will master a large set of materials. If the judgments are greater than actual performance, overconfidence has occurred (Destan & Roebers, 2015).

You do not have to spend much time with a six-year-old to see evidence of overconfidence. Many young children will assert that they possess skills that they could not possibly have yet. For example, some time ago, I played chess with a six-year-old relative. I assured him before we started that I knew he was a good chess player and I would not go easy on him. He assured me that he would win every game. His overconfidence was such that he thought he could reliably beat an experienced adult chess player.

Metacognition researchers have examined this issue in a number of important experiments. For example, Shin, Bjorkland, and Beck (2007) asked children in kindergarten to estimate how many pictures they would be able to remember out of a set of 15 pictures. Following judgment and study, the children tried to recall the names of the pictures they had seen. They then repeated the process on a new set of pictures. Despite the experience and the feedback they received on the earlier sets, their judgments of learning were equally overconfident on all trials. Not only were they overconfident on the first set, but they did not learn from the feedback that their actual performance was likely to be lower, and they continued to give high judgments. Such overconfidence is not unusual—it has been demonstrated in a variety of situations in children (see Dunlosky & Metcalfe, 2009; Sellers & Bjorklund, 2014).

Shin et al. (2007) argued that—in children at any rate—overconfidence is adaptive. Young children must learn how to do a great many things, many of which they will fail at initially. Consider whether or not my six-year-old relative would have wanted to play chess with me if he was certain that he would lose every game. Overconfidence provides children with a psychological buffer to deal with failure. Even though they may not be successful, they still think they will be the next time. To support this position, Shin et al. pointed out that those children who showed the greatest level of overconfidence in the initial trial also showed the greatest level of improvement in their actual performance. Indeed, Destan & Roebers (in press) find no deficits in children who are more overconfident than those who are less overconfident.

In this chapter, we have discussed the development of memory strategies and the development of metamemory. These two concepts are closely related. Recall that memory strategies are the conscious activities a person engages in to assist the remembering of information, whereas metamemory is the awareness and knowledge of our own memory. Defined in this way, metamemory should provide information that would be helpful to the development of memory strategies. Siegler (1999) argued that some memory strategies are based on simple associations—that is, children continue to engage in behaviors that have been successful. However, Siegler also argued that other memory strategies are based on metamemory. To support this proposition, Cavanaugh and Borkowski (1980) found that elementary school–age students who demonstrated greater metamemory knowledge also showed a more effective use of memory strategies.

A GUIDE TO DEVELOPING MEMORY SKILLS IN YOUNG CHILDREN

Memory is often viewed as an innate ability; some people are good at it, others are poor at it, and these abilities cannot be changed. However, the research suggests otherwise. People of all ages can train their memories, using strategies and metamemory to facilitate their learning. Moreover, practice itself improves the efficiency of memory systems.

This is certainly true for young children. We have seen in this chapter that memory conversations between parents and children can strengthen children's episodic memory (Peterson et al., 2007). Cultural differences in autobiographical memory clearly reflect cultural leaning, not innate differences among ethnic groups (Wang & Fivush, 2005). By and large, episodic memory is not trained in the school setting, as is semantic memory for information, such as the concepts and categories that are relevant in school. Nonetheless, frequent rehearsal of information from episodic memory helps to build a strong episodic memory system.

Although some of the improvement in memory across childhood has to do with the maturation of the child's brain (Bauer, 2002) and the speed of cognitive processing (Hale, 1990), much of it has to do with the learning of memory strategies and the development of metacognition (Dunlosky & Metcalfe, 2009). Certainly, in the later elementary school years, memory strategies can be taught, and children who use them learn faster (Pressley & Hilden, 2006).

Coffman et al. (2008) compared two groups of teachers in a naturalistic study. One group of teachers seldom referred to memory strategies and ways in which their first-grade children could learn faster. This group of teachers focused on content rather than process. A second group of teachers often referred to such strategies. Although this group also focused on content, they paid more attention to process. When Coffman et al. tested these children at the end of first grade, the ones in the process-oriented classrooms acquired new information more quickly.

SUMMARY

In later childhood, memory becomes more adult-like. In practice, that means that children switch to a meaning-based approach to encoding. Thus, whereas suggestibility decreased as children age, false memories that arise from meaning-based processes, such as in the DRM paradigm, actually increase. Metacognition also develops over the childhood years. The beginning of metamemory parallels the beginnings of theory of mind. Children around the age of five years pass the false-belief test. At about the same age, children start making accurate metamemory judgments. Metamemory judgments, such as judgments of learning, improve over the first few years of grade school. Metamemory control also improves over this period. Overconfidence is often seen in young children's judgments. Improvement in metamemory predicts improvement in memory recall in children, suggesting that metamemory is important to the development of memory.

MEMORY: FOUNDATIONS AND APPLICATIONS

Section Quiz

1. Research on the Deese-Roediger-McDermott paradigm (DRM) shows that
   a. Older children show more critical intrusions than younger children
   b. Older children show fewer critical intrusions than younger children
   c. Older children show the same amount of critical intrusions than younger children
   d. Older children never show critical intrusions, whereas they occur continuously with younger children

2. Otgaar, Smeets, and Peters (2012) repeatedly asked children ages seven to nine about a true event (their first day of school) and a false event (a visit to a burn treatment center). They found that
   a. Children only showed false memories for the true event. They always rejected the false event
   b. Giving more of such information in the form of semantic memory scripts increased the likelihood of false memories
   c. The older children showed less correct recall but more false memories
   d. The younger children could only remember the false event

3. The awareness that other individuals have separate states of awareness different from that of our own is known as
   a. Metacognition
   b. Meta-awareness
   c. Theory of mind
   d. Theory of metamemory

4. Shin, Bjorkland, and Beck (2007) asked children in kindergarten to estimate how many pictures they would be able to remember out of a set of 15 pictures. They found that
   a. Children could draw all 15 pictures
   b. Children showed underconfidence in their ability to recall the pictures
   c. Children with disabilities were more underconfident than those without disabilities
   d. Children generally showed overconfidence in their ability to remember the pictures

1. a
2. b
3. c
4. d

KEY TERMS

conjugate reinforcement technique

false-belief test

imitation

memory conversations

memory efficiency view

memory strategies view

metamemory

nonnutritive sucking

novelty preference

overconfidence in judgments

theory of mind

visual recognition

REVIEW QUESTIONS

1. Describe three methods that are used to investigate memory in infancy. How does each method attribute learning to the growing infant?

2. Why is episodic memory nearly impossible to examine in infants younger than one year?

3. What is meant by the terms *memory strategies* and *memory efficiency*? How does each shape the development of memory in young children?

4. Describe a study that supports the idea that young children have episodic memory. Does this study support the idea that young children can remember over the childhood amnesia barrier?

5. What are memory conversations? How do they shape the development of episodic memory in young children?

6. Why is testimony from young children not considered reliable? What evidence supports this claim?

7. Why do older children show more false memories in the DRM paradigm?

8. What is meant by the term *theory of mind*? How is it tested in young children?

9. At what age do children start making accurate judgments of learning? Do judgments of learning accuracy continue to improve with age?

10. What is meant by the term *overconfidence?* How might it be adaptive for young children to be overconfident?

ONLINE RESOURCES

1. For more on eye tracking in infants, go to http://www.psychology.uiowa.edu/labs/maclab/.

2. For more information on Judy DeLoache's research, go to http://www.faculty.virginia.edu/deloache/.

3. For more on the relation of early childhood memory and later childhood amnesia, go to http://www.apa.org/science/about/psa/2004/12/bauer.aspx.

4. For more on Qi Wang's research, go to http://www.human.cornell.edu/bio.cfm?netid=qw23.

5. For more on the high-profile case in California in which a woman who ran a child care center was accused of sexually molesting numerous children, go to http://www.law.umkc.edu/faculty/projects/ftrials/mcmartin/mcmartin.html.

6. For the transcript of an interview with Dr. Ceci, go to http://www.pbs.org/wgbh/pages/front line/shows/terror/interviews/ceci.html.

7. For more on this topic and its relation to eyewitness memory, go to http://www.nsf.gov/news/news_summ.jsp?org=NSF&cntn_id=111230.

8. For more on Dr. Otgaar's research, go to http://www.personeel.unimaas.nl/henry.otgaar/.

Go to **study.sagepub.com/schwartz3e** for additional exercises and study resources. Select **Chapter 11, Memory in Childhood** for chapter-specific resources.

CHAPTER 12

Memory in Older Adults

Jane Y is 80 years old. She retired nine years ago after teaching art education at the high school level for over 50 years. She also taught art instruction at the local community college and wrote a book on that subject, which is still used in the public schools in her state. Since retiring, she has kept active by gardening, reading a novel a week, taking courses at the local community college in the "seniors in education" program with her husband, also retired, and babysitting her various grandchildren whenever possible. What bothers Jane is that she seems to be forgetful. She forgets appointments, she forgets whether she has reordered her cholesterol medicine, and she sometimes pauses before calling each grandchild by the right name. She visited a highly respected neurologist in the closest big city, who did a scan of her brain and told her everything looked good and that she should not worry about her memory. The doctor told her that being a little forgetful is normal for someone her age. Nonetheless, the worries persist.

Should Jane be concerned? Is Jane simply more aware of the failures of her memory when they occur, or is she really more forgetful than she was when she was younger? Is her forgetfulness a harbinger of bad things to come? Is poor Jane Y going senile or succumbing to Alzheimer's disease? Should she be worried despite the clean bill of health given to her by the neurologist? Is there anything she can do to restore her memory to its youthful vigor and strength? These are just some of the questions seniors ask themselves when they feel that their memory is "not as good as it once was" (see Figure 12.1).

In our society, many young people of college age may have little opportunity to interact with older adults. Even grandparents may live in another state or another country. An interesting activity for students in a memory course is to find an older adult (perhaps someone 70 or older) and ask them questions about their memory, their worries about the future of their memory, and how they compensate for perceived shortcomings in their memory. In contrast, students may also choose to interview a person in middle age (perhaps someone in their late 40s or 50s) and ask them if they have noticed any changes in their ability to learn new information and retrieve it.

For most of us, preserved memory function is seen as vital to maintaining health and competence as we get older. The ability to remember is crucial to many aspects of human life. Memory provides us with our sense of identity, an ability to keep track of the things that are vital to our survival (money, food, medicines, clothing, etc.), and a way of avoiding deception (older adults are often the target of scammers). Thus, the prospect of having

Figure 12.1 Healthy older adults have functional memory systems.

Creatas Images/Thinkstock.

diminished memory abilities can cause concern in even the least hypochondriacally challenged older adult. So it should come as no surprise that many older adults are themselves most concerned with memory loss. When they find themselves unable to recall a specific word or event when called upon to do so, they worry about the consequences. Indeed, they may worry that each memory failure is an omen of further decline to come. Thus, it is important to separate fact from fiction in this chapter. Again, our focus is on the science of memory; in this case, that means examining the empirical findings on aging and memory.

It is important to note that older adults are individuals and as in every domain of psychology, there are individual differences. In this sense, one should never judge an individual's memory abilities by his or her age. The distributions overlap, and any individual older adult may outperform an individual younger adult. In cognitive psychology, we do our best to make generalizations about trends and patterns while remembering that individual differences exist. Of course, certain factors lead some older adults to have more memory loss than others, but that does not negate the point that individual differences matter in this area. For example, education and verbal ability mitigate age-related declines (Manly, Touradji, Tang, & Stern, 2003).

This chapter will discuss the developmental changes that occur in normal, healthy older adults. In contrast, Chapter 10 considered the many forms of memory loss that accompany brain damage. Many of these forms of brain damage, particularly an increased risk of stroke and increased likelihood of developing Alzheimer's disease, are associated with being older. These conditions and illnesses can be devastating to older adults. But most old adults have healthy brains, albeit older brains, and most seniors will never develop Alzheimer's. (For a comparison of healthy and unhealthy brains, go to www.sage pub.com/schwartz3e.[1]) Our focus in this chapter is in normal aging, not pathological processes.

Certainly, in our culture, we have a stereotype of older adults as being more forgetful and having memory deficits relative to younger adults (Zacks & Hasher, 2006). How many movies have you seen in which a joke is made about an older person forgetting a vital piece of information? What this chapter will consider is in what domains older adults really have worse memories than their juniors and in what ways they are equal or superior to those younger than themselves.

As memory scientists, we want to know: Is this stereotype true? Are memory deficits associated with old age? Do all older adults experience them or only some people? It is probably unavoidable in U.S. (and other Western) culture not to have some negative stereotypes about memory and cognition in older adults. You might consider writing down some of your own preconceptions before continuing with the text. Then, you can compare your views before reading the chapter to your views afterward. Most readers of this book are younger adults, but college students hopefully will become senior citizens in time. Thus, the issues involved in memory and aging will eventually affect all of us.

Table 12.1	Most Older Adults Have Healthy Memories

Memory declines
Working memory
Encoding into and retrieval from episodic memory
Source monitoring
Prospective memory
Memory stays constant or improves
Implicit memory
Metamemory
Lexical knowledge
Semantic memory

By this point, you should also know that memory comes in many flavors—that is, multiple memory systems (e.g., working memory, episodic memory, lexical memory, semantic memory). You should also know that there are many processes involved in producing and retrieving memories (encoding, retrieval, source monitoring, etc.). Thus, it is sensible to suspect that older adults may have declines in some aspects of memory (e.g., ease of retrieval) but may have no declines or may even have advantages in other areas (general semantic knowledge). In reviewing the science, we will see areas in which older adults show declines relative to their younger peers (Salthouse, 2016). But we will also examine areas in which age-related declines are seldom seen in normal aging. In some ways, in fact, older adults outperform younger adults (word knowledge, for example).

Table 12.1 lists some of the areas in which older adults can expect declines relative to their younger peers or to when they themselves were younger. It also lists areas in which age either has little to no effect (implicit memory and metamemory) or improvements continue with age (semantic memory and lexical knowledge). Each of these areas will be discussed at length. First, however, the theories that guide memory and aging research will be introduced. These theories attempt to explain how memory changes in older adults and why it does so. These theories are developmental in nature, seeking to explain the changes that occur in memory as we grow older.

THEORIES OF AGING AND MEMORY

Processing Speed

Processing speed theory postulates that age-related declines occur because older people's cognitive processing does not work as quickly as that of younger adults. Because the speed

Processing speed: Age-related declines are caused because older people's cognitive processing does not work as fast as that of younger adults.

of processing slows down, people take longer to learn new information and to retrieve information already stored in memory. Both slowed encoding and retrieval can result in relatively weaker memory performance. This general slowing leads to deficits in those memory-specific domains that require encoding of new information and rapid retrieval of existing information. The processing view does not predict deficits in memory performance that is untimed and does not require recall. For example, self-paced recognition tests should not show any deficits.

This view likens memory to a physical skill. In general, younger adults have quicker reflexes and stronger muscles than do older adults. As one grows older, one loses quickness, and it takes longer to build muscle. The processing-speed hypothesis suggests that cognitive processes likewise slow down. Although encoding and retrieval abilities decrease, this view also suggests that when older adults have ample time to study or process information, their performance may be no weaker than those of younger adults. In fact, in many cognitive tasks, older adults can perform just as accurately as younger adults, but each response takes them a bit more time.

Studies that measure reaction time show age-related declines (Hess & Smith, 2016; McCabe & Hartman, 2008). For example, in tasks in which participants must make speeded decisions, such as lexical decision tasks, older adults will perform more slowly than younger adults (see Figure 12.2). Salthouse (1996) asked younger and older adults to make perceptual comparisons as fast as possible. These involved deciding whether two letters in different fonts (c, C) were the same or whether two pictures were the same. The

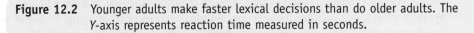

Figure 12.2 Younger adults make faster lexical decisions than do older adults. The Y-axis represents reaction time measured in seconds.

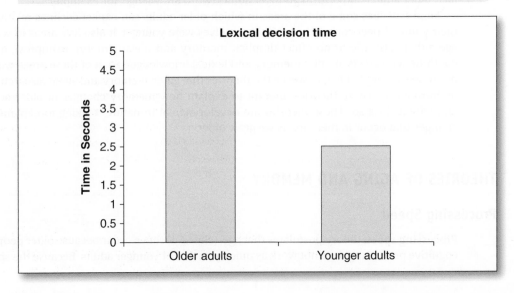

Figure 12.3 Recognition as a function of age and speed of tempo. The *Y*-axis represents percent recognized.

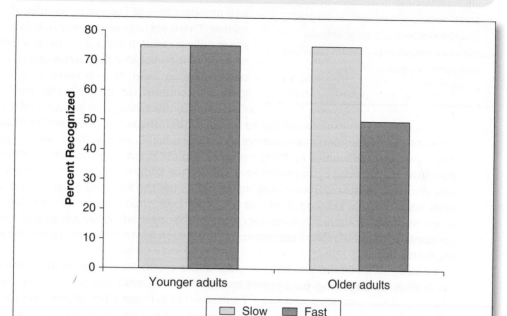

participants were expected to make these judgments as fast as they possibly could. When reaction times were examined, there was a consistent advantage for younger adults over older adults. Speed of processing also predicted performance on a host of memory tasks within each age group. Those older adults who were faster at the perceptual comparison tasks also did better in working memory and episodic memory tasks (Salthouse, 1996).

For any theory to be useful, it must be predictive across a range of situations. The processing-speed theory meets this expectation. Consider memory for music. Older adults, relative to younger adults, have more difficulty recognizing melodies when they are played at a fast tempo than when they are played at a slower tempo (Dowling, Bartlett, Halpern, & Andrews, 2008). When the melody is played slowly, there are no differences in recognition between younger and older adults, but when the music is sped up, older adults cannot follow it as well, and their performance goes down relative to the younger adults (see Figure 12.3). Indeed, on a great many other cognitive tasks, younger adults can react more quickly (see Salthouse, 1996). (For more on Dr. Salthouse's research, go to www .sagepub.com/schwartz3e.²)

Inhibition Theory

Inhibition theory argues that older adults relative to younger adults have a lessened ability to block out irrelevant stimulation. This means that the memory declines seen in old age are a consequence of poor attentional processes. Younger adults can more easily block out

Inhibition theory: The ability to block out irrelevant stimulation decreases with age, so the memory declines seen in old age are a consequence of poor attentional processes. *Inhibition* also means the ability to suppress retrieval of irrelevant information.

competing sources of information, such as background noise, and focus on the task at hand. Older adults, by contrast, cannot direct their attention as well among a host of competing sources of information. This is perhaps why parents tell their teenage or college children to put away the headphones while studying—because the parents can no longer concentrate on learning with music in the background. By contrast, listening to music may be less distracting for the teenager or college student.

Inhibition also means the ability to suppress the retrieval of irrelevant information. For example, when older adults attempt to retrieve a name, such as the name of a grandchild, they have difficulties in inhibiting other names (of other grandchildren). Thus, the grandparent may need extra time to sort through the additional names that are accidentally retrieved, or the older adult may inadvertently use the wrong name. It is not that the older adult does not know the name of his or her grandchild; it is just that it is harder to suppress the other names that are also retrieved. Younger adults are less plagued by the accidental retrieval of related but incorrect information because they are better at inhibiting distractors.

Evidence of inhibition problems in older adults comes from directed forgetting studies. In **directed forgetting**, participants are asked to remember some information but are

Directed forgetting: The inhibition in memory that occurs when people are asked to forget some information but not other information.

explicitly told to forget other information (Bjork & Woodward, 1973). Directed forgetting experiments require participants to first study some items, usually a list of words, and then try to forget them. After participants study the words, the experimenters "apologize" and tell the participants that they gave the participants the wrong list. Forget

that list, the researchers say, because you need to study this other list. Surprisingly, most people will succeed at this task, and recall of the to-be-forgotten list is worse than it is for control lists that receive the same study but are not subject to the forgetting instructions.

Because younger adults are better at inhibition, it is possible that younger adults are better at directed forgetting than are older adults. Indeed, younger adults are better able to inhibit the to-be-forgotten words. In a directed-forgetting situation, that means that younger adults will be better able to forget the to-be-forgotten items. This leads to the ironic effect that older adults have better recall for the to-be-forgotten items than do the younger adults (Andrés, Van der Linden, & Parmentier, 2004; Colombel, Tessoulin, Gilet, & Corson, 2016).

A powerful demonstration of the success of inhibition theory to explain age-related memory declines comes from Darowski, Helder, Zacks, Hasher, and Hambrick (2008). Darowski et al. asked younger and older participants to read short texts. Some of these texts contained irrelevant and distracting words embedded in otherwise meaningful sentences. For example, consider the following sentence: "Jane Goodall has studied chimpanzee behavior for many years at Gombe Stream National Park in the African nation of Tanzania."

Hopefully, this is an easy and informative sentence. Now compare your fluency in reading that sentence as compared to this one: "Jane Goodall *clerk* has studied *Kansas* chimpanzee *definition* behavior *lunch* for many *clones* years at Gombe *blanket* Stream National *whisker* Park in the *pine* African nation *reverse* of Tanzania." Obviously, the insertion of irrelevant words in italics makes the sentence more difficult to decipher. With some work, most of us can figure out what the sentence about Jane Goodall is about. However, Darowski et al. found that older adults were more affected by the irrelevant stimuli than were younger adults. Their reading times were slower than those of younger adults, and they remembered less from the passages than did younger adults. In essence, the younger adults were better able to screen out or inhibit the irrelevant words, allowing them to process the information in the sentences. The older adults struggled with the irrelevant stimuli, though, eventually, they too could understand the sentences. Thus, deficits in inhibition, like slower processing speed, may account for some of the age-related declines in memory.

In an interesting study, Colombel et al. (2016) first classified older adults by their inhibition ability in order to see how such abilities affected both correct recall and false memory. Older adults were classified as good at inhibition and poor at inhibition based on their ability do inhibition tasks, such as the Stroop effect. Once participants were classified as either being good or poor at inhibition, they were given a DRM task. However, there were two versions of the DRM task. In the standard DRM task, participants were asked to recall the items they saw on the list. However, in the "inclusion" task, participants were asked to generate anything the list made them think of. Thus, critical intrusions are errors in the standard version, but not in the inclusion task. Although there were no differences between good and poor inhibitors on the inclusion task, poor inhibitors recalled less and generated more critical intrusions on the standard version. What this means is that when there was no need to inhibit responses, those older adults who were poor at inhibition did just as well in memory as those who were good at inhibition. However, when inhibition was necessary, memory in older adults suffered. Thus, this study supports the view that inhibition failure may contribute to reduced memory in older adults.

Decline in the Strategic Use of Memory

A third theory of memory and aging argues that declines in memory are a function of a declining use of appropriate memory strategies (e.g., Castel, McGillivray, & Friedman, 2012; Naveh-Benjamin, Cowan, Kilb, & Chen, 2007 Otani et al (2008)). This means that older adults are less likely to explicitly use strategies that will help their encoding and retrieval, such as elaboration, imagery, mnemonics, and appropriate distribution of study time. This theory is based on the finding that older adults have control deficits with respect to working memory that might interfere with strategy use. Craik, Morris, and Gick (1990) claimed that older adults engage in less self-initiated strategies. When instructed to use memory strategies, they will, but left on their own, they use them less often than do younger adults. Naveh-Benjamin et al. (2007) showed that older adults used less chunking than did younger adults in a working memory task. They suspected that relative impairment in the frontal lobe may lead to fewer memory strategies being used and a decrease in metamemory ability. (For more on this topic, go to study.sagepub.com/schwartz3e.[3])

However, this view is no longer in favor. In particular, many studies now show that metamemory shows no or few declines in older adults. Hertzog (2016) argued that there are domains in which older adults show decreased metamemory but in general, preserved metamemory abilities allow older adults to maintain high functioning. With respect to both judgments of learning and feelings of knowing, older adults are as accurate as younger participants. For example, Sacher, Landré, and Taconnat (2015) showed that memory performance affected feeling-of-knowing accuracy, but variations in feeling of knowing did not predict memory performance in older adults. Moreover, Castel et al. (2012) showed that, as people age, they direct their cognitive processes in more value-directed ways. Older adults control their learning in such a way as to master the most important or high-value information, even if this comes at the expense of less valuable information. Thus, older adults will remember what symptoms to tell the doctor even if they later forget what items to pick up at the grocery store. This value-relevant processing is adaptive given older adults' relative impairment in encoding and retrieval. Thus, metamemory monitoring and control remain excellent among older adults, and preserved metamemory function suggests that older adults continue to maintain good strategic use of memory (Hertzog, 2016).

As in most issues in human memory, the answer is complex. Therefore, age-related memory declines are likely to be because of a combination of slower processing speed and reduced ability to inhibit irrelevant stimuli, although probably not because of declining use of memory strategies. With that in mind, we will turn our focus to specific components of memory and how they are affected by aging.

SECTION SUMMARY AND QUIZ

Many older adults are concerned about deficits in memory, and there are popular beliefs that memory declines in old age. However, the research shows that although some declines occur, mostly associated with episodic memory, other memory domains, such as semantic and lexical memory, remain intact. Three theories have been advanced to account for declines in memory. Decline in processing speed is supported by reaction time studies, which show slower reaction times for older adults; working memory shows age-related declines because of decreases in processing speed. Inhibition theory is supported by data that show that older adults have a more difficult time dividing their attention and blocking out irrelevant stimuli. The third theory is that memory declines because of the failure of older adults to use appropriate memory strategies, but few data support this idea.

Section Quiz

1. In which of the following domains is there evidence for declines in memory with normal aging?
   a. Metamemory and semantic memory
   b. Implicit memory and metamemory
   c. Episodic memory and prospective memory
   d. None of the above

2. The theory that postulates that age-related declines occur because older people's cognitive processing does not work as quickly as that of younger adults is known as
   a. Inhibition theory
   b. Relational theory
   c. Processing speed theory
   d. Decline in the strategic use of memory

3. Colombel et al. (2016) classified older adults by their inhibition ability in order to see how such abilities affected both correct recall and false memory. They found that
   a. Older adults showed fewer false memories than younger adults
   b. Older adults did not retrieve the critical intrusions
   c. When inhibition was necessary, memory in older adults suffered relative to younger adult controls
   d. All of the above are true

4. Darowski et al. (2008) asked younger and older participants to read short texts. Some of these texts contained irrelevant and distracting words embedded in otherwise meaningful sentences. They found that
   a. Older adults were more affected by the irrelevant stimuli than were younger adults
   b. Younger adults were more affected by the irrelevant stimuli than were older adults
   c. The irrelevant stimuli were just that—irrelevant to memory
   d. Older adults were so thrown off by the irrelevant stimuli that they could not remember the meaning of the sentences

1. c
2. c
3. c
4. a

AGE-RELATED CHANGES IN WORKING MEMORY

Working memory is the short-term memory system that maintains information for conscious introspection over relatively short time intervals (up to 15 seconds). Although working memory is generally considered a separate neurocognitive system from long-term memory systems, information must be held in working memory during encoding and during retrieval. Therefore, it is possible, and indeed many researchers have argued, that deficits in working memory in older adults are also responsible for the deficits seen in long-term memory (Craik & Byrd, 1982; Salthouse, 2000; Sander, Lindenberger, & Werkle-Bergner, 2012). These deficits in working memory may arise from the general reduction in processing speed seen in older adults. Slower working memory, in turn, may mean that information is less likely to reach the long-term memory systems.

To review, working memory is composed of three major systems (see Chapter 3). The phonological loop maintains information about auditory stimuli, whereas the visuospatial sketchpad maintains information about visual stimuli. When task difficulty increases or simultaneous processing is required, the central executive allocates attentional resources to the appropriate system. It is the central executive system that seems to be most negatively affected by age. In working memory tasks that require central executive components (i.e., directing attention among competing stimuli), older adults find themselves at a disadvantage. In dual-processing tasks, older adults are impaired relative to younger adults (Rhodes, Parra, & Logie, 2016; Sander et al., 2012). Central executive deficits may also be the function of reduced ability to inhibit competing sources of information. Because in dual tasks participants must figure out a manner in which to attend to two or more competing sources, being able to inhibit one while focused on the other is important. Deficits in the ability to inhibit competing sources will show up as executive deficits.

In some working memory tasks, particularly those that tap the phonological loop, older adults perform just as well as younger adults. Consider the standard digit span task. A participant hears a list of numbers and must repeat them back immediately in order, as in the famous magic number seven experiment (Miller, 1956). Most young adults can maintain about seven items in working memory. However, older adults do just as well as younger adults in this task (Dixon & Cohen, 2003). It is likely that because the digit span task mostly uses the phonological loop, it requires little input from central executive processes in working memory. This leads to equivalent performance between healthy old and young participants.

However, in tasks for which the central executive is an important component, older adults perform less well than younger adults. Consider the following experiment by Göthe, Oberauer, and Kliegl (2007), which nicely illustrates the central-executive deficits in older adults. Göthe et al. compared younger and older adults on two tasks. One task was a visuomotor task, in which participants had to mentally track the location of an arrow as it moved to various marked locations on a computer screen. When the arrow reached a predetermined location, the participants were expected to press the space bar. This task is fairly easy to do, but it does require attention. When older and younger adults were tested on this task, both were able to learn it and perform it at a criterion level, although younger adults were faster at learning it than were the older adults. Nonetheless, once mastery had occurred, there were no differences as a function of age.

The second task was a simple numerical task, to add a number to a preexisting sum each and every time the participant heard a tone. Certain tones were associated with certain numbers. Thus, a high-pitched tone might mean eight, whereas a low-pitched tone might mean five. A high-pitched tone followed by a low-pitched tone would mean a sum of 13. Another high-pitched tone would mean 21. This task employed the phonological loop, as the participants had to maintain the sums in their head without writing them down. Again, the task is relatively easy but requires attention and some problem-solving ability. Both older and younger adults learned this task with equal ease, although younger adults were faster in performing the task, consistent with their general advantage in processing speed. Again, though, we see no differences in accuracy between the younger and older adults.

Note that the first task involved using the visuospatial sketchpad, and the second task required the use of the phonological loop. Thus, both tasks involve working memory processes. In each task, despite a speed advantage for the younger adults, the older adults were able to learn the task and perform it accurately. Once the task had been learned, there were no differences in performance between the older and younger adults—as long as the tasks were done individually.

A second group of participants, both old and young, were asked to learn the two tasks simultaneously and then asked to perform the tasks simultaneously. After considerable practice, the younger adults were able to learn the tasks and to perform them simultaneously without any costs in speed at either task. This took much more practice than had been necessary to learn each task individually—but the younger adults did learn to perform the tasks at the same time as fast as they could perform each task when doing it alone. However, not one of the older adults could reach this level of performance! The demands on their central executive were just too great. Whereas the older adults were as good as the younger adults when the tasks were learned alone, they were at a huge disadvantage when the tasks were required to be learned together. In fact, the older adults could only complete the study by alternating from one task to the other, whereas the younger adults appeared to be successfully dual tasking, essentially doing both tasks at once. Göthe et al. (2007) concluded that the results reflect differences in executive control on working memory tasks. Many other studies have found similar findings between old and young adults in dual-task performance (see Riby, Perfect, & Stollery, 2004).

This experiment appears complicated and removed from real-world experience. If you did not entirely understand the procedures and conclusions, reread the above paragraph and make sure you understand what Göthe et al. (2007) were doing. Study it until you understand—your professor just may ask a question about it on the next exam. But in fact, it has some real-world applications too! Think about how often you engage in dual tasks, trying to do two or more things at once. Dual tasking has become an everyday part of life. Perhaps you have listened to music while studying for class or watched a football game on television while cooking for your family. Many students now routinely have their phones or computers tuned to a social media site even when they are in class. Perhaps the most ubiquitous dual processing occurs when we drive. Driving a car is a visuomotor task; it requires your eyes on the road and your hands on the steering wheel. However, it leaves your mouth and ears free to do other things. Many of us listen to music or talk on our cell phones while we are driving. Research suggests that speaking on a cell phone can cause driving failures even in young adults (Bergen, Medeiros-Ward, Wheeler, Drews, & Strayer, 2013; Strayer & Drews, 2007), as attentional resources must be redistributed from driving to talking. The Göthe et al. (2007) study suggests that older adults might be even more at risk when trying to talk and drive at the same time because they have a reduced ability to allocate attention to multiple sources. Older people may be just as good at driving (and just as good at speaking) as younger adults are. But when the two tasks are combined, their performance may suffer relative to younger adults (Bergen et al., 2013).

Cell phone use while driving is an obvious application of the dual-task findings, but there are other implications for older adults as well. Consider the busy life of a medical doctor. She might have to examine MRI scans while simultaneously giving advice to a resident walking alongside. The data on dual-task performance suggest that older doctors might want to do one task, then the other task, in a linear fashion to remain competent. The resident, on the other hand, still in his late 20s, might be able to do both. The point here is that older adults can do tasks equally well as younger adults but that multitasking can be more difficult.

To summarize, older adults have deficits in working memory, but these deficits tend to be related to reduced capacity of the central executive. The visuospatial sketchpad and the phonological loop are less affected by age-related declines.

SEMANTIC MEMORY

Aging has little effect on **semantic memory** tasks. Most studies point to the preserved nature of representation of information in semantic memory. Indeed, in studies in which general knowledge is tested (politics, history, sports, etc.), older adults typically outperform younger adults (Dixon, Rust, Feltmate, & See, 2007). Moreover, older adults are often better able to encode information into semantic memory than younger adults. Metcalfe et al. (2015) in an aptly named paper, "On Teaching Old Dogs New Tricks," found that older adults were better able to correct errors after feedback on a semantic memory task

> **Semantic memory:** The neurocognitive memory system that encodes, stores, and retrieves information concerning knowledge of the world.

than were younger adults. This was especially true for answers that were originally given with low confidence. In the experiment, older and younger adults answered general-information questions, such as "Who was the second president of the United States?" (John Adams). After making a response, the participants received feedback, including the correct answer. When participants made high-confidence errors, both younger and older adults were as likely to later remember the correction, but older adults were more likely to remember the correction to low-confidence answers, thereby demonstrating an advantage for older-adult memory (Metcalfe et al., 2015).

In another study, Carmichael and Gutchess (2016) looked at the ability of younger and older adults to avoid errors in semantic memory retrieval. In the study, Carmichael and Gutchess gave participants categorized lists (e.g., tools: hammer, nail, wrench, screwdriver) and later asked for recall of those items. Like in the DRM paradigm, participants will sometimes include an exemplar of the category that was not presented originally (e.g., "saw"). When participants were warned about this possibility, older adults improved in their ability to avoid intrusions, whereas younger adults did not, although the improvement only brought the older adults up to the levels that the younger adults were at anyway. Nonetheless, this study shows that older adults are better able to use warnings to improve their semantic memory. In sum, semantic memory is not impaired in normal aging. Indeed, it improves with respect to correcting errors and avoiding errors.

EPISODIC MEMORY

"I can't remember whether I took my blood pressure pill or not." "I forgot my lunch date with my cousin Estelle." "I forgot to turn the stove off, and if it wasn't for my son coming over to visit, I might have burned the house down." "I don't remember if I fed the dog this afternoon." These are some of the complaints older adults have about their memory problems. You will note that all of these are failures of episodic memory. **Episodic memory** is the domain of memory in which older adults most often complain of declines. In fact, these self-perceptions are validated by the research. Even in healthy older adults, episodic memory declines do occur, both in encoding and

> **Episodic memory:** The neurocognitive memory system that encodes, stores, and retrieves memories of our personal individual experiences.

retrieval (Morcum, 2016). But what is the nature of these declines? Even within episodic memory, performance is preserved in some areas while it declines in others. For example, Mohanty, Naveh-Benjamin, and Ratneshwar (2016) showed that preserved semantic memory skills could be used to improve episodic memory in older adults. In the study, participants were encouraged to use meaning-based and relational processing to encode brand logos with brand names (e.g., "Fifteen minutes could save you 15% percent on car insurance—GEICO"). The test was later one of remembering the pairings. The results found that meaningful processing eliminated the aging deficit relative to younger adults. Thus, when older adults use semantic-memory strategies, they can improve their episodic memory. We now turn to some core issues in episodic memory and aging.

Recall Versus Recognition in Episodic Memory

Recall involves the ability to produce the correct answer by generating that answer from retrieval. Recognition, on the other hand, only requires one to match a presented stimulus to one's memory of the original. In general, recognition is therefore considered the easier test, as it can be done on the basis of familiarity without necessarily requiring specific recollection of the original event. Familiarity seems to be unaffected by aging, but recollection is impaired in aging (Healey & Kahana, 2016). Therefore, it is likely that recognition will be relatively spared in older adults, whereas recall may show impairments. In general, the research supports this, suggesting that the ability to recall information declines with age but that recognition performance remains relatively stable (see Figure 12.4). This is true for information learned earlier, such as autobiographical memory, and for new learning. That older adults do as well as younger adults on recognition tests of newly learned information suggests that encoding processes can be as good in older adults as they are in younger adults. However, because recall involves the inhibition of competing responses, it will show more age-related deficits. In other words, older adults are encoding information; it is just more difficult for them to access that information relative to younger adults. Although the total amount of information recalled declines, the accuracy of older adults' memory reports does not decline. We will look at each of these claims in turn.

Most studies find that older adults show roughly equivalent performance on recognition tests relative to younger adults. For example, Rhodes, Castel, and Jacoby (2008) asked both older and younger adults to study pairs of faces with the goal of being able to recognize that the two faces went together. In each pair, the participants studied a paired male and female face. Later, the participants were given a recognition test. The cue was one of the faces from the male-female pairs, and the test choices were two faces, one of which was the actual pair complement seen at the time of study. The participant chose the face that matched his or her memory for the original pair. Older adults and younger adults

Figure 12.4 Typical results when older and younger adults are compared on recall and recognition tests. The *Y*-axis is percentage correct on either recall or recognition.

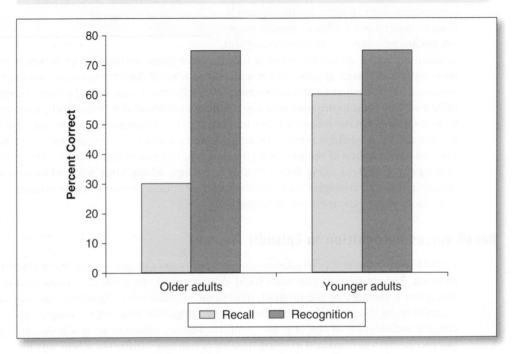

performed at the same level in this task, with both groups performing well at identifying the matching face. Thus, this study demonstrates the similar performance of older and younger adults in a recognition task.

However, when recall tests are used to evaluate episodic memory, older adults typically have deficits relative to younger adults. In general, the findings here show that starting around age 40, adults tend to do progressively worse at recall tests than those younger than them. The effect may not be statistically large, but it is found in nearly every study. In one study, Dunlosky and Hertzog (1998) asked older and younger adults to study unrelated word pairs (e.g., *cat–fork*). Participants studied the items until all participants had mastered the items; this took a bit longer for the older participants. Later, when they returned for a recall test, the younger participants recalled more of the target words than did the older participants, even though all participants had initially learned all of the associations. In another study, Koen and Yonelinas (2016) asked older adults and younger adults to view a list of items that they had either previously seen or not previously seen and decide which was which—a standard old-new recognition test. After deciding if an item was old or not, participants were then asked if they recollected the item or sensed its familiarity, a remember/know judgment. The remember/know judgments were used to estimate the differences that older and younger adults used to recognize the targets. Koen and Yonelinas found that older adults were much more reliant on familiarity than were younger adults, consistent with the view that recall is a function of recognition and relatively impaired in older adults.

Memory Accuracy in Episodic Memory

Although the total amount of information in recall decreases in older adults, the accuracy of what older adults recall is not impaired relative to younger adults. What does this mean? Well, if a younger adult recalls 20 words from a list, but two items are errors, he or she has a 90% hit rate. If the older adult remembers only 10 items, but nine of those are correct, the older adult has the same hit rate—90%. Thus, even though the older adult has remembered fewer correct items, his or her accuracy remains the same. In simple free recall and cued recall tests, older adults and younger adults exhibit the same level of accuracy (Rhodes & Kelley, 2005).

Consider the implications of the above findings for eyewitness testimony. Because younger adults remember more details, they make better witnesses for the initial phases of investigation. The police investigators may get more leads from younger witnesses, although a greater number of these leads may be errors. However, in a courtroom, an older witness is as likely to remember as accurately as the younger witness. Thus, what an older witness reports during testimony is as likely to be as accurate as the testimony of a younger adult. Dahl et al. (2015) showed older adults a film and then asked them questions about the events in the film. They found high rates of accuracy for participants in their 60s and 70s, but that accuracy declined for people in their 80s. However, the octogenarians showed little overconfidence, suggesting that that they were generally aware that their memory performance would not be ideal.

There is a caveat here—older adults are more susceptible to misleading and deceptive information, and this has a greater effect on their accuracy than it does on younger adults (Rhodes & Kelley, 2005). Thus, as with young children, investigators must be careful not to make suggestive statements to their oldest witnesses. As long as one is certain that the witnesses were not tampered with, however, then the older witness is as good as the younger witness.

FALSE MEMORY IN OLDER ADULTS

When nonsuggestive methods are used, older adults demonstrate memory accuracy equivalent to that of younger adults. However, older adults are more susceptible to a host of memory illusions caused by suggestive statements, misattribution of source, and associative meaning. We will consider each of these causes of memory illusions in this section.

Suggestibility

One of the major sources of false memories is suggestibility. A generation of research has shown that misleading information can affect people's memory for an event (Loftus, 1979, 2004). These findings were discussed in detail in Chapter 8. In the misinformation paradigm, a person witnesses a crime by watching videotape or some other media and then later receives information about the event, often via a questionnaire, some of whose questions contain misleading information. The misinformation effect comes about because people are more likely to falsely remember the event if they have received misinformation.

Older adults are more likely to make errors based on misleading suggestions. In one study using the classic misinformation paradigm, Karpel, Hoyer, and Toglia (2001) showed older and younger participants a slideshow depicting a crime. Later, the participants were given questions about the event. Some of the questions included misleading information, such as "Did you see the thief kick the garbage can in anger?" when no garbage can had been present in the slideshow. Following questioning, the participants were given a recognition test in which they had to select the correct answer from alternatives. In the recognition test, older participants showed a bigger misinformation effect than did younger participants. The older adults were more likely to misremember, for example, that they had seen a garbage can. Thus, older adults are more likely to demonstrate false memories when misinformation is presented. (For more on this topic, go to study.sagepub.com/schwartz3e.[4])

Misattribution of Source

Source memory refers to the ability of an individual to remember from whom or where (that is, what source) he or she learned something. For example, you may know that your cousin is coming to visit next week. That is the basic memory; that you heard this information from your mother is the source of that memory. Remembering that you heard it from your mother is source memory. Many studies have shown that older adults have a deficit in source monitoring. For example, they are more likely to think that an imagined event was real and more likely to confuse the source of a real memory (Henkel, Johnson, & De Leonardis, 1998).

> **Source memory:** The ability of an individual to remember from whom or where (that is, what source) he or she learned something.

Source-monitoring deficits in older adults are widespread. For example, older adults have a more difficult time than younger adults in distinguishing perceptually similar sources as well as conceptually similar sources. As an example of a perceptual source-monitoring error, one might remember hearing a story from one person who has a similar voice to that of the person who actually told the story. If making a conceptual source-monitoring error, one might remember reading a story in one newspaper rather than the paper where the story actually appeared. Older adults are also more likely to make source errors if their attention is divided (Henkel et al., 1998). However, these source errors do not extend to all kinds of tasks. One study found that when older and younger adults had to make judgments of whether statements were true based on where they had heard the statements (i.e., from someone they knew was telling the truth or someone they knew was lying), older adults performed just as well as younger adults (Rahhal, May, & Hasher, 2002).

This last study is important, because it is well known that scammers often target older adults, thinking that they are easier to deceive. Given the prevalence of identity theft in today's digital world, attributing falsehood to remembered statements that are, in fact, false is important. That older adults are not more likely to think a false statement is true than do younger adults is fortunate. It suggests that older adults may not be more vulnerable than younger adults to scams that capitalize on a person's willingness to believe others.

Nonetheless, source errors can have negative consequences for older adults. If their memory for taking their medicine today is based on a memory of taking their pills today, older adults may jeopardize their health by not taking their medicine. Moreover, if they cannot correctly attribute medical advice to their doctor and instead think it comes from the gossipy neighbor, they may follow incorrect health plans. Older adults, like younger adults, must be especially vigilant to attend to source in order to avoid these errors.

Interestingly, one source of such false memories in older adults is misidentifications in perception. When older adults misperceive an object, they will often forget the correction that then leads them to correctly identify the object. Thus, if an object is incorrectly identified as a hairdryer when, in fact, it is an electric drill, older adults are more prone to remember their original misperception than a subsequent correction than are younger adults. When younger adults are corrected, in contrast, they remember the correct information. In one experiment, Vannucci, Mazzoni, Marchetti, and Lavezzini (2012) found that false identifications of objects led to false memories in older adults, even when the older adults received feedback as to what the object was initially. This suggests that older adults forget the source of the correct information (that is, the feedback) and instead remember the initial misperceived source.

Associative Meaning

Associative meaning concerns the links that form among related concepts in semantic memory and how these associations can influence episodic memory. This avenue to false memories has typically been studied with the Deese-Roediger-McDermott (DRM) procedure, discussed in Chapter 8. Researchers have compared the rate of critical intrusions in the DRM procedure in younger and older participants. To review, participants study a list of words, all of which are related to an absent critical intrusion. Many people will falsely report the critical intrusion as being on the list. A large number of studies support the conclusion that older adults are more likely to recall the critical intrusion than are younger adults (e.g., Colombel et al., 2016). In addition, when participants are warned of the likelihood of misremembering a critical lure, older adults are less able to resist recalling it anyway than are younger adults (Carmichael, & Gutchess, 2016; Jacoby & Rhodes, 2006; McCabe & Smith, 2002), consistent with a general deficit in inhibiting incorrect alternatives.

SECTION SUMMARY AND QUIZ

Working memory is composed of three major systems. The phonological loop maintains information about auditory stimuli, whereas the visuospatial sketchpad maintains information about visual stimuli. Working memory, particularly central executive functions in working memory, declines in older adults. However, other memory abilities are preserved in older adults. Semantic memory is generally unaffected by age-related declines. Indeed, some studies suggest that semantic memory continues to improve in normal healthy aging. Episodic memory does show age-related declines, particularly when tested with recall rather than recognition. Moreover, older adults show more source memory errors than do younger adults and do not do as well on prospective memory tests. As a consequence of source memory errors and declines in episodic memory, older adults are more at risk of creating false memories than are younger adults.

Section Quiz

1. Göthe et al. compared younger and older adults on two tasks, a visual task and an auditory task. They found that
   a. Younger adults out-performed older adults in terms of accuracy
   b. Younger adults scored better on the visual task, but older adults did better on the auditory task
   c. Both groups were equivalent, suggesting that there are no differences in working memory as a function of age
   d. When participants were asked to learn the two tasks simultaneously and then asked to perform the tasks simultaneously, younger adults significantly outperformed older adults

2. Carmichael and Gutchess (2016) looked at the ability of younger and older adults to avoid errors in semantic memory retrieval. They found that
   a. When participants were warned about this possibility of making false memories, older adults improved in their ability to avoid intrusions
   b. Older adults showed an increased rate of false memories, regardless of warnings
   c. Semantic memory was impaired in older adults but episodic memory was not
   d. None of the above

3. Which of the following statements is true?
   a. Older adults tend to show deficits in episodic memory relative to younger adults
   b. Older adults tend not to show deficits in semantic memory relative to younger adults
   c. Accuracy in memory is defined not in terms of the total amount recalled but the percentage recalled that is correct
   d. All of the above are true

4. Karpel, Hoyer, and Toglia (2001) showed older and younger participants a slideshow depicting a crime. They found that
   a. Older adults were not impaired relative to younger adults
   b. In a recognition test, older participants showed a bigger misinformation effect than did younger participants

c. In the recognition test, older participants showed a smaller misinformation effect than did younger participants

d. Only when short-term memory was tested were the younger adults better than the older adults

1. d
2. a
3. d
4. b

METAMEMORY IN OLDER ADULTS

Metamemory is our knowledge and awareness of our own memory. In the last chapter, we discussed how metamemory develops in children. In this section, we will examine metamemory in older adults. To review, metamemory consists of two main functional components: monitoring and control. **Monitoring** is the awareness or knowledge of whether our cognitive systems are successfully engaging in a particular task. Thus, if a person is confident that he or she is going to remember something, that confidence reflects his or her metacognitive monitoring. **Control** is the behaviors a person engages in to ensure encoding or retrieval. Thus, an older adult who wants to remember more of what he reads in the newspaper may choose to read more slowly than he used to and read without music playing in the background as he used to.

> **Monitoring:** Our ability to reflect on and become aware of what we know and what we do not know.

> **Control (in metamemory):** Our ability to regulate our learning or retrieval based upon our own monitoring.

An important component of metamemory concerns beliefs that we have about our own memory systems. If people, for example, believe that they remember everything they read based on a single reading, they may be less inclined to reread chapters in advance of an exam. If, however, they believe that they are not good at remembering names, they may make an extra effort to learn them. If older adults believe that they are having memory difficulties, they may make adjustments in the way they encode information. On the other hand, older people who believe that their memory is impaired may also choose not to try to remember new information. Thus, it is important to assess memory beliefs among older adults and then determine to what extent these beliefs correlate with actual memory performance. It is also important to consider how the beliefs themselves affect memory.

Dunlosky and Metcalfe (2009) summarized the results of numerous studies that assess older adults' beliefs about memory. These studies confirm a few assertions that many of us might assume to be self-evident with respect to memory and aging. They confirm that older adults believe that their memories are not as good as those of younger people, that their memories are not as good as they used to be when they were younger, and that they have less control over the efficiency of their memory than they did when they were younger. Thus, in terms of older adults' metacognitive beliefs about memory, Dunlosky and Metcalfe conclude that they tend to be pessimists, believing in memory decline. However, as we have seen, memory does not universally decline in old age. Many areas of memory, such as semantic and lexical memory, remain intact in healthy older adults.

Does it matter that older people think that their memories are better or worse than they once were or compared to those of other people? Yes, it does. It turns out that older adults make decisions based on their self-perception of their own memory abilities (Castel et al., 2012). Consider two older adults—one who is confident in his or her memory ability and another who is not. The confident individual may be more likely to engage in memory-intensive pursuits, such as crossword puzzles or senior learning courses, than the person who is less confident (Castel et al., 2012; Dunlosky & Metcalfe, 2009). Moreover, older adults who believe that their memory is impaired may be less likely to engage in strategic memory behaviors, believing that it is pointless to work to remember something (Lachman & Andreoletti, 2006). Thus, there is some value in promoting better memory beliefs among older adults; if they believe their memory is better, they will work harder to remember information. Working harder to learn and remember is obviously beneficial to people of any age. Of course, overconfidence is not desirable, but the belief that, with effort, information can be learned and mastered is certainly within the grasp of every healthy older adult.

Metamemory is also concerned with the monitoring of learning on individual to-be-learned items. Metamemory judgments can be made to assess whether we have learned a particular item or whether we think we are going to retrieve information. These are measured by the various judgments introduced in Chapter 9.

Judgments of Learning

One of the common metamemory judgments is the judgment of learning. **Judgments of learning** are made at the time of study and are predictions of the likelihood of remembering that item in the future. Generally, high judgments of learning indicate a prediction that the item will be remembered, whereas low judgments of learning indicate a prediction that the item will not be remembered. Judgments of learning are important for several reasons. First, in younger adults, they have been shown to be highly accurate in some circumstances but less accurate in others. Judgments of learning have also been shown to be highly predictive of study behavior. People use judgments of learning to allocate their study efforts to the difficult or to the easy items, depending on study constraints. Therefore, if we can direct people to situations in which their judgments of learning are predictive of performance, then their study behaviors will be effective.

> **Judgments of learning:** Judgments made during study of whether the item has been learned.

Older adults, in general, believe that their memory ability is worse than it used to be when they were younger. But that is a global judgment. Do these beliefs affect older adults' ratings of individual items? We can use judgments of learning to ask whether older adults also feel that they are less likely to remember each item. Furthermore, it is of interest if older adults are more, equal, or less accurate in their judgments relative to younger adults.

If metamemory is largely intact in older adults, one might expect that older adults will give lower judgments of learning to most items, reflecting their impaired ability to learn, but that their accuracy will remain high and equivalent to that of younger adults, reflecting their preserved metamemory (Price, McElroy, & Martin, 2016; Tauber & Rhodes, 2012). We now turn to some empirical studies that have addressed these issues.

Hertzog, Kidder, Powell-Moman, and Dunlosky (2002) asked younger and older adults to study word pairs. Some of the word pairs were related (e.g., *cat–dog*), whereas other word pairs were unrelated (e.g., *buffalo–rocket*). During the study, both the younger and older adults made judgments of learning on the likelihood of recalling the second word when given the first word later as a cue. Subsequently, the participants were given a recall test for all of the pairs. Not surprisingly, given that all participants had the same amount of study time, the younger adults remembered more of the pairs than did the older adults. In keeping with this finding, the older adults gave lower judgments of learning overall than did the younger adults. Indeed, when Hertzog et al. looked at the accuracy of the judgments at predicting recall, the older adults showed just as good accuracy as the younger adults, and their accuracy equally benefited from a delay between study and test. This means that those items that were given high judgments of learning tended to be recalled, and those given low judgments of learning tended to be forgotten, and this ability to accurately predict performance was equivalent for both groups. A number of other studies have also confirmed the observation that older adults' judgment of learning accuracy is equivalent to that of younger adults (see Dunlosky & Metcalfe, 2009; Figure 12.5). Moreover, research suggests that older adults use the same strategies to determine their judgments of learning as do younger adults (Hines, Hertzog, & Touron, 2015; Price et al., 2016; Tauber & Rhodes, 2012). The bottom line here is that older adults' lower judgments of learning are adaptive: They remember fewer items than do younger adults, but because they know they will remember less, their judgments are just as accurate as the younger adults' judgments.

The above results support the claim that older adults are just as good as younger adults in determining what they will learn and what they will not learn. This ability to predict one's performance is the essence of metacognitive monitoring. However, monitoring is only half of the metamemory equation. For metamemory to be functional, older adults must be able to use their monitoring accuracy as input for making sound decisions about learning and remembering; this is metacognitive control. If older adults know that a particular item is difficult, will they spend more time studying that item than easier items? Will they do this similarly to or differently than younger adults?

Most people in the field agree that the research shows that older adults are just as accurate in monitoring as are younger adults. However, there is debate in the field as to whether or not older adults show a control deficit relative to younger adults (Hertzog & Dunlosky, 2011). On the one hand, older adults often show a lower negative correlation between their judgments of learning and their allocation of study time. On the other hand, because older adults do not encode and retrieve as well as younger adults, it may be adaptive for them to study easier items than harder items. We examine a study that looks at metacognitive control based on judgments of learning in older adults.

Souchay and Isingrini (2004) asked a group of younger adults and a group of older adults to study a list of paired associates. For each pair, the participants also made a judgment of learning. After making judgments of learning for all the pairs, the participants were given an opportunity to restudy items. In the restudy phase, participants had control over how much time they would spend on each item. In other words, this study phase was self-paced. The question was whether older adults would restudy the items in the same way that younger adults did. And if older adults differed from the younger adults, would they be more or less successful in directing that control?

Souchay and Isingrini (2004) found that the younger adults remembered more of the word pairs than did the older adults, as was expected. They also found that the older adults were equally accurate at predicting their performance as were the younger adults, also in keeping with other studies. The critical measurement in this experiment, though, was the relation of the judgments of learning to the amount of time for which each item was restudied. Assuming that easy items require less study and more difficult items require more study, people should study items that are given lower judgments of learning for more time than the items given high judgments of learning. A difficult pair, such as *refuse–button*, will receive a lower judgment of learning but require more time to associate in memory than an easier pair, such as *black–sheep*. Souchay and Isingrini found a negative correlation between judgments of learning and study time for both older and

Figure 12.5 Judgment of learning accuracy is equivalent for younger and older adults. The *Y*-axis represents the correlation between predictions of performance and actual performance.

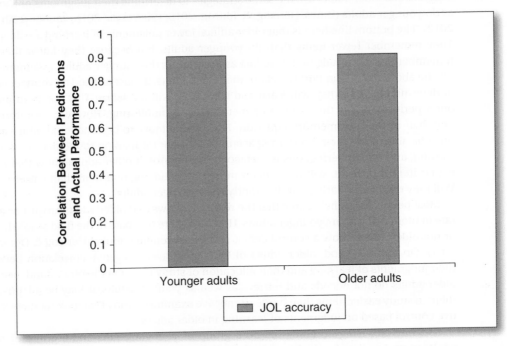

SOURCE: Based on Hertzog, Kidder, Powell-Moman, and Dunlosky (2002).

younger adults, but the effect was larger among the younger adults. Younger adults spent more time restudying the items with the lowest judgments of learning relative to the older adults, whereas older adults were more likely to choose items with higher judgments of learning for restudy.

Does this mean that the older adults have a deficit in metacognitive control. If the items are particularly difficult, it is possible that no amount of restudy will guarantee that they will be remembered. Thus, especially difficult items, despite their low judgments of learning, should be avoided during restudy. Indeed, it is more efficient to restudy a known item to ensure you will not forget it than to study an item you have no chance of learning. Given the general better ability of younger adults to encode novel associations relative to older adults, there will be more of these self-judged impossible pairs for the older adults than for the younger adults. Avoiding the study of these difficult items will lower the correlation for the older adults but not for the younger adults, who may think these items are learnable. However, the older adults are adaptively concentrating their study on relatively easier items that they might, in fact, be better able to remember. (Such items were referred to as the region of proximal learning in Chapter 9.) Thus, it is also possible to interpret the results of Souchay and Isingrini (2004) as supporting the hypothesis that older adults are as good at metacognitive control as are younger adults.

TOTs and Aging

Many studies show that, as people age, they experience more tip-of-the-tongue states (TOTs; see Brown, 2012). Indeed, many older adults can find TOTs to be a frustrating condition. Increased numbers of TOTs can occur because of two possible reasons. First, it may be that older adults have more retrieval failures for known words. This is consistent with the findings that older adults have difficulties in recall even though they recognize information quite well. Second, older adults may be more aware of the retrieval failures they do have, consistent with the findings that older adults are more sensitive or pay more attention to memory failures and consistent with their beliefs about memory. There are data that suggest both of these hypotheses come into play. The first theory is in line with the various memory declines that we have discussed in this chapter. Many studies show that the number of TOTs increases with age, as the ability to rapidly retrieve words declines (Brown, 2012; Heine, Ober, & Shenaut, 1999). The second view—that an increase in TOTs is because of increasing self-consciousness about memory failures—is consistent with the view that older adults have strong metamemory beliefs concerning the decline of their memory. A third theory has also been advanced to explain the increase in TOTs with age. This view suggests that older adults experience more TOTs, because they have bigger semantic memories. Because they know more, there are more items for which TOTs can occur (Dahlgren, 1998; Schwartz & Frazier, 2005). Indeed, Dahlgren showed that TOTs increased with vocabulary scores to a greater extent than TOTs increased with respect to age. Regardless of the explanation, all researchers agree that older adults experience more TOTs than do younger adults.

From a metamemory perspective, TOTs serve an important function. TOTs alert the person that an unretrieved item may be stored in memory but is temporarily inaccessible.

When the older adult is alerted that the item is still in memory, that person can engage in a number of memory strategies to trigger retrieval. If awareness of the block did not occur, the person would not be able to engage in these behaviors. Therefore, experiencing more TOTs is an advantage that older adults have. To investigate this issue, it is important to know whether older adults' TOTs are accurate at predicting later memory recall. If TOTs are accurate at predicting future recall, then TOTs can be considered an adaptive adjustment to the increase in memory failures in older adulthood. Indeed, analysis of people's ability to resolve (recall the originally unrecalled item) shows that older adults are better at resolving TOTs than are younger adults (see Schwartz & Metcalfe, 2011). Thus, with respect to metamemory, TOTs can be seen as another area in which older adults have preserved metamemory, at least as well, if not better than, younger adults.

We can draw on studies that use feeling-of-knowing judgments to address retrieval failures in older adults (Souchay & Isingrini, 2012). In feeling-of-knowing experiments, people first attempt recall. If they are unable to recall the target word, they are asked to make a feeling-of-knowing judgment, which is a prediction of future recognition. Then, they receive a multiple-choice recognition test and must pick out the correct target from a number of other items. In younger adults, feeling-of-knowing judgments are highly accurate at predicting correct recognition. Most of the research suggests that older adults are also highly accurate at feeling-of-knowing judgments. For example, Souchay, Moulin, Clarys, Taconnat, and Isingrini (2007) found that feeling of knowing for semantic memory is as accurate in older adults as it is in younger adults, though there was a slight deficit in accuracy with older adults with respect to episodic memory materials. Thus, as with judgments of learning, older adults are equally able to use metamemory monitoring to arrive at accurate predictions of memory performance.

To summarize: Healthy older adults perform just as well in metamemory tasks as do younger adults. Their accuracy in predicting performance is as good as that of younger adults in judgments of learning, TOTs, and feelings of knowing. Some evidence suggests that older adults have slight deficits in control, but it may also be the case that good metamemory control may be shown differently for older adults who do have weaker abilities to encode new information. Older adults correctly believe that their memory is not as good as that of younger adults. Unfortunately, this may lead to decisions to avoid learning or remembering contexts, which may have negative outcomes. Nonetheless, the general message here is that metamemory is an area of preserved function in older adulthood.

USE IT OR LOSE IT: MAINTAINING MEMORY ABILITY IN OLDER ADULTS

Is the decline in memory in old age inevitable, or can older adults engage in behaviors to preserve their memory? The answer is no and yes. First, all of us do lose a bit in terms of the speed of our responses as we get older. In fact, this aspect of cognition can be shown to start declining in adults in their 30s. There is no single thing a person can do to preserve his or her memory, nor does any combination of the activities described below ensure that memory will not decline. Moreover, age-related diseases that affect memory may occur regardless of the behaviors that older adults engage in to prevent them. However, numerous studies show statistically that certain behaviors tend to alleviate some age-related memory declines (Bielak, 2010; Binder et al., 2016).

Education and lifestyle are buffers against memory declines and other cognitive declines in old age. Those who are more educated maintain cognitive skills longer and later into older adulthood. Shimamura, Berry, Mangels, Rusting, and Jurica (1995), for example, found that college professors (a group that certainly qualifies as educated) showed no decline in story recall as a function of age, although they did show declines in working memory tasks. It is likely that the declines in working memory simply reflect diminished speed of processing, which even the educated cannot avoid. However, a lifetime of learning provides many associative structures with which to process new stories or other kinds of semantic-memory information. Thus, the college professors showed no declines in their recall of these stories. More educated adults are also less likely to experience some forms of abnormal aging, such as Alzheimer's disease, than are their less educated peers. Physical fitness is also correlated with fewer declines. Older adults who exercise routinely show greater cognitive abilities as well (Dixon et al., 2007).

However, older adults without advanced degrees who cannot exercise regularly need not despair. Other behaviors appear to be related to a decreased likelihood of excessive declines of memory and cognitive skill. Those older adults who engage in mental activity regularly are also less prone to memory loss. Salthouse (2006) called this the **use-it-or-lose-it hypothesis**, because older adults who engage in complex mental activity on a regular basis are more likely to preserve function, whereas those who do not engage in complex mental activity are more likely to suffer declines. Mental activities can include reading the newspaper, performing in musical groups, doing crossword puzzles, or taking college-level courses, to name a few. The tasks simply need to be challenging. In one important study, for example, the researchers tracked a group of nuns as they grew older (Snowdon, 2003). The nuns who spent more time engaged in mentally demanding exercises, such as crossword puzzles, maintained cognitive function to an older age and were also less likely to develop Alzheimer's disease than were the nuns who engaged in less cognitive activity. Given that all the nuns had similar habits (pun very much intended) in terms of diet, living arrangements, and personal health, it is likely that the mental activity was driving the effect rather than some other unidentified correlate of mental activity. (For more on this research, go to study.sagepub.com/schwartz3e.[5])

> **Use-it-or-lose-it hypothesis:** Older adults who engage in complex mental activity on a regular basis are more likely to preserve function, whereas those who do not are more likely to suffer declines.

Binder et al. (2016) focused on improving memory and cognitive performance by working on attentional control. In their study, older adults were divided into four groups. Three groups did a training regimen in which they worked on a number of cognitive functions separately, including inhibition, visuomotor function, and spatial navigation. The fourth group worked on all three simultaneously. Each group completed 50 training sessions at one session per day. Not surprisingly, at a six-month follow-up, the group that practiced all three tasks performed better across a range of cognitive tasks than did the groups that only practiced one skill. Thus, similar to the use-it-or-lose-it hypothesis, this study shows that focusing on cognitive weaknesses, such as the relative impairment of cognitive control in aging, can lead to improvements in performance.

Memory rehabilitation refers to interventions that clinical neuropsychologists use to promote memory performance in memory-impaired individuals. Some research sug-

> **Memory rehabilitation:** Interventions that clinical neuropsychologists use to promote memory performance in memory-impaired individuals.

gests that memory training can improve memory in older adults, just as it can in younger adults. If older adults practice memory skills, such as chunking, using encoding strategies, and processing for meaning, they should be able to improve memory, just as younger adults do. For long-term memory, this is generally true. Craik et al. (2007) found that memory training led to improvements in the recall of stories. However, Craik et al. also found out that working memory practice does not lead to significant improvement in working memory tasks in older adults. This study suggests that aspects of memory that are primarily dictated by processing speed, such as working memory tasks, are less easily changed, because older adults probably cannot increase processing speed. But tasks that rely on strategic or controlled processing, such as story recall, can be improved by greater attention to strategic use of memory. However, McDaniel and Bugg (2012) argued that the assumptions of memory rehabilitation are incorrect. From a multiple memory systems perspective, they argued that specific memory training may enhance that particular form of memory in that older adult but will have limited generalizability to tasks that tap other memory systems. (For more on memory rehabilitation, go to www .sagepub.com/schwartz3e.[6])

MNEMONIC TIPS FOR OLDER ADULTS

First, metamemory is just as good in older adults as it is in younger adults. Thus, older adults can use their metamemory as a guide to what has already been learned and what requires further study. When an older adult needs to learn something new, he or she should self-test and make judgments of learning. If the person has not learned it, he or she will benefit from restudy. If the person has already learned it, he or she can have confidence that the item is now known. The person may require more restudy than a younger peer but may get to the same level of learning eventually. If the older person spends more time restudying than do younger persons, he or she may even wind up outperforming them. If the older adult is having retrieval difficulties, he or she should remember that a TOT is not just a time to be frustrated. It means that recalling the item is likely if the older adult figures out the right cues to retrieve the answer. So the person should keep working at the task before giving up. Thus, the first mnemonic tip is to let metamemory be the guide.

Second, semantic memory and lexical memory are not impaired in normal aging. Therefore, even though an older adult may take a split second more to retrieve information than formerly, the older adult still has a lifetime's worth of learning at his or her disposal. Thus, the person may still have a competitive advantage over a younger adult who may still have to learn what the older adult already knows.

Third, "know thy weaknesses." As an older adult, it takes more time and is more difficult to encode new information, particularly episodic knowledge. Older adults should compensate for this by taking the slow and steady approach. Older adults should plan to spend more time trying to learn the information that they will need to know. They should write it down just to be sure and go back to it more often. But they should not give up: Older adults do learn and remember, and deficits in episodic memory are usually relatively minor. Thus, older adults can compensate for their deficits. They should take special care with routine but important aspects of memory. For example, a problem many older adults report is not remembering whether they have already taken their medications that day. This routine activity is easily forgotten, but the problem is easily remedied. Older adults should keep a log by their medicine cabinet. After they take their medications, they should check off that medication for that day. This externalizes the memory; it is down on paper, so there is no longer any need to trust one's slightly rusty episodic memory. Indeed, most drugstores now sell commercially produced and inexpensive pill organizers to help people remember which medicines to take when.

Fourth, mnemonic techniques are effective in older adults as well as in younger adults. Older adults can learn and successfully apply mnemonic techniques, and they will create equal boosts in memory performance relative to younger adults. In one study, Robertson-Tchabo, Hausman, and Arenberg (1976) taught older adults the method of loci. As discussed in Chapter 6, the method of loci involves associating to-be-learned items with locations in a well-known spatial layout. The researchers found that all of the older adults were able to learn the technique and deploy it successfully to improve their recall. Unlike the proverbial old dog, old folks can learn new tricks! Furthermore, Price, Hertzog, and Dunlosky (2008) also showed that older adults benefit from training in and use of imagery mnemonics, although older adults often underestimate the effectiveness of this training. Thus, older adults, especially those who become concerned about problems in memory, can avail themselves of mnemonic techniques.

THE NEUROSCIENCE OF MEMORY AND AGING

Significant changes occur in the brain even in normal adults as they age. The changes are widespread, and therefore it is difficult to pin down exactly which brain areas cause the functional changes associated with memory and aging. Nonetheless, a tremendous amount of research is directed toward this area, and some progress has been made. As it turns out, many of the brain regions known to be associated with memory show changes as the brain itself ages (Damoiseaux et al., 2016; Raz et al., 2012).

The **hippocampus** has long been known to be a part of the memory circuit, particularly with respect to encoding into episodic memory. A number of studies have shown that hippocampi show a general shrinkage in older adults. Indeed, Head, Rodrigue, Kennedy, and Raz (2008) showed that hippocampal volume (that is, the size of the hippocampus) was correlated with episodic memory performance in older adults. The smaller the hippocampal volume was, the greater the

Hippocampus: An area of the brain associated with learning and memory.

memory deficit seen. Other studies have come to similar conclusions (e.g., Jernigan et al., 2001). Damoiseaux et al. (2016) found that the connectivity from the hippocampus to other areas of the brain is diminished by aging, and this reduction in connections between areas may be associated with decreased memory. Thus, one effect of aging is that the hippocampus may shrink, thereby causing deficits in encoding.

One of the recent foci of research into the neuroscience of memory and aging is considering how changes in white-matter tracts affects cognition in older adults. White-matter tracts refer to the bundles of axons that connect neurons in one area of the brain to another. Current research shows that shrinkage of these white-matter tracts occurs in a number of areas in the aging brain, and that this shrinkage is associated with decreased memory function (Persson, et al., 2016). Thus, looking for neurological ways to keep these white-matter tracts intact may benefit older adult memory, if such solutions are possible.

Areas in the prefrontal lobe have been shown to be associated with a number of memory functions, including working memory and memory for source information, two areas in which older adults often exhibit declines (Dulas & Duarte, 2016). The prefrontal areas are particularly vulnerable to minor damage in older adults, in terms of both the reduction of volume and small structural damage. Both may result from mini-infarcts, strokes that the person does not even notice. Furthermore, Head et al. (2008) correlated decreased prefrontal tissue with problems in working memory. Decreased prefrontal volume was also associated with failures to inhibit competing sources of information, another age-related decline. Rabbitt et al. (2007) found that decreased prefrontal volume was correlated with deficits in retrieving information from episodic memory. Dulas and Duarte showed that diminished abilities in executive control of memory were also associated with reduction in prefrontal volume. However, in these studies that measure volume reduction, age, and memory performance, once the volume reduction is factored out, age has no continued influence on memory performance. Thus, it is the reduction of cortical space that really predicts memory decline rather than age per se. Nonetheless, it is becoming increasingly clear that age-related declines in memory are based on selective reduction of size and efficiency in the areas of the brain responsible for those memory functions.

White matter tracts: The bundles of neurons that connect one area of the brain to another.

At present, nothing can be done about reduced cortical volume, but it is possible that this will be a tractable issue for medical science in the future. If medical science could find ways to prevent the reduction of cortical volume or reverse it, ameliorating some of the effects of age-related memory problems might be possible.

SUMMARY

Monitoring is the awareness or knowledge of whether our cognitive systems are successfully engaging in a particular task. Control is the behaviors a person engages in to ensure encoding or retrieval. Thus, an older adult who wants to remember more of what he reads in the newspaper may choose to read more slowly than he used to and read without music playing in the background as he used to. Metamemory monitoring is unimpaired in older adults, although metamemory control may show some deficits. The use-it-or-lose-it hypothesis refers to the view that older adults must remain cognitively active if they want to keep their memory and cognition at successful levels. Older adults can benefit from memory rehabilitation and from mnemonic techniques. Memory rehabilitation refers to interventions that clinical neuropsychologists use to promote memory performance in memory-impaired individuals. This section offered a number of specific mnemonic tips that can help healthy older adults remember more and do so more efficiently. Reduction of volume of areas critical to memory, such as the hippocampus and the prefrontal cortex, is correlated with age-related memory declines.

Section Quiz

1. Which of the following statements is true?
   a. Older adults believe that their memories are not as good as those of younger people
   b. Older adults believe that their memories are not as good as they used to be when they were younger
   c. Older adults who believe that their memory is impaired may be less likely to engage in strategic memory behaviors
   d. All of the above are true

2. Hertzog, Kidder, Powell-Moman, and Dunlosky (2002) asked younger and older adults to study word pairs. They found that
   a. Older adults showed impaired accuracy of their judgments of learning
   b. Older adults remembered few of the word pairs, but predicted that they could remember all of them
   c. Older adults showed accuracy equivalent to younger adults, and their accuracy equally benefited from a delay between study and test
   d. All of the above are true

3. In Snowdon's famous study with nuns, it was shown that
   a. Cognitive activity throughout life was associated with an increased likelihood of developing Alzheimer's disease
   b. Cognitive activity throughout life was associated with a decreased likelihood of developing Alzheimer's disease
   c. Nuns who were in the habit of doing memory competitions also did better in Scrabble tournaments
   d. All of the above are true

4. Which of these statements about the aging brain is true?
   a. Decrease in the size of white-matter tracts is associated with decreased memory ability
   b. Decrease in the size of the periaqueductal glutamin is associated with decreased memory ability

c. The brains of older adults are indistinguishable from those of younger adults

d. All of the above are true

1. d
2. c
3. b
4. a

KEY TERMS

control (in metamemory)

directed forgetting

episodic memory

hippocampus

inhibition theory

judgments of learning

memory rehabilitation

monitoring

processing speed

semantic memory

source memory

use-it-or-lose-it hypothesis

white-matter tracts

REVIEW QUESTIONS

1. What stereotypes exist with respect to the effects of aging on memory? What parts of the stereotype are true, and what parts are false?

2. Describe two memory components that decline in healthy older adults and two memory components that remain stable in these adults.

3. What is the processing-speed theory? What memory phenomena does it predict?

4. What is the inhibition theory of memory decline? What memory phenomena does it predict?

5. What working memory components are spared in aging, and what components suffer declines in memory? Describe an experiment that supports this view.

6. What evidence exists to suggest that older adults are more susceptible to false memories? What mechanisms can account for this?

7. What are metamemory beliefs? How do they change among older adults?

8. Souchay and Isingrini (2004) examined the effects of aging on metamemory control of self-paced study. What did they find?

9. What does the phrase "use it or lose it" mean with respect to memory and aging? What evidence is relevant to testing this theory?

10. What areas of the brain are associated with which memory problems in older adults?

ONLINE RESOURCES

1. For more on normal aging, go to http://memory.ucsf.edu/brain/aging/overview/.

2. For more on Dr. Salthouse's research, go to http://www.faculty.virginia.edu/cogage/? s = timothy + salthouse.

3. For more on Dr. Naveh-Benjamin's research on memory and aging, go to http://macal.missouri .edu/researchers.html.

4. For more on the misinformation effect and aging, go to https://www.babylab.ucla.edu/wp-content/uploads/sites/8/2016/09/Gredeback_etal.pdf

5. For advocates of the use-it-or-lose-it hypothesis, go to http://www.memorylossonline.com/ use_it_or_lose_it.htm.

6. For more on memory rehabilitation, go to http://www.apa.org/research/action/memory -changes.aspx.

Go to **study.sagepub.com/schwartz3e** for additional exercises and study resources. Select **Chapter 12, Memory in Older Adults** for chapter-specific resources.

CHAPTER 13

Memory Improvement and Learning Efficiency

A User's Guide

Learning and remembering are ubiquitous human activities. Learning starts almost from the moment a child is born, and evidence now suggests it occurs in the developing fetus. In Western countries, most children are in school settings by the time they are three, with formal instruction already taking place. Indeed, studies now show that children who do not attend pre-K are "behind" when they get to first grade. And this is just the beginning of lifelong learning. Many years of formal schooling ensue—and then functioning in today's world requires constant retraining, regardless of whether you are a plumber, a nurse, an auto mechanic, or an experimental psychologist. For example, an auto mechanic who trained in the late 1970s is likely to be still working today. However, the increased computerization of auto mechanics and the introduction of hybrid and cleaner engines means that repairing today's cars requires knowledge that did not exist in 1979, thus requiring continual re-training. Learning should extend even into retirement. Retired people may retrain to learn how to use cell phones and set up their computer printers. To accomplish all this, people must learn, and to learn efficiently means to learn and accomplish more. In this chapter, some evidence-based methods of improving memory are discussed.

In almost all nations in the world, most children engage in some form of formal education. In most Western countries, many young adults then attend college with the goal of learning new skills and new knowledge. In 2013, approximately 21 million people were enrolled in U.S. higher education institutions (National Center for Education Statistics, 2016). In addition, millions of people every year receive formal on-the-job training; thus, education is a part of business as well. And it does not stop there—consider the five branches of the U.S. military, which train additional tens of thousands every year, from recruits in basic training to enlisted men and women in specialist training to potential officers in the elite military academies. In terms of money, billions of dollars are spent annually to promote learning and remembering in the United States alone (and the United

States spends less of its gross domestic product on education than many other Western countries do). Thus, making learning more efficient is financially expedient and vital to national security as well.

Consider all the informal learning that goes on every day—in businesses, in homes, and often on our computers, as we are forever connected to the Internet. Many people assert that we now need to know more than ever before in our information age. Think about some of the things you may not have known about a few years ago—as they did not exist—that have nothing to do with formal training or education. These include but are not limited to how to rent movies over the Internet, how to set up your own web page, how to set your new digital watch, and where to find the best bargains in the new mall in your town. If you are a sports fan, you may have learned Stephen Curry's scoring average; if you follow celebrity gossip, you may have just learned on what day Oprah Winfrey was born. Then there are your daily activities: Did you remember to call your mother and tell her about your aunt's visit? Did you remember to tell your boyfriend or girlfriend about the concert tickets you just bought? Our lives are filled with acts of learning and remembering.

Given how much time we all spend learning and remembering, you might expect that at some point, you might get some specific instruction in how to maximize your learning and memory abilities. Unfortunately, such instruction is usually lacking (Roediger & Pyc, 2012). Very seldom do high school age students receive specific instructions in how best to master new material. Even when such instruction is given, it is usually done as an "extra," communicating to the typical high school student that his or her attention is not required. Even some college courses on human memory often skip the topic of memory improvement—you will not find an equivalent chapter in most other textbooks on this topic. There are, however, some excellent new books on the topic. One great book-length treatment of memory improvement is Brown, Roediger, and McDaniel's (2014) book, which you can find in the reference section and in a link at the end of the chapter.

It is the goal of the last chapter of this book to remedy that oversight on the part of our educational system. This chapter is intended as a guide to memory improvement and learning efficiency. It will outline how one can improve the efficiency of one's learning as well as the science behind these assertions. It cannot, however, guarantee improvement. Each individual will need to figure out what works best for him or her and then apply that technique assiduously. However, following some of the principles outlined in this book and emphasized in this chapter will certainly be part of any person's success at improving memory. But before we start, let me reiterate one of the key themes of memory improvement: Memory improvement does not come for free—it requires work and intelligent application.

Thus, hard work is incumbent even on the "memory elite." In this chapter, we will discuss memory performers—these are people with truly fantastic innate memory abilities. Yet, they too must work hard to maximize their memory performance (Foer, 2011). So, yes, there are clearly individual differences in the ability to learn, process information, and remember it later, but even the most intelligent and gifted must work to learn. This chapter will provide some guidelines as to how to make the work you put in give you the most learning for the time spent. In other words, this chapter offers tips as to how to make your study time more efficient. It does so by reviewing and summarizing the various mnemonic tips that you have already read in the earlier chapters.

Over the course of the first 12 chapters, 21 mnemonic improvement hints have been offered to help you bolster your ability to learn and remember. All 21 can be found in abbreviated form in Table 13.1 at the end of this chapter. However, by now, you should recognize that 21 hints puts quite a bit of strain on a person's memory to remember. Could you list all 21 hints? It is likely that few readers of this book can, despite the fact that you studied each one before your exams for your memory course. The paradox here is that to use the mnemonic hints, you must be able to remember them. And 21 hints are a lot to retain. In addition, each hint applies under slightly different situations, so you also have to remember which hint is appropriate under which set of circumstances. Proposed here is a way to organize the 21 hints into just four broad principles, which are a lot easier to remember.

The first principle is to **process for meaning**. As you learn new material, focus on what it means. Several of the hints are related to the importance of meaning-based processing in learning. For example, Mnemonic Improvement Hint 4.1 advises you to use elaborative encoding. By relating new information to knowledge we already have, we focus on the meaning of the stimuli. A corollary of this principle is that we need to avoid distraction. When we are distracted, we no longer direct attention to meaning in terms of what we want to learn and remember. When our attention is distracted, it is more difficult to focus on meaning. Think of this in terms of being on a social media site during a class. The comings and goings of your friends on Snapchat engage your attention, and you lose the thread of the professor's lecture, even though the words are still entering your ears. So, one can improve the efficiency of learning by limiting distractions. In practice, this may mean putting one's cell phone away or closing one's Facebook connection.

> **Process for meaning:** As you learn new material, focus on what it means.

The second principle is to engage in **retrieval practice**. Many of the hints promote the generation and retrieval of a particular item as a strong reinforcer of that learning. Think of Mnemonic Improvement Hint 4.2, the generation effect. By generating the item that we need to learn, we strengthen the memory trace much more than by reading the item, leading to a strong boost in long-term retention. Retrieval practice can be interpreted as self-testing, though we benefit from formal testing as well. In the section on retrieval practice, we will also introduce the concept of encoding variability, a method that capitalizes on increasing the number of retrieval cues to improve memory efficiency. More and more research shows just how effective retrieval practice can be for helping us learn more efficiently (Mulligan & Picklesimer, 2016).

> **Retrieval practice:** Generate and practice the items you need to remember from memory rather than simply read or restudy them. Retrieval practice means self-testing.

The third principle is to use **metamemory**. Metamemory refers to our awareness and knowledge of our own memories. By careful and deliberate monitoring of what you have learned and what you still need to know, you can guide your learning

> **Metamemory:** Our knowledge and awareness of our own memory processes.

in efficient ways. For example, Mnemonic Improvement Hint 1.3 reminds you that memory does not come for free—you have to work at it. This metacognitive knowledge compels you to spend more time engaged in study behaviors. We will also present research that identifies failures of metamemory. Thus, using metamemory to improve learning efficiency is fraught with potential problems. One must understand the advantages and disadvantages of using metamemory in order to improve learning efficiency. But by being aware of metamemory failures, we can compensate for them.

Finally, the fourth principle is that **distributed learning or practice** is superior to massed learning or practice. This means that spreading out your studying over time is superior to cramming. This goes against the folk wisdom that you can always prepare last minute by cramming. With busy schedules, students have a tendency to cram, but this strategy shortchanges them. While cramming is better than nothing, it is a remarkably inefficient way of learning. A little distributed practice goes a long way toward improved memory efficiency. Mnemonic Improvement Hint 1.2 embodies this principle.

> **Distributed learning or practice:** Spacing one's study over time can lead to faster acquisition of information.

Many cognitive psychologists interested in learning efficiency would concur with these four broad principles (see Brown et al., 2014; Roediger & Pyc, 2012; Willingham, 2009). (For a related approach to memory improvement, based on Daniel Willingham's ideas, go to www.sage pub.com/schwartz3e.[1])

Let's examine each of these principles in detail.

1. PROCESS FOR MEANING

Think about the "washing clothes" story introduced in Chapter 5. Bransford and Johnson (1972) asked two groups of participants to read a story. One group had few clues as to what the story was about, whereas the other group knew the title of the story, namely, "Washing Clothes." The participants who knew the title remembered more details from the story than those who did not have the title, even though both groups had the same amount of time to learn the material. Why did the title group do better? Because the group that knew the title was better able to process for meaning. The title provided meaning and therefore structure to the otherwise confusing passage. The title allowed the reader to process the confusing sentences in terms of what they actually meant, because it facilitated tapping existing knowledge bases with which to associate the new material. Thus, the meaning implied in the title led to efficient memory. Both groups had the same amount of study time, but the group that was also better able to process for meaning remembered more from the story.

Now apply this to the learning one typically does in a college course. In a college course, facts (e.g., "Berlin is the capital of Germany") are usually less crucial than concepts ("Berlin was made the capital after the unification of Germany in 1990 following the fall of the Berlin Wall in 1989. Berlin was also the capital of a united Germany before the end of World War II. What do these facts tell us about German nationalism?"). In our technological, urban Western world, meaning is far more a significant aspect of our world than sensory characteristics. Thus, our teachers generally focus on meaning, and—this is critical—we are mostly tested on meaning-based material. Textbook authors do not put some terms in bold and dark lettering like **this** because we want you to remember which words are in boldface. We use boldface, because those words carry important meaning in a particular section and we want to draw your attention to them. Similarly, your diving instructor does not care if you remember whether he or she was wearing a blue wetsuit or a black wetsuit during your practice dive. Rather, the instructor wants you to remember why you need to ascend slowly (avoiding decompression sickness), why you can stay only a few minutes at depths of over 100 feet (buildup of nitrogen in the blood), and why you can remain much longer when diving at 30 feet (less buildup of nitrogen). Thus, in general, processing for meaning works because it conforms to the demands of your teacher, who will generally emphasize meaning.

A review of the mnemonic hints in Table 13.1 will demonstrate how many are related to the principle of "process for meaning." Mnemonic Improvement Hints 4.1 to 4.4, 6.1 to 6.3, 7.1, and 11.1 all make use of process for meaning to one degree or another. Hints 4.1 through 4.4 are all about processing for meaning. Thus, one of the most reliable ways of improving your memory is to focus on levels of processing—specifically, processing for meaning.

Consider the mnemonic improvement hint that advises you to organize what you are learning (4.3). Organization has a long and distinguished history of helping memory (Tulving, 1962). The best way to organize material is in relation to oneself in a strategy known as **subjective organization** (Tulving, 1962). Thus, in studying, you may want to reorganize the information given to you and make up your own organization. For a budding musician, using musical principles to organize biology or history may be helpful. For a musician, written music is a well-learned and meaningful body of knowledge that

> **Subjective organization:** In studying, you may want to reorganize the information given to you and make up your own organization.

can be used as an organizing principle for scaffolding new information, such as the bones of the body. Conversely, a doctor attempting to learn the cello as an adult may want to use this process in reverse. The names of the bones may help the doctor as an organizational scheme for remembering musical notation.

Indeed, research shows that when students are forced to organize the material themselves, they remember more than when someone else provides the organization. This is true even when the external organization derives from an expert on the subject matter. In one experimental demonstration, Mannes and Kintsch (1987) gave one group of students well-organized outlines of material on which they would be tested. The outlines, prepared by professionals, provided a logical and coherent manner in which to study for the test. A second group was given a disorganized outline. It contained all of the same facts and did not contain any errors, but there was no logical and coherent sequence to it. There were two interesting outcomes. First, students judged the organized outlines as more helpful and liked them better than the disorganized ones. Second, the first group did better on simple memory tasks, such as recognition, but the second group learned in a deeper, more flexible way that gave them an advantage when they were asked to solve problems and make inferences. Why? Well, the second group of students had to employ

Figure 13.1 Students learned more when the review sheet was disorganized but free of errors. The *Y*-axis represents the number of items recalled.

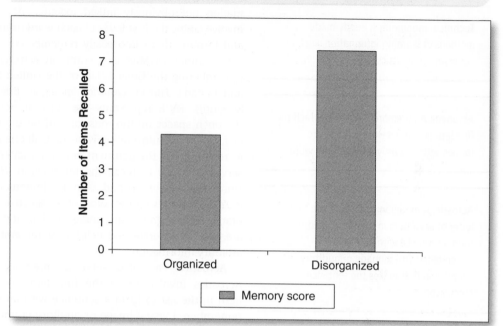

SOURCE: Based on Christina and Bjork (1991).

their own personalized organizational strategies to learn the material rather than rely on the already prepared outlines. This forced them into using self-organization and focusing on the meaning of the stimuli in a way not required of the other students. The self-organization that they supplied led to better performance than the logical, professional, but impersonal outline provided by the experimenters. This study demonstrates the need for students to organize material themselves into meaningful patterns (see Christina & Bjork, 1991; see Figure 13.1).

This presents a conundrum for teachers. If a teacher wants students to like him or her and give good evaluations, that teacher should provide them with careful, well-organized notes and outlines. This will make the students feel like they are learning easily. However, if the teacher wants the students to learn more, he or she will give them disorganized outlines that will force them to learn the material themselves. The students will be less satisfied with the teaching but will understand more information from the class.

Technical Mnemonics

A few technical mnemonics take advantage of subjective organization. These mnemonics can often be quite useful in remembering arbitrary lists. By and large, they employ simple meaning-based schemes that are useful for the memory of items unrelated to that scheme. **Technical mnemonics** refer to ready-made methods of learning information.

Technical mnemonics: Ready-made methods of learning information, such as acronyms or acrostics.

Acronym: A mnemonic device in which the first letters of each word in a list are formed into an easily remembered word.

Acrostic: A mnemonic in which the first letter of each item in the list is used to form a sentence with an easily remembered visual image or auditory connection that makes the sentence memorable.

Acronyms can be used to help learn lists of information not obviously linked together. Acronyms involve taking the first letter of each word from a list and forming them into easily remembered words. For example, HOMES is a common acronym for remembering the Great Lakes of the United States and Canada (Huron, Ontario, Michigan, Erie, and Superior). FACE represents the musical notes in the open spaces on the musical staff on the treble clef. When the information is needed, all one needs to remember is the acronym, and each letter then serves as a cue to recall the information. *H* cues Huron, *O* cues Ontario, and so on. The famous, if silly, ROY G BIV stands for the colors of the spectrum (red, orange, yellow, green, blue, indigo, violet). Acronyms are easy to generate and helpful for remembering arbitrary information.

Acrostics can also serve as memory aids. Acrostics involve using the first letter of each item in the list to form a sentence with an easily remembered visual image or auditory connection that makes the sentence memorable. When the information needs to be retrieved, it can be unpacked from the acrostic. For example, a famous acrostic is "Every Good Boy Does Fine." The first letter specifies the musical note on the line in the treble clef in musical notation. "Beautiful People Wear Clothes" is an acrostic to remember that Broca's area (*B*) of the brain is involved with the production (*P*) of language and Wernicke's area (*W*) is responsible for comprehension (*C*) of language.

Both of these mnemonics employ organizational principles that may be lacking in the material itself. For example, the naming of the parts of the brain is an historical accident— nor is the logic apparent in the names of the Great Lakes. When we devise our acronym or acrostic, we supply organization that helps us encode that information.

Avoid Distraction to Enhance Meaning and Retention

In our culture, there is constant buzz about the advantages and disadvantages of our technological innovations. Parents lament how much time their kids spend texting, while they themselves spend endless hours talking and driving, a far more dangerous choice. As professors, when we look out at our classes, we seldom see eyes watching us anymore. Students' attention is buried in their laptops, cell phones, and tablets. Our goal here is not to pass judgment on the current status of technology and our culture but to give you an advantage in learning efficiently. And the data here are quite clear: Divided attention prevents processing for meaning, which lowers one's memory efficiency (Hollis & Was, 2016).

Thus, an easy way to improve your learning is to leave the electronics behind when you attend a lecture and turn off your cell phone when you study. The data on this point will be reviewed here.

Smith, Isaak, Senette, and Abadie (2011) examined the effects of texting while studying. They divided participants into two groups, one of which was not allowed to use cell phones and a second group that was encouraged to text while studying. The participants studied DRM lists—that is, lists of related items associated with an absent word known as the critical intrusion. After studying the lists, participants were first given a recognition test of items from the list. The results were clear. Recognition performance was much higher in the non-distracted group than in the distracted group. It is worth noting, however, that texting did not increase the likelihood of false memories in this study. However, Otgaar, Peters, and Howe (2012) found that divided attention both lowered correct recall and increased false recall in the DRM paradigm in adults. The bottom line, of course: Texting while studying hurts performance!

These data are consistent with many studies that show that divided attention or distraction can interfere with memory performance across a wide range of memory tests. Brewer, Ball, Knight, Dewitt, and Marsh (2011), for example, found that participants with divided attention showed an impairment on prospective memory tests. This means that when one is distracted, such as by texting or doing other activities, one is less likely to remember the things one needs to do, such as an appointment. Parker, Dagnall, and Munley (2012) showed that divided attention interfered with category-cued recall, a paradigm similar to the kinds of learning one does for a school-related test. It is likely that at least some of the reduced performance seen in divided-attention tasks is because participants are no longer able to direct their attention to the meaning of the to-be-learned material. When they are no longer focusing on meaning, their ability to encode those items is reduced. Thus, a very practical bit of advice is that, when you really want to learn something, avoid being distracted by competing stimuli.

There are also effects of chronic distraction on memory. People who frequently place themselves in situations in which they are multitasking are putting themselves at risk of creating long-lasting problems with memory efficiency. This was recently tested by Uncapher, Thieu, and Wagner (2016). They found that chronic multitaskers performed worse on working-memory tests and long-term memory tests even when they were not multitasking. Thus, even when trying to focus on a single-task, chronic multitaskers looked for distractions, and these distractions lowered their ability to learn and remember.

2. ENGAGE IN RETRIEVAL PRACTICE

The second broad principle in improving memory is to test oneself. Across a large range of situations, self-testing, classroom testing, and other forms of testing lead to strong memory traces and more long-term retention than simply restudying or rereading material. Across many experiments and classroom studies, the advantages of retrieval practice are now well documented. Retrieval practice can help the learning of introductory psychology, foreign language vocabulary, general knowledge facts, visual materials, and middle-school science (Carpenter et al., 2016; Rawson & Dunlosky, 2011; Roediger & Pyc, 2012; Trumbo et al., 2016).

Retrieval practice means to learn by testing oneself—that is, making yourself retrieve information. Retrieval practice is currently an important topic of cognitive research, but it is also an easily applied principle of learning and remembering. Research shows that a trial of testing oneself is superior to a trial of restudy (see Kornell & Bjork, 2007). As an example, consider a student who must memorize a lengthy passage from a Shakespeare play. Once the information has been studied to the point at which the student is beginning to memorize the lines but is still shaky with them, he or she can consider two options: (1) Continue to read over the lines or (2) practice saying them, and when he or she makes a mistake, get feedback from a listener. A volume of research demonstrates that retrieval practice or the generation of the lines themselves produces quicker learning than reading them. Likewise, learning a new vocabulary word in French is quicker when you repeatedly test yourself (as in, *monkey*—?) than when you simply read the association (*monkey–le singe*). The act of retrieving creates stronger associations between cues and targets than does simply restudying the items (Carpenter et al., 2016; Karpicke & Roediger, 2008; see Figure 13.2).

Consider a landmark study in this domain. Roediger and Karpicke (2006) focused attention on the advantages of retrieval practice. They asked participants to read short prose passages concerning scientific information. One group of participants simply restudied the items several times. A second group read the same passage but then was asked to recall information about the story on three practice tests. One week later, the participants returned and were retested on the information. The testing group outperformed the restudy group. In fact, the testing group recalled 50% more information than did the restudy group. This study clearly shows how important testing yourself is to acquiring information.

Retrieval practice can either be self-initiated or provided to students by instructors. For example, many teachers will provide practice quizzes for material in the class for which you are reading this book. Though students generally see these quizzes as opportunities to find out how prepared they are, taking the quizzes is also an effective learning tool. Research again shows that taking such practice tests is more effective than restudying (McDaniel, Roediger, & McDermott, 2007). In another study, Campbell and Mayer (2009) tested college students during classes. In one condition, students in an educational psychology class received a PowerPoint presentation that included questions. Another set of PowerPoints included only statements. The students who saw the questions later remembered more from the lecture than those who had only read statements. In yet another study, Trumbo et al. (2016) showed that quiz performance in an introductory psychology course improved for the students who were assigned to a retrieval-practice condition.

The effects of retrieval practice on efficient learning also hold up in light of a number of features that might affect real students. For example, an interesting feature of the testing effect is that even generating a wrong answer leads to better retention of the correct answer, if there is feedback, than simply restudy the item. Huesler and Metcalfe (2012) asked participants to study cue-target word pairs. Some participants reread the items, whereas other students generated the targets. If a participant reported an incorrect target, the researchers gave him or her corrective feedback. They found that participants who generated the wrong answer remembered more correct answers later than those who had simply read the answer. This addresses one of the criticisms of self-testing: Some have suggested that it does not work in the real world, because students might retrieve and therefore study the wrong information. However, as long as students have access to the correct answer, generating an incorrect answer is not a problem and indeed, is better than restudying. Metcalfe and Finn (2011) even showed that high-confidence wrong answers, once corrected, lead to good recall of the actual target, provided that the wrong answer was generated. In this experiment, if a participant reported with high confidence that Sydney was the capital of Australia, he or she would later better recall that it is actually Canberra relative to a wrong answer generated with less confidence. Thus, students need not fear generating wrong answers in practice, as doing so produces better learning than does restudying correct answers.

Although retrieval practice can have profound benefits for learning, most people, by and large, are unaware of the huge advantage it affords on learning. People have poor metacognitive knowledge concerning the advantages of retrieval practice. Bjork, Dunlosky, and Kornell (2013) pointed out that even students who self-test to determine their level of preparation are often unaware of the positive consequences of self-testing on learning. Some student may self-test to help determine which items they need to restudy but are not aware that the self-testing actually is studying. Moreover, Jönsson, Hedner, and Olsson (2012) did not find that judgments of learning were higher for retrieval practice items than for studied items. This means that even after self-testing, we do not feel like those items are more well learned than those we just read, even though they are. It is therefore incumbent on memory scientists to spread the word: Retrieval practice helps. Use it (Brown et al., 2014; Roediger & Pyc, 2012)!

Earlier we discussed a paradigm called the **generation effect**, which is consistent with the notion of retrieval practice. In the generation effect, a person generates the to-be-remembered target either by following a rule (e.g., generate a word that rhymes with *head* and starts with a *b*) or by simply reading the association (e.g., *head–bed*). The data show that participants remember the generated associations better than the read associations (Slamecka & Graf, 1978). Again, the act of producing the to-be-remembered item oneself produces cues, which will later be useful in recall.

> **Generation effect:** Memory is better when we generate associations ourselves than when we simply read them.

Thus, a generalization we can make about memory improvement is the following: Test thyself. Repeatedly generating target answers and testing your knowledge base produces the cues that lead to good memory later. This is a pretty easy rule to follow. Most textbooks have test banks that go along with them or review questions at the end of the chapter. The memory-conscious student can employ these educational tools. Ten minutes spent answering the review questions at the end of this chapter will promote better long-term learning of the material than 10 minutes spent rereading various sections. If questions are not provided by your textbook, you can make flashcards—either on regular index cards or the equivalent in computer files—that have a question on one side and the answer

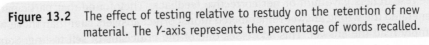

Figure 13.2 The effect of testing relative to restudy on the retention of new material. The *Y*-axis represents the percentage of words recalled.

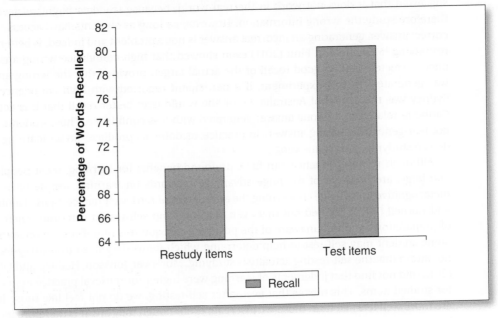

SOURCE: Based on Karpicke and Roediger (2008).

on the back. Try answering the question before you check the back. This strategy will allow you to benefit from the generation effect. Making your own flashcards has an additional advantage: Writing down the questions and the answers when you make the cards provides an additional study trial. (For more on the advantages of self-testing and other mnemonic techniques, go to study.sagepub.com/schwartz3e.[2])

Retrieval Cues and Encoding Variability

A related technique that can be used to improve memory efficiency is to create good retrieval cues for oneself. By making a variety of good retrieval cues, one may later have the right hook to retrieve a particular memory or fact. Think about the following familiar situation. You are in your English literature class. You are sitting in front of a blank piece of paper. Your exam essay is to write a short description of the character Horatio in Shakespeare's play *Hamlet* and comment on his influence on the protagonist, so you are trying to remember something about the character of Horatio. But you are drawing a blank. You know you read the play, and you think you got the gist out of it: A man is trying to avenge his father's murder but gets bogged down in uncertainty about whether to believe a ghost. But there were so many funny names that it was hard to keep track of them all.

Was Horatio one of the friends who betrayed Hamlet to his evil uncle? Or was Horatio Polonius's son? The failure here is not one of learning but one of retrieval. You do not have the correct retrieval cue. If the question had contained information about Horatio's role, such as "Hamlet's friend Horatio, who also witnessed seeing the ghost, influences Hamlet in certain ways," this would have instantly triggered the associations of Hamlet's close friend and his role in the play, and then you would have been able to tackle the essay without any difficulty. Armed with the extra information that functions as a retrieval cue, you would now be able to write a stellar essay.

Cues are bits of information provided by either the external environment or your own imagination. Cues are triggers that help us recall the information that is associated with them. As we discussed in Chapter 4, the right cue can bring back a long-lost memory. You might not have thought of the vacation you took to the woodlands of Minnesota when you were a child for a long time. But when your father or mother says, "Remember when we were staying at the fishing lodge, and you caught a large trout?" this cue then elicits your memory of struggling to land the feisty fish. You may not have known you could remember this event until your parent provided the correct retrieval cue.

Students can also rely on the structuring of retrieval cues in a number of different ways. If we learn in such a way that we know what the relevant retrieval cues will be later, we can perform better by ensuring that those retrieval cues are present at the time of test. This means controlling the encoding environment so that it produces usable cues that will be present at the time of retrieval. **Encoding variability** means that multiple encoding conditions produce good recall, because encoding under a variety of conditions provides lots of different cues, which can then be taken advantage of at the time of retrieval. By chance, it is more likely that one of these conditions will be present at the time of retrieval than if the encoding had taken place under homogeneous conditions. Thus, encoding variability produces good memory (Verkoeijen, Rikers, & Özsoy, 2008).

> **Encoding variability:** The principle that if you study an item of information under several mental and physical conditions, you will be more likely to remember it than if you had studied for the same amount of time or number of trials but under uniform conditions.

The encoding variability principle claims if you study an item of information under several different mental and physical conditions, you will be more likely to remember it than if you had studied for the same amount of time or number of trials but under uniform conditions. So, if you want to remember a particular piece of information (i.e., Julius Caesar lived from 100 BCE to 44 BCE), it is best to study it under a variety of conditions, such as when you are tired and angry, in your dorm room and in the library. Then, when you are asked about the facts of Julius Caesar's life in your history class, you have a number of different cues to remember this information. You may be tired when you take the test, in which cases the cues acquired when you studied when tired will be useful. You may be feeling angry for one reason or another when you take the test, and therefore your "angry" cues will be useful. Consider the scenario when you study only when you are well rested, happy, and in your dorm room. You may establish a series of cues that are associated with each of those states. When you take the exam, you may be tired, unhappy about something or other, and in the classroom. Not having studied in different states will leave you with fewer retrieval cues to rely on than if you had studied under more diverse conditions. Therefore, you can use encoding variability to study more efficiently and boost memory performance (Soraci et al., 1999).

Encoding variability ensures that you will have created a range of cues for the information. At the time of test, the **encoding specificity** principle applies—that is, if retrieval conditions match encoding conditions, recall will be maximized. The problem is that you may not always know what the retrieval conditions will be. It may be that the test will take place on a sunny day in which you are a bit tired but feel good about the world. The test may also take place on a rainy day in which you are agitated and angry, because you just had an argument with

> **Encoding specificity:** Retrieval of information from memory will be maximized when the conditions at retrieval match the conditions at encoding.

your boyfriend or girlfriend. If you studied under both sets of conditions—that is, encoding variability—you will be able to make use of the encoding specificity principle at the time of test, as either condition at test was preceded by study in the same condition.

Encoding variability can be taken advantage of to improve the efficiency of one's learning. It also can be combined with retrieval practice, which likewise improves the efficiency of one's learning. As with processing for meaning, both encoding variability and retrieval practice require active learning on the part of the student or other learner. One must plan one's study and engage with the material. Indeed, much research is ongoing to understand why retrieval practice is such a powerful learning enhancer (Carpenter et al., 2016). We now turn to the next memory improvement principle, which also emphasizes the advantages of active learning.

SECTION SUMMARY AND QUIZ

This chapter focuses on how each of us can improve our memory by learning and remembering more efficiently. Four major principles have been emphasized: (1) Process for meaning, (2) employ retrieval practice, (3) use metamemory, and (4) make use of distributed practice. Each of these individually can improve learning efficiency, and certainly in combination, they can make your learning and remembering far more efficient. In this chapter, the various mnemonic improvement hints given throughout the book are organized according to these four memory principles. Process for meaning covers a number of topics. First, it implies that elaborative encoding or distinctive encoding lend to more efficient learning. Processing for meaning also means avoiding activities that distract one from using meaning-based strategies. Thus, multitasking and other distractions cause us to not process information meaningfully, leading to less efficient learning. Retrieval practice is an important efficiency tool. A block of time devoted to self-testing (or retrieval practice) leads to better long-term retention than rereading the information. Encoding variability means that, if you study an item of information under several mental and physical conditions, you will be more likely to remember it than if you had studied for the same amount of time or number of trials but under uniform conditions.

Section Quiz

1. Which of the following is not a principle of memory efficiency?
   a. Process for meaning
   b. Use metamemory
   c. Use distributed learning
   d. Employ visual mnemonics whenever possible

2. In studying, that you may want to reorganize the information given to you and make up your own organization is known as
   a. Self-retrieval
   b. The self-testing effect
   c. Subjective organization
   d. Inferential reorganization

3. Roediger and Karpicke (2006) asked participants to read short prose passages concerning scientific information. One group of participants simply restudied the items several times. A second group read the same passage but then was asked to recall information about the story on three practice tests. They found that
   a. The group that recalled information during study did best on the final test
   b. The group that restudied information during study did best on the final test
   c. Only groups that received encoding variability improved on the task
   d. None of the above are true

4. Which of the following would be considered encoding variability?
   a. Engaging in retrieval practice immediately after first studying information
   b. Using technical mnemonics, such as acronyms, to help learn arbitrary information
   c. Studying the same material when you are in a number of different moods, so that one of those moods will match the one you will be in when you are tested
   d. Rejecting technical mnemonics and avoiding distraction

1. d
2. c
3. a
4. c

3. USE METAMEMORY

The importance of metamemory is generally underestimated in memory improvement programs and books. These books emphasize imagery and other memory tricks and seldom mention the important role of conscious control over the learning environment.

However, cognitive psychology is showing an increasing understanding of the role that metamemory plays in ordinary learning and remembering and the role it plays in memory improvement (Kornell & Finn, 2016; Schwartz & Efklides, 2012). *Metamemory* means our awareness and knowledge of our own memories. This awareness ("I know this material really well") and knowledge ("I am good at remembering names," or "I know very little about dog shows") can be used to structure our learning and remembering. For example, when asked to recall the mailing address of your third cousin twice removed, you may know immediately that you do not know this bit of information. This awareness can spur a number of responses. You can look up the address on the Internet or call another cousin to get it. But your awareness of your lack of knowledge allows you to make a decision. A student studying vocabulary can quickly assess whether he or she has learned all of the items. On the basis of this assessment, he or she can then decide either to continue studying or to get a good night's rest. Metamemory can play a role in memory improvement both at the time of encoding and at the time of retrieval.

The message of this section is the following. Studies show that metamemory is good at distinguishing difficult items from easy ones. Thus, we can use our metamemory judgments to determine which items need to be studied more and which items need to be studied a bit less. However, our metamemory tends to be overconfident so that we overestimate the likelihood that we will remember and underestimate the likelihood that we will forget. This may lead us to not study enough. So, although we may use our judgments of learning to determine which items to study, we should not rely on them to determine how long or in what manner to study (Kornell & Finn, 2016; Schwartz & Efklides, 2012).

Judgments of Learning as Mnemonic Improvement Tools

Judgments of learning are made during study and concern the likelihood of remembering an item later. As discussed in Chapter 9, judgments of learning are both accurate at predicting future performance and useful as a guide to which items to restudy. Consider the use of judgments of learning in encoding. While studying, you can assess how well you have learned particular items. For example, while studying for a Spanish vocabulary test, you can make judgments of learning on English Spanish word pairs (e.g., *railroad–el ferrocarril*). Making judgments of learning can offer a number of distinct memory advantages. First, if you use the delayed judgment of learning effect (that is, wait a few minutes after studying the item and then cue yourself with only the cue word, in this case, the English word), you can make more accurate judgments of learning as well as benefit from the retrieval practice (Jönsson et al., 2012). Second, making judgments of learning provides you with feedback as to what you have learned and what you have not. Having made judgments of learning for the various items, you are now in a position to decide what you need to restudy. You probably do not need to study further those items to which you gave high judgments of learning. However, those items that you gave lower judgments of learning need more time and more study trials (Kornell et al., 2011).

Judgments of learning: Judgments during study of whether the item has been learned already.

How does this improve memory? The act of making a judgment of learning itself appears not to improve memory more than the equivalent amount of time spent studying the item, although this has been the subject to debate within the field (see Dunlosky & Metcalfe, 2009; Jönsson et al., 2012). Instead, judgments of learning can be used to improve memory by allowing us to direct our time, energy, and effort toward those items for which we need the most study. Consider if you studied all the items a second time for an equal amount of time each. You would essentially be wasting study time on the easy items that you have already mastered and might not study the more difficult items enough. Instead, by making judgments of learning and knowing which are easier and more difficult items, you can concentrate your study on the items you need to learn. Thus, in the same amount of time, you can learn more information by not focusing on items you already know.

The output of judgments of learning can also inform our learning in a second manner. It can allow us to adaptively control our study behavior, depending on our goals and our circumstances. For one class, for example, you may be aiming for an *A* because you really want to do well in that class. In another class, you may be satisfied to just get by, perhaps because it is a general requirement and not part of your major, perhaps because it is just plain difficult, and perhaps because it is less interesting. Thus, the goal of one class is perfection, but for the other class, it is just to master enough to pass the course. You can use judgments of learning to adjust to these different goals. In the class where you want the *A*, you must study even the most difficult items, but in the other class, you might just study the easier items and perhaps a few difficult items to earn a *C*. Interestingly, this approach to study has now been formalized into a model of memory study called the **region of proximal learning**, developed by Janet Metcalfe and her colleagues (see Metcalfe & Kornell, 2005; Xu & Metcalfe, 2016). (For more on this topic, go to study.sagepub.com/schwartz3e.[3])

> **Region of proximal learning:** A theory of metamemory that advances that an adaptive learning strategy is to study those items that have not yet been learned but are not too difficult—those at the leading edge of difficulty.

According to this theory, we maximize our learning by studying at the leading edge of difficulty. We maximize our learning by studying the easiest of the items we have not mastered yet. We do not need to restudy the items we have learned already—this would be an inefficient use of our time. Also, we do not exactly know how much time we will have to prepare or how much time we would need to master the highest-difficulty items, so we might sacrifice too much time if we focus on the most difficult items first. So we study the least difficult of the ones we have not yet mastered. Figure 13.3 shows this triage of study material. But then we should direct our attention to those items that we think we can master in the shortest amount of time and retain for the longest. We can only do so by focusing on the judgments of learning we have made about these items.

We seldom know exactly how much time we need to study or how much time we have to study. You do not know ahead of time that you will have to drive to the airport to pick up your cousin or that a friend will need to speak to you after a bad breakup with a boy-friend or girlfriend. Thus, at times, our ability to learn or prepare for a test will be cut off before we are satisfied. If our study time turns out to be limited, and we cannot study all

Figure 13.3   The region of proximal learning stipulates that the most efficient manner of studying is to study the easiest items we have not yet learned. This is illustrated by the relation of judgments of learning (JOLs) to study time decisions in this figure.

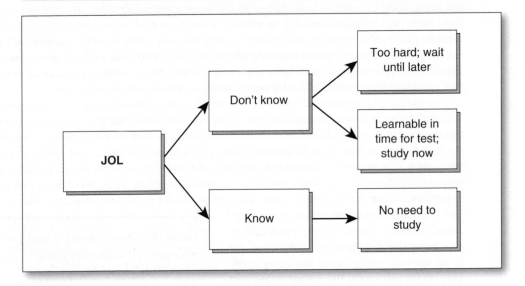

the items, we are better off learning as many items as possible in the time that we have. Thus, by focusing on the easiest of the not-yet-mastered items, we will learn more of these items than if we had started with the most difficult of the not-yet-mastered items and then progressed to easier items. If it turns out we have enough time to focus on the most difficult items, then we can do so, but these items are attempted only once all other items have been learned.

Thus, judgments of learning can be used as a screen to determine the difficulty of items, given that easy items require less study than difficult items. Moderately difficult items ought to be studied before the most extremely difficult items. Depending on how much total study time you have, you can master more and more of the difficult items. The efficient way to study is to always study the easiest item not yet learned so as to master the most amount of the material if your study time is suddenly curtailed.

Stability Bias

One of the original authors of the region of proximal learning model, Nate Kornell, has more recently described a phenomenon that limits the usefulness of the proximal-learning model. He and his colleagues called the phenomenon **stability bias** (Kornell, 2011). Stability bias is an inherent flaw in how metacognition works. Stability bias leads to poor judgments and poor decision-making. Thus, being aware of stability bias may allow you to account for it or overcome it. Stability bias means that we tend to underestimate the advantages of further study and underestimate future forgetting based on what we can retrieve now. Thus, stability bias has two components: We discount the advantages of future studying, and we discount the likelihood that we will forget what we remember now. Thus, if I have now learned that Canberra is the capital of Australia, I will underestimate the likelihood that I will forget that fact later and underestimate the helpfulness of future study. This has important implications for the usefulness of judgments of learning as study tools.

> **Stability bias:** Underestimating future forgetting and overestimating future remembering based on what we can retrieve now.

To test the idea of stability bias, Kornell and Bjork (2009) conducted 12 experiments. Participants were instructed to study some paired associates one time and other paired associates four times, and then they took a cued-recall test. Not surprisingly, recall increased across the learning trials, with more trials leading to better recall performance. But judgments of learning did not track this; judgments of learning given on individual paired associates did not increase across the learning sessions. This means that participants were, by and large, unaware of the strengthening of each memory trace that came from further study, though, of course, they knew that, in general, continued study means more learning. They just did not apply that understanding to individual items. If students do not see the advantage of further study on individual items, they may choose not to study, even though continued study would improve performance. This tendency leads to the proverbial complaint among students that they studied really hard but did not do well on the test. This experience may be, in part, fueled by the failure to anticipate the benefits of continued study. "Studying hard" does not mean studying enough.

Stability bias also means that we underestimate forgetting—that is, we do not anticipate how much information we will forget over time. For example, Koriat, Bjork, Sheffer, and Bar (2004) examined people's abilities to anticipate forgetting. Two groups of participants studied paired associates and then made judgments of learning. One group's judgments of learning were directed at a test to be taken in 10 minutes, whereas the other group's judgments of learning were directed at a test to be taken one week later. Despite the difference in the anticipated retention interval, the judgments of learning were identical. At test, those in the one-week retention interval group recalled fewer items than those in the 10-minute retention interval group. The judgments of learning did not predict the certainty of forgetting, especially over longer retention intervals. In sum, stability bias demonstrates both a failure to appreciate the value of continued study and a failure to anticipate forgetting. To counter the effects of stability bias and overconfidence, learners should continue to study learned items by engaging in retrieval practice, in addition to attacking unlearned items.

To summarize, judgments of learning are useful in distinguishing between easy items and difficult items (Schwartz & Efklides, 2012). This is helpful, as it allows us to make control decisions about what to study. Given different time constraints, we might want to focus more on easy items or difficult items. The region of proximal learning model suggests that we study the easiest items not yet mastered. This will maximize our learning by allowing the most learning to take place per unit of time. However, the stability bias suggests that our judgments of learning are overconfident. We discount forgetting and also underestimate the advantages of overlearning. Thus, an efficient learner will also restudy items that he thinks are already learned to avoid the pitfall of stability bias. So the take-home message here is that judgments of learning can be successfully used to distinguish between easy and difficult items, but that we need to study even after we feel like we have learned the material.

These aspects of metamemory involve the continuous monitoring of one's own knowledge and the continuous use of this monitoring to make informed decisions about learning and memory. This approach to memory improvement is called **self-regulated learning**. Research shows that self-regulated learning is superior to learning in which others, even experts, decide which items a person should study (Kornell & Bjork, 2008). This is because only each individual can know which items are distinctive (and therefore easy) or confusing for that individual. We now turn to the next broad principle that drives memory improvement.

> **Self-regulated learning:** The continuous monitoring of one's own knowledge and the continuous use of this monitoring to make informed decisions about learning and memory.

4. DISTRIBUTE YOUR PRACTICE

Distributed practice means that long-term retention is enhanced when we spread out our study over time as compared to studying all at once. This particular principle applies across many learning domains, not just studying for exams or mastering a new language. Distributed practice is superior to massed practice in learning new skills, varying from playing a musical instrument, typing, sewing, playing basketball, and even driving a tank. However, this section will focus on the advantages of distributed practice for encoding information, such as school-related learning, into long-term memory (Paik & Ritter, 2016; Roediger & Pyc, 2012).

> **Distributed practice:** Spacing study out over time.

Avoid Cramming: Massed Versus Distributed Practice

Every college student has found herself in this situation. It is the night before the big test, and you have not yet even started reading the textbook chapters that will be covered on the exam. Because of other commitments, you have also missed several class sessions. So you are essentially starting to prepare for this exam from scratch! Students call this "cramming." It is a staple of college life, yet it is a remarkably inefficient manner of learning. The memory improvement tip offered here is to avoid cramming.

The technical term for cramming is *massed practice*. **Massed practice** means that all study occurs in one block of time. Now, massed practice has its place. It should not be completely rejected. In fact, massed practice can be employed with

> **Massed practice:** Studying entirely in one block of time.

some success right before an exam (or performance). The practice immediately before the exam will leave studied information highly accessible, and this may help on test performance. Think of the time you quickly glanced over your notes just before a professor started handing out exams. You may have noticed something in your notes that turned up on the exam. The disadvantage of massing is that, although it may render a few items highly accessible, it does little for availability. Because a student cramming for an exam is focused on a short-term issue—passing the test—the long-term goal of learning tends to be forgotten. Thus, students often fall into a pattern of cramming because it gets them through their tests, but then they remember little of the course once it is over. If you have not studied, you have no choice and must mass your study before the test. However, you can learn more effectively and do as well on the test by distributing your study. The point here for students is that cramming is remarkably inefficient. You can learn more—and do better on your tests—in less time if you used distributed practice.

Massed practice promotes little long-term retention of the practiced material. Cramming may result in enough learning to get you a passing grade on the test, but you will have to restudy it all over again to prepare for the cumulative final, almost as if the material was brand-new. More important in the long run is that you will not remember the information later—in the real world—when it might come in handy. A useful rule is that massed practice promotes accessibility—a good thing if the material is already well learned and you are about to be tested on it. But distributed practice promotes availability—a good thing if you want the information to be in your memory when you may need it later. In this sense, distributed practice is more efficient; it creates more total learning than does massed practice in less time.

Distributed practice means that practice is spread out over time. In this way, distributed practice is based on the **spacing effect**; two trials produce better retention if they are separated by more time than if they are closer together. For the college student, distributed practice means that you might spend 30 minutes every morning reading your textbook and perhaps 15 minutes reviewing the major concepts. If you do this, you may need only a short study session the night prior to the exam, because you will have already mastered the material. The short study session accomplishes the same goal as cramming would; it renders the material accessible for the test situation. Thus, you will do better on the test than the crammers and remember the information years from now. In addition, when your friends are busy cramming and feeling really stressed, you can go out for dinner with other friends, get a good night's sleep, be relaxed the next day, and still do better than your cramming friends on the exam—and then go to the beach or to a party while your crammer friends are sleeping off the all-nighter. The only negative side effect of distributing your practice? Your friends will be jealous! (For more on the differences between massed and distributed practice, go to study.sagepub.com/schwartz3e.[4])

Ample research supports this assertion (except the part about jealous friends and partying at the beach). In one study that employed methods very much akin to the learning students must do for school, Kornell (2009) asked participants to study difficult, GRE-type

> **Spacing effect:** More learning occurs when two study trials on the same information are spread out over time than when they occur successively.

words and their more common synonyms (e.g., *effulgent–brilliant*). Each word definition was presented on a computerized version of a flashcard. The "flashcards" had the difficult word on one side, and if you pressed a key, you could see the "back" of the flashcard, which had the definition or more common word. Kornell used this paradigm to compare learning under massed or distributed practice.

Kornell's (2009) participants were divided into two groups. One group learned by massing first, the other group by distributing practice first. In both the massed and the spaced conditions, participants studied each definition four times throughout the course of study. However, in the distributed condition, the group studied one big stack of flash-cards, thereby maximizing spacing. A particular word definition was not restudied until all of the other definitions had already been studied. In the massed condition, the group studied four small stacks of flashcards and was tested after each one. Thus, there was much less time between two successive study sessions of the same word definition. The total number of items was the same for the big stack of flashcards and the four smaller ones. Therefore, the difference was the amount of spacing between successive studying of a particular definition.

Kornell (2009) found that the distributed items led to better cued recall than did the massed items. And the distributed condition produced about 50% more items recalled. This is a huge effect! Imagine it: Just by employing this one memory improvement technique, you can improve your memory ability by 50%! And it is remarkably consistent across individuals. The advantage of distribution over massing was present in over 90% of the students tested. Thus, the effects of distributed practice are strong and consistent across individuals. Regardless of whether we use old-fashioned index cards or computer programs to help us learn efficiently, the spacing effect is important. Kornell's study is one of a long line of studies that demonstrates just how much better distributed practice is than massed practice. What makes Kornell's study particularly compelling is that it deals directly with materials that many students must master—if they want to be accepted into graduate school—and it deals with the manner in which many students do study.

In another study, Landauer and Bjork (1978) attempted to maximize the advantages of both massed and distributed practice by using both in a study paradigm. They devised what they called optimum rehearsal patterns. In their study, Landauer and Bjork compared standard spaced practice to something they called **expanded retrieval practice**. Expanded retrieval practice means that you initially space your study of a particular item very close together to maximize learning and the advantages of retrieval practice, but then your subsequent trials get further and further apart. Thus, you might study *book–le livre*, then study the same item again. Then, you might intersperse three other French English word pairs before you study *book–le livre* again. Next, you might intersperse eight more French English word pairs before you study *book–le livre* again. In this way, you continually remind yourself of the items and keep the pairs easily accessible but don't waste study time by short spacing.

Expanded retrieval practice: Initially spacing study of a particular item very close together to maximize learning and the advantages of retrieval practice but then spacing subsequent trials further and further apart.

The expanded retrieval practice takes advantage of the effects of cramming—that is, that studied items become easily accessible in the early phases of study—and then it takes advantage of distributed practice through the expanding spacing, which allows for restudy and permanent storage in an efficient way. This phenomenon is also one of a select few in memory science that has inspired a limerick:

You can get a great deal from rehearsal

If it just has the proper dispersal

You would just be an ass

To do it en masse

Your remembering would turn out much worsal.

—Bjork (1988, p. 399)

A caveat to the advantages of distributed practice (spacing effect) over massed practice is that people prefer to mass their practice. Indeed, in Kornell's (2009) study, even though 90 % of people did better when using distributed practice, 72 % *thought* that they did better when massing their practice. Logan, Castel, Haber, and Viehman (2012) showed that judgments of learning were not affected by massing or spacing, even though spacing led to much better recall. This metamemory error can be persuasive. In another study, Baddeley and Longman (1978) also showed that distributed practice produced better learning, in this case, in a program to teach employees to type on typewriters quickly and accurately. However, the employees who learned via a massed program rated their learning experience as more positive than those who had learned via distributed practice. Thus, it is important for those who want to maximize their memory efficiency to keep distributed practice in mind when they begin learning, because it is both counterintuitive and less pleasant than massed practice.

What is common to all of these studies, regardless of the stimuli, specifics of the experiment, or time course of the spacing is that distributed practice leads to better recall performance than does massed practice. For the person who wants to maximize his or her learning efficiency, this is valuable information, especially given how much distributed practice goes against our natural grain. Like all the other memory efficiency themes in this chapter, using distributed practice requires an active learner who is willing to plan and use his or her intelligence. The reward in learning efficiency, however, can be quite large.

SECTION SUMMARY AND QUIZ

Four major principles have been emphasized: (1) process for meaning, (2) employ retrieval practice, (3) use metamemory, and (4) make use of distributed practice. Each of these individually can improve learning efficiency, and certainly in combination, they can make your learning and remembering far more efficient. In this section, we focus on the use of metamemory and the use of distributed practice. Judgments of learning can be useful in helping us guide our study. However, they should be used to determine which items are easy and which items are difficult. They should not be used to determine how long or in what manner to study. This is because of the stability bias-—which causes us to underestimate the advantages of future learning and discount the likelihood of forgetting. Distributed practice means that long-term retention is enhanced when we spread out our study over time as compared to studying all at once. Many studies have shown that distributed practice is superior to mass practice. Thus, even though students prefer massed study, if they wish to improve their learning efficiency, they should switch to distributed practice.

Section Quiz

1. The theory of metamemory that advances that an adaptive learning strategy is to study those items that have not yet been learned but are not too difficult—those at the leading edge of difficulty is known as the
   a. Judgment of learning theory
   b. Region of proximal learning
   c. Strategic agenda theory
   d. The labor-in-vain effect

2. Cameron has been studying for an exam. After considerable study, he attempts to evaluate his learning. Because he does not think he is benefiting from continuing to study and is confident he knows all the items that he will be tested on, he stops studying. What issue of memory efficiency should Cameron be concerned about?
   a. Stability bias
   b. The Kornell effect
   c. The region of proximal learning
   d. People's preference for massed practice

3. Kornell (2009) asked participants to study difficult, GRE-type words and their more common synonyms (e.g., *effulgent–brilliant*). He found that
   a. More than 90% of students did better with massed practice
   b. More students preferred distributed practice to massed practice
   c. Students learned about the same using massed and distributed practice
   d. All of the above are false

4. Two trials produce better retention if they are separated by more time than if they are closer together is known as
   a. Massed practice
   b. The judgment-of-learning effect
   c. Stability bias
   d. The spacing effect

1. b
2. a
3. d
4. d

MYTHS AND METHODS TO AVOID

A few widely practiced mnemonic techniques and memory improvement strategies are not based on good science and in some cases, may work against good memory performance. These will be described briefly, because it is as important to avoid the bad techniques as it is to embrace good techniques in many endeavors, memory included.

First, there is no such thing as a memory drug—at least, not as of yet. If you go to your local health food store, you may see ginkgo biloba advertised as a memory-enhancing herbal supplement. However, there is no scientific evidence that ginkgo biloba actually boosts memory (Canter & Ernst, 2007). Though harmless, perhaps, it will not give your memory the boost that the advertisements on the bottles claim. Beck et al. (2016) found that, while harmless, ginkgo biloba did not improve memory or cognitive functioning in elderly adults. Many students rely on caffeine to help them study. Caffeine does allow one to remain alert for longer, but there is no evidence that it helps memory abilities. In fact, if anything, people who have caffeine in their bloodstreams are less efficient learners than those who do not have caffeine in their blood (Mednick et al., 2008). So drink your cappuccino if you like it, but do not expect it to help you remember material when you take the exam. (For more on this topic, go to www.sage pub.com/schwartz3e.[5])

Second, there is no science behind the claim that you can learn new information by subliminal methods or by playing tapes while you sleep (Druckman & Bjork, 1991). Subliminal learning means receiving information below the threshold of consciousness. Although such subliminal presentation can affect some behaviors (e.g., implicit memory), it does not seem to promote the learning and remembering of explicit information, such as the knowledge we acquire in college courses. Furthermore, there is no research to support the claim that playing tapes while sleeping will have any positive impact on later learning or remembering (Willingham, 2009).

A Note About Imagery-Based Mnemonics

You will note that imagery-based mnemonics have been largely left out of this chapter. Indeed, the principle upon which they are based—namely, that use of perceptual imagery can boost memory—runs counter to the first principle reviewed in this chapter (process for meaning). Don't let this confuse you. Memory is complex, and the more techniques we use, the more efficient memory can become. Therefore, processing for meaning and using imagery-based mnemonics will be superior to using either strategy by itself. In some cases, imagery techniques, such as the method of loci, will help you do this. Imagery-based mnemonics can be quite useful in remembering lists of arbitrary items, names, and especially new language vocabulary (see Verhaeghen & Marcoen, 1996).

Thus, by careful and intelligent use of these memory principles, it is possible to improve your memory. Repetition and distributed practice are important to the learning process—so we'll repeat them again: (1) Process for meaning, (2) engage in retrieval practice, (3) use metamemory wisely, and (4) distribute your practice.

MNEMONISTS

For the overwhelming majority of us, even when we follow all the recommendations in this chapter, memory will still be hard work and take time. However, through a combination of innate ability and practice, some people have extraordinary memory. By and large, these people use memory techniques similar to the ones described in this chapter, but they often heavily rely on imagery, particularly variants of the method of loci, and remember new information much more quickly than do the rest of us (Foer, 2011). In this section, we will consider some of these famous **mnemonists** and how they remember or remembered so well.

> **Mnemonists:** People with extraordinary memory. One becomes a mnemonist through a combination of innate ability and practice.

S

The famous Russian psychologist A. R. Luria wrote a book about his study of a young Russian man named Solomon Sherashevsky (Luria, 1968/1987). Luria referred to his subject by his initial, S, but since Mr. Sherashevsky was also a public memory performer, there is no need for anonymity. Sherashevsky was born into an educated Jewish Russian family, growing up learning Hebrew and Yiddish as well as Russian. He would later use his multilingual abilities to help him remember large lists when giving demonstrations of his memory.

As Luria described the development of this mnemonist, Mr. Sherashevsky was working as a reporter for a newspaper in Soviet-era Moscow when his editor noticed that, despite the fact that Sherashevsky never took notes, he seemed to remember everything: his assignment, the assignments of other reporters, indeed everything the editor said. On the urging of his editor, Sherashevsky visited the neuropsychologist Luria, who then began probing his memory in a collaboration that lasted years. In one study, Luria showed that he could give Sherashevsky a list of 70 items just one time and Sherashevsky could repeat the list *in any order!*

One thing that became clear to Luria was that Sherashevsky's great memory was in part dependent on his unusual sensory characteristics. Sherashevsky had a condition called **synesthesia**. Synesthesia means that sensory qualities from one sense (e.g., vision) are perceived as being sensory qualities in another sense (e.g., sound), in addition to the actual modality that they are perceived in (Brogaard, Marlow, & Rice, 2016). Synesthesia does not involve hallucinations; people with it know where the perceptions are coming from in the environment and behave normally in most circumstances. However, they have interesting perceptual responses. Many people with synesthesia, for example, see words as having colors. Thus, the word *image* may be purple, but the word *book* may be bright red. They know that the word *image* may be printed in any particular color, and they perceive that, too. But when they read the word *image,* a sensation of "purpleness" appears. Most people with this condition

> **Synesthesia:** Sensory qualities from one sense (e.g., vision) are perceived as being sensory qualities in another sense (e.g., sound) in addition to the actual modality that they are perceived in.

consider it an advantage, and many of them use it to become successful artists (see Ward, 2008). (For more on synesthesia, go to study.sagepub.com/schwartz3e.[6])

Sherashevsky employed his synesthesia to remember just about everything throughout his life. He could remember a single list memorized for Luria a year later without any loss of details. He claimed to be able to remember events from very early in his infancy, well before the offset of childhood amnesia in most people. Sherashevsky parlayed his memory abilities into a career, as he toured Russia showing off his memory abilities. But Luria claimed there was also a price to pay: Because of his vivid synesthesia and attention to sensory details, Sherashevsky would often become confused about the meaning of even the simplest stories. Sherashevsky was an intelligent man who could eventually figure out the meanings, but it was difficult for him at times, because the sensory characteristics would always overwhelm the meaning intended by the storyteller. Thus, a particular metaphor by an author would elicit a synesthesiac reaction from him, which was often counter to the intended meaning of the metaphor. He also picked up on the slightest errors in text—such as when a blue coat is later referred to as "navy." The change in color would completely throw off his imagery of the story. Such conflicts were confusing to Sherashevsky.

Most of the empirical work done by Luria concentrated on Sherashevsky's extraordinary ability to encode meaningless information on the very first trial, such as his ability to hear and then recall a long list of numbers. Luria did express interest in Sherashevsky's seeming inability to forget information from autobiographical memory. However, Luria did not extend his research into this domain. Recently, there have been a number of cases of people reported with superior autobiographical memory, including people who claim to be able to remember everything they have done on every day of their life. In one case, Parker, Cahill, and McGaugh (2006) studied a woman who reported "total recall"; she claimed to remember every event from her life. Parker et al. could find no events that their mnemonist participant could not remember from her life, who claimed to have exerted no effort in encoding the events of her life; in fact, there were events that she wished that she could forget, but she simply could not. However, documented cases of such superior autobiographical memory are rare indeed. (For more on the case investigated by Parker et al., go to www.sagepub .com/schwartz3e.[7])

Many other mnemonists have been studied by experimental psychologists. Some seem similar to Sherashevsky in that they have synesthesia (Yaro & Ward, 2007), or their exceptional abilities are unique to numbers (Takahashi, Shimizu, Saito, & Tomoyori, 2006; Thompson, Cowan, & Frieman, 1993). It is worth pointing out the title of one of the most recent scientific reports on a mnemonist—namely, "One Percent Ability and Ninety-nine Percent Perspiration" (Takahashi et al., 2006), which suggests that even individuals who claim to have great memory, demonstrate great memory, and may work as professional mnemonists need to put a great deal of work into it. This is described in detail in the book by Joshua Foer, which describes his journey from being ordinary journalist to the U.S. memory champion (Foer, 2011).

Exceptional memory has actually become a competitive sport. Every two years, at the Memory Olympics, participants compete in remembering names, remembering digits, and many other memory-dependent games. Maguire, Valentine, Wilding, and Kapur (2003) were able to study some of these competitors using fMRI. Relative to control participants, the "Olympians" showed more activity in areas of the right prefrontal cortex, which are associated with spatial memory and navigation. This is consistent with the report by more than 90% of the memory experts that they use the method of loci to aid their memory. (For more on memory competitions, go to study.sagepub.com/schwartz3e.[8])

SUMMARY

This chapter focuses on how each of us can improve our memory by learning and remembering more efficiently. Four major principles have been emphasized: (1) process for meaning, (2) employ retrieval practice, (3) use metamemory, and (4) make use of distributed practice. Each of these individually can improve learning efficiency, and certainly in combination, they can make your learning and remembering far more efficient. In this chapter, the various mnemonic improvement hints given throughout the book are organized according to these four memory principles. Moreover, it is possible to contrast normal memory and how to make it efficient with the exceptional memory seen in rare individuals. For the most part, these individuals combine a natural gift for or interest in memory with the same principles that improve normal memory. The author personally wishes each and every reader the best of luck in applying these cognitive principles to your own learning and remembering.

Table 13.1   Twenty-Two Mnemonic Tips

- Mnemonic Improvement Tip 1.1: **Overlearn:** Study past the point where you have mastered the material. Promotes long-term retention.
- Mnemonic Improvement Tip 1.2: **Use the spacing effect or distributed practice.** Space your study over time—don't study all at once. Promotes long-term retention.
- Mnemonic Improvement Tip 1.3: **Learning takes work.** There is no magic bullet for memory. Good memory requires hard work. Requires strategic planning.
- Mnemonic Improvement Tip 1.4: **External cues can help.** Structure your environment to help you remember. Promotes prospective memory and memory for ordinary objects.
- Mnemonic Improvement Tip 3.1: **Use chunking.** Group information in working memory. Promotes good short-term retention.
- Mnemonic Improvement Tip 3.2: **Practice working memory tasks.** Train your working memory, perhaps by practicing digit span tasks. Promotes good short-term retention.
- Mnemonic Improvement Tip 4.1: **Deep processing.** Use elaborative encoding. Promotes rapid encoding of new information.
- Mnemonic Improvement Tip 4.2: **Leverage the generation effect.** Produce your own associations and practice recalling the items you need to remember. Promotes rapid encoding of new information.
- Mnemonic Improvement Tip 4.3: **Organize the information.** Apply meaningful categories to to-be-learned material. Promotes rapid encoding of new information.
- Mnemonic Improvement Tip 4.4: **Use distinctiveness to advantage.** Focus on a distinctive aspect of to-be-learned information. Promotes rapid encoding of new information.
- Mnemonic Improvement Tip 4.5: **Use retrieval cues.** Create powerful retrieval cues that are strongly associated to the information. Ensures access to learned information.

- Mnemonic Improvement Tip 4.6: **Leverage the encoding specificity principle.** Match your learning environment, internal and external, to the expected testing environment. Ensures access to learned information.
- Mnemonic Improvement Tip 6.1: **Use the method of loci.** Use a well-learned landscape to encode new items. Promotes rapid encoding of new information.
- Mnemonic Improvement Tip 6.2: **Use the keyword technique.** Make visual images that link to-be-learned items. Promotes rapid encoding of new information.
- Mnemonic Improvement Tip 6.3: **Use the pegword technique.** Use both visual and auditory imagery to learn new items. Promotes rapid encoding of new information.
- Mnemonic Improvement Tip 7.1: **Keep a memory diary.** Record events from your life every day. Promotes good retention of autobiographical events.
- Mnemonic Improvement Tip 8.1: **The cognitive interview.** Use the three principles of cognitive interviewing (context reinstatement, different temporal patterns, different spatial patterns) when retrieving eyewitness events. Allows for maximum retrieval of event detail.
- Mnemonic Improvement Tip 8.2: **Close your eyes.** Allows you to recall more details from episodic memories without a cost in false memories.
- Mnemonic Improvement Tip 9.1: **Make judgments of learning.** Assess what you know and don't know. Use this self-knowledge as a guide to what to study. Promotes rapid encoding of new information.
- Mnemonic Improvement Tip 9.2: **Work within your region of proximal learning.** Study easy or difficult items based on time constraints and learning goals. Maximizes study efficiency.
- Mnemonic Improvement Tip 11.1: **Engage in memory conversations.** Have frequent discussions with young children (and other adults) about past events. Promotes good retention and recall of autobiographical events.

KEY TERMS

acronym	generation effect	retrieval practice
acrostic	judgments of learning	self-regulated learning
distributed learning or practice	massed practice	spacing effect
	metamemory	stability bias
encoding specificity	mnemonists	subjective organization
encoding variability	process for meaning	synesthesia
expanded retrieval practice	region of proximal learning	technical mnemonics

REVIEW QUESTIONS

1. What are the four broad principles of memory improvement?

2. Why is distraction considered an example of divided attention? What is the effect of divided attention on encoding?

3. What is subjective organization? What evidence exists that subjective organization is superior to other forms of organization?

4. What is encoding variability? How can it be employed to improve memory?

5. What is retrieval practice? How can it be employed to improve memory?

6. How can students use judgments of learning to improve the efficiency of their study? What are the potential drawbacks of relying on judgments of learning?

7. When is massed practice helpful? Why is distributed practice generally a better study strategy?

8. Kornell (2009) conducted a study to examine the differences between massed and distributed practice. What was his methodology, and what did he demonstrate?

9. What is the difference between distributed practice and expanding rehearsal? When might expanding rehearsal be superior to distributed practice?

10. What is a mnemonist? How do the memories of mnemonists differ from those of normal individuals?

ONLINE RESOURCES

1. For a related approach to memory improvement, go to Daniel Willingham's website at http://www.danielwillingham.com.

2. For more on the advantages of self-testing and other mnemonic techniques, go to http://bps-research-digest.blogspot.com/2008/02/how-to-study.html.

3. For more on the region of proximal learning, go to http://www.columbia.edu/cu/psychology/metcalfe/Research.html.

4. For more on the differences between massed and distributed practice, go to http://www.psychologicalscience.org/index.php/publications/observer/2011/april-11/how-should-students-study-tips-advice-and-pitfalls.html.

5. It is likely that memory-enhancing drugs are not far off in the future. For more on this topic, go to http://www.newyorker.com/reporting/2009/04/27/090427fa_fact_talbot. Also see http://www.scientificamerican.com/article.cfm?id = the-quest-for-a-smart-pil.

6. For more on synesthesia, go to http://www.syn.sussex.ac.uk.

7. For more on the case investigated by Parker et al., go to https://www.wired.com/2009/03/ff-perfectmemory/

8. To learn more about the USA memory championships, go to http://www.usamemorychampionships.com.

Go to **study.sagepub.com/schwartz3e** for additional exercises and study resources. Select **Chapter 13, Memory Improvement: A User's Guide** for chapter-specific resources.

Glossary

Absolute judgment: in a sequential lineup (a show-up), the witness matches the particular face to his or her memory of the face seen and decides if this particular face matches the memory. (Chapter 6)

Accessibility: that part of our stored memories that we can retrieve under the present conditions. (Chapters 4 and 9)

Acronym: a mnemonic device in which the first letter of each word from a list is formed into an easily remembered word. For example, *HOMES* is a common acronym for remembering the Great Lakes of the United States and Canada (*Huron, Ontario, Michigan, Erie,* and *Superior*). (Chapter 13)

Acrostic: a mnemonic that involves taking the first letter from each item in the list and forming a sentence with an easily remembered visual image or auditory connection that makes the sentence memorable. (Chapter 13)

Action potential: the electrochemical process of transmission in an axon. (Chapter 2)

Active suppression: a theory that explains repression. People may deliberately force themselves to not remember the event. (Chapter 8)

Agenda-based regulation: participants initially develop a plan of study, which includes both their study goals and their study constraints. (Chapter 9)

Allocation of study time: the decisions participants make about which items to study during an experiment. (Chapter 9 and 13)

Alzheimer's disease: one of many dementia-type illnesses that are more common in older adults than they are in younger adults. Memory is the first deficit detected in this disease. (Chapters 2 and 10)

Amnesia: memory deficits acquired through brain damage. (Chapters 2 and 10)

Amnesic syndrome: characteristic of the amnesic syndrome patient is specific impairment of encoding new information into both episodic and semantic memory, while most other cognitive functions remain intact. (Chapter 10)

Amount of information: the quantity of information retrieved while recalling an episodic event. (Chapter 8)

Amygdala: a part of the brain critical in emotional learning, fear, and memory. (Chapter 2)

Amyloid plaques: masses of unwanted proteins, which interfere with normal brain function. (Chapter 10)

Analog representation: a theory that argues that we store visual images in a manner similar to actual pictures. (Chapter 6)

Anosognosia: the failure to become aware of a cognitive deficit. (Chapter 10)

Anterograde amnesia: an inability to form new memories following brain damage. (Chapters 2 and 10)

Articulatory suppression: a concurrent task that prevents participants from engaging in rehearsal within the phonological loop. (Chapter 3)

Associative model: we represent information in semantic memory in terms of connections among units of information. A node is the unit of memory, which is then connected to other nodes. (Chapter 5)

Availability: all information present in the memory system. (Chapters 4 and 9)

Axon: the part of the neuron that sends information to other neurons. (Chapter 2)

Behaviorism: a school of psychology that focused on only the relation of environmental inputs and the observable behavior of organisms, including human beings. (Chapter 1)

Benzodiazepines: drugs that are used usually because of their effects on anxiety, insomnia, and muscle relaxation. However, they are also strong amnesia-inducing drugs, especially within the episodic memory domain. (Chapters 2 and 10)

Bizarre imagery: forming strange visual images based on to-be-learned information can lead to good memory for that information. (Chapter 6)

Capacity: the amount of information that can be maintained in working memory. (Chapter 3)

Capgras syndrome: patients come to believe that other people have been duplicated and that two sets of identical people may exist. It is caused by brain damage. (Chapter 10)

Category: mental construct referring to a set of objects or ideas that are grouped together or are associated with each other. (Chapter 5)

Central executive: the attentional mechanism of working memory. (Chapter 3)

Cerebral cortex: the outer layer of the brain most associated with higher cognitive and emotional functioning. (Chapter 2)

Characteristic features: according to feature comparison theory, characteristic features generally accompany an instance of the category but are not required. (Chapter 5)

Childhood amnesia: (also known as infantile amnesia) refers to the observation that adults have almost no episodic memories from the first 3 to 5 years of their lives. (Chapter 7)

Childhood amnesia—age-related changes in self-concept: the view that childhood amnesia is caused by the lack of development of a coherent psychological self. (Chapter 7)

Childhood amnesia—influence of language on memory development: the view that childhood amnesia is caused by the growth of language ability in the young child, which provides the structure and narrative schemas necessary to support episodic memories. (Chapter 7)

Childhood amnesia—neurological transitions in memory systems: the view that childhood amnesia is caused by changes in the brain as it matures. (Chapter 7)

Childhood amnesia—psychodynamic view: the view that childhood amnesia is caused by active repression. (Chapter 7)

Cholinergics: drugs prescribed to patients with Alzheimer's disease that alleviate memory loss in early phases of the disease. (Chapter 2)

Chunk: basic unit of information in working memory. A chunk may be decomposable into more information. (Chapter 3)

Classical conditioning: a situation in which a relation exists between a stimulus (e.g., a ringing bell) and an outcome (e.g., getting food); the organism demonstrates behavior or response (e.g., salivating) that shows that the organism has learned the association between the stimulus and the outcome. (Chapter 1)

Clinical neuropsychology: the practice of helping brain-damaged patients recover and cope with their injuries. (Chapter 2)

Coexistence hypothesis: a theory that explains the misinformation effect. Participants form one memory about the original event and then form a second memory of reading questions or reading a summary after the event. (Chapter 8)

Cognitive interview: a protocol designed to help police investigators obtain the maximum amount of information from witnesses with the least likelihood of inducing false memories. (Chapter 8)

Cognitive maps: mental representations of the external world. Based on our spatial representation of the world. (Chapter 6)

Cognitive neuroscience: the study of the role of the brain in producing cognition. (Chapter 1)

Cognitive psychology: an approach to psychology that emphasizes hidden mental processes. (Chapter 1)

Coherence: the processes that yield autobiographical memories that are consistent with the working self. (Chapter 7)

Collaborative memory: working together with other people to remember information. (Chapter 13)

Concept: mental construct that contains information associated with a specific idea. (Chapter 5)

Concurrent tasks: tasks to be done simultaneously. (Chapter 3)

Confabulation: when amnesic patients lie about their past. They do not know they are not telling the truth because of deficits in source monitoring. (Chapter 10)

Conjugate reinforcement technique: a ribbon is attached to the infant's foot, which will eventually be attached to a mobile placed overhead. When the infant moves or kicks her foot, it will make the mobile move and jiggle. After a delay, the infant is again given the opportunity to move the mobile. If the infant does so in less time, learning has occurred. (Chapter 11)

Consolidation: a neurological process whereby memory traces are made permanent in a person's long-term memory. (Chapter 10)

Contextual associations: an explanation for the retrieval of critical intrusions in the DRM. It states that all of the presented words are linked or associated to, in some way, the critical intrusion. (Chapter 8)

Control (in metamemory): our ability to regulate our learning or retrieval based upon our own monitoring. (Chapters 9 and 12)

Correspondence: the match between the retrieved memory and the actual event from the past. (Chapters 7 and 8)

Critical intrusion: the false memory created by a list in which all of the words are related or associated with the absent but suggested word. (Chapter 8)

Cross-language semantic priming: the effect that priming a word in one language has on a related word in another language in bilinguals or multilinguals. (Chapter 5)

Cue familiarity: stored information about the cue or the degree to which we recognize that the cue influences our metamemory judgment about the to-be-remembered target. (Chapter 9)

Cue-only judgments of learning: upon seeing only a cue word, the participant judges the likelihood of later being able to recall the target when presented with its cue. (Chapter 9)

Cue-target judgments of learning: upon seeing a target word and cue word, the participant judges the likelihood of later being able to recall the target when presented with its cue. (Chapter 9)

Cue-word technique: an ordinary word is provided to participants, who are asked to provide the first memory—from any point in their life—that the word elicits. (Chapter 7)

Cued recall: occurs when we are given a specific cue to remember a specific memory. (Chapter 1)

Declarative memory: any memory that can be verbalized; includes both episodic and semantic memory. (Chapter 5)

Deep brain stimulation (DBS): A device is implanted directly into the brain, which then sends electrical impulses to specific regions of the brain; used exclusively implanted for medical reasons.

Deep processing: when we process more deeply, that is, using elaborative or meaningful processing, we are more likely to remember the information processed. (Chapter 4)

Deese-Roediger-McDermott (DRM) procedure: used to induce false memories for items on word lists. It involves presenting associates to an unpresented word in the list. The unpresented word is often recalled because of its associations to the other words. (Chapter 8)

Defining features: according to feature comparison theory, defining features are required for any example of a particular category. (Chapter 5)

Déjà vu experience: the experience we get when we think we have seen or heard something before but objectively know that we have not. (Chapter 9)

Dendrites: the part of the neuron that receives information from other neurons or from sensory receptors. (Chapter 2)

Dependent variables: the observations that we measure or record in response to the independent variable. (Chapter 1)

Developmental amnesia: a congenital memory deficit, usually restrictive to episodic memory. (Chapter 4)

Diary studies: the experimenters or participants record events from their own lives and keep track of events over long periods of time. Later, their memory for these events can be tested. (Chapter 7)

Diencephalon: the part of the brain that includes the thalamus and hypothalamus. It serves as an important relay point in the human memory circuit. (Chapters 2 and 10)

Digit span task: a task in which a person must remember a list of digits presented by an experimenter. (Chapter 3)

Direct-access theories: hold that the judgments we make are based on the same processes that allow us to remember in the first place. That is, metamemory judgments measure the strength of the stored memory even if that memory cannot be recalled. (Chapter 9)

Directed forgetting: the inhibition in memory that occurs when people are asked to forget some information but not other information. (Chapters 4 and 12)

Disputed memories: when we feel a memory is our own when it actually corresponds to an event in another's past. (Chapter 7)

Dissociation: brain damage (or an experimental variable) can affect one cognitive system but leave another one intact. (Chapter 4)

Dissociative amnesia: a condition in which only the traumatic event or events closely related to that trauma are not remembered. (Chapter 10)

Dissociative fugue: the psychogenic amnesia in which the patient forgets his or her personal identity in addition to access to his or her autobiographical past. (Chapter 10)

Distinctiveness: focusing on distinctive aspects of a stimulus causes comparatively good memory performance for that item. (Chapter 4)

Distributed practice: spacing out study over time. (Chapters 1 and 13)

Distributional information: the patterns of speech that co-occur, that is, an aspect of language that always accompanies another. (Chapter 5)

Double-blind procedure: in an experiment, neither the tester nor the participant know what condition that participant is in. (Chapter 1)

Dual-store view (or separate store) of bilingual representation: the view that meaning is represented separately for each language in the lexical memory of a bilingual. (Chapter 5)

Duration of information in working memory: the amount of time information will remain in working memory if not rehearsed. (Chapter 3)

Ease-of-learning judgments: estimates of how likely an item will be remembered in advance of actual studying and predictions about how difficult that item will be to learn. (Chapters 9 and 13)

Echoic memory: auditory sensory memory. (Chapter 3)

EEG (electroencephalography): using electrodes to measure the electrical output of the brain. (Chapters 1 and 2)

Elaborative rehearsal: processing the meaning of information in working memory. (Chapters 3 and 4)

Electroconvulsive therapy (ECT): an effective treatment for depression that involves delivering a strong electric shock to the head of a patient. It creates periods of retrograde amnesia. (Chapter 10)

Empirical evidence: the product of scientific research. To be empirical evidence, it must be verifiable, that is, another scientist should be able to get the same results if he or she does the same or similar experiment. (Chapter 1)

Enactment effect: performed tasks are remembered better than those that are simply read about. (Chapter 4)

Encoding: the learning process, that is, how information is initially encountered and learned. (Chapter 4)

Encoding specificity: retrieval of information from memory will be maximized when the conditions at retrieval match the conditions at encoding. (Chapters 4 and 13)

Encoding variability: this principle claims that if we study an item of information under several different mental and physical conditions, we will be more likely to remember it than if we had studied for the same amount of time or trials but under uniform conditions. (Chapter 13)

Engram: the hypothetical physical unit of storage of a memory. (Chapter 2)

Episodic buffer: coordinates overlap between the auditory and visual systems. (Chapter 3)

Episodic memory: the neurocognitive memory system that encodes, stores, and retrieves memories of our personal, individual experiences. (Chapters 4 and 12)

Errorless learning: a technique that trains a patient to learn a particular fact or skill while preventing that person from making errors during training. (Chapter 12)

Event-related potential: the averaged EEG pattern across many trials of EEG recordings in response to a particular class of stimulus. (Chapter 2)

Event-specific memories: individual events stored in episodic memory. (Chapter 7)

Exemplar theory: categories are classified by maintaining a large number of specific instances of a category (exemplars) that are associated with each other in semantic memory. (Chapter 5)

Expanded retrieval practice: expanded retrieval practice means that initially we space our study of a particular item very close together to maximize learning and the advantages of retrieval practice, but subsequent trials get further and further apart. (Chapter 13)

Experiment: set of observations that occur under controlled circumstances determined by the experimenter. (Chapter 1)

Eyewitness memory: memory for the events that transpire in a single event, usually a crime. (Chapters 6 and 8)

Failure to rehearse: a theory that explains repression. It argues that because memories of childhood trauma are highly negative, often private, and potentially embarrassing, they are not likely to be rehearsed often. (Chapter 8)

False-belief test: a child learns something that another person does not have the opportunity to learn. The child must then decide whether the other person knows what he or she knows. Three-year-olds seldom succeed, whereas most 5-year-olds have mastered this task. (Chapter 11)

False memories: memories that people have that do not correspond to events as they actually happened. (Chapter 8)

False memory induction procedure: inducing false memories of events in participants by repeatedly asking them about events they never experienced. (Chapter 8)

Family resemblance: membership in a category may be defined by each item's general similarity to other members in the category rather than by a specific list of features. (Chapter 5)

Fast mapping: the rules that allow a child to rapidly learn the meaning of words in his or her language. (Chapter 5)

Feature comparison theory: membership in a category may be defined by each item's correspondence to a list of features for any particular category. (Chapter 5)

Feeling-of-knowing judgments: estimations of the likelihood that an unrecalled item will be recognized. (Chapter 9)

Field memories: autobiographical and visual memories in which we see the memory as if we were looking at the event through our own eyes. (Chapter 7)

Flashbulb memories: highly confident personal memories of surprising events. To study them, researchers have focused on the memory of public tragedies. (Chapters 4 and 7)

fMRI (functional magnetic resonance imagery): magnetic fields create a three-dimensional image of the brain that can capture both the structure and function of the brain. (Chapters 1 and 2)

Forced-choice recognition: a person must identify the answer from a series of possible answers. (Chapter 1)

Forgetting curve: a graph that traces the decline of memory performance over time. (Chapter 1)

Free recall: recall in which participants must generate memories with minimal or no cuing of the memories. (Chapter 1)

Frontal lobe: the most anterior part of the cerebral cortex. Associated with higher emotion, decision making, metacognition, and memory. (Chapter 2)

Frontal lobe amnesia: patients show some evidence of anterograde amnesia, although it tends to be much less severe than in other patients. They may also show anosognosia and confabulation. (Chapter 10)

Fusiform face area (FFA): a part of the brain in the inferior-temporal cortex that appears to specialize in face recognition. (Chapter 6)

Fuzzy-trace theory: an explanation for the retrieval of critical intrusions in the DRM. It states that when items are encoded, they are not encoded literally but rather in terms of their meaning, a reasonable hypothesis given what we know about long-term memory. (Chapter 8)

General events: include the combined, averaged, and cumulative memory of highly similar events. Also include extended events, which are long sequences of connected episodic events. (Chapter 7)

Generation effect: memory is better when we generate associations ourselves than when we simply read them. (Chapters 4 and 13)

Hemifield neglect: a condition in which patients ignore one half of the visual world. It occurs because of damage to the right parietal lobe. Also known as **unilateral neglect.** (Chapter 6)

Hippocampus: an area of the brain associated with learning and memory. Damage can cause anterograde amnesia. (Chapters 2, 10, and 12)

Hypnosis: increases the number of false memories without increasing the number of accurate memories. (Chapter 8)

Hypothalamus: an area of the brain associated with basic emotions. (Chapter 2)

Iconic memory: visual sensory memory. (Chapter 3)

Imagery: the experience of retrieving a memory that is mostly visual or experienced primarily as a sensory experience. Can also refer to the representation of those memories. (Chapter 6)

Imagination inflation: researchers induce false memories by simply having the participant imagine the event. (Chapter 8)

Imitation: mimicking the actions of another. (Chapter 11)

Implicit memory: the preserved ability to perform tasks that are influenced by a past event without the person being aware of the event experience. (Chapter 10)

Implicit memory tests: tests that draw on the non-conscious aspects of memory. (Chapter 1)

Incidental learning: people encode information not by actively trying to remember but rather as by-product of perceiving and understanding the world. (Chapter 4)

Independent variables: the factors that the experimenter manipulates among different conditions. (Chapter 1)

Indirect or inferential theories: hold that we use a variety of clues, cues, tricks, and heuristics to estimate the strength of an item in memory, which we cannot measure directly. (Chapter 9)

Inhibition: mechanism that actively interferes with and reduces the likelihood of recall of particular information. (Chapter 4)

Inhibition theory: older adults do not have a good ability to block out irrelevant stimuli. Thus, the memory declines seen in old age are a consequence of poor attentional processes. Inhibition is also the ability to suppress the retrieval of irrelevant information. (Chapter 12)

Intentional learning: people actively engage in learning information because they know that their memories may be tested. (Chapter 4)

Interference: new information enters working memory and displaces information already present. (Chapter 3)

Irrelevant speech effect: the observation that the phonological loop is mildly impaired when background talking is going on. (Chapter 3)

Judgments of learning: predictions made during study of whether we will remember the studied items later. (Chapters 1, 9, 12, and 13)

Keyword technique: involves creating an image that links two items in memory. With respect to language learning, it means creating an image that links the word in the language you know to the word in the language you are learning. (Chapter 6)

Korsakoff's disease: a severe form of amnesia brought on by long-term alcoholism. Characterized by anterograde amnesia, retrograde amnesia, anosognosia, and confabulation. (Chapter 10)

Labor in vain: when extra study does not guarantee that difficult items will be mastered. (Chapter 9)

Lemma: a hypothetical entity containing only semantic and syntactical information without any information concerning the phonology of the word. (Chapter 5)

Levels of categorization: categories are nested structures in which the level of organization is important in defining the category. There are three such levels: basic, subordinate, and superordinate. (Chapter 5)

Levels of processing: more meaningful handling of information leads to better encoding of that information. (Chapter 4)

Lexeme: the level of representation that stores the phonology of a word, that is, how the word sounds. (Chapter 5)

Lexical decision task: a cognitive task in which participants judge whether a string of letters is a word as quickly as they can. (Chapter 5)

Lexical memory (lexicon): our mental dictionary; a representational system for the words of our language. (Chapter 5)

Lexicon: our mental dictionary. (Chapter 5)

Lifetime periods: the idiosyncratic, personal ways in which we organize our autobiographical past. These lifetime periods are usually organized by a common theme and may overlap in the physical time periods that they cover. (Chapter 7)

Limbic system: set of brain structures located just beneath the cerebral cortex. It includes the hypothalamus, the hippocampus, and the amygdala and functions as an important area for both memory and emotion. (Chapter 2)

Magnetoencephalography (MEG): a technology that allows researchers to measure brain activity by detecting magnetic fields that the brain produces.   (Chapters 1 and 2)

Maintenance rehearsal: repeating information over and over. (Chapters 3 and 4)

Mammillary bodies: a subcortical region of the brain associated with learning. Damage can cause anterograde amnesia. (Chapter 10)

Massed practice: studying in one block of time rather than spreading out study. (Chapters 1 and 13)

Medial temporal lobes: a cortical area of the brain in the temporal lobes associated with learning and memory. Damage can cause anterograde amnesia. (Chapters 2 and 10)

Memory appropriation: an amnesiac may be able to retrieve an event based on someone else's repeated retelling of the event. (Chapter 10)

Memory compensation: rather than trying to answer a question about the past, an amnesiac talks instead about the issues that have arisen from amnesic syndrome. (Chapter 10)

Memory conversations: the talk between a parent and a child concerning past events. The discussions we have with others about the past. Normal individuals frequently have memory conversations. (Chapters 10 and 11)

Memory efficiency view: holds that memory improves in young children because of increases in speed and efficiency in learning new information and storing it in long-term memory. (Chapter 11)

Memory importation: when amnesiacs describe a memory from before their injury as if it had happened after. (Chapter 10)

Memory rehabilitation: the interventions that clinical neuropsychologists use to promote improved memory performance in memory-impaired individuals. (Chapters 10 and 12)

Memory strategies view: the conscious activities a person engages in to assist the remembering of information. (Chapter 11)

Metacognition: our knowledge and awareness of our own cognitive processes. (Chapter 9)

Metacognitive control: self-regulation directed at memory. (Chapters 9 and 13)

Metamemory: our knowledge and awareness of our own memory processes. (Chapters 1, 9, 11, and 13)

Method of loci: using visual imagery, the learner associates a list of new to-be-learned items with a series of well-known physical locations. (Chapter 6)

Method of vanishing cues: this technique uses the spared implicit memory of amnesiacs to help them learn new skills. (Chapter 10)

Misinformation effect: presenting postevent misinformation about a witnessed event can obscure, change, or degrade the memory of the original event. (Chapter 8)

Mnemonists: people with extraordinary memory. One becomes a mnemonist through a combination of innate ability and practice. (Chapter 13)

Monitoring: our ability to reflect on and become aware of what we know and what we do not know. (Chapters 9 and 12)

Mood congruence: people are more likely to remember events or information that are positive when they are in a positive mood and more likely to remember events or information that are negative when they are in a negative mood. (Chapter 4)

Morphology: how words are constructed within a particular language. (Chapter 5)

Multiple sclerosis: a disease caused by the loss of myelin along human axons. (Chapter 2)

Neurofibrillary tangles: twisted amyloid plaques around neurons that cause destruction of those neurons. (Chapter 10)

Neuroimaging: a set of techniques that allow researchers to make detailed maps of the human brain and assign functions to particular regions in the brain. (Chapters 1 and 2)

Neurons: biological cells that specialize in the transmission and retention of information. (Chapter 2)

Neuropsychology: the study of patients with brain damage. (Chapter 1)

Neurotransmitters: chemicals (such as dopamine) that cross the synapse and induce an electric flow in the next neuron. (Chapter 2)

Nonnutritive sucking: a natural reflexive behavior biologically necessary for obtaining milk. Infants suck differentially to the presence of a novel stimulus compared to a familiar stimulus. A novel stimulus usually elicits an increase in sucking, most likely because the stimulus is new and exciting. (Chapter 11)

Nonsense syllables: meaningless words (e.g., *wob*) that can be given to participants to study so as to avoid the effect of meaning on memory. (Chapter 1)

Observer memories: autobiographical memories in which we take the vantage point of an outside observer and see ourselves as actors in our visual memory. (Chapter 7)

Occipital face area (OFA): an area of the occipital lobe that has been identified as crucial to face recognition. (Chapter 6)

Old/new recognition: participants have to decide whether an item was on a study list. (Chapter 1)

Olfactory bulb: the primary organ in the brain for processing odors. (Chapter 2)

Open-ended questions: retrieval questions that contain very few cues and thus allow participants to describe their memory without suggestions. Open-ended questions limit the possibility of introducing inadvertent misinformation. (Chapter 8)

Operant conditioning: organisms learn to emit responses or behaviors (e.g., pressing a bar) in response to a stimulus to achieve desirable outcomes (e.g., getting food) or avoid undesirable outcomes (e.g., getting an electric shock). (Chapter 1)

Organization: imposing a meaningful structure on to-be-learned material. (Chapter 4)

Orienting tasks: direct the participant's attention to some aspect of the stimuli—either deep or shallow—but do not alert the participant to the potential of a later memory test. (Chapter 4)

Overconfidence in judgments: overestimating the likelihood that a to-be-learned item or set of items will be remembered. (Chapters 9, 11, and 13)

Overlearning: studying after material has been thoroughly learned. (Chapter 1)

Own-race bias: people are, by and large, better at recognizing faces from their own "race" than from other racial groups. (Chapter 6)

Paired-associate learning: learning the association between two items, such as in language learning (e.g., learning the association *monkey–le singe*). (Chapter 1)

Part-set cueing: occurs when people study some but not all of the information in a set of already-learned information. (Chapter 4)

Pegword technique: a mnemonic technique that takes advantage of our natural auditory memory system as well as our visual imagery system. We associate new items with words in a known rhyme scheme. (Chapter 6)

PET (positron emission tomography): radioactive chemicals are placed in the blood, allowing scientists to obtain a three-dimensional image of the intact brain. (Chapter 1)

Phonological loop: auditory working memory. (Chapter 3)

Phonology: the study of sounds and how they are used in a language. (Chapter 5)

Photographic memory: very strong visual memories that have a strong feeling of being images. (Chapter 6)

Posttraumatic stress disorder: psychological problems caused by exposure to extremely dangerous or stressful situations. (Chapter 10)

Prefrontal cortex (prefrontal area): the part of the frontal lobe most associated with higher emotions (e.g., jealousy, respect) and memory. (Chapter 2)

Primacy effect: the observation that memory is usually superior for items at the beginning of a serial position curve; thought to be caused by the encoding of those items into long-term memory. (Chapter 3)

Primary memory: a term used to mean short-term memory. (Chapter 3)

Primary visual cortex: the first area in the occipital cortex that processes visual images. (Chapter 6)

Process for meaning: focus on the meaning of new material during learning. (Chapter 13)

Processing speed: age-related declines are caused because the older person's cognitive processing does not work as quickly as that of younger adults. (Chapter 12)

Pronunciation time: the amount of time it would take to say aloud the items being rehearsed in working memory. (Chapter 3)

Propositional representation: storing visual images in terms of a language-like code. (Chapter 6)

Prosopagnosia: an acquired deficit in face recognition caused by brain damage. (Chapter 6)

Prospective memory: memory for the things we need to do in the future. (Chapters 1 and 4)

Prototype theory: states that prototypes form the central characteristic in our representation of categories. A prototype is defined as the most typical member of a particular category. (Chapter 5)

Psychogenic amnesia: a broad term that covers all forms of amnesia that are not directly linked to disruption or injury to the brain. (Chapter 10)

Psycholinguistics: the study of the psychological processes involved in human language. (Chapter 5)

Random assignment: any particular participant is equally likely to be assigned to any of the conditions in an experiment. (Chapter 1)

Reaction time: the measured amount of time required to perform a particular task. (Chapter 1)

Reading fluency: the ability to read at speeds sufficient to process and understand written material. (Chapter 3)

Reality monitoring: our ability to distinguish whether our memory is of a real event or of an imagined event. (Chapters 1 and 8)

Recall: generating the target memory based on cues, without seeing or hearing the actual target memory. (Chapter 1)

Recency effect: the observation that memory is usually superior for items at the end of a serial position curve; thought to be caused by the maintenance of those items in working memory. (Chapters 1 and 3)

Recognition: identifying the target memory from presented item(s). (Chapter 1)

Recovery of repressed memories: the ability to recover previously forgotten memories that had been repressed. (Chapter 8)

Reduplicative paramnesia: a condition in which patients believe that places or locations have been duplicated and that the two locations exist simultaneously. It is caused by brain damage. (Chapter 10)

Region of proximal learning: a theory of metamemory that advances that an adaptive strategy is to study those items that have not yet been learned but are not too difficult. We maximize our learning by studying at the leading edge of difficulty, that is, by studying the easiest items we have not yet mastered. (Chapters 9 and 13)

Rehearsal: actively maintaining items in working memory by repeating them over and over (maintenance rehearsal) or by elaborating on the relation of item to some other concept (elaborative rehearsal). (Chapter 3)

Rehearsal prevention task: a task that prevents a participant from maintaining information in working memory. (Chapter 3)

Relative judgment: in a lineup, participants match their memory of whom they saw during an event to each of the presented faces in the lineup and then try to determine which is the closest match. (Chapter 6)

Remember/know judgments: tasks in which participants determine the feeling of memories by assigning them categories of "remember" or "know." (Chapter 4)

Reminiscence bump: the spike in recalled memories corresponding to late adolescence to early adulthood, or roughly between the ages of 16 and 25. (Chapter 7)

Repetition priming: the effect of presenting a stimulus on the processing of that same stimulus at a later date. Amnesiacs show repetition priming even when they do not consciously recall the target. (Chapter 10)

Representation: the storage of information in memory when that information is not in use. (Chapters 4 and 6)

Repression: the active forgetting of highly emotional memories, usually from childhood. (Chapters 8 and 10)

Retention interval: the amount of time that transpires between the learning of an event or material and when recall for that event or material occurs. (Chapter 1)

Retrieval: the process of how we activate information from long-term memory and access it when we need it. (Chapter 4)

Retrieval bias: a technique used to make some information easier to recall than other information. (Chapter 8)

Retrieval cues: we use information present in our current environment, that is, retrieval cues, to trigger our memories of past events. (Chapter 4)

Retrieval-induced inhibition: the interference of recently retrieved information with retrieval of other related information. (Chapter 4)

Retrieval of related information: when we retrieve information related to a target, that information can influence our metamemory judgment for learning or remembering the target. (Chapter 9)

Retrieval practice: learning by self-testing. That is, making oneself retrieve information is a superior method of learning than simply rereading that information. (Chapter 13)

Retrograde amnesia: loss of the ability to retrieve memories of events prior to brain damage. (Chapters 2 and 10)

Retrospective confidence judgments: estimations that a retrieved answer is indeed correct. (Chapter 9)

Ribot's law: newer memories are more affected by retrograde amnesia than are older memories. (Chapter 10)

Right hemisphere/left hemisphere: the brain is divisible into two symmetrical halves, oriented in the left-right direction. (Chapter 2)

Savings score: the reduction in time required to relearn a previously mastered list. (Chapter 1)

Schema: generalized knowledge about an event, a person, or a situation. (Chapter 5)

Scripts: well-learned sequences of events associated with common activities. (Chapter 5)

Second-language acquisition: occurs when a person has already mastered his or her native language and then begins learning a second language. (Chapter 5)

Self-reference effect: the observation that linking to-be-learned information to personally relevant information about oneself creates strong encoding. (Chapter 4)

Self-regulated learning: the continuous monitoring of one's own knowledge and the continuous use of this monitoring to make informed decisions about learning and memory. (Chapter 13)

Semantic categories: meaning affects our cognitive maps. For example, people tend to think of borders between countries as being more straight than they are. (Chapter 6)

Semantic memory: the neurocognitive memory system that encodes, stores, and retrieves information concerning knowledge of the world. (Chapters 4, 5, and 12)

Semantic priming: the effect of one word or idea on the processing of a related word or idea. A related word will activate a target item and allow it to be processed more quickly. (Chapter 5)

Sensory memory: a very brief memory system that holds literal information for a fraction of a second to allow cognitive processing. (Chapter 3)

Sentence verification task: participants are asked to decide as quickly as possible whether a sentence is true or false. (Chapter 5)

Sequential lineup (show-up): procedure used to identify a suspect in which a witness must decide whether each of a successive list of suspects was the person seen at the crime. (Chapter 6)

Serial position curve: the observation that participants remember items well from the beginning and end of a list but not from the middle. (Chapter 3)

Shallow processing: when we process more shallowly, that is, using maintenance rehearsal or processing for sensory characteristics, we remember less of the information processed. (Chapter 4)

Shepard and Metzler's (1971) mental rotation experiment: an early experiment on visual imagery that showed that representation is analog. (Chapter 6)

Short-term memory: an older term used to describe the memory system that holds information for a short period of time, up to 15 seconds. (Chapter 3)

Short-term memory amnesia: deficits in keeping larger amounts of information stored or rehearsed in working memory. (Chapter 10)

Simultaneous lineup (lineup): a procedure used to identify a suspect in which a witness must decide whether a suspect is present among several potential suspects. (Chapter 6)

Single-store view of bilingual representation: there is a common semantic level of representation—that is, meaning is shared in bilinguals. The shared semantic representational system then connects to lemma-level representations for each language. (Chapter 5)

Source amnesia: deficits in correctly attributing the source of a memory. (Chapter 10)

Source judgments: our attributions of where or from whom we learned something. (Chapter 1)

Source memory: refers to the ability of an individual to remember from whom or where (that is, what source) he or she learned something. (Chapter 12)

Source monitoring: our ability to distinguish among the sources of our retrieved memories, in both the external and internal world. (Chapter 8)

Spacing effect: more learning occurs when two study trials on the same information are spread out over time than when they occur successively. (Chapters 1 and 13)

Speech errors: errors in ordinary speech. (Chapter 5)

Spreading activation: refers to the transfer of activation from one node to an associated node. (Chapter 11)

Stability bias: we tend to underestimate future forgetting and overestimate future remembering based on what we can retrieve now. (Chapter 13)

State-dependent memory: the application of encoding specificity to internal human states such as drug states or mood states. (Chapter 4)

Subjective organization: in studying, reorganizing the information in a personally significant way so as to improve learning efficiency. (Chapter 13)

Substantia nigra: a part of the brain that produces dopamine. In Parkinson's disease, this brain region does not produce enough dopamine. (Chapter 2)

Suggestibility: the tendency to incorporate information from sources other than the original witnessed event. These other sources may be potentially misleading. Other sources include other people, written materials, or pictures. (Chapter 8)

Survival processing: processing information in terms of its value to survival in the wild is a surprisingly effective manner in which to encode information. (Chapter 4)

Synapses: gaps between the axon of one neuron and the dendrite of the next neuron in which transmission occurs via neurotransmitters. (Chapter 2)

Synesthesia: sensory qualities from one sense (e.g., vision) are perceived as being sensory qualities in another sense (e.g., sound) in addition to the actual modality that they are perceived in. (Chapter 13)

Taxonomic constraint: states that words refer to categories that share meaning. (Chapter 5)

Technical mnemonics: ready-made methods of learning information such as acronyms or acrostics. (Chapter 13)

Temporal lobe: a part of the cerebral cortex associated with learning, memory, audition, and language. (Chapter 2)

Terminal buttons: the ends of axon that hold neurotransmitters. (Chapter 2)

Thalamus: an area of the brain heavily connected to other areas of the brain. It appears to serve as a routing center, connecting disparate parts of the brain. (Chapter 4)

Theory of mind: the awareness that other individuals have separate states of awareness different from our own awareness. (Chapter 11)

Tip-of-the-tongue states (TOTs): feelings that an unrecalled item will be recalled soon. (Chapter 9)

Trace impairment view: a theory that explains the misinformation effect. In this view, the original memory is altered by the misinformation. (Chapter 8)

Traditional method: words are translated from the speaker's native language into the new language. Grammar is taught in the native language, and reading and writing are emphasized. (Chapter 5)

Transcranial direct current stimulation (tDCS): low current electricity is applied directly to the scalp in a continuous fashion. Used for both research and medical reasons.

Transcranial magnetic stimulation (TMS): a small magnetic pulse to create a small pulse of electricity, which temporarily changes function in a small area of the brain.

Transfer-appropriate processing: retrieval will be stronger when the cognitive processes present at the time of retrieval are most similar to the ones that were present at the time of encoding. (Chapter 4)

Transient global amnesia: a rare form of amnesia in which the amnesic affects are shortlived, usually on the order of hours. (Chapter 10)

Traumatic brain injuries: sudden and devastating injuries to the brain. (Chapter 2)

Use-it-or-lose-it hypothesis: older adults who engage in complex mental activity on a regular basis are more likely to preserve function, whereas those who do not engage in complex mental activity are more likely to suffer declines. (Chapter 12)

Verbal facilitation: hearing verbal descriptions makes it easier to remember visual features. (Chapter 6)

Verbal fluency: the ability to talk without pausing or stopping. (Chapter 3)

Verbal overshadowing: hearing a verbal description makes it more difficult to remember visual features. (Chapter 6)

Visual recognition: infants look selectively at novel stimuli over familiar stimuli. (Chapter 11)

Visuospatial sketchpad: visual working memory. (Chapter 3)

von Restorff effect: advantage in memory that distinctive items have over less distinctive items. (Chapter 4)

Whole-object assumption: young infants appear to innately know that words usually refer to an entire object, rather than parts of it or parts of the object and adjacent objects. (Chapter 5)

Word: in psycholinguistics, a word means the smallest unit of grammar that represents a full meaning. (Chapter 5)

Word fragment completion: in this task, a participant is given some letters of a word but not all of them and must figure out the word. (Chapter 10)

Word length effect: longer words are more difficult to maintain in working memory than are shorter words. (Chapter 3)

Working memory: the neural structures and cognitive processes that maintain the accessibility of information for short periods of time in an active conscious state. (Chapter 3)

Working self: the monitoring function that controls the retrieval of information from the levels of representation. The working self includes the goals and self-images that make up our view of ourselves. (Chapter 7)

References

Abel, M. T., & Bäuml, K.-H. (2016). Retrieval practice can eliminate list method directed forgetting. *Memory & Cognition, 44*,15–23.

Abelson, R. P. (1981). Psychological status of the script concept. *American Psychologist, 36*, 715–729.

Addis, D., R., Roberts, R. P., & Schacter, D. L. (2011). Age-related neural changes in autobiographical remembering and imagining. *Neuropsychologia, 49*, 3659–3669.

Addis, D. R., Knapp, K., Roberts, R. P., & Schacter, D. L. (2012). Routes to the past: Neural substrates of direct and generative autobiographical memory retrieval. *Neuroimage, 59*, 2908–2922.

Aggleton, J. P. (2008). Understanding anterograde amnesia: Disconnections and hidden lesions. *Quarterly Journal of Experimental Psychology, 61*, 1441–1471.

Ait-Ghezala, G., Mathura, V. S., Laporte, V., Quadros, A., Paris, D., Patel, N., . . . Mullan, M. (2005). Genomic regulation after CD40 stimulation in microglia: Relevance to Alzheimer's disease. *Molecular Brain Research, 140*, 73–85.

Akdoğan, E., Izaute, M., Danion, J.-M., Vidailhet, P., & Bacon, E. (2016). Is retrieval the key? Metamemory judgment and testing as learning strategies. *Memory, 13*, 1390–1395.

Alea, N., & Wang, Q. (2015). Going global: The functions of autobiographical memory in cultural context. *Memory, 23*, 1–10.

Alloway, T. P., Gathercole, S. E., Adams, A.-M., Willis, C., Eaglen, R., & Lamont, E. (2005). Working memory and phonological awareness as predictors of progress towards early learning goals at school entry. *British Journal of Developmental Psychology, 23*, 417–426.

Altgassen, M., Ariese, L., Wester, A. J., & Kessels, R. P. C. (2016). Salient cues improve prospective remembering in Korsakoff's syndrome. *Journal of Clinical Psychology, 55*, 123–136.

Amaral, D., & Lavenex, P. (2007). Hippocampal neuroanatomy. In P. Andersen, R. Morris, D. Amaral, T. Bliss, & J. O'Keefe (Eds.), *The hippocampus book* (pp. 37–115). Oxford, UK: Oxford University Press.

Amendola, K. L., & Wixted, J. T. (2015). Comparing the diagnostic accuracy of suspect identifications made by actual eyewitnesses from simultaneous and sequential lineups in a randomized field trial. *Journal of Experimental Criminology, 11*, 263–284.

Anderson, M. C. (2007). Inhibition: Manifestations in long-term memory. In H. L. Roediger III, Y. Dudai, & S. M. Fitzpatrick (Eds.), *Science of memory: Concepts* (pp. 295–299). New York: Oxford University Press.

Anderson, M. C., Bjork, R. A., & Bjork, E. L. (1994). Remembering can cause forgetting: Retrieval dynamics in long-term memory. *Journal of Experimental Psychology: Learning, Memory, and Cognition, 20*, 1063–1087.

Anderson, M. C., & Green, C. (2001). Suppressing unwanted memories by executive control. *Nature, 410*, 366–369.

Anderson, M.C., & Huddleston, E. (2012). Towards a cognitive and neurobiological model of motivated forgetting. In Belli, R. F. (Ed.), *True and false recovered memories: Toward a reconciliation of the debate* (Vol. 58). New York: Springer.

Anderson, M. C., Ochsner, K. N., Kuhl, B., Cooper, J., Robertson, E., Gabrieli, S. W., . . . Gabrieli, J. D. E. (2004). Neural systems underlying the suppression of unwanted memories. *Science, 303*, 232–235.

Anderson, N., & Craik, F. I. M. (2000). Memory in the aging brain. In E. Tulving & F. I. M. Craik (Eds.), *The Oxford handbook of memory* (pp. 411–426). New York: Oxford University Press.

Andrés, P., Van der Linden, M., & Parmentier, F. B. R. (2004). Directed forgetting in working memory: Age-related differences. *Memory, 12,* 248–256.

Arbuckle, T. Y., & Cuddy, L. L. (1969). Discrimination of item strength at time of presentation. *Journal of Experimental Psychology, 81,* 126–131.

Arndt, J. (2012). The influence of forward and backward associative strength on false recognition. *Journal of Experimental Psychology: Learning, Memory, and Cognition, 38,* 747–756.

Arndt, J. (2015). The influence of forward and backward associative strength on false memories for encoding context. *Memory, 23,* 1093–1111.

Artioli, F., Cicogna, P. C., Occhionero, M., & Reese, E. (2012). "The people I grew up with": The role of sociodemographic factors in early memories in an Italian sample. *Memory, 20,* 189–197.

Atkinson, R. C., & Shiffrin, R. M. (1968). Human memory: A proposed system and its control processes. In K. W. Spence & J. T. Spence (Eds.), *The psychology of learning and motivation: Advances in research and theory* (Vol. 2, pp. 89–195). New York: Academic Press.

Bacon, E., Schwartz, B. L., Paire-Ficout, L., & Izaute, M. (2007). Dissociation between the cognitive process and the phenomenological experience of the TOT: Effect of the anxiolytic drug lorazepam on TOT states. *Cognition and Consciousness, 16,* 360–373.

Baddeley, A. (2012). Working memory, theories models and controversy. *The Annual Review of Psychology, 63,* 12.1–12.29.

Baddeley, A. D. (1986). *Working memory.* Oxford, UK: Clarendon.

Baddeley, A. D. (2000). The episodic buffer: A new component of working memory? *Trends in Cognitive Sciences, 4,* 417–423.

Baddeley, A. D. (2007). *Working memory, thought and action.* Oxford, UK: Oxford University Press.

Baddeley, A. D., & Hitch, G. J. (1974). Working memory. In G. Bower (Ed.), *Recent advances in learning and memory* (Vol. 8, pp. 47–90). New York: Academic Press.

Baddeley, A. D., & Longman, D. J. A. (1978). The influence of length and frequency of training session on the rate of learning to type. *Ergonomics, 21,* 627–635.

Baddeley, A. D., & Wilson, B. A. (2002). Prose recall and amnesia: Implications for the structure of working memory. *Neuropsychologia, 40,* 1737–1743.

Baddeley, A.D., Lewis, V., & Vallar, G. (1984). Exploring the articulatory loop. *Quarterly Journal of Experimental Psychology Section A. 36,* 233–352

Badham, S. P., & Maylor, E. A. (2016). Antimnemonic effects of schemas in young and older adults. *Aging, Neuropsychology, and Cognition, 23,* 78–102.

Bahrick, H. P. (1984). Semantic memory content in permastore: Fifty years of memory for Spanish learned in school. *Journal of Experimental Psychology, 113,* 1–29.

Bailey, D. J., & Saldanha, C. J. (2015). The importance of neural aromatization in the acquisition, recall, and integration of song and spatial memories in passerines. *Hormones and Behavior, 74,* 116–124.

Barber, S. J., Rajaram, S., & Aron, A. (2010). When two is too many: Collaborative encoding impairs memory. *Memory & Cognition, 38,* 255–264.

Barber, S. J., Rajaram, S., & Fox, E. B. (2012). Learning and remembering with others: The key role of retrieval in shaping group recall and collective memory. *Social Cognition, 30,* 121–132.

Barnhardt, T. M., Choi, H., Gerkens, D. R., & Smith, S. M. (2006). Output position and word relatedness effects in a DRM paradigm: Support for a dual-retrieval process theory of free recall and false memories. *Journal of Memory and Language, 55,* 213–231.

Barrouillet, P., & Camos, V. (2015). *Working memory: Loss and reconstruction.* New York: Psychology Press.

Barsalou, L. W. (2003). Situated Simulation in the Human Conceptual System. *Language and Cognitive Processes, 18,* 513–562.

Bartlett, F. C. (1932). *Remembering: A study in experimental and social psychology*. Cambridge, UK: Cambridge University Press.

Basden, B. H., Basden, D. R., & Morales, E. (2003). The role of retrieval practice in directed forgetting. *Journal of Experimental Psychology: Learning, Memory, and Cognition, 29*, 389–397.

Bauer, P. (2015). A complementary processes account of the development of childhood amnesia and a personal past. *Psychological Review, 122*, 204–231.

Bauer, P. J. (2002). Long-term recall memory: Behavioral and neuro-developmental changes in the first two years of life. *Current Directions in Psychological Science, 11*, 137–141.

Bauer, P. J., & Larkina, M. (2014). Childhood amnesia in the making: Different distributions of autobiographical memories in children and adults. *Journal of Experimental Psychology: General, 143*, 597–611. http://dx.doi.org/10.1037/a0033307

Baugerud, G. A., Howe, M. L., Magussen, S., & Melinder, A. (2016). Maltreated and non-maltreated children's true and false memories of neutral and emotional word lists in the Deese/Roediger–McDermott task. *Journal of Experimental Child Psychology, 143*, 102–110.

Bäuml, K.-H. T., & Samenieh, A. (2012). Influences of part-list cuing on different forms of episodic forgetting. *Journal of Experimental Psychology: Learning, Memory, and Cognition, 38*, 366–375.

Bays, R. B., Zabrucky, K. M., & Foley, M. A. (2015). Imagery induction processes differentially impact imagination inflation. *Imagination, Cognition and Personality, 35*, 5–25.

Bearce, K. H., & Rovee-Collier, C. (2006). Repeated priming increases memory accessibility in infants. *Journal of Experimental Child Psychology, 93*, 357–376.

Beck, S. M., Ruge, H., Schindler, C., Burkart, M., Miller, R., Kirschbaum, C., & Goschke, T. (2016). Effects of ginkgo biloba extract EGb 761® on cognitive control functions, mental activity of the prefrontal cortex and stress reactivity in elderly adults with subjective memory impairment—A randomized double-blind placebo-controlled trial. *Human Psychopharmacology: Clinical and Experimental, 31*, 227–242.

Bell, R., Röer, J. P., & Buchner, A. (2015). Adaptive memory: Thinking about function. *Journal of Experimental Psychology: Learning, Memory, and Cognition, 41*, 1038–1048.

Belleville, S., Caza, N., & Peretz, I. (2003). A neuropsychology argument for a processing view of memory. *Journal of Memory and Language, 48*, 686–403.

Bellezza, F. S. (1996). Mnemonic methods to enhance storage and retrieval. In E. L. Bjork & R. A. Bjork (Eds.), *Memory* (pp. 345–380). San Diego, CA: Academic Press.

Belli, R. F. (2012). Introduction: In the aftermath of the so-called memory wars. In R.F. Belli (Ed.), *True and false recovered memories: Toward a reconciliation 1 of the debate, Nebraska symposium on motivation*. New York: Springer Science + Business Media.

Belli, R. F., Windschitl, P. D., McCarthey, T. T., & Winfrey, S. E. (1992). Detecting memory impairment with a modified test procedure: Manipulating retention interval with centrally presented event items. *Journal of Experimental Psychology: Learning, Memory, and Cognition, 18*, 356–367.

Benjamin, A. S., & Diaz, M. (2008). Measurement of relative metamnemonic accuracy. In J. Dunlosky & R. A. Bjork (Eds.), *Handbook of memory and metamemory* (pp. 73–94). New York: Psychology Press.

Bennett, D. A., Schneider, J. A., Tang, Y., Arnold, S. E., & Wilson, R. S. (2006). The effect of social networks on the relation between Alzheimer's disease pathology and level of cognitive function in old people: A longitudinal cohort study. *Lancet: Neurology, 5*, 406–412.

Bennetts, R. J., Butcher, N., Lander, K., Udale, R., & Bate, S. (2015). Movement cues aid face recognition in developmental prosopagnosia. *Neuropsychology, 29*, 855–860.

Benoit, R. G., Hulbert, J. C., Huddleston, E., & Anderson, M. C. (2015). Adaptive top–down suppression of hippocampal activity and the purging of intrusive memories from consciousness. *Journal of Cognitive Neuroscience, 27*, 96–111.

Benoit, R. G., & Schacter, D. L. (2015). Specifying the core network supporting episodic simulation and episodic memory by activation likelihood estimation. *Neuropsychologia, 75*, 450–457.

Benoit, R. B., Hulbert, J. C., Huddleston, E., & Anderson, M. C. (2015). Adaptive top–down suppression of hippocampal activity and the purging of intrusive memories from consciousness. *Journal of Cognitive Neuroscience, 27,* 96–111.

Benson, D. F., Gardner, H., & Meadows, J. C. (1976). Reduplicative paramnesia. *Neurology, 26,* 147–151.

Beran, M. J., Brandl, J., Perner, J., & Proust, J. (2012). *Foundations of metacognition.* New York: Oxford University Press.

Bergen, B., Medeiros-Ward, N., Wheeler, K., Drews, F., & Strayer, D. (2013). The crosstalk hypothesis: Why language interferes with driving. *Journal of Experimental Psychology: General, 142,* 119–130.

Bergen, P. S., Thompson, P. J., Baxendale, S. A., Fish, D. R., & Shorvon, S. D. (2000). Remote memory in epilepsy. *Epilepsia, 41,* 231–239.

Bergström, Z. M., Vogelsang, D. A., Benoit, R. G., & Simons, J. S. (2015). Reflections of oneself: Neurocognitive evidence for dissociable forms of self-referential recollection. *Cerebral Cortex, 25,* 2648–2657.

Bermejo-Pareja, F., Benito-León, J., Vega, S., Medrano, M. J., & Román, G. C. (2008). Incidence and subtypes of dementia in three elderly populations of central Spain. *Journal of the Neurological Sciences, 264,* 63–72.

Bernstein, D. M., & Loftus, E. F. (2009). The consequences of false memories for food preferences and choices. *Perspectives on Psychological Science, 4,* 135–139.

Berntsen, D., & Rubin, D. C. (2004). Cultural life scripts structure recall from autobiographical memory. *Memory & Cognition, 32,* 427–442.

Berntsen, D., & Rubin, D. C. (2006). Emotion and vantage point in autobiographical memory. *Cognition & Emotion, 20,* 1193–1215.

Berntsen, D., Staugaard, S. R., & Sørensen, L. M. T. (2013). Why am I remembering this now? Predicting the occurrence of involuntary (spontaneous) episodic memories. *Journal of Experimental Psychology: General, 142,* 426–444.

Beuhring, T., & Kee, D. W. (1987). Developmental relationships among metamemory, elaborative strategies, and associative memory. *Journal of Experimental Child Psychology, 44,* 377–400.

Bielak, A. A. M. (2010). How can we not 'lose it' if we still don't understand how to 'use it'? Unanswered questions about the influence of activity participation on cognitive performance in older age—A mini-review. *Gerontology, 56,* 507–519.

Binder, J. C., Martin, M., Zöllig, J., Röcke, C., Mérillat, S., Eschen, A., . . . Shing, Y. L. (2016). Multi-domain training enhances attentional control. *Psychology and Aging, 31,* 390–408.

Bisiach, E., & Luzzatti, C. (1978). Unilateral neglect of representational space. *Cortex, 14,* 129–133.

Bjork, R. A. (1988). Retrieval practice and the maintenance of knowledge. In M. M. Gruneberg, P. E. Morris, & R. N. Sykes (Eds.), *Practical aspects of memory II* (pp. 396–401). London: John Wiley.

Bjork, R. A. (1992). William Kaye Estes as mentor, colleague, and friend. In A. Healy, S. Kosslyn, & R. Shiffrin (Eds.), *From learning theory to connectionist theory* (Vol. 1, pp. vii–x) *and From learning processes to cognitive processes: Essays in honor of William K. Estes* (Vol. 2, pp. viii–xi). Hillsdale, NJ: Lawrence Erlbaum.

Bjork, R. A., & Bjork, E. L. (1992). A new theory of disuse and an old theory of stimulus fluctuation. In A. F. Healy, S. M. Kosslyn, & R. M. Shiffrin (Eds.), *From learning processes to cognitive processes: Essays in honor of William K. Estes* (Vol. 2, pp. 35–67). Hillsdale, NJ: Lawrence Erlbaum.

Bjork, R. A., & Woodward, A. E. (1973). Directed forgetting of individual words in free recall. *Journal of Experimental Psychology, 99,* 22–27.

Bjork, R. A., Dunlosky, J., & Kornell, N. (in press). Self-regulated learning: Beliefs, techniques, and illusions. *Annual Review of Psychology.*

Blake, A. B., Nazarian, M., & Castel, A. D. (2015). The Apple of the mind's eye: Everyday attention, metamemory, and reconstructive memory for the Apple logo. *The Quarterly Journal of Experimental Psychology, 68,* 858–865.

Blake, M. L. (2016). Cognitive-communication deficits associated with right hemisphere brain damage. In M. L. Kimbarow (Ed.), *Cognitive communication disorders* (2nd ed., pp. 129–185). San Diego, CA: Plural Publishing.

Bland, C. E., Howe, M. L., & Knott, L. (in press). Discrete emotion-congruent false memories in the DRM paradigm. *Emotion*.

Blaney, P. H. (1986). Affect and memory: A review. *Psychological Bulletin, 99*, 229–246.

Blumen, H. M., & Rajaram, S. (2008). Influence of re-exposure and retrieval disruption during group collaboration on later individual recall. *Memory, 16*, 231–244.

Boduroglu, A., Pehlivanoglu, D., Tekcan, A. I., & Kapucu, A. (2015). Effects of self-referencing on FOK accuracy and recollective experience. *Memory, 23*, 736–747. http://dx.doi.org/10.1080/09658211.2014.925927

Bonni, S., Veniero, D., Mastropasqua, C., Ponzo, V., Caltagirone, C., Bozzali, M., & Koch, C. (2015). TMS evidence for a selective role of the precuneus in source memory retrieval. *Behavioral Brain Research, 282*, 70–75.

Botvinick, M. (2007). Conflict monitoring and decision making: Reconciling two perspectives on anterior cingulate function. *Cognitive, Affective and Behavioral Neuroscience, 7*, 356–366.

Boucard, C. C., Rauschecker, J. P., Neufang, S., Berthele, A., Doll, A., Manoliu, A., . . . Mühlau. M (2016). Visual imagery and functional connectivity in blindness: A single-case study. *Brain Structure and Function, 221*, 2367–2374.

Bower, G. H. (2000). A brief history of memory research. In E. Tulving & F. I. M. Craik (Eds.), *The Oxford handbook of memory* (pp. 3–32). New York: University Press.

Bowers, J. S. (2009). On the biological plausibility of grandmother cells: Implications for neural network theories in psychology and neuroscience. *Psychological Review, 116*, 220–251.

Boyacioğlu, R., & Barth. M. (2013). Generalized INverse imaging (GIN): Ultrafast fMRI with physiological noise correction. *Magnetic Resonance in Medicine, 70*, 962–971.

Brainerd, C. J., Wright, R., Reyna, V. F., & Mojardin, A. H. (2001). Conjoint recognition and phantom recollection. *Journal of Experimental Psychology: Learning, Memory, and Cognition, 27*, 307–327.

Brandt, J., & Rich, J. B. (1995). Memory disorders in the dementias. In A. D. Baddeley, B. A. Wilson, & F. N. Watts (Eds.), *Handbook of memory disorders* (pp. 243–270). New York: John Wiley.

Bransford, J. D., & Johnson, M. K. (1972). Contextual prerequisites for understanding: Some investigations of comprehension and recall. *Journal of Verbal Learning and Verbal Behavior, 11*, 717–726.

Brewer, G. A., Ball, B. H., Knight, J. B., Dewitt, M. R., & Marsh, R. L. (2011). Divided attention interferes with fulfilling activity-based intentions. *Acta Psychologica, 138*, 100–105.

Brewer, W. F., & Treyens, J. C. (1981). Role of schemata in memory for places. *Cognitive Psychology, 13*, 207–230.

Brogaard, B., Marlow, K., & Rice, K. (in press). Do synesthetic colors grab attention in visual search? *Review of Philosophy and Psychology*.

Brookmeyer, R., Johnson, E., Ziegler-Graham, K., & Arrighi, M. H. (2007). Forecasting the global burden of Alzheimer's disease. *Alzheimer's and Dementia, 3*, 186–191.

Brooks, L. (1968). Spatial and verbal components of the act of recall. *Canadian Journal of Psychology, 22*, 349–368.

Brown, A. S. (1991). A review of the tip-of-the-tongue experience. *Psychological Bulletin, 109*, 204–223.

Brown, A. S. (1998). Transient global amnesia. *Psychonomic Bulletin & Review, 5*, 401–427.

Brown, A. S. (2004). *The déjà vu experience*. New York: Psychology Press.

Brown, A. S. (2012). *The tip of the tongue state*. New York: Psychology Press.

Brown, C., & Lloyd-Jones, T. J. (2005). Verbal facilitation of face recognition. *Memory & Cognition, 33*, 1442–1456.

Brown, J. (1958). Some tests of the decay theory of immediate memory. *Quarterly Journal of Experimental Psychology, 10*, 12–21.

Brown, R., & Kulik, J. (1977). Flashbulb memories. *Cognition, 5*, 73–99.

Brown, R., & McNeill, D. (1966). The "tip of the tongue" phenomenon. *Journal of Verbal Learning and Behavior, 5*, 325–337.

Brown, P. C., Roediger, H. L., & McDaniel, M. A. (2014). *Make it stick: The science of successful learning.* Cambridge, MA: Harvard University Press.

Bruce, V., Burton, M., & Hancock, P. (2007). Remembering faces. In R. C. L. Lindsay, D. F. Ross, J. D. Read, & M. P. Toglia (Eds.), *The handbook of eyewitness psychology: Vol II. Memory for people* (pp. 87–100). Mahwah, NJ: Lawrence Erlbaum.

Brunel, F. F., & Nelson, M. R. (2003). Message order effects and gender differences in advertising persuasion. *Journal of Advertising Research, 42*, 330–341.

Buchanan, J. P., Gill, T. V., & Braggio, J. T. (1981). Serial position and clustering effects in a chimpanzee's free recall. *Memory & Cognition, 9*, 651–660.

Buján, A., Galdo-Alvarez, S., Lindin, M., & Diaz, F. (2012). An event-related potentials study of face naming: Evidence of phonological retrieval deficit in the tip-of-the-tongue state. *Psychophysiology, 49*, 980–990.

Burt, C. D. B., Kemp, S., & Conway, M. A. (2001). What happens if you retest autobiographical memory 10 years on? *Memory & Cognition, 29*, 127–136.

Burt, C. D. B., Kemp, S., & Conway, M. A. (2003). Themes, events, and episodes in autobiographical memory. *Memory & Cognition, 31*, 317–325.

Butler, A. C., & Roediger, H. L., III. (2007). Testing improves long-term retention in a simulated classroom setting. *European Journal of Cognitive Psychology, 19*, 514–527.

Bywaters, M., Andrade, J., & Turpin, G. (2004). Determinants of the vividness of visual imagery: The effects of delayed recall, stimulus affect and individual differences. *Memory, 12*, 479–488.

Cabeza, R., & Nyberg, L. (1997). Imaging cognition: An empirical review of PET studies with normal subjects. *Journal of Cognitive Neuroscience, 9*, 1–26.

Cai, Z. G., Pickering, M. J., Yan, H., & Branigan, H. P. (2011). Lexical and syntactic representations in closely related languages: Evidence from Cantonese–Mandarin bilinguals. *Journal of Memory and Language, 65*, 431–445.

Calkins, M. W. (1894). Association: I. *Psychological Review, 1*, 476–483.

Campbell, J., & Mayer, R. E. (2009). Questioning as an instructional method: Does it affect learning from lectures? *Applied Cognitive Psychology, 23*, 747–759.

Campbell, R., & Conway, M. A. (1995). *Broken memories: Case studies in memory impairment.* Malden, MA: Blackwell.

Canter, P. H., & Ernst, E. (2007). Ginkgo biloba is not a smart drug: An updated systematic review of randomized clinical trials testing the nootropic effects of G. biloba extracts in healthy people. *Human Psychopharmocology, 22*, 265–278.

Caramazza, A., & Miozzo, M. (1997). The relation between syntactic and phonological knowledge in lexical access: Evidence from the tip-of-the-tongue phenomenon. *Cognition, 64*, 309–343.

Carmichael, A. M., & Gutchess, A. (2016). Using warnings to reduce categorical false memories in younger and older adults. *Memory, 24*, 853–863.

Carney, R. N., & Levin, J. R. (2011). Delayed mnemonic benefits for a combined pegword-keyword strategy, time after time, rhyme after rhyme. *Applied Cognitive Psychology, 25*, 204–2011.

Carpenter, S. K., Lund, T. J. S., Coffman, C. R., Armstrong, P. I., Lamm, M. H., & Reason, R. D. (2016). A classroom study on the relationship between student achievement and retrieval-enhanced learning. *Educational Psychology Review, 28*, 353–375.

Castel, A. D., McGillivray, S., & Friedman, M. C. (2012). Metamemory and memory efficiency in older adults: Learning about the benefits of priority processing and value-directed remembering. In M. Naveh-Benjamin & N. Ohta (Eds.), *Memory and aging: Current issues and future directions* (pp. 245–270). New York: Psychology Press.

Catarino, A., Kupper, C. S., Werner-Seidler, A., Dalgleish, T., & Anderson, M. C. (2015). Failing to forget: Inhibitory-control deficits compromise memory suppression in posttraumatic stress disorder. *Psychological Science, 26,* 604–616.

Cavanaugh, J. C., & Borkowski, J. G. (1980). Searching for the metamemory-memory connections: A developmental study. *Developmental Psychology, 16,* 441–453.

Caza, N., & Belleville, S. (2008). Reduced short-term memory capacity in Alzheimer's disease: The role of phonological, lexical, and semantic processing. *Memory, 16,* 341–350.

Ceci, S. J., & Bronfenbrenner, U. (1985). "Don't forget to take the cupcakes out of the oven": Prospective memory, strategic time-monitoring, and context. *Child Development, 56,* 152–164.

Ceci, S. J., Papierno, P. B., & Kulkofsky, S. (2007). Representational constraints on children's suggestibility. *Psychological Science, 18,* 503–509.

Chang, F., Bauman, M., Pappert, S., & Fitz, H. (2015). Do lemmas speak German? A verb position effect in German structural priming. *Cognitive Science, 39,* 1113–1130.

Charest, I., Kriegeskorte, N., & Anderson, M. C. (2015). Retrieval induces adaptive forgetting of competing memories via cortical pattern suppression. *Nature Neuroscience, 18,* 582–589.

Chen, T., Michels, L., Supekar, K., Kochalka, J., Ryali, S., & Menon, V. (2015). Role of the anterior insular cortex in integrative causal signaling during multisensory auditory–visual attention. *European Journal of Neuroscience, 41,* 264–274.

Chiroro, P. M., Tredoux, C. G., Radaelli, S., & Meissner, C. A. (2008). Recognising faces across continents: The effect of within-race variations on the own-race bias in face recognition. *Psychonomic Bulletin & Review, 15,* 1089–1092.

Chiu, C.-Y. P., Schmithhorst, V. J., Brown, R. D., Holland, S. K., & Dunn, S. (2006). Making memory: A cross-sectional investigation of episodic memory encoding in childhood using fMRI. *Developmental Neuropsychology, 29,* 321–340.

Chomsky, N. (1986). *Knowledge of language.* New York: Praeger Special Studies.

Christina, R. W., & Bjork, R. A. (1991). Optimizing long-term retention and transfer. In D. Druckman & R. A. Bjork (Eds.), *In the mind's eye: Enhancing human performance* (pp. 23–56). Washington, DC: National Academy Press.

Clancy, S. (2005). *Abducted: How people come to believe they were kidnapped by aliens.* Cambridge, MA: Harvard University Press.

Clare, L., Wilson, B. A., Carter, G., & Hodges, J. R. (2003). Cognitive rehabilitation as a component of early intervention in Alzheimer's disease: A single case study. *Aging and Mental Health, 71,* 15–21.

Clark, A., Nash, R. A., Fincham G., & Mazzoni, G. (2012). Creating non-believed memories for recent autobiographical Events. *PLoS ONE, 7*(3), e32998. doi:10.1371/journal.pone.0032998

Clark-Foos, A., Brewer, G., & Marsh, R. L. (2015). Judging the reality of others' memories. *Memory, 23,* 427–436.

Cleary, A. M., & Claxton, A. B. (2015). The tip-of-the-tongue heuristic: How tip-of-the-tongue states confer perceptibility on inaccessible words. *Journal of Experimental Psychology, 41*(5), 1533–1539.

Cleary, A. M., Brown, A. S., Sawyer, B. D., Nomi, J. S., Ajoku, A. C., & Ryals, A. J. (2012). Familiarity from the configuration of objects in 3-dimensional space and its relation to déjà vu: A virtual reality investigation. *Consciousness and Cognition: An International Journal, 21,* 969–975.

Cleveland, E. S., & Reese, E. (2008). Children remember early childhood: Long-term recall across the offset of childhood amnesia. *Applied Cognitive Psychology, 22,* 127–142. http://dx.doi.org/10.1002/acp.1359

Cochran, K. J., Greenspan, R. L., Bogart, D. F., & Loftus, E. F. (2016). Memory blindness: Altered memory reports lead to distortion in eyewitness memory. *Memory & Cognition, 44,* 717–776.

Coffman, J. L., Ornstein, P. A., McCall, L. E., & Curran, P. J. (2008). Linking teachers' memory-relevant language and the development of children's memory skills. *Developmental Psychology, 44,* 1640–1654.

Cohen, G. (1996). *Memory in the real world*. Hove, UK: Psychology Press.

Cole, S. N., Morrison, C. M., Barak, O., Pauly-Takacs, K., & Conway, M. A. (2016). Amnesia and future thinking: Exploring the role of memory in the quantity and quality of episodic future thoughts. *British Journal of Clinical Psychology, 55,* 206–224.

Collins, A. M., & Loftus, E. (1975). A spreading activation theory of semantic memory. *Psychological Review, 82,* 407–428.

Collins, A. M., & Quillian, M. R. (1969). Retrieval time from semantic memory. *Journal of Verbal Learning and Verbal Behavior, 8,* 240–247.

Colombel, F., Tessoulin, M., Gilet, A.-L., & Corson, Y. (2016). False memories and normal aging: Links between inhibitory capacities and monitoring processes. *Psychology and Aging, 31,* 239–248.

Cona, G., Scarpazza, C., Sartori, G., Moscovitch, M, & Bisiacchi, P. S. (2015). Neural bases of prospective memory: A meta-analysis and the "Attention to Delayed Intention" (AtoDI) model. *Neuroscience and Biobehavioral Reviews, 52,* 21–37.

Conrad, R., & Hull, A. J. (1964). Information, acoustic confusion and memory span. *British Journal of Psychology, 55,* 429–432.

Conway, M. A. (2005). Memory and the self. *Journal of Memory and Language, 53,* 594–628.

Conway, M. A., & Loveday, C. (2015). Remembering, imagining, false memories & personal meanings. *Consciousness and Cognition: An International Journal, 33,* 574–581.

Conway, M. A., & Pleydell-Pearce, C. W. (2000). The construction of autobiographical memories in the self-memory system. *Psychological Review, 107,* 261–288.

Conway, M. A., Anderson, S. J., Larsen, S. F., Donnelly, C. M., McDaniel, M. A., McClelland, A. G., . . . Logie, R. H. (1994). *The formation of flashbulb memories. Memory & Cognition, 22,* 326–343.

Conway, M. A., Cohen, G., & Stanhope, N. (1992). Very long-term memory for knowledge acquired at school and university. *Applied Cognitive Psychology, 6,* 467–482.

Conway, M. A., Pleydell-Pearce, C. W., Whitecross, S. E., & Sharpe, H. (2003). Neurophysiological correlates of memory for experienced and imagined event. *Neuropsychologia, 41,* 334–340.

Conway, M. A., Wang, Q., Hanyu, K., & Hasque, S. (2005). A cross-cultural investigation of autobiographical memory: On the universality and cultural variation of the reminiscence bump. *Journal of Cross-Cultural Psychology, 36,* 739–749.

Cowan, N. (2001). The magical number 4 in short-term memory: A reconsideration of mental storage capacity. *Behavioral and Brain Sciences, 24,* 87–185.

Corkin, S. (2002). What's new with the amnesic patient H.M.? *Nature Reviews Neuroscience, 3,* 153–160.

Corkin, S., Amaral, D. G., Gonzalez, R. G., Johnson, K. A., & Hyman, B. T. (1997). H.M.'s medial temporal lobe lesions: Findings from magnetic resonance imaging. *Journal of Neuroscience, 17,* 3964–3979.

Corrigan, J. D. (2015). TBI at the Centers for Disease Control and Prevention. *The Journal of Head Trauma Rehabilitation, 30,* 147.

Corson, Y., Mahé, A., Verrier, N., Columbel, F., & Jagot, L. (2011). Variations d'encodage et faux souvenirs en rappel. *Canadian Journal of Experimental Psychology, 65,* 285–293.

Costa, A., Peppe, A., Zabberoni, S., Serafini, F., Barban, F., Scalici, F., . . . Carlesimo, G. A. (2015). Prospective memory performance in individuals with Parkinson's disease who have mild cognitive impairment. *Neuropsychology, 29,* 782–791.

Craik, F. I. M., & Byrd, M. (1982). Aging and cognitive deficits: The role of attentional resources. In F. I. M. Craik & S. Trehub (Eds.), *Aging and cognitive processes* (pp. 191–211). New York: Plenum.

Craik, F. I. M., & Lockhart, R. S. (1972). Levels of processing: A framework for memory research. *Journal of Verbal Learning and Verbal Behavior, 12,* 671–684.

Craik, F. I. M., & Tulving, E. (1975). Depth of processing and the retention of words in episodic memory. *Journal of Experimental Psychology: General, 104,* 268–294.

Craik, F. I. M., Morris, R. G., & Gick, M. L. (1990). Adult age differences in working memory. In G. Vallar & T. Shallice (Eds.), *Neuropsychological impairments of short-term memory* (pp. 247–267). New York: Cambridge University Press.

Craik, F. I. M., Winocur, G., Palmer, H., Binns, M. A., Edwards, M., Bridges, K., . . . Stuss, D. T. (2007). Cognitive rehabilitation in the elderly: Effects on memory. *Journal of the International Neuropsychological Society, 13,* 132–142.

Crowder, R. G. (1992). Eidetic memory. In L. R. Squire (Ed.), *Encyclopedia of learning and memory.* New York: Macmillan.

Curci, A., & Luminet, O. (2009). Flashbulb memories for expected events: A test of the emotional-integrative model. *Applied Cognitive Psychology, 23,* 98–114.

Curci, A., Lanciano, T., Maddalena, C., Mastandrea, S., & Sartori, G. (2015). Flashbulb memories of the Pope's resignation: Explicit and implicit measures across differing religious groups. *Memory, 23,* 529–544.

Cutler, B. L., Penrod, S. D., & Dexter, H. R. (1990). Juror sensitivity to eyewitness identification evidence. *Law and Human Behavior, 14,* 185–191.

Dahl, J. J., Kingo, O. S., & Krojgaard, P. (in press). The magic shrinking machine revisited: The presence of props at recall facilitates memory in 3-year-olds. *Developmental Psychology.*

Dahl, M., Allwood, C. M., Scimone, B., & Rennemark, M. (2015). Old and very old adults as witnesses: Event memory and metamemory. *Psychology, Crime, & Law, 21,* 764–775.

Dahlgren, D. J. (1998). Impact of knowledge and age on tip-of-the-tongue rates. *Experimental Aging Research, 24,* 139–153.

Dalrymple, K. A., Elison, J. T., & Duchaine, B. (in press). Face-selective and domain-general visual processing deficits in children with developmental prosopagnosia. *Quarterly Journal of Experimental Psychology.*

Daneman, M., & Carpenter, P. A. (1980). Individual differences in working memory and reading. *Journal of Verbal Learning and Verbal Behavior, 19,* 450–466.

Daneman, M., & Hannon, B. (2001). Using working memory theory to investigate the construct validity of multiple-choice reading comprehension tests such as the SAT. *Journal of Experimental Psychology, 130,* 208–223.

D'Angelo, M. C., & Humphreys, K. R. (2015). Tip-of-the-tongue states reoccur because of implicit learning, but resolving them helps. *Cognition, 142,* 166–190.

Damoiseaux, J. S., Viviano, R. P., Yuan, P., & Raz, N. (2016). Differential effect of age on posterior and anterior hippocampal functional connectivity. *Neuroimage, 133,* 468–476.

Danion, J. M. (1994). Drugs as a tool for investigating memory. *European Neuropsychopharmacology, 4,* 179–180.

Darowski, E. S., Helder, E., Zacks, R. T., Hasher, L., & Hambrick, D. Z. (2008). Age-related differences in cognition: The role of distraction control. *Neuropsychology, 22,* 638–644.

Daselaar, S. M., Rice, H. J., Greenberg, D. L., Cabeza, R., LaBar, K. S., & Rubin, D. C. (2008). The spatio-temporal dynamics of autobiographical memory: Neural correlates of recall, emotional intensity, and reliving. *Cerebral Cortex, 18,* 217–229.

De Barbaro, K., Clackson K., & Wass, S. (2016). Stress reactivity speeds basic encoding processes in infants. *Developmental Psychobiology, 58,* 623–639.

De Gelder, B., Tamietto, M., Pegna, A. J., & Van den Stock, J. (2015). Visual imagery influences brain responses to visual stimulation in bilateral cortical blindness. *Cortex: A Journal Devoted to the Study of the Nervous System and Behavior, 72,* 15–26.

de Graaff, S., Verhoeven, L., Bosman, A. M. T., & Hasselman, F. (2007). Integrated pictorial mnemonics and stimulus fading: Teaching kindergartners letter sounds. *British Journal of Educational Psychology, 77,* 519–539.

Deese, J. (1959). On the prediction of occurrence of particular verbal intrusions in immediate recall. *Journal of Experimental Psychology, 58,* 17–22.

Dekle, D. J. (2006). Viewing composite sketches: Lineups and showups compared. *Applied Cognitive Psychology, 20,* 383–395.

DeLoache, J. S., Cassidy, D. J., & Brown, A. (1985). Precursors of mnemonic strategies in very young children's memory. *Child Development, 56,* 125–137.

DeLozier, S., & Rhodes, M. G. (2015). The impact of value-directed remembering on the own-race bias. *Acta Psychologica, 154,* 62–68.

Demiray, B., & Freund, A. M. (2015). Michael Jackson, Bin Laden and I: Functions of positive and negative, public and private flashbulb memories. *Memory, 23,* 487–506.

Demirtas-Tatlidede, A., Vahabzadeh-Hagh, A. M., & Pascual-Leone, A. (2013). Can noninvasive brain stimulation enhance cognition in neuropsychiatric disorders? *Neuropharmocology, 64,* 566–578.

Dempster, F. N. (1981). Memory span: Sources of individual and developmental differences. *Psychological Bulletin, 89,* 63–100.

Desmond, J. E., Chen, S. H. A., & Shieh P.B. (2005). Cerebellar transcranial magnetic stimulation impairs verbal working memory. *Annals of Neurology,* 553–560.

Destan, N., & Roebers, C. M. (2015). What are the metacognitive costs of young children's overconfidence? *Metacognition and Learning, 10,* 347–374.

Dewhurst, S. A., & Conway, M. A. (1994). Pictures, images, and recollective experience. *Journal of Experimental Psychology: Learning, Memory, and Cognition, 20,* 1088–1098.

Diard-Detoeuf, C., Desmidt, T., Mondon, K., & Graux, J. (2016). A case of Capgras syndrome with one's own reflected image in a mirror. *Neurocase, 22,* 168–169.

Dick, A. S., Bernal, B., & Tremblay, P. (2014). The language connectome: New pathways, new concepts. *The Neuroscientist, 20,* 453–467.

Dickson, R. A., Pillemer, D. B., & Bruehl, E. C. (2011). The reminiscence bump for salient personal memories: Is a cultural life script required? *Memory & Cognition, 39,* 977–991.

Dixon, R. A., & Cohen, A. L. (2003). Cognitive development in adulthood. In R. M. Lerner, M. A. Easterbrooks, & J. Mistry (Eds.), *Handbook of psychology* (pp. 443–461). Hoboken, NJ: John Wiley.

Dixon, R. A., Rust, T. B., Feltmate, S. E., & See, S. K. (2007). Memory and aging: Selected research directions and application issues. *Canadian Psychology, 48,* 67–76.

Do Lam, A. T. A., Axmacher, N., Fell, J., Staresina, B. P., Gauggel, S., Wagner, T., . . . Weis, S. (2012). Monitoring the mind: The neurocognitive correlates of metamemory. *PLoS ONE, 7,* 1.

Dowling, W. J., Bartlett, J. C., Halpern, A. R., & Andrews, M. W. (2008). Melody recognition at fast and slow tempos: Effects of age, experience, and familiarity. *Perception & Psychophysics, 70,* 496–502.

Druckman, D., & Bjork, R. A. (Eds.). (1991). *In the mind's eye: Enhancing human performance.* Washington, DC: National Academy Press.

Duchaine, B. & Yovel, G. (2015). A revised neural framework for face processing. *Annual Review of Vision Science, 1,* 393–416.

Dulas, M. R., & Duarte, A. (2016). Age-related changes in overcoming proactive interference in associative memory: The role of PFC-mediated executive control processes at retrieval. *Neuroimage, 132,* 116–128.

Duñabeitia, J. A., Carreiras, M., & Perea, M. (2008). Are coffee and toffee served in a cup? Orthophonologically mediated associative priming. *Quarterly Journal of Experimental Psychology, 61,* 1861–1872.

Dundas, E. M., Plaut, D. C., & Behrmann, M. (2013). The joint development of hemispheric lateralization for words and faces. *Journal of Experimental Psychology: General, 142,* 348–358.

Dunlosky, J., & Ariel, R. (2011). The influence of agenda-based and habitual processes on item selection during study. *Journal of Experimental Psychology: Learning, Memory, and Cognition, 37,* 899–912.

Dunlosky, J., & Bjork, R. A. (2008). The integrated nature of metamemory and memory. In J. Dunlosky & R. A. Bjork (Eds.), *Handbook of memory and metamemory: Essays in honor of Thomas O. Nelson* (pp. 11–28). New York: Psychology Press.

Dunlosky, J., & Hertzog, C. (1998). Aging and deficits in associative memory: What is the role of strategy production? *Psychology and Aging, 13,* 597–607.

Dunlosky, J., & Metcalfe, J. (2009). *Metacognition.* Thousand Oaks, CA: Sage.

Dunlosky, J., & Nelson, T. O. (1992). Importance of the kind of cue for judgments of learning (JOL) and the delayed-JOL effect. *Memory & Cognition, 20,* 373–380.

Dunlosky, J., & Nelson, T. O. (1994). Does the sensitivity of judgments of learning (JOLs) to the effects of various study activities depend on when JOLs occur? *Journal of Memory and Language, 33,* 545–565.

Dunlosky, J., & Tauber, S. (2016). *Oxford handbook of memory.* New York: Oxford University Press.

Dunlosky, J., Serra, M., & Baker, J. M. C. (2007). Metamemory applied. In F. Durso, R. S. Nickerson, S. T. Dumais, S. Lewandowsky, & T. J. Perfect (Eds.), *Handbook of applied cognition* (2nd ed., pp. 137–159). Hoboken, NJ: John Wiley.

Dunning, D., & Stern, L. B. (1992). Examining the generality of eyewitness hypermnesia: A close look at time delay and question type. *Applied Cognitive Psychology, 6,* 643–658.

Eacott, M. J., & Crawley, R. A. (1998). The offset of childhood amnesia: Memory for events that occurred before age 3. *Journal of Experimental Psychology: General, 127,* 22–33.

Ebbinghaus, H. (1964). *Memory: A contribution to experimental psychology.* New York: Dover (Original work published in 1885)

Eich, E. (1984). Memory for unattended events: Remembering with and without awareness. *Memory & Cognition, 12,* 105–111.

Eich, E. (2008). Mood and memory at 26: Revisiting the idea of mood mediation in drug-dependent and place-dependent memory. In M. A. Gluck, J. R. Anderson, & S. M. Kosslyn (Eds.), *Memory and mind: A Festschrift for Gordon Bower* (pp. 247–260). New York: Psychology Press.

Eich, E., & Metcalfe, J. (1989). Mood dependent memory for internal versus external events. *Journal of Experimental Psychology: Learning, Memory and Cognition, 15,* 443–455.

Eich, J., Weingartner, H., Stillman, R., & Gillian, J. (1975). State-dependent accessibility of retrieval cues and retention of a categorized list. *Journal of Verbal Learning and Verbal Behavior, 14,* 408–417.

Eimas, P., Siqueland, E. R., Jusczyk, P., & Vigorito, J. (1971). Speech perception in infants. *Science, 171,* 303–306.

Eimas, P. D., & Quinn, P. C. (1994). Studies on the formation of perceptually-based basic-level categories in young infants. *Child Development, 65,* 903–917.

El Asam, A., & Samara, M. (2015). The cognitive interview: Improving recall and reducing misinformation among Arab children. *Journal of Forensic Psychology, 15,* 449–477.

Elbers, L. (1985). A tip-of-the-tongue experience at age two? *Journal of Child Language, 12,* 353–365.

Ellis, N. C., & Hennely, R. A. (1980). A bilingual word-length effect: Implications for intelligence testing and the relative ease of mental calculation in Welsh and English. *British Journal of Psychology, 71,* 43–52.

Elsabagh, S., Hartley, D. E., Ali, O., Williamson, E. M., & File, S. E. (2005). Differential cognitive effects of Ginkgo biloba after acute and chronic treatment in healthy young volunteers. *Psychopharmacology, 179,* 437–446.

Engle, R. W. (2002). Working memory capacity as executive attention. *Current Directions in Psychological Science, 11,* 19–23.

Engvig, A., Fjell, A. M., Westlye, L. T., Moberget, T., Sundseth, O., Larsen, V. A., & Walhovd, K. B. (2010). Effects of memory training on cortical thickness in the elderly. *Neuroimage, 52,* 1667–1676.

Er, N. (2003). A new flashbulb memory model applied to the Marmara earthquake. *Applied Cognitive Psychology, 17,* 503–517.

Ericsson, K. A. (2003). Exceptional memorizers: Made, not born. *Trends in Cognitive Sciences, 7*(6), 233–235.

Ericsson, K. A., Chase, W. G., & Faloon, S. (1980). Acquisition of a memory skill. *Science, 208,* 1181–1182.

Evans, J. J., Wilson, B. A., Schuri, U., Andrade, J., Baddeley, A. D., Bruna, O., . . . Taussik, I. (2000). A comparison of errorless learning and trial-and-error learning methods for teaching individuals with acquired memory deficits. *Neuropsychological Rehabilitation, 10,* 67–101.

Faul, M., Xu, L., Wald, M. M., & Coronado, V. G. (2010). *Traumatic brain injury in the United States: Emergency department visits, hospitalizations and deaths 2002–2006.* Atlanta, GA: Centers for Disease Control and Prevention, National Center for Injury Prevention and Control. Retrieved from http://www.cdc.gov/traumaticbraininjury/pdf/blue_book.pdf

Fazio, L. K., & Marsh, E. J. (2006). Older, not younger, children learn more false facts from stories. *Cognition, 106,* 1081–1089.

Feinberg, T. E., & Farah, M. J. (2000). A historical perspective on cognitive neuroscience. In M. J. Farah & T. E. Feinberg (Eds.), *Patient-based approaches to cognitive neuroscience* (pp. 3–20). Cambridge, MA: MIT Press.

Finn, B. (2008). Framing effects on metacognitive monitoring and control. *Memory & Cognition, 36,* 813–821.

Finnbogadóttir, H. & Berntsen, D. (2013). Involuntary future projections are as frequent as involuntary memories, but more positive. *Consciousness and Cognition, 22,* 272–280.

Fisher, R. P., & Craik, F. I. M. (1977). Interaction between encoding and retrieval operations in cued recall. *Journal of Experimental Psychology: Human Learning and Memory, 3,* 701–711.

Fisher, R. P., & Geiselman, R. E. (1992). *Memory-enhancing techniques for investigative interviewing: The cognitive interview.* Springfield, IL: Charles C Thomas.

Fisher, R. P., & Schreiber, N. (2007). Interview protocols for improving eyewitness memory. In M. P. Toglia, J. D. Read, D. F. Ross, & R. C. L. Lindsay (Eds.), *The handbook of eyewitness psychology: Vol I. Memory for events* (pp. 53–80). Mahwah, NJ: Lawrence Erlbaum.

Fivush, R., McDermott-Sales, J., Goldberg, A., Bahrick, L., & Parker, J. (2004). Weathering the storm: Children's long-term recall of Hurricane Andrew. *Memory, 12,* 104–118.

Flavell, J. H., Miller, P. H., & Miller, S. A. (1993). *Cognitive development* (3rd ed.). Upper Saddle River, NJ: Prentice Hall.

Fleischman, J. (2002). Phineas Gage: A gruesome but true story about brain science. New York: Houghton Mifflin.

Foer, J. (2011). *Moonwalking with Einstein.* New York: Penguin Books.

Foley, M. F., & Foley, H. J. (2007). Source monitoring about anagrams and their solutions: Evidence for the role of cognitive operations information in memory. *Memory & Cognition, 35,* 211–217.

Frazier, J. L. (2010). False belief drawing.

Freud, S. (1953). Three essays on the theory of sexuality. In J. Strachey (Ed.), *The standard edition of the complete psychological works of Sigmund Freud* (Vol. 7, pp. 125–148). London: Hogarth. (Original work published 1905)

Friedman, A., Montello, D. R., & Burte, H. (2012). Location memory for dots in polygons versus cities in regions: Evaluating the category adjustment model. *Journal of Experimental Psychology: Learning, Memory, & Cognition, 38,* 1336–1351.

Gabbert, F., Hope, L., Carter, E., Boon, R., & Fisher, R. (2016). The role of initial witness accounts within the investigative process. In G. Oxburgh, T. Myklebust, T. Grant, & R. Milne (Eds.), *Communication in investigative and legal contexts: Integrated approaches from forensic psychology, linguistics and law enforcement* (pp. 107–131). Hoboken, NJ: Wiley-Blackwell.

Gagne, C. L., & Shoben, E. J. (2002). Priming relations in ambiguous noun-noun combinations. *Memory & Cognition, 30,* 637–646.

Gardiner, J. M. (2002). Episodic memory and autonoetic consciousness. In A. Baddeley, M. Conway, & J. Aggleton (Eds.), *Episodic memory: New directions in research* (pp. 11–30). New York: Oxford University Press.

Garrett, B. (2009). *Brain & behavior: An introduction to biological psychology* (2nd ed.). Thousand Oaks, CA: Sage.

Garrett, M. (1992). Disorders of lexical selection. *Cognition, 42,* 143–180.

Garrido, M. I., Barnes, G. R., Sahani, M., Dolan, R. J. (2012). Functional evidence for a dual route to amygdala. *Current Biology, 22,* 129–134.

Geraerts, E., Raymaekers, L., & Merckelbach, H. (2008). Recovered memories of childhood sexual abuse: Current findings and their legal implications. *Legal and Criminological Psychology, 13,* 165–176.

Gerbier, E., Toppino, T. C., & Koenig, O. (2015). Optimising retention through multiple study opportunities over days: The benefit of an expanding schedule of repetitions. *Memory, 23,* 943–954.

Germano, C., Kinsella, G. J., Storey, E., Ong, B., & Ames, D. (2008). The episodic buffer and learning in early Alzheimer's disease. *Journal of Clinical and Experimental Neuropsychology, 30,* 613–638.

Gianico, J. L., & Altarriba, J. (2008). An introduction to bilingualism: Principles and processes. In J. Altarriba & R. R. Heredia (Eds.), *An introduction to bilingualism: Principles and processes* (pp. 71–103). Mahwah, NJ: Lawrence Erlbaum.

Glanzer, M., & Cunitz, A. R. (1966). Two storage mechanisms in free recall. *Journal of Verbal Learning & Verbal Behavior, 5,* 351–360.

Godden, D. R., & Baddeley, A. D. (1975). Context-dependent memory in two natural environments: On land and under water. *British Journal of Psychology, 66,* 325–331.

Goldsmith, M., & Koriat, A. (2008). The strategic regulation of memory accuracy and informativeness. In A. Benjamin & B. Ross (Eds.), *The psychology of learning and motivation* (Vol. 48, pp. 1–60). Amsterdam: Academic Press.

Goldsworthy, M. R., Pitcher, J. B., & Ridding, M. C. (2015). Spaced noninvasive brain stimulation: Prospects for inducing long-lasting human cortical plasticity. *Neurorehabilitation and Neural Repair, 29,* 714–721.

Gollan, T. H., & Brown, A. S. (2006). From tip-of-the-tongue (TOT) data to theoretical implications in two steps: When more TOTs means better retrieval. *Journal of Experimental Psychology: General, 135,* 462–483.

Goodwin, D. W., Powell, B., Bremer, D., Hoine, H., & Stern, J. (1969). Alcohol and recall: State-dependent effects in man. *Science, 163,* 1358–1360.

Gopnik, A., & Wellman, H. M. (2012). Reconstructing constructivism: Causal models, Bayesian learning mechanisms, and the theory theory. *Psychological Bulletin, 138,* 1085–1108.

Göthe, K., Oberauer, K., & Kliegl, R. (2007). Age differences in dual-task performance after practice. *Psychology and Aging, 22,* 596–606.

Grill-Spector, K., Knouf, M., & Kanwisher, N. (2004). The fusiform face area subserves face perception, not generic within-category identification. *Nature Neuroscience, 7,* 555–562.

Groninger, L. D. (1971). Mnemonic imagery and forgetting. *Psychonomic Science, 23,* 161–163.

Guasch, M., Sanchez-Casas, R., Ferre, P. &Garcia-Albea, J. E. (2011). Effects of the degree of meaning similarity on cross-language semantic priming in highly proficient bilinguals. *Journal of Cognitive Psychology, 23,* 942–961.

Habib, R., McIntosh, A. R., Wheeler, M. A., & Tulving, E. (2003). Hemispheric asymmetries of memory: The HERA model revisited. *Trends in Cognitive Science, 7,* 241–245.

Haense, C., Kalbe, E., Herholz, K., Hohmann, C., Neumaier, B., Krais, R., & Heiss, W.-D. (2012). Cholinergic system function and cognition in mild cognitive impairment. *Neurobiology of Aging, 33*(5), 867–877.

Hagwood, S. (2007). Memory power: You can develop a great memory: America's grand master shows you how. New York: Free Press.

Hainselin, M., Quinette, P., Desgranges, D., Martinaud, O., de la Sayette, V., Hannequin, D., . . . Eustache, F. (2012). Awareness of disease state without explicit knowledge of memory failure in transient global amnesia. *Cortex: A Journal Devoted to the Study of the Nervous System and Behavior, 48,* 1079–1084.

Hale, S. (1990). A global developmental trend in cognitive processing speed. *Child Development, 61,* 653–663.

Hanley, J. R., & Chapman, E. (2008). Partial knowledge in a tip of the tongue state about two and three word proper names. *Psychonomic Bulletin & Review, 15*, 156–160.

Harley, T. A. (2008). *The psychology of language: From data to theory* (3rd ed.). New York: Taylor & Francis.

Harnishfeger, K. K., & Pope, R. S. (1996). Intending to forget: The development of cognitive inhibition in directed forgetting. *Journal of Experimental Child Psychology, 62*, 292–315.

Harris, J. E., & Wilkens, A. J. (1982). Remember how to do things: A theoretical framework and an illustrative experiment. *Human Learning, 1,* 123–126.

Hart, J. T. (1965). Memory and the feeling-of-knowing experience. *Journal of Educational Psychology, 56*, 208–216.

Hartshorn, K., & Rovee-Collier, C. (1997). Infant learning and long-term memory at 6 months: A confirming analysis. *Developmental Psychobiology, 30*, 71–85.

Hartzell, J. F., Tobia, M. J., Davis B., Cashdollar, N. M., & Hasson, U. (2015). Differential lateralization of hippocampal connectivity reflects features of recent context and ongoing demands: An examination of immediate post-task activity. *Human Brain Mapping, 36*, 519–537.

Harvey, D. Y., & Burgund, E. D. (2012). Neural adaptation across viewpoint and exemplar in fusiform cortex. *Brain and Cognition, 80*, 33–44.

Hasinki, A. E., & Sederberg, P. B. (2016). Trial-level information for individual faces in the fusiform face area depends on subsequent memory. *Neuroimage, 124*, 526–535.

Hatano, A., Ueno, T., Kitagami, S., & Kawaguchi, J. (in press). Why verbalization of non-verbal memory reduces recognition accuracy: A computational approach to verbal overshadowing. *PLoS ONE*.

Hayne, H. (2004). Infant memory development: Implications for childhood amnesia. *Developmental Review, 24*, 33–73.

Head, D., Rodrigue, K. M., Kennedy, K. M., & Raz, N. (2008). Neuroanatomical and cognitive mediators of age-related differences in episodic memory. *Neuropsychology, 22*, 491–507.

Healey, M. K., & Kahana, M. J. (2016). A four-component model of age-related memory change. *Psychological Review, 123*, 23–69.

Heaps, C. M., & Nash, M. (2001). Comparing recollective experiences in true and false autobiographical memories. *Journal of Experimental Psychology: Learning, Memory, and Cognition, 27*, 920–930.

Hege, A. C. G., & Dodson, C. S. (2004). Why distinctiveness information reduces false memories: Evidence for both impoverished relational-encoding and distinctiveness heuristics accounts. *Journal of Experimental Psychology: Learning, Memory, and Cognition, 30*, 787–795.

Heine, M. K., Ober, B. A., & Shenaut, G. K. (1999). Naturally occurring and experimentally-induced tip-of-the-tongue experiences in three adult age groups. *Psychology and Aging, 14*, 445–457.

Helmes, E., & Østbye, T. (2015). Associations between benzodiazepine use and neuropsychological test scores in older adults. *Canadian Journal on Aging, 34*, 207–214.

Helstrup, T. (2004). The enactment effect is due to more than guesses or beliefs. *Scandinavian Journal of Psychology, 45*, 259–263.

Henkel, L. A., Johnson, M. K., & De Leonardis, D. M. (1998). Aging and source monitoring: Cognitive processes and neuropsychological correlates. *Journal of Experimental Psychology: General, 127*, 251–268.

Hennig-Fast, K., Meister, F., Frodl, T., Beraldi, A., Padberg, F., Engel, R. R., . . . Meindl, T. (2008). A case of persistent retrograde amnesia following a dissociative fugue: Neuropsychological and neurofunctional underpinnings of loss of autobiographical memory and self-awareness. *Neuropsychologia, 46*, 2993–3005.

Henri, V., & Henri, C. (1898). Earliest recollections. *Popular Science Monthly, 53*, 108–115.

Hermanowicz, N. (2002). A blind man with Parkinson's disease, visual hallucinations and Capgras syndrome. *Journal of Neuropsychiatry & Clinical Neurosciences, 14*, 462–463.

Hertzog, C. (2016). Aging and metacognitive control. In J. Dunlosky & S. K. Tauber (Eds.), *The Oxford handbook of metamemory* (pp. 537–558). New York: Oxford University Press.

Hertzog, C., & Dunlosky, J. (2011). Metacognition in later adulthood: Spared monitoring can benefit older adults' self-regulation. *Current Directions in Psychological Science, 20*, 167–173.

Hertzog, C., Kidder, D., Powell-Moman, A., & Dunlosky, J. (2002). Monitoring associative learning: What determines the accuracy of metacognitive judgments? *Psychology and Aging, 17*, 209–225.

Herz, R. (2007). *The scent of desire: Discovering our enigmatic sense of smell*. New York: HarperCollins.

Herz, R. S. (2004). A naturalistic analysis of autobiographical memories triggered by olfactory, visual, and auditory stimuli. *Chemical Senses, 29*, 217–224.

Herz, R. S. (2005). Odor-associative learning and emotion: Effects on perception and behavior. *Chemical Senses, 30*, 250–251.

Hess. T. M., & Smith, B. T. (2016). Linkages between age-related changes in the costs of cognitive engagement, motivation, and behavior. In T. S. Braver (Ed.), *Motivation and cognitive control* (pp. 339–360). New York: Taylor & Francis.

Hickin, H., Mehta, B., & Dipper, L. (2015). To the sentence and beyond: A single case therapy report for mild aphasia. *Aphasiology, 29*, 1038–1061.

Hicks, J. L., Marsh, R. L., & Cook, G. I. (2005). Task interference in time-based, event-based, and dual intention prospective memory conditions. *Journal of Memory and Language, 53*, 430–444.

Higham, T., Basell, L., Jacobi, R., Wood, R., Bronk Ramsey, C., & Conard, N. J. (2012). Testing models for the beginnings of the Aurignacian and the advent of figurative art and music: The radiocarbon chronology of Geißenklösterle. *Journal of Human Evolution, 62*, 664–676.

Hines, J. C., Hertzog, C., & Touron, D. R. (2015). Younger and older adults weigh multiple cues in a similar manner to generate judgments of learning. *Aging, Neuropsychology, and Cognition, 22*, 693–711.

Hinkebein, J. H., Callahan, C. D., & Gelber, D. (2001). Reduplicative paramnesia: Rehabilitation of content-specific delusion after brain injury. *Rehabilitation Psychology, 46*, 75–81.

Hirst, W., Johnson, M. K., Kim, J. K., Phelps, E. A., Risse, G., & Volpe, B. T. (1986). Recall and recognition in amnesiacs. *Journal of Experimental Psychology: Learning, Memory, & Cognition, 12*, 445–451.

Hirst, W., Phelps, E. A., Buckner, R. L., Budson, A. E., Cuc, A., Gabrieli, J. D. E., & Johnson, M. K. (2009). Long-term memory for the terrorist attack of September 11: Flashbulb memories, event memories, and the factors that influence their retention. *Journal of Experimental Psychology: General, 138*, 161–176.

Hirst, W., Phelps, E. A., Meksin, R., Vaidya, C. J., Johnson, M. K., Mitchell, K. J., . . . Olsson, A. (2015). A ten-year follow-up of a study of memory for the attack of September 11, 2001: Flashbulb memories and memories for flashbulb events. *Journal of Experimental Psychology: General, 144*, 604–623.

Holliday, R. E., Reyna, V. F., & Brainerd, C. J. (2008). Recall of details never experienced: Effects of age, repetition, and semantic cues. *Cognitive Development, 23*, 67–78.

Hollis, B. R., & Was, C. A. (2016). Mind wandering, control failures, and social media distractions in online learning. *Learning and Instruction, 42*, 104–112.

Howe, M. L. (2006). Distinctiveness effects in children's memory. In R. R. Hunt & J. Worthen (Eds.), *Distinctiveness and human memory* (pp. 237–257). New York: Oxford University Press.

Howe, M. L., & Courage, M. L. (1993). On resolving the enigma of infantile amnesia. *Psychological Bulletin, 113*, 305–326.

Howe, M. L., Toth, S. L., & Cicchetti, D. (2011). Can maltreated children inhibit true and false memories for emotional information? *Child Development, 82*, 967–981.

Howells, S. R., & Cardell, E. A. (2015). Semantic priming in anomic aphasia: A focused investigation using cross-modal methodology. *Aphasiology, 29*, 744–761.

Huesler, B. J., & Metcalfe. J. (2012). Making related errors facilitates learning, but learners do not know it. *Memory & Cognition, 40*, 514–527.

Huff, M. J., Bodner, G. E., & Fawcett, J. M. (2015). Effects of distinctive encoding on correct and false memory: A meta-analytic review of costs and benefits and their origins in the DRM paradigm. *Psychonomic Bulletin & Review, 22*, 349–365.

Hunt, R. R. (1995). The subtlety of distinctiveness: What von Restorff really did. *Psychonomic Bulletin & Review, 2*, 105–112.

Hunter, G. (2011). Transient global amnesia. *Neurologic Clinics, 29*, 1045–1054.

Hunter, R. C., & Eimer B. N. (2012). *The art of hypnotic regression therapy: A clinical guide*. Norwalk, CT: Crown House.

Huttenlocher, J., Hedges, L. V., & Duncan, S. (1991). Categories and particulars: Prototype effects in estimating spatial location. *Psychological Review, 98*, 352–376.

Hyman, I. E., Jr., Husband, T. H., & Billings, F. J. (1995). False memories of childhood experiences. *Applied Cognitive Psychology, 9*, 181–197.

Hyman, I. E., Jr., & Pentland, J. (1996). The role of mental imagery in the creation of false childhood memories. *Journal of Memory and Language, 35*, 101–117.

Izaute, M., & Bacon, E. (2006). Effects of the amnesic drug lorazepam on complete and partial information retrieval and monitoring accuracy. *Psychopharmacology, 188*, 472–481.

Jack, F., & Hayne, H. (2007). Eliciting adults' earliest memories: Does it matter how we ask the question? *Memory, 15*, 647–663.

Jack, F., & Hayne, H. (2010). Childhood amnesia: Empirical evidence for a two-stage phenomenon. *Memory, 18*, 831–844.

Jack, F., Simcock, G., & Hayne, H. (2012). Magic memories: Young children's verbal recall after a 6-year delay. *Child Development, 83*, 159–172.

Jackson, J. W., & Rose, J. (2013). The stereotype consistency effect is moderated by group membership and trait valence. *The Journal of Social Psychology, 153*, 51–61.

Jacoby, L. L. (1991). A process dissociation framework: Separating automatic from intentional uses of memory. *Journal of Memory and Language, 30*, 513–541.

Jacoby, L. L., & Rhodes, M. G. (2006). False remembering in the aged. *Current Directions in Psychological Science, 15*, 49–53.

Jacobs, C., & Silvanto, J. (2015). How is working memory content consciously experienced? The 'conscious copy' model of WM introspection. *Neuroscience and Biobehavioral Review, 55*, 510–519.

James, W. (1890). *The principles of psychology*. New York: Henry Holt.

Janata, P. (2001). Brain electrical activity evoked by mental formation of auditory expectations and images. *Brain Topography, 13*, 169–193.

Janata, P., Tomic, S. T., & Rakowski, S. K. (2007). Characterisation of music-evoked autobiographical memories. *Memory, 15*, 845–860.

Jernigan, T. L., Archibald, S. L., Fennema-Notestine, C., Gamst, A. C., Stout, J. C., Bonner, J., & Hesselink, J. R. (2001). Effects of age on tissues and regions of the cerebrum and cerebellum. *Neurobiology and Aging, 5*, 356–368.

Johansen, M. K., Savage, J., Fouquet, N., & Shanks, D. R. (2015). Salience not status: How category labels influence feature inference. *Cognitive Science, 39*, 1594–1621.

Johnson, M. K., Hashtroudi, S., & Lindsay, S. (1993). Source monitoring. *Psychological Bulletin, 114*, 3–28.

Jones, G., & Macken, B. (2015). Questioning short-term memory and its measurement: Why digit span measures long-term associative learning. *Cognition, 144*, 1–13.

Jones, L. L. (2012). Prospective and retrospective processing in associative mediated priming. *Journal of Memory and Language, 66*, 52–67.

Jonides, J. (1995). Working memory and thinking. In E. E. Smith & D. N. Osherson (Eds.), *An invitation to cognitive science: Vol. 3. Thinking* (pp. 215–265). Cambridge, MA: MIT Press.

Jonides, J., Lacey, S. C., & Nee, D. E. (2005). Processes of working memory in mind and brain. *Current Directions in Psychological Science, 14*, 2–5.

Jonides J., Lewis, R. L., Nee, D.E., Lustig, C.A., Berman, M.G., Moore, K.S. (2008). The mind and brain of short-term memory. *Annual Review of Psychology, 5*, 193–224.

Jönsson, F. U., Hedner, M., & Olsson, M. J. (2012). The testing effect as a function of explicit testing instructions and judgments of learning. *Experimental Psychology*, *59*, 251–257.

Jou, J. (2008). Recall latencies, confidence and output positions of true and false memories: Implications for recall and metamemory theories. *Journal of Memory and Language*, *58*, 1049–1064.

Juckel, G., Karch, S., Kawohl, W. Kirsch, V. Jäger L. Leicht, G., . . . Möller, H. J. (2012). Age effects on the P300 potential and the corresponding fMRI BOLD-signal. *Neuroimage*, *60*, 2027–2034.

Juhascik, M. P., Negrusz, Faugno, D., Ledray, L., Green, P., Lindner, A., Haner, B., & Gaensslen, R. E. (2007). An estimate of the proportion of drug-facilitation of sexual assault in four U.S. localities. *Journal of Forensic Science*, *52*, 1396–1400.

Kail, R. (1991). Processing time declines exponentially during childhood and adolescence. *Developmental Psychology*, *27*, 259–266.

Kalenzaga, S., Sperduti, M., Anssens, A., Martinelli, P., Devauchelle, A.-D., Gallarda, T., . . . Piolino, P. (2015). Episodic memory and self-reference via semantic autobiographical memory: Insights from an fMRI study in younger and older adults. *Frontiers in Behavioral Neuroscience*, *8*, 449.

Kanwisher, N. (2004). The ventral visual object pathway in humans: Evidence from fMRI. In L. M. Chalupa & J. S. Werner (Eds.), *The visual neurosciences* (pp. 1179–1190). Cambridge, MA: MIT Press.

Kao, Y.-C., Davis, E. S., & Gabrieli, J. D. E. (2005). Neural correlates of actual and predicted memory formation. *Nature Neuroscience*, *8*, 1776–1783.

Kaplan, M. (2005). Benzodiazepines and anxiety disorders: A review for the practicing physician. *Current Medical Research and Opinion*, *6*, 941–950.

Kaplan, R. L., Van Damme, I., Levine, L. J., & Loftus, E. F. (2016). Emotion and False Memory. *Emotion Review*, *8*, 8–13.

Karpel, M. E., Hoyer, W. J., & Toglia, M. P. (2001). Accuracy and qualities of real and suggested memories: Nonspecific age differences. *Journals of Gerontology Series B: Psychological Sciences and Social Sciences*, *56*, P103–P110.

Karpicke, J. D., & Roediger, H. L., III (2008). The critical importance of retrieval for learning. *Science*, *319*, 966–968.

Kazanas, S. A., & Altarriba, J. (2015). The survival advantage: Underlying mechanisms and extant limitations. *Evolutionary Psychology: An International Journal of Evolutionary Approaches to Psychology and Behavior*, *13*, 360–396.

Kelley, W. M., Macrae, C. N., Wyland, C. L., Caglar, S., Inati, S., & Heatherton, T. F. (2002). Finding the self? An event-related fMRI study. *Journal of Cognitive Neuroscience*, *14*, 785–794.

Kensinger, E. A., & Schacter, D. L. (2006). When the Red Sox shocked the Yankees: Comparing negative and positive memories. *Psychonomic Bulletin & Review*, *13*, 757–763.

Keppel, G., & Underwood, B. J. (1962). Proactive inhibition in short-term retention of single items. *Journal of Verbal Learning and Verbal Behavior*, *1*, 153–161.

Kessels, R. P. C., & de Haan, E. H. F. (2003). Implicit learning in memory rehabilitation: A meta-analysis on errorless learning and vanishing cues methods. *Journal of Clinical and Experimental Neuropsychology*, *25*, 805–814.

Khalil, R. B., & Richa, S. (2014). When affective disorders were considered to emanate from the heart: The Ebers Papyrus. *The American Journal of Psychiatry*, *171*, 275.

Kihlstrom, J. F., & Schacter, D. L. (1995). Functional disorders of autobiographical memory. In A. D. Baddeley, B. A. Wilson, & F. N. Watts (Eds.), *Handbook of memory disorders* (pp. 337–364). New York: John Wiley.

Kirsch, I., Mazzoni, G., & Montgomery, G. H. (2007). Remembrance of hypnosis past. *American Journal of Clinical Hypnosis*, *49*(3), 171–178.

Kisilevsky, B. S., & Brown, C. A. (2016). Comparison of fetal and maternal heart rate measures using electrocardiographic and cardiotocographic methods. *Infant Behavior & Development*, *42*, 142–151.

Kisilevsky, B. S., Hains, S. M. J., Lee, K., Xie, X., Huang, H., Ye, H. H., . . . Wang, Z. (2003). Effects of experience on fetal voice recognition. *Psychological Science, 14*, 220–224.

Kızılöz, B. K., & Tekcan, A. I. (2013). Canonical categories in flashbulb memories. *Applied Cognitive Psychology, 27*, 352–359.

Klein, S. B. (2012a). Self, memory, and the self-reference effect: An examination of conceptual and methodological issues. *Personality and Social Psychology Review, 16*, 283–300.

Klein, S. B. (2012b). A role for self-referential processing in tasks requiring participants to imagine survival on the savannah. *Journal of Experimental Psychology: Learning, Memory, and Cognition, 38*, 1234–1242.

Klingberg, T., Forssberg, H., & Westerberg, H. (2002). Training of working memory in children with ADHD. *Journal of Clinical & Experimental Neuropsychology, 24,* 781–791.

Koen, J. D., & Yonelinas, A. P. (2016). Recollection, not familiarity, decreases in healthy ageing: Converging evidence from four estimation methods. *Memory, 24,* 75–88.

Kondo, Y., Suzuki, M., Mugikura, S., Abe, N., Takahashi, S., Iijima, T., & Fujii, T. (2005). Changes in brain activation associated with use of a memory strategy: A functional MRI study. *Neuroimage, 24*(4), 1154–1163.

Kondo, Y., Suzuki, M., Mugikura, S., Abe, N., Takahashi, S., Iijima, T., & Fujii, T. (2004). Changes in brain activation associated with the use of a memory strategy: A functional MRI study. *Neuroimage, 15,* 1154–1163.

Konishi, Y., Okubo, K., Kato, I., Ijichi, S., & Nishida, T. (2012). A developmental change of the visual behavior of the face recognition in the early infancy. *Brain & Development, 34,* 719–722.

Kopelman, M. D. (2002). Disorders of memory. *Brain: A Journal of Neurology, 125,* 2152–2190.

Kopelman, M. D., & Bright, P. (2012). On remembering and forgetting our autobiographical pasts: Retrograde amnesia and Andrew Mayes's contribution to neuropsychological method. *Neuropsychologia.*

Koppel, J., & Bernsten, D. (2016). The reminiscence bump in autobiographical memory and for public events: A comparison across different cueing methods. *Memory, 24,* 44–62.

Koriat, A. (2008). Easy comes, easy goes? The link between learning and remembering and its exploitation in metacognition. *Memory & Cognition, 36,* 416–428.

Koriat, A., & Goldsmith, M. (1996). Monitoring and control processes in the strategic regulation of memory accuracy. *Psychological Review, 103,* 490–517.

Koriat, A., & Levy-Sadot, R. (2001). The combined contributions of the cue-familiarity and accessibility heuristics to feelings of knowing. *Journal of Experimental Psychology: Learning, Memory, and Cognition, 27*(1), 34–53.

Koriat, A., & Lieblich, I. (1974). What does a person in a "TOT" state know that a person in a "don't know" state doesn't know. *Memory & Cognition, 2,* 647–655.

Koriat, A., & Shitzer-Reichert, R. (2002). Metacognitive judgments and their accuracy: Insights from the processes underlying judgments of learning in children. In P. Chambres, M. Izaute, & P. J. Marescaux (Eds.), *Metacognition: Process, function, and use* (pp. 1–18). Dordrecht, the Netherlands: Kluwer Academic.

Koriat, A., Bjork, R. A., Sheffer, L., & Bar, S. (2004). Predicting one's own forgetting: The role of experience-based and theory-based processes. *Journal of Experimental Psychology: General, 133,* 643–656.

Kornell, N. (2009). Optimising learning using flashcards: Spacing is more effective than cramming. *Applied Cognitive Psychology, 23,* 1297–1317.

Kornell, N. (2011). Failing to predict future chances in memory: A stability bias yields long-term overconfidence. In A. S. Benjamin (Ed.), *Successful remembering and successful forgetting: A festschrift in honor of Robert A. Bjork* (pp. 365–386). New York: Psychology Press.

Kornell, N., & Bjork, R. A. (2007). The promise and perils of self-regulated study. *Psychonomic Bulletin & Review, 14,* 219–224.

Kornell, N., & Bjork, R. A. (2008). Optimising self-regulated study: The benefits—and costs—of dropping flashcards. *Memory, 16,* 125–136.

Kornell, N., & Bjork, R. A. (2009). A stability bias in human memory: Overestimating remembering and underestimating learning. *Journal of Experimental Psychology: General, 138*, 449–468.

Kornell, N. & Finn, B. (2016). Self-regulated learning: An overview of theory and data. In J. Dunlosky, S. K. Tauber (Eds.), *The Oxford handbook of metamemory* (325–340). New York: Oxford University Press.

Kornell, N., & Metcalfe, J. (2006). Study efficacy and the region of proximal learning framework. *Journal of Experimental Psychology: Learning, Memory, & Cognition, 32*, 609–622.

Kornell, N., Rhodes, M. G., Castel, A. D., & Tauber, S. K. (2011). The ease of processing heuristic and the stability bias: Dissociating memory, memory beliefs, and memory judgments. *Psychological Science, 22*, 787–794.

Koshino, H., Kana, K., Keller, T. A., Cherkassky, V. L., Minshew, N. J., & Just, M. A. (2008). fMRI investigation of working memory for faces in autism: Visual coding and underconnectivity with frontal areas. *Cerebral Cortex, 18*, 289–300.

Kosslyn, S. M. (1975). Information representation in visual images. *Cognitive Psychology, 7*, 341–370.

Kosslyn, S. M. (2005). Mental images and the brain. *Cognitive Neuropsychology, 22*, 333–347.

Kosslyn, S. M. (2010). Where is the "spatial" hemisphere? In *The cognitive neuroscience of mind: A tribute to Michael S. Gazzaniga* (pp. 39–58). Cambridge, MA: MIT Press.

Kosslyn, S. M., Alpert, N. M., & Thompson, W. L. (1995). Indentifying objects at different levels of hierarchy: A positron emission tomography study. *Human Brain Mapping, 3*, 107–132.

Kosslyn, S. M., Ball, T. M., & Reiser, B. J. (1978). Visual images preserve metric spatial information: Evidence from studies of mental scanning. *Journal of Experimental Psychology: Human Perception and Performance, 4*, 47–60.

Kosslyn, S. M., Ganis, G., & Thompson, W. L. (2006). Mental imagery and the human brain. In Q. Jing, M. R. Rosenzweig, G. D'Ydewalle, H. Zhang, H.-C. Chen, & K. Zhang (Eds.), *Progress in psychological science around the world: Vol 1. Neural, cognitive, and developmental issues* (pp. 195–209). London: Psychology Press.

Kraha, A., Talarico, J. M., & Boals, A. (2014). Unexpected positive events do not result in flashbulb memories. *Applied Cognitive Psychology, 28*, 579–589.

Kril, J. J., & Harper, C. G. (2012). Neuroanatomy and neuropathology associated with Korsakoff's syndrome. *Neuropsychology Review, 22*, 72–80.

Kroll, J. F., Bobb, S. C., Misra, M., & Guo, T. (2008). Language selection in bilingual speech: Evidence for inhibitory processes. *Acta Psychologica, 128*, 416–430.

Kroll, N. E., Schepeler, E. M., & Angin, K. T. (1986). Bizarre imagery: The misremembered mnemonic. *Journal of Experimental Psychology: Learning, Memory, and Cognition, 12*, 42–53.

Kuchinke, L., van der Meer, E., & Krueger, F. (2009). Differences in processing of taxonomic and sequential relations in semantic memory: An fMRI investigation. *Brain and Cognition, 69*, 245–251.

Küntay, A. C., Gulgoz, S., & Tekcan, A. I. (2004). Disputed memories of twins: How ordinary are they? *Applied Cognitive Psychology, 18*, 405–413.

Kwok, S. C., Shallice, T., & Macaluso, E. (2012). Functional anatomy of temporal organization and domain-specificity of episodic memory retrieval. *Neuropsychologia, 50*, 2943–2955.

Lachman, M. E., & Andreoletti, C. (2006). Strategy use mediates the relationship between control beliefs and memory performance for middle-aged and older adults. *Journal of Gerontology: Series B: Psychological Sciences and Social Sciences, 61B*, P88–P94.

Laguna-Camacho, A. & Booth, D. A. (2015). Meals described as healthy or unhealthy match public health education in England. *Appetite, 87*, 283–287.

Lah, S., & Miller, L. (2008). Effects of temporal lobe lesions on retrograde amnesia: A critical review. *Neuropsychological Review, 18*, 24–52.

Lampinen, J. M., Leding, J. K., Reed, K. B., & Odegard, T. N. (2006). Global gist extraction in children and adults. *Memory, 14*, 952–964.

Lanciano, T., & Curci, A. (2012). Type or dimension? A taxometric investigation of flashbulb memories. *Memory, 20*, 177–188.

Landauer, T. K., & Bjork, R. A. (1978). Optimum rehearsal patterns and name learning. In M. M. Gruneberg, P. E. Morris, & R. N. Sykes (Eds.), *Practical aspects of memory* (pp. 625–632). London: Academic Press.

Laney, C., Morris, E. K., Bernstein, D. M., Wakefield, B. M., & Loftus, E. F. (2008). Asparagus, a love story: Healthier eating could be just a false memory away. *Experimental Psychology, 55*, 291–300.

Langerock, N., Vergauwe, E., & Barrouillet, P. (2014). The maintenance of cross-domain associations in the episodic buffer. *Journal of Experimental Psychology, 40*, 1096–1109.

Large, M.-E., Cavina-Pratesi, C., Vilis, T., & Culham, J. C. (2008). The neural correlates of change detection in the face perception network. *Neuropsychologia, 46*, 2169–2176.

Larsen, S. T., & Thompson, C. P. (1995). Reconstructive memory in the dating of personal and public news events. *Memory & Cognition, 23*, 780–790.

Laughery, K. R., Welte, J. W., & Spector, A. (1973). Acoustic and visual coding in primary and secondary memory. *Journal of Experimental Psychology, 99*, 323–329.

Leding, J. K. (2011). Need for Cognition and false recall. *Personality and Individual Differences, 51*, 68–72.

Leding, J. K. (2012). False memories and persuasion strategies. *Review of General Psychology, 16*, 256–268.

Lee, K., Shinbo, M., Kanai, H., Nagumo, Y. (2011). Reduplicative paramnesia after a right frontal lesion. *Cognitive and Behavioral Neurology, 24*, 35–39.

Leichtman, M. D., & Ceci, S. J. (1995). The effects of stereotypes and suggestions on preschoolers' reports. *Developmental Psychology, 31*, 568–578.

Leshikar, E. D., Dulas, M. R., & Duarte, A. (2015). Self-referencing enhances recollection in both young and older adults. *Aging, Neuropsychology, and Cognition, 22*, 388–412.

Lesk, V. E., & Womble, S. P. (2004). Caffeine, priming, and tip of the tongue: Evidence for plasticity in the phonological system. *Behavioral Neuroscience, 118*, 453–461.

Levelt, W. M. J. (1989). *Speaking: From intention to articulation*. Cambridge, MA: MIT Press.

Levitin, D. J. (2006). *This is your brain on music: The science of a human obsession*. New York: Penguin.

Li, P., Jia, X., Li, X., & Li, W. (2016). The effect of animacy on metamemory. *Memory and Cognition, 44*, 696. doi: 10.3758/s13421-016-0598-7

Liesefeld, H. R., & Zimmer, H. D. (2013). Think spatial: The representation in mental rotation is nonvisual. *Journal of Experimental Psychology: Learning, Memory, and Cognition, 39*(1), 167–182.

Lilienfeld, S. O., Lynn, S. J., Ruscio, J., & Beyerstein, B. J. (2010). *50 great myths of popular psychology: Shattering widespread misconceptions about human behavior*. New York: Wiley-Blackwell.

Lindner, I., & Henkel, L. A. (2015). Confusing what you heard with what you did: False action-memories from auditory cues. *Psychonomic Bulletin & Review, 22*, 1791–1797.

Linton, M. (1986). Ways of searching and the contents of memory. In D. C. Rubin (Ed.), *Autobiographical memory* (pp. 50–67). New York: Cambridge University Press.

Litman, J. A., Hutchins, T. L., & Russon, R. K. (2005). Epistemic curiosity, feeling-of-knowing, and exploratory behaviour. *Cognition and Emotion, 19*, 559–582.

Loftus, E. F. (1974). Reconstructing memory: The incredible eyewitness. *Psychology Today, 8*, 116–119.

Loftus, E. F. (1979). *Eyewitness testimony*. Cambridge, MA: Harvard University Press.

Loftus, E. F. (1992). When a lie becomes a memory's truth: Memory distortion after exposure to misinformation. *Current Directions in Psychological Science, 1*, 121–123.

Loftus, E. F. (2004). Memory of things unseen. *Current Directions in Psychological Science, 13*, 145–147.

Loftus, E. F., & Davis, D. (2006). Recovered memories. *Annual Review of Clinical Psychology, 2*, 469–498.

Loftus, E. F., & Ketcham, K. (1991). *Witness for the defense; the accused, the eyewitness, and the expert who puts memory on trial*. New York: St. Martin's.

Loftus, E. F., & Ketcham, K. (1994). *The myth of repressed memory*. New York: St. Martin's.

Loftus, E. F., & Palmer, J. C. (1974). Reconstruction of automobile destruction: An example of the interaction between language and memory. *Journal of Verbal Learning and Verbal Behavior, 13,* 585–589.

Loftus, E. F., & Pickrell, J. E. (1995). The formation of false memories. *Psychiatric Annals, 25,* 720–725.

Loftus, E. F., & Zanni, G. (1975). Eyewitness testimony: The influence of the wording of a question. *Bulletin of the Psychonomic Society, 5,* 86–88.

Loftus, E. F., Coan, J. A., & Pickrell, J. E. (1996). Manufacturing false memories using bits of reality. In L. M. Reder (Ed.), *Implicit memory and metacognition* (pp. 195–220). Hillsdale, NJ: Lawrence Erlbaum.

Loftus, E. F., Miller, D. G., & Burns, H. J. (1978). Semantic integration of verbal information into a visual memory. *Human Learning and Memory, 4,* 19–31.

Loftus, G. R. (1983). The continuing persistence of the icon. *Behavioral and Brain Sciences, 6,* 28.

Logan, J. M., Castel, A. D., Haber, S., & Viehman, E. J. (2012). Metacognition and the spacing effect: The role of repetition, feedback, and instruction on judgments of learning for massed and spaced rehearsal. *Metacognition and Learning, 7,* 175–195.

Logie, R. H. (1986). Visuo-spatial processing in working memory. *Quarterly Journal of Experimental Psychology, 38A,* 229–247.

Lorayne, H., & Lucas, J. (1974). *The memory book: The classic guide to improving your memory at work, at school, and at play.* New York: Ballantine.

Lucchelli, F., & Spinnler, H. (2007). The case of lost Wilma: A clinical report of Capgras delusion. *Neurological Science, 28,* 188–195.

Luo, Y., Baillageon, R., Brueckner, L., & Munakata, Y. (2003). Reasoning about a hidden object after a delay: Evidence for robust representations in 5-month old infants. *Cognition, 88,* B23–B32.

Luria, A. R. (1987). *The mind of a mnemonist: A little book about a vast memory.* Cambridge, MA: Harvard University Press. (Original work published 1968)

Lynch, S., & Yarnell, P. R. (1973). Retrograde amnesia: Delayed forgetting after concussion. *American Journal of Psychology, 86,* 643–645.

Lynn, S. J., Krackow, E., Loftus, E. F., Locke, T. G. & Lilienfeld, S. O. (2015). Constructing the past: Problematic memory recovery techniques in psychotherapy. In S. O. Lillienfeld, S. J. Lynn, & J. M. Lohr (Eds.), *Science and pseudoscience in clinical psychology* (2nd ed., pp. 210–244). New York: Guilford Press.

Lynn, S. J., Laurence, J.-R., Kirsch, I. (2015). Hypnosis, suggestion, and suggestibility: An integrative model. *American Journal of Clinical Hypnosis, 57,* 314–329.

Mace, J. H., Bernas, R. S., & Clevinger, A. (2015). Individual differences in recognising involuntary autobiographical memories: Impact on the reporting of abstract cues. *Memory, 23,* 445–452.

MacLeod, C. M., Pottruff, M. M., & Forrin, N. D. (2012). The next generation: The value of reminding. *Memory & Cognition, 40,* 693–702.

Madsen, H. B., & Kim, J. H. (2016). Ontogeny of memory: An update on 40 years of work on infantile amnesia. *Behavioral Brain Research, 298,* 4–14.

Maguire, E. A., Valentine, E. R., Wilding, J. M., & Kapur, N. (2003). Routes to remembering: The brains behind superior memory. *Nature Neuroscience, 6,* 90–95.

Manly, J. J., Touradji, P., Tang, M., & Stern, Y. (2003). Literacy and memory decline among ethnically diverse elders. *Journal of Clinical and Experimental Neuropsychology, 25,* 680–690.

Mannes, S. M., & Kintsch, W. (1987). Knowledge organization and text organization. *Cognition and Instruction, 4,* 91–115.

Maras, K. L., & Bowler, D. M. (2012). Context reinstatement effects on eyewitness memory in autism spectrum disorder. *British Journal of Psychology, 103,* 330–342.

Marcel, A. J. (1983). Conscious and unconscious perception: An approach to the relations between phenomenal experience and perceptual processes. *Cognitive Psychology, 15,* 238–300.

Marche, T. A., & Brainerd, C. J. (2012). The role of phantom recollection in false recall. *Memory & Cognition, 40,* 902–917.

Marcon, J. L., Susa, K. J., & Meissner, C. A. (2009). Assessing the influence of recollection and familiarity in memory for own- and other-race faces. *Psychonomic Bulletin & Review, 16,* 99–103.

Marelli, M., Aggujaro, S., Molteni, F., & Luzzatti, C. (2012). The multiple-lemma representation of Italian compound nouns: A single case study of deep dyslexia. *Neuropsychologia, 50,* 852–861.

Maril, A., Simons, J. S., Mitchell, J. P., Schwartz, B. L., & Schacter, D. L. (2003). Feeling-of-knowing in episodic memory: An event-related fMRI study. *NeuroImage, 18,* 827–836.

Maril, A., Simons, J. S., Weaver, J. J., & Schacter, D. L. (2005). Graded recall success: an event-related fMRI comparison of tip of the tongue and feeling of knowing. *NeuroImage, 24,* 1130–1138.

Marsh, R. L., & Hicks, J. L. (1998). Event-based prospective memory and executive control of working memory. *Journal of Experimental Psychology: Learning, Memory, & Cognition, 24,* 336–349.

Marsh, R. L., Hicks, J. L., & Cook, G. I. (2006). Task interference from prospective memory interferes covaries with contextual associations of fulfilling them. *Memory & Cognition, 34,* 1037–1045.

Martin, N., & Dell, G. S. (2007). Common mechanisms underlying perseverative and non-perseverative sound and word substitutions. *Aphasiology, 21,* 1002–1017.

Massimini, M., Ferrarelli, F., Huber, R., Esser, S. K., Singh, H., & Tononi, G. (2005). Breakdown of cortical effective connectivity during sleep. *Science, 309,* 2228–2232.

Mavridis, I. N. (2015). Deep brain stimulation for psychiatric disorders: Are nucleus accumbens and medial forebrain bundle two branches of the same tree? *Neuroscience and Biobehavioral Review, 56,* 345–346.

Mazzoni, G., & Laurence, J-R., & Heap,. M. (2014). Hypnosis and memory: Two hundred years of adventures and still going! *Psychology of Consciousness: Theory, Research, and Practice, 1,* 153–167.

Mazzoni, G., & Lynn, S. J. (2007). Using hypnosis in eyewitness memory: Past and current issues. In M. P. Toglia, J. D. Read, D. F. Ross, & R. C. L. Lindsay (Eds.), *The handbook of eyewitness psychology: Vol I. Memory for events* (pp. 321–338). Mahwah, NJ: Lawrence Erlbaum.

Mazzoni, G., & Memon, A. (2003). Imagination can create false autobiographical memories. *Psychological Science, 14,* 186–188.

McCabe, D. P., & Smith, A. D. (2002). The effects of warnings on false memories in young and older adults. *Memory & Cognition, 25,* 838–848.

McCabe, J., & Hartman, M. (2008). An analysis of age differences in perceptual speed. *Memory & Cognition, 36,* 1495–1508.

McCabe, J. A. (2015a). Learning the brain in introductory psychology: Examining the generation effect for mnemonics and examples. *Teaching of Psychology, 42,* 203–210.

McCabe, J. A. (2015b). Location, location, location! Demonstrating the mnemonic benefit of the method of loci. *Teaching of Psychology, 42,* 169–173.

McCloskey, M., & Zaragoza, M. (1985). Misleading postevent information and memory for events: Arguments and evidence against the memory impairment hypothesis. *Journal of Experimental Psychology: General, 114,* 1–16.

McDaniel, M. A., & Bugg, J. M. (2012). Memory training interventions: What has been forgotten? *Journal of Applied Research in Memory and Cognition, 1,* 45–50.

McDaniel, M. A., & Einstein, G. O. (2007). *Prospective memory: An overview and synthesis of an emerging field.* Thousand Oaks, CA: Sage.

McDaniel, M. A., Maier, S. F., & Einstein, G. O. (2002). Brain-specific nutrients: A memory cure? *Psychological Science in the Public Interest, 3,* 12–38.

McDaniel, M. A., Roediger, H. L., III, & McDermott, K. B. (2007). Generalizing test-enhanced learning from the laboratory to the classroom. *Psychonomic Bulletin & Review, 14,* 200–206.

McDaniel, M. A., Umanath, S., Einstein, G. O., & Waldum, E. R. (in press). Dual pathways to prospective remembering. *Frontiers in Human Neuroscience.*

McIsaac, H. K., & Eich, E. (2004). Vantage point in traumatic memory. *Psychological Science, 15,* 248–253.

McNamara, T. P. (2005). *Semantic priming: Perspectives from memory and word recognition*. New York: Psychology Press.

McNamara, T. P., & Altarriba, J. (1988). Depth of spreading activation revisited: Semantic mediated priming occurs in lexical decisions. *Journal of Memory and Language, 27*, 545–559.

McWhirter, L, Carson, A., & Stone, J. (2015). The body electric: A long view of electrical therapy for functional neurological disorders. *Brain: A Journal of Neurology, 138*, 1113–1120.

Medin, D. L., & Rips, L. J. (2005). Concepts and categories: Memory, meaning, and metaphysics. In K. J. Holyoak & R. J. Morrison (Eds.), *The Cambridge handbook of thinking and reasoning* (pp. 37–72). New York: Cambridge University Press.

Mednick, S. C., Cai, D. J., Kanady, J., & Drummond, S. P. A. (2008). Comparing the benefits of caffeine, naps, and placebo on verbal, motor, and perceptual memory. *Behavioral Brain Research, 193*, 79–86.

Medved, M. I. (2007). Remembering without a past: Individuals with anterograde memory impairment talk about their lives. *Psychology, Health, & Medicine, 12*, 603–616.

Megreya, A. M., Memon, A., & Havard, C. (2012). The headscarf effect: Direct evidence from the eyewitness identification paradigm. *Applied Cognitive Psychology, 26*, 308–315.

Meissner, C. A., Brigham, J. C., & Kelley, C. M. (2001). The influence of retrieval processes in verbal overshadowing. *Memory & Cognition, 29*, 176–186.

Meissner, C. A., Sporer, S. L., & Susa, K. J. (2008). A theoretical review and meta-analysis of the description-identification relationship in memory for faces. *European Journal of Cognitive Psychology, 20*, 414–455.

Melnyk, L., Crossman, A. M., & Scullin, M. H. (2007). The suggestibility of children's memory. In M. Toglia, J. D. Read, & R. C. L. Lindsay (Eds.), *Handbook of eyewitness memory* (Vol. 1, pp. 401–451). Mahwah, NJ: Lawrence Erlbaum.

Mervis, C. B., Catlin, J., & Rosch, E. (1976). Relationships among goodness-of-example, category norms, and word frequency. *Bulletin of the Psychonomic Society, 7*, 283–284.

Metcalfe, J. (2002). Is study time allocated selectively to a region of proximal learning? *Journal of Experimental Psychology: General, 131*, 349–363.

Metcalfe, J. (2011). Desirable difficulties and studying in the region of proximal learning. In *Successful remembering and successful forgetting: A festschrift in honor of Robert A. Bjork* (pp. 259–276). New York: Psychology Press.

Metcalfe, J., & Casal-Roscum, L., & Radin, A., & Friedman, D. (2015). On teaching old dogs new tricks. *Psychological Science, 26*, 1833–1842.

Metcalfe, J., & Finn, B. (2008). Familiarity and retrieval processes in delayed judgments of learning. *Journal of Experimental Psychology: Learning, Memory, & Cognition, 34*, 1084–1097.

Metcalfe, J., & Finn, B. (2011). People's hypercorrection of high-confidence errors. Did they know it all along? *Journal of Experimental Psychology: Learning, Memory, and Cognition, 37*, 437–448.

Metcalfe, J., & Kornell, N. (2005). A regional of proximal learning model of metacognitively guided study-time allocation. *Journal of Memory and Language, 52*, 463–477.

Metcalfe, J., & Schwartz, B. L. (2016). The ghost in the machine: Self-reflective consciousness and the neuroscience of metacognition. In J. Dunlosky & S. Tauber (Eds). *Oxford handbook of metamemory* (pp. 407–424). New York: Oxford University Press.

Metzger, R. L., Warren, A. R., Shelton, J. T., Price, J., Reed, A. W., & Williams, D. (2008). Do children "DRM" like adults? False memory production in children. *Developmental Psychology, 44*, 169–181.

Meyer, D. E., & Schvaneveldt, R. W. (1971). Facilitation in recognizing pairs of word: Evidence of a dependence between retrieval operations. *Journal of Experimental Psychology, 90*, 227–234.

Meyer, D. E., & Schvaneveldt, R. W. (1976). Meaning, memory structure, and mental processes. *Science, 192*, 27–33.

Mickes, L., & Wixted, J. T. (2015). On the applied implications of the "verbal overshadowing effect." *Perspectives on Psychological Science, 10*, 400–403.

Miles, S. J., & Minda, J. P. (2012). Perceptual fluency can be used as a cue for categorization decisions. *Psychonomic Bulletin & Review, 19*, 737–742.

Miller, G. A. (1956). The magical number seven, plus or minus two: Some limits on our capacity for processing information. *Psychological Review, 63*, 81–97.

Miller, J. P., Sweet, J. A., Baily, C. M., Munyon, C. N., Luders, H. O., & Fastenau, P. S. (2015). Visual-spatial memory may be enhanced with theta burst deep brain stimulation of the fornix: A preliminary investigation with four cases. *Brain: A Journal of Neurology, 138*, 1833–1842.

Miller, T. M., & Geraci, L. (2011). Training metacognition in the classroom: The influence of incentives and feedback on exam predictions. *Metacognition and Learning, 6*, 303–314.

Mohanty, P., Naveh-Benjamin, M., & Ratneshwar, S. (2016). Beneficial effects of semantic memory support on older adults' episodic memory: Differential patterns of support of item and associative information. *Psychology and Aging, 31*, 25–36.

Moldovan, C. D., Ferré, P., Demestre, J., & Sánchez-Casas, R. (2015). Semantic similarity: Normative ratings for 185 Spanish noun triplets. *Behavior Research Methods, 47*, 788–99.

Momennejad, I., & Haynes, J-D. (2012). Human anterior prefrontal cortex encodes the 'what' and 'when' of future intentions. *Neuroimage, 61*, 139–148.

Moon, Y., Moon, W.-J., & Han, S.-H. (in press). The structural connectivity of the recurrent transient global amnesia. *Acta Neurologica Scandinavica*.

Moradi, A. R., Heydari, A. H., Abdollahi, M. H., Rahimi-Movaghar, W., Dalgleish, T., & Jobson, L. (2015). Visual false memories in posttraumatic stress disorder. *Journal of Abnormal Psychology, 124*, 905–917.

Morcum, A. M. (2016). Mind over memory: Cuing the aging brain. *Current Directions in Psychological Science, 25*, 143–50.

Moscovitch, M. (1989). Confabulation and the frontal system: Strategic vs. associative retrieval in neuropsychological theories of memory. In H. L. Roediger & F. I. M. Craik (Eds.), *Varieties of memory and consciousness: Essays in honour of Endel Tulving* (pp. 133–160). Hillsdale, NJ: Lawrence Erlbaum.

Moss, A. S., Monti, D. A., & Newberg, A. (2013). Working memory and meditation. In T. Packiam Alloway & G. Alloway (Eds). *Working memory: The connected intelligence* (pp. 261–273). New York: Psychology Press.

Mueller, M. L., Dunlosky, J., & Tauber, S. K. (2016). The effect of identical word pairs on people's metamemory judgments: What are the contributions of processing fluency and beliefs about memory? *Quarterly Journal of Experimental Psychology, 69*, 781–799.

Mulligan, N. W., & Picklesimer, M. (2016). Attention and the testing effect. *Journal of Experimental Psychology, 42*, 938–950.

Murdock, B. B. (1962). The serial position effect of free recall. *Journal of Experimental Psychology, 64*, 482–488.

Murre, J. M., & Sturdy, D. P. (1995). The connectivity of the brain: Multi-level quantitative analysis. *Biological Cybernetics, 73*, 529–545.

Myers, N. A., & Perlmutter, M. (1978). Memory in the years from two to five. In P. A. Ornstein (Ed.), *Memory development in children* (pp. 191–218). Hillsdale, NJ: Lawrence Erlbaum.

Nairne, J.S. (2010). Adaptive memory: Evolutionary constraints on remembering. In B. H. Ross (Ed.), *The psychology of learning and motivation* (Vol. 53, pp. 1–32). Burlington: Academic Press.

Nairne, J. S., Thompson, S. R., & Pandeirada, J. N. S. (2007). Adaptive memory: Survival processing enhances retention. *Journal of Experimental Psychology: Learning, Memory, & Cognition, 33*, 263–273.

Nakabayashi, K., Lloyd-Jones, T. J., Butcher, N., Liu, C. H. (2012). Independent influences of verbalization and race on the configural and featural processing of faces: A behavioral and eye movement study. *Journal of Experimental Psychology: Learning, Memory, and Cognition, 38*, 61–77.

Nash, R. A., Wade, K. A., & Lindsay, D. S. (2009). Digitally-manipulated memory: Effects of doctored videos and imagination in distorting beliefs and memories. *Memory & Cognition, 37*, 414–424.

National Center for Education Statistics. (2016). *Digest of education statistics: 2013*. Retrieved from http://nces.ed.gov/programs/digest/d11/index.asp

Naveh-Benjamin, M., & Ayres, T. J. (1986). Digit span, reading rate, and linguistic relativity. *Quarterly Journal of Experimental Psychology, 38*, 739–751.

Navah-Benjamin, M., Cowan, N., Kilb, A., & Chen, Z. (2007). Age-related differences in immediate serial recall: Dissociating chunk formation and capacity. *Memory & Cognition, 35*, 724–737.

Neisser, U. (1967). *Cognitive psychology*. New York: Appleton.

Nelson, K. (1989). *Narratives from the crib*. Cambridge, MA: Harvard University Press.

Nelson, T. O. (1984). A comparison of current measures of the accuracy of feeling of knowing predictions. *Psychological Bulletin, 95*, 109–133.

Nelson, T. O., & Leonesio, R. J. (1988). Allocation of self-paced study time and the "labor-in-vain" effect. *Journal of Experimental Psychology: Learning, Memory, & Cognition, 14*, 676–686.

Nelson, T. O., & Narens, L. (1990). Metamemory: A theoretical framework and new findings. In G. Bower (Ed.), *The psychology of learning and motivation* (Vol. 26, pp. 125–141). San Diego, CA: Academic Press.

Neuschatz, J. S., Wetmore, S. A., Key, K., Cash, D., Gronlund, S. D., & Goodsell, C. A. (in press). Comprehensive evaluation of showups. In M. Miller & B. Bornstein (Eds.), *Advances in psychology and law*. New York: Springer.

Nickerson, R. S. (1984). Retrieval inhibition from part-set cueing: A persistent enigma in memory research. *Memory & Cognition, 12*, 531–552.

Nickerson, R. S., & Adams, J. J. (1979). Long-term memory for a common object. *Cognitive Psychology, 11*, 287–307.

Nicolas, S. (2006). La mesure de la mémoire. *L'essentiel cerveau & Psycho, 6*, 1–4.

Nicolas, S., Barnes, M. E., & Murray, D. J. (2015). A French description of German psychology laboratories in 1893 by Victor Henri, a collaborator of Binet. *Psychological Research/Psychologische Forschung, 79*, 361–370.

Nigro, G., & Neisser, U. (1983). Point of view in personal memories. *Cognitive Psychology, 15*, 467–482.

Oates, J. M., Peynircioğlu, Z. F., & Bates, K. B (2015). Is event-based prospective memory resistant to proactive interference? *Current Psychology: A Journal for Diverse Perspectives on Diverse Psychological Issues*.

Oates, J.M., Peynircioğlu, Z.F. & Bates, K.B. (2016). *Current Psychology, 35*, 632–637. doi:10.1007/s12144-015-9330-1

O'Conner, M., Lebowitz, B. K., Ly, J., Panizzon, M. S., Elkin-Frankston, S., Dey, S., . . . Pearlman, C. (2008). A dissociation between anterograde and retrograde amnesia after treatment with electroconvulsive therapy: A naturalistic investigation. *Journal of ECT, 24*, 146–151.

O'Doherty, D. C. M., Chitty, K. M., Saddiqui, S., Bennett, M. R., & Lagopoulos, J. (2015). A systematic review and meta-analysis of magnetic resonance imaging measurement of structural volumes in posttraumatic stress disorder. *Psychiatry Research: Neuroimaging, 232*, 1–33.

Okamoto, M., Wada, Y., Yamaguchi, Y., Kyutoku, Y., Clowney, L., Singh, A. K., & Dan, I. (2011). Process-specific prefrontal contributions to episodic encoding and retrieval of tastes: A functional NIRS study. *Neuroimage, 54*, 1578–1588.

Olszewska, J. M., Reuter-Lorenz, P. A., Munier, E., & Bendler, S. A. (2015). Misremembering what you see or hear: Dissociable effects of modality on short- and long-term false recognition. *Journal of Experimental Psychology, 41*, 1316–1325.

Ornstein, P. A., Haden, C. A., & Elischberger, H. B. (2006). Children's memory development: Remembering the past and preparing for the future. In E. Bialystok & F. I. M. Craik (Eds.), *Lifespan cognition: Mechanisms of change* (pp. 143–161). New York: Oxford University Press.

Otani, A. (1992). Memory in hypnosis. *The Advocate, 16*, 111–121.

Otani, H., Kato, K., Von Glahn, N. R., Nelson, M. E., Widner, R. L., Jr., & Goernert, P. N. (2008). Hypermnesia: A further examination of age differences between young and older adults. *British Journal of Psychology, 99*, 265–278.

Otgaar, H., Candel, I., Merckelbach, H., & Wade, K. (2009). Abducted by a UFO: Prevalence information affects young children's false memories for an implausible event. *Applied Cognitive Psychology, 23,* 115–125.

Otgaar, H., Howe, M. L., Brackmann, N., & Smeets, T. (2016). The malleability of developmental trends in neutral and negative memory illusions. *Journal of Experimental Psychology: General, 145,* 31–55.

Otgaar, H., Peters, M., & Howe, M. L. (2012). Dividing attention lowers children's but increases adults' false memories. *Journal of Experimental Psychology: Learning, Memory, and Cognition, 38,* 204–210.

Otgaar, H., Smeets, T., & Peters, M. (2012). Children's implanted false memories and additional script knowledge. *Applied Cognitive Psychology, 26,* 709–715.

Otgaar, H., Verschuere, B., Meijer, E. H., & Van Oorsouw, K. (2012). The origin of children's implanted false memories: Memory traces or compliance? *Acta Psychologica, 139,* 397–403.

Otsuka, Y., & Osaka, N. (2015). High-performers use the phonological loop less to process mental arithmetic during working memory tasks. *Quarterly Journal of Experimental Psychology, 68,* 878–886.

Otsuka, Y., & Osaka, N. (2005). Working memory in the elderly: Role of prefrontal cortex. *Japanese Psychological Research, 48,* 518–529.

Oudman, E., Nijboer, T.C.W., Postma, A., Wijnia, J. W., & Van der Stigchel, S. (2015). Procedural learning and memory rehabilitation in Korsakoff's syndrome—A review of the literature. *Neuropsychology Review, 25,* 134–148.

Oudman, E., Van der Stigchel, S., Nijboer, T. C. W., Wijnia, J. W., Seekles, M. L., & Postma, A. (2016). Route learning in Korsakoff's syndrome: Residual acquisition of spatial memory despite profound amnesia. *Journal of Neuropsychology, 10,* 90–103.

Oxburgh, G., Myklebust, T., Grant, T., & Milne, R. (2016). *Communication in investigative and legal contexts: Integrated approaches from forensic psychology, linguistics and law enforcement.* Hoboken, NJ: Wiley-Blackwell

Paik, J., & Ritter, F. R. (2016). Evaluating a range of learning schedules: Hybrid training schedules may be as good as or better than distributed practice for some tasks. *Ergonomics, 59,* 276–290.

Paivio, A. (1969). Mental imagery in associative learning and memory. *Psychological Review, 76,* 241–263.

Parker, A., Dagnall, N., & Munley, G. (2012). Encoding tasks dissociate the effects of divided attention on category-cued recall and category-exemplar generation. *Experimental Psychology, 59,* 124–131.

Parker, E. S., Cahill, L., & McGaugh, J. L. (2006). A case of unusual autobiographical remembering. *Neurocase, 12*(1), 35–49.

Parkin, A. J., Bindschaedler, C., Harsent, L., & Metzler, C. (1996). Pathological false alarm rates following damage to the left frontal cortex. *Brain & Cognition, 32,* 14–27.

Parra, M. A., Saarimaki, H., Bastin, M. E., Londono, A, C., Pettit, L., Lopera, F., . . . Abrahams, S. (2015). Memory binding and white matter integrity in familial Alzheimer's disease. *Brain: A Journal of Neurology, 138,* 1355–1369.

Patihis, L., & Loftus, E. F. (2016). Crashing memory 2.0: False memories in adults for an upsetting childhood event. *Applied Cognitive Psychology, 31,* 41–50.

Plaut, C., & McClelland, J. L. (2010). Locating object knowledge in the brain: Comment on Bowers's (2009). attempt to revive the grandmother cell hypothesis. *Psychological Review, 117,* 284–290.

Paz-Alonso, P. M., & Goodman, G. S. (2008). Trauma and memory: Effects of post-event misinformation, retrieval order and retrieval interval. *Memory, 16,* 58–75.

Perez, O., Mukamel, R., Tankus, A., Rosenblatt, J. D., Yeshurun, Y., & Fried, I. (2015). Preconscious Prediction of a Driver's Decision Using Intracranial Recordings. *Journal of Cognitive Neuroscience, 27,* 1492–1502.

Perfect, T. J. (2002). When does eyewitness confidence predict performance? In T. J. Perfect & B. Schwartz (Eds.), *Applied metacognition* (pp. 95–120). Cambridge, UK: Cambridge University Press.

Perfect, T. J., Wagstaff, G. F., Moore, D., Andrews, B., Cleveland, V., Newcombe, S., . . . Brown, L. (2008). How can we help witnesses to remember more? It's an (eyes) open and shut case. *Law and Human Behavior, 32,* 314–324.

Pergolizzi, D., & Chua, E. F. (2015). Transcranial direct current stimulation (tDCS) of the parietal cortex leads to increased false recognition. *Neuropsychologia, 66,* 88–98.

Perner, J. (2000). Memory and the theory of mind. In E. Tulving & F. I. M. Craik (Eds.), *The Oxford handbook of memory* (pp. 285–314). New York: Oxford University Press.

Perner, J., & Roessler, J. (2012). From infants' to children's appreciation of belief. *Trends in Cognitive Science, 10,* 519–525.

Perrin, D., & Rousset, S. (2014). The episodicity of memory: Current trends and issues in philosophy and psychology. *Review of Philosophy and Psychology, 5,* 291–312.

Persson, N., Ghisletta, P., Dahle, C. L., Bender, A. R., Yang, Y., Yuan, P., Daugherty, A. M., & Raz, N. (2016). Regional brain shrinkage and change in cognitive performance over two years: The bidirectional influences of the brain and cognitive reserve factors. *Neuroimage, 126,* 15–26.

Peterson, C. (2012). Children's autobiographical memories across the years: Forensic implications of childhood amnesia and eyewitness memory for stressful events. *Developmental Review, 32,* 287–306.

Peterson, C., McDermott Sales, J., Rees, M., & Fivush, R. (2007). Parent-child talk and children's memory for stressful events. *Applied Cognitive Psychology, 21,* 1057–1075.

Peterson, L. R., & Johnson, S. F. (1971). Some effects of minimizing articulation of short-term retention of individual verbal items. *Journal of Verbal Learning and Verbal Behavior, 10,* 346–354.

Peterson, L. R., & Peterson, M. J. (1959). Short-term retention of individual verbal items. *Journal of Experimental Psychology, 58,* 193–198.

Pezdek, K., Finger, K., & Hodge, D. (1997). Planting false childhood memories: The role of event plausibility. *Psychological Science, 8,* 437–441.

Philippot, P., Baeyens, C., Douilliez, C., & Francart, B. (2004). Cognitive regulation of emotion: Application to clinical disorders. In P. Philippot & R. S. Feldman (Eds.), *The regulation of emotion* (pp. 71–97). Mahwah, NJ: Lawrence Erlbaum.

Pinker, S. (1994). *The language instinct: How the mind creates language.* New York: HarperCollins.

Pinker, S. (1999). *Words and rules: The ingredients of language.* New York: Basic Books.

Pinker, S. (2012). False fronts in the language wars. *Slate, 5.31.2012.*

Plaut, C., & McClelland, J. L. (2010). Locating object knowledge in the brain: Comment on Bowers's (2009). attempt to revive the grandmother cell hypothesis. *Psychological Review, 117,* 284–290.

Poort, E. D., Warren, J. E., & Rodd, J. M. (2016). Recent experience with cognates and interlingual homographs in one language affects subsequent processing in another language. *Bilingualism, 19,* 206–212.

Popov, V., & Hristova, P. (2015). Unintentional and efficient relational priming. *Memory & Cognition, 43,* 866–878.

Porter, S., Yuille, J. C., & Lehman, D. R. (1999). The nature of real, implanted, and fabricated memories for emotional childhood events: Implications for the recovered memory debate. *Law and Human Behavior, 23,* 517–537.

Pressley, M., & Hilden, K. (2006). Cognitive strategies. In D. Kuhn & R. Siegler (Eds.), *Handbook of child psychology* (6th ed., pp. 511–556). Hoboken, NJ: John Wiley.

Price, H. L., & Connolly, D. A. (2008). Children's recall of emotionally arousing repeated events: A review and call for further investigation. *International Journal of Law and Psychiatry, 31,* 337–346.

Price, J., McElroy, K., & Martin, N. J. (2016). The role of font size and font style in younger and older adults' predicted and actual recall performance. *Aging, Neuropsychology, and Cognition, 23,* 366–388.

Price, J., Hertzog, C., & Dunlosky, J. (2008). Age-related differences in strategy knowledge updating: Blocked testing produces greater improvements in metacognitive accuracy for younger than older adults. *Aging, Neuropsychology, and Cognition, 15,* 601–626.

Prince, S. E., Tsukiura, T., & Cabeza, R. (2007). Distinguishing the Neural Correlates of Episodic Memory Encoding and Semantic Memory Retrieval. *Psychological Science, 18,* 144–151.

Proust, M. (1928). *Swann's way*. New York: The Modern Library.

Provost, A., & Heathcote, A. (2015). Titrating decision processes in the mental rotation task. *Psychological Review, 122,* 735–754.

Pylyshyn, Z. W. (2003). Return of the mental image: Are there pictures in the brain? *Trends in Cognitive Science, 7,* 113–118.

Quas, J. A., Rush, E. B., Yim, I. S., Edelstein, R. S., Otgaar, H. & Smeets, T. (2016). Stress and emotional valence effects on children's versus adolescents' true and false memory, *Memory, 24,* 696–707, DOI: 10.1080/09658211.2015.1045909

Quiroga, R. Q. (2013). Gnostic cells in the 21st century. *Acta Neurobiologiae, 73,* 463–471.

Quiroga, R. Q., Reddy, L., Kreiman, G., Koch, C., & Fried, I. (2005). Invariant visual representation by single neurons in the human brain. *Nature, 435,* 1102–1107.

Rabbitt, P., Mogapi, O., Scott, M., Thacker, N., Lowe, C., Horan, M., . . . Lunn, D. (2007). Effects of global atrophy, white matter lesions, and cerebral blood flow on age-related changes in speed, memory, intelligence, vocabulary, and frontal function. *Neuropsychology, 21,* 684–695.

Rabin, J. S., & Rosenbaum, R. S. (2012). Familiarity modulates the functional relationship between theory of mind and autobiographical memory. *Neuroimage, 62,* 520–529.

Race, E., & Verfaellie, M. (2012). Remote memory function and dysfunction in Korsakoff's syndrome. *Neuropsychology Review, 22,* 105–116.

Racette, A., & Peretz, I. (2007). Learning lyrics: to sing or not sing. *Memory & Cognition, 35,* 242–253.

Rahhal, T. A., May, C. P., & Hasher, L. (2002). Truth and character: Sources that older adults can remember. *Psychological Science, 13,* 101–105.

Ramachandran, V. S. (2011). *The tell-tale brain: A neuroscientist's quest for what makes us human.* New York: Norton & Co.

Ramachandran, V. S., & Blakeslee, S. (1998). *Phantoms in the brain.* New York: William Morrow.

Raposo, A., Mendes, M., & Marques, J. F. (2012). The hierarchical organization of semantic memory: Executive function in the processing of superordinate concepts. *Neuroimage, 59,* 1870–1878.

Rasmussen, K. G., Johnson, E. K., Kung, S., Farrow, S. L., Brown, S. K., Govrik, M. N., & Citronowicz, R. I. (2016). An open-label, pilot study of daily right unilateral ultrabrief pulse electroconvulsive therapy. *The Journal of ECT, 32,* 33–37.

Rathbone, C. J., Ellis, J. A., Baker, I., & Butler, C. R. (2015). Self, memory, and imagining the future in a case of psychogenic amnesia. *Neurocase, 21,* 727–737.

Rawson, K. A., & Dunlosky, J. (2011). Optimizing schedules of retrieval practice for durable and efficient learning: How much is enough? *Journal of Experimental Psychology: General, 140,* 283–302.

Raz, N. Yang, Y. Q., Rodrigue, K. M., Kennedy, K. M., Lindenberger, U., & Ghisletta P. (2012). White matter deterioration in 15 months: Latent growth curve models in healthy adults. *Neurobiology of Aging, 33,* e1–e5.

Reder, L. M. (1987). Selection strategies in question answering. *Cognitive Psychology, 19,* 90–138.

Reder, L. M., & Ritter, F. E. (1992). What determines initial feeling of knowing? Familiarity with question terms, not with the answer. *Journal of Experimental Psychology: Learning, Memory, and Cognition, 18,* 435–451.

Redondo, M. T., Beltrán-Brotóns, J. L., Reales, J. M., & Ballesteros, S. (2015). Word-stem priming and recognition in Type 2 diabetes mellitus, Alzheimer's disease patients and healthy older adults. *Experimental Brain Research.*

Reid, C. A., Green, J. D., Wildschut, T., & Sedikides, C. (2015). Scent-evoked nostalgia. *Memory, 23,* 157–166

Reisberg, D., & Heuer, F. (2004). Memory for emotional events. In D. Reisberg & F. Heuer (Eds.), *Memory and emotion* (pp. 3–41). New York: Oxford University Press.

Rhodes, M. G. (2016). Judgments of learning: Methods, data, and theory. *Oxford handbook of metamemory.* (pp. 65–80). New York: Oxford University Press.

Rhodes, M. G., & Castel, A. D. (2008a). Memory predictions are influenced by perceptual information: Evidence for metacognitive illusions. *Journal of Experimental Psychology: General, 137,* 615–625.

Rhodes, M. G., & Castel, A. D. (2008b). Metacognition and part-set cuing: Can interference be predicted at retrieval? *Memory & Cognition, 36,* 1429–1438.

Rhodes, M. G., Castel, A. D., & Jacoby, L. L. (2008). Associative recognition of face pairs by younger and older adults: The role of familiarity-based processing. *Psychology and Aging, 23,* 239–249.

Rhodes, M. G., & Kelley, C. M. (2005). Executive processes, memory accuracy, and memory monitoring: An aging and individual difference analysis. *Journal of Memory and Language, 52,* 578–594.

Rhodes, M. G. & Tauber, S. K. (2011). The influence of delaying judgments of learning on metacognitive accuracy: A meta-analytic review. *Psychological Bulletin, 137,* 131–148.

Rhodes, S., Parra, M.A., & Logie, R. H. (2016). Ageing and feature binding in visual working memory: The role of presentation time. *The Quarterly Journal of Experimental Psychology, 69,* 654–668.

Riby, L. M., Perfect, T. J., & Stollery, B. T. (2004). The effects of age and task domain on dual task performance: A meta-analysis. *European Journal of Cognitive Psychology, 16,* 868–891.

Rindal, E. J., DeFranco, R. M., Rich, P. R., & Zaragoza, M. S. (2016). Does reactivating a witnessed memory increase its susceptibility to impairment by subsequent misinformation? *Journal of Experimental Psychology: Learning, Memory, and Cognition, 42,* 1544–1558.

Rimmele, U., Davachi, L., & Phelps, E. A. (2012). Memory for time and place contributes to enhanced confidence in memories for emotional events. *Emotion, 12,* 834–846.

Risacher, S. L., Wang, Y., Wishart, H. A., Rabin, L. A., Flashman, L. A., McDonald, B. C., West, J. D., Santulli, R. B., & Saykin, A. J. (2013). Cholinergic enhancement of brain activation in mild cognitive impairment during episodic memory encoding. *Frontiers in Psychiatry, 4,* 105.

Robertson-Tchabo, E. A., Hausman, C. P., & Arenberg, D. (1976). A classical mnemonic for older learners: A trip that works. *Educational Gerontology, 1,* 215–226.

Robinson, J. A. (1992). First experience memories: Contexts and function in personal histories. In M. A. Conway, D. C. Rubin, H. Spinnler, & W. A. Wagenaar (Eds.), *Theoretical perspectives on autobiographical memory.* Dordrecht, the Netherlands: Kluwer Academic.

Robinson, J. A., & Swanson, K. L. (1993). Field and observer modes of remembering. *Memory, 1,* 169–184.

Rochat, P. (2003). Five levels of self-awareness as they unfold early in life. *Consciousness and Cognition, 12,* 717–731.

Roediger, H. L., III (1980). Memory metaphors in cognitive psychology. *Memory & Cognition, 8,* 231–246.

Roediger, H. L., III, & Crowder, R. G. (1976). A serial position curve in recall of United States presidents. *Bulletin of the Psychonomic Society, 8,* 275–278.

Roediger, H. L., III, & Karpicke, J. D. (2006). Test-enhanced learning: Taking memory tests improves long-term retention. *Psychological Science, 17,* 249–255.

Roediger, H. L. III & Magdalena, A. (2015). Collective memory: A new arena of cognitive study. *Trends in Cognitive Sciences, 19,* 359–361.

Roediger, H. L., III, & McDermott, K. B. (1995). Creating false memories: Remembering words not presented in lists. *Journal of Experimental Psychology: Learning, Memory, and Cognition, 21,* 803–814.

Roediger, H. L., III, & Pyc, M. A. (2012). Inexpensive techniques to improve education: Applying cognitive psychology to enhance educational practice. *Journal of Applied Research in Memory and Cognition, 1,* 242–248.

Roediger, H. L., III, Watson, J. M., McDermott, K. B., & Gallo, D. A. (2001). Factors that determine false recall: A multiple regression analysis. *Psychonomic Bulletin & Review, 8,* 385–407.

Rogers, T. B., Kuiper, N. A., & Kirker, W. S. (1977). Self-reference and the encoding of personal information. *Journal of Personality and Social Psychology, 35,* 677–688.

Rogers, T. T., & McClelland, J. L. (2004). *Semantic cognition: A parallel distributed processing approach.* Cambridge, MA: MIT Press.

Rosch, E. (1975). Cognitive representations of semantic categories. *Journal of Experimental Psychology: General, 104,* 192–233.

Rosch, E., & Mervis, C. B. (1975). Family resemblances: Studies in the internal structure of categories. *Cognitive Psychology, 7,* 573–605.

Rosch, E., Mervis, C. B., Gray, W. D., Johnson, D. M., & Boyes-Braem, P. (1976). Basic objects in natural categories. *Cognitive Psychology, 8,* 382–439.

Rosenbaum, R. S., Kohler, S., Schacter, D. L., Moscovitch, M., Westmacott, R., Black, S. E., . . . Tulving, E. (2005). The case of K. C.: Contributions of a memory-impaired person to memory theory. *Neuropsychologia, 43,* 989–1021.

Rosenbaum, S. R., Casidy, B. N., & Herdman, K. A. (2015). Patterns of preserved and impaired spatial memory in a case of developmental amnesia. *Frontiers in Human Neuroscience, 9,* 196.

Rovee-Collier, C., & Cuevas, K. (2009). The development of infant memory. In M. Courage & N. Cowan (Eds.), *The development of memory in infancy and childhood* (pp. 11–42). Hove, UK: Psychology Press.

Rovee-Collier, C., & Cuevas, K. (2008). The development of infant memory. In M. Courage & N. Cowan (Eds.), *The development of memory in childhood* (pp. 11–42). Hove, UK: Psychology Press.

Rubin, D. C., & Umanath, S. (2015). Event memory: A theory of memory for laboratory, autobiographical, and fictional events. *Psychological Review, 122,* 1–23.

Ruchkin, D. S., Grafman, J., Cameron, K., & Berndt, R. S. (2003). Working memory retention systems: A state of activated long-term memory. *Behavioral and Brain Sciences, 26,* 709–777.

Russ, M. O., Mack, W., Grama, C.-R., Lanfermann, H., & Knoff, M. (2003). Enactment effect in memory: Evidence concerning the function of the supramarginal gyrus. *Experimental Brain Research, 149,* 497–504.

Russell, R., Duchaine, B., & Nakayama, K. (2009). Super-recognizers: People with extraordinary face recognition ability. *Psychonomic Bulletin & Review, 16,* 252–257.

Ryan, D. R., & Caplan, D. (2016). "Cat-gras" delusion: A unique misidentification syndrome and a novel explanation. *Neurocase, 22,* 251–256.

Ryan, M. P., Petty, C. R., & Wenzlaff, R. M. (1982). Motivated remembering efforts during tip-of-the-tongue states. *Acta Psychologica, 51,* 137–147.

Rypma, D., & D'Esposito, M. (2003). A subsequent-memory effect in dorsolateral prefrontal cortex. *Cognitive Brain Research, 16,* 162–166.

Sacher, M., Landré, L., & Taconnat, L. (2015). Age-related differences in episodic feeling-of-knowing arise from differences in memory performance. *Memory, 23,* 119–126.

Sacks, O. (1985). *The man who mistook his wife for a hat.* New York: Simon & Schuster.

Sahin-Acar, B., & Leichtman, M. D. (2015). Mother–child memory conversations and self-construal in Eastern Turkey, Western Turkey and the USA. *Memory, 23,* 69–82.

Salame, P., & Baddeley, A. (1989). Effects of background music on phonological short-term memory. *Quarterly Journal of Experimental Psychology, 41A,* 107–122.

Salthouse, T. A. (1996). The processing-speed theory of adult age differences in cognition. *Psychological Review, 103,* 403–428.

Salthouse, T. A. (2000). Aging and measures of processing speed. *Biological Psychology, 54,* 35–54.

Salthouse, T. A. (2006). Mental exercise and mental aging. *Perspectives on Psychological Science, 1,* 68–87.

Salthouse, T. A. (2016). Continuity of cognitive change across adulthood. *Psychonomic Bulletin & Review, 23,* 932–939.

Sanbonmatsu, D. M., Strayer, D. L., Biondi, F., Behrends, A. A., & Moore, S. M. (2016). Cell-phone use diminishes self-awareness of impaired driving. *Psychonomic Bulletin & Review, 23,* 617–623.

Sander, M. C., Lindenberger, U., & Werkle-Bergner, M. (2012). Lifespan age differences in working memory: A two-component framework. *Neuroscience and Biobehavioral Reviews, 36,* 2007–2033.

Sarver, D. E., Rapport, M. D., Kofler, M. J., Raiker, J. S., & Friedman, L M. (2015). Hyperactivity in attention-deficit/hyperactivity disorder (ADHD): Impairing deficit or compensatory behavior? *Journal of Abnormal Child Psychology, 43*, 1219–1232.

Schaal, N. K., Javadi, A.-H., Halpern, A. R., Pollok, B., & Banissy, M. J. (2015). *European Journal of Neuroscience, 42*, 1660–1666.

Schachtel, E. G. (2000). On memory and childhood amnesia. In U. Neisser & I. E. Hyman Jr. (Eds.), *Memory observed: remembering in natural contexts*. New York: Worth. (Original work published 1947)

Schacter, D. L. (1996). *Searching for memory: The brain, the mind, and the past*. New York: Basic Books.

Schacter, D. L. (2001a). Forgotten ideas, neglected pioneers: Richard Semon and the story of memory. Philadelphia, PA: Psychology Press.

Schacter, D. L. (2001b). *The Seven sins of memory: How the mind forgets and remembers*. New York: Houghton Mifflin Company.

Schacter, D. L. (2007). Memory: Delineating the core. In H. L. Roediger, Y. Dudai, & S. M. Fitzpatrick (Eds.), *Science of memory: Concepts* (pp. 23–27). New York: Oxford University Press.

Scharinger, C., Soutschek, A., Schubert, T., & Gerjets, P. (2015). When flanker meets the n-back: What eeg and pupil dilation data reveal about the interplay between the two central-executive working memory functions inhibition and updating. *Psychophysiology, 52,* 1293–1304.

Schmolck, H., Buffalo, A. E., & Squire, L. R. (2000). Memory distortions develop over time: Recollections of the O. J. Simpson verdict after 15 and 32 months. *Psychological Science, 11*, 39–45.

Schneider, W., & Löffler, E. (2016). The development of metacognitive knowledge in children and adolescents. In J. Dunlosky & S. K. Tauber (Eds.), *The Oxford handbook of metamemory* (491–518). New York: Oxford University Press.

Schneider, W., & Ornstein, P. A. (2015). The development of children's memory. *Child Development Perspectives, 9*, 190–195.

Schneider, W., & Pressley, M. (1997). *Memory development between two and twenty* (2nd ed.). Hillsdale, NJ: Lawrence Erlbaum.

Schneider, W., Vise, M., Lockl, K., & Nelson, T. O. (2000). Developmental trends in children's memory monitoring: Evidence from a judgment-of-learning task. *Cognitive Development, 15*, 115–134.

Schnyer, D. M., Verfaellie, M., Alexander, M., LaFleche, G., Nicholls, L., & Kaszniak, A. W. (2004). A role for right medial prefrontal cortex in accurate feeling-of-knowing judgments: Evidence from patients with lesions to frontal cortex. *Neuropsychologia, 42*, 957–966.

Schreiber Compo, N., Evans, J. R., Carol, R. N., Villalba, D., & Ham, L.S. (2012). Intoxicated eyewitnesses: Better than their reputation? *Law and Human Behavior, 36*, 77–86.

Schreiber Compo, N., Gregory, A. H., & Fisher, R. P. (2012). Interviewing behaviors in police investigators: A field study of a current US sample. *Psychology, Crime, & Law, 18*, 359–375.

Schröter, P., & Schroeder, S. (2016). Orthographic processing in balanced bilingual children: Cross-language evidence from cognates and false friends. *Journal of Experimental Child Psychology, 141*, 239–246.

Schulkind, M. D. (2004). Serial processing in melody identification and the organization of musical semantic memory. *Perception & Psychophysics, 66*, 1351–1362.

Schwartz, B. L. (2001). The relation of tip-of-the-tongue states and retrieval time. *Memory & Cognition, 29*, 117–126.

Schwartz, B. L. (2008). Working memory load differentially affects tip-of-the-tongue states and feeling-of-knowing judgment. *Memory & Cognition, 36*, 9–19.

Schwartz, B. L., & Brown, A. S. (2014). *Tip-of-the-tongue states and related phenomena*. Cambridge University Press.

Schwartz, B. L., & Cleary, A. M. (2016). Tip-of-the-tongue states, déjà vu and other metacognitive oddities. In J. Dunlosky & S. Tauber (Eds), *Oxford Handbook of Metamemory* (pp. 95–108). New York: Oxford University Press.

Schwartz, B. L., & Efklides, A. (2012). Metamemory and memory efficiency: Implications for student learning. *Journal of Applied Research in Memory and Cognition, 1,* 145–151.

Schwartz, B. L., & Frazier, L. D. (2005). Tip-of-the-tongue states and aging: Contrasting psycholinguistic and metacognitive perspectives. *Journal of General Psychology, 132,* 377–391.

Schwartz, B. L., & Krantz, J. H. (2016). *Sensation and perception.* Thousand Oaks, CA: Sage.

Schwartz, B. L., & Metcalfe, J. (2011). Tip-of-the-tongue (TOT) states: Retrieval, behavior, and experience. *Memory & Cognition, 39,* 737–749.

Schweickert, R., & Boruff, B. (1986). Short-term memory capacity: Magic number or magic spell? *Journal of Experimental Psychology: Learning, Memory, and Cognition, 12,* 419–425.

Scoboria, A., Mazzoni, G., & Josee, J. L. (2008). Suggesting childhood food illness results in reduced eating behavior. *Acta Psycologica, 128,* 304–309.

Scullin, M. K., & Bugg, J. M. (2012). Failing to forget: Prospective memory commission errors can result from spontaneous retrieval and impaired executive control. *Journal of Experimental Psychology: Learning, Memory, and Cognition.*

Seamon, J. G., Bohn, J. M., Coddington, I. E., Ebling, M. C., Grund, E. M., Haring, C. T., Jang, S.-J., Kim, D., Liong, C., Paley, F. M., Pang, L. K., & Siddique, A. H. (2012). Can survival processing enhance story memory? Testing the generalizability of the adaptive memory framework. *Journal of Experimental Psychology: Learning, Memory, and Cognition, 38,* 1045–1056. doi: 10.1037/a0027090

Sellers II, P. D., & Bjorklund, D. F. (2014). The development of adaptive memory. In B. L. Schwartz, M. L. Howe, M. P. Toglia, and H. Otgaar (Eds). *What is adaptive about adaptive memory.* New York: Oxford University Press.

Semkovska, M., Noone, M., Carton, M., & McLoughlin, D. M. (2012). Measuring consistency of autobiographical memory recall in depression. *Psychiatry Research, 197,* 41–48.

Shallice, T., & Warrington, E. K. (1970). Independent functioning of verbal memory stores: A neuropsychological study. *Quarterly Journal of Experimental Psychology, 22,* 261–273.

Shang, Q., Huang, Y., & Ma, Q. (2015). Hazard levels of warning signal words modulate the inhibition of return effect: Evidence from the event-related potential P300. *Experimental Brain Research, 233,* 2645–2653.

Shaw, J., & Porter, S. (2015). Constructing rich false memories of committing crime. *Psychological Science, 26,* 291–301.

Sheen, M., Kemp, S., & Rubin, D. (2001). Twins dispute memory ownership: A new false memory phenomenon. *Memory & Cognition, 29,* 779–788.

Sheng, M., Sabatini, B., & Südhof, T. C. (2012). *The synapse.* New York: Cold Spring Harbor Press.

Shepard, R. N., & Metzler, J. (1971). Mental rotation of thee-dimensional objects. *Science, 171,* 701–703.

Sheridan, C. J., Matuz, T., Draganova, R., Esweran, H., & Preissl, H. (2010). Achievements and challenges in the study of prenatal and early postnatal brain responses: A review. *Infant and child development, 19,* 80–93.

Sherman, S. M., & Kennerley, J. (2014). The organisation of musical semantic memory: Evidence from false memories for familiar songs. *Memory, 22,* 852–860.

Sherry, D. F., & Hoshooley, J. S. (2009). The seasonal hippocampus of food-storing birds. *Behavioural Processes, 80,* 334–338.

Shettleworth, S. J. (2010). *Cognition, evolution, and behavior* (2nd ed.). New York: Oxford University Press.

Shettleworth, S. J. (2012) *Fundamentals of comparative cognition.* New York: Oxford University Press

Shimamura, A. P. (2008). A neurocognitive approach to metacognitive monitoring and control. In J. Dunlosky & R. A. Bjork (Eds.), *Handbook of metamemory and memory* (pp. 373–390). New York: Psychology Press.

Shimamura, A. P. (2014). Remembering the Past: Neural Substrates Underlying Episodic Encoding and Retrieval. *Current Directions in Psychological Science, 23*, 257–263.

Shimamura, A. P., & Squire, L. R. (1986). Memory and metamemory: A study of the feeling-of-knowing phenomenon in amnesic patients. *Journal of Experimental Psychology: Learning, Memory, and Cognition, 12*(3), 452–460.

Shimamura, A. P., Berry, J. M., Mangels, J. A., Rusting, C. L., & Jurica, P. J. (1995). Memory and cognitive abilities in university professors: Evidence for successful aging. *Psychological Science, 6*(5), 271–277.

Shingaki, H., Park, P., Ueda, K., Murai, T., & Tsukiura, T. (2016). Disturbance of time orientation, attention, and verbal memory in amnesic patients with confabulation. *Journal of Clinical and Experimental Neuropsychology, 38*, 171–182.

Shipstead, Z., Harrison, T. L., & Engle, R. W. (2015). Working memory capacity and the scope and control of attention. *Attention, Perception, & Psychophysics, 77*, 1863–1880.

Shipstead, Z., Lindsey, R. B., Marshall, R. L., & Engle, R. W. (2014). The contributions of maintenance, retrieval and attention control to working memory capacity. *Journal of Memory and Language, 72*, 116–141.

Shipstead, Z., Redick, T. S., & Engle, R. W. (2012). Is working memory training effective. *Psychological Bulletin, 138*, 628–654.

Shin, H., Bjorklund, D. F., & Beck, E. F. (2007). The adaptive nature of children's overestimation in a strategic memory task. *Cognitive Development, 22*, 197–212.

Shlomo, B., DeGutis, J. M., D'Esposito, M., & Robertson, L. C. (2007). Too many trees to see the forest: Performance, event-related potential, and functional magnetic resonance imaging manifestations of integrative congenital prosopagnosia. *Journal of Cognitive Neuroscience, 19*, 132–146.

Shobe, K. K., & Schooler, J. W. (2001). Discovering fact and fiction: Case-based analyses of authentic and fabricated memories of abuse. In G. M. Davies & T. Dalgleish (Eds.), *Recovered memories: Seeking the middle ground* (pp. 95–151). Chichester, UK: John Wiley.

Siegler, R. S. (1999). Strategic development. *Trends in Cognitive Science, 3*, 430–435.

Simcock, G., & Hayne, H. (2002). Breaking the barrier? Children fail to translate their preverbal memories into language. *Psychological Science, 13*, 225–231.

Simner, J., & Ward, J. (2006). The taste of words on the tip of the tongue. *Nature, 444*, 438.

Simons, J. S., Scholvinck, M. L., Gilbert, S. J., Frith, C. D., & Burgess, P. W. (2006). Differential components of prospective memory? Evidence from fMRI. *Neuropsychologia, 44*, 1388–1397.

Singer, M., Fazaluddin, A., & Andrew, K. N. (2011). Distinctiveness and repetition in item recognition. *Canadian Journal of Experimental Psychology/Revue canadienne de psychologie experimentale, 65*, 200–207.

Slamecka, N. J., & Graf, P. (1978). The generation effect: Delineation of a phenomenon. *Journal of Experimental Psychology: Human Learning and Remembering, 4*, 592–604.

Slotnick, S. D. (2012). The cognitive neuroscience of memory. *Cognitive Neuroscience, 3*(3-4), 139–141.

Slotnick, S. D., & Schacter, D. L. (2006). The nature of memory related activity in early visual areas. *Neuropsychologia, 44*, 2874–2886.

Slotnick, S.D., Thompson, W. L., & Kosslyn, S. M. (2012). Visual memory and visual mental imagery recruit common control and sensory regions of the brain. *Cognitive Neuroscience, 31*, 14–20.

Smith, E. E., Shoben, E. J., & Rips, L. J. (1974). Structures and process in semantic memory: A featural model for semantic decisions. *Psychological Review, 81*, 214–241.

Smith, J. D., & Ell, S. W. (2015). One giant leap for categorizers: One small step for categorization Theory. *PLoS One, 10*(9).

Smith, S. M. (1994). Frustrated feelings of imminent recall: On the tip-of-the-tongue. In J. Metcalfe & A. P. Shimamura (Eds.), *Metacognition: Knowing about knowing* (pp. 27–46). Cambridge, MA: MIT Press.

Smith, S. M., & Moynan, S. C. (2008). Forgetting and recovering the unforgettable. *Psychological Science, 19*, 462–468.

Smith, T. S., Isaak, M. I., Senette, C. G., & Abadie, B. G. (2011). Effects of cell-phone and text-message distractions on true and false recognition. *Cyberpsychology, Behavior, and Social Networking, 14*, 351–358.

Snowdon, D. A. (2003). Healthy aging and dementia: Findings from the nun study. *Annals of Internal Medicine, 139*, 450–454.

Son, L., & Vandierendonck, A. (Eds.). (2007). *Bridging cognitive science and education: Learning, memory, and metacognition.* New York: Psychology Press.

Son, L. K., & Metcalfe J. (2000). Metacognitive and control strategies in study-time allocation. *Journal of Experimental Psychology: Learning, Memory, & Cognition, 26*, 204–221.

Son, L. K., & Metcalfe, J. (2005). Judgments of learning: Evidence for a two-stage model. *Memory & Cognition, 33*, 1116–1129.

Soraci, S. A., Carlin, M. T., Checile, R. A., Franks, J. J., Wills, T., & Watanabe, T. (1999). Encoding variability and cuing in generative processing. *Journal of Memory and Language, 41*, 541–559.

Souchay, C., & Isingrini, M. (2004). Age-related differences in the relation between monitoring and control of learning. *Experimental Aging Research, 30*, 179–193.

Souchay, C., & Isingrini, M. (2012). Are feeling-of-knowing and judgment-of-learning different? Evidence from older adults. *Acta Psychologica, 139*, 458–464.

Souchay, C., Moulin, C. J. A., Clarys, D., Taconnat, L., & Isingrini, M. (2007). Diminished episodic memory awareness in older adults: Evidence from feeling of knowing and recollection. *Consciousness and Cognition, 16*, 769–784.

Spellman, B. A., Bloomfield, A., & Bjork, R. A. (2008). Measuring memory and metamemory: Theoretical and statistical problems with assessing learning (in general) and using gamma (in particular) to do so. In J. Dunlosky & R. A. Bjork (Eds.), *Handbook of memory and metamemory: Essays in honor of Thomas O. Nelson* (pp. 95–116). New York: Psychology Press.

Sperling, G. (1960). The information available in brief visual presentations. *Psychological Monographs: General and Applied, 74*, 1–29.

Sporer, S. L. (1991). Deep-deeper-deepest? Encoding strategies and the recognition of human faces. *Journal of Experimental Psychology: Learning, Memory, and Cognition, 17*, 323–333.

Standing, L. (1973). Learning 10,000 pictures. *Quarterly Journal of Experimental Psychology, 25*, 207–222.

Steblay, N. K., Dysart, J. E., & Wells, G. L. (2011). Seventy-two tests of the sequential lineup superiority effect: A meta-analysis and policy discussion. *Psychology, Public Policy, and Law, 17*, 99–139.

Sternberg, S. (1969). Memory scanning: Mental processes revealed by reaction time experiments. *American Scientist, 57*, 421–457.

Strange, D. Sutherland, R., Sharman, S. J., & Garry, M. (2006). Event plausibility does not affect children's false memories. *Memory, 14*, 937–951.

Strange, D., Wade, K., & Hayne, H. (2008). Creating false memories for events that occurred before versus after the offset of childhood amnesia. *Memory, 16*, 475–484.

Strayer, D. L., & Drews, F. A. (2007). Cell-phone-induced driver distraction. *Current Directions in Psychological Science, 16*, 128–131.

Strayer, D. L., Watson, J. M., & Drews, F. A. (2011). Cognitive distraction while multitasking in the automobile. In B. Ross (Ed.), *The psychology of learning and motivation* (pp. 29–58). Burlington: Academic Press.

Storm, B. C., & Jobe, T. A. (2012). Remembering the past and imagining the future: Examining the consequences of mental time travel on memory. *Memory, 20*, 224–235.

Sun, R. (2012). Memory systems within a cognitive architecture. *New Ideas in Psychology, 2*, 227–240.

Sutcliffe Cleveland, E., & Reese, E. (2008). Children remembering early childhood: Long term recall across the offset of childhood amnesia. *Applied Cognitive Psychology, 22*, 127–142.

Takahashi, M., Shimizu, H., Saito, S., & Tomoyori, H. (2006). One percent ability and ninety-nine percent perspiration: A study of a Japanese memorist. *Journal of Experimental Psychology: Learning, Memory, and Cognition, 32*, 1195–1200.

Talarico, J. M., & Rubin, D. C. (2003). Confidence, not consistency, characterizes flashbulb memories. *Psychological Science, 14,* 455–461.

Talarico, J. M., & Rubin, D. C. (2007). Flashbulb memories are special after all; in phenomenology, not accuracy. *Applied Cognitive Psychology, 21,* 557–578.

Tan, S-L., Pfordresher, P. & Harre, R. (2010). *Psychology of music: From sound to significance.* New York: Psychology Press.

Tannenbaum, C., Paquette, A., Hilmer, S., Holroyd-Leduc, J., & Carnahan, R. (2012). A systematic review of amnestic and non-amnestic mild cognitive impairment induced by anticholinergic, antihistamine, GABAergic and opioid drugs. *Drugs & Aging, 29,* 639–659.

Tauber, S. K., & Rhodes, M. G. (2012). Multiple bases for young and older adults' judgments of learning in multitrial learning. *Psychology and Aging, 27,* 474–483.

Teasdale, J. D., Dritschel, B. H., Taylor, M. J., Proctor, L., Lloyd, C. A., Nimmo-Smith, I., & Baddeley, A. D. (1995). Stimulus-independent thought depends on central executive resources. *Memory & Cognition, 23*, 551–559.

Tekcan, A. I., Ece, B., Gulgoz, S., & Er, N. (2003). Autobiographical and event memory for 9/11: Changes across one year. *Applied Cognitive Psychology, 17*, 1057–1066.

Tessler, M., & Nelson, K. (1994). Making memories: The influence of joint encoding on later recall by young children. *Consciousness & Cognition, 3,* 307–326.

Thomas, A. K., Lee, M., & Hughes, G. (2016). Introspecting on the elusive: The uncanny state of the feeling of knowing. In J. Dunlosky & S. K. Tauber (Eds.), *The Oxford handbook of metamemory* (pp. 81–94). New York: Oxford University Press.

Thomas, M. H., & Wang, A. Y. (1996). Learning by the keyword mnemonic: Looking for long-term benefits. *Journal of Experimental Psychology: Applied, 2,* 330–342.

Thomas-Antérion, C. (2012). L'amnésie dissociative: Une rare situation de voyage dans le temps perdu. *Annales Médico-Psychologiques, 170,* 181–184.

Thompson, C. P., Cowan, T. M., & Frieman, J. (1993). *Memory search by a memorist.* Hillsdale, NJ: Lawrence Erlbaum.

Thompson, D. M., & Tulving, E. (1970). Associative encoding and retrieval: Weak and strong cues. *Journal of Experimental Psychology, 86*, 255–262.

Thompson, R., Emmorey, K., & Gollan, T. H. (2005). "Tip of the fingers" experiences by deaf signers. *Psychological Science, 16,* 856–860.

Thompson-Schill, S. L., Ramscar, M., & Chrysikou, E. G. (2009). Cognition without control: When a little frontal lobe goes a long way. *Current Direction in Psychological Science, 18*, 259–263.

Thomsen, D. K., & Berntsen, D. (2008). The cultural life script and life story chapters contribute to the reminiscence bump. *Memory, 16,* 420–435.

Thomsen, D. K., Jensen, T., Holm, T., Oleson, M. H., Schnieber, A., & Tonnesvang, J. (2015). A 3.5 year diary study: Remembering and life story importance are predicted by different event characteristics. *Consciousness and Cognition: An International Journal, 36*, 180–195.

Thomsen, D. K., Olesen, M. H., Schnieber, A., Jensen, T., & Tonnesvang, J. (2012). What characterizes life story memories? A diary study of freshmen's first term. *Consciousness and Cognition: An International Journal, 21,* 366–382.

Tincoff, R., & Jusczyk, P. W. (1999). Some beginnings of word comprehension in 6-month-olds. *Psychological Science, 10,* 172–175.

Tiwari, G. K. (2012). The misinformation effect and fate of witnessed minutiae. *Indian Journal of Community Psychology, 8,* 134–142.

Tom, A. C., & Tversky, B. (2012). Remembering routes: Streets and landmarks. *Applied Cognitive Psychology, 26,* 182–193.

Toppino, T. C., & Cohen, M. S. (2010). Metacognitive control and spaced practice: Clarifying what people do and why. *Journal of Experimental Psychology: Learning, Memory, and Cognition, 36,* 1480–1491.

Trumbo, M. C., Leiting, K. A., McDaniel, M. A., & Hodge, G. K. (2016). Effects of reinforcement on test-enhanced learning in a large, diverse introductory college psychology course. *Journal of Experimental Psychology: Applied, 22,* 148–160.

Tsivilis, D., Vann, S. D., Denby, C., Roberts, N., Mayes, A. R., Montaldi, D., & Aggleton, J. P. (2008). The importance of the fornix and mammillary bodies for human memory: A disproportionate role for recall versus recognition. *Nature Neuroscience, 11,* 834–842.

Tulving, E. (1962). Subjective organization in free recall of "unrelated" words. *Psychological Review, 69,* 344–354.

Tulving, E. (1972). Episodic and semantic memory. In E. Tulving & W. Donaldson (Eds.), *Organization of memory* (pp. 381–403). New York: Academic Press.

Tulving, E. (1983). *Elements of episodic memory.* New York: Oxford University Press.

Tulving, E. (1985). Memory and consciousness. *Canadian Journal of Psychology, 26,* 1–12.

Tulving, E. (1993). What is episodic memory? *Current Directions in Psychology, 3,* 67–70

Tulving, E. (2002). Episodic memory and common sense: how far apart. In A. Baddeley, M. Conway, & J. Aggleton (Eds.), *Episodic memory: New direction in research* (pp. 269–287). New York: Oxford University Press.

Tulving, E., & Lepage, M. (2000). Where in the brain is awareness of one's past? In D. L. Schacter & E. Scarry (Eds.), *Memory, brain, and belief* (pp. 208–228). Cambridge, MA: Harvard University Press.

Tulving, E., & Pearlstone, Z. (1966). Availability versus accessibility of information in memory for words. *Journal of Verbal Learning and Verbal Behavior, 5,* 381–391.

Tulving, E., & Schacter, D.L. (1990). Priming and human memory systems. *Science, 247,* 301–306.

Tushima, W.T., Geling, O., & Arnold, M. (2016). Effects of two concussions on the neuropsychological functioning and symptom reporting of high school athletes. *Applied Neuropsychology: Child, 5,* 9–13.

Tversky, B. (2000). Remembering spaces. In E. Tulving & F. I. M. Craik (Eds.), *The Oxford handbook of memory* (pp. 363–378). New York: Oxford University Press.

Ueno, D., Masumoto, K., Sutani, K., & Iwaki, S. (2015). Latency of modality-specific reactivation of auditory and visual information during episodic memory retrieval. *Neuroreport, 26,* 303–308.

Uncapher, M. R., Thieu, M., & Wagner, A. D. (2016). Media multitasking and memory: Differences in working memory and long-term memory. *Psychonomic Bulletin & Review, 23,* 483–490.

Usher, J. A., & Neisser, U. (1993). Childhood amnesia and the beginnings of memory for four early life events. *Journal of Experimental Psychology: General, 122,* 155–165.

Vaidya, C. J., Gabrieli, J. D., Keane, M. M., & Monti, L. A. (1995). Perceptual and conceptual memory processes in global amnesia. *Neuropsychology, 9,* 580–591.

Vallar, G., & Baddeley, A. D. (1984). Fractionation of working memory: Neuropsychological evidence for a phonological short-term store. *Journal of Verbal Learning and Verbal Behavior, 23,* 151–161.

Van Abbema, D. L., & Bauer, P. J. (2005). Autobiographical memory in middle childhood: Recollections of the recent and distant past. *Memory, 13,* 829–845.

Vannucci, M., Mazzoni, G., Marchetti, I., & Lavezzini, F. (2012). "It's a hair-dryer . . . No, it's a drill": Misidentification-related false recognitions in younger and older adults. *Archives of Gerontology and Geriatrics, 54,* 310–316.

Vargha-Khadem, F., Gadian, D. G., Watkins, K. E., Connelly, A., Van Paesschen, W., & Mishkin, M. (1997). Differential effects of early hippocampal pathology on episodic and semantic memory. *Science, 277,* 376.

Vendetti, M., Castel, A. D., & Holyoak, K. J. (2013). The floor effect: Impoverished spatial memory for elevator buttons. *Attention, Perception & Psychophysics, 75*, 633–643.

Verhaeghen, P., & Marcoen, A. (1996). On the mechanism of plasticity in young and older adults after instructions in the method of loci: Evidence for an amplification model. *Psychology & Aging, 11*, 164–178.

Verkoeijen, P. P. J. L., Rikers, R. M. J. P., & Ozsoy, B. (2008). Distributed rereading can hurt the spacing effect in text memory. *Applied Cognitive Psychology, 22*, 685–695.

Vilkki, J., Servo, A., & Surma-aho, O. (1998). Word list learning and prediction of recall after frontal lobe lesion. *Neuropsychology, 12*, 268–277.

von Restorff, H. (1933). Über die Wirkung von Bereichsbildungen im Spurenfeld [The effects of field formation in the trace field]. *Psychologie Forschung, 18*, 299–234.

Wade, K. A., Green, S. L., & Nash, R. A. (2010). Can fabricated evidence induce false eyewitness testimony? *Applied Cognitive Psychology, 24*, 899–908.

Wagenaar, W. A. (1986). My memory: A study of autobiographical memory over six years. *Cognitive Psychology, 18,* 225–242.

Wagoner, B. (2013). Bartlett's concept of schema in reconstruction. *Theory & Psychology, 23*, 553–575.

Wang, A. Y., & Thomas, M. H. (1995). The effect of keywords on long-term retention: Help or hindrance. *Journal of Educational Psychology, 87*, 468–475.

Wang, Q. (2006). Earliest recollections of self and others in European Americans and Taiwanese young adults. *Psychological Science, 17*, 706–714.

Wang, Q., & Fivush, R. (2005). Mother-child conversations of emotionally-salient events: Exploring the functions of emotional reminiscing in European-American and Chinese families. *Social Development, 14*, 473–495.

Wang, Q., Peterson, C., & Hou, Y. (2010). Children dating childhood memories. *Memory, 18, 7*, 754–762,

Wang, X., & Forster, K. (2015). Is translation priming asymmetry due to partial awareness of the prime? *Bilingualism: Language and Cognition, 18*, 657–669.

Ward, J. (2008). *The frog who croaked blue: Synesthesia and the mixing of the senses.* Oxford, UK: Routledge.

Warker, J. A., & Dell, G. S. (2015). New phonotactic constraints learned implicitly by producing syllable strings generalize to the production of new syllables. *Journal of Experimental Psychology: Learning, Memory, and Cognition, 41*, 1902–1910.

Warrington, E. K., & Shallice, T. (1969). The selective impairment of auditory short-term memory. *Brain, 92*, 885–896.

Washburn, D. A., Beran, M. J., & Smith, J. D. (2016). Metamemory in a comparative context. In J. Dunlosky & S. Tauber (Eds). *Oxford handbook of metamemory* (pp. 269–288). New York: Oxford University Press.

Watson, J. B. (1913). Psychology as the behaviorist views it. *Psychological Review, 20,* 158–177.

Watson, J. M., Bunting, M. F., Poole, B. J., & Conway, A. R. A. (2005). Individual differences in susceptibility to false memory in the Deese-Roediger-McDermott paradigm. *Journal of Experimental Psychology: Learning, Memory, and Cognition, 31*, 76–85.

Waugh, N. C., & Norman, D. A. (1965). Primary memory. *Psychological Review, 72*, 89–104.

Weaver, C. A., III. (1993). Do you need a "flash" to form a flashbulb memory? *Journal of Experimental Psychology: General, 122*, 39–46.

Weingartner, H. J., Joyce, E. M., Sirocco, K. Y., Adams, C. M., Eckardt, M. J., George, T., & Lister, R. G. (1993). Specific memory and sedative effects of the benzodiazepine triazolam. *Journal of Psychopharmacology, 7*, 305–315.

Weldon, D. A. (2015). Cognitive neuroscience: A progress report. *PsycCritiques*. In press.

Wells, G. L., Dysart, J. E., & Steblay, N. K. (2015). The flaw in Amendola and Wixted's conclusion on simultaneous versus sequential lineups. *Journal of Experimental Criminology, 11*, 285–289.

Wells, G. L., Steblay, N. K., & Dysart, J. E. (2012). Eyewitness identification reforms: Are suggestiveness-induced hits and guesses true hits? *Perspectives on Psychological Science, 7*, 264–271.

Wenk, G. L. (2003). Neuropathologic changes in Alzheimer's disease. *Journal of Clinical Psychiatry, 64*, 7–10.

Werker, J. F., & Tees, R. C. (1999). Influences on infant speech processing: Toward a new synthesis. *Annual Review of Psychology, 50*, 509–535.

White, R. (2002). Memory for events after twenty years. *Applied Cognitive Psychology, 16*, 603–612.

White, R. (2011). *How to improve your memory in just 30 days.* Melrose, FL: Laurenzana Press.

Wijnia, J. W., van de Wetering, B. J. M., Zwart, E., Nieuwehuis, K. G. A., & Goossensen, M. A. (2012). Evolution of Wernicke-Korsakoff syndrome in self-neglecting alcoholics: Preliminary results of relation with Wernicke-delirium and diabetes mellitus. *The American Journal of Addictions, 21*, 104–110.

Willander, J., & Larsson, M. (2006). Smell your way back to childhood: Autobiographical odor memory. *Psychonomic Bulletin & Review, 13*, 240–244.

Willander, J., & Larsson, M. (2007). Olfaction and emotion: The case of autobiographical memory. *Memory & Cognition, 35*, 1659–1663.

Williams, L. M. (1995). Recovered memories of abuse in women with documented child sexual victimization histories. *Journal of Traumatic Stress, 8*, 649–673.

Willingham, D. T. (2009). What will improve student's memory? *American Educator, 32*, 17–25.

Wilson, B. A. (2009). *Memory rehabilitation: Integrating theory and practice.* New York: Guilford.

Wilson, B. A., & Wearing, D. (1995). Broken memories: Case studies in memory impairment. In R. Campbell & M. A. Conway (Eds.), *Broken memories: Case studies in memory impairment* (pp. 14–30). Malden, MA: Blackwell.

Wilson, B. M., Mickes, L., Stolarz-Fantino, S., Evrard, M., & Fantino, E. (2015). Increased false-memory susceptibility after mindfulness meditation. *Psychological Sciences, 26*, 1567–1573.

Wilson, T. L., & Brown, T. L. (1997). Reexamination of the effect of Mozart's music on spatial-task performance. *Journal of Psychology: Interdisciplinary and Applied, 131*, 365–370.

Wimmer, H., & Perner, J. (1983). Beliefs about beliefs: Representation and constraining function of wrong beliefs in young children's understanding of deception. *Cognition, 13*, 103–128.

Wise, N. (2016). The Capgras delusion: An integrated approach. *Phenomenology and the Cognitive Sciences, 15*, 183–205.

Wixted, J. T., Mickes, L., Clark, S. E., Gronlund, S. D., & Roediger, H. L. III. (2015). Initial eyewitness confidence reliably predicts eyewitness identification accuracy. *American Psychologist, 70*, 515–526.

Wolfe, J. M., Horowitz, T. S., & Michod, K. O. (2007). Is visual attention required for robust visual memory? *Vision Research, 47*(7), 955–964.

Wollen, K. A., Weber, A., & Lowry, D. (1972). Bizarreness versus interaction of mental images as determinants of learning. *Cognitive Psychology, 3*, 518–523.

Wright, A. A., Santiago, H. C., & Sands, S. F. (1984). Visual serial position curves in SPR tasks. *Journal of Experimental Psychology: Animal Behavior Processes, 10*, 513–529.

Wu, L.-I., & Barsalou, L. W. (2009). Perceptual simulation in conceptual combination: Evidence from property generation. *Acta Psychologica, 132*, 173–189.

Xu, J., & Metcalfe. J. (2016). Studying in the region of proximal learning reduces mind wandering. *Memory & Cognition, 44*, 681–695.

Yamada, M., Muria, T., & Ohigashi, Y. (2003). Postoperative reduplicative paramnesia in a patient with a right frontotemporal lesion. *Psychogeriatrics, 3*, 127–131.

Yang, L., Truong, L., Fuss, S., & Bislimovic, S. (2012). The effects of ageing and divided attention on the self-reference effect in emotional memory: Spontaneous or effortful mnemonic benefits? *Memory, 20*, 596–607.

Yaro, C., & Ward, J. (2007). Searching for Shereshevskii: What is superior about the memory of synaesthetes? *Quarterly Journal of Experimental Psychology, 60,* 681–695.

Yates, F. A. (1966). *The art of memory.* London: Routledge & Kegan Paul.

Young, G. (2008). Capgras delusion: An interactionist model. *Consciousness and Cognition, 17,* 863–876.

Yuille, J. C., & Cutshall, J. L. (1986). A case study of eyewitness memory of a crime. *Journal of Applied Psychology, 71,* 291–301.

Zacks, R. T., & Hasher, L. (2006). Aging and long-term memory: Deficits are not inevitable. In E. Bialystok & F. I. M. Craik (Eds.), *Lifespan cognition: Mechanisms of change* (pp. 162–177). New York: Oxford University Press.

Zaragoza Scherman, A., Salgado, S., Shao, Z., & Bernsten, D. (2015). Life span distribution and content of positive and negative autobiographical memories across cultures. *Psychology of Consciousness: Theory, Research, and Practice, 2,* 475–489.

Zucco, G. M., Aiello, L., Turuani, L, & Koster, E. (2012). Odor-evoked autobiographical memories: Age and gender differences along the life span. *Chemical Senses, 37,* 179–189.

Author Index

Subject Index

Absolute judgment, 190
Acetylcholine, 41
Acronyms, 424
Acrostics, 424
Action potentials, 39–40
Active retrieval suppression, 265, 269–270
Agenda-based regulation, 309
Aging-related memory issues. *See* Older adult memory
Alcohol effects, 60
Alcoholism-associated amnesia, 332
Alien abduction memories, 249, 261, 376
Alprazolam, 60
Alzheimer's disease, 37, 319, 347–350
   awareness and, 324
   causes, 349
   diffusion tensor imaging, 56
   prevention and treatment, 349–350
   working memory and, 97
Amnesia, 318–319
   anterograde, 321–323. *See also* Anterograde amnesia
   benzodiazepine effects, 60–62, 326–327
   brain damage effects, 59–60
   case studies, 320–321, 329
   childhood amnesia, 216–223
   coping strategies, 325–326
   defining, 319
   developmental, 106
   dissociative, 345–346
   frontal syndrome, 336–338
   hippocampal damage and. *See* Hippocampus
   Korsakoff's disease, 332–336
   movie depictions, 318, 344
   psychogenic, 344–347

retrograde, 328–331. *See also* Retrograde amnesia
short-term memory, 339–340
source monitoring errors, 337
See also Amnesic syndrome; Memory disorders
Amnesic syndrome, 322
   awareness in, 324–326, 334
   coping strategies, 325–326
   implicit memory in, 323–324
   See also Amnesia; Anterograde amnesia; Korsakoff's disease
Amount of information, 280
Amygdala, 47, 244
Amyloid plaque, 349
Analog representation, 174–175, 177
Animal models, 23, 45
   theory of mind, 379
   working memory, 68
Anomic aphasia, 146
Anosognosia, 327, 334, 335
Anterior cingulate, 95, 115, 295, 304, 337
Anterograde amnesia, 318, 321–323
   Alzheimer's disease, 348
   benzodiazepine effects, 326–327
   frontal syndrome, 336–337
   Korsakoff's disease and, 333
   neuropsychology cases, 59–60, 320–321
   transient global amnesia, 338–339
   See also Amnesia; Amnesic syndrome
Aricept, 61
Aristotle, 34
Articulatory suppression, 85–86, 87

Associative models, 5, 9–10, 142–144
   semantic priming, 144–146
   spreading activation, 142–143, 146–147
   See also Semantic memory
Atavan, 60
Attention-deficit/hyperactivity disorder (ADHD), 97
Auditory cortex, 63
Auditory memory, pegword mnemonic technique, 202–203
Auditory recognition in infants, 357–358
Auditory sensory memory, 68–69
Auditory working memory. *See* Phonological loop
Autism, 56
Autobiographical memory, 103, 207–209
   childhood amnesia, 216–223
   Conway's theory of representation, 209–215, 234
   correspondence concept, 215, 251
   cue-word technique, 234–235
   cultural differences, 368
   developmental transitions, 376
   diary studies and, 232–234
   disputed memories, 239–240
   episodic memory and, 103, 208
   field and observer memories, 238
   flashbulb memories, 207–208, 224–230
   in early childhood, 367
   involuntary memories, 238–239
   mnemonists, 443
   music and, 62–63, 240
   neuroscience of, 241–244
   odor and, 240–241

About the Author

Bennett L. Schwartz is Professor of Psychology and Fellow of the Honors College at Florida International University. A native of Long Island, New York, he earned both his bachelor's degree (1988) and PhD (1993) from Dartmouth College in Hanover, New Hampshire. He then moved to Florida International University in Miami, Florida, where he has been ever since. He does research on metamemory, human memory, and nonhuman primate memory. He has published over 50 journal articles in these areas. He has authored, co-authored, or edited six books. He is past president of the Southeastern Workers in Memory (2006), and he has served on the editorial boards of several journals in cognitive and comparative psychology, currently including the *Animal Cognition and Journal of Applied Research in Memory and Cognition*. He teaches courses in memory, cognitive psychology, sensation and perception, and interdisciplinary honors courses.